D0204137

THE
VISUAL
NATURE
OF
COLOR

Into the same rivers we step and we do not step;
we are and we are not.

Heraclitus

THE VISUAL NATURE OF COLOR

PATRICIA SLOANE

DESIGN PRESS

ACKNOWLEDGMENTS

Research for this book was partially supported by a fellowship from the John Simon Guggenhelm Memorial Foundation, and the New York City Technical College of The City University of New York.

For their suggestions and encouragement, I would like to thank Robert Motherwell, Rudolph Arnhelm, David Ecker, Jerome Hausman, Robert Ginsberg, Pamela Dohner, Linda Venator, Kurt Wildermuth, and Nancy Green.

First Edition, First Printing

Copyright © 1989 by Patricia Sloane
Printed in the United States of America
Designed by Gilda Hannah

Reproduction or publication of the content in any manner, without express permission of the publisher, is prohibited. The publisher takes no responsibility for the use of any of the materials or methods described in this book, or for the products thereof.

Library of Congress Cataloging in Publication Data

Sloane, Patricia.
    The visual nature of color.

    Bibliography: p.
    Includes Index.
    1. Color in art. 2. Color (Philosophy) 3. Color—
Psychological aspects. I. Title.
ND1488.S55 1989   701'.8   88-33624
ISBN 0-8036-5500-X

Design Press offers posters and The Cropper, a device for cropping artwork, for sale. For information, contact Mailorder Department. Design Press books are available at special discounts for bulk purchases for sales promotions, fund raisers, or premiums. For details contact Special Sales Manager. Questions regarding the content of the book should be addressed to:

DESIGN PRESS
Division of TAB BOOKS Inc.
10 East 21st Street
New York, NY 10010

Contents

Preface

Color and vision are inseparable. What we see is composed of colors, though the question "what is color?" yields inconclusive answers. The study of color is not an academic discipline in its own right, and many disciplines claim pieces of it. Physics owns the question of how color is caused, leaving to philosophy and psychology inquiry about whether color is chimerical and how we interpret what we see. The relationship between color and form is touched on in the philosophy of design. Geometry tells us what forms are and hints at what color is not.

The issue of beauty or harmoniousness in color combinations, and whether the terms can be defined, are addressed in the writings of artists and the literature of art education. These questions also involve disciplines as diverse as aesthetics and colorimetry.

We learn from the biological sciences that the colors of living organisms are functional, that life on earth would be different if the chlorophyll of plants was not green, if human blood was not red. Astronomy and cosmology, growing ever closer to particle physics, consider what the colors of the stars and sky suggest about the origin of the universe and about the origin of colors.

The social sciences offer theories about color names, about the relationship between the experiences of seeing color and the words used to describe what we see. Clues to the early history of human ideas about color are also revealed by the etymology of key color terms, the history of what these terms have meant and their cognates—words from which they may have been derived.

Finding the means to combine the theories

of these diverse disciplines is less the task of Sisyphus than that of Isis, collecting the fragments of the corpse of Osiris so that they could be reassembled and brought back to life. Who could be qualified for such a task? Nobody—or anybody, because we all know what we see.

Those who have contributed to our understanding of color or wrote at length about it represent these different disciplines. Robert Boyle and Sir Isaac Newton regarded themselves as natural philosophers, though we call them physicists. Johann Wolfgang von Goethe was a poet. Thomas Young was a physician. M.E. Chevreul was a chemist who served for a time as the director of a dye factory. William Ewart Gladstone was Queen Victoria's prime minister. Albert H. Munsell was an art educator. Wilhelm Ostwald, who shared Munsell's hope of simplifying the use of color for industry, began a second career as a color theorist after retiring as a professor of physical chemistry.

Those interested in color should read Vincent van Gogh's letters, Eugène Delacroix's journals, and the many statements and manifestos by painters that point a way to new understandings. The literature of color, or of popular beliefs about color, also includes the writings of Ludwig Wittgenstein, Dante, T.S. Eliot, and virtually any author who often refers to color or shares ideas about colors in the course of discussing another subject.

Nobody looks at color with what used to be called the innocent eye. To look without preconceptions is impossible. Color is something we see, but we adjust our thoughts about it to conform to traditional and very ancient beliefs passed from one generation to the next. We recognize these popular ideas about color, woven into the reasoning of the theorists as into our own. But familiar ideas are not necessarily good ideas, about to bear scrutiny.

If the literature of color is a collection of fragments, can the fragments be fit together to make sense? One conception of truth relies on the metaphor of the montage, derived from cinematography. By this reasoning, each discipline regards color from its own point of view, beginning from its own premises. Truth is approached by imagining the several points of view laid atop one another like a montage; the inquirer looks into the heart of the matter through the layers of the montage. Thus, color is in one sense what the physicist tells us. In other senses, it is what artists, philosophers, psychologists, and workers in other areas say. In total, color is to be understood as an aggregate of all the points of view about it.

I find this manner of reasoning more confusing than helpful. Color is a singular phenomenon. If it is to be chopped into pieces called points of view, the points of view must be consistent within themselves and consistent with one another. The pieces of the jigsaw puzzle must fit together. We cannot assume that all points of view are equal or that they all meet the tests of logical consistency and consistency with what we see.

Color is a visual phenomenon. As a society, we need to sharpen our skills at visual thinking, at reasoning about what we see in an intelligent manner. Artists are trained to think in visual terms, but the skill is too important to be taught just to artists. In this post-humanist age, we need to become seriously interested in understanding what we see, an endeavor more noble, necessary, and interesting than understanding who we are.

In this book I attempt to make sense of familiar theories about color. I originally meant to show only that discarding worn, meaningless, or literary ideas could lay a foundation for newer, better ideas that were genuinely visual. I think I have gone farther and suggested that visual thinking is a necessity, not a nicety.

PART ONE

Color and Language

If one says "Red" (the name of a color) and there are 50 people listening, it can be expected that there will be 50 reds in their minds. And one can be sure that all these reds will be very different.

Josef Albers, Interaction of Color

CHAPTER 1

Learning to Use Color Names

I know what colour is because I know red when I see it; I know what red is . . . . Of course the colour red is not the word "red."

R. Rhees, "Can There Be A Private Language?"

Aristotle rejected an argument by comparing it to the misguided reasoning of a "a man born blind arguing about colors" (*Physics* 2.1.11). Aristotle's simile draws its authority from the common knowledge that color is a visual experience. Persons who have never been able to see have access to color phenomena only indirectly. In theory, those not born blind can speak with authority: they could learn about colors because they could see them.

Whether the average person believes he or she has learned much about color is another matter. Individuals who say they understand the mysteries of, say, computers or macrobiotic cooking probably outnumber those willing to make the same claim about color. But the ubiquitous disclaimers cannot be taken at face value. Even people who say they know nothing about color know that colors are not sounds or smells.

A normal adult usually can provide a general name (for example, red, green, or brown) for any color. He or she recognizes finer variations, to which more esoteric cognomens are correctly or incorrectly applied (vermilion, viridian, mahogany). We assume anyone understands that no two colors look alike. Therefore, color coding is used on household appliances and industrial machinery. Instructions explain this coding by telling what to expect if a red light blinks and a green light does not. Or conditions are identified under which the blue lever ought to be pressed. Users are not expected to ask how to distinguish blue levers from yellow levers.

Everyone is supposed to know how to do that.

The aberrants, if any, who do not know, cannot depend on equipment manuals for help. Written descriptions cannot sufficiently clarify the differences people see between yellow and blue. If these perceptual differences could be translated into words without loss of anything essential, Aristotle's hypothetical blind person, and all others blind from birth, would have no difficulty understanding how blue levers differ from yellow ones.

People know more about color than they realize. How is the information acquired? As Bertrand Russell pointed out, human beings are taught to understand color names (a skill different from that of distinguishing colors) through *ostensive definition*, the process of teaching the meaning of a word without explaining it in terms of other words.[1] To teach color names, the learner is shown colors. An adult can point out blue objects to a child while repeating the word "blue." The child will eventually understand that the word refers to a class of related colors: the aggregate of all colors that might be called blue. More blues exist than those of the objects the adult uses as examples. If an intelligent child asks how many, the adult has no answer and may change the subject.

Ostensive definition cannot be the most primitive means through which children learn. It requires prior familiarity with at least five ideas. First, although perception is private, communicating about it is possible. Second, communicating differs from perceiving. Third, language is one of several tools for communicating. Fourth, pointing (as in pointing to a color) can have a purpose. Fifth, people attribute importance to purposes.

The child must additionally understand that objects have names, the circumstance that links the word *chair* with certain masses, tactilely apprehensible aggregates of corporeality in the external world. To be capable of ostensive learning of color names, the child must realize that objects have names and that certain relationships are explained in terms of negatives. Although an adult points to objects in showing colors, the names of colors should not be confused with those of colored objects. A blue chair is not correctly called a blue. Nor is blueness a physical part of the chair in the same sense as one of its legs.

A child who progresses to this point is prepared to acquire competence in use of the small group of commonplace words regarded as color names proper. The greater number of these names are monosyllabic: red, orange, yellow, green, blue, violet or purple, brown, white, black, gray, tan, pink, and so forth. Indigo might be included for its currency in Great Britain, although less often used in the United States. These words are the *primal color names*, or simply primals, the small group of descriptive terms with which everyone is familiar.

The word white (like the word night) is evidently of ancient etymological origin and cannot be traced to earlier words meaning anything different. Among the remaining primals, about half are derived from the names of objects characterized by distinctive colors. But yellow, brown, blue, black, and gray show complex etymological relationships.

Yellow, akin to a Sanskrit word meaning both yellowish and glowing, is also akin to an Old Irish word for white. Brown is akin to Old High Gothic *brun*, which means both brown and shining and is used in this manner in *Beowulf*. Blue and black are both related to *bael* (OE, fire). Blue is akin to a Latin word for yellow, and black to a Latin word for burning and a Sanskrit word for radiance.[2] Other primal color names derive from the names of objects: red, green, violet, pink, tan, purple, orange, indigo.

Red is from Sanskrit *rudhira*, blood. Green (Old English *grene*) derives from *growan*, to grow, a reference to green growing plants. Violet and pink are from names of flowers. Tan is from *tannum* (Middle Latin), the bark of oak trees crushed to make tannin. Purple is from *purpura*, Latin for purple fish or sea creature, a reference to the mollusk (*Purpura lapillus*) whose secretion was used to make Tyrian purple dye. Orange is from the Sanskrit *naranga*, for the fruit. Indigo comes from Greek *indikon*, literally, Indian, a reference to dye made in India from the Indigo plant (*Indigofera tinctoria*).

Color names borrowed from other languages may be used differently than in the original tongue. Cerulean, from the Latin name for dark blue, is used in English to identify blues that are greenish or turquoise (and not necessarily dark). Among synonyms for red, carmine and crimson can be traced to an Arabic word for crimson, thence to a Sanskrit term meaning produced by a worm, apparently a reference to a natural coloring matter. Cochineal, a color name with an etymologically similar derivation, refers to a dye made from the dried body of an insect (*Dactylopius coccus*) that lives on cacti in Central America.

Errors in use of the primal color names (for example, misidentifying green by calling it white) are exceedingly rare. Because of their brevity, these names lend themselves to forming compounds for describing intermediary colors. The compounds should not be overly long. Bluish green, along with such variants as blue green or blue-green, has a commonly understood meaning. Pinkish bluish brownish purplish white communicates less effectively, even as a name for a color mixed from pink, blue, brown, purple, and white.

A human being might live out his or her life making use of no color names beyond the primals. Dictionaries of color names illustrate, however, that thousands of others exist, often used for subtle intermediary colors. One tiny subset of nonprimal names identifies colors in terms of subjective effects they might have on viewers. *Shocking pink* is incomprehensible unless the term means that this variety of pink

shocks or startles. *Electric blue* similarly refers to an effect that somebody assumed was electrifying to observers.

Like about half of the primals, the largest group of nonprimal color names consists of terms derived from the names of objects, such as olive and avocado. Color names drawn from object names are abbreviated similes, and describing color through simile is the syntactical norm in some non-Indo-European languages. In the type of compression common in English, lengthy concatenations collapse to succinct alternates: "a color like that of Burgundy wine" becomes *burgundy* or *burgundy red*. When an object name inspires a color name, the definition of the color name is a simile. *Burgundy* is correctly defined as a color like that of Burgundy wine.

Colors are usually named after objects regarded as good examples of that color (figure 1-1). Occasionally the connection seems remote, in English as in other languages. W. H. R. Rivers, studying the Mabuiag of New Guinea, found "a great tendency to invent names for special colors." But he puzzled over why one native coined a name for a bright blue by comparing it to the color of water muddied from washing mangrove roots (Segall, Campbell, and Herskovits 1966, 42). This may be no more mystifying than why the English color name *magenta* is borrowed from the battle of Magenta (1859), at which the Austrians were put to rout by the French and the Sardinians.

To understand color names taken from object names, the prospective learner must master a further layer of syntactical convention. Colors are not objects, and color names are not the names of objects. But object names can acquire a secondary meaning as the names of colors. The color of a chair can be called olive, although a chair is not an olive. The subtlety of this proposition is beyond the grasp of a child too immature to realize that a single word can have more than one meaning or that what a word means may be contextual.

Fig. 1-1. Color names derived from object names.

alabaster	café-au-lait	curry	lavender	peach	sanguine[12]
almond	canteloupe	delphinium	lead	pearl	sapphire
amber	caramel	ebony	lemon	periwinkle	scarlet[13]
amethyst	cardinal	ecru[3]	lilac	persimmon	shrimp
apricot	carrot	eggplant	lily	pewter	sienna
aquamarine	cerise[5]	emerald	lime	pimento	silver
aureolin[1]	chalk	fawn	lobster	pink	slate
avocado	charcoal	flame	madder[8]	pistachio	smoke
azure[2]	chartreuse	flamingo	magenta	pitch	straw
banana	cherry	flesh	mahogany	plum	strawberry
beige[3]	chestnut	fuchsia	marigold	poppy	sulfur
bisque	chocolate	gamboge[6]	maroon[9]	porcelain	tangerine
blackberry	chutney	garnet	mauve	primrose	taupe[14]
blueberry	cinnamon	geranium	melon	puce[10]	teal
bone	citron	gold	mint	pumpkin	terra cotta
brandy	clay	grape	mole	purple[11]	toast
brass	coal	gunmetal	mulberry	raspberry	tobacco
brick	cochineal	heather	mustard	raven	tomato
bronze	cocoa	heliotrope[7]	oak	rose	turquoise
buckskin	coffee	henna	oatmeal	ruby	ultramarine
buff[4]	copper	hyacinth	olive	russet	umber[15]
burgundy	coral	ivory	orange	rust	violet
buttercup	cranberry	jade	orchid	saffron	walnut
butterscotch	cream	jet	palomino	salmon	watermelon
camel	currant	lapis lazuli	paprika	sand	

Notes: (1) from aureole (halo). (2) from Persian word for lapis lazuli. (3) refers to color of unbleached wool. (4) color of leather made from buffalo skins. (5) French word for cherry. (6) from the name Cambodia; refers to coloring matter made from the yellowish resin from a tree (*Garcinia hanburyi*) native to that locale. (7) plant name. (8) from a plant that produces dye of that color. (9) from French word for chestnut. (10) from French word for flea. (11) from the name of a mollusk from which purple dye was obtained in ancient times. (12) synonym for bloody. (13) from Persian word for a rich cloth. (14) from French word for mole. (15) from the region Umbria.

During the early twentieth century, proposals for simplifying and standardizing names of colors, in part for the convenience of industrial users, were put forth by Albert H. Munsell, Wilhelm Ostwald, and other color theorists. The systems generally eliminate color names drawn from the names of objects. Or, declining to dignify the matter by discussion, theorists proceeded as if words such as *lemon* and *olive* were not bona fide color names in the same sense as *red* and *brown* were. Yet real color names are neither more nor less than words people use to name colors. Few differences can be identified between the primal and nonprimal names, except that more complicated language conventions need to be mastered to understand the latter. References to objects are often references to certain parts of those objects only, or to the object under certain conditions.

Among miscellaneous examples, *ebony* is an allusion to the black wood of the ebony tree, not its green leaves. But *cherry* refers to the fruit of its tree. *Chestnut* means the brown of ripe chestnuts, not the green of those that are immature. *Olive* refers to green or brown olives, not those that are black. *Flame* means the red of a wood fire, not the blue flame of a gas stove. *Wine* usually means the color of red wine.

Tulip is rarely used as a color name; the flower exists in many colors. Yet *rose*, in both English and French, has acquired a widely familiar meaning as the color of, so to speak, rose-colored (or pink) roses, never those that are yellow or white. *Violet*, similarly, is the color of purple violets, although the flower can also be blue, yellow, or white.

Flowers provide some of the more esoteric examples of unusual associations. *Madder*, a color name used for paints (rose madder, madder lake), is not related to the yellow flowers of the madder plant. The allusion instead is to the red dye manufactured from the plant's root. *Saffron* is not the color of the saffron flower, a purple crocus. The word refers to the yellow-orange of the dried stigmas of the flower.

Color names borrowed from object names need not always allude to the color of the named object. In a subclass, the object cited is a geographical entity: a city, district, or nation associated with a particular color or colored pigment. Although sienna and Naples yellow are color names derived from names of artists' pigments, each of the pigments is named after a place (respectively, Siena, Naples) once noted for its manufacture.

A variant linkage between color name and geographical name turns on allusion to artifacts and works of art from the indicated locale. *Chinese red* points to the reds in Chinese lacquer work; *Pompeiian red*, to the red backgrounds of wall paintings at the Villa of the Mysteries, the Villa Boscoreale, and a few other Roman houses at Pompeii. In an alternate that cites the name of an artist rather than that of a place where works of art were created, *Raphael blue* is the color of Mary's robe in several of Raphael's paintings of the Madonna and Child. Color names that allude to works of art bear a time stamp, because they cannot be of earlier vintage than the art to which they refer. The color called Raphael blue must have been known by some other name to Raphael's predecessors.

Human beings can learn to use a word in a conventional manner without knowing its derivation. Umber is understandable as a name for dark brown, even for those uninformed about either the central Italian district of

Umbria or the etymological linkage between the place name and the color name. Similarly, those who know nothing about the art of China, Pompeii, or Raphael can learn the conventions for use of *Chinese red, Pompeiian red,* and *Raphael blue.*

The rules by which color names are derived from object names are complex and intersect with rules for the use of adjectives and nouns. The English language includes two groups of compound words that couple the name of a color with that of an object. Sequence functions as a determinant. If the color name follows the object name, the compound is a color name (sky blue, grass green, midnight black, blood red, lemon yellow). Although exceptions can be cited (see below), usually no compound is a color name if the order is reversed, as in redbird, bluebird, blackbird, whitefish, goldfish, and bluegrass.

Sky blue is a color name, although *blue sky* is not. *Sky blue* is not synonymous with *blue*; it names a narrower range. *Grass green* is the name of a type of green, although *bluegrass* is the name of a type of grass. Within the framework of existing convention, *bluegrass*, although a type of grass, could reasonably acquire an additional meaning as the name of a color resembling that of bluegrass. Red lead, identified as a color name in color-name dictionaries, was evidently the name of a substance (red oxide of lead, Pb_3O_4) before being adapted as the name of a color.

Although colors are often named after objects, objects are rarely named after colors *Rouge* (the cosmetic) is from the French word for red, a borrowing that has acquired new meaning in passing from one language to another. In the dubious argument of the painter and color theorist Moses Harris (1731–85), "the word orange seems indeed as if the colour took its name from the fruit, but the fruit took its name from the colour, for the proper name of the fruit is the orange citron" (Harris [1766] 1963, 8). If *orange* is a contraction of orange citron, then strictly speaking the fruit is not named after the color. And *orange* is generally fruit before color. *Naranja* (Spanish) seems to allude to the shape (rather than color) of oranges, because the word can also mean a cannonball of the same size as an orange.

People, or groups of them, are named after colors more often than are other objects. Examples, however, are infrequent. The name of the Hindu deity Krishna comes from the Sanskrit word for black. In English, Black, Brown, Green, Gray, and White, along with such variant spellings as Browne, Greene, and Grey, are commonplace family names. Pink, yellow, purple, and orange (although Holland has its House of Orange) are almost never used for this purpose. Red, a common nickname for those with auburn hair, is rarely a given name or surname.

Among groups larger than family units, race (described by anthropologists as if it were an extension of family, clan, or tribe) provides the most striking example in which the names of objects (of groups of humans) are borrowed from those of colors. Like the practice of adopting color names for family names, that of imagining humanity as a whole subdivided into black, brown, red, white, and yellow race exists on a nebulous borderline between naming and coding. In medicine, a few pathologies named after colors refer to abnormal hues seen in the human body in those conditions, usually in the skin. Among examples, *jaundice* comes from the French word for yellow, and *cyanosis*, which describes the blueness of "blue babies," is from *kyanosis*, a Greek word for dark blue.

Although rarely named after colors, objects are often either coded or symbolized by means of colors or color names. The usage can be arbitrary, in the sense that the color need not reveal anything about the object. For example, red is assigned a value of 2 and white has a value of 9 in the colored bands used to code

Figure 1-2. Color coding used to indicate the ohmic value of carbon resistors (resistance given in ohms). Four colored bands encircle the resistor. The two near the end indicate the first two digits of the ohmic value. The third indicates the number of zeros to add to these digits. The fourth indicates the tolerance. (After Donald E. Herrington, *How to Read Schematic Diagrams* (New York: Bobbs Merrill, 1962) p. 23.)

Color	Digit	Multiplier	Tolerance (+ or −)
Black	0	1.00	20.00%
Brown	1	10.00	1.00%
Red	2	100.00	2.00%
Orange	3	1000.00	3.00%
Yellow	4	10000.00	GMV
Green	5	100000.00	5.00%
Blue	6	1000000.00	6.00%
Violet	7	10000000.00	12.50%
Gray	8	.011	30.00%
White	9	.101	10.00%
Gold		.102	5.00%
Silver		.012	10.00%
No color			20.00%

the ohmic value of carbon resistors (figure 1-2). Because colors have no correlation with numbers or ohms, the coding could easily have been reversed.

Theories about the origin of color names, like those about the origin of mathematics, are schematic and conjectural. The most familiar proposes two historical stages in the development of color vocabularies. Among primitive peoples, the color of an object is said to be described by comparing it to that of another object of similar color, adopted as the implied norm. Green items, say, are identified as the color of (green) leaves. In a later development, human beings coin color names that are abstract, that do not refer to objects.

As Segall, Campbell, and Herskovits have pointed out (1966, 40), for Grant Allen and other nineteenth-century theorists "color terms develop first where color distinguishes among objects that are otherwise similar. Where colors and objects go together uniformly, the object name suffices. The availability of pigments and dyes facilitates the development of abstract color words that are applicable to the color no matter upon what object it is found. Color terms are initially metaphorical extensions of what are originally object names, or else of pigment and dye names.

Variations of these theories persist, because identifying colors by simile has been shown to be common among primitive peoples. That the practice itself is primitive is unlikely. In the English language, our largest group of color names consists of condensed or abbreviated similes. Describing a color as ''like (green) leaves'' is not significantly different from identifying the colors of objects by those words listed in figure 1-1. Each names a color but also (because simile is implied) an object available as an example of the color. Use of simile is more than just commonplace in naming colors in English. It remains the standard means of inventing color names, as ubiquitous as jargon, as irrepressible as graffiti.

Many of our comparisons are of recent vintage. *Electric blue*, as a color name, cannot predate the term *electricity*. *Fire engine red*, *tomato red*, and *tobacco brown* are similarly time stamped. So is *pistachio*, which refers to the color of pistachio ice cream, not pistachio nuts.

Avocado became popular as a color name, particularly among American manufacturers of kitchen appliances, during the period when this tropical fruit acquired wide commercial distribution. Avocado is not used as a color name for office furniture, and innovative color names are more common in industries in which changing fashion is a factor. Writers of advertising copy for department stores can be expected to tantalize prospective customers in coming decades with such stylish offerings as bath towels of intergalactic blue and underwear of astronaut green. Whatever criticism might be made about such coinages, people will understand what they mean.

Use of simile in naming colors is not unusual in English. The form is sophisticated for its purpose, rather than primitive. Beyond

this, nineteenth-century analyses are questionable on two points. First, it cannot be true that color names originally developed to permit a distinction to be made between objects alike in form but different in color. If that were the case, there would never have been a need to identify grass as green: no item exists that looks exactly like grass except that it happens to be purple, red, orange, or blue.

Second, the etymological record does not support the conjecture that the earliest color names referred to objects while more modern names are abstract. A better argument can be made that the circumstances are the reverse. As noted earlier, the color names blue, yellow, white, black, and brown are of such ancient etymological origin that they cannot be traced to earlier words that have any other meaning. Later color names, which unvaryingly point to objects, are abstract only in the limited sense that they can be shown to be extrapolations from (or abstractions based on) the names of objects.

Early theorists might have considered such color names as *red, green*, and *maroon* unconnected to objects, hence abstract. But the disjunction is nominal. Each of these words comes from the name of an object, though in a language other than English. Because borrowing color names from object names is so common, uncertainty surrounds even *blue, yellow, white, black, gray,* and *brown*. Although these six names cannot be shown to be derivatives from object names, this is insufficient evidence that they are not. Their origins may be lost in antiquity.

During the past 150 years, advances in pigment and dye technology set a course for modern art and revolutionized public taste. The catalyst was an English teenager, William Henry Perkin (1838–1907), who in 1856 synthesized mauve from coal tar, evidently in an inspired blunder. The dye-making technology based on Perkin's discovery swept the world. Even before the first exhibition of Impressionist painting, Navaho rug weavers were using the aniline dyes synthesized in chemical laboratories. Traditional vegetable dyes were put aside because their colors were less bright.

The commercial success of aniline dyes may have led Grant Allen, whose *Colour-Sense* was published in 1879, to overestimate both the historic importance and the modernity of dyeing and coloring processes. From the Paleolithic painters onward, every human society known has used staining or coloring materials. We cannot reasonably ask whether a society without pigments or dyes would be more likely to identify colors by pointing to objects. The question is whether such a society exists or has ever existed.

Staining and coloring with found or manufactured materials is a primitive impulse in the life of the individual, as in that of the human race. Smearing of feces by children, investigated in the psychoanalytic literature, provides an early experience in changing the color of a surface by applying colored material to it. It also provides experience in use of the human (or primate) hand to manipulate objects. The attention of modern children is redirected to wax crayons and coloring books. Paper is provided, to which children—but also chimpanzees—enjoy applying paint. A later improvement of motor skills allows children to be taught writing, a specialized form of applying color to a surface.

Bertrand Russell suggested that the more ordinary color names, such as *red*, can only be learned ostensively, but "the less common ones, such as vermilion, may be described by their similarities and differences" (Russell 1948, 69). If vermilion is called a fiery red, the description, although ambiguous, conveys some information to anyone who has seen red. Theoretically, the learning process could proceed in reverse order, with common names taught by reference to those that are unusual. If a person is familiar with vermilion, red can be described as either a color of the same type as vermilion but not always so fiery, or the color class to which vermilion belongs.

Sensibility to color depends on vision before vocabulary. Recognizing a color without knowing a particular, rather than generic, name for it is a common, annoying experience. It causes little practical difficulty. Magenta pieces of paper can be sorted from vermilion ones, even by persons who never knew, or cannot remember, the words *magenta* and *vermilion*. Awareness that vermilion is a type of red is not enough to enable a person to determine which of several red color chips is vermilion. And an observer who believes that a certain object is vermilion may find that not everyone agrees. The red in question, others may say, is not fiery enough to be called vermilion.

A child requires considerable sophistication to understand these everyday mysteries. Color names are applied according to visual criteria. But people often disagree about application of the criteria. The child, if able to grasp this final subtlety, will have come a long way since the day someone pointed to a chair and pronounced the word "blue."

CHAPTER 2

Color as a Continuum

Looked at from the point of view of an individual thinker, the act of naming is the first step in knowledge. At the very beginning of modern logic, Thomas Hobbes rightly said: "Reason is attained by industry, first in apt imposing of names."

Daniel Sommer Robinson, The Principles of Reasoning

Color is a continuum because it forms the fabric of visual homogeneousness: of the uninterrupted expanse of what I see. In a more immediate sense, color is a continuum because any two colors are separated by a range of intermediary colors (figure 2-1). The number of these intermediaries may be infinite if the color continuum is analogous to the number continuum and we follow the reasoning of the mathematician Georg Cantor (1845–1918). Because the number of fractions between any two consecutive integers is infinite, Cantor's work implies that the number series has neither a beginning nor an end. For anyone who imagines making a tally of every color variation, the model is serendipitously apt. The question is not whether the job of counting all the colors in the world could be completed, but how anyone could find a way to begin.

In practice, the fineness of the intermediary ranges in the color continuum is limited by human perception. The constraint is acknowledged in those colorimetric studies that propose the minimum unit of a just-noticeable difference (just noticeable to human beings) between two nearly alike colors. The possibility cannot be ruled out that a race with more exquisite visual acuity would see differences between two reds that all human beings believe are alike.

Precisely because a just-noticeable difference is relative to an observer, people vary in ability to discriminate within the color continuum. Some individuals are better than others at deciding whether colors are identi-

Figure 2-1. Color as a continuum. The Munsell solid arranges colors according to the parameters of hue, value, and chroma.

Green		
	Extremely	Greenish Blue-green
	Very	Greenish Blue-green
		Greenish Blue-green
		Blue Green
		Green blue
		Bluish Green-Blue
	Very	Bluish Green-Blue
	Extremely	Bluish Green-Blue
Blue		

cal. The skill is partly innate, partly acquired, partly dependent on temperamental factors: on whether the observer has the confidence to make a careful evaluation and to express a considered judgment.

The ability to recognize that red is not blue, virtually universal among those of normal vision and comprehension, implies the further understanding that differences among colors can be regarded as quantitative. Relying on a mathematical metaphor that may not be appropriate, color difference can impress an observer as either great or small. Some colors match, others almost do, still others bear little resemblance to one another.

Among many similarities between the color continuum and the number continuum, the name of each is a coinage of convenience for an entity we cannot locate. Like the idea of number as a continuum, the idea of the many shades of color organized in a hierarchy is a mental construction. It develops from the everyday recognition that an unknown number of colors lies chromatically "between" other colors, an encounter with that which exceeds measure. Just as the number series continues forever and the sky has no discernible edges, the number of shades of bluish green between blue and green is indeterminable.

Names and the Continuousness of Color

Naming the other living creatures is the first task Adam performed in the Garden of Eden. Although presented in the biblical story (Gen. 2:19) as a gesture of dominion, the more immediate purpose of naming is to facilitate talking about the entities to which names have been given. The Bible offers no clue about how Adam decided which names to use. His descendants apply names according to what is perceived as discrete. *Horse* and *cow* are different names because a horse is not a cow. Nor does one animal blend into the other, except in the mystical sense that the universe can be regarded as a unified whole.

The key problem in naming members of a continuum is that there may be no members that can be separated from the whole. Nor does language offer a mechanism that allows names to blend into one another, as the individual colors blend in the color continuum. The familiar expedient is to pretend, to defer to utility by talking as if we could divide the unity of a continuum into multiplicities.

If a society is to develop a workable system of color names, the arbitrary points at which the color continuum is to be "cut" (or imagined as segmented) must be determined as exactly as possible. To avoid tempting everyone to form his or her own opinion about whether blue and red are different colors, the determination is best sustained through consensus. Consensus is also required on the rules for matching segments with names. Should blue be called *blue*? Or should it be called *yellow*?

Everyday experience teaches that these tasks are difficult to accomplish, or we quickly arrive at an impasse from which logic cannot extricate us. Two observers may agree that one color is blue and another is green. Even beginning from, so to speak, the same premises, they may not agree on the name for a third color "between" the first two. What one observer calls *bluish green*, another may insist is *greenish blue*.

Absence of agreement reflects uncertainty about naming, rather than about sorting colors. Viewers who differ about whether to call a color *greenish blue* or *bluish green* usually will not disagree about how to arrange blue-green color chips in a row according to relative degree of blueness or greenness. What can be seen in looking at color has a simplicity without correspondence in language. We understand what we see, but search for words to explain what is understood.

Whether a shade of color is greenish blue (by implication, a type of blue), or bluish green (a type of green) cannot be settled by determining the point at which the blue segment of the color continuum ends and the green begins. Beginnings and endings within the continuum are located where people want to place them. A more subtle constraint is that because temporality (the passing of time) is implied, the color continuum has no point at which, in any physical or experiential sense, color stops belonging to the class blue and begins belonging to the class green.

Language consists of a series of little boxes called words. Color is not a series of little boxes. Language and color match up poorly, which is why color names are usually regarded as ambiguous, often frustrating to use and difficult to understand. Among a few dissenting voices, the philosopher Rudolph Carnap contended that color names are not difficult to use, communicate with more than usual effectiveness, and function as reasonably unequivocal descriptive devices.

Carnap argued that language is an abstraction and that two types of language exist. The first, an incomplete code, cannot convey com-

prehensive information about objects. Carnap mentioned, as an example, a black-and-white photograph of city buildings, incomplete in failing to record the colors of the buildings. Color names illustrate the more successful type of language, conveying complete information. If you hear the word *blue*, Carnap pointed out, "you immediately imagine blue" (Carnap 1966, 114).

Carnap's argument raises the question of whether blue is a clearly defined entity. Can we visualize the color by, in a manner of speaking, translating it into a mental picture? I prefer more limited assumptions. On hearing the word *blue*, the listener understands that the term is a generic name for a class of colors, the class containing many individual shades of blue. In Russell's reminder of the truism, these "many shades [have] different names; there is navy blue, aquamarine, peacock blue, and so on" (Russell 1948, 126).

Because the number of shades of blue is indeterminable, the question is how to imagine all of them at the same time, an existentially absurd endeavor. Relying on the familiar manner in which dictionaries define blue, a set of instructions for imagining every blue might advise imagining one portion of the spectral continuum or hue continuum: the range of colors in the rainbow running from those blues that are most green to those that are most purple.

The simplicity of the prescription is treacherous. Every blue includes a greater number than those of the solar spectrum, because the spectral continuum fails to span all dimensions of the color continuum. Variation can be found among blues beyond whether they tend toward green or toward purple, their immediate spectral neighbors. Blues can vary according to whether light or dark, bright or muted, matte or shiny.

The color solid developed by the American

painter and educator Albert H. Munsell is a three-dimensional construction (other color solids have come from other theorists). Its purpose is to provide a model for relationships within the color continuum (figure 2-2). The Munsell solid arrays color samples according to hue, value, and chroma. Hue is "that quality by which we distinguish one *color family from another*, as red from yellow, or green from blue or purple." Value is "that quality by which we distinguish a *light color from a dark one*. Color values are loosely called tints and shades, but these terms are frequently misapplied. A tint should be a light Value, and a shade a dark Value, but the word shade has become a general term for any type of color so that a shade of yellow may prove to be lighter than a tint of blue." Chroma refers to the strength of a color, "that quality of color by which we distinguish a strong color from a weak one; the degree of departure of a color sensation from that of white or gray; the intensity of a distinctive Hue; color intensity" (Munsell [1905] 1961, 15–16).

Like color atlases, which array graded color swatches in grids on multiple pages, the color solid implies a three-dimensional color continuum. Dimensions beyond three may exist, although we do not know how to incorporate a fourth or further spatial dimension into the model graphically. Colors, for example, can vary in shininess of surface. The Munsell system acknowledges this parameter but suggests no way to incorporate it into the three-dimensional color solid.

Despite the preferences of compilers of dictionaries, any three-dimensional color solid is superior to the hue continuum as a model of the color continuum. The challenge for prospective imaginers is to visualize the array of shades of blue as they appear in a model of this type. The blues lie on an infinity of colored planes arranged on three axes. We must picture the planes behind one another (as arranged in color solids) but also not behind

one another (to expedite seeing all of them at once).

Imagining cannot rise to the task because of the contradiction in terms. There is no such thing as a visual image of the concealed interior of an opaque solid (here, a color solid). Nobody could ever see such a thing or know what it would look like. The visual or visualizable has limitations, which is why we cannot imagine how nothing would look if it could be seen.

Proposing that we "imagine blue," Carnap refrained from conjecturing about what pictures might come to mind on hearing the word *color*. To direct an artist to take a canvas and color it "color" is meaningless. The task cannot be performed because, as the name of a genus or class, color has no direct visual or pictorial equivalent.

The color that corresponds to *blue* is as elusive as that corresponding to *color*, for similar reason. *Blue* is generic. It names a range of colors rather than an individual shade we can isolate with the eye or in the mind's eye. By encompassing every member of its class, *blue* fails to point to any particular blue. We cannot direct an artist to take a canvas and paint it (generic) blue, let alone with the further stipulations that the desired color be every blue but no particular blue. No object can be every member of its class yet at the same time no particular member.

The hypothetical artist might, at least theoretically, divide the canvas into compartments, color each a different shade of blue, and thereby include every blue. But every blue (which is what blue means) has no visual equivalent unless we can be certain about which colors are unambiguously blue. The greenish blues (which are blue) would have to be separated from the bluish greens (which are green). The purplish blues would have to be separated from the bluish purples, the whitish blues from the bluish whites, and so forth.

The task cannot be accomplished. Consensus would be required, and no consensus of any firmness is available. For this reason, it is beyond human capability to speak authoritatively to the question of how many colors, and which, are properly included under the rubric *every blue*. The term is experientially meaningless, a convenient fiction. The artist dividing the canvas into compartments, each to be colored a different blue, would have no way of determining how many compartments to provide.

I doubt we imagine blue according to any definition of that generic color that is more than nominal. Another way of understanding the trains of thought that occur when people hear color names is to assume that the mind wends its way into symbolism, the game of pursuing an elusive object by appropriating another object as its surrogate. Thus, a hypothetical listener hears "blue," a word recognized as the name of a color class. The class includes, as Russell has indicated, a large, but unknown, number of varieties of blue. The listener seeks a single blue to imagine (the thrust is toward specificity, not generalization), relying on context for clues. If the admiral wore a blue uniform and the sky was blue, the same blue cannot be meant in both cases. If the listener finds no pointer toward finer categories, he or she selects a single shade of blue that seems pure or typical, thus appropriate as a representative for the class. The barriers to imagining this single shade are less formidable than those to imagining blue in general.

A counterargument rests on the truism that a word can have more than one meaning. *Blue* can name a broad class of colors but also particular members of the class. Perhaps imagining any single shade *is* imagining blue, though in the particularized sense of the word. The appeal of the counterargument is that many people, unconcerned with fine distinction, habitually use the name *blue* for any variety of the color. The usage conforms to conventions similar to those that allow us to substitute generic terms for proper names as a form of address.

Among generic or class names people use when addressing one another, the more formal are called titles: Doctor, Professor, Madame President. Syntactically similar alternates are less socially acceptable. They range from the marginally discourteous ("Mister!") to the overtly hostile (racial, ethnic, and gender slurs). The class name, used as a surrogate for the proper name, is understood *not* to be the name of the individual being addressed. We all know that nobody's name is Madame President or Mister.

Names for individual shades of color are similarly acknowledged to differ from the generic name of the class. The individual questioned on why any and every blue is being called "blue" can reasonably be expected to confess awareness that specific names exist for particular blues. The likelihood is that the namer cannot recall them, is uncertain of how to apply them, or for some reason lacks interest in offering them. Everyone knows, or appears to agree, that words such as *blue* are generic, apply to broad classes of color, and are not the names of the individual members of their respective classes.

The expediency of using the class name for the individual member, with the proviso that it is understood to be "not really the proper name," sheds light on the survival, in English, of the enormous number of color names collected in specialized dictionaries. Some of the names are rarely used, and many people profess uncertainty about the meaning of others. Is peacock blue equivalent to dark cerulean? Does cerulean differ from turquoise? A large repertory of infrequently used color names is easy to dismiss as superfluous, a type of linguistic appendix with no identifiable utility.

I prefer to believe the body of names serves a purpose, because we realize it exists. By existing (or by being known to exist), it assumes the potential for satisfying the uniquely human requirement that every object of interest to human beings have a name. No parallel requirement exists that everyone know or use all the names. My not knowing the name of every human being or of every species of animal does not interfere with my conviction that it is appropriate for each to have one.

Names, including color names, can be operationally defined as a recognition of the discrete: an acknowledgment that an entity exists apart from or (more likely) in imagination can be extrapolated from the unity of everything in the universe other than itself.

CHAPTER 3

Understanding Color Names

And how important it is to know how to mix on the palette those colours which have no name and yet are the real foundation of everything.

Vincent van Gogh, *Complete Letters*

Carnap's argument in favor of the sufficiency of color names takes issue with the proverbial wisdom that any picture is worth a thousand words. In opposing blue and a photograph of buildings, he tells us a single word communicates more than a picture. A picture of buildings, whether monochrome or colored, communicates more information than the word *buildings*. A blue color swatch communicates information the color name does not convey. The swatch shows definitively, as words cannot, which variety of blue is meant.

When more than one person must interpret a color name, words alone cannot identify which color is intended. Color standardizing addresses problems that arise in industry as a result. To ensure, for instance, that the blue in all American flags is similar, manufacturers must agree on what blue means in this case. The agreement, which cannot be verbal, is formalized through the production of swatches: pieces of paper painted or printed in the color to be standardized. Visual comparison between swatch and object tests whether the blue of flags on the assembly line matches the necessary shade. The deaf can make this comparison as easily as can anyone else, even those born profoundly deaf who never have heard anyone pronounce "blue."

Visual comparisons are more accurate than those made by instruments (Evans 1948, 203) and facilitate color matching more effectively than any attempt to interpret statements that include color names. Consider the commercial requirements that vitamin C pills not be too yellow, or that gray file cabinets rolling off an assembly line match the color of those manufactured last year. Accomplishing these goals requires the use of swatches, because words cannot communicate sufficiently. How yellowish is too yellow? Showing, rather than telling, avoids misunderstanding.

In the manufacture of American flags, the assumption can be made that *thirteen* will mean the same thing to different persons at different times and places, but *blue* will not. We do not need standards to show how *thirteen* (as in thirteen stripes) should be interpreted. But we need them for *blue*. The codability of color names—their adequacy in conveying information about that to which they refer—is low compared to that of names and notations for numbers.

Efforts to achieve greater specificity, although of practical value, do not eliminate the problem. Colors properly called *dark cerulean blue* are not as numerous as those properly called *blue*. Dark cerulean blue, nonetheless, has a large number of subsets or varieties. Hundreds or thousands of colors are acceptably identified as *dark cerulean blue*, but the colors fail to match one another.

The codability of some color names is so low we cannot be certain they communicate (or cause the listener to imagine) anything. Few people conjure up a vivid mental picture on hearing ''fuscous.'' The additional information that fuscous is a standard color name used in ornithology would not be very helpful. Fuscous is a type of brown, displayed in a sample swatch in Frank M. Chapman's *Handbook of Birds of Eastern North America*. In describing the colors of the feathers of birds, ornithologists must not confuse fuscous with rufous, another variety of brown.

The limited usefulness in knowing that fuscous and rufous are both brown suggests a need to qualify Russell's assertion that children can be taught unusual color names by reference to those that are common. Because there are tens of thousands of browns, teaching the difference between rufous and fuscous can only be accomplished by showing the colors. Words do not convey enough information, or do not convey the right information. Ostensive definition is more than a technique by which children can be taught a basic vocabulary of color names. It is also the only adequate means of making fine discriminations between colors and communicating them among people. Color names are useful to the extent that they relieve human beings of the nuisance of carrying packages of color samples with them wherever they go.

Dictionaries of color names have been compiled and reveal a large repertory. Robert Ridgway, curator of the Department of Birds of the United States Museum, published a color dictionary in 1886 and an illustrated edition in 1912. It includes 1,113 painted color samples identified by name. Munsell notations have been published for the samples. The Maerz and Paul *Dictionary of Color* includes 4,000 color names keyed to 7,000 samples. The National Bureau of Standards has published *The Inter-Society Color Council Dictionary*, and European dictionaries have come from the British Colour Council, the Royal Horticultural Society, and the Sociéte Francaise des Chrysanthemistes.

Many of the names in color-name dictionaries are not widely familiar, used in a consistent manner, or often employed. If language attains highest utility when used with greatest economy (when every object has a name of its own and no object has two names), each name ought to apply to only one range of color. Reality falls short of this ideal. The twenty-four color names in the list below, all referring to varieties of red orange, are not synonyms; they identify more than one range of color. Nor are they names for twenty-four different ranges; overlaps occur in some cases. Without color samples, nobody would be able to explain what he or she regarded as the proper use of each name.

vermilion	Japanese red
carnelian	Spanish red
persimmon	Naples red
flame red	Mars red
red lead	scarlet
Egyptian red	cochineal
Pompeiian red	turkey red
Chinese red	red earth
crimson	Morocco red
poppy	Venetian red
lacquer red	Indian red
madder red	English red

Although the twenty-four names for varieties of orange-red do not all refer to the same shade, a given shade of color is sometimes known by dozens of popular names. *The Inter-Society Color Council Dictionary* lists sixty-nine for the range of color standardized as *moderate reddish orange* (ISCC-NBS color no. 37). More than a hundred are given for others (figure 3-1).

Inter-Society Color Council compilations reveal that *vermilion* is used, but not consistently, for the color range standardized as *moderate reddish orange* (color no. 37). Dissenters reserve *vermilion* for *strong reddish orange* (color no. 35), a more intense orange. The lack of consensus suggests data has been collected from members of the general public, who are often uncertain about how to use unusual color names. But the information in this case comes from color name dictionaries; the lack of agreement is that of authorities. In nontechnical dictionaries, lapses in cross-referencing of color words are common. The *American College Dictionary* identifies *henna*

Figure 3-1. Names for ISCC standard color no. 182 (moderate blue).
Sources: 1-72, Maerz and Paul (1930); 73-86, Plochere (1948); 87-105, Ridgway (1912); 106-19, Taylor, Knoche and Granville (1950); 120-25, Textile Color Card Association (1941).

1. air blue	26. diva blue	51. nikko	76. coronet blue	101. marine blue
2. Antwerp blue	27. Dresden blue	52. orient blue	77. cosmic blue	102. Orient blue
3. Armenian stone	28. Dumont's blue	53. pilot blue	78. cruise blue	103. oxide blue
4. Asmalte	29. Dutch azure	54. pompadour green	79. deep water	104. Prussian blue
5. blue de Lyons	30. empire blue	55. porcelain	80. Lake Como	105. Vanderpool's
6. blue ashes	31. enamel blue	56. powder blue	81. Lake Louise	106. bright cerulean
7. blue aster	32. English blue	57. queen blue	82. Neopolitan night	107. bright navy
8. bluebell	33. eschel blue	58. queen's blue	83. palace blue	108. cerulean blue
9. blue bice	34. flaxflower blue	59. Raphael	84. queen blue	109. Copen blue
10. bluebird	35. gentian	60. rapids	85. Riviera	110. dark blue
11. bluet	36. Harlem blue	61. resolute	86. theatrical blue	111. deep blue
12. blue ultramarine ash	37. Hungarian blue	62. royal blue	87. alizarine blue	112. deep cerulean
13. blue verditer	38. Infanta	63. Sander's blue	88. Antwerp blue	113. Delft blue
14. Britanny	39. jay blue	64. Saunder's blue	89. Blanc's stone	114. Della Robbia blue
15. cadet blue	40. king's blue	65. Saxony blue	90. cadet blue	115. Dutch blue
16. cathedral blue	41. Lambert's blue	66. smalt	91. Chapman's blue	116. lapis lazuli
17. celestial	42. laundry blue	67. smaltino	92. chessylite blue	117. medium blue
18. centre blue	43. lime blue	68. triumph blue	93. China blue	118. sky blue
19. ceramic	44. Limoges	69. Tuileries	94. Columbia blue	119. strong blue
20. chessylite blue	45. Madonna	70. virgin	95. dark cadet blue	120. bluebird
21. China blue	46. mineral blue	71. wireless	96. dusky greenish blue	121. hydrangea blue
22. cobalt glass	47. mosaic blue	72. zaffre blue	97. Eton blue	122. lustre blue
23. commelina blue	48. mountain blue	73. bohemian blue	98. gendarme blue	123. Majolica blue
24. copper blue	49. Murillo	74. ceramic	99. Hortense blue	124. old China
25. Daphne	50. national blue	75. classic blue	100. jay blue	125. Peking blue

as a name for a reddish orange dye. An entry for *henna* as a color name identifies it as reddish brown, leaving open the question of whether *henna* is the correct name for the color of articles dyed with henna.

Among manufacturers of artist's oil paints, no two use exactly the same color names or apply them to the same shades of color (figure 3-2). We must look at the paint in the tubes to find out whether Rembrandt's Chinese vermilion or its Dutch vermilion is more similar to Grumbacher's vermilion (Chinese). Winsor & Newton's cadmium yellow pale may or may not closely match Grumbacher's cadmium yellow light.

The National Bureau of Standards, which has an interest in industrial color standards, sponsored a study of color names in 1932. The immediate inspiration was that "E. N. Gathercoal, member of the U.S. Pharmacopoeial Revision Committee, protested the selection of color names used to describe chemicals and drugs . . . in particular, the term: 'blackish white' " (National Bureau of Standards n.d. *b*, 1). The case provides an example of failure to understand a compound color name, although its components were familiar.

Gathercoal knew, because everyone knows, what *white*, *black*, and the derivative *blackish* means. This did not explain blackish white to his satisfaction. Perhaps he thought of the colors as opposites, a condition that implies blackish white is a contradiction in terms. Or, unlike Carnap's hypothetical listener hearing the word *blue*, Gathercoal might have been unable to imagine anything upon encountering the color name *blackish white*.

As first chairman of the Inter-Society Color Council (ISCC), organized to facilitate exchange of information about color among industrial and scientific groups, Gathercoal supervised the preparation of what was to be an improved method of cataloging and naming colors. The National Bureau of Standards published the ISCC-NBS system in 1939, revis-

Figure 3-2. Color (pigment) names used by three manufacturers of artist's oil paints. Even among manufacturers of artist's oil paints, pigment names tend to be used loosely.

Name of Paint	1	2	3
alizarin crimson	x	x	x
alizarin crimson, golden	x		
alizarin carmine			x
aureolin		x	
brown madder	x	x	x
burnt umber	x	x	x
cadmium orange	x	x	
cadmium red		x	
cadmium red lightest	x		
cadmium red extra pale			x
cadmium red light	x		
cadmium red medium	x		
cadmium red deep	x	x	
cadmium red extra deep			x
cadmium lemon		x	
cadmium yellow light	x		
cadmium yellow pale		x	
cadmium yellow extra pale		x	
cadmium yellow medium	x	x	x
cadmium yellow deep	x	x	x
cadmium yellow orange			x
cadmium green		x	
cadmium green light		x	
cerulean blue	x	x	
cerulean			x
chromium oxide green	x		
oxide of chromium		x	
oxide of chrome mat			x
cambridge blue		x	
cambridge green		x	
cambridge red		x	
cambridge violet		x	
cambridge yellow		x	
cobalt blue		x	
cobalt blue light	x		x
cobalt blue deep	x		x
cobalt rose	x		
cobalt violet light	x		x
cobalt violet deep	x		x
cobalt violet dark		x	
cobalt green deep			x
cobalt green light		x	x
chrome yellow deep			x
chrome yellow lemon			x
chrome yellow light			x
Chinese vermilion			x
vermilion Chinese	x		
Dutch vermilion			x

1 = Grumbacher
2 = Winsor & Newton
3 = Rembrandt

ing it to its present form a decade later. Among criteria, Gathercoal aimed for a system "sufficiently commonplace to be understood, in a

Figure 3-3. Names of the 267 major color classes in the ISCC-NBS method of designating colors.

1. vivid pink
2. strong pink
3. deep pink
4. light pink
5. moderate pink
6. dark pink
7. pale pink
8. grayish pink
9. pinkish white
10. pinkish gray
11. vivid red
12. strong red
13. deep red
14. very deep red
15. moderate red
16. dark red
17. very dark red
18. light grayish red
19. grayish red
20. dark grayish red
21. blackish red
22. reddish gray
23. dark reddish gray
24. reddish black
25. vivid yellowish pink
26. strong yellowish pink
27. deep yellowish pink
28. light yellowish pink
29. moderate yellowish pink
30. dark yellowish pink
31. pale yellowish pink
32. grayish yellowish pink
33. brownish pink
34. vivid reddish orange
35. brilliant reddish orange
36. deep reddish orange
37. moderate reddish orange
38. dark reddish orange
39. grayish reddish orange
40. strong reddish brown
41. deep reddish orange
42. light reddish brown
43. moderate reddish brown
44. dark reddish brown
45. light grayish reddish brown
46. grayish reddish brown
47. dark grayish reddish brown
48. vivid orange
49. brilliant orange
50. strong orange
51. deep orange
52. light orange
53. moderate orange
54. brownish orange
55. strong brown
56. deep brown
57. light brown
58. moderate brown
59. dark brown
60. light grayish brown
61. grayish brown
62. dark grayish brown
63. light brownish gray
64. brownish gray
65. brownish black
66. vivid orange yellow
67. brilliant orange yellow

68. strong orange yellow
69. deep orange yellow
70. light orange yellow
71. moderate orange yellow
72. dark orange yellow
73. pale orange yellow
74. strong yellowish brown
75. deep yellowish brown
76. light yellowish brown
77. moderate yellowish brown
78. dark yellowish brown
79. light yellowish brown
80. grayish yellowish brown
81. dark grayish yellowish brown
82. vivid yellow
83. brilliant yellow
84. strong yellow
85. deep yellow
86. light yellow
87. moderate yellow
88. dark yellow
89. pale yellow
90. grayish yellow
91. dark grayish yellow
92. yellowish white
93. yellowish gray
94. light olive brown
95. moderate olive brown
96. dark olive brown
97. vivid greenish yellow
98. brilliant greenish yellow
99. strong greenish yellow
100. deep greenish yellow
101. light greenish yellow
102. moderate greenish yellow
103. dark greenish yellow
104. pale greenish yellow
105. grayish greenish yellow
106. light olive
107. moderate olive
108. dark olive
109. light grayish olive
110. grayish olive
111. dark grayish olive
112. light olive gray
113. olive gray
114. olive black
115. vivid yellow-green
116. brilliant yellow-green
117. strong yellow-green
118. deep yellow-green
119. light yellow-green
120. moderate yellow-green
121. pale yellow-green
122. grayish yellow-green
123. strong olive green
124. deep olive green
125. moderate olive green
126. dark olive green
127. grayish olive green
128. dark grayish olive green
129. vivid yellowish green
130. brilliant yellowish green
131. strong yellowish green
132. deep yellowish green
133. very deep yellowish green
134. very light yellowish green

135. light yellowish green
136. moderate yellowish
137. dark yellowish green
138. very dark yellowish green
139. vivid green
140. brilliant green
141. strong green
142. deep green
143. very light green
144. light green
145. moderate green
146. dark green
147. very dark green
148. very pale green
149. pale green
150. grayish green
151. dark grayish green
152. blackish green
153. greenish white
154. light greenish gray
155. greenish gray
156. dark greenish gray
157. greenish black
158. vivid bluish green
159. brilliant bluish green
160. strong bluish green
161. deep bluish green
162. very light bluish green
163. light bluish green
164. moderate bluish green
165. dark bluish green
166. very dark bluish green
167. vivid greenish blue
168. brilliant greenish blue
169. strong greenish blue
170. deep greenish blue
171. very light greenish blue
172. light greenish blue
173. moderate greenish blue
174. dark greenish blue
175. very dark greenish blue
176. vivid blue
177. brilliant blue
178. strong blue
179. deep blue
180. very light blue
181. light blue
182. moderate blue
183. dark blue
184. very pale blue
185. pale blue
186. grayish blue
187. dark grayish blue
188. blackish blue
189. bluish white
190. light bluish gray
191. bluish gray
192. light bluish gray
193. bluish black
194. vivid purplish blue
195. brilliant purplish blue
196. strong purplish blue
197. deep purplish blue
198. very light purplish blue
199. light purplish blue
200. moderate purplish blue
201. dark purplish blue

202. very pale purplish blue
203. pale purplish blue
204. grayish purplish blue
205. vivid violet
206. brilliant violet
207. strong violet
208. deep violet
209. very light violet
210. light violet
211. moderate violet
212. dark violet
213. very pale violet
214. pale violet
215. grayish violet
216. vivid purple
217. brilliant purple
218. strong purple
219. deep purple
220. very deep purple
221. very light purple
222. light purple
223. moderate purple
224. dark purple
225. very dark purple
226. very pale purple
227. pale purple
228. grayish purple
229. dark grayish purple
230. blackish purple
231. purplish white
232. light purplish gray
233. purplish gray
234. dark purplish gray
235. purplish black
236. vivid reddish purple
237. strong reddish purple
238. deep reddish purple
239. very deep reddish purple
240. light reddish purple
241. moderate reddish purple
242. dark reddish purple
243. very dark reddish purple
244. pale reddish purple
245. grayish reddish purple
246. brilliant purplish pink
247. strong purplish pink
248. deep purplish pink
249. light purplish pink
250. moderate purplish pink
251. dark purplish pink
252. pale purplish pink
253. grayish purplish pink
254. vivid purplish red
255. strong purplish red
256. deep purplish red
257. very deep purplish red
258. moderate purplish red
259. dark purplish red
260. very dark purplish red
261. light grayish purplish red
262. grayish purplish red
263. white
264. light gray
265. medium gray
266. dark gray
267. black

general way, by the whole public'' (National Bureau of Standards n.d. *a*, 1). The ISCC-NBS system is intended to be sufficient for the task of cataloging ten million colors, computed to be the number that the unaided human eye can differentiate.

The system identifies 267 major classes of color, each of which has a name (figure 3-3). Numbers indicate distinctions within a class, a necessary device because ten million names are not available. In response to Gathercoal's rallying cry, the offending *blackish white* has gone its way. *Blackish red, reddish black*, and other relatives escaped the purge. The project had no consulting epistemologist who might have inquired what *-ish* contributes when appended to a color name, as in reddish, blackish, or pinkish.

Larger in scale than other similar endeavors, the ISCC system illustrates the range of problems arbiters encounter in selecting appropriate names for colors. Despite Gathercoal's call for clarity, the names are among the project's lesser triumphs. As has been consistent among modern systems for simplifying color naming, nonprimal names derived from object names were eliminated, with the exception of olive in this case. Less typically, the ISCC abandoned use of the more popular primals, such as *red, blue*, or *brown*, as single names for major classes of color. All subvarieties, except black and white, are identified by compound terms in which the primals are supplemented by adverbs and adjectives. Figure 3-4 lists the hierarchy of qualifiers developed by Deane B. Judd.

The ISCC favored constructions such as *grayish yellowish pink* (color no. 32), intended as a replacement for color names such as *salmon* or *bisque*. Which is superior is debatable. People usually recognize the subset of color to which salmon applies, having learned to recognize it from seeing the fresh, canned, or smoked fish in restaurants, fish stores, supermarkets, and delicatessens. *Grayish yellowish pink* is a less accessible commodity: the ISCC color can be seen only by obtaining the appropriate color swatches. The question is less whether the public can understand the ISCC-NBS system than how the system can be useful to either specialists or non-specialists in its present form.

An apparent intention is to replace color names derived from object names (such as salmon) by compounds based on a minimal vocabulary. The ISCC stopped short of the extreme, and the method reduces easily *ad absurdem*. The system might consistently eliminate, say, gray and pink because these colors are not elemental, although the names are primal color names. Gray is a combination of black and white; pink, of red and white. *Grayish yellowish pink* reduces to *blackish whitish yellowish whitish red*, which, in theory, ought to mean the same thing. But color names do not necessarily communicate more effec-

Figure 3-4. System of modifiers for ISCC color names. (After Judd 1979, 219.)

very pale (very light, weak)	very light	very brilliant (very light, strong)	
pale (light, weak)	light	brilliant (light, strong)	
weak	moderate	strong	vivid (very strong)
dusky (dark, weak)	dark	deep (dark, strong)	
very dusky (very dark, weak)	very dark	very deep (very dark, strong)	

tively if compounded from a limited repertory of common terms. Understanding *moderate* and *blue* does not explain *moderate blue*.

Carnap's theorem of the fundamental intelligibility of color names falters when applied to the behemoth apparatus of the ISCC system. Not everyone imagines the intended color upon hearing *grayish yellowish pink*. The ISCC prudently took this into account by recommending that a sample of the color be exhibited, even to respondents familiar with gray, yellow, and pink. Exhibiting a large number of samples is more to the point. If ten million colors exist, each of the 267 ISCC classes, including *grayish yellowish pink*, includes on average thirty-five thousand discernible shades of that color.

Judd's system of modifiers for color names, incorporated into the ISCC system, relies on a hierarchical arrangement of ten words, any of which can be modified by *very: pale, light, brilliant, weak, moderate, strong, dusky, dark,* and *deep* (see figure 3-4). The words are simple (everyone uses them), but not necessarily useful for identifying colors. *Brilliant* and *vivid* are synonyms or nearly synonyms, as are *dark, dusky,* and *deep,* or *pale, light,* and *weak. Moderate* is poorly chosen in that the name *moderate blue* (color no. 182) implies that this variety of blue is only moderately blue. The intention might reasonably be to identify the range as moderately light, moderately dark, moderately greenish, moderately purplish, or moderately grayish. Possibly it is moderately something. It cannot, however, be moderately blue, an inconsistency in terms unless further explained.

Reliance on *very,* an unsatisfactory qualifier for a color name, is similarly problematic, as in differentiation between *pale violet* (color no. 214) and *very pale violet* (color no. 213). *Very* is devoid of objective meaning. My opinion of what constitutes *very* (as in *very nice*) can never exactly match yours.

A side effect of the preference for qualifiers is the length of many ISCC color names. *Light grayish purplish red* is spelled with twenty-three letters, three short of the length of the alphabet. A decade before the ISCC project was begun, T. S. Eliot caused muttering about pedantry by opening a poem titled "*The Hippopotamus*" with the elephantine *polyphiloprogenitive.* Even that infamously long word contains 13 percent fewer letters than *light grayish purplish red,* probably intended as a replacement for color names such as *mauve* or *taupe.*

By 1965 minor improvements to the ISCC-NBS system had provided what Kenneth L. Kelly proclaimed to be "the last missing link in our complete universal color language" (National Bureau of Standards n.d. *a,* 6). From the late nineteenth century onward, attempts to systematize the naming of colors have typically been introduced by the same announcement. The author or mover was galvanized upon confronting, in the morass of putatively unsatisfactory color names, one example that especially provoked ire (*blackish white*). This led to the revelation that the world, often the no-nonsense manufacturing world, was in need of a more rational method for naming colors. Never accomplished before, the task is now brought to fruition. The author is self-congratulatory, often with a lavishness more appropriate to discovery of an elixir for immortality.

One of the utilities of the systems is to teach that the fabled difficulties in naming colors are not so bad as we thought. To complain that *salmon* is vague is injudicious if the best available substitute is *grayish yellowish pink.* Whether to apply science (or what is dignified by that name) to the task of assigning names to colors is an insufficiently aired question. I can muster no enthusiasm for a rational color naming system if, without improvement in clarity, it purges language of the poetry of such names as *vermilion, viridian, cerulean,* and *turquoise.* Clear or not, these mellifluous words are a pleasure to use, as *grayish yellowish pink* is not. They guide us in the right direction, toward the love of color that inspires us to observe it and learn about it.

The portentous lengthiness of ISCC names is more than a sentimental issue. Color names, like all words, are used by including them in sentences. How is Homer's "rosy-fingered dawn" to be recast by those who believe that bureaucratic concatenations like *very light pale moderate reddish orange* are of greater utility than *rose*? A comparison of the ISCC system with that of Albert H. Munsell, its predecessor, suggests color cataloging systems have grown progressively more ponderous in the name of simplicity.

Munsell introduced his system in 1905, proclaiming that "COLOR ANARCHY IS REPLACED BY SYSTEMATIC COLOR DESCRIPTION" (Munsell [1905] 1961, 24). Munsell found intolerable the continued countenancing of such notations as *topazy yellow* and aimed to eliminate ambiguous color names. In contrast to the 267 major colors of the Inter-Society Color Council, Munsell's list has 10. He avoided qualifiers of the ilk of *very* and *moderate*. No suffixes trail like cabooses: *yellow green* is preferred to *yellowish green*.

A literature primarily by members of the Optical Society of America documents the permutations that led from the leanness of Munsell's familiar system to its more weighty, less widely known, successor.[1] In Germany, similar revisions of the Ostwald system led to DIN 6164 (May 1962), a color chart devised by Manfred Richter and used for German industrial color standards.

In the American system, the drove of appellatives derived from Munsell's terse *blue green* includes ISCC *vivid bluish green, strong bluish green, dark bluish green, very dark bluish green, moderate bluish green*, and so forth. Munsell, given his preference for brevity, might have wondered about them, or about whether a color name like ISCC *grayish yellowish pink* improved on the despised *topazy yellow*.

Putatively simplified color-naming systems share an oddity in common with Esperanto. None has been placed in wide usage, which suggests the claimed simplicity is suspect. Even the developers of the ISCC system find it unwieldy for expository use, as can be seen in the voluminous writings of Deane B. Judd (1900–72), president of the Munsell Color Foundation and associated for forty-three years with the colorimetric section of the National Bureau of Standards. Describing a scene the reader is to imagine, Judd identified its colors as *olive-drab, purple, green, blue, purplish-black, blue-green*, and *pale green* (Judd 1979, 485). Among these seven descriptive terms, only *pale green* (color no. 149) and unhyphenated *purplish black* (color no. 235) are bona fide ISCC-NBS color names.

The lack of user-friendliness in the ISCC-NBS system, and to a lesser extent in earlier systems by Munsell and Ostwald, derives in part from the wanton discarding of widely known traditional color names. Either *cerulean* or *turquoise* is a less ambiguous color name than *greenish blue*. *Vermilion* means more than *yellowish red* or *red orange*. The wholesale discarding of color names derived from object names (the largest class of popular names for colors) raises the question of why these names are viewed with distaste.

The most likely answer is that color names derived from object names are contracted similes, and high school English teachers deplore simile. Walt Whitman is said to have addressed notes to himself warning "avoid simile!" Metaphor is held to be preferable, evidently because simile implies pointing, a gesture to which aversion is widespread. Every infant is instructed not to point, as if doing so were either stupid or impolite.

Color, however, is the special case in which pointing (ostensive definition) is integral to adequate communication. Showing Chapman's color swatches for rufous and fuscous is the correct way to make clear the difference between the two browns. Not pointing to the samples is impractical. The niceties of etiquette run counter, in this instance, to the more consequential need for communication.

Although we are taught to regard simile as an inferior construction for such purposes as writing poetry, it supports a special logic in naming colors. The collapsed simile in any color name derived from an object name implies a hidden imperative that is, so to speak, to the point. *Lemon* as a color name means more than just a color like that of a lemon. It means the observer should look at a lemon if uncertain about the exact color. The name implies, in other words, the ostensive.

Color names drawn from object names are finely tuned to their purpose, because each is a reminder of where to look for a sample of the color. The nuance is sensed in folk wisdom. Although devalued as not real color names, words such as *eggshell, avocado,* and *turquoise* are commonly used and continue to survive.

The submerged imperative is rarely or never obeyed, in the sense that nobody goes to a jewelry store to examine coral necklaces if uncertain about what the color name *coral* means. What the hidden imperative acknowledges is less an immediate need to take action than the nature of color itself: of what is definitive in regard to it. We all know that ultimately the only way is to look.

Anyone unable to discover by other means what the color coral looks like could acquire the information by regarding a piece of coral as a color sample. The utility of the imperative in the simile is expressive, and it expresses what we know to be true. The bottom line for color is the need to look, at some point, in order to learn anything about it.

CHAPTER 4

The Limits of Language and the Logic of Color

We are up against trouble caused by our way of expression.
Ludwig Wittgenstein, The Blue and Brown Books

Language is used to report perceptual experience, and all languages are arbitrary or conventional. In what came to be called the Whorf-Sapir hypothesis, Benjamin Whorf and Edward Sapir argued that perception may be limited or controlled by the forms of language (Sapir 1921, 1949; Whorf [1956] 1967). A much-cited illustration tells us that the Eskimos have dozens of words used to describe types of snow. Because this must enable them to find, so to speak, more to say, Eskimos ought to be more sensitive to snow than others with more limited vocabularies.

I have never discussed snow with an Eskimo. Without prejudice to their knowledge of the topic, generalizing broadly along this line is unwise. That a language includes many words to describe a given phenomenon does not necessarily mean speakers will become refined in observation of that phenomenon. Thousands of color names exist in the English language. More limited vocabularies for identifying color are reported for some non-Indo-European tongues. No doubt we have many more names for colors than the Eskimos have for snow. This large repertory does not inspire speakers of English to become especially expressive on the topic of color or confident that they have much to say. Sensibility to color among the peoples of the world, judging from the use of color in their art, has no correlation with the number of color names in their individual languages.

To assess the effect of language, more has to be considered than gross numbers of words. We need to know how many speakers of the language know the words, how often the words are used, and how clear the meaning of each word is. The previous chapter contains a list of twenty-four common names for varieties of orange-red. Few people use more than two or three, because these words are ambiguous as color labels. No consensus exists, even among experts, about exactly which shades of orange-red ought to be called, say, *vermilion*. The lack of consensus reflects subjective elements built into all color names.

Vermilion originally meant a certain red pigment. Later, the name was applied to any color resembling that of the pigment. How close a resemblance is required is anyone's guess. *Pompeiian red*, another name for a variety of orange-red, must have been coined by somebody who visited the Villa of the Mysteries at Pompeii. A large fresco in that villa shows human figures against a red background that has faded since the villa was excavated. Pompeiian red means a red resembling—how closely?—the red of the fresco. For those who have never visited Pompeii or who never saw the red of the fresco before it faded, the color name means the red of the fresco as it appears in color reproductions in books, or the red of a swatch labeled *Pompeiian red*.

Speakers familiar with the etymology of the words might think of the pigment or the fresco when using *vermilion* or *Pompeiian red*. Many speakers of English do not know the history of these words. *Vermilion* means a color identified to them by that name or any similar color.

One effect of this vagueness of language is that exact shades of color are difficult to identify in words. Does this affect our perception of fine color differences? I think not. People understand the futility of describing a color as, say, a somewhat pale vermilion with a slightly blue-gray tinge. When an exact match for a color is important, color swatches or samples are used. People understand the problem and the visual solution. They sidestep the limita-

tions of language when dealing with color variations too subtle to translate into words.

Whether or not language directs perception, people use it to talk about color. Speakers of English can include color names in two classes of statements. The first refers to color only nominally. Although the word *color* and individual color names may be uttered, statements are being made about words or about rules of language. Consider the proposition that color is the name of a class containing particular colors, including black, green, red, and so forth. The assertion is not about color, but about how its name should be used. It conveys to the listener that the rules for the English language are violated if the word *color* is used to identify the class containing all chairs rather than that containing all colors.

Statements of the second type refer properly to color as an object of perception. They pertain to the viewer's visual experiences. The criterion for distinguishing between statements about language rules and statements about colors rests in the domain in which verification can be sought. If *color* is the name of the class that includes red and blue among its members and if these individual members are said to be colors, confirmation can be found by observing how people talk. A person asked to name colors is likely to mention green and yellow, but not tables or refrigerators.

A statement about color as object is verified by considering how colors look. The task requires that the observer monitor his or her perceptions. To test the assertion that black is darker than white, I look at the colors to determine whether this is how they appear to me. Because the domain of verification is visual, I pay little or no attention to what other people say. No statement can be verifiable in both domains at once, because no language rule is intended as a statement about objects or about human perceptions of them. Nor are statements of the second type conventional, even in instances where nearly everyone agrees.

That *black* refers to one color and *white* to another or that *dark* has a meaning is convention. For persons of normal eyesight and comprehension to report that black looks darker than white is not, properly speaking, convention, but rather, consensus. Convention changes when people develop new ideas about how to talk or behave. For consensus to change, people must acquire new beliefs about what they understand to be true.

A theory that language forms affect the forms of perception amounts to a proposal that consensual opinions about perception (about, say, the perception of color) might be affected by a change in convention: a rose by any other name might not be a rose—or it might be, if we consider the passing into obsolescence of individual conventions for color naming. The colors once called *cochineal* and *aureolin* look no different today, although rarely identified by the names that were formerly used.

Having a Concept of Color

Language rules govern use of the word *color* and of the names of individual colors. Each name refers to a circumscribed range. *Red* is no synonym for *green*. *Light blue* does not properly describe objects that can be called *dark blue*. *Purple* is not to be equated with *black*. A complete listing constitutes a subset of the catalog of rules for arranging words in sentences.

A catalog of this type can never explain everything people believe about the use of language. Using words, including color terms, correctly implies not only constructing proper sentences but uttering these sentences under circumstances considered appropriate. It implies the world external to language in which these appropriate circumstances occur. We routinely rely on this criterion when making judgments about whether a given individual has a concept of color, a reliable understanding of its nature.

We need not, and do not, go around asking others whether they have a concept of color or demanding that the claim be substantiated by those who say that they do. The person with a concept of color indicates, through speech and action, an awareness that color can only be experienced visually. No individual can be said to have a clearly defined concept of color if wanting in this insight. A blind person might be said to have a concept of color, albeit a concept limited by the condition, if aware that color is a phenomenon the blind are unable to experience. Even that small wisdom would save the individual from the error of Aristotle's hypothetical blind person, who insisted on arguing about colors with those who could see.

Relying on this criterion (which is a criterion for appropriate behavior), tests can be devised to determine whether a person behaves as if he or she has a concept of color. I can imagine a test in which the person is asked to name the color of some object he or she has not seen, perhaps a table concealed in another room. To pass the test, the subject must *not* try to answer before doing at least one of three things: look at the object, receive a report from another person who looked, or acquire access to a surrogate for first-hand visual experience, say, a color photograph.

A color photograph would not help a blind observer answer the question, because cameras cannot perform the human function of looking, any more than computers can perform the human function of thinking. Cameras do, however, produce photographs at which human observers can look. Whether the person answers the question about the color of the table is irrelevant to the test. The critical point is that he or she show awareness that some questions about color are requests for reports about visual experience. They can be answered only by determining what the colors of objects look like.

The imaginary test is tempting to dismiss

as trivial or nonsensical. It offends our hope that a concept, including a concept of color, is more grand, more complex, than an insight on such a primitive level. Despite this objection, the proposed test is consistent with the manner in which people judge one another. Imagine a lecture on color by a speaker with outstanding credentials who was regarded as unusually erudite. The listeners would not be impressed if they detected in this lecturer a lack of awareness that questions about the colors of objects cannot be answered until the objects are seen. We take it for granted that color is a visual phenomenon, that no conceptual understanding of its nature can exist in absence of this acknowledgment. No person with normal powers of reasoning fails to understand that color is something we see.

Color is also something at which, if not prevented by visual impairment, we can choose to look or not look. Looking with insufficient care is commonplace, a lapse rarely treated charitably if noticed. I lose confidence in theoretical proposals about color if the theorist does not use his or her eyes or makes statements that conflict with the evidence I obtain by using my own eyes. Would anyone, to give the simple-minded example, trust any of the ideas about color presented by a person who insisted that white is darker than black?

Sorting Criteria

Visual experience, although not conventional in itself, is reported (and, prior to that, sorted) according to conventional formats. Bright red and bright green can be called similar if the sorting criterion is brightness, dissimilar if it is hue. According to other criteria, the viewer may legitimately conclude red and green are similar in some ways, dissimilar in others.

By varying the sorting criterion, a different form of interpretation (or a different emphasis) is imposed on a visual experience assumed to be approximately similar for all. A preference or distaste for any individual criterion might develop within a society, thus becoming a convention of that society. But a sorting criterion is not a perception.

Hans Hahn (1879–1934), a member of the Vienna Circle, commented extensively on color while discussing language and logic. He attributed to convention the practice of calling some objects red and others blue ([1933] 1966, 222-35). Hahn cannot have understood the nature of the convention if he meant we arbitrarily bestow the name *blue* as fancy dictates. Blue objects are called *blue* because they display that characteristic; red objects are *red* because they are that color. Conventional color names are conventionally used to report perceptually apprehended color differences. They are incorrectly used under other circumstances. If asked to identify the color of a coffee cup, I look at the cup to make the determination. It would be unconventional to give ''red'' as an answer if the coffee cup was visibly blue.

Because names are arbitrary and conventions change, blue objects might be called *red*, and red objects might be called *blue*. A language would not likely evolve in which the name *red* was used for some red objects and some blue ones and *blue* was used for some red objects and some blue ones. No one would know how to use such a language without information about which red objects and which blue ones belong in each class. Perhaps all large objects could be called *red* and all small objects *blue*, irrespective of redness or blueness. In that case, one criterion for sorting (redness, blueness) would be replaced by another (largeness, smallness). The substitution is similar to classifying people on Monday according to height, on Tuesday according to yearly income. Red, in such a language, would mean large, or a large red or blue object.

One of many color games proposed by the philosopher Ludwig Wittgenstein turns on an ornate articulation of sorting criteria:

> Imagine this game: A shows B different patches of colours and asks him what they have in common. B is to answer by pointing to a particular primary color . . . . If in this game A showed B a light blue and a dark blue and asked what they had in common, there would be no doubt about the answer. If then he pointed to pure red and pure green, the answer would be that these have nothing in common. But I can easily imagine circumstances under which we should say that they had something in common and would not hesitate to say what it was.
>
> Imagine a use of language (a culture) in which there was a common name for green and red on one hand, for yellow and blue on the other. Suppose, for example, that there were two castes, one the patrician caste, wearing red and green garments, the other, the plebian, wearing blue and yellow garments. Both yellow and blue would always be referred to as plebian colours, green and red as patrician colours. Asked what a red patch and a green patch have in common, a man of our tribe would not hesitate to say they were both patrician (Wittgenstein 1958, 134).

In the course of his game, Wittgenstein switched rules by changing the question to be answered. Initially, the player must determine what red and green look like. Later, the consideration is who wears these colors. In the first instance, the report is about perceptions. In the second, the player supplies an interpretation by telling what the colors represent. They represent, in Wittgenstein's game, either the modality of the patrician or the colors of clothing worn by that caste.

Life, as Wittgenstein argued, is gamelike. But human beings play multiple games simultaneously. Knowing that red and green represent patrician status has no bearing on the separate awareness that the colors do not look alike. Anyone taught to play Wittgenstein's second game would not be impeded from also continuing to play the first. Everyday experience offers several parallels. Although red and green are not indicators of patrician social status, convention associates them with Christmas in societies with a Christian population. A conviction that the two colors belong together as a symbol for a holiday season will not persuade that they also belong together if the criterion for sorting is hue similarity.

Among sorting criteria appropriate to other contexts, red and green traffic lights mean stop and go. A red light on an elevator indicates the elevator is going down. Adhering to whatever interpretation is contextually appropriate has less to do with how the colors are seen than with the sorting criterion of the moment. Red can imply anger, virility, or communism. Green suggests envy, inexperience, money, or Saint Patrick's Day. Green can point to the Irish or any group that adopts the color as its emblem. It can suggest the environmental concerns of the German political party that calls itself the Greens.

Wittgenstein favored the view that perception—not just interpretation—is conventionally determined, therefore easily susceptible to modification. He argued that if, say, light blue and dark blue were known by the dissimilar names *Oxford* and *Cambridge,* people would say they saw no similarity between them. The generalization is too broad. Names can create a bias for or against the named object or color, which is why *daffodil yellow* sounds more appealing than *pus yellow*. But pairs of color names as different in sound and spelling as *Oxford* and *Cambridge* exist. Viewers shown the pairs of colors, or familiar with them, recognize a visual similarity. Dark brown and chestnut, cerulean and turquoise, vermilion and crimson, ocher and mustard, are examples.

Names for similar colors need not be similar words, a special case of the language convention that synonyms and near synonyms need not be spelled or pronounced similarly. In most cases they are not. The flaw in Wittgenstein's argument about Oxford and Cambridge blue is the assumption that a determination can be made about whether colors look similar by investigating whether they have similar names. This is no more reasonable than asserting that the paintings of Monet must be similar to those of Manet or that Austria should resemble Australia. The proper domain of verification is visual, because statements about how colors look are conventionally understood to be reports about perception. They are not properly understood if thought to be statements of language rules.

Red and Not-Red

Defining a concept of color as an awareness of its visual nature amounts to categorizing color as a percept, to be encountered by experience. This implies that knowledge of color is a posteriori, after the fact. Nobody can know (or nobody can know firsthand) about experience he or she has not had. The nature of the perceptual world cannot be anticipated, though we can and should think about what was seen after the act of perception. We cannot assume that what we see will conform to what reason suggests. Human ability to reason, like human language, has limits. One limit is that we are unable to see the future. Nobody knows the color of a color swatch sealed in an envelope until someone sees it.

Consider the puzzlement of a hypothetical epistemologist who lives on an unnamed planet in an inaccessible galaxy. This distant neighbor subscribes to terrestrial philosophy journals. The journals convey an impression that earthly colors all come in pairs, like the animals in Noah's ark. Red finds its counterpart in not-red, blue in not-blue, and so forth. The epistemologist has not been able to locate an example of not-red, a matter of concern. If many shades of red are available, an equal number of shades of not-red should exist. The epistemologist has begun to suspect the range of colors does not exist, but wonders, if this is the case, why it provokes lively discussions. She wants to test the hypothesis that some discussions about color are not about color in any visual or experiential sense. They reflect a semantic confusion in which questions about language rules are mistakenly classified as questions about visual experience.

The philosophical literature on not-red is more extensive than that on not-blue, not-yellow, or not-taupe. It seeks criteria for distinguishing not-red from red, evidently of greater importance than distinguishing red or not-red from yellow. Little is in print about distinguishing red or not-red from not-chickens. Questions about the not-colors, several examined by Wittgenstein, usually concern the circumstances under which they can be seen: "Could it perhaps be imagined that where I see blue, this means that the object I see is not blue . . . ?" (Wittgenstein 1967, 103). "But may not someone who is observing a surface be quite preoccupied with the question whether it is going to turn green or not green?" (Wittgenstein 1967, 19).

A viewer may indeed become preoccupied with whether a surface "is going to turn green or not green." But asking *whether or not* green is the color the surface will become is syntactically preferable and less likely to cause confusion. "The surface is not green" means the surface is an unspecified color, which only subordinately cannot be specified to be green. As Bertrand Russell pointed out, "When, as a judgment of perception, we disbelieve 'This is red,' we are always perceiving that it is some other color" (Russell 1948, 124).

Not-red is a nonvisual concept, one of many that make reasoning about color more difficult than it otherwise might be. *Whether* is a sensible term, in harmony with the nature of the phenomenological world. Because I am unable to anticipate the future, I might reasonably wonder *whether* the next car to come over the hill will be green. Interjecting fancies about not-green surfaces and not-green automobiles adds nothing of substance to the question and sows confusion about its nature.

The not-colors apparently arose through false analogy with the proposition, in logic, that any statement is either true or not true. The logical proposition is often illustrated by examples that use color names: Either it is true that the table is red, or it is not true that the table is red. The coupled statements are not interchangeable with that other familiar pair: either the table is red or the table is not red. The first set of statements concerns the truth of a proposition. The second concerns the color of an object.

In the first set of statements, "not true" has a meaning, because not true is synonymous with false. What "not red" means, other than "unspecified," is less clear. The term implies classes as divergent as all colors in the world other than red or all entities in the world other than the color red. That the table is not red is a trivial truth about its color. It hides the necessary antecedent, the greater truth, that the table is yellow, purple, light blue, or any shade that we do not call red.

Considered as units in a classification system, each of the not-colors is an empty category, devoid of attributes other than its emptiness and its name. One category is not-red, another, not-green, and so forth. Not-red, which is not the name of a color, is also not self-sufficient as a label for a color condition.

Blue is not adequately described as not-red, because blue is also not green, not black, not silver, not mahogany, and so forth through the full range of colors. An explanation of the difference between red and not-red cannot lead to greater understanding of what *red* means. It might produce insight into what the word *not* means, but reveals nothing about color by so doing.

If not-red were genuinely a recondite philosophical issue, it could safely be left to Wittgenstein and a few other specialists. I regard it as no philosophical question at all, just one of many examples of a looseness of expression in talking about colors that drifts into the academic world from everyday life. The looseness is traditional, a matter of acculturation. We are not encouraged to discriminate carefully between statements about the perception of color and statements about rules for using words.

The bias is at a cost. Many intelligent, educated people, though nothing is wrong with their eyes, never learn to think visually, to reason in an orderly manner about visual phenomena. They become distracted by semantic issues without recognizing that the issues are semantic. When not-red is accorded the status of a color, as in, say, comparing it with red, a parallelism is mistakenly assumed between colors and logical classes. Logic, a proper tool for determining the truth or falsity of a statement, cannot be used to make determinations about the colors of objects. It lacks a facility for dealing with the visual continuum: with what we see or with what objects look like.

Not-red might be an amusing piece of nonsense were it not taken too seriously too often. Hans Hahn found that "nothing is both red and not red. This is the law of contradiction"([1933] 1966, 228). The law of contradiction states that A and not-A cannot both be true at the same time. Red and not-red are poor examples of its operation. Some objects are neither red nor not-red because they are partly red. A table painted with blue and red stripes is not properly called a red object: it is only partly red. Nor is it properly called not-red: it is only partly not-red.

Color, which by nature is a continuum, is not structured in terms of parity. For several reasons, no viable classification system can begin with the premise that any object is either red or not-red. A red/not-red system assumes that all red objects share the same color, a wrongly drawn parallel with the assumption, in logic, that all true statements share the same truth. More than one shade of red occurs in the experiential world. Language, more refined than logic in this case, has forms that facilitate comparison among different reds. To say that "the red of the first necktie is very different from that of the second, but almost matches that of the third" is syntactically allowable and meaningful.

Color and Logic

What do they mean, these discussions of not-red, of Wittgenstein's surface that might turn not-green? Like the imaginary epistemologist from another galaxy, none of us has ever seen not-red or not-green. At best, each term is meaningless, a negative definition. If color is something we see, inventing colors that cannot be seen serves no useful purpose. I can go to a hardware store and ask for the paint that is not-red, though this is saying too little. I do better, maintain more control, if I ask for the color I want.

If asking about the difference between red and not-red is nonsensical, why is it done? Why does the question sound sober and familiar, as if serious issues are being raised? The answers lie, I think, in cultural attitudes about the visual sense that affect the way we reason about color and about everything else. The Greek philosophers passed along the bad habit of imagining the universe as a collection of

opposites, the units in each pair linked in a symmetrical complementarity that mimics the complementarity of logical classes.

William M. Ivins, Jr., pointed out that, "intuitionally the Greeks were tactile-minded. . . . Whenever they were given the choice between a tactile or a visual way of thought, they instinctively chose the tactile one" (Ivins 1946, 9). The Greek conception of a primary substance, or matter, is even "the reduction of the tactile-muscular intuitions to a sort of basic philosophical principle."

The Greek conception of logic, which remains our conception, is cut from the same pattern. If an intimation of truth, it resembles the truth of the hand. Exploring the world, the hand discovers two states. It bumps into things or it does not, with no other possible condition. Matter is not space. In metaphorical extensions of this given, what is true is not false, and right is not wrong. Switches are on or off. Answers are yes or no.

In the age of the computer, reasoning based on what Ivins calls tactile-muscular intuition nevertheless remains the state of the art. Classical ideas about the emptiness of space and the non-emptiness of matter have gone their way, both the ideas of the classical Greeks and those of classical (Newtonian) physics. But the assumption that the natural world exhibits parity—that its building blocks come in pairs—continues as a cornerstone of quantum mechanics and other branches of modern physics. The assumption is rarely helpful at any level in relation to color or visual perception.

Consider the familiar assertion that black is the opposite of white. Black/white is not a parallel construction to red/not-red. One set of purported opposites pairs two colors. The other consists of a single color contrasted with a hypothetical entity. In each case, the asserted oppositeness finds its paradigm in logic, which holds that classes have opposites or complements. For every class K, there exists its complement, not-K. The logical assumption supports the language rule that the word *not* may be placed in front of any color name. The construction is semantically allowable. But is it meaningful? Does it lead to greater understanding or just to nonsense?

As in the complementarity assumed between color and form, or attributed to colors opposite one another on the color wheel, the ubiquitous assumption that black has an opposite (for every *K*, a not-*K*) has not produced consensus about where to find that opposite. For the philosopher Daniel Sommer Robinson, "the opposite of black, is not, as we usually think, white, but non-black . . . *non-black* is the absolute or exact opposite of black" (Robinson 1947, 25). Because black is often characterized as not a color, its opposite can as reasonably be the doubly negative not-not-a-color. Beyond the merit of the several answers to the question, some more existentially absurd than others, the difficult assumption is that colors can be presumed to have opposites, as if they were logical classes.

The statement "black is the opposite of white" is a contradiction in terms. It says that the opposite of a given color is another color. If black and white are not colors, it says that the opposite of a not-color is another not-color. "Black is the opposite of not-black" creates the need for a definition of not-black. If not-black (or nonblack) is an umbrella term covering every color except black, we have said that the opposite of a color is all other colors.

If not-black means every item in the world other than black, the sense of the assertion is the truism that nothing is anything except itself. If not-black is a hypothetical construct (not a percept), then the opposite of a color is hypothetical. This last has the virtue of suggesting that colors, like hummingbirds, may not have opposites.

The tendency to structure thought in terms of sets of opposites underlies nearly all confused reasoning about color. But it also runs aground at other points. Although we think of finite and infinite as opposites, mathematicians have difficulty dealing with infinite sets. The rules for handling them are not just the opposite of rules for managing sets that are finite. Color is obdurately resistant to analysis in terms of parity. Ideas about it that are incoherent, nonvisual, often begin with an assumption that one aspect of color is opposite to some other.

Ivins traces to the Greeks our cultural preference for reasoning in terms of polarities, for tactile concepts at the expense of those that are visual. But the devaluing of visual experience also has Judeo-Christian antecedents. The most influential aspect of monotheism is not, I think, the idea of one god. This god, importantly, is invisible, suggesting that things we are unable to see can outweigh in importance what is seen. Historically, the assumption contributed to the devaluing of visual sensibility—or affirmed a devaluing that had already occurred. The Bible does not provide careful descriptions of what things look like.

All sense experience, not just visual experience, eventually came to be devalued. The thread runs through Western philosophy, which tells us the senses are unreliable. I suspect this means that the eye, if able to see correctly, ought to be able to see God. In the West, we have not had the counterbalancing concept of the third eye. This inner eye sees invisible worlds, the metaphysics of what might lie beyond surfaces. It leaves to the external eye the task of understanding the world that is visible.

Doubting Colors

The deadening of visual sensibility displays itself in many ways. We rarely have a strong sense of when words refer to colors and when they refer to something else. A search under *color* in the card catalog of any library of respectable size turns up a literature that considers the difference between the statements "it looks red" and "it is red." Nothing is called red that never looks red, a rule of language. So anything that is red will look red to at least one viewer on at least one occasion. Does the difference between the two statements tell us about color or the perception of color? I think not. It reveals societal value judgments, again expressed primarily through rules of language.

"It looks red" is a psychological report, equivocal about the color of the object but definite about the observer's state of mind. The observer is not certain about the color of the object. "It looks red" is the functional equivalent of "it looks red, but I'm not sure," or "I think it's red, though I might be mistaken." The viewer's uncertainty reduces to uncertainty about a logical proposition. The statement that the object is red is either true or false. Isn't the answer one or the other? How can anyone look and not know?

In what has been called the tie-shop argument, Wilfred Sellars has theorized about why uncertainty might arise. Objects look different colors under different kinds of light. A necktie that looks one color in a tie shop looks another color under daylight illumination. "It looks red" implies that the object might not look red under more optimal or normal lighting conditions. But optimal or normal conditions have not been established or do not exist. Because the color of any object varies with lighting conditions, no object is the same shade of red under all conditions. Because illumination is never perfectly even, neither is any object exactly the same color over all parts of its surface. An object that looks red when the lights are on looks gray or black in the darkness. If, in a visual or phenomenological sense, objects have no absolute colors, what is the observer's dilemma about?

The issue is a societal expectation as old as the phrasing "it looks red." The construction assumes the existence of an objective, real, or normal world in which objects show their "real" colors. Imagine asking the observer to decide once and for all whether the object that "looks red" *is* red. To be certain, the observer would want to know the real color of the object, to see the object under normal or average lighting, and so forth. These and all similar conditions cannot be met. They assume a world that does not exist, that has a stability lacking in our own.

"It looks red" is a linguistic mistake, though traditional. It expresses a lack of harmony with the existential world of visual experience. It cannot help us to understand what we see, because it effectively asserts we ought to be seeing something else. The construction is too deeply embedded in language to be easily eliminated. Its appearance in poems is instructive. In *Inferno*, Dante described the Rock of Purgatory, red in the rays of the setting sun. Is the rock red, or does it just look red?

T. S. Eliot's youthful improvements on Dante's passage in "The Death of Saint Narcissus" included the addition of a gray rock and firelight that reddens the red rock:

> Come in under the shadow of this gray
>   rock,
> And I will show you something different
>   from either
> Your shadow sprawling over the sand at
>   daybreak, or
> Your shadow leaping behind the fire
>   against the red rock:

How many gray rocks are in the Eliot passage? For a literary commentator, there might be two. Eliot's red rock, as well as Dante's, might be regarded as a poetic compression. Yet I doubt we improve the poetry, or the sense, in either case, by assuming the poet meant to say that the red rock just looks red. As a logical proposition, if a rock looks red under certain conditions, it *is* red under those conditions.

The conception of a rock that looks red but

really is not red is a semantic confusion possible only in a society in which the evidence of the senses is routinely mistrusted. As a visual phenomenon, color is of the moment, because we see (and live) only in the present moment. Eliot's rock, as he said, is red when seen by firelight. It might be another color under other conditions. But those are other conditions.

Looks like clouds the singular nature of phenomenological reality. To make sense of the conception, we need to assume a real or normal world that reveals truths purportedly hidden in ordinary phenomenological experience. We do better, I think, to take the visual world as it is, freeing ourselves, where possible, of ideas that refer to what it ought to be. No other way exists of coming to terms with visual experience, including the experience of seeing color.

CHAPTER 5

Knowing How to Identify Color

Colour is something "out there," resistant to the eye. It is, so to speak, the vitality that shows upon the surface of an object, tinging as does the life-blood our skins.

Adrian Stokes, Colour and Form

Color, among its several functions, can be defined as the name of a class. This implies that the class can be identified and the items belonging in it isolated. It need not imply that everyone ought to know how to do so. Human beings, however, arrive at virtual unanimity regarding which items are colors. Because of the overwhelming consensus, a test for ability to separate the names of colors from those of noncolors would be fatuous (figure 5-1). Few test takers will achieve less than perfect scores.

People rarely argue about whether red is a color. Questions occasionally arise about black, white, gray, and the metallic colors. Even in these cases, I think most people would make the reasonable choice. If asked to sort colors from noncolors, they would group black, white, or silver with red, orange, and green, rather than with motorboats, cows, derby hats, or other items that are properly not colors.

In a refinement of the ability, few adults make errors in identifying black, white, brown, or gray, as well as red, orange, yellow, and other major hues. The competence should not be taken for granted. People are not usually adroit at estimating weight, velocity, temperature, or time of day. No person of normal eyesight and comprehension fails to learn to identify colors. The question of whether the ability can be lost is more clouded.

The Visual Agnosias
In a group of brain diseases called the visual agnosias, perception and ability to speak are

Figure 5-1. Separating colors and noncolors. Object names that also identify colors are easily separated from those that do not.

apricot	brown	charcoal	cup	grenade	plate	table
avocado	cabinet	chartreuse	curtain	horse	red	vermilion
banana	camel	chicken	dog	magenta	rocket	violet
bed	car	child	flag	monkey	ruler	white
black	carousel	church	giraffe	motorcycle	saucer	window
blue	cerise	computer	gray	orange	shell	yacht
bomb	chair	cow	green	pitcher	stool	yellow

not generally impaired, but a condition arises that is usually described as loss of ability to understand the meaning of color names. Agnosiacs follow a private logic of their own, and their color-naming practices have been described by Norman Geschwind (Geschwind 1969, 4:98–136). The selective amnesias of the patients assume different forms. One man, observed by Efron, substituted color names for object names, which the examiner believed had been forgotten. The man used *silver* as a name for keys, an incorrect reference to their material or a correct reference to their color (Efron 1969, 4:137–73).

The larger group of agnosiacs of more immediate interest retains the ability to sort by color, but conditionally. They cannot separate blue objects from yellow ones unless the task is presented without using color names (Geschwind 1969, 121). Agnosiacs in this group are said to have no comprehension of what blue, yellow, and other color names mean. Because we legitimately ask how a person would show understanding of the meaning of color names, case reports raise as many questions about the tests administered as about the patient's performances.

No standard psychological test has been developed to evaluate understanding of color or of color names, and color blindness is not easy to identify either. To bridge the gap in the social sciences, ad hoc testing methods are widely used that reflect the assumptions of the designer of the test. Little can be learned about anyone's conception of color or understanding of color names by having the individual sort colored poker chips or other similarly neu-

tral items. Under environmental conditions, colors are often chosen (or sorted) for complex, indirect reasons. A customer in a cafeteria selecting chocolate ice cream instead of vanilla, or tomato juice rather than orange juice, gives attention to color as an indicator of taste, the prime criterion in this case.

Agnosiacs apparently are tested for understanding of only a few color names, notably red, green, and blue, the colors of poker chips. This leaves unanswered the question of how the patients handled, if at all, words such as turquoise, brick, salmon, scarlet, or lime. Unless the term is defined with great care, what type of knowledge (or behavioral skill) would be lost by an individual afflicted by amnesia for color names is unclear. Many or most words used to name colors have more than one meaning.

By their nature, color names derived from object names function as color names only when colors are what they are being used to name: *lemon* can identify either object or color, for example. Among the primal color names, nearly all have additional meanings that are metaphorical. We speak of feeling blue, of being in the pink, of seeing red, of being in the red, in the black, or green with envy. We understand the meaning of yellow coward, purple prose, blue laws, green recruits, the scarlet letter, scarlet women, or once in a blue moon.

A patient who selectively forgets the meaning of color names might show this in any of a variety of ways, each implying a different aberration. A person who uses the word *olive* correctly, except as the name of a color (or except as the name of an object), has a selective amnesia for some meanings of some words. An individual who forgets all meanings of the word *olive*, because one of those meanings names a color, may have an amnesia for all meanings of some words. If the condition is accurately described, the individual, in an improbable pathology, would correctly understand the word *apple* (which cannot be the name of a color), but have no comprehension of *orange* (which can be).

An agnosiac, in another possibility, may have no difficulty using words such as *olive*, whether for color name or object name. But, as the literature reports, he or she may lack understanding of *blue, green,* or *yellow*, again an improbable pathology. Of immediate concern, the defect would be limited to forgetting the names of the primal colors. It cannot be regarded as an equivalent for forgetting the names of all colors.

The literature provides no way of surmounting the absence of some kinds of data. Can the agnosiac remember what lightness means when it refers to the weight of an object, but not if a reference to the object's color? What response would be elicited by instructions to sort items according to whether their color was shiny or dull? If an agnosiac confused red with blue, would he or she describe sadness as feeling red rather than feeling blue? Can an agnosiac, or anyone else, remember how to order a glass of Burgundy wine in a restaurant but forget that the color name *burgundy* refers to the color of the wine?

Reports about agnosiacs, despite conclusions to the contrary by the authors, rarely suggest the patients have forgotten color names. They appear to have forgotten, instead, the rules for determining which name to use. A patient observed by Geschwind gave wrong answers when asked the colors of objects, substituting "red" when he should have said "green."[1] But the patient evidently responded to questions about color with color names. He never gave nonsensical answers such as "the color of the poker chip is music." The behavior suggests that what the patient remembered about color exceeded what had been forgotten.

Relying on data Geschwind provides, the patient understood what a color is and had an unimpaired concept of color. He knew that color is a visual phenomenon and that objects had to be looked at before answering questions about their colors. Because even agnosiacs are not reported to be willing to sort red poker chips from green in the dark, the patient was aware that determining the colors of objects requires the presence of illumination.

The patient also realized that colors have names. He knew some of those names and apparently had no difficulty pronouncing them. He understood that color names were to be chosen, from those he knew, in response to the examiner's questions. Importantly, he did not use the same name for every color. He evidently understood that one purpose in using different names is to acknowledge differences among colors.

The patient's difficulty was limited to an inability to correctly judge which color name, from among those he knew, would have been most correct or appropriate. Geschwind's patient may have forgotten that color names are not applied to colors at random (blue is not called yellow). He may have lost the ability to sort or to distinguish between an order that is random and another that is hierarchical according to some criterion.

He may have forgotten the sorting criteria for determining which name went with which color, as opposed to sorting criteria in general. Or he may have garbled the sequence, for unknown reasons. The distinctions between these several failures in comprehension are subtle. But they point to differences as vast as those between not remembering a person's name and not realizing people have names.

Because Geschwind's patient was able to judge, visually, the difference between red and green, some disturbance in his sense of order or appropriateness (choosing the right name for the circumstances) is implied. This is a selective inability to use language correctly. Why color names alone are confabulated is not clear, nor can we be certain this is the case. The literature does not suggest extensive testing to determine whether agnosiacs also confuse names for animals, people, streets, or other items. A question that bears on societal expectations is why it is considered abnormal to mix up the names when asked to identify colors but not when asked to identify state capitals.

Geschwind, explaining the agnosias, suggested "the patient with a colour-naming disturbance can give only a poor account of his colour-experience or indeed none at all since his speech area has little or no access to information about the colour-experience of the visual cortex" (Geschwind 1969, 133). More recent work with patients in whom right and left brain hemispheres have been separated by severing the corpus callosum (usually to relieve epileptic seizures) indicates that speech is localized in the left brain. Visual and spatial understanding, required for understanding of color, is localized in the right. Either hemisphere is capable of independent functioning, although not in the same way. Split-brain patients may be able to copy simple geometrical forms with the left hand (controlled by the right brain) more skillfully than with the right.

Damage to localized areas of the brain has been correlated with specific behavioral malfunctionings. Injury to Broca's area, in the lower rear part of the left brain's frontal lobe, causes aphasia, difficulty in speaking or inability to speak. Injury to Wernicke's area, straddling the parietal and temporal lobes in the rear center part of the left brain, leaves speech syntactically normal but senseless. If, however, certain kinds of information are stored in local-

ized areas of the brain that can be identified, color information poses a problem. How would the conception of, say, coolness be classified or stored? Coolness refers to a condition of temperature, but we also speak of cool colors.

In English, though not in all languages, words occur that are not considered names of colors, though these words function syntactically as if they were. Colors can be sorted according to whether, say, light, dark, or pastel. Yet light, dark, and pastel are not considered to be color names. Other terms applicable to colors are subjective. A subject can be asked to sort colors according to whether, say, beautiful or interesting, which again are not names of colors. How are these terms understood, and these sorting tasks performed, by agnosiacs? If they cannot sort colors according to whether, say, light or beautiful, should the impediment be classified as a forgetting of color names? Is a broader difficulty in using speech implied? These questions are for the medical community. Yet answering them requires a clearer understanding of the nature of color names, how colors are described in English, and how color-sorting tasks are performed.

Assume, say, that color information is stored in two areas of the brain, one handling visual information about how colors look, the other, information about how words are used in making statements about color. The difficulty of agnosiacs seems to lie in the second area. The area, however, spans out to include any conception that might be used in sorting colors. A subject can be asked to sort colors according to whether, say, the color has been seen recently, is fashionable this year in clothing, or is used in traffic signs.

Any word in the English language might be used in talking about colors or in giving instructions about how they should be sorted and labeled. The primal color names, although they are the words most often used for label-

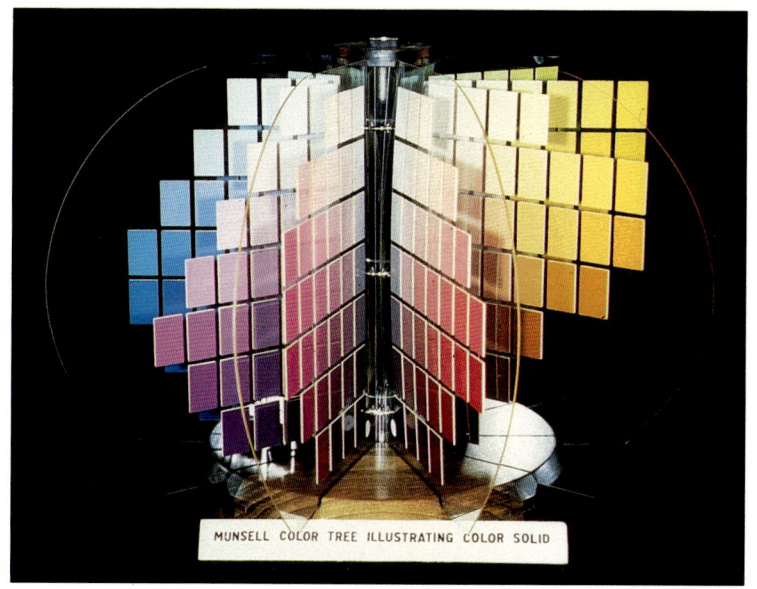

The Munsell Color Tree. (Courtesy, Munsell Color, 2441 N. Calvert St., Baltimore, MD 21218.) The Munsell parameters for ranking color are hue, value, and chroma. The Ostwald parameters are hue, black content, and white content. In both systems, dullness or shininess of surface is acknowledged as a fourth quality, which cannot be incorporated into a three-dimensional model.

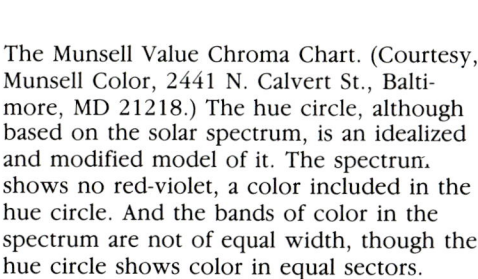

The Munsell Value Chroma Chart. (Courtesy, Munsell Color, 2441 N. Calvert St., Baltimore, MD 21218.) The hue circle, although based on the solar spectrum, is an idealized and modified model of it. The spectrum shows no red-violet, a color included in the hue circle. And the bands of color in the spectrum are not of equal width, though the hue circle shows color in equal sectors.

White has traditionally been equated with light, and black with its absence. But the gray scale is as stylized as the hue circle. White light is brighter than any white paint, and the experience of seeing darkness is different from that of seeing black paint.

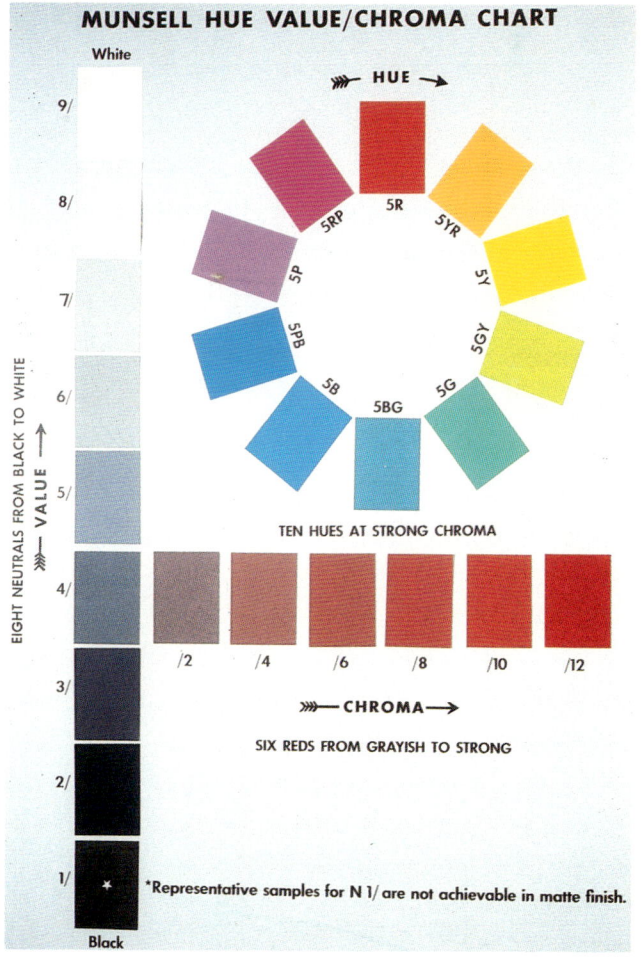

MUNSELL HUE VALUE/CHROMA CHART

TEN HUES AT STRONG CHROMA

SIX REDS FROM GRAYISH TO STRONG

*Representative samples for N 1/ are not achievable in matte finish.

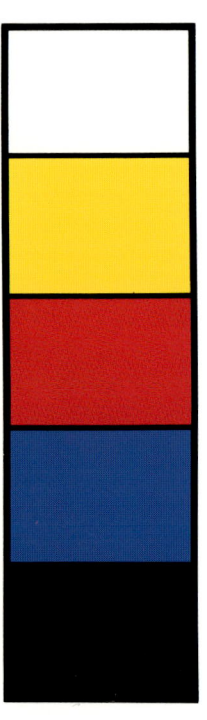

Combined Hue-Value Scale (after Kandinsky). (Illustration by Pamela Dohner.) Although the achromatic colors (black, white, gray) have no hue, the hues can be ranked according to value, their degree of lightness or darkness. In Kandinsky's arrangement, yellow falls near white because both are light. Blue falls near black because both are dark. Red occupies an intermediary position, and is neither very light nor very dark.

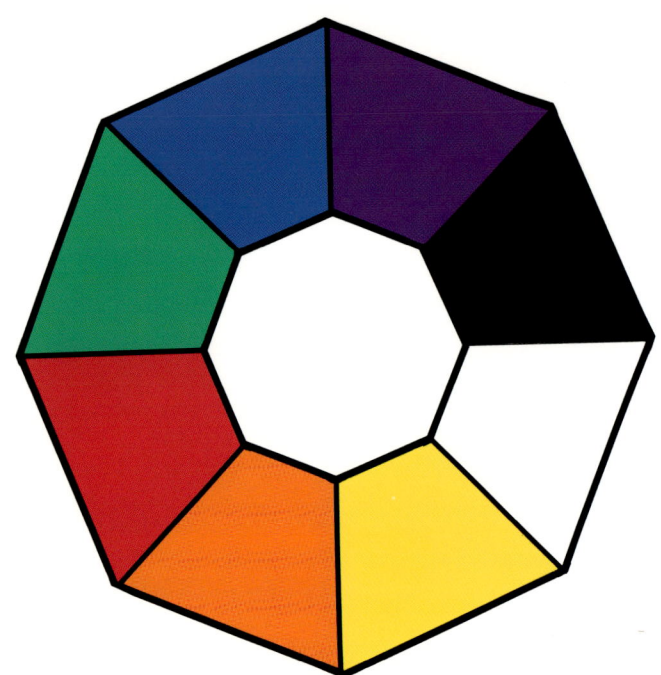

Combined Hue-Value Circle. (Illustration by Pamela Dohner.) In this combined hue-value circle designed by the author, black, white, and the spectral hues are ranked by degree of darkness around the perimeter of the circle. Each color is opposite a color of high contrast to itself, although no color is opposite to its complementary color. The strongest value contrast is between black and white; the strongest hue contrast, red and green.

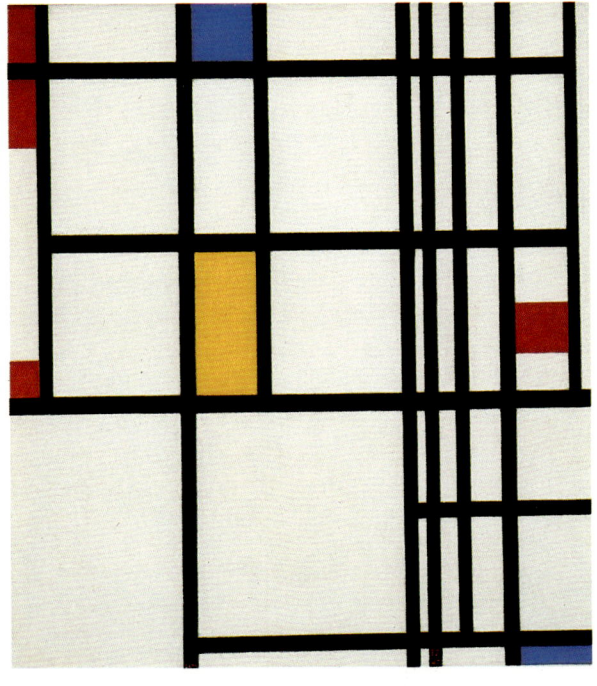

Piet Mondrian, *Composition in Red, Blue, and Yellow,* 1937-42. Oil on canvas, 23¾ × 21⅛ in. (Collection, The Museum of Modern Art, The Sidney and Harriet Janis Collection.) Over a period of years, Mondrian gradually reduced his palette to the five colors he regarded as pure: red, blue, yellow, black, and white.

Kenneth Campbell, *Untitled,* 1949.
Casein on paper, 31.5 × 22.3 in (80.01 ×
56.64 cm). (Photograph by Bob Rubrick.)
Forms affect colors by limiting their areas.
This hard-edge geometrical abstraction uses
a relatively large number of relatively small
shapes. The effect would have been different with, say, the same colors but only
four or five large shapes. And it also would
have been a vastly different painting if
done entirely in, say, shades of green. The
perennial question of whether form is
more important than color has no answer,
other than that a change in either is a significant change.

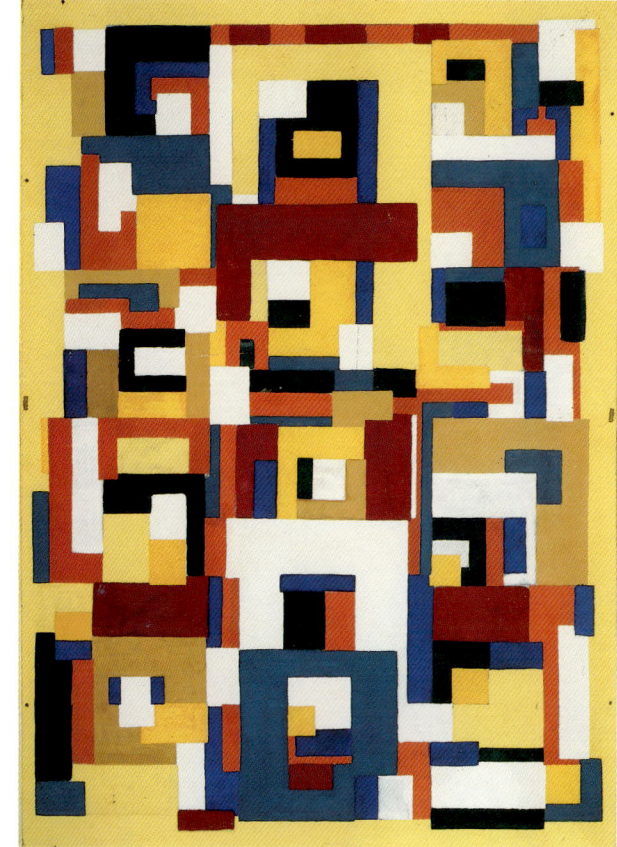

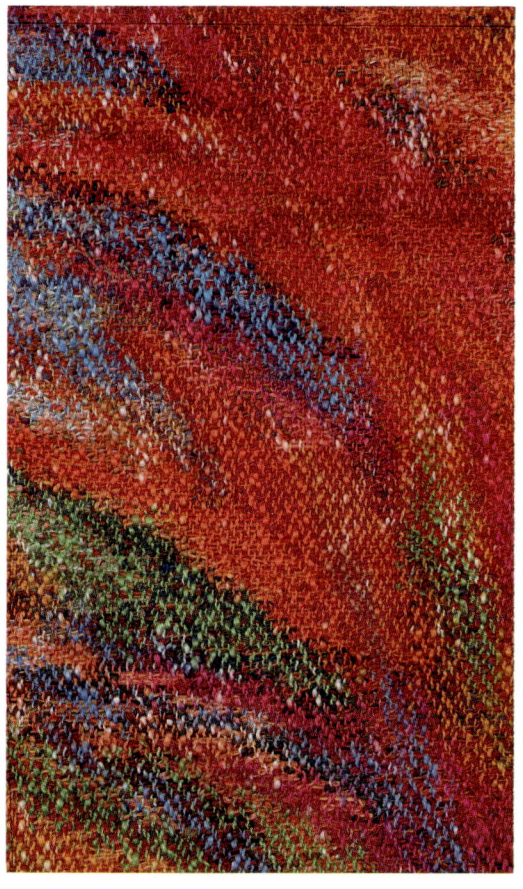

Betty Vera, *Hot Planet,* 1988. Cotton
tapestry with painted warp, discontinuous weft inlays, and broken twill
weave, 36 × 36 in (91.44 × 91.44 cm).
(Photograph by Betty Vera.) In this
tapestry, the artist selected saturated
middle-value hues that have little light-
dark contrast. If reproduced in black
and white, the design would almost disappear. The contrasts are of warm-cool,
and of hue changes.

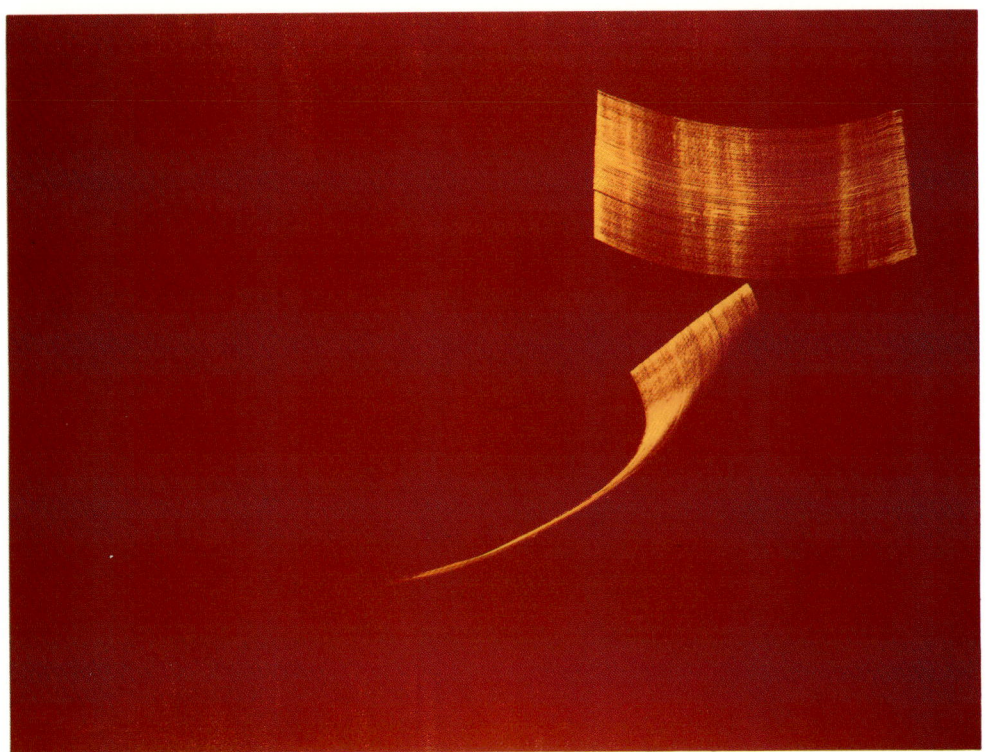

Al Alcopley, *Approach,* 1987. Oil on canvas, 50 × 68 in (127 × 172.72 cm). (Photograph by Bob Rubrick.) A painting, like anything else we see, can be thought of as a matrix or aggregate of color spots, an arrangement of pigments on a surface. The color itself can become an image, icon, or subject.

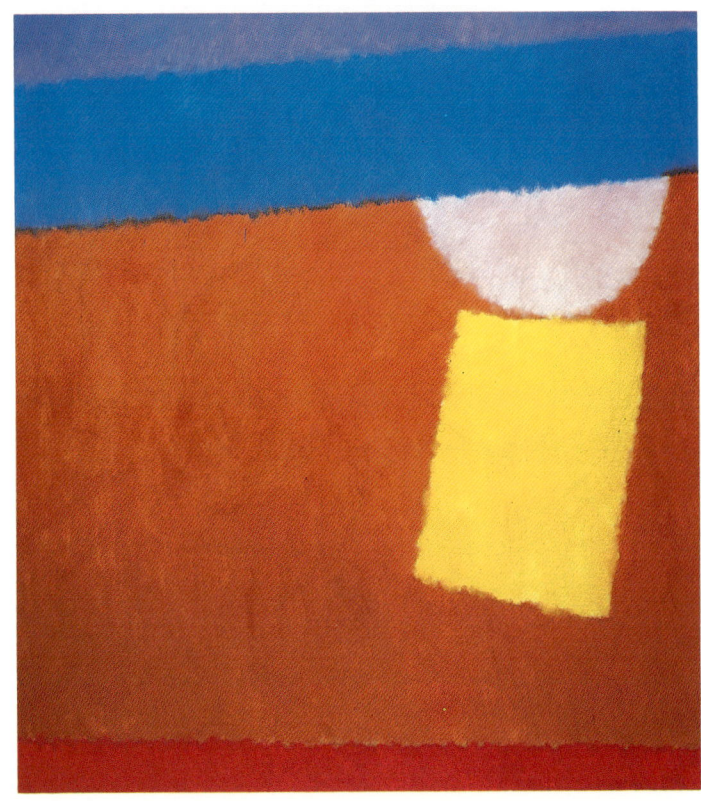

Herman Cherry, *Day and Night,* 1987. Oil on canvas, 66 × 60 in (167.64 × 152.40 cm). (Courtesy of White Pine Gallery, New York City. Photograph by R. Cherry.) Like style, artists' use of color is individualistic. In this painting, day and night are associated not with black and white but with an arrangement in which pink takes the place of green, and all spectral hues other than green are included.

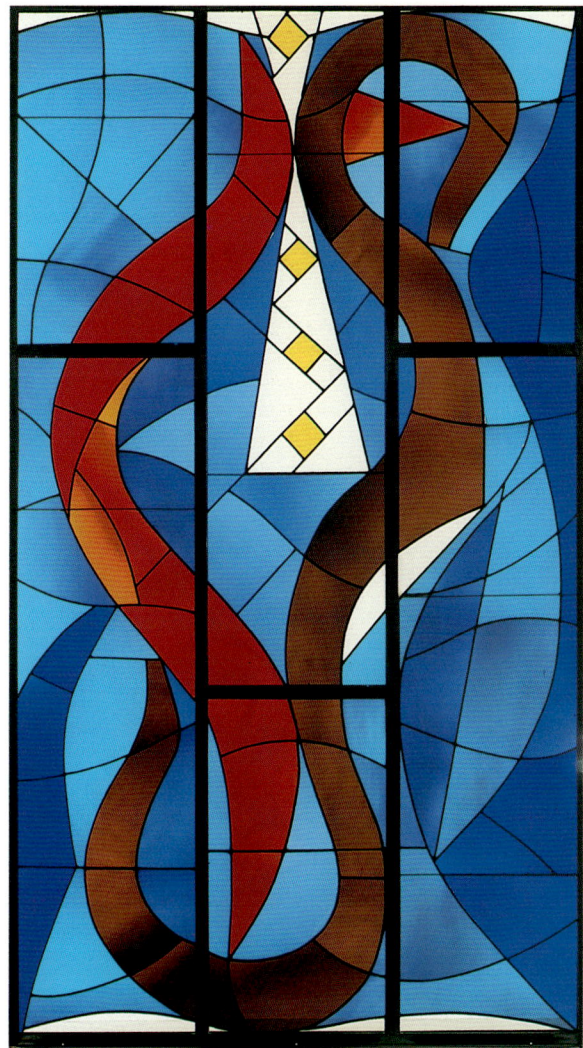

Nina Tryggvadottir, *Untitled,* 1956. Oil on masonite, 49.2 × 24.2 in (124.97 × 61.47 cm). Shapes are always referential, even those shapes that only refer to the forms of geometry. The irregular shapes in this painting are biomorphic; the austere blue-green, black, and white of this abstraction suggest a rocky landscape.

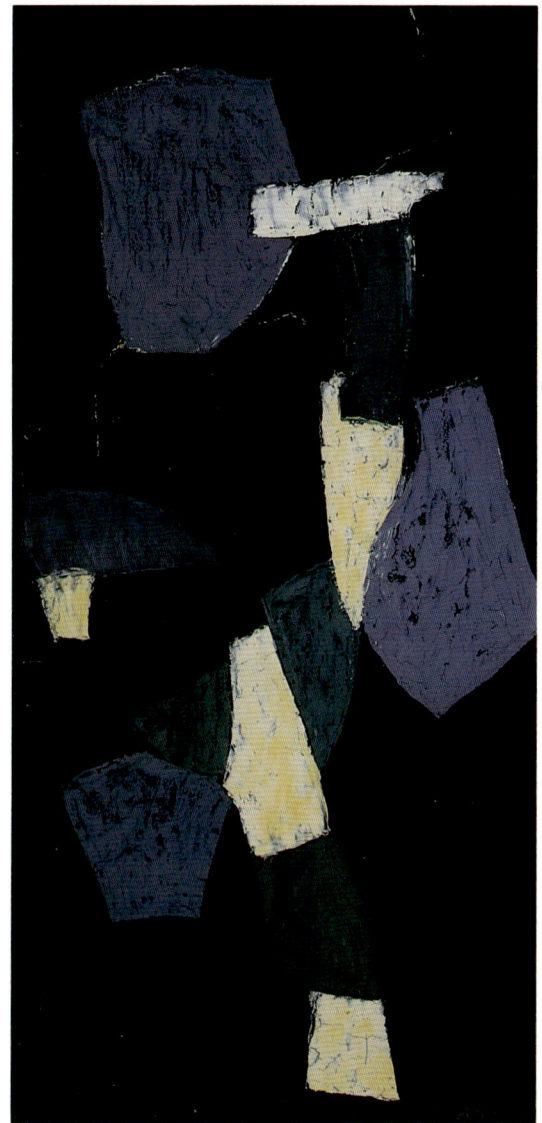

Jeanne Bultman, *Istanbul—Nightfall Rising ,* 1979. Stained glass fabricated from collage by Fritz Bultman, 84 × 48 in (213.36 × 121.92 cm). (Photograph courtesy of Jeanne Bultman.) Media dictate their own conventions, limiting the ways in which colors and shapes can be used. Stained-glass color is filtered light, rather than light reflected from surfaces. To view it, light is required behind the work of art but not necessarily in front of it. The black lines between the colors are a necessity rather than an aesthetic choice; the channels of lead support the pieces of glass. Closed forms are the natural forms of stained glass, and of the paper collage on which this piece is based.

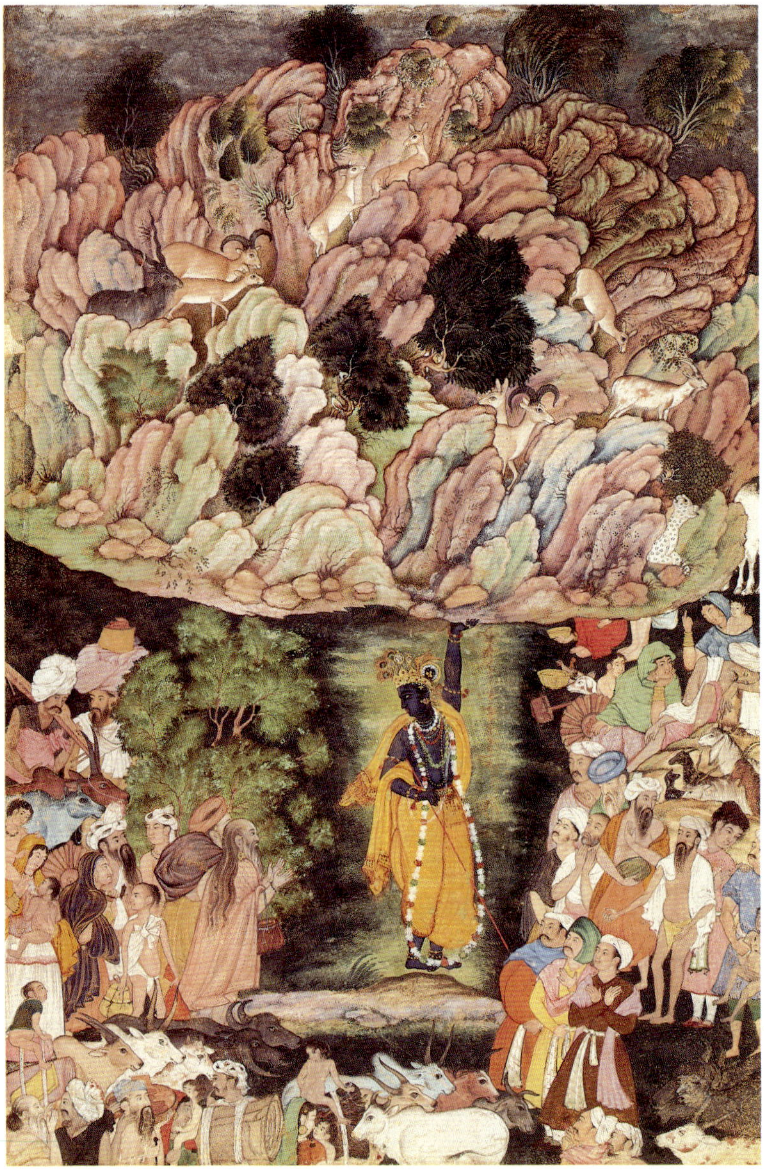

Mughal, Harivamsa (The Genealogy of Hari): *Krishna Lifts Mount Govardhan,* c. 1590. Opaque watercolor on paper, 11.375 × 7.875 in (28.9 × 20 cm). (The Metropolitan Museum of Art, Purchase, Edward C. Moore, Jr. Gift, 1928. (29.63.1).) The color combinations in this painting are related to those in El Greco's *View of Toledo,* but the moods are quite different, partly because of the difference in subject matter, partly because the color is pale.

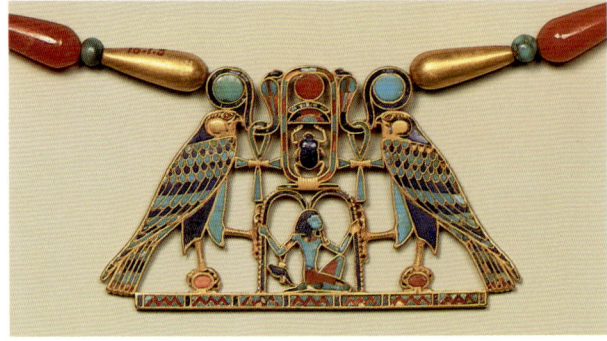

Egyptian, *Pectoral of Senwosret II.* (Detail). Gold, amethyst, turquoise, feldspar, carnelian, lapiz lazuli, and garnet. Pectoral, 3.25 × 1.75 in (8.2 × 4.5 cm). (The Metropolitan Museum of Art, Rogers Rund and Henry Walters Gift, 1916. (16.1.3).) The colors in this piece of jewelry are the colors of metals and precious and semiprecious stones. Here opacity, translucence, and transparency come into play.

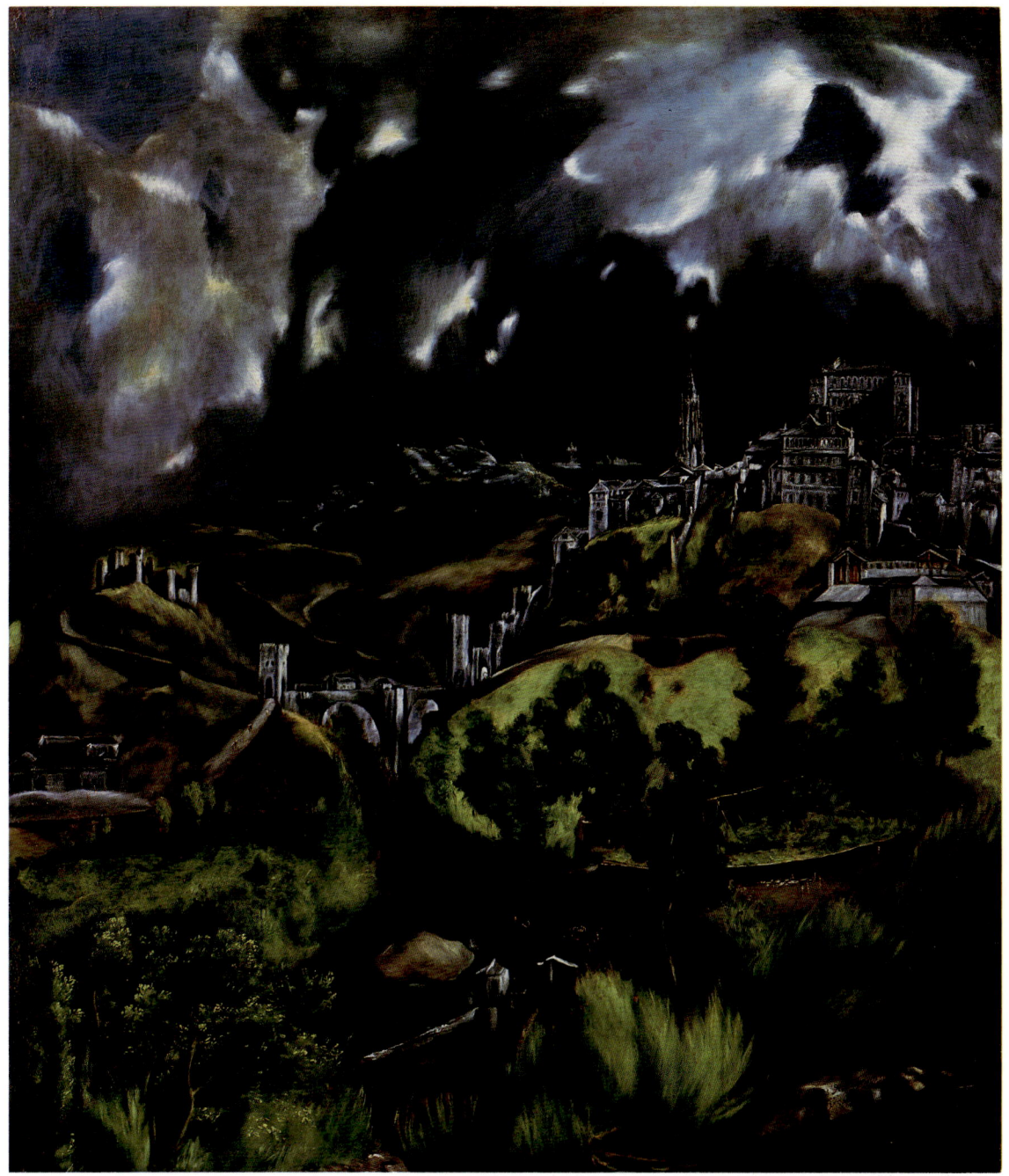

El Greco (Domenicos Theatocopoulos), *View of Toledo*. Oil on canvas, 47.75 × 42.75 in (121.3 × 108.6 cm). (The Metropolitan Museum of Art, Bequest of Mrs. H. O. Havemeyer, 1929. The H. O. Havemeyer Collection. (29.100.6).) Colors and deep shadows create a stormy, moody effect, perhaps because we associate the colors with natural phenomena and link these phenomena to emotions or states of mind. Subject matter can strengthen or dilute the effect. And some paintings more than others invite us to consider the state of mind of the artist who chose the colors and arranged them.

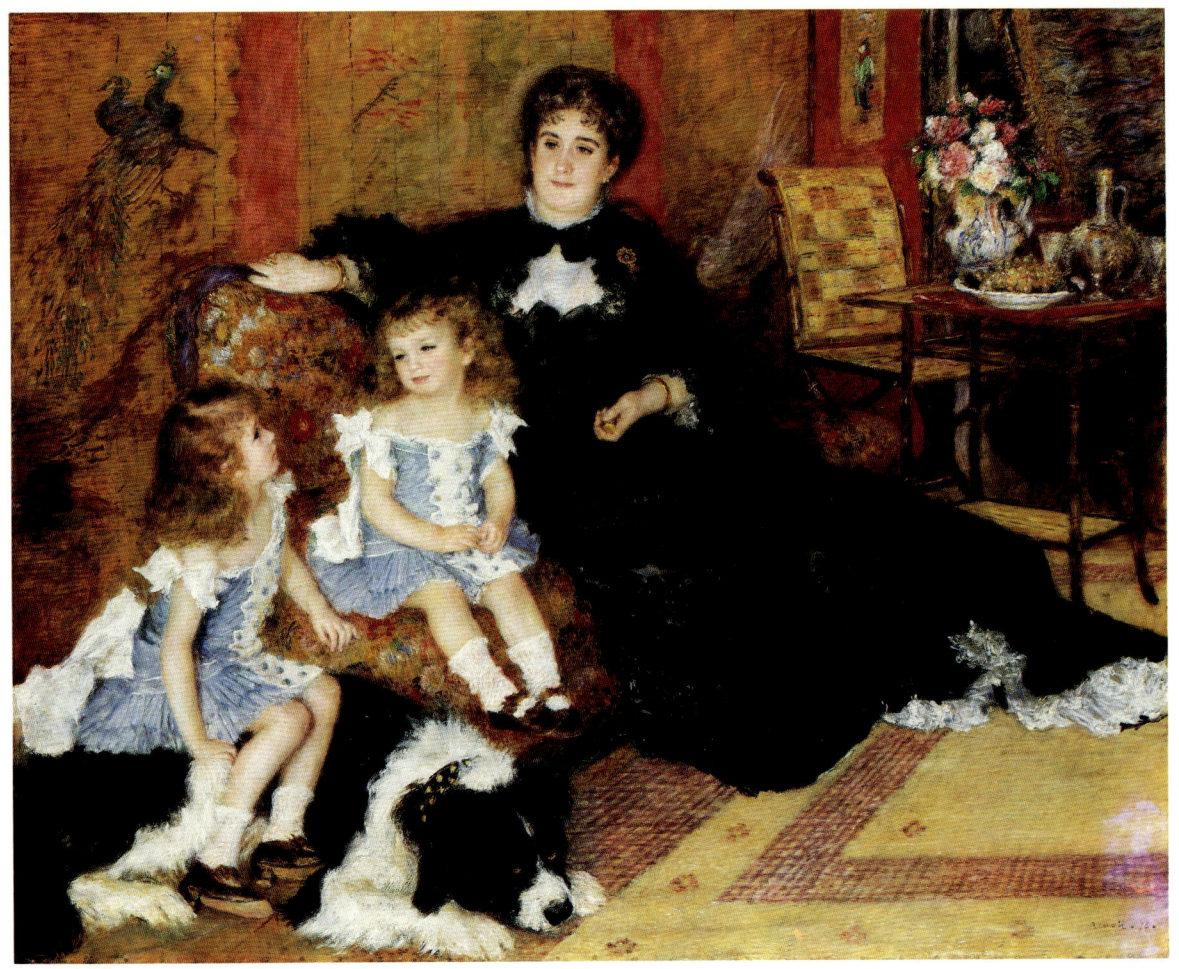

Renoir, *Madame Charpentier and Her Children,* 1878. Oil on canvas, 60.5 × 7.125 in (153.7 × 190.2 cm). (The Metropolitan Museum of Art, Wolfe Fund, 1907. Catherine Lorillard Wolfe Collection. (07.122).) Blue is said to recede, a characteristic of cool colors. But in this painting, the pale blue of the children's dresses is set off by the warmer tones of the background, and by its proximity to the strong black-white contrast of the mother's clothing and the dog.

ing colors, are never the only correct identifiers. The color labeled yellow can also be correctly classified as light, bright, warm, or the color of daffodils. A certain yellow may be lemon yellow, chrome yellow, or any of the many nonprimal names for different yellows. The picture of the abilities of agnosiac patients should be filled out by determining their general level of verbal competence, a necessary background to assessing impediments in labeling colors. In one conceivable type of impediment, an agnosiac might misuse, say, the color name *yellow* but be able to identify yellow as a light or bright color. The agnosiac might be able to describe colors by simile, identifying, say, which color looked like the sky or which was the color of grass.

So far as is known, agnosiac patients have no physical reason for the specialized lack of access Geschwind attributed to them. What is needed is a clearer picture of what they lack access to. The terms *color experience* or *account of color experience* are not easy to define. Is it an account of a color experience if I say my favorite color is blue? Because of the structural and syntactical peculiarities of the English language, a selective amnesia for color names cannot occur. Therefore, it cannot be the basis of a pathology, or it cannot be an accurate behavioral description of that pathology. If color names were to disappear from the English language, we would lose at the same time many names of objects, many metaphorical expressions, the de facto color names (pastel, dark), and many conceptions applicable to color but also used to label other items (beautiful).

Forgetting Color Names

The term *forgetting* is used arbitrarily, a looseness that bears on studies of memory. An agnosiac is said to have forgotten color names, but a patient with anorexia is not said to have forgotten how to eat. As lack of access to infor-

mation about color experience implies, an analogue for the behavior of Geschwind's patient is that of a normal person wearing a blindfold, compelled to make guesses at the colors of objects because the objects cannot be seen. Another analogue is a person asked to label colors according to whether they were, say, puce, taupe, or aureolin. If the person did not know the meaning of these color names, random guesses and errors might be made.

Geschwind's patient apparently looked at the objects before answering, a significant detail because it ties his behavior to the behavior of anyone else. The patient is not reported to have said he could not identify the colors of the objects he had looked at. Nor did he say he had forgotten color names. He lacked awareness of having forgotten. Or he resisted accepting this as his condition, if it was his condition.

Perhaps, like the rest of us, Geschwind's patient found it inconceivable that anyone could look at an object and be unable to name its color correctly. Chimpanzees who learned to use sign language, under the tutelage of Beatrice and Robert Gardner at the University of Nevada, were taught the signs for the principal colors and used them correctly. If the brain has a special method for storing words and concepts that cannot be forgotten or are almost never forgotten, the names of the primal colors, though not other color names, might fall in this group. *Color* might be an unforgettable concept. It had not been forgotten by Geschwind's patient, which is why he was able to answer the questions put to him.

Although the criteria for unforgettable concepts have not been defined, we often assume they exist. Freud, writing on pain and pleasure, never considered the possibility that anyone could forget the nature of these conditions or even what the words meant. Pain and pleasure precede language. Organisms low on the evolutionary scale move toward some things and away from others, actions we interpret in terms of what the organism likes or dislikes. Mammals, say cats, react to pain and pleasure with sounds and body language that human beings understand perfectly. Nobody mistakes a suffering cat or an angry cat for a contented cat.

Pain and pleasure, we might theorize, are unforgettable because reaction to these conditions is integral to the life process. Organisms do not forget they are alive. Describing pain or pleasure in words is an afterthought, a late development in the evolutionary process. But color, or the light condition we call color, falls into the same category. Many organisms low on the evolutionary scale move toward light or away from it, or selectively respond to light of certain colors.

Whether plants can feel pain or pleasure is a highly controversial question, often dismissed as ridiculous although some people talk to their plants. That plants respond to color and light, however, is firmly established and many of the mechanisms are understood. In, for example, the process called phototropism, plants grow toward the light. Cells on the side of the plant stem away from the light multiply more rapidly, the mechanism by which the process operates.

That a plant might forget how to grow toward the light is inconceivable. We would classify such a plant as a damaged plant or a dead plant, not a plant with amnesia. Living organisms cannot forget how to respond to light, because they cannot forget how to live and still continue living. Because light is a different color from darkness, a mechanism for discriminating between colors (or between light and darkness) is implied, even for tulips, amoebas, and other organisms that do not have eyes. The eye, like the brain, is a centralized organ of great refinement that evolved to control decentralized mechanisms that preceded it.

I conclude we cannot forget what color is, or forget, say, how to notice a light in the dark-

ness. The responses of Geschwind's patient are consistent with this. He knew what color was, knew questions were being asked about it, and understood he was expected to answer the questions. He gave wrong answers.

Memory and Value Judgment

Selective amnesia (or selective forgetting) is accepted as normal when it occurs in the general population. Everyday examples include forgetting how to use logarithms or remembering people's faces but not their names. The lapse implies a selective failure of will: an aversion to paying attention to what does not seem important.

An elderly person with severe memory problems may forget what everyone considers important. A living relative may be addressed by the name of a person known many years ago, as if the conception of time had collapsed. A person with Alzheimer's disease may forget what happened five minutes ago or may forget the need to put clothes on before going out in the street. Value judgment by an observer is a central issue in memory, because strict societal rules determine what is allowably forgotten and what we expect will be remembered. A job interviewer in a business office may forget the names of unsuccessful job applicants. That interviewer should not forget the name of his or her employer. Nor should the interviewer forget the name of his or her spouse.

The absentminded, like the poor, are always among us. Although small boys have no difficulty remembering the batting average of major league ball players, an adult population perennially unable to remember how to use the names *vermilion, carnelian, magenta, chartreuse,* and *mauve* is not difficult to collect. Many people misuse, confuse, or forget color names other than the primals. The ineptitude escapes notice because commonplace, an indicator of societal priorities. Few except students in art schools are actively encouraged to develop a refined ability to name, observe carefully, match, or mix colors.

Those who misuse many of the less familiar color names shed light on what otherwise presents itself as an uncanny aspect of the agnosias: unimpaired skill at sorting, combined with inability to name correctly. Nobody needs to know the words *vermilion* and *magenta* to sort vermilion and magenta color swatches. Naming and sorting are unrelated skills, and we should not expect otherwise in agnosiacs.

Geschwind's patient who confused red and green displayed a different magnitude of impairment from that of an individual who confuses vermilion and viridian. Whether or not red, like *color*, is an unforgettable concept, errors are not expected in use of the primal color names, which even signing chimpanzees learn to handle correctly. If encountered in the course of everyday affairs, an individual whose vision was not anomalous but who misapplied the words *red* and *green* would be regarded as retarded. Yet gender-based stereotypes cannot be ignored and reflect societal value judgments.

The man unable to remember unusual color names is as familiar a figure as the woman unable to remember the names of the parts of an automobile engine. Interest in color passes widely as either feminine or effeminate, a code that questions whether it has a value, whether remembering information about color is important. When a hostile art critic describes a painter as merely a colorist, a work of art as merely colorful, a world of attitudes is conveyed by the word *merely*. This world of attitudes bears on the central issue in the agnosias. With due respect for the strange symptoms of the patients, interpretations of these symptoms are also strange. The patients are interviewed by medical personnel who share the expectations and misapprehensions about color common through our society. They expected the

word *red* to be used correctly by the patients, but doubtless would have been more forgiving about, say, the words *carnelian* or *cerise*. Why? Rules exist, and we follow the rules. But none of us can say what they are or why we make value judgments as we do.

What goes on in the minds of agnosiacs may be no more curious than what goes on in our own minds. I am less interested in why women like color, if in fact they like color, than in the train of metaphorical association that suggests the interest would be appropriate. We cling stubbornly to the bad habit of attributing gender to what is neither masculine nor feminine. The nearest analogue may be the alchemists, who superstitiously imagined that the union of chemical elements could be meaningfully compared to human coitus. The association never led the alchemists to any insight of scientific significance. It catered to a vainglorious idea, shared by both men and women: that the world is a mirror of human concerns. The cosmos, viewed in this manner, reduces to a collection of opposites reflecting the oppositeness attributed to male and female.

Color Names and Object Names

Although thousands of color names exist, the average adult uses very few. Anyone asked to list all the names of objects he or she could think of and then all the names of colors would produce a longer list of object names than of color names. Yet I doubt that seeing a difference between two shades of cerulean blue is more difficult than seeing a difference between a chair and a sofa. The disparity in vocabulary mirrors human value systems rather than the nature of the phenomenological world. Form differences are regarded as more significant than color differences.

The bias, unexamined, infects scientific theory, much like the outlaw computer programs, called viruses, that infect and disrupt modern computer programs. Hermann Rorschach, without examining his reasoning or its traditional sources, went so far as to suspect that only defectives and artists paid more attention to color than to form when given the inkblot test. Rorschach inkblot test scores are not available for, say, Newton, Goethe, Munsell, or Ostwald. Would they, too, have paid more attention to color, at the expense of form, than Rorschach regarded as appropriate?

As Rorschach realized, paying attention to color rather than form is unconventional, a deviation from societal rules. But the development of human thought depends on entertaining ideas that are different and new, that are not just a recyling of ideas from the past, not just a rehash of what everyone thinks. The presumed propriety of preferring form to color is conventional, an old way that may not be a better way or may not be suitable for all circumstances. A plant would be in trouble if it decided not to grow toward the sun or if it decided to grow in the direction of forms that, say, included right angles.

The preference for placing form above color finds serendipitous support in constraints set by language. Children learn the names of forms or objects before learning color names, a route that cannot be avoided. Understanding that the blueness of a chair is not the chair requires prior understanding of what a chair is. An individual cannot correctly name colors but lack understanding of what an object is. Learning to identify colors, like learning to count, requires an understanding that objects can be considered to have attributes. I hazard a guess that among those of low intelligence, low literacy, or low educational level, difficulty in naming colors and in counting exceeds difficulty in naming objects.

What is forgotten by patients with visual agnosias is less interesting than what is remembered. Even agnosiacs know what a color is, which is why Geschwind's patient gave color names, though the wrong color names, in response to the questions put to him. Asking how agnosiacs and others make the determination amounts to seeking an operational understanding of how color is identified as color. Three answers to the question are old enough to have been thought upon by Plato and Aristotle. First, color is a visual percept. Second, color is either an attribute of light or a phenomenon caused by light waves. The third answer, related to the first, is that color, as visual percept, is something other than visually perceived form.

PART TWO

Color and Light

We can take up the subject of the study of color in two quite different ways; namely, as a subject in physics or as a subject in art. If we consider it from the point of view of physics we are dealing with exact laws of light and optics, and may proceed on a basis of fairly well-established facts.

Walter Sargent, The Enjoyment and Use of Color

Whereas the world of naive men is somewhat confused, and reveals its subjective character in any critical discussion of its properties, in the world of the physicist no confusion and no contradiction are tolerated.

Wolfgang Kohler, Gestalt Psychology

Light of Day, Dark of Night

There is a degree of light which surfeits, a want of it which
starves the visual organ.

Horatio Greenough, Form and Function

Suppose, Ananda, there is no light and they are unable to see
things, does that mean that they cannot see the darkness? If it
is possible to see darkness when it is too dark to see things,
it simply means there is no light; it does not mean they
cannot see.

The Surangama Sutra

Color is caused by light, a familiar assertion. We explain what it means in either of two ways, according to
whether light is ordinary daylight or light as
it is described in the physical sciences. Neither
explanation suffices if light is considered in the
alternative sense. Neither addresses the curious question of whether light exists in isolation from color or apart from its own colors.

Light of Day

If light means daylight, objects exhibit many
colors during the daytime. They appear
indistinguishable from one another in color
(although not colorless) at night. All cats, we
are proverbially told, are black in the dark. For
the ophthalmologist Ernest Fuchs, "the functioning of the color sense is more or less
dependent on the illumination. The brighter
the light, the more color there is in the world"
(Fuchs [1908] 1924, 243). For Claude Bragdon,
the underlying basis of theory was that "the
sun is the affector, the eye is the receptor"
(Bragdon 1932, 122). For Robert Boyle, "the
Beams of Light, Modify'd by the Bodies
whence they are sent (Reflected or Refracted)
to the Eye, produce there that kind of Sensation, Men commonly call Colour" (Boyle
[1664] 1964, 90).

It is more difficult to agree that "if the illumination sinks below a certain limit the perception of colors fails altogether" (Fuchs
[1908] 1924, 90). Color vision, inseparable
from vision, achieves widest scope (the greater
number of colors can be seen) within a circum-

scribed range. With sufficient light, we see many colors. Dimming the light reduces the number of colors perceived, though never to none. When light is absent, the color of the darkness remains. All looks black.

We do not know whether long-term deprivation of light causes permanent impairment of vision. Goethe argued that acuity improves, and that prisoners confined in the dark learn to see without light, at least dimly. Excessive illumination is obviously harmful, the reason for not looking into lights of blinding brightness or at eclipses of the sun. Color vision is also adversely affected by oscillation from one condition to another, the reason eye strain is caused by strobe lights. And changes occur in the color balance of human vision as a result of aging or certain diseases.

In his essay "Nature" Ralph Waldo Emerson (1803-82) found "no object so foul that intense light will not make it beautiful" (Emerson [1836] 1969, 8). Leonardo da Vinci (1452–1519) was less convinced that strong light flatters colors. In one chapter of his treatise on painting, he finds "colors situated in a light space will show their natural beauty in proportion to the brightness of that light" (Rigaud [1802] 1957, 145). Elsewhere, "polished and glossy surfaces show least of their genuine color... The parts which receive the light do not show their natural color" (Rigaud [1802] 1957, 137). Light will not enhance the colors of objects if reflected from their surfaces in a manner that produces excessive sheen, glossiness, highlight, or glare. These effects, each of which can be given an optical explanation, consist of a greater than optimal amount of reflected light. The excess may exist throughout the field (glare) or over a small portion (highlight). In photography, where highlights and glare are rarely desirable or acceptable, methods of controlling them include photographing through polarizing filters.

Fuch's equating of brighter light with more color relies on the assumption that the illuminating light is white or nearly white. The full range of yellows cannot be seen under a light, however bright, that is blue. Beyond this, bright light causes harsh shadows, and diffused light is kinder to colors. Most color films for cameras, like most human beings, distinguish fine nuances of colors less effectively on a sunny day at noon. A gray day provides better conditions, as does morning or evening light.

Dark of Night

If colors are brought out by daylight or require its presence to some degree, light, in this sense, causes color. The causative relationship is said to have been proved by establishing it scientifically. Nature's puzzles rarely unravel easily, and the nature of proof, including scientific proof, has inspired extensive debate. Setting aside those issues, scientific theory explains, or proposes to explain eventually, the nature of human experience in the everyday world, including the perceptual experience of seeing color. The presumption is that human beings are able to give an accurate report of the experiences science will explain. A reason for resisting that assumption in the case of color is that many conventionalized ways of reporting the perceptual experience are nominal.

It is not true, for example, that objects have no color in the dark. They simply all look the same color, the reason they cannot be distinguished from one another or from their environment. That is immediately fatal to the argument that light causes color or is identifiable as its sole cause. The color of the dark of the night is seen when illumination is not present. Furthermore, the color common to the environment and all nonfluorescent objects in the dark is poorly described as black. In many cases, the tonality is so much closer to charcoal gray that the term *visual gray* has been used (Stokes 1937, 22). In astronomy, the corresponding phenomenon is called *airglow*, a narrower word referring to the deviation from absolute blackness observable in the night sky.

One conjecture attributes airglow, described as a weak glow, to stray radiant energy from the sun. Possibly, interpreting the night sky as aglow is a rationalization of visual experience. Defeating any expectation to the contrary, the color of the sky at night is not black. Even in rural areas removed from bright city lights, it is only nominally black, which implies no more than that human beings have lapsed into the habit of calling it black.

The nonblackness of the nocturnal skyscape has a counterpart in the nonblackness of enclosed rooms. Indoors or out, black nights are not black, nor do all cats look black in the dark. All cats look gray in the dark, even black cats. Light is not a sole cause for color if we see the gray of the darkness and do not cease seeing in light's absence. The most intense, the most nearly absolute, blacks are not caused by the absence of light. They are caused by its presence. The color of black patent leather and of other extremely dark objects—colors that are blacker than the black of night—are seen in daylight but not in the dark.

The darkness is often mottled or reticulated, sometimes in two tones of gray. Traversing it in stately procession are minuscule spots or flashes of white, orange, and pale blue. These markings, called phosphenes by modern researchers, were identified by Helmholtz as the *"self-light* or *intrinsic light* of the retina" (Helmholtz [1856-66] 1962, 2:12). They move horizontally across the field from left to right, perhaps because we are habituated to reading (therefore, to scanning) in that direction.

The absence of landmarks familiar in an illuminated environment may explain the charac-

teristics of the visual gray. Colors in daylight seem to be located "out there," attributes of the surfaces of objects rather than of human neurological processes. Because no horizon line crosses it (we assume that horizons are "out there"), the visual gray appears closer: not so close as to be inside the eye or within the eyelids, yet no more than a few inches or feet away. To Stokes, the visual gray gave an impression of being soft, perhaps because, like the blue of the sky, not associated with the hardness of objects.

The deviation from absolute black, sometimes conjectured to be caused by spontaneous neural discharge, may be a function of the absence of what M. E. Chevreul called simultaneous contrast. Colors are brought out by light, but also by juxtaposition to other colors that look different. Black looks most dark (or most black) next to white or next to light or bright colors. Color contrast is absent in the darkness, and what is caused by absence of light is absence of color differentiation, not absence of color.

The familiar question of whether everyone sees colors in the same way assumes its own light in this monochrome context. If one person saw the darkness as gray, another as green, another as yellow, the fundamental nature of the experience would be unchanged: nobody can see objects in the dark because they look the same color as their environment, whatever that color might be or might be called.

Undifferentiated Color

Fear of the dark is explained in terms of childish imaginings of demons and hobgoblins. The terror has a visual source before literary sources, and its cause is how darkness looks. Absence of color differentiation is known to disturb some people. Walter Cohen noted anxiety among subjects in tests that were "attempts to study the effects of uniform stimulation over the entire visual field," or *Ganzfeld* (Cohen 1966, 306). The German term means whole field or entire field. Typically, subjects are exposed to dimly illuminated, one-color environments (the usual color is white) in which no forms can be seen. Cohen's observers were asked to peer inside a translucent sphere that had its interior illuminated from the outside. "The most representative description of the homogeneous *Ganzfeld* is that of close, impenetrable fog. The experience is a unique one, and most 0's [observers] have difficulty in describing the field in terms usually associated with visual phenomena" (Cohen 1966, 313). The fog was reported as "a hazy insipid yellow," or "misty, like being in a lemon pie" (Cohen 1966, 309). Cohen's subjects found the experience unpleasant, and "anxiety and fear of blindness under somewhat similar conditions also were reported by Hochberg, Triebel and Seaman."

Calling a field of color a fog implies that objects ought to be present or are concealed by the "fog." What is expressed is resistance to the idea that we can see without seeing forms. Form is equated with meaning and structure and can suggest logic, an association founded on the idea that forms can be described in terms of geometry, and geometry is said to be logical.

The conception of form as a visual, intellectual, or psychological necessity is wrong-headed but commonplace. Its simplest expression is a demand for more than one color, familiar in responses to works of art. When first exhibited, paintings by Barnett Newman and others in which a canvas is covered with a single color were found unsettling by some viewers. Form-seeking resistance to monochrome apparently also explains why experiments in sensory deprivation disorient subjects untrained in meditation, and why meditation is difficult to learn. The darkness within can be as unsettling as the dark of the night, evidently for the same reason.

Nocturnal inability to distinguish forms removes the comfort of the daytime environment in which we orient ourselves to the accretions of space-time we have grown accustomed to interpreting as corporeal objects. Goethe believed that confrontation with structureless color, including the color of the night, created a sense of deprivation. The color field of the darkness can suggest invasion by the inchoate but also respite from the confines of structure. Potentially terrifying in one case, it frees the spirit in the other.

Night is frightening, and its imagined hobgoblins are memorialized in folk tales from around the world. I regard the hobgoblins as a pictorial expression of the idea that a formless world of color is irrationally different from the world of everyday experience. The color conditions of night are so different from those of daytime that the most bizarre encounters seem possible. Seeing "nothing" is a confrontation with the primitive Ur-vision, with what human beings see when ostensibly nothing is to be seen.

Brown is often identified as the most commonly occurring of all terrestrial colors. But black, including the entire range of nominal blacks and near blacks, is observed more often. Black, whether absolute or nominal, is the color of night, including the expanses of unending night between the stars in the sky.

Look Back Time

The uncertain nature of the relationship between black (which is a color), darkness (a quality of black) and nothingness (a metaphysical concept) is touched on in the so-called look back time of contemporary cosmology and astronomy. The idea of look back time is founded on the reasoning that light from the quasars at the edge of the known universe, unusually bright celestial objects at distances approaching fifteen billion light years, must have begun traveling toward earth an enormously long time ago. What we see, for this reason, must be interpreted as an image of what used to exist: of the way the universe looked in a distant past when galaxies began to form. Look back time tells us about the structure of the universe but also about the nature of visual imagery.

The quasars, according to one theory, are young galaxies, formed after a period of darkness that followed the big bang, the cataclysmic explosion by which the universe was created. The quasars, if this theory is correct, probably no longer exist, except as images formed by the light and other radiant energy they emitted billions of years ago. Beyond a limit estimated at fifteen billion light years, the sky looks uniformly black and contains no celestial objects. We are looking so far back into time (or into four-dimensional space-time) that there is nothing to see, other than the darkness that existed before the quasars.

Why does empty space look dark or black, rather than "looking" (if this is possible) imperceivable? It is the familiar question of why, in the story of the Creation, God's first act is the creation of light (Genesis 1:3) but prior to that "darkness was upon the face of the deep." Why does God create the world out of darkness and not out of absolute nullity?

Black, Nothing, and Look Back Time

I doubt that the question of the relationship, if any, between black and nothing is semantic as it arises in cosmological look back time. If blackness permeated the unpopulated space-time of the early universe, which had no stars to radiate light, we need not assume that nothing existed. In visual terms, the black color of the darkness existed, as did the darkness, in whatever form this formlessness possessed in isolation from its color.

Equating either with a vacuity leads to problems with words, prototypes for the semantic tangles about the color black that crop up in several disciplines. If, say, the universe was originally a black *nothing*, what expanded or exploded to create the big bang? The modern explanation that the expansion of the universe means the expansion of the spaces between the stars is not entirely informative. How did an original black *nothing* become the space that expanded?

The Causes of Nothing

Cultural commitment to the concept of causality leads us to believe that any colored image we see has a cause. The causative *something* may vary from light waves reflected by objects (as when I see a red apple) to human neurological processes (as when I hallucinatorily see what is not there). Images that are black in color fail to consistently conform to this paradigm. Seeing a black pair of shoes, like seeing a red pair of shoes, is agreed to be caused by something: likely, by the presence of shoes of that color. But the black of the sky or of the night is uniquely said to have no cause, which is what being caused by nothing implies.

Unless either causality or nothingness can be redefined, curious questions will continue to intrude. One is how an effect (black) can be created by an entity (nothing) presumably devoid of properties, including the property of being able to cause an effect. Another is why nothing causes no effect in some cases but the effect of black color in others.

If the black color of the sky cannot be attributed to nothing, it must be something. Several possibilities occur for what that something might be. Word drifts back from cosmological circles that a missing mass cannot be located in the universe, which appears to include things we cannot see (Hawking 1988, 45). Black, in the night or in the sky, may be the color of a form of radiant energy antecedent to, or more primitive than, light: the color, say, of space-time, or of the radio waves that surround us in space and are thought to be remnants of the big bang.

The enigma of black reduces to the questions of what we mean by absence of light, and why the condition is assumed to imply an absence of anything. Whatever the answers, the status of black, in explanations of color, is a Gordian knot that defies attempts to untie it. Part of the tangle is caused by the double standard about the color that acculturation imposes. Some people say nothing can be seen in the dark. If asked to admit that the color of the darkness can be seen, they reply either that this is not a color or that the blackness is what they mean by nothing. Yet nobody seriously believes that black is a definition of nothing that can stand scrutiny. Black is the name of a color.

Look Back Time as Perspective

Cosmological look back time, although not customarily identified in this manner, is a four-dimensional space-time perspective, a superset of the more familiar perspective of three-dimensional space. Look back time is a visual phenomenon. It looks as it does because of how we see.

In terrestrial space, objects look progressively smaller as they recede into the distance. The phenomenon, called perspective, is rarely recognized as an everyday example of the relativity of either space or the extension of images in two-dimensional visual space. But it provides a perfect illustration of what Einstein concluded through mathematical, rather than visual, reasoning. No coordinate system is privileged, because the universe has no fixed center. We imagine ourselves at the center of the universe, because practical reasons exist for doing so. I need to know how far a door is from me, though I know the door is not the same distance from other people.

Absence of a privileged coordinate system implies that perspective is a factor in vision,

and objects do not have "normal" ways they ought to look. The size and shape an object displays for a viewer depends on the interval of space between object and viewer and on the orientation of the object. For an architect at a drafting board, a building can be drawn in correct perspective from any of an infinite number of points of view. No point of view is more normal than any other.

Human beings and animals recognize objects seen in unfamiliar orientations, but human beings both understand and resist the infinity of possibilities. We maintain mental picture books in which each object is remembered in the single aspect considered normal. Paleolithic painters depicted animals only in side view, although they saw and recognized living animals from many perspectives. Egyptian and Sumerian artists combined "typical" views of different parts of the human body, evolving composite figures; head and legs are seen in side view although the chest is seen in front view.

Today, thousands of years later, twentieth-century art students often have difficulty learning to draw the human figure from unusual points of view. The most difficult are orientations in which relative sizes of body parts are transposed. The student is able to see that in some circumstances the model's hand can look larger than his or her head. This is hard to accept because it offends the conception of what is normal.

Perspective is a universal phenomenon because nothing escapes from it. It has small effects as well as large. Roman painters, courageous enough to attempt its depiction (it was largely ignored by the artists of earlier cultures), were reluctant to recognize its all-pervasiveness. An anonymous painter from Pompeii failed to realize that if two legs of a table are the same length when measured by a ruler, the leg farther from the viewer will look shorter to that viewer.

Although most people sense this and other

similarly minute perspective effects, few have occasion to think about them. A Roman painting with the perspective inadvertently reversed (with "wrong perspective" by modern standards) looks wrong to the modern viewer. But many people cannot immediately identify what disturbs them or how they would modify the painting to make its perspective look "right."

Moving from tables to extraterrestrial spaces, the assumption inherent in the four-dimensional perspective of look back time—which concerns time as well as astronomically large spaces—is that celestial objects we see at great distances are old, because light from them has required time to arrive. What we see today is the way these objects used to look, millions or billions of years ago. This idea, too, demands generalization, because the earth and its objects (as the cosmological principle implies) cannot be materially or functionally different from the rest of the universe.

Like rays of light from the quasars, rays reflected from the proverbial yellow chair in my room take time to travel to my eye. In absolute terms the time is so brief I can ignore it for practical purposes. An interval, nonetheless, must be assumed. It can neither be reduced to zero nor eliminated.

The curious implication of this infinitesimal interval is that every color I see, or every set of colors combined to form an image of an object, must be understood as an image of the way the perceived object used to look. Arguing around this is impossible, even if "used to" implies how the object looked billionths upon billionths of a nanosecond ago. I am subtly separated from the things that I see, because at the moment I see their images the objects are slightly older.

I understand this to imply that all colored images I see are those of objects from a different time than my own. We can see only into the past although we live in the present. All time is look back time, which is intuitively understood. The understanding intrudes in intimations of alienation or separation, or in the mythic urge to look into the future, feelings that reflect genuine insight into the nature of the physical world. The loneliness of God is the loneliness of human beings. We dream through our nights alone and die alone. We also see alone and live alone, each subject to our own personal technicolor visions in the privacy of our own unique coordinate system.

Black as an Absolute

If anything causes a greater amount of conceptual difficulty than the habit of equating black, including the black of the sky or of the night, with nothing, it is the custom of regarding the color as an absolute. Most people find it easy to understand that a color name such as *red* refers to a range of colors, rather than a single variety of shade. Vermilion, magenta, alizarin, and crimson are names for types of red, subcategories within the larger category. Black and white similarly refer to ranges of color, although this is more difficult to grasp. Terms such as *near black* and *off-white* misleadingly imply that no shade of color is black or white unless an extreme or absolute in that range.

That all black objects are not identical in color (and therefore are not all absolute black) can be easily demonstrated by collecting a dozen and comparing them. The difference between tonalities in this range is played on in the black paintings of Ad Reinhardt. Each is a sixty-inch square of canvas divided into nine (three by three) squares. Each of the nine embedded squares is painted a different shade of black. None of the nine blacks is an exact color match for any of the others.

Similar games, as easily played at the other extreme of the value scale, are familiar throughout the history of art. From Jan Vermeer's *Young Woman Standing at a Virginal* (National Gallery, London) to Kazimir Malevich's *White on White* (Museum of Modern Art, New York), innumerable paintings play on the point that all whites are not color matches for one another. Like *black* or any other color name, *white* is a label applied to a range of thousands of closely similar colors.

Achromaticity

Words confuse about color as often as they elucidate because language is inherently limited or because human confusions are incorporated into it. In English, one locus of difficulty about both black and white lies in the double meaning of *color*. In its broader sense, the word names the class to which any and every color belongs. In its narrower, *color* is a synonym for *chroma*: the redness, blueness, greenness, or other hue quality that makes it possible to distinguish one spectral hue from another.

In thinking of black as color in one sense but not in another, we rarely reflect on the oddity of using *color* to refer, at one and the same time, both to some colors (the spectral colors) but also to any and all colors. To stabilize the ambiguous position of black, white, and gray (the color obtained by mixing black and white), the term *achromatic colors* came to be applied. A syntactical peculiarity in itself, *achromatic color* perpetuates the idea that black, white, and gray are colors without color. The coinage is unfortunate.

Black, Blue, and Sky

Among the chromatic colors, as Goethe and others have remarked, blue is the most similar to black, not just because it is dark. Generations of housewives have added bluing to laundry because many people appear to believe that a white that is slightly blue looks more genuinely white than one that is yellowish, grayish, reddish, greenish, brownish. There is a visual affinity, in other words, between blueness and the color quality called achromaticity, seen in black, gray, and white.

Speakers of some languages use a common name for blue and black, which led early anthropologists to assume no difference could be seen between the colors. Discounting that extravagant conjecture, a refined visual observation is involved. Blue and black look similar, by any ordinary visual criterion. At the dark end of the value scale, navy blue and black are more easily confused than any other two colors, particularly at a distance. At the pale end, relationships are more ambiguous. Light gray looks more similar to or is more easily confused with a light blue of similar value than a similarly pale pink or yellow. But light violet may be more similar in color to light gray than light blue is.

CHAPTER 7

Light and Dark in Perspective

Sight being, as I conceive, in the eyes, and he who has eyes
wanting to see; color being also present in them, still unless there
be a third nature specially adapted to the purpose, the owner of
the eyes will see nothing and the colors will be invisible.

Of what nature are you speaking?

Of that which you term light, I replied.

Plato, The Republic

olor, unlike form, cannot be reduced to geometry, which is able to present in visual terms ideas that remain abstract if expressed arithmetically. Plane geometry is a primitive geography of two-dimensional universes. Supplemented by the laws of perspective, it introduces the topography of the picture plane and the visual field. But theorems memorized in high school are not always consistent with perceptual experience. Those theorems convey rules about forms drawn or projected on planar surfaces. They rarely acknowledge backgrounds, the negative spaces surrounding forms. Plane geometry is as silent about the nature of its implied universe—a picture plane—as it is about the origin of the Euclidean point.

Something and Nothing

Because the spaces enclosed by their perimeters are treated as if divorced from those outside, the shapes of Euclidean geometry float in a sea of nothingness. We imagine the stars in the sky in a similar manner, white objects adrift in empty space. Art contributes further images of something displayed in a field of nothing, a primitive assessment of the nature of visual phenomenology. Most painters before the Romans drew human and animal figures against blank backgrounds. Black curtainlike expanses are suspended behind the sitters in fifteenth-century Netherlandish portrait paintings. Like the blank backgrounds, the black curtains deny the continuousness of two-dimensional pictorial space by asserting a private dimension of their own.

Although the inconsistency is not always easy to grasp, all such vignettes deviate from visual experience. They express the duality that Ivins called the tactile-muscular ambience (Ivins 1946). Unlike the objects I touch, those I see, whether red triangles or white chickens, are not located in emptiness. Each is surrounded by an environment continuous with itself, similarly reducible to a simple or complex pattern of color spots. We acquire or fortify incomplete conceptions of two-dimensional universes when we study geometry. The Greeks sing siren songs from their graves, pursuing us with their unsophisticated conviction that tactile experience is the model for all experience.

As in the popular idiom, "a nothing person," an object labeled *nothing* is summarily dismissed from attention, the subjective or operational meaning of an otherwise incomprehensible term. Euclidean geometry ignores the spaces around forms. And cosmologists and astronomers were not originally concerned with studying the blackness or nothingness between stars. Interest centered on investigations of any *something*, whether cosmic rays, radio waves, or light waves, possibly or actually traversing the void. The recent bubble theory of the nature of the universe is exceptional in this regard. Its foundation is the long-neglected negative space: the shape of the interstellar blackness as we perceive it from earth.

Although usually less visual than geometry, arithmetic rises to finer metaphor in this case. The cipher or zero, invented by medieval Hindu or Arab mathematicians, expresses the idea that an entity cannot be ignored just because *nothing* is the label applied to it. By acknowledging a difference between 15 and 105—by recognizing that *nothing* does not mean no effect—the cipher enabled modern computation.

The interesting visual and conceptual aspect of this computation is the elusiveness of zero, a metaphorical link between color and number. Just as no amount of lowering of light can reduce vision to nothing (we always see the color of the darkness), an infinite number of repetitions of the process of dividing will not reduce a numerical quantity to zero. In subtraction, where zero can be arrived at, it proves to be a bridge rather than an abyss: the point of transition between the positive and negative numbers.

If the zero or cipher has a counterpart in the two-dimensional universe, I prefer to imagine it as the vanishing point of a perspective system, which, like a Euclidean point, can be located but never perceived. No visual analogue exists for silence, because seeing implies seeing color, and we never see *nothing*. In art, the concept of negative space, the spaces around forms, became important during the late nineteenth and early twentieth centuries. An understanding of negative space makes it possible to deal with a two-dimensional matrix, say, the picture plane of a painting, without the preconception that some parts of the composition are important and others are not.

Reasoning based on tactile rather than visual experience remains a more widespread kind of reasoning. It begins with eliminating what is nothing, not significant. The job is to discover what is significant. In visual thinking, everything is significant, a paradigm based on the experience of seeing color. For the functioning eye, color is all-pervasive. It permeates all parts of the visual field at all times.

I am not surprised that in mathematics the cipher or zero was a non-Western invention. We rarely reason effectively about anything, including color, that we regard as formless or inchoate, as unimportant or as nothing. I find some students unable to grasp the concept of negative space. They list the names of objects they see in paintings and insist, against all reason, that nothing else is included by the artist. Often such a student is highly intelligent with an overdeveloped conscience, a person who "has standards" and takes society's imperatives seriously. Separating what will be looked at from what will be ignored is a habit that cannot be transcended.

Visual thinking is sometimes called creative thinking, as if there were any purpose to thinking that is not creative. I think of the visual paradigm as more than an aesthetic nicety useful in understanding the visual arts. Most of our better ideas, are based on a visual, not tactile, paradigm.

Visual thinking is thinking for the present. No other kind of thinking releases us from unthinking recycling of the misconceptions of earlier peoples. In tactile sorting of the significant from the insignificant, where will the standards come from? We inherit them from the past, condemning ourselves to live out our lives as if we had been born a hundred or a thousand years ago. A great many misconceptions and poorly thought out conceptions about color are traditional. They should be subjected, one by one, to a scrutiny that is visual, that does not allow the possibility that vast areas of phenomenological experience can be unimportant, insignificant, nothing.

Color in Perspective

Color might be defined as the mode in which time and space appear within the confines of a planar or two-dimensional universe. More than one color exists. We see an array of spots of different colors, an ambience often explained by saying that we see color and form. But forms cannot be seen at night. And forms or shapes, in a two-dimensional matrix, always reduce to arrays of color spots. I prefer to imagine that the basic visual elements are color and perspective, or colors in perspective.

What any human being sees at any given instant is a portion of time and space, limited by the spatio-temporal perspective of that observer. Comparable parameters govern representation in those visual arts that are two-dimensional. To represent, or depict, a moment of time and space in a painting, I do not use time and space. What are manipulated are the colors of paints, again, to create a perspective.

To assess visual experience and the place of color in this experience, we need to consider all that we see at night, not just how objects look in the daytime. Astronomy and cosmology have a great deal to teach us about color and in fact are studies of colors, although we rarely try to integrate findings in these disciplines into our understanding of color in general. As Hawking noted, for the vast majority of stars, "there is only one characteristic feature we can observe—the color of their light" (Hawking 1988, 37). The data of astronomy and cosmology (except radio waves) are acquired largely from observation of the varicolored image we call the sky and the colored spectra formed by light emitted from distant stars. The much-popularized red shift is an observed color phenomenon. It provides our sole evidence for the expansion of the universe and, beyond that, for the big bang theory, which holds that the origin of the universe was a cataclysmic explosion.

T. S. Eliot penned marvelously biting words when he heard that the universe was expanding. He wondered how anyone knew. But an expanding universe is the most coherent explanation, perhaps the only conceivable explanation, for why the spectra of light from distant stars is shifted toward the red end of the visible light spectrum. The red shift increases with distance, implying a limit beyond which no visible light can reach us from stars. This is not because the stars are so far away, but because they are moving away from us so rapidly. The edge of the visible universe is reasonably defined as a color phenomenon: the distance at which the red shift becomes so extreme that light from more distant stars cannot reach us.

The tactile habit of thinking in terms of polarities gives a gratuitously violent theory of how the universe began, though the evidence presented would fit more modest theories as well. If all celestial bodies are moving apart from one another (or if the spaces between the stars are expanding), this need not imply that the process began with a cataclysmic explosion. The beginning might as easily have resembled a pebble dropping unnoticed into water or, as in recent theory, the foaming of a silent sea of black bubbles.

The celestial bubbles, discovered in mapping of a large sector of the sky, consist of starless expanses of approximately ovoid shape. The edges of the ovoid shapes are marked by the galaxies squeezed between them. Whether or not it proves out, the bubble theory is genuinely visual. It takes account of the entire sky, rather than assuming that stars are to be taken seriously as *something* and the black spaces between them to be disregarded as *nothing*. The bubble theory does not assume violence—a war of opposites—where no evidence of violence is to be seen.

Cosmologists are unlikely to classify themselves as investigators of colors. And those astronomers, say, Fred Hoyle, who stress the importance of observation of the stars to the development of human thought rarely mention that we could not observe the stars if we had hands and not eyes. Nor do they mention that a race of color-blind human beings would have had no way to see the red shift.

Long before people observed the stars with scientific detachment, they used them as a form of celestial entertainment. Perhaps they stared at the sky with the fascination modern children give to television screens. People imagined one dot joined to the next to form the pictures we now call constellations. They

spun yarns about how, say, the mythological giant Orion came to be placed in the sky as a constellation of stars. Later the constellations were thought of as guides for navigators. But the pictures in the sky were not originally picked out to help navigators, and the navigators did not need the stories. Possibly the idea of drawing pictures on surfaces was inspired by the game of drawing pictures in the sky by imagining lines linking the dots of the stars.

Today the stars are viewed with more sobriety. The modern understanding is that the images in the sky are not images, not chimerical. They are neither just colors, pictures, nor essentially visual phenomena. The spots and dots seen through telescopes are accounted for by celestial objects believed to be "there." We may pass lightly over the embarrassing question of whether the blackness surrounding these objects is similarly there. The assumption that it is remains difficult to reconcile with the status of interstellar blackness as nullity: as an image of, so to speak, what is not there.

Meteorites fall to the earth, and rockets can be dispatched to the planets, so the question of whether objects in the solar system (by extension, other celestial objects) are verifiably there appears to be laid to rest. The quasars, however, tell a different story and represent a different class of visual image. Afloat in their four-dimensional space-time perspective, the quasars were there at one time, a time irreconcilable with our own. As cinematography similarly suggests, the bare fact that we collectively see something and can take photographs of it does not prove it is there.

Astonishingly, objects—and not, as we imagine, images—may be the more ephemeral class of entity. The images of quasars seen through telescopes today have endured for fifteen billion years. This life span is longer than that enjoyed by the quasars in the form in which we presently see them. In visual terms, the most interesting aspect of the images of quasars is the failure of correspondence between image and object. If we could instantaneously transport ourselves to the spot where we see the quasar, it evidently would not be there. This failure of correspondence has a visual parallel in the more limited world of terrestrial perspective.

Just as seeing a quasar does not prove it is there, seeing an elephant progressively diminish as it walks off into the distance does not prove that the elephant is shrinking. That objects look smaller when farther away has been pointed to—incorrectly, I think—as evidence of the unreliability of the senses. Perspective effects, in elephants or quasars, are visual evidence of the absence of any privileged coordinate system: of the relativity of space and time, or of the role of vantage point in determining how the world looks. More important than whether the walking elephant is shrinking in any absolute sense is that the elephant is not shrinking from its point of view, however tiny it may appear to have become to a conscientious observer.

Time, Perspective, and the Colors of Objects

If an evanescent panorama of perspectival effects is what we see when looking out into space and time and these effects reduce to arrangements of color spots, are colors subject to what are loosely known as the laws of perspective? On earth, distant objects look bluish or blue-gray and more pale than nearby objects. The poorly explained effect has long been known as aerial perspective. Although attributed by Leonardo da Vinci and others to the effect of air, which is said to look blue in thick layers, the explanation is not entirely satisfactory.

Beyond the effect being explained, no corroborating evidence is available that air has a slightly bluish color or that the blueness is proportional to the thickness of the layer. Furthermore, distant objects look more pale, and

not just more blue-gray, than those that are nearer. They also display a lesser degree of either color contrast or tonal (light-dark) contrast. These effects are not explained by the presumed blueness of air. Nor can they be replicated by looking through blue-tinted glass.

A more problematical area is that if aerial perspective is caused by the blueness of air, it is not, strictly speaking, an effect attributable to distance. Indeed, the color effect may be accidental. We are left to assume that on a planet where the atmosphere is slightly orange, distance objects would look orange rather than blue.

Whether or not aerial perspective should be regarded as a perspectival effect, a modification caused by distance, it has no parallel among the colors of extraterrestrial spaces. The moon and stars look more white than blue-gray, though the same atmosphere intervenes between them and us as between any viewer and distant scenery. Because of the red shift, light from distant galaxies looks progressively more red rather than more blue. Only if the universe were shrinking, theory implies, could this red shift be replaced by a violet shift or a blue shift.

Is the red shift itself a color-perspective effect? If caused by the speed at which distant galaxies move away from us, and not by their absolute distance, one might say no: the color of light received from distant stars does not depend on their distance. The argument could be yes on another basis. Distant galaxies move away more rapidly than those that are near and are more red-shifted. Speed and distance in this case are inseparable.

A crude perspective of color value (lightness or darkness) can be identified in astronomy and cosmology. If two identical stars are at different distances, the ratio of their brightness (a color relationship) is said to be in inverse proportion to the squares of their distances. This rule for the perspective of visual brightness, of little interest except to astronomers, parallels the more familiar rules for the perspective of visual size. Beyond this, the colors of radiant celestial objects too close to be strongly affected by the red shift reveal little about the distances of these objects. Color, however, conveys a great deal of other information. The chemical composition of stars can be determined from their spectra. And color, as Leonardo da Vinci and his contemporaries recognized, is a more reliable measure of the absolute surface temperature of celestial objects than either their brightness when observed from earth or tactile sensations of warmth they induce.

Human beings reason by analogy, and often the better analogy incorporates more keen observation about the phenomenological world. Thus, Leonardo complained that, "some say that the sun is not hot because it is not the colour of fire but is much paler and clearer. To these we may reply that when liquified bronze is at its maximum of heat it most resembles the sun in colour and when it is less hot it has more of the colour of fire" (Leonardo 1939, 281). Leonardo would not have been surprised at one classification system used in astronomy today. It ranks stars according to their surface temperature, estimated from their spectra or colors (Gallant 1961).

Ranking of Star	Color	Surface Temperature
O	greenish white	35,000° C +
B	bluish	15,000–35,000° C
A	white	7,500–11,000° C
F	yellowish	6,000–7,500° C
G	yellow	5,100–6,000° C
K	orange	3,600–5,100° C
M	orange-red	3,000–3,500° C
R	orange-red	c. 2,300° C
N	orange-red	c. 2,600° C
S	orange-red	c. 2,600° C

The sun is a G star, Sirius an A star, and Betelgeuse an M star on this scale. An oddity of the scale is its inconsistency with the scale of wavelengths of visible light. The hottest stars are not, so to speak, white-hot. They are not reddish, the spectral extreme that extends into infrared. Nor are they bluish or violet (the other extreme). The green cast of the hottest stars suggests a preponderance of radiation median between red and violet, the extremes of the electromagnetic scale for visible light.

Within terrestrial limits, as in the sky, a simple increase in space interval has little effect on color but modifies form considerably. A nearby elephant, compared to another farther away, looks more different in size than in color. A perspective of colors in time can be identified, however. I mean by this that the colors of those objects in the world that reflect light are unendingly changing rather than fixed. Attributed to variations in illumination, the effect implies changes within time, the dimension required to allow illumination to vary.

Examples of the phenomenon suggest that objects have no real colors, because no fixed point can be located in the evanescent panorama. What color is, say, a red rubber ball illuminated by purple light? Questions of this type elude answer, other than that the color of any object varies in its color according to changes in lighting conditions over an interval of time.

Under a blue light, a green light, a purple light, the colors in an environment change, approaching the hue of the illumination. The phenomenon is not limited to circumstances in which the variation in light is extreme. Colors that appear to match under the yellowish cast of artificial illumination often look dissimilar or are discovered to be mismatches when viewed under outdoor light. Experience teaches the folk wisdom that color matching ought to be done in daylight.

Light from the sun changes in color quality throughout the day. The blue cast of early morning and evening veils the environment in that tonality, causing red objects to look bluish. Sunlight at noon is golden, although not so yellowish as tungsten light. Further variations, many studied by the French Impressionist painters, run according to seasonal cycle, latitude and longitude (Mediterranean sunlight differs from that of the Arctic), or the transient weather conditions that provide both gray days and golden days.

This dizzying continuum of permutations presents a barrier to identifying the colors of objects. A particular red object may look one color in daylight, a different shade under artificial light, another under blue light, yet another under green. The object apparently has no real color—or no constant color in isolation from its environment. The colors of objects, however, are not entirely dependent on illumination, which speaks against the possibility of explaining them solely in terms of the light falling on them. There is no light under which black velvet can be made to look chrome yellow.

Developing Color Standards

Newton's belief that colors reside in light, and not on the surfaces of objects, must have been inspired by the chimerical quality of surface colors, a scintillation with an extraterrestrial counterpart in the twinkling of the stars in the sky. We cannot even assume that a color swatch being used for comparison will invariably look the same color irrespective of the illumination. How can stability be imposed on this flux? Can the task be accomplished?

If normal or standard lighting conditions were established, the real colors of objects might be defined as those exhibited under those normal conditions. Accomplishing this requires seeking out the type of illumination that is most invariant in color. The task presents considerable practical problems. Sunlight is too changeable for the purpose. Ordi-

nary electric light bulbs shed a yellowish light, becoming more yellowish with age. The 3,400°K photoflood bulbs and 3,200°K tungsten bulbs used in photography similarly give light that varies in color according to the age of the bulb, a matter of concern in cinematography. The color of these bulbs is also affected by spikes and surges in electric voltage.

Of all commonly available types of bulbs, quartz lights show the smallest degree of color variability. The color of an object might be defined as the color the object exhibits when illuminated by a specified number of quartz lamps, of specified wattages, placed at specified distances. Quartz bulbs are expensive, the reason they are not used for all-purpose illumination. The costliness would limit any standard based on their use. The inch and the centimeter are successful standards because rulers can be produced cheaply and distributed widely. A large ruler-using population has therefore learned to measure in inches and feet or centimeters and meters. The same population cannot be expected to accustom itself to thinking of the colors objects present when viewed by quartz lights. The lamps are too expensive to become as widely available as rulers.

The ambiguity built into color names has a positive aspect in this case. As Monet's paintings of the facade of Rouen cathedral show, with considerable poetic license, an object varies in color over the course of a day. A red apple lying in a field is not the same red from morning to evening. Because illumination is not perfectly even, the apple is also not uniform in color over its entire surface at any single moment. But the color name *red* is so loose and covers such a wide range of color variations that we may safely conclude the apple is red. The greater number of color variations on the apple's surface will probably fall in that class. *Red* names a range of colors, not a single shade or variety of the color. But a red object is many shades of red, a nice matching between color names and the colors of the objects to which they refer.

Colors Created by Light

Color is often thought of as a skin or surface on objects. But natural light phenomena include effects only loosely associated, if associated at all, with the surfaces of objects. These effects include the colors of oil slicks and rainbows (or those of the sky and the night). Colors in oil slicks and soap bubbles are given their most convincing explanation as interference patterns. These patterns are created when different wavelengths of light, some reflected from the upper surface of the film and some from the lower, impinge on one another.

The Tyndall blues, explained in terms of diffraction, account for many of the blue colors seen in beetles, butterflies, birds, and mammals. Named after the Irish physicist John Tyndall, who discussed the phenomenon in 1869, they provide another example of the ubiquitous visual affinity between blue and black. The Tyndall blues might as appropriately have been called the Tyndall blacks. They are typically created when a layer of melanin, a black pigment, is overlaid by translucent ridges, scales, or other structures that scatter light. A blue wing feather from a blue jay, for example, contains no blue pigment. When crushed, the feather is reduced to a black, not blue, powder.

Why the scattering of light over a black pigment ought to look blue rather than, say, red, is suggested by a chart of reflectances of artists' pigments compiled by the Fogg Art Museum (see figure 23-4). Black is called a reflector of no light, too loose an assessment. Any black other than absolute black would reflect some light, raising the question of what color or colors this feebly reflected light would be. The Fogg Art Museum compilations indicate that the wavelength most profusely reflected by

ivory black pigment lies in the blue range. The pigment looks black rather than blue because so little blue light is reflected. Some blacks have a brownish cast rather than bluish. But, so far as I know, no browns in the animal world, where the color is common, are created by a mechanism similar to that which accounts for the Tyndall blues.

Rainbows

Among natural light phenomena, the rainbow and related forms of the solar spectrum are unique in presenting colors in an invariant order. We do not know when the discovery was first made that artificial "rainbows" could be created. But, as Koyré pointed out, study of all manner of spectra, including those formed by prisms, began in antiquity. It continued throughout the Middle Ages and the Renaissance, proliferating during the seventeenth century (Koyré 1965, 3).[1] Leonardo da Vinci advised the seeker of spectra to examine "the roots of radishes which have been kept a long time at the bottom of wells or other stagnant water." In the water, each radish root is "surrounded by a sequence of colours like those of the rainbow" (Leonardo 1939, 26).

Prior to Newton, spectra, whether seen around radish roots or through prisms, were not regarded as central to any general theory of color. Robert Boyle (1627–91), with more typically scattered reasoning, conjectured that white animals might be more common in cold climates, presumably because the temperate or tropical sun "brought out" more colors. In *Experiments and Considerations Touching Colours*, Boyle listed six major and additional minor hypotheses current among his contemporaries (Boyle [1664] 1964, 85).

One theory, attributed to Aristotle, "derives Colours from the Mixture of Light and Darkness," a recycling of the belief that the world can be explained as an interplay of opposites. A second theory, accounting for colors in terms of a sulphurous principle in bodies, had been borrowed from alchemy. In the updated version current in Boyle's day, the colors of objects are explained by their relative proportions of salt, sulphur, or mercury.

A third proposal is that colors are caused, as Plato suggested, by corpuscles emitted by bodies. The model of the universe developed by René Descartes (1596–1650) follows this format. Revolving globules of etherial matter produce different colors according to the speed of their whirling (*Principia* 3:52).

Rapidly spinning particles, Descartes declared, give a sensation of red. Slower ones produce yellow; the slowest account for green and blue. Why did Descartes believe the most rapidly spinning articles would be red? He must have been inspired by the traditional symbolic association of red with blood, fire, passion, and states of high energy. Green and blue tend to be associated with spirituality, peacefulness, or passivity.

In other theories that predate Newton's experiments, colors are created by "an internal light of the more lucid parts of the object" (Boyle [1664] 1964, 84). A variation of the internal light hypothesis held that color, as if a permeating miasma, is "a corporeal Effluvium issuing out of the Colour'd Body" (Boyle [1664] 1964, 85). Robert Hooke (1635–1703), who began his career as Boyle's assistant, proposed that "colour is nothing but the disturbance of light by the communication of the pulse to other transparent mediums, that is, by the refraction thereof" (Whittaker [1910] 1951, 1:16).

Hooke, who later was to argue bitterly with Newton, declared in his address to the Royal Society (1671) that "blue is an impression on the Retina of an oblique and confus'd pulse of light, whose weakest part precedes, and whose strongest part follows . . . . Red is an impression on the Retina of an oblique and confus'd pulse of light, whose strongest part precedes, and whose weakest follows."

CHAPTER 8

Newton

Even Galileo himself was not the *perfect* scientific man. Perfection was reached only in the person of Isaac Newton.

J. W. N. Sullivan, The Limitations of Science

Today the proposition that color depends on light has accumulated ornate accretions. The idea is rarely defended (although it might be defended) by observing that at night, or in the absence of light, color is limited to the color of the darkness. Daylight or some other form of illumination is required to see other colors or to see more than just one color. Possibly, "light causes color" means no more than that. But we give greater weight to scientific explanations that to everyday understandings. The line of reasoning regarded as more authoritative begins with the experiments of Sir Isaac Newton (1642–1727), Urfather of modern color theory.

In 1666 Newton, at the time a university undergraduate, passed sunlight through a glass prism. He proposed a theory of colors based on the spectrum cast on his wall. Newton's conclusions were initially published in "A Letter of Mr. Isaac Newton . . . Containing his New Theory about Light and Colors." The letter catalyzed a bitter controversy with Robert Hooke, recorded in an extended correspondence preserved in *Philosophical Transactions of The Royal Society* (80:3075). A final exposition is included in *Opticks* (1704), which Newton published more than three decades after his original experiments.

The Inherent and the Phenomenological

Disagreement between Hooke and Newton turned on Hooke's belief that colors are caused when light is disturbed by refraction: the bending of rays that occurs when light passes from one transparent medium to another of differing density, say, air to water or air to glass. Color, like the heat generated by friction (or like the colors of bruises), was to be explained as the incidental by-product of a physical event.

Hooke's theory can be construed to imply that glass prisms create solar spectra by inflicting damage, or irreversible change, on the light passing through them. Newton proved no irreversible transformation occurs. In an experiment admired for its simplicity, he directed the spectral rays through a second prism that was inverted. They recombined to produce a beam of white light. Newton theorized that white light is not changed into colored rays by prisms. It is, instead, inherently colored. The proposition was subjected to more sophisticated scrutiny centuries after Newton's death (Whittaker [1910] 1951, 1:14). So was Newton's famous remark that "the Rays to speak properly are not coloured" (Newton [1704] 1952, 124).

Newton's criticism of Hooke followed Hooke's criticism of Descartes. Hooke regarded light as a motion. Descartes called it a tendency to motion. What is the difference between white light that is actually the white light it appears to be (Hooke) and white light that is inherently colored (Newton)? Because Newton's light is not colored but "inherently" colored (it might become colored at some future time), the distinction is so exquisitely fine as to be semantic. When the inherent fails to make itself manifest, it remains non-phenomenological.

No such thing exists as an object—in this case, a light beam—that looks one color but is really another. Statements that seem to say otherwise characteristically mean that the object shows one set of colors under certain conditions but another set of colors under other conditions. Light is white if not passed though a prism, but it exhibits the spectral colors after passing. Arguing that one or the other of these manifestations is more normal, real, or consequential is arbitrary. No basis exists for assuming that an object's real (or verifiable) state for a given set of conditions ought to be constant for all others.

Newton demonstrated that light undergoes no irreversible change in passing through prisms. But Hooke may have been equally correct in insisting the light was changed, although not irreversibly. During the twentieth century, Whittaker and others were to take up the argument that spectra cannot be seen (or do not exist) until light passes through a prism or other refracting device. The prism, in effect, manufactures the colors.

Hooke's argument (or Whittaker's) also implies that colors are not made manifest by light. Instead, the sun, by radiating light, manufactures the colors we see by day. The remaining puzzle is what manufactures the color of the dark of the night. One possibility is human consciousness, an answer impossible to integrate with conventional understandings of the nature of the physical world. Another answer, no easier, is that the dark of the night is a priori, a color that exists without being manufactured in any ordinary sense of the word.

Whether the colors of the spectral rays are inherent in light or arise through its modification is a seventeenth-century variation on that question human beings never tire of asking: whether colors are real or illusory, enduring objects or transient effects. One way of putting the question to the test is to procure a set of real (nonillusory) colors. If the two sets of colors can be compared, we should be able to determine whether the colors we see look different from the colors in the other set, the set of real colors.

Unfortunately, no set of colors is available other than those we see. The imaginary test and the question it proposes to answer are each equally misguided. The sense of the question is not improved by asking whether colors are actually there, as opposed to just perceivably (ephemerally) there. Can we determine whether a color is actually there by looking carefully at the color? I think not. Sorting criteria—rules of language—are involved. No visual criterion can be identified that shows the difference between a color that is there and one that just appears as if it were. Color cannot be shown to be either there or not there and shares this characteristic with virtually everything else.

Language, before it affects perception, affects scientific theorizing about what we see. Newton was courageous enough to take a position in a difficult area. He found that "Colours are not *Qualifications of light* derived from Refractions, or Reflections of natural Bodies (as 'tis generally believed) but *Original and connate properties*, which in divers Rays are divers. Some Rays are disposed to exhibit a red colour and no other: some a yellow and no other, some a green and no other, and so of the rest. Nor are there only Rays proper and particular to the more eminent colours, but even to all their intermediate gradations" (*Phil. Trans.*, 6 [19 February 1671-72]: 3075).

Newton's reasoning is a modified version of a theory Boyle traced to ancient Greece, where "the Peripatetic Schools, although they dispute amongst themselves divers particulars concerning Colours . . . seem Unanimously enough to Agree, that Colours are Inherent and Real Qualities, which the light doth but Disclose, and not concurr to Produce" (Boyle [1664] 1964, 84). A critical difference is that Newton regarded colors as properties of light, rather than of colored objects.

When Newton tried to analyze the spectral rays further, he found this could not be accomplished. Each ray seemed elemental. Passing the ray through additional prisms had no effect on its color. Neither could the colors of the rays be changed by other means.[1] Rays of some colors showed another type of uniqueness, in that their colors could not be repli-

cated. Newton reports that he mixed blue and yellow spectral rays to produce green (some commentators have questioned whether this is possible) but found the green dissimilar in hue to the singular ray of spectral green.

Rays could be mixed and unmixed at will. A test for whether a colored beam was monochromatic was to pass it through a prism. If it were an amalgamation of beams, these would separate. If the ray was light of only one color, it would emerge from the prism a single beam.

The Nature of Light

The exchange of letters between Newton and Hooke is an episode in an extended controversy about the nature of light. The underlying questions, originally raised by the pre-Socratic philosophers, became so closely entangled in color theory they will probably never be extricated. The questions concern whether light is corporeal and the relationship between light (radiant energy) and matter.

Two opposing views became classical and were repeatedly recycled. The first, in its earliest formulation, assesses light as a stream of particles or corpuscles emitted by incandescent bodies. The counterargument focuses squarely on the issue of substantiality. If light consists of corporeal particles, it was argued, these would collide when beams of light crossed. But if the environmental scale of the particles were exceedingly small, the probability of collision might not be statistically consequential, and its occurrence might not be detectable by instruments. The orbits of comets cross those of planets without collision necessarily occurring. And the chance for collision of molecules need not be assumed to be significantly increased when one stream of water intersects another. Thus, a mere absence of evidence of collision is not sufficient to disprove corporeal particles.

The classical alternate to the particle

hypothesis is that light is a wave phenomenon. The main counterargument is that waves, say, those in water or air, require a medium through which they travel. Light, which crosses a vacuum when it arrives from the stars, apparently transcends the need for a corporeal conducting medium.

To account for propagation in a vacuum, the wave theory was shored up by proposing that space might be permeated by a wave-transmitting vehicle designated the aether. Part of the reason for hypothesizing the aether was that empty space (incorporeality) was assumed to be a vacant receptacle devoid of physical characteristics. Yet vacuums had been known since ancient times, and today their characteristics are regularly exploited in vacuum pumps and similar devices.

The aether was never isolated, in the sense that no light-conducting medium was proved to permeate vacuums or to be separable from them. The usual conclusion, that nothing exists in a vacuum (the aether could not be found), is questionable on two counts. Empirically, we know interstellar space is not absolutely empty, a finding at odds with the traditional wisdom that the universe can be divided into empty and nonempty parts or that the difference between emptiness and nonemptiness is significant. Conceptually, the absence of etheriality "in" vacuums implies that the etherial element being sought, the medium that conducts light, must be the vacuum itself. The corporeal (matter) and the incorporeal (the vacuum) are not necessarily different in every respect. Each is capable of transmitting waves, if light is a wave phenomenon. Each also can be transparent and, if so, will allow light to pass.

The classical argument about whether light is particle or wave was never resolved. An uneasy reconciliation was reached through Bohr's complementarity principle (1928). Supplemented by Heisenberg's uncertainty principle, complementarity became a cornerstone of what came to be called the Copenhagen interpretation of quantum theory. The wave and corpuscular descriptions were held to be complementary ways of explaining light, both needed to understand the phenomenon (complementarity).[2] But (uncertainty) no experiment can demonstrate both at the same time (Jenkins and White, 1957, 617).

More exactly, the uncertainty principle suggests the experimenter will be equally successful in finding whichever configuration the experiment is designed to display. The concept has simple visual parallels. In one class of optical illusion, ambiguous cubes look alternately concave and convex. By focusing attention, the viewer can will which way the cubes ought to look. But the cubes cannot be seen as both concave and convex at the same time.

At very high frequencies, say, in the X-ray range, radiant energy behaves as if corpuscles, but at low frequencies, as if a wave. Because wave properties predominate in the visible light sector, scientific explanations of color generally rely on reference to wavelengths of light, measured in either millimicrons (nanometers) or angstrom units. If radiant energy is to be described in terms of the corpuscular theory in its modern form, it is assumed to consist of massless particles called photons, which belong to a larger class of particles called bosons. Photons are ejected from atoms in aggregates called quanta (hence, quantum theory). The different colors of light are correlated with different energy levels in the photons. In the visible light sector, those responsible for red have about half the energy of those that account for blue.

The varying energy levels of the photons suggest Descartes's whirling globules, moving particles colored according to their energy levels. A difference is that each of the Cartesian particles revolves on its axis. The more intricate choreography of the photon, shown arbitrarily traveling in a straight line in the Feynman diagrams used in quantum mechanics, allows it to transcend time (it can move backward as well as forward in time) and to be transformed into an electron or a positron. These peregrinations through time cast doubt on whether the relationship between light and color is as simple as is usually assumed, and on whether light moves in the ordinary sense of the word.

Newton denied Hooke's accusation that he was a proponent of the doctrine of the corporeality of light. Any incandescent body, Newton argued, emits corpuscles, which excite waves in the aether, a reconciliation of sorts between the wave and corpuscular theories.

> If by any means those [aether vibrations] of unequal bigness be separated from one another, the largest beget a Sensation of a *Red* colour, the least or shortest of a deep *Violet*, and the intermediate ones, of intermediate colours; much after the manner that bodies, according to their several sizes, shapes, and motions, excite vibrations in the Air of various bignesses, which, according to those bignesses, make several Tones in Sound (*Phil. Trans.* 7:5088).

After Newton, rearticulations of the wave theory were presented by Christiaan Huygens (1629–95), by the English physician Thomas Young (1773–1829), and by Augustin Fresnel (1788–1827). James Clerk Maxwell (1831–79) reinterpreted the light wave as a form of electromagnetic wave, related to X rays, radio waves, and microwaves. Max Planck (1858–1947), discoverer of the quantizing of energy, provided one answer to the question of why Maxwell's theory found favor. It had an immediate utility. Irrespective of whether electromagnetic theory was true in any absolute sense, it allowed optics and electrodynamics to be connected. The single set of laws it generated explained phenomena in

either field. For Planck, the remaining task was to amalgamate mechanics into the system (Planck n.d., 145).

In addition to inventing the Maxwell discs used for many years to demonstrate color mixing and devising the Maxwell triangle still popular in adapted form in colorimetric studies, Maxwell left about a dozen papers on color. Although he is said to have considered his papers on color the most important of his works, his reinterpretation of the light wave as an electromagnetic phenomenon brought the study of color in physics to an abrupt halt. Some questions were never asked again because a definitive answer was thought to have been found. Others were relegated to psychology and other life sciences, or to philosophy and aesthetics. From the seventeenth century until the twentieth, the word *color* is used with precipitously declining frequency in the literature of the physical sciences. Russell complained, forty years ago, that it could be avoided entirely. The result was a gradual curtailing, over the centuries, of questions that legitimately could be asked.

During the seventeenth century Robert Boyle had no hesitation about inquiring why and how red looks different from green (Boyle [1664] 1964, 91). The query lies far afield from the physical sciences today. Or it might be disposed of by the modern scientific answer that red differs from green because each derives from a different sort of radiant energy: in classical theory, from light with a different wavelength; in quantum theory, either from a probability wave with a measurably different wavelength or from photons with a different energy level.

The modern answer, however framed, is circular, because colors are defined in physics in terms of radiant energy. If the wavelength of red light is agreed to differ from that of green, this does not speak to the question of why this should cause the two colors to look different. Nor does it explain why they look different in the way they do. The visual question is similarly evaded by recourse to other disciplines that give attention, say, to how light affects the visual pigments in the retina of the eye. Nor is it touched by explanations that regard color as illusory or subjective, a mass hallucination of some sort.

The hope of unifying relativity theory and quantum theory remains unrealized. But the new understandings they brought to physics upset classical assumptions, including several integral to the explanation of color. Absolute space and absolute time fell by the wayside, with crashes so resounding it was scarcely noticed that the aether had been discarded too. In part because of the loss of absolute time, causality became dubious. What was missing was the further reasoning that would have allowed it to be extricated from classical explanations of color, as in the assertion that light causes color. If no absolute time exists, an assertion that any A causes any B is meaningless or needs further explanation.

Some ideas about time and light were retained—both are still said to move—that have never been fully reconciled with the explanation of color. If color can be equated with light, and light moves, why do we regard or perceive color as unmoving?

In the new world of subatomic particles, known primarily through experiments with particle accelerators, distinctions between matter and energy blur. Or the distinction we have grown accustomed to making is shown to be arbitrary. Like positive and negative space in a painting, objects are integrated with the space around them. They may be inseparable from it, or accretions of it.

Waves, indistinguishable from particles, are referred to as probability waves, and in essence are mathematical abstractions. Photons and fellow wave-particles, in incessant collision with one another, change their forms as they oscillate in time. Fritjof Capra (1975) compared this ceaseless activity to a cosmic dance of creation and destruction. The electromagnetic force, carried by the photon (the particle still thought to account for color and light), is one of four primary forces. The others are the strong nuclear force, the weak nuclear force, and gravitation, each theorized to be carried by a different form of subatomic particle. The strong nuclear force, which prevents the positively charged protons in an atomic nucleus from repelling one another, is carried by mesons; the weak nuclear force, which accounts for radioactive decay and the emission of beta particles (electrons) by radioactive nuclei, may be carried by a weak boson; the gravitational force, by a graviton, perhaps.

In the proliferation of new theories and new particles, many old questions remain untouched. One is what it means to say black is an absence, irrespective of whether the absence is of light, light waves, electromagnetic waves, probability waves, quanta, photons, or quarks. Another is why light is thought to have an existence apart from color, if one is unvaryingly to be found in the same location as the other. This is not the same question as that of whether color exists apart from light.

A new question, because the chemical properties of the elements can be traced to the electrons in their atoms, is why color changes of a chemical nature differ from those that are nonchemical. The statement that, say, orange and yellow can be mixed to form yellow-orange implies that no chemical interaction occurs among the substances mixed. In an example of chemical interaction, copper is orange (or copper-colored). Sulfur crystals are yellow. Oxygen is a colorless gas. Each is a chemical constituent of copper sulfate, which for some reason is blue.

We are apparently to conclude that the blueness of copper sulfate can be explained in terms of the arrangement of its molecules. Beyond that, why a substance with yellow and orange constituents should be blue is a mystery. Color changes in chemical reactions follow no known rules. And they differ greatly from changes observable in nonchemical combining of pigments, dyes, lights, or other colored substances. The neglected question of why this disparity exists is pressing if both color and chemical properties are to be traced to the activities of atoms.

Pending solution of the puzzles of the subatomic world, Newtonian physics, like Euclidean geometry, is said to provide sufficiently close approximations for everyday use. Most of its basic assumptions are no longer state of the art. But apples still fall out of trees, oblivious to the news that gravity, no longer a force, is now considered a distortion of the curvature of space-time in the presence of objects. Continuing to explain color in terms of obsolete theory, however, is as misguided as navigating a ship by Ptolemaic astronomy, though it could probably be done.

An older difficulty, long shunted aside, is that classical physics never provided a sufficiently coherent explanation of color, even on its own terms. There are too many points at which theory cannot be induced to conform with what we see. The inconsistencies trickle down to the largely unsatisfactory formulations of conventional color theory, which relies loosely on classical physics.

Transparency, Translucency, Opacity

Vacuums, including the interstellar vacuum we call the sky, have traditionally been regarded as tracts of emptiness, isolated as if by an invisible wall from the nonempty portions of the universe. Interpenetration was inconceivable. Emptiness ceases to be emptiness if it has something in it. Today we know that putatively empty interstellar space contains a variety of items. These range from organic compounds (about a hundred have been identified) to—perhaps—black holes, regions of

intense gravitation from which even light cannot escape. Whatever the nature of interstellar space, a web of assumptions about its presumed nullity explains the attention given to the problem of how waves of light could pass through it. I can think of more interesting questions than whether an aether exists.

One is why centuries of debate on invisible waves versus invisible particles has overwhelmed everyday observation of a commonplace visual phenomenon. Ordinary human beings have taken for granted for millennia, on the matter of transmission of light, that it passes through anything transparent (including vacua), but never through what is opaque. The question of how light, whether wave or particle, is transmitted may reduce less to the question of how media differ from vacuums (or corporeality from incorporeality) than to that of how transparency differs from opacity.

The semantics, as often, is revealing. Transparent means transparent to light; opaque means opaque to light. Translucency, an intermediate state, permits passage of light, but not necessarily in a sufficiently coherent form to permit passage of clear images of objects. A recognizable continuum from the entirely transparent, through progressively more clouded degrees of translucency to entire opacity, seems correlated with the physical conditions of objects.

Transparency (ability to transmit light) is a functional equivalent for colorlessness, whether in vacuums or in material objects. Opacity (inability to transmit light) is a functional equivalent for color. No such thing occurs as an opaque object that is not, at the same time, a colored object. The converse, however, is not the case: color, as in stained-glass windows, is not necessarily opaque. But its perceived intensity depends on opacity. Paintings made with opaque watercolor (gouache) look different from those made with transparent watercolor. Ability to reflect light (therefore, to appear strongly colored) is a direct function of degree of opacity.

Vacuums, so far as we know, are always transparent. And light itself is transparent to light, which is why light beams can cross. Among inorganic substances, gases are generally more transparent than liquids, which are more transparent than solids. A transparent solid, say, glass, is typically opaque when reduced to a powder, a phenomenon explained in terms of scattering of light by the surfaces of the particles. Thickness of layer is usually significant: a thin sheet of glass might be transparent, a large block of the same type of glass translucent. Thick or thin, glass can also be opaque, and when opaque is unvaryingly colored, whether white, black, red, or some other color.

Among organic substances, some change from transparent to opaque under certain conditions. The change may be irreversible. A transparent egg white becomes opaque when cooked. The lens of the eye loses its transparency when cataracts form. Honey crystallizes when chilled and becomes opaque in the process. The honey, however, returns to its previous translucency when warmed.

The question of what causes light is the mirror image of that of what causes transparency, translucency, and opacity. In both color theory and the physical sciences, the notoriety of the first question has almost submerged the second. Among a multitude of scales devised to measure weight, temperature, and other continuum phenomena, I know of none that enables grading the degrees of translucency between absolute transparency and absolute opacity. Yet a scale of capability to transmit light is also a scale between color (opacity) and its absence (transparency). The question of what causes opacity is also the question of why light does not interact similarly with every material object it meets.

The concepts are interesting to play with and probably have their own logic. Nothing can be both entirely opaque and entirely transparent at the same time. The conditions preclude one another. Anything other than an entirely transparent state is evidently unique to matter, because vacuums are not known to be either opaque or translucent. We might imagine that matter behaves like a louvered window. The louvers can exclude light entirely, pass it entirely, or allow it to pass partially. Polarizing filters, used on cameras, operate in very much this manner. A pair of these filters, one superimposed on the other so that they can be rotated on a common center, are either opaque or transparent depending on how rotated. Unlike the filters, most objects are always opaque, always translucent, or always transparent. Like the colors of objects, their transparency or translucency is presumably to be explained by the arrangement of their molecules.

An absolutely transparent object is absolutely colorless, displaying only the colors of the objects behind it. Some opacity is a prior condition for color. Or color, which was once thought to be an attribute of objects, can also be explained as a secondary attribute to their opacity, their imperviousness to light. The continuum of opacity–transparency evidently extends beyond the visible light sector of the electromagnetic spectrum. Lead stops X rays, although other substances are not opaque to these rays. Some subatomic particles pass through anything. For them, nothing is opaque.

The question of whether transparency/opacity is inherent in objects or caused by light reflects the similar question about color. Because transparency cannot be distinguished from opacity in the darkness, each might be called an effect caused by light. More commonly either is regarded as an attribute integral to an object, an inconsistent reasoning.

Although a pane of window glass is assumed to remain transparent at night, its transparency cannot be confirmed under that set of conditions. Like all cats, all panes of glass look black (or gray) in the dark.

Would a better explanation of color and light evolve if attention were given to the question of why some objects are transparent and other opaque? We choose our questions for scientific study selectively. On the matter of the transmission of light, the preference has traditionally been for invisible waves and invisible particles rather than the phenomena we see. The impact on the explanation of color has been regrettable. The explanations run around in circles.

In successive reworkings of hypotheses about its cause, not its nature, color has been defined in physics in terms of light and light in terms of waves. The waves were identified as an electromagnetic phenomenon, which Planck and Einstein discovered to be quantized: to consist of energy emitted in discrete packets rather than as an inchoate stream. Between 1905 and the present, successive peeks behind the quantum to find the basic building blocks of the universe revealed the photon, fermion, boson, hadron, lepton, gluon, pion, meson, positron, muon, and other denizens of what has been dubbed the zoo of hundreds of subatomic particles. These particles may be reducible to quarks, a still lower sublevel of particle that also comes in many varieties. The fascinating ferment has not yet yielded the final word on what lies behind quarks. We should not await the answer with high expectation that it will reveal anything previously unnoticed about color.

The incessant discovering and hypothesizing of particles has been accompanied by a prophesying of qualities for these particles through mathematical means. We are advised not to inquire what these qualities are, other than that they exist or are conjectured to exist and have been assigned interesting tags. An early example of labeling was regretted. The unfortunately named *spin* of an electron, we are often reminded, should not be considered a spin in any ordinary sense. Unlike Descartes's whirling globules, an electron has no axis on which to spin. Spin is now more often interpreted as a form of symmetry. Some particles are believed to look the same from all directions, like a steel ball bearing. Others, like a coin with two faces, have to be flipped twice to present the same face, and there are other variations.

To avoid more misunderstandings of the kind caused by the electron's spin, and as a replacement for Latin and Greek, whimsical or nonsensical names have become the fashion. *Charm* is the tag bestowed on a predicted quality of some or all quarks, which are thought to come in at least six *flavors*. In addition to charm, the quark flavors are *up, down, strange, bottom*, and *top* (Hawking 1988, 65). Each flavor is available in three *colors*, named as red, yellow, and blue or red, green, and blue. The jokiness would have left Bertrand Russell uneasy. The use of color names for predicted but unknown qualities is meant to imply, in this case, that *red, yellow, green,* and *blue* are no more seriously likely than *charm* to be fundamental characteristics of the physical world. The real joke might be that no firm foundation exists for that assumption.

CHAPTER 9

The Cause of
Color and Light

Suppose I say, for instance, "By red light I mean light of such-and-such a range of wave lengths." In that case the statement that light of such wave lengths makes me see red is a tautology, and until the nineteenth century people were uttering meaningless noises when they said that blood is red, because nothing was known of the correlation of wave lengths with sensations of color. This is absurd. It is obvious that "red" has a meaning independent of physics, and that this meaning is relevant in collecting data for the physical theory of colors, just as the pre-scientific meaning of "hot" is relevant in establishing the physical theory of heat.

Bertrand Russell, Human Knowledge, Its Scope and Limits

Although color is said to be caused by light, an even more frequent answer to the proverbial question connects that idea with another considered equally self-evident. Color is caused by light and is seen. In an unwieldly concatenation of the two ideas, color is "the evaluation by the visual sense of that quality of light (reflected or transmitted by a substance) which is basically determined by its spectral composition" (*American College Dictionary*, 1957).

If color is something that is seen, it requires the eye. If it is an effect caused by light, independence from the eye is suggested, a capability for existing alone. It cannot be both true and not true that the seeing eye is a necessity for color. To smooth over the inconsistency, color might be regarded as dependent on the eye in one sense but not in another. Because this is just a vernacular way of acknowledging the paradox, it contributes nothing towards its resolution. Color, like any phenomenon, is singular. It either exists or does not, which is incompatible with existing in multiple senses. A simpler understanding is that the two propositions contradict one another. At least one is false, incomplete, incoherently stated, or syntactically meaningless.

The difficulty is more likely to lie with the familiar assertion that light causes color. It leads to too many inconsistencies, whether it refers to ordinary daylight or light as its veils are progressively lifted through the ever-changing definitions of contemporary physics. The origin of the idea is prescientific. Human beings said color depended on light, rather than on a functioning eye, long before classical physics evolved with its idealized conception of objective light waves rippling through an objective world contemplated by an objective mind.

Our ancestors also had alternate theories. As Robert Boyle's seventeenth-century compilation shows, they thought color might be caused by invisible waves or equally invisible flying corpuscles. It might be explained as an interplay of undefined forces (say, a mingling of opposites) or the machinations of vaguely lightlike effluvia. Today these ancient schemes impress as loose language framing wildly conjectural hypotheses. They also sound uncomfortably similar to state-of-the-art explanations in the contemporary physical sciences. Defining black as an absence of electromagnetic manifestations in the wavelength range of the visible light sector—or worse, as an absence of probability waves, photons, or quarks—cannot address the more dubious aspects of defining anything as an absence of anything. What is absent when black is seen is immaterial. We want to know what is present.

The classical question of whether color is in eyes, objects, or light is probably simplistic, as are monolithic conceptions of causality. If a single cause must be identified, the eye may well have an edge. Light cannot be the cause for color, because people with ordinary vision do not cease seeing in its absence—we see the darkness. More important, light cannot be the sole cause. Unless the need for a functioning eye is admitted, we cannot explain why the blind are unable to see.

The model of an objective world is familiar from classical physics. It rests on three assumptions, each considerably tempered in relativity theory and quantum theory. The first is that objectivity is within the reach of human beings. The second is that we transcend subjectivity by deciding to do so, by an act of faith. The third is that the gesture is beneficial because it leads to a higher truth.

In explanations of color, these assumptions support the perennial insistence that what we see is not to be trusted and what cannot be seen is real. Medieval artists painting pictures of angels may have believed that angels existed. Early theorists on light, color, and natural philosophy undoubtedly believed the universe is full of invisible waves, particles, and miasmas. We smile at the innocence of these ancient imaginings, as at the ideas of the alchemists. But why does modern theory sound similar to ancient theory? The same old invisible waves and particles reappear in more ornate dress.

One explanation for the similitude is that the pre-Socratic Greeks and other early thinkers had an intuitive understanding of the nature of the physical world, which has been elaborated on in succeeding centuries. They knew nothing about electrons, mesons, gluons, and pions. But they correctly sensed that invisible waves and particles were there, which is exactly what they told us.

This suggests that essential truth arises spontaneously from within human consciousness. What rises with it are ideas that are not true, as in the case of phlogiston and the aether. So we are obliged to separate ideas that are useful from those that are not. I wonder if we can explain what we see without inventing what cannot be seen.

The notion that truth lies beyond human limits is a staple of philosophy and theology. It takes issue with the more modest assumption that the only truth available to human beings lies in the human condition. Perceptual experience, because individual, impresses us as a subjectively tainted ephemera, to be excluded from the objective world of classical physics. Russell argued that the exclusion is ''a peculiarity: Physics never mentions percepts except when it speaks of empirical verification of its laws; but if its laws are not concerned with percepts, how can percepts verify them?'' (Russell 1948, 20). The question is rhetorical; the answer is that they cannot.

Explaining red as light with a wavelength of 650 millimicrons is incomplete. It includes no indication of how to locate or identify the red being explained. A complete statement ought to say that the red that we see (the only way red can be encountered by human beings) is accounted for by a particular wavelength. That statement, however, is inconsistent for the context. A model of the world that purports to be objective is devoid of any sentient creature able to see anything. By excluding human sensations, an objective world excludes human beings, because no way exists to separate one from the other. Within this unpopulated realm, the phrase "that we see" is meaningless, as is any terminology that similarly acknowledges sensual experience. Thus, "Physics, per se, has nothing to say about sensations; and if it uses the word 'color' (which it need not do), it will wish to define it in a way which is logically independent of sensation" (Russell 1948, 261).

A lengthy passage by Max Planck addresses the metaphysical problem of reconciling inconsistencies in the explanation of color and light. *Light*, as the term is used in physics, is to be understood to possess qualia different from those of light as an experiential phenomenon.

> The first problem of physical optics, the condition necessary for the possibility of a true physical theory of light, is the analysis of all the complex phenomena connected with light, into objective and subjective parts. The first deals with those phenomena which are outside, and independent of, the organ of sight, the eye. It is the so-called light rays which constitute the domain of physical research. The second part embraces the inner phenomena, from eye to brain, and this leads us into the realms of physiology and psychology.

It is not at all self-evident, from first principles, that the objective light rays can be completely separated from the sight sense, and that such a fundamental separation involves very difficult thinking cannot better be proved than by the following fact. Johann Wolfgang von Goethe was gifted with a very scientific mind (though little inclined to consider analytical methods), and would never see a detail without considering the whole, yet he definitely refused, a hundred years ago, to recognize this difference. Indeed, what assertion could give a greater impression of certainty to the unprejudiced than to say that light without the perceptive organ is inconceivable? But, the meaning of the word light in this connection, to give it an interpretation that is unassailable, is quite different from the light ray of the physicist.

> Though the name has been retained for simplicity, the physical theory of light or optics, in its most general sense, has as little to do with the eye and light perceptions as the theory of the pendulum has to do with sound perception. This ignoring of the sense-perceptions, this restricting to objective real phenomena, which doubtless, from the point of view of immediate interest, means a considerable sacrifice made to pure knowledge, has prepared a way for a great extension of the theory. This theory has surpassed all expectations, and yielded important results for the practical needs of mankind (Planck n.d., 139).

For Planck, the two forms of light are comparable to apples and oranges. One can be seen and the other is inaccessible to perception. But this amounts to burying the question in words. If light, as the term is understood in physics, cannot be equated with the light of day, identifying one as an explanation for the other is a meaningless syntactical exercise. It embroiders on the assertion that color (and, in Planck's reasoning, light) is caused by something other than itself.

If the statement "color is caused by light" is true in any conventional sense, black should not be identifiable as a color not caused by light. Apart from whether true, "color is caused by light" may not be syntactically meaningful. The statement asks us to assume something called light that, unlike other entities, can be separated from its own color. As Russell's argument implies, that this separation can be accomplished is unlikely, however convenient the assumption in some cases.

Those of my generation encountered Planck's quaint nineteenth-century objective world as a rite of passage, a revelation of elementary school science class. The objective world was a science fiction ghost world, from which human beings had been banished. Spirits composed of pure thought read instruments with cool detachment and never made mistakes—or the instruments were studied by other instruments. The wonders of this world included light that could not be seen because it had been separated from the dross of subjective experience. But how can we find objective light if it cannot be seen, if it exists "outside, and independent of, the organs of sight?"

Asserting that light exists in an unseen objective form shores up its respectability as a causal explanation of color. The visible is shown to have invisible forces behind it, and the invisible is what counts. If asked what causes a green color patch I see, I am not expected to answer "green paint." The correct answer is objective light, the Planckian light I cannot see, although I should know it is there. If it were not there, how could I answer the question "what causes color?"

These curious assumptions about causality have a further dimension today. We are asked to assume that causality can be a meaningful concept in the explanation of color yet dubious elsewhere in the physical sciences. The double standard is untenable. If time is relative and if subatomic particles move backward and forward in time, we cannot assume a linear hierarchy in which the phenomena we identify as causes lead to (or antecede) those we identify as effects.

We do not need the virtually incomprehensible computations of contemporary physics to suggest that causality is a concept with only limited usefulness, whether in the assertion "light causes color" or anywhere else.[1] The four-year-old child who asks "why?" and who responds to any answer provided with yet another "why?" is discovering the nature of the infinite regress. Reasons, like horizons, can never be reached. They continually recede as we approach closer to where they had previously seemed to be. Even the prime antecedent—the idea of God, fate, or big bang as the reason behind everything—is not impervious to "why?"

In the visible light sector of the electromagnetic spectrum, wavelength is said to correlate with hue, ranging from approximately 780 millimicrons (red) to 380 millimicrons (violet). This correlation is unlike that of, say, the thermometer, which measures a smooth transition from extreme cold to extreme heat. The sectors of the electromagnetic spectrum are unlike one another. Ultraviolet rays pass into X rays, which have different physical characteristics. No intermediate range of rays has some of the characteristics of X rays combined with some of the characteristics of ultraviolet rays.

In the visible light sector, the colors of the electromagnetic spectrum are those of the rainbow, arranged in the same order. Wavelength does not correlate with those visual attributes of hue that can be identified. The brightest part of the spectrum is yellow, near the center. Yellow-green, also near the center, is said to be the range in which the finest hue discriminations can be made. The pair of complementary hues with the smallest difference in color value is red and green. The pair with the greatest is yellow and purple. None of these visual effects can be genuinely correlated with wavelength.

Russell's objection to the exclusion of percepts reaches to the heart of one difficulty with explanations of color that rely on classical physics. Imagine that a scientist from another galaxy knew that certain wavelengths of light were supposed to look green. The scientist was unable to verify that this was correct because he or she had no idea of the meaning of the word *green* or of the nature of the difference supposed to exist between green and red. How could this visitor be edified about what red and green look like if no samples were available to show?

The task evidently cannot be accomplished: color is apparently so innate to the sensory realm that words are insufficient to convey its nature to those who have never seen it. Yet people regularly learn about items that they will never see. And dictionaries exist because word definitions are not only possible but adequate to the purpose in most cases.

Dictionaries are able to describe an elephant as a large quadruped with tusks and a trunk. Yet they are limited to defining colors either by simile or in terms of light waves, a conceit that is a simile of another variety. "Blue," for example, has been called "a color whose hue is [like] that of the clear sky or [like] that of the portion of the spectrum lying between green and violet" (*Webster's Third New International Dictionary*). Dictionaries are not reduced to defining *elephant* by telling what the beasts resemble or where some of them can be located.

Nor are we asked to accept, as sufficient to the question, that an elephant is an aggregate of molecules, as is a cat or a mouse. That

would be considered an absurd definition, because inappropriate or too general. Yet, quite regularly, colors are said to be wavelengths of light, probability waves, quanta, photons, bosons, quarks, or similar subatomic units. Our ability to describe elephants vastly exceeds our ability to describe colors.

The exclusion of percepts from physics is a secondary phenomenon. Physics purports to examine reality, however that might be defined. Percepts, by unspoken agreement, are usually excluded from our conception of an objective reality. For this reason, the question of whether color exists in light, in the eye, in objects, in some or all of these, or (as Plato imagined) in none of them superficially resembles the bogus enigma of whether the sound of the crash exists when a tree falls in the forest. The intended question is whether human consciousness can be the criterion for reality or for those realities accessible to human beings. It is culturally biased in that only the unheard sound is assumed to be conjectural. The thought experiment of Schrödinger's cat raises the question in quantum theory: We are asked whether a cat, unseen by any observer able to verify its condition, can be regarded as alive or dead for any observer other than itself. We are not invited to consider whether (or why) the cat—or the tree, the forest, or the event of the fall—should be assumed to really exist in the absence of a verifying observer. Events and objects are assumed to be real, but perceptions of them may not be. Alfred North Whitehead reported that Galileo, to whom the puzzle of the tree was put in a more complicated manner, "considered this question, and at once pointed out that, apart from eyes, ears, or noses, there would be no colours, sounds, or smells" (Whitehead [1925] 1953, 55).

Russell would have approved of the answer, which is consistent with the Copenhagen interpretation of quantum theory. Unlike classical physics, this holds that the observer is part of any experiment and that reality cannot exist in the absence of a verifying observer. A reality that depends on the observer comes close to implying that the only reality *is* that of the observer. The dilemma might be resolved by assuming the possibility of multiple observers. We can also ask what *reality* is intended to imply.

A simpler approach to the question about the falling tree is familiar to modern schoolchildren. The answer depends on how *sound* is defined. The word can mean the sound waves assumed to have been caused by the fall (if the fall occurred). Or it can mean the effect of these waves on a listening ear or recording device.

The question of whether color is in the eye, in light, or elsewhere is only partially analogous to that of the subjectivity or objectivity of any sound caused by the fall of the tree. The explanation of sound as a wave phenomenon is considerably more coherent than the approximately parallel reading of color as a wave of another sort. This can be seen by turning to the particulars of how light is held to cause red-violet, brown, blue, and black.

CHAPTER 10

Red-Violet, Blue, Brown, and Optical Mixture

If red and violet be mingled, there will be generated according to their various Proportions various Purples, such as are not like in appearance to the Colour of any homogeneal Light, and of these Purples mix'd with yellow and blue may be made other new Colours.

Sir Isaac Newton, Opticks

Purples and magentas do not exist, they are a figment of our perception.

Anton Wilson, "Film Feedback"

While other societies have developed different methods of naming, the major colors of the rainbow or solar spectrum are usually identified today as *red, orange, yellow, green, blue,* and *violet*. Newton included *indigo*, a seventh hue intermediary between blue and violet. The major spectral colors, sometimes called major hues, exist in a continuum relationship. Between, say, blue and green a range of intermediaries is found. These are called *bluish greens* or *greenish blues*, according to whether they more nearly resemble green or blue. The relationships among the major hues are familiarly shown in diagrammatic form.

None of these commonplace concepts is incompatible with scientific theory, whether in its classical or more recondite forms. Phys-icists, like everyone else, identify the spectral hues as red, orange, yellow, green, blue, and violet. They agree about the continuum nature of the range and that a diagram can be constructed.

Diagrams of Hue Relationships

What kind of diagram best shows the relationship among the hues? If color is regarded as an effect of light waves, one kind of diagram is used. If classified as a percept, another kind of diagram is required. The two diagrams are incompatible. If the nature of the relationship among the hues is correctly shown by one, it cannot be correctly shown by the other because one is linear and the other circular (figure 10-1).

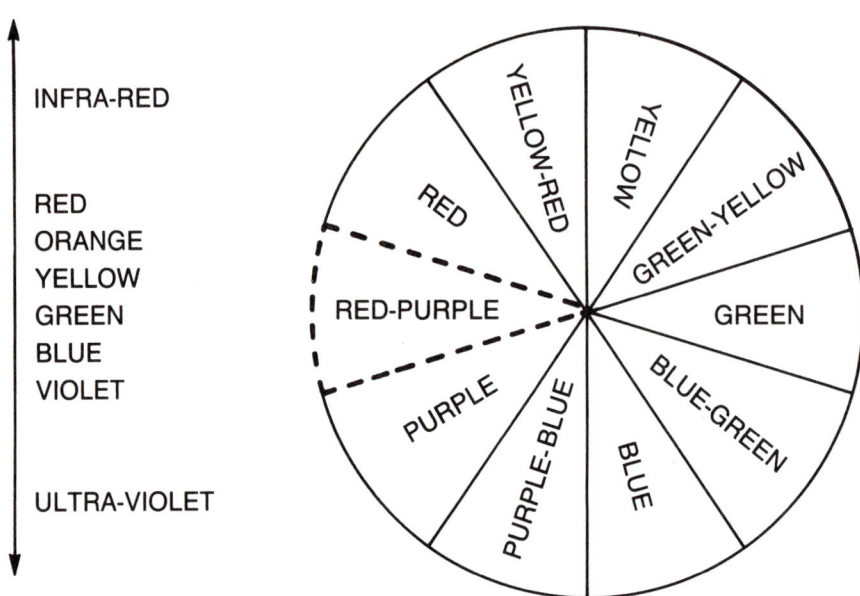

Figure 10-1. The electromagnetic scale and the color wheel. The electromagnetic wave scale and the color wheel are topologically inconsistent because one is linear and the other is circular.

The diagram familiar from classical physics is unmodified by more recent developments. Following Maxwell's reasoning, it assumes that variation in color among the spectral hues is correlated with variation in wavelength of light. The range of wavelengths accounting for visible light (color) is only a short segment of the electromagnetic scale. The scale also includes gamma rays, X rays, ultraviolet, infrared, radar, radio and television waves, microwaves, and any other form of radiant energy.

The visible light portion of the scale consists of wave lengths from roughly 380 to 780 millimicrons (3,800-7,800 angstrom units). The lower extreme consists of violet light (380 millimicrons); the upper extreme, of red light (780 millimicrons). Beyond red lies infrared. Beyond violet lies ultraviolet. Infrared and ultraviolet are said to be invisible to human beings, though Helmholtz reports that some people can see ultraviolet. Orange, yellow, green, and blue, between red and violet, appear in the visible light sector in the order in which they can be seen in the rainbow. In electromagnetic theory, the color or visible light sector is part of a "longer" scale, properly diagrammed as a line segment for this reason.

Color as Percept

When color is regarded as something we see, a percept or visual phenomenon, a different diagram is used. This second diagram is the familiar color wheel or color circle. Newton, credited with its invention, "became surprised to see [the spectral colors emerge from the prism] in an *oblong* form, which, according to the received laws of Refraction, I expected should have been circular" (*Phil. Trans.* 6:3075). On the color wheel, red and violet, no longer representing extremes, lie adjacent to one another.

The compelling argument for the color wheel's arrangement is experiential. We see a continuum of colors intermediary between red and violet. These colors have such names as *reddish violet* and *violet-red*, though Newton preferred to call them *purples*. Infrared, ultraviolet, and the wave phenomena lying beyond each are not included in the color wheel. The relationship among the hues is regarded as circular.

Red-violet is left in an ambiguous position by the disparity between the color wheel and the electromagnetic wave scale. Although a hue variation recognized on the color wheel, it has no place on the electromagnetic spectrum or in scientific theory. No way exists to add red-violet to the scale of wavelengths. Red-violet belongs at the top of the electromagnetic scale and also at the bottom. Yet it cannot be added in both places without violating the linear nature of the scale. In scientific theory, red grades into infrared, and violet grades into ultraviolet. As we see color, red-violet provides a transition between red and violet.

Circular and Linear Diagrams

The color wheel and the electromagnetic scale suggest that the entity called color can be subdivided into half a dozen major hues. The relationship among the hues is analogous to the perimeter of a circle (it can be diagrammed in circular form). But it is also analogous to a line (it can be diagrammed as a line segment). This is a logical inconsistency and a topological incongruency. Because circular means nonlinear (and linear mean noncircular), no set of relationships can be both circular and linear at the same time. If, say, biological evolution is regarded as a linear (hierarchical) transition from lower to higher life forms, we cannot consistently assert that its nature is also circular (cyclic): that higher forms, say, mammals, will eventually develop into forms lower on the evolutionary scale, say, protozoa.

The Second Continuum

In diagramming the relationships among the hues, the locus of the topological incongruity is the relationship between red and violet. These colors either should or should not be envisioned as extremes, as opposite ends of a linear scale. In topological terms, lines and circles are related. A line segment can be created by cutting the perimeter of a circle, just as a circle can be created by joining the ends of a line segment (figure 10-2).

Imagine the color wheel severed at that point on its perimeter where red and violet meet. The question is whether one or two color continua lie between red and violet. Are two different cities (call them red and violet) joined by two roads or just one?

If color is to be equated with wavelength (if the relationship between the spectral hues is linear), a single continuum or road is implied. It consists of orange, yellow, green, and blue, those hues assigned wavelengths between the

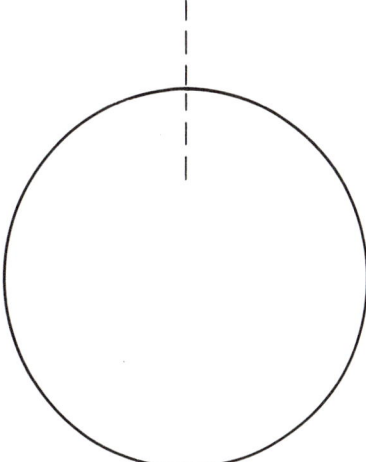

Figure 10-2. Transforming a circular diagram into a linear diagram. A circle can be transformed into a line by cutting it—or a line segment cannot both meet itself end to end to form a circle and not meet itself at the same time.

extremes of red and violet. What we see tells us, however, that two roads exist, recognized in the circular arrangement of the hues on the color wheel. The continuum additional to orange, yellow, green, and blue consists of those colors commonly said to lie between red and violet: the range of red-violet colors.

Which diagram provides a more accurate model for color relationships? I conclude the color wheel is correct and the diagram of wavelengths is incomplete. By failing to include red-violet colors, it implies they do not or cannot exist. This is incorrect because we see a large range of red-violet colors. How are we able to see them if they are not on the scale?

Conjecture runs rampant on this question. Red waves and violet waves, we are told, probably mix in the eye in some manner. This mixing enables us to see red-violet colors or to imagine we see them. Unlike other hue variations, they cannot be correlated with any range of wavelengths of light. To buttress these suppositions, we are asked to make a curious assumption: the red-violet colors are not really colors, or do not really exist (as colors). Thus, theory continues, we can salvage the idea all colors or variations of hue can be correlated with wavelengths of light. Red-violets do not fit in the picture because they are not really there.

The explanation, now woven into folklore, is too slapdash to take seriously. The thesis of optical mixing in this sense is untenable. There is no such thing as colors we see that are not hallucinatory but nevertheless do not exist. No way can be found to give a reasonable explanation of what such a statement could mean. Because color is a visual phenomenon, the criterion for whether a color exists *is* whether that color can be seen.[1]

Any attempt to dispose of the initial difficulty leads to others that are worse. Consider the hypothesis that we actually see yellow but only imagine red-violet. To define this idea, the difference must be identified, if any, between a color that exists—yellow—and another seen alongside it that does not—red-violet. Confusions proliferate if Newton's experiment is repeated with tubes of red and violet paint. Red and violet both exist and are each part of the electromagnetic spectrum. Yet mixing the two colors of paint produces red-violet, a "nonexistent" color. Adding to the red-violet paint small quantities of other existing colors—yellow, green, brown—produces mixed colors that partly exist and partly do not.

What meaning can we extract from these bizarre propositions about the nature of red-violet? If color itself is illusory, what can it mean to classify red-violet as more illusory than, say, orange or green? No matter how rearranged, the argument that shades of color in the red-violet range are "figments of perception" falsifies the theory it purports to sustain. All colors or all hue variations cannot be explained in terms of wavelengths of light if the range of red-violet colors requires a different explanation.

Putting forward optical mixture as the alternate explanation for red-violet colors is tantamount to an admission that the color wheel is correct and the diagram of wavelengths is incomplete. Two color continua lie between red and violet in the experiential world. The ideal world of classical physics can include neither red-violet nor variations on colors in that range: it is assumed to include no human eye in which red and violet waves might mix.

Circular and Linear Relationships

In electromagnetic theory, which became a cornerstone of classical physics, red-violet was sacrificed to preserve an idea that cannot be reconciled with visual observation. The relationship among the hues, as Newton recognized, is circular rather than linear. Theory does not match observation, and the degree of disparity is unusual. I can think of no other instance in which the quality to be measured by a linear scale appears not to be linear, therefore, to be incapable of measurement by that kind of scale.

The quality experienced as heat is measured by the thermometer. The thermometer, which is linear, shows hot and cold as polarities, with a single continuum between these extremes. The linearity of the thermometer and its single continuum are compatible with perception. We cannot imagine, and have never experienced, any condition intermediary between hot and cold except for a transitional warmness. There is no other intermediary continuum that is dissimilar to warmness.

Many further examples could be listed. Pitch, which the ear perceives in sounds, is envisioned as linear. Sounds range from low pitched to high pitched, and perception again agrees with theory. Extremes of high-pitched sound do not grade into low-pitched sound as they grow progressively higher.

Weight ranges from light to heavy, a linear conception. Objects that are becoming heavier do not, at a certain point, circle back to become lighter. Heat, pitch, and weight are each properly diagrammed by a line segment, not a circle. In none of these instances is theory inconsonant with perception on the question of whether linearity or circularity characterizes the set of relationships.

The linear nature of the electromagnetic scale introduces more than just ideas about the hues that are irreconcilable with visual experience. The scale implies conditions about color that are impossible to imagine because they make no sense topologically. A line segment, for example, has two ends, although the perimeter of a circle has none. Because of this two-endedness, line segments are used to construct diagrams that serve as visual analogues for hierarchical relationships.

In these relationships, a range exists between dissimilar extremes. The extremes can be explained in terms of polarities, say, more–less, bigger–smaller, longer–shorter, or better–worse. Each end of the line segment is labeled to correspond to one of the extremes. For the diagram to be useful, a correlation should exist with an imaginable, even if never experienced, extreme in perceptual experience.

The heat, pitch, and weight scales can be correlated in this manner. Therefore, no conceptual barrier exists to envisioning the extension of each. I can imagine more heat than I have ever felt, higher pitched sounds than I have ever heard, weights heavier than I can lift. The wavelength scale, unlike these other scales, cannot be correlated with extremes in the perceptual experience of color. Imagining the linear extension of the scale is impossible. Red is not perceived as more color than violet, though its wavelength is longer. Nor does red look longer or brighter—it cannot be characterized by a superlative of any quality found to a lesser degree in violet. Red just looks different from violet, and either looks different from yellow.

If human beings were able to see by infrared light, which has a longer wavelength than red, we cannot say that this experience would make available more color or more extreme color than we are able to see now. I can only imagine that infrared might look different from the colors we presently see, just as each of these colors looks different from any other color.

The high and low extremes of the visible light sector of the electromagnetic wavelength scale cannot be correlated with extremes of visual experience. Red is not an opposite to violet, in the sense that hot might be thought an opposite of cold, high pitched of low pitched, or heavy of light. Nor is color linear or binary. We find color, in electromagnetic theory, forced to a pattern it does not fit, the exact reason the range of red-violet colors appears to have been mislaid.

For Newton, "the received laws of Refraction" suggested a circular relationship among the hues. But Maxwell, in devising the electromagnetic scale, was interested in another set of relationships. He hoped to show that light, radio waves, X rays, and other phenomena could all be explained as forms of radiant energy of varying wavelength. Red-violet fell victim to the synthesis, and the electromagnetic scale, for this reason, falls short in its explanation of the hues.

Can we retain the hue circle and discard the electromagnetic scale? The hue circle has no room for infrared, ultraviolet, and other forms of radiant energy beyond the visible light sector. In theory, the electromagnetic scale might be adjusted. No barrier exists to a line segment on which two points are joined by two lines (figure 10-3). Negative numbers, from -380 to -780, could be used for the red-violet sector. But this introduces the conception of negative wave lengths, which is untenable. And whether a monochromatic beam can be

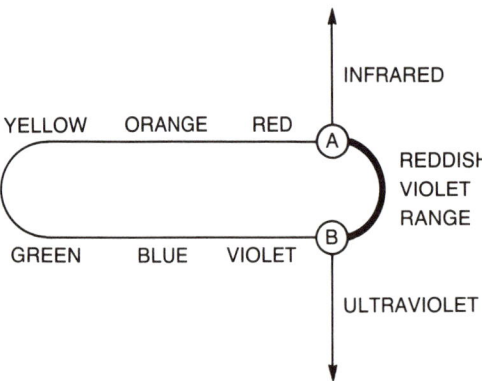

Figure 10-3. Alternate construction for the visible light sector of the electromagnetic wave scale. Two points on the electromagnetic wave scale, *A* and *B*, are placed at 380 and 780 millimicrons, the extremes of the color, or visible light, sector. *A* and *B* are assumed to have two discrete circuits, or paths, between them. This arrangement allows room not only for the spectral colors presently on the scale but also for the red-violet range, which is presently excluded.

produced which is red-violet in color is not clear.

Seeing Ultraviolet

The status of red-violet, in electromagnetic theory, is no more curious than that of ultraviolet and blue. Wavelengths in the ultraviolet range, like those in the infrared range, are said to be imperceptible to human beings. The lens of the human eye filters them out, a mechanism suggesting that ultraviolet rays are damaging and the retina is sensitive to them.

Despite the filtering (which appears to be partial), experimental evidence is available that human beings, and not just some insects, are able to see by ultraviolet light. The literature is divided only on the question of whether the capability is commonplace. Some writers said that it is (Jenkins and White 1957, 202). Others contended the ability is limited to persons who have had the natural lens of the eye removed, as in cataract operations.

Irrespective of the size of the human population involved, those able to see by ultraviolet light do not perceive its color as violet, purple, lavender, or any of the other shades misleadingly suggested by its name. The color is described as bluish gray. Helmholtz filled this out by observing that when ultraviolet rays are of low intensity, "their color is indigo-blue, and with higher intensity bluish gray" (Helmholtz [1909] 1962, 2:66).

The color of ultraviolet rays has a bearing on the location of blue. Although red-violet has no place on the electromagnetic spectrum, the blue range, which should be found at one place, occupies two. The perceptual experience of seeing bluish gray (or indigo-blue) may indicate that waves from the blue sector of the scale have entered the viewer's eye. It can also indicate, relying on Helmholtz, that the viewer is seeing ultraviolet, waves from a different range that is not adjacent to blue. Why should wavelengths from the ultraviolet range look blue, indigo-blue, or bluish gray? Why should they resemble blue more than they resemble violet?

That waves from more than one range look blue suggests a disruption of what is usually regarded as a one-to-one relationship between the visible hue continuum and the electromagnetic continuum. But phenomenological reality is more complex than theory, and whether all sectors of the electromagnetic spectrum exist in a smooth linear relationship is not certain. The red extreme of the visible light sector passes into infrared, radar, and short radio waves. In 1917, Nichols and Tear produced infrared with wavelengths up to 0.42 millimeters; radio waves down to 0.22 millimeters (Jenkins and White 1957, 203).

That this could be accomplished suggests an overlap between these two sectors. Wave phenomena in the zone of overlap (0.42–0.22 millimeters) can be either radio waves or infrared. Or wavelengths that in theory ought to have been infrared were shown to be radio waves and vice versa. The apparent disruption in the far infrared sector of the scale suggests parallels with the apparent bifurcation of blue (or indigo-blue) at the other extreme.

The earth's atmosphere filters out ultraviolet rays, as does the lens of the human eye. This filtering suggests that the rays, linked to the formation of skin cancers, are damaging to the retina in large amounts. In that case, a visual pigment adapted to responding to ultraviolet rays would be superfluous, though it might occur as an evolutionary relic. Ultraviolet rays entering the human eye must interact with the mechanism for seeing blue or for seeing blue and violet. Helmholtz describes the visual sensation as indigo-blue, and Newton named indigo as a seventh hue between blue and violet.

My dictionary identifies blue as the color "between green and violet in the spectrum." Blue arguably is also the color lying beyond violet, in the range called ultraviolet. Indigo-blue or blue-gray are the colors human beings see, if they see anything, when encountering wavelengths in the ultraviolet range.

The Cause of Brown

Newton differentiates between "all the Colours in the Universe which are made by Light" and those that depend "on the Powers of Imagination . . . as when by the power of Phantasy we see Colours in a Dream, or a Madman sees things before him which are not there; or when we see Fire by striking the Eye, or see Colours like the Eye of a Peacock's Feather, by pressing our Eyes in either corner whilst we look the other way" (Newton [1730] 1952, 161). The colors made by light include those of natural bodies, and "every Body reflects the Rays of its own Colour more copiously than the rest" (Newton [1730] 1952, 179). Newton demonstrated this by his seventeenth experiment, which tests the reflective powers of vermilion (cinnabar) and ultramarine pigment under red and blue lights.

Each pigment looked brighter under the light that resembled it in color. It looked darker or duller under the other light. Newton's observation that the experiment works best with objects of "the fullest and most vivid Colours" (Newton [1730] 1952, 180) ought to have warned of the danger of generalizing to "all the Colours in the Universe" other than those thought to be phantasmagorical.

Vermilion, a red pigment, reflects primarily red light. Ultramarine, a blue pigment, reflects primarily blue light. But neither pigment reflects light of a single color or single wavelength. The deviation is the basis for modern spectrophotometry and colorimetry, which assess the multiple colors of light that most surfaces reflect. Newton's understanding of his seventeenth experiment implies that ideal red and blue objects can exist, functioning as ideally selective reflectors of red and blue light. But the objects of the world are imperfect reflectors that fail to conform to theory in this form.

Multiple reflectance is at the heart of why Newton's conclusions from his seventeenth experiment cannot be expanded to explain the colors of brown or metallic-colored objects. No sense exists in which any brown or metallic object "reflects the Rays of its own Colour." Brown and, say, copper are not included in the visible light portion of the electromagnetic spectrum. Brown spectral rays do not exist, nor do silver, bronze, copper, or gold spectral rays.

In modern colorimetry, the issue of how brown is to be related to the colors of the spectrum has been addressed by reinterpreting it as a supersaturated yellow. The reinterpretation is unconvincing on epistemological grounds. *Supersaturated*, a term borrowed from chemistry, has no clear meaning in relation to color. In chemistry, it refers to the behavior of liquids in which substances are dissolved. How are we to *supersaturate* a ray of light? Furthermore, that all browns look similar to yellow is not a viable assumption. Many browns are greenish, reddish, orange, even purplish.

Optical Mixing

Browns are usually classified in color theory not as supersaturated yellows but as tertiary colors, mixtures that include each of the primary colors. No monochromatic wavelength exists for any brown, just as none exists for red-violet. Instead, the browns, chromatic grays, and other colors that approach brown or neutral are created by mixtures of varying wavelengths. The explanation wobbles when we are told the mixture occurs in the eye, that ubiquitous explanation of too much. Eyes are presumed not to be present in the classical model of the physical world.

Mixing in the eye has become the default explanation for color, put forward to explain how we see colors that cannot be correlated with a single spectral wavelength. The super-

ficiality of the explanation can be gauged by its vagueness. What mixing in the eye (in what part of the eye?) implies is unclear, though it suggests the bare minimum that the rays enter the eye simultaneously. Why should a mixing internal to the eye differ from an external aggregating? If rays of light mix in the eye to enable us to see brown, taupe, olive, russet, and similar colors, no barrier should exist to bundling the same rays outside the eye to produce beams of monochromatic light in these colors. Yet this cannot be done.

The easier conclusion is that the generalizations that can be drawn from Newton's seventeenth experiment are limited. The colors of some substances, say ultramarine and cinnabar, can be explained by assuming they reflect rays of their own color. The colors of most substances, objects, or surfaces cannot be explained in this manner. More than one wavelength of light is reflected, and the electromagnetic spectrum may include no monochrome wavelength matching the color of that object. The large range of colors called brown is far beyond the scope of Newton's explanation. Brown color in objects cannot be correlated with a component in light that matches the color of the object and is reflected from the object's surface.

Optical Mixture

Mixing in the eye is put forward too often as an explanation for color phenomena it does not explain. I do not mean to call into question, however, what the Impressionist and neo-Impressionist painters regarded as optical mixture (*mélange optique*). The term, borrowed from Maxwell and Rood, refers to an observable visual phenomenon. Its foundation is that no visual analogue can be found for emptiness, just as none can be found for silence. We see color throughout the visual field even when the limits of visual acuity are exceeded.

Two colors on a spinning Maxwell disc, for example, can be rotated too fast for either to be seen individually. Unlike the rapidly moving wings of a hummingbird, the colors on the Maxwell disc do not become invisible. Instead, the observer perceives a third color, classified as an optical mixture of the colors spinning on the disc.

A similar phenomenon occurs when objects are so small that they pass below the threshold of conscious perception. A building made of tan bricks and brown bricks may be too far away to allow its individual bricks to be seen. The building becomes neither invisible nor no color, even if the color spots that correspond to its bricks lie below the threshold of vision. It presents a color of its own, again assumed to be an optical mixture of the colors of the individual bricks.

After a century of critiques of Impressionist and neo-Impressionist painting, the term *optical mixture* is too firmly entrenched in the English language to be dislodged. But it may be redundant. To regard the single color presented by a spinning Maxwell disc as a mixture implies it must be a mixture of something

else, of the colors of the disc at rest, which are assumed to be the real colors of the disc.

As in the Newton-Hooke argument about whether the spectral colors are inherent in light, we need not assume that objects possess normal colors that they display under normal conditions. Because color in objects is contextual, the dark sky of night is as normal as the blue sky of day. The color of the disc when spinning is its real (and only) color for that condition.

Arguing that a distant building, which appears to be a single color, is actually multicolored (or made of multicolored bricks) is as arbitrary as arguing that the building is really made of protons, neutrons, and electrons, which human beings would see if we were small enough. The lesson of optical mixture is that color is unitary in nature. The seeing eye always sees colors but never more than one at any given time and place. The visual field can be modeled as a two-dimensional matrix, a grid of boxes resembling a piece of graph paper. We might imagine that the boxes are tiny, each box contains a color, and no box is able to contain two colors at the same time.

CHAPTER II

Achromatic Colors and Mirrors

> Black is a real sensation, even if it is produced by entire absence of light. The sensation of black is distinctly different from the lack of all sensation. A spot in the field of view which sends no light to the eye looks black; but no light comes to the eye from objects that are behind it, whether they are dark or bright, and yet these objects do not look black, there is simply no sensation so far as they are concerned.
>
> Erwin von Helmholtz, Treatise on Physiological Optics

Intimations of the negative and backward characterize most statements about black, the retrograde color which is variously nothing, not caused by light, or not caused by the phenomena that account for light. Like brown, silver, or red-violet, black confutes Newton's conclusions from his seventeenth experiment. No sense exists in which a black object, or any object that is achromatic in color, reflects "Rays of its own Colours." To smooth out these discrepancies, further negatives flesh out the picture.

The Cause of Black

The popular assertion that black is not a color rests on the syllogism that light waves cause colors, yet do not cause black, which conse-quently cannot be a color. I submit in place of this confused reasoning that, because black *is* a color, light waves do not cause all colors. The more usual or more popular train of thought forces an untenable conclusion. It implies that black is a noncolor produced when light acts as a noncause, a conceptual morass in which negative events result in nega-tive consequences. If causality is to be assumed and black is not caused by light, a categorical hiatus is created unless its formation can be attributed to some other agency.

As both Helmholtz and the Buddha have wisely observed, seeing black is not tanta-mount to not seeing. Black is a color, as is white or gray, by any reasonable visual criterion. In common with all other colors, black is exclusive to the visual field. We see it and do not hear it. Like any color, black meets the criterion of exclusivity in spatiotemporal location: I cannot see black at the same time and place I see yellow.

The turgidity of popular lines of reasoning about black conveys its own message. We must look to culture before science to understand the conception of this color. Salvaging the presumed oppositeness of black and white, an idea originally inspired by primitive recognition of the difference between night and day, is integral to our conception of oppositeness in general. The salvage job forces us to sustain a conception of black inconsistent with visual experience.

Recognizing that black is a color—because we see it as a color—raises questions about the generalization that colors can be correlated with wavelengths, thence questions about whether electromagnetic theory provides an adequate explanation of color. Recognizing black as a color—assessing it according to visual criteria—casts in doubt the presumed oppositeness of black and white. Oppositeness of color is not a visual concept.

When the world is interpreted as a collection of opposites (black and white are among the pairs of opposites), each pair is imagined to consist of a positive member poised against a negative twin. In psychological association and in symbolism, positives may be freely interchanged, as may negatives. Black, for this reason, is said to symbolize (or suggest) night, darkness, the void, Satan, evil. In our society black is rarely associated with day, light, salvation, God, goodness, or other concepts more intimately linked with white. Gray has few symbolic associations, an omission I consider significant. A world seen predominantly in terms of black or white, true or false, allows little room for the continuum of ambiquities, for that which is more or less true, or neither exactly black or white.

Among the traditional pairs of opposites, form/color is virtually indistinguishable from form/space. Although great care is needed in distinguishing between two-dimensional and three-dimensional space, color and space are both devoid of corporeality but exhibit dimension or extension. The valence of form is positive, perhaps because Plato idealized the forms of geometry. The valence of color is negative. In the familiar web of symbolic associations, form is "real." It is structured, analyzable, intellectual (perhaps because associated with geometry), rational, and consequently masculine. Color (or color qua space) is chimerical, unreal, unstructured, unanalyzable (hence, suggestive of chaos), emotional, irrational, and consequently feminine.

Over the centuries, layers of additional association have been piled atop these. Angular forms are said to be masculine, curved forms feminine, as if gender should be attributed to geometrical shapes. Among noncorporeal entities, light is regarded as immaterial but real. Colors are immaterial but unreal, presumably because they are secondaries that are classified as effects of light. Hue is opposed to [color] value, the rationale for differentiating between chromatic and achromatic colors. Among the achromatic colors, black, reduced to no more than an antipode for white, is defined almost totally in negatives. It is not a color, not caused by light, and it is interpreted as nothing when seen at night or in interstellar space. Factors more profound than the foibles of fashion explain why the walls of houses and apartments are often painted entirely white but rarely entirely black.

Anyone so inclined may write sonnets in praise of colors, including black. But the negative member of each opposed pair is subtly devalued, flagged as less worthy of respect or of serious attention. Oppositeness is a value system. And color, primarily because other than form (or because of its association with space), drifts to the negative side of the balance. Even if acknowledged to be good to look at, it may be dismissed as just decorative, as in early critiques of the use of color in the paintings of Henri Matisse.

Within these stereotyped limits, color is not often expected to be of significant interest to serious thinkers, or even to manly men. Although the merits of draftsmanly (form-oriented) versus painterly (color-oriented) painting styles have historically been considered at greater length than so trivial a topic deserves, I do not mean to imply these issues are often debated. Rarely are they even given much thought. But we live out our stereotypes as we sense them, often teetering on the edge of reducing human potential to a cartoon.

Trivial in the instance but telling in the aggregate, thoughtless comments about color are made even by those who we assume have thought about it more deeply than others. Newton discoursed on "the more eminent colors" without explaining his criteria for color eminence. Maxwell's list of the colors of the spectrum and their corresponding wavelengths is apocryphal for its omission of violet and its tortured use of common color names (figure 11-1). Bluish green is not usually regarded as a less blue variety of blue-green. Scarlet is ordinarily ranked as a subclass of red, not, as Maxwell has it, as a major hue name of the level of red or orange. These small oddities suggest a degree of societally determined indifference to color or to visual experience.

The indifference is difficult to comprehend because inconsistent with the human condition, with what the mass of human beings really feel and think. The prospect of blindness evokes terror. Freud equated loss of the eyes with castration, pointing to, say, *Oedipus Rex* as evidence of the severity of the punishment, fitting for only the gravest sins. For the protagonist of Rudyard Kipling's *The Light That Failed*, loss of the ability to see meant loss of a reason for living. We are not genuinely indifferent to what we see. We care greatly whether we see.

Figure 11-1. The spectral colors and their wavelengths according to James Clerk Maxwell. Note that Maxwell's wavelength units are inch units rather than millimicrons, and should be multiplied by 10^{-8}. (After Maxwell [1890] 1965, 425).

Spectral Color	Wavelength
red	2,450
scarlet	2,328
orange	2,240
yellow	2,154
yellow-green	2,078
green	2,013
green	1,951
bluish green	1,879
blue-green	1,846
greenish blue	1,797
blue	1,755
blue	1,721
blue	1,688
indigo	1,660
indigo	1,630
indigo	1,604

Oppositeness was originally a philosophical concept, not a scientific discovery. But it long ago became incorporated into theory in the physical sciences, assuming a position so central it survived even the demise of Newton's absolute space and absolute time. Today, parity is regarded as a fundamental feature of the subatomic world, as if an orderly God had ordained that everything ought to come in pairs.

In contemporary physics, manifestations of parity include the charges of subatomic particles (positive, negative, or no charge), which cause them to attract or repel one another. Each particle is said to be paired with an antiparticle so opposite to itself that it may even insist on moving in an opposite direction through time. A chance meeting of particle and antiparticle results in the annihilation of both. What else would opposites do?

The photon, which is said to account for light and color, fits uneasily into this system. The photon is described as without mass, without charge, and as its own antiparticle. The semantic question is how functioning as one's own antiparticle—one's own opposite—differs from having no antiparticle. I conclude that the possibility that all particles may not have antiparticles is regarded as threatening, and tortuous explanations are constructed to avoid considering the possibility. Can the photon annihilate its antiparticle on meeting it, if the photon is its own antiparticle?

Absorbers and Reflectors of Light

Black and white are sometimes explained in terms of an interaction between light and objects. Thus, the ideal black object is said to be a perfect absorber of light. The ideal white object is a perfect reflector. The ideal transparent (colorless) object is a perfect transmitter. The definitions survive because they make the behavior of light eminently easy to understand. We all know the diagrams in which waves, usually represented by arrows, are shown bouncing from surfaces as if they were volleyballs.

As is generally true of idealized conceptions, the parameters are too simplistic to help us understand visual phenomena. Black cats look black in the daytime, ostensibly from absorbing all light that falls on them, but as gray as everything else in the dark when no light is present that they might absorb. A blackboard ought to be more efficient absorber of light than a white wall. But either surface makes an equally effective movie screen. Under some circumstances, neither is more absorptive than the other.

The status of white as ideal reflector is as dubious as that of black as ideal absorber. A mirror is a more likely candidate for the title, because what it reflects is more complete or

coherent. A white surface reflects only light. A mirror reflects light reflected from the surfaces of the objects in front of it, in a manner allowing us to see images of these objects. Mirrors are typically silver, not white. Color, rather than substance, is critical.

Ordinary household mirrors are "silvered" with mercury. Aluminum compounds coat movie screens, the legendary "silver screen." Although all highly polished surfaces are reflective, the best mirrors are created by objects that are either silver or metallic in color. The polished shield used as a mirror is a familiar fixture in myth, as in the Greek tale of the slaying of the Gorgon. The roofs of houses, to enable them to reflect light, are given coatings of silver-colored substances, known to be more effective than white. Can any empirical reason be found for classifying white, not silver or a mirror, as the ideal reflector? I doubt it. The conventional reasoning is meant to sustain the theory that colors have opposites, and that white, not silver, is the opposite of black.

Causes of Transparency

Although Munsell complained about the ambiguity of color names, terms that refer to achromatic or transparent conditions are equally ambiguous. Misuse of the terms, or confusing usage, is common and institutionalized. Physics has its study of black bodies. These are not necessarily black, raising the question of why they are known as black bodies. The mutilation of language might be traceable to Max Planck, whose conception of "the black heat rays emitted from a stove" attributed color (which we see) to heat, which cannot be seen (Planck n.d. 143).

Planck's blurring of the distinction between colorless and black probably rests on the reasoning that black is proverbially not a color. Hence it can appropriately be associated with heat, which, because it cannot be seen, is also, in its way, not a color. The Inter-Society Color Council, sailing in an opposite direction but navigating as erratically, decided to extend the gamut of standard color names "by substituting colorless for white," a usage that deprives us of a label for transparent conditions (National Bureau of Standards n.d.*a.*, 1).

The word *white* is misused so often that even Helmholtz or his translator floundered. We are told of König's discovery that some individuals can detect no difference between yellow, blue, and "a colorless mixture," whether colorless in the sense of black, white, or transparent (Helmholtz [1909] 1962, 2:404).

Students in beginning painting classes, reasoning similarly, have been known to ask what color paint to buy "to paint glass." The question implies that, say, blue paint, yellow paint, and glass paint might exist. Although this, of course, is not the case, the inquiry is not wholly without sense. Colorlessness is a color condition: no object can be entirely blue and entirely colorless or transparent at the same time. Beyond this, many people have difficulty understanding the phenomenological nature of transparency.

If an object (say, a pane of glass) can be said to look transparent or colorless, it looks neither black nor white. The colors seen when looking at colorless objects are those of the objects behind them. This aspect of transparency is difficult to reconcile with the dark color of the sky at night. Vacuums, including the vacuum of interstellar space, ought to be the most ideally transparent of all objects. In theory, they contain little or nothing that could impede light or reflect it.

What and where, therefore, is the blackness of the sky? If not to be understood as the color of what lies beyond the transparency, then the colorlessness of interstellar space is dissimilar to that of, say, sheets of glass. A primitive regarding the night sky and reasoning by analogy with transparent objects on earth might reasonably assume that the blackness is the color of whatever lies immediately outside the universe. The sky might be regarded as, say, a black curtain or sphere with a fire burning outside. The stars are glimpses of that fire, seen through holes in the curtain or sphere.

Twentieth-century creation myth paints a more grandiose picture, raising new questions without answering old ones. The universe, we are told, has no "outside," a consequence of the curvature of space-time. The question, in that case, is why this curvature, or light traveling through it, ought to result in a black color. We have no reason to believe that interstellar space is anything other than transparent. Yet the way it looks, or the color it presents, cannot be explained by analogy with transparent objects on earth, which transmit the colors of the objects behind them.

We are limited to just a few possibilities in conjecturing about why the sky looks black. All return to the question of what causes black. Prevailing wisdom identifies black as the condition of default for human vision: the color that appears when there is ostensibly nothing to see. Yet black does not appear to be categorically different from other colors, as one might expect if a switch were either on or off. In another inconsistency, we see black objects in the daytime and explain their blackness by assuming that they absorb all light. Interstellar space looks black, yet ought to be a transmitter, not an absorber, of light. Vacuums look transparent rather than black, at least in small volumes.

If the black of the night sky is not to be understood as an accident of human neurology, the edge of the universe is what looks black. In current theory the universe is finite. We are encouraged to regard it as a closed box, elastic and expanding as if it were a balloon being inflated. The box is formed by the curvature of space-time, a twentieth-century reinterpretation of the celestial dome imagined by ancient peoples or of the spheres that enclose the universe in Ptolemaic astronomy.

The expansion of the box creates a presumption that anything outside it may be growing correspondingly smaller. But if nothing can escape from the box, whether anything lies outside is irrelevant. Is the box itself transparent or opaque? If the curvature of its surface is transparent (or cannot be seen), the blackness of the sky lies outside the box, a remarkable possibility that implies we can see what lies outside the universe.

Because the box is closed, anything inside that bumps into its curvature is deflected and might at some later point enter a human eye. This raises the question of whether the blackness we see could be something deflected by this curvature, perhaps a previously unrecognized component of light. If so, this might salvage the theory that all colors are accounted for by waves or particles that enter an eye, most often after being deflected by objects. This direction of conjecture implies that the curvature of space-time looks black or behaves in a manner similar to any other black object. The curvature of space-time cannot, however, absorb light. That contingency requires us to assume that light could leak out of an otherwise closed universe.

Coding Colors by Wavelengths

The electromagnetic spectrum is schematic in its explanation of color because many colors are not on the scale. Nevertheless, the commonplace assertion that "color can be defined in terms of light" passes as unimpeachable. From this follows the familiar suggestion, whether meant to be implemented or only theoretical, that color names could be eliminated from language if light-wave notations were used in their place. Red, in a classification system of this type, would be described as a wave of 650 millimicron wavelength, blue, 450 to 500 millimicrons, and so forth.

The system seems admirably exact if it is not examined in detail. We are left to understand that the reason for not putting it into use is that habituation to less excellent methods for designating colors makes it difficult for human beings to change their ways. Despite any aura of technological exactitude, however, no system for naming colors by wavelengths would be workable. Too many serious impediments occur. The electromagnetic spectrum, for example, is devoid of wavelengths (therefore, of wavelength notations) for colors in the red-violet range and in other ranges as well.

The two perceptual continua between red and violet (electromagnetic theory acknowledges only one) present another sort of obstacle. If the wavelength notation for red is 650 millimicrons, and that of violet is 400, 525 millimicrons ought to be halfway between. But we have no way of determining on which continuum. The median number might indicate yellow-green, with a wavelength halfway between those for red and violet. Or it might as validly point to red-violet, similarly between red and violet but on an alternate continuum.

Correlation between hue variation and wavelength fails with both red-violet and the blue-to-ultraviolet range. Even if this failure of correspondence could be overcome, most colors cannot be explained in terms of hue alone. They therefore have no place on the electromagnetic wavelength scale, no wavelengths and no wavelength notations. The excluded group includes gray, white, black, brown, pink, all tints and tones, any color that deviates from spectral purity (say, a slightly brownish yellow), fluorescent colors, iridescent colors, and metallics, as well as such recent innovations as dayglo colors and the colors of anodized aluminum. The electromagnetic scale is a hue scale, and color has other dimensions in addition to hue.

The electromagnetic wavelength scale does not accommodate color value (lightness and darkness), which creates impediments to notating the achromatic colors by wavelengths. Black, if attributable to absence of light, consists of an absence of wavelengths. One possibility is to notate it as 0, which skirts the problem that absence of light is an improperly framed concept, irrespective of the merits of the theory on which it relies.

A more immediate problem is that the only black that can be understood as an entire absence of light (null notation) is an absolute black. If this absolute exists, it must be a single shade of color, not a range of colors. The large number of different blacks that we see, which are not absolute blacks, might be regarded off blacks or near blacks, each properly labeled as *black* though not as *absolute black*. Each must reflect, or be accounted for by, a few wavelengths rather than none. Thus zero (0) could not be a proper notation.

A system that notated the range of blacks or near blacks in terms of the light they reflected would be difficult to correlate, incidentally, with the manner in which colors are presently named. Ivory black artists' pigment has been shown to be a weak reflector of predominantly blue light (see figure 23-4). In a notational system based on wavelengths, ivory black would be classified with the blues, although we call it black.

If reflectance of light is to be used as the criterion in naming colors, any color other than absolute black can be classified as a very dark variety of blue, green, red, or some other chromatic color. The Impressionist painters, following this logic, contended that artists had no need for black paint, because black objects could be represented without it. Although this is perfectly true, it fails to take full account of how we process what we see. Two black color swatches will be recognized as black before one is noticed to be, say, slightly greenish and the other slightly reddish.

Is the immediate recognition of the swatches as black a matter of vision or of acculturation? I suspect we must recognize it as visual, because it can be placed in a phenomenological perspective. A respective redness and greenness in two black swatches seen from a viewing distance of 18 inches will be less noticeable from a distance of 150 feet. We recognize black immediately and may under certain conditions also notice the direction in which this black deviates from absolute black. I conclude that the names *black* and *white* have a visual function and refer to more than just the concepts of darkness and light.

That reflectance can vary in degree is sufficient to suggest that notating by wavelength cannot be a complete system. Imagine that a bright blue and a black both reflect a certain wavelength of blue light but in different amounts. No way of differentiating between these colors is provided by a system that takes note only of the wavelength of the reflected blue light. Unlike hue, color value (lightness/darkness) and chromaticity (saturation of hue) cannot be correlated with wavelength.

White

The notational problems presented by white are similar to those for black but more complicated. Absent from the solar spectrum and unassigned to any wavelength, white is regarded as a mixture of *all* wavelengths, a less exact quantifier than *many*. Because of this multiple reflectance, a theory of how to notate a mixture of wavelengths is required. The need similarly exists in the case of any color that reflects more than a single wavelength of light, say, a black that reflected some red light and some blue. The problem of developing a notational method for mixtures is not easy. It has not been solved in, say, chemical nomenclature, which otherwise is marvelously intricate.

White, like black, is a range of numerous shades. All of these shades other than absolute white might be regarded as off-whites and can incline toward virtually any color other than white. Whites can be yellowish, bluish, brownish, or grayish. The need, therefore, is to write notations for a mixture that will not always include exactly the same components. The achromatic grays, because mixtures of black and white, again are a special case. They would have to be notated as mixtures of nothing (no wavelengths) and everything (all wavelengths), a similarly stupendous technical problem.

The problem of how to notate a mixture, or how to take account of multiple reflectance, might appear to be solved in the familiar tables of tristimulus values (figure 11-2). These tables, developed with the aid of a colorimeter, do not, however, measure light reflected from a surface. They measure the relative amounts of red, blue, and green required to obtain a match for a spectral color for a statistically determined average viewer.

The spectrophotometer comes closer. A color sample is successively illuminated with beams of given wavelengths, usually spaced at 10-millimicron differences in wavelength. The reflectance of the sample for each individual

Figure 11-2. Tristimulus values of the spectral colors (abridged).
Adopted in 1931 by International Commission on illumination.

Wavelength (millimicrons)	X (red)	Y (green)	Z (blue)	Wavelength (millimicrons)	X (red)	Y (green)	Z (blue)
380	0.0014	0.0000	0.0065	580	0.9163	0.8700	0.0017
385	0.0022	0.0001	0.0105	585	0.9786	0.8163	0.0014
390	0.0042	0.0001	0.0201	590	1.0263	0.7570	0.0011
395	0.0076	0.0002	0.0362	595	1.0567	0.6949	0.0010
400	0.0143	0.0004	0.0679	600	1.0622	0.6310	0.0008
405	0.0232	0.0006	0.1102	605	1.0456	0.5668	0.0006
410	0.0435	0.0012	0.2074	610	1.0026	0.5030	0.0003
415	0.0776	0.0022	0.3713	615	0.9384	0.4412	0.0002
420	0.1344	0.0040	0.6456	620	0.8544	0.3810	0.0002
425	0.2148	0.0073	1.0391	625	0.7514	0.3210	0.0001
430	0.2839	0.0116	1.3856	630	0.6424	0.2650	0.0000
435	0.3285	0.0168	1.6230	635	0.5419	0.2170	0.0000
440	0.3483	0.0230	1.7471	640	0.4479	0.1750	0.0000
445	0.3481	0.0298	1.7826	645	0.3608	0.1382	0.0000
450	0.3362	0.0380	1.7721	650	0.2835	0.1070	0.0000
455	0.3187	0.0480	1.7441	655	0.2187	0.0816	0.0000
460	0.2908	0.0600	1.6692	660	0.1649	0.0610	0.0000
465	0.2511	0.0739	1.5281	665	0.1212	0.0446	0.0000
470	0.1954	0.0910	1.2876	670	0.0874	0.0320	0.0000
475	0.1421	0.1126	1.0419	675	0.0636	0.0232	0.0000
480	0.0956	0.1390	0.8130	680	0.0468	0.0170	0.0000
485	0.0580	0.1693	0.6162	685	0.0329	0.0119	0.0000
490	0.0320	0.2080	0.4652	690	0.0227	0.0082	0.0000
495	0.0147	0.2586	0.3533	695	0.0158	0.0057	0.0000
500	0.0049	0.3230	0.2720	700	0.0114	0.0041	0.0000
505	0.0024	0.4073	0.2123	705	0.0081	0.0029	0.0000
510	0.0093	0.5030	0.1582	710	0.0058	0.0021	0.0000
515	0.0291	0.6082	0.1117	715	0.0041	0.0015	0.0000
520	0.0633	0.7100	0.0782	720	0.0029	0.0010	0.0000
525	0.1096	0.7932	0.0573	725	0.0020	0.0007	0.0000
530	0.1655	0.8620	0.0422	730	0.0014	0.0005	0.0000
535	0.2257	0.9149	0.0298	735	0.0010	0.0004	0.0000
540	0.2904	0.9540	0.0203	740	0.0007	0.0003	0.0000
545	0.3597	0.9803	0.0134	745	0.0005	0.0002	0.0000
550	0.4334	0.9950	0.0087	750	0.0003	0.0001	0.0000
555	0.5121	1.0002	0.0057	755	0.0002	0.0001	0.0000
560	0.5945	0.9950	0.0039	760	0.0002	0.0001	0.0000
565	0.6784	0.9786	0.0027	765	0.0001	0.0000	0.0000
570	0.7621	0.9520	0.0021	770	0.0001	0.0000	0.0000
575	0.8425	0.9154	0.0018	775	0.0000	0.0000	0.0000

wavelength can be measured and compared with the reflectance of a standard white for that same wavelength. The spectrophotometer cannot directly measure reflectance for the various wavelengths of a mixed light, say, ordinary daylight. Its procedures are therefore necessarily ponderous.

Imagine that a certain color swatch reflected certain percentages of red, orange, yellow, green, blue, and violet wavelengths, and this was determined by a spectrophotometer. Why would listing these statistics be more simple than just calling the swatch *white*? The same swatch will look slightly different in color on another occasion when the illumination has changed. The swatch will require a new set of spectrophotometric measurements. Indeed, the swatch needs an infinite number of sets of measurements, to account for all possible lighting conditions. Are we all to carry around spectrophotometers to determine the measurements applicable for the moment?

Exactitude of measurement is not always necessary or practical, the exact reason that objects, including colors and people, have names. I have been known by the same name since birth. People who address me by my name have no need to know, say, my blood pressure, number of brain cells or hemoglobin cells, or other items that could be measured. Rarely would their having this information on hand be useful. Even the Internal Revenue Service, which wants to know everything, wisely does not inquire about my cholesterol count.

Although I have been known by the same name all the days of my life, a reasonable argument could be made that I have not always been the same person. Over a seven-year period, all cells in the human body are replaced, and the cells in my body today are not exactly the same cells present yesterday. Human beings, like the colors we see, are not static. Measurements are just the measurements of the moment, plotting points in a coordinate system without halting the continuous changes occurring in that system.

I am not disturbed that a color swatch is not always the same. I am not always the same either, because this is the nature of phenomenological reality. A hope of getting at the facts once and for all, by measurement, is not realistic. No constant facts that might be ascertained about either colors or people exist.

The reason that we do not presently have in operation a system for identifying colors by wavelengths is that no such system can be complete, coherent, or even desirable. The task is impossible in theory and would not be useful in practice. All colors cannot be explained in terms of wavelengths: no wavelengths have been assigned to pink, brown, silver, black, and other nonspectral colors. All spectral hues cannot be explained in terms of wavelength, given, say, the double location of blue and the missing wavelength notation for red-violet, which in theory ought to be a spectral color because it consists of a mixture of red and violet, each of which is a spectral color.

CHAPTER 12

Color Causes Light

All vision is colour vision, for it is only by observing differences of colour that we distinguish the forms of objects. I include differences of brightness or shade among differences of colour.

James Clerk Maxwell, Scientific Papers

I express variety of illumination through an understanding of the differences in the values of colors, alone and in relation.

Henri Matisse, Matisse Speaks to his Students

The notion that color is really light is too firmly entrenched in popular belief and the physical sciences to be dislodged by the less difficult assumption that light is really color. But if color cannot be completely explained as an inference from the experience of seeing light, it cannot be just a name for perceived effects caused by light waves. The task of explaining light (a name for certain perceived color effects) as an inference from the experience of seeing color is less fraught with difficulty.

I shall play the devil's advocate by asking what light is and by proposing that it does not exist—or it exists only as a convenient fiction, a label applied to color effects under some circumstances. In an ideal language—a code in which every object has a name and no object

has two names—the word *light* could then be eliminated if *color* were used in its place.

Because this bears on how causality (as in "light causes color") is envisioned, imagine an observer looking at the sun and receiving a certain visual sensation. The event is conventionally explained by assuming that an entity called *light* travels from the sun to the observer's eye. The explanation is circular. The only immediate evidence for the existence of the light, said to have caused the experience, is that the viewer had a visual experience the presence of light is intended to explain. On another planet, a simpler race of human beings might say that the sun, rather than light streaming from it, causes any sensations experienced when looking at the sun. They could argue that they had discovered a greater truth, because if light causes the sensation, the sun causes the light.

I am interested in the diagrammatic manner in which the event is typically imagined. The popular conception of light was entangled with that of lines—including lines representing trajectories of particles—long before Maxwell pictured the electromagnetic spectrum as a line with indeterminate ends. Drawing lines to represent rays, especially in halos, is a familiar device in medieval and early Renaissance art as well as in drawings by children. Rays of light (or their paths) continue to be depicted as lines in diagrams used as illustrations for modern texts on optics.

We think in diagrams, which breed their own confusion, reflecting what we believe rather than what we see. If asked to imagine light traveling from the sun to an observer's eye, most people visualize it in the form of lines connecting the two. Or the lines might be arrows, to indicate that the light has a direction. Human beings have long been accustomed to imagining any relationship between objects in terms of a causal connection—of links that can be shown in graphic form. No observer of an observer watching the sky would have noticed lines or arrows descending from the sun into anyone's eyes.

The behavioral psychologist B. F. Skinner believed "man's first experience with causes probably came from his own behavior: things moved because he moved them. If other things moved, it was because someone else was moving them, and if the mover could not be seen, it was because he was invisible "(Skinner 1972, 5). The invisible "he" subsequently became an invisible force. We draw diagrams to show what the invisible force is doing, and these diagrams become our private truths.

Causality of the push-pull variety presents too simpleminded a picture of the phenomenological world. Yet even laboratory animals recognize that actions have consequences. Pushing one button rather than another may result in punishment or reward. Human beings probably imagined lines representing causal connections between objects long before those lines came to be regarded, in some cases, as symbolic equivalents for rays of light.

Lines used for graphic purposes have their own history, separate from the history of those marks that developed into systems of writing. At some unknown early date, human beings picked· out the constellations by imagining lines connecting one star to another in the night sky. They learned to imagine connections where none existed and to represent these connections as lines. Outline drawings in Paleolithic caves show a recognition that lines have a greater potential than functioning as images of lines or of anything else that looks linear. Outline drawings, imagined in the sky or marked on cave walls, were the first abstract art, if only because objects do not have outlines wrapping their surfaces like black wires.

Outline drawings are usually regarded as tracings of shapes, unconnected to the colors of objects. Calling them juncture drawings would be thought peculiar. Yet we find (or invent) the outline of an object by looking at the juncture between the aggregate of color spots associated with the object and those associated with its surroundings. In drawing rays of light, outlines, paths, trajectories, or circuits, lines are manufactured that cannot be correlated with other, similar black lines that can be located in the natural world. Perhaps these imaginary lines were inspired by the horizon, the line separating earth and sky that we see but cannot reach or touch.

Whatever light is, it is not the lines so often drawn to represent it. Nor is it the intimations of causal connection that the lines incidentally convey. Above all, light is not the isolated ray, a thin white line usually surmounted by a dove, that we remember as a familiar accessory in Renaissance paintings of the Annunciation. Rays of light seen in side view are not, we are told, what they seem. What is seen is the scattering of the light by dust particles suspended in the air. The ray itself is effectively invisible from that oblique angle.

Instantaneous Propagation

Until the seventeenth century, the propagation of light was thought to be instantaneous. The Italian astronomer G. D. Cassini (1625–1712) noticed variations in the elapsed time between eclipses of Jupiter's moons, according to whether the planet was approaching or receding from earth. Ole Roemer (1644–1710) recognized the cause of the discrepancy as the varying times required for light to traverse the distance. Roemer made the first computation of the speed of light in 1675, 140,000 miles per second. The modern figure is 186,282 miles per second, a velocity that in theory cannot be exceeded.

Although instantaneous propagation ostensibly has been discarded in contemporary physics, it may instead have been displaced. A staple of relativity theory is that a clock (or time) slows down according to the velocity with which it moves. At the speed of light, time stands still. This is usually interpreted to mean that time is a null dimension from, so to speak, the point of view of a photon.

A ray of light reaching the earth from the edge of the universe may have taken, by our manner of reckoning, fifteen billion years to arrive. If we had been able to ride on one of the light particles (a photon travels at the speed of light because it *is* light), theory holds that the journey would have been accomplished instantaneously. As Gribbin pointed out, "for a photon time has no meaning. . . . A photon of the cosmic background radiation has, from our point of view, been traveling through space for perhaps fifteen thousand million years since the Big Bang in which the universe as we know it began, but to the photon itself the Big Bang and our present are the same time" (Gribbin 1984, 190).

A curiosity of this modern picture of the relativity of time is that it raises the question of whether light—a photon—is capable of movement in any ordinary sense. Because motion is an event that happens to forms in time, nothing moves in a formless void. Motion is similarly inconceivable without time, the dimension within which it occurs.

The photon thought it moved from here to there in no time at all. But it must also have concluded (if it is a logician-photon) that *here* is synonymous with *there*. The logic of the syllogism is that the photon cannot change its position.

What contemporary physics has brought us to in its conception of light, space-time, and color-qua-light is the notion of a photon trapped in a world of its own in which time has collapsed, carrying space along with it if one is continuous with the other. Motion is paradoxically impossible and instantaneous at the same time. This, at least, is how a photon looks to a human being through the filter of relativity theory, without prejudice to how human affairs might appear to a photon.

The speed of sound was surpassed during the 1950s at the cost of many lives. In retrospect, the barrier was just mechanical or aerodynamic. The speed of light is less approachable. Equaling it implies hurtling into a world of immobility, in which space is inaccessible (or instantaneously accessible) because of the absence of time in which movement through it could occur. The four-dimensional time-space continuum is compressed to a Euclidean point, a one-dimensional (or nondimensional) universe. The metaphysics is intriguing.

The presumed cessation of time for a particle moving at the speed of light implies that the nominally four-dimensional time-space continuum of the photon lacks one of its dimensions. The obvious parallel is color, which, as we perceive it, is similarly devoid of a dimension: the colored images of the visual field have no depth. Can one dimension be transformed into another?

Perhaps it can. Both relativity theory and quantum theory allow theoretically for travel through time. The technique allowed by relativity theory "involves distorting the fabric of space-time so that in a local region of space-time the time axis points in a direction equivalent to one of the three space directions in the undistorted region of space-time. One of the other space directions takes on the role of time, and by swapping space for time such a device would make true time travel, there and back again, possible" (Gribbin 1984, 193). Space-time can be distorted by a strong gravitational field.

I am less interested in time travel than in the interchange of one dimension for another. Interchangeability of dimensions other than time is self-evident. In the case of a cube or other volumetric form, which measurement is regarded as its height, which width, and which depth is arbitrary. Motion may be as impossible in the depthless world of the color spot as in the timeless world of the photon. The lines and arrows used in diagrams mislead about the nature of motion on any type of planar surface. They tempt us to assume that a color spot can move laterally from here to there. How does this differ, if it differs, from the spot dematerializing in one place and materializing in another? One answer to Zeno's paradox about the arrow, said not to move because it only rests consecutively at points in space, is that this *is* the nature of motion, especially on a planar surface.

What Light Looks Like

To ask whether light exists as a perceptual phenomenon amounts to asking for a description of what it looks like. If not the spurious beam that is just illuminated dust particles, light may be, say, the glow around incandescent objects. But this glow, because invariably a color phenomenon, does not require assuming the independent existence of an entity called *light* that is separable from color.

Beyond that some objects glow, always with a glow of some color, attempts to reason about what light looks like lead to either paradox or a tangle of words. Illumination, for example, is said to be the vehicle that enables seeing to occur. But illumination is also identified as that which is seen, a merging of cause and effect. Light acts upon photographic plates but cannot itself be photographed. Although light accounts for the formation of images, no such thing exists as an image of light. Images are limited to those of illuminated or illuminating objects. If we see by perceiving images, this suggests we cannot see light or seeing it is a radically different experience from seeing anything else.

I need not assume a table enters my eye when perceived. But when light is seen, the experience is explained by saying light has entered my eye. When a crowd convenes, the aggregate amount of light that enters everyone's eyes causes no measurable drop in the general illumination. Yet if the same crowd were confined in a subway car in summer, their aggregate body heat would affect the temperature of the immediate environment.

A river can be observed without touching it. But the only way to observe light or to collect information about it is to interfere with its travels. A photographic plate, a measuring instrument, or an eye must intercept it by blocking its path. The body of human knowledge about light is a collection of inferences about these impacts, an exquisitely restricted investigatory domain. Light is assumed to be continuously traveling through space when nobody sees it or when allowed to pursue its route without interruption. If we theorize that unseen light circles the universe to return to the spot from which it left, an impact of light with itself is implied. But the expansion of the universe, by changing the location of the point of origin, would cause the path described by the light to be a spiral. However, light cannot be seen when it is not being looked at, whether the nonlooking is by eyes or by instruments. Therefore, no way exists of demonstrating that such interphenomena (in effect, nonphenomenological phenomena) can occur.

Unseen light, precisely because it cannot be seen, cannot be elevated to more than an assumption. Even the need for the assumption can be eliminated by expanding Whittaker's argument. If Newton's prism can be thought to have manufactured the spectral colors, an eye or instrument can be thought to manufacture the light it sees or records.

Never encountered and seldom discussed, unseen light seems destined to haunt imagination, if only in the form of those imagined lines streaming down from the sun: lines symbolizing that which cannot acquire phenomenological reality until it encounters an eye or instrument. Unseen light is a conceptual necessity, hence its ghostly persistence. We need to believe it exists. It shores up the otherwise dubious proposition that light can be shown to exist at all. If devoid of an unseen state, light exists only in the form of an impact, less an object than a nonentity.

If light does not exist, a conceptual error was made at any early date in human history. People saw the phenomenon of color and mistakenly gave it two names. Sometimes they called it *light*, and sometimes they called it *color*. Compounding the error, the phenomenon also received a third name: sometimes it was called *vision*, although everything visible is just an array of color spots.

Sensing that a single phenomenon should not have three names, people eventually tried to right the balance. But they went about it in the wrong way. They tried to eliminate the word *color*, though this is the most useful and most comprehensive of the three terms. People failed to recognize that whenever they saw what they called *light*, they were seeing color effects. So they said light causes color, rather than color causes light.

Sometimes people said that vision causes color, which they explained to mean that color is an accident of human neurology. Again, they had cause and effect reversed. Had they said that color causes vision, the mechanism would have been more clear. Less time would have been wasted debating nonsensical questions that grew from these confusions about words.

Is this what occurred? The answer depends on whether anything about light and vision is verifiable yet not reducible to a color phenomenon, to the sensory experience of seeing colors. In the case of light, a large superstructure of theory consistently tries to separate it from color, to prove that one is not the same as the other.

To the ancient Greeks, light was not a name for certain color effects they saw but was a separate entity attributable to invisible waves or particles. In modern theory, light has many attributes different from those of color. The issue is whether those different attributes are verifiable. Color is regarded as, say, unmoving, while light moves. What does movement mean in this case? Does theory tell us about what occurs or just about what could occur?

Relativity theory and quantum theory are said to transcend many puzzles about the nature of light by positing a world of events. We are not encouraged to inquire about the material nature, if any, of the objects, if any, that participate in the events. As in the Buddha's Fire Sermon, all that appears to be substantial is discovered to be phantasmagoria. We find ourselves in the picture as empty spaces residing in empty spaces, a vision at least as plausible as that of unseen light forever frustrated in its attempt to encircle a rapidly expanding universe.

Because large pictures need to be balanced with simpler understandings, I am not fond of A. S. Eddington's insistence that a table that appears to be solid may, paradoxically, be composed of emptiness: of subatomic particles colliding in interparticular vastness. This may be a serious misunderstanding of the nature of paradox. In the absence of privileged coordinate systems, all perspectives are coequal and coexistent. Therefore, Eddington's table, if made of bosons, fermions, or quarks, is at the same time made of wood, at least from our human perspective. We assume too much in believing we can set this human perspective aside at will. The theory that supports Eddington's argument is a theory that says we cannot. That a speeding automobile can be reduced to probability waves is unlikely to be more real or objective than that certain effects may be anticipated if the automobile runs out of gas.

Modern theory, although Eddington would not have agreed, allows us to have our cake and eat it too. We can believe in invisible worlds of unseen particles and forces without discarding the world that we see. Each is a different perspective, a different coordinate system. And modern theory defends the validity of multiple coordinate systems. If I were the size of an electron, doubtless the world would look different. But I am not the size of an electron.

If the universe is assumed to exist, no part of the world of theory speaks to the question of how we can separately verify that light exists. Is *light* just another name for color? The question reduces to whether light can be separated from its own colors, a separation presumably accomplished only when the light is not seen.

I am willing to risk believing that a chair is there when I am not looking at it. I have reasons for making the assumption. I believe, until told otherwise, that the chair is not affected by my looking at it. The experience of seeing the chair is not interactive. But unseen light is a phenomenon of a different order. We are told light *is* affected by our looking at it, and the experience is interactive. When I see light, my eye stops the light from traveling further. The light acts on the eye by entering it; the eye acts on the light by stopping it.

These interactions suggest that light that is never seen cannot be similar to light as we know it. The unseen light has never endured the metamorphosizing meeting with an eye or the similarly interactive impact with a measuring instrument. Having never, so to speak, crashed, the virginal rays must be as different from the light we see as a speeding automobile is from a car crash. Furthermore, the usual aids to extrapolation are lacking. I can assess the severity of a car crash because I know what cars look like if not wrecked. Because nothing can be known of the form light assumes before meeting the receptor, the severity of the crash cannot be gauged.

Once light is stopped, no way exists of starting it up again. It vanishes, apparently without trace, into the barrier that stopped it. Unlike water squeezed from a sponge, it cannot be separated from the absorbing eye or instrument. Although light is said to be radiant energy, once stopped, it no longer has (or is) energy. The rays that entered Newton's prism emerged, perhaps because the prism was transparent. Those that collide with eyes are never seen again. They presumably catalyze events in the pathway between eye and brain.

What arguments can be given to prove that light is an independent entity, not just another name for color? The historical argument says that people have always talked about light. This suggests the existence of some entity for which they had invented a name. Yet incubi, the philosopher's stone, and the aether suggest we cannot assume things exist just because people have talked about them.

Judging by their more frequent occurrence in ancient literary works, words referring to light effects are of earlier vintage than color names. They more often cannot be traced to earlier words meaning anything different than they do. I conclude that the first color effect people noticed, or thought seriously about, was the difference between day and night. They coined words referring to light and to darkness, an absence of light. Later, they made more refined observations about color differences in the daytime, the differences, say, between red and blue. This type of phenomenon was called color, with little or no recognition that day, night, and all phenomena associated with light and darkness were also color phenomena.

Aristotle conjectured that colors were created by a mixture of the opposites of darkness and light. He never carried this further by asking whether light/darkness and color are a single phenomenon. Perhaps by Aristotle's day the habit of distinguishing between light effects and color effects was too firmly entrenched to be easily questioned. Munsell, Ostwald, and all other modern color theorists have had to address the issue more directly. They realized color could not be explained through hue alone. Color value—lightness and darkness—had to be taken into account. They said nothing, however, about the relationship between, say, the light of day and the darkness of night and lightness/darkness as color phenomena. By this time it was assumed that physicists talked about the nature of light, and color theorists considered only lightness and darkness of color.

The inconsistency was noticed from time to time, although the arguments were not carried to the conclusion toward which they pointed. The painter Henri Matisse and the physicist James Clerk Maxwell pointed out that brightness and shade can be classified as variation in color, although traditionally identified as variations in illumination. A light in the darkness is seen as a spot of white color. If no white spot appears, there is said to have been no light.

The dependence of light on the presence of color suggests analogies with motion, which depends on the presence of forms. Motion cannot be seen in isolation from forms, and visible light cannot be perceived in isolation from color. Each, in this sense, is dependent on something else that precedes it. The psychologist Rudolph Arnheim asks the essential question about illumination: "Is there such a thing, and under what conditions is it observed?" (Arnheim 1956, 297).

I prefer the answer that light or illumination is never, strictly speaking, observed. It can be explained as an abstract idea around which observations of color, or some kinds of observations about color, are organized. Motion, in a similar manner, can be explained as an abstract idea around which certain observations about forms or objects can be organized. The statement that a chair has been moved, for example, explains the observation that the chair is now located a measurable distance from where it was at a previous moment. We cannot say the chair has been moved if, as a matter of fact, chairs do not exist. Motion presupposes the objects that move.

Any statement about light that refers to its appearance in the phenomenological world can be recast as a statement about color. The difference between night and day can be specified by a catalog of the colors observed under the respective conditions. At night, no color is seen other than that of the darkness. During the day, all colors are visible, including black and gray. Without exception, describing differences in light means describing observable changes in colors.

The concept of motion is as redundant as that of light, in that it just explains changes in the spatiotemporal location of forms. In vision, these forms can be reduced to their images, to the array of color spots we see. Maxwell was eminently correct in observing that in the visual field, form, motion, illumination, and all other phenomena can be identified as color phenomena.

Because images are two-dimensional, color is more coherently understood as a two-dimensional matrix. Only the world we touch has a third dimension, and touch is not vision. In three-dimensional terms, however, an intriguing question arises about light. Motion is an event that happens to forms, and light is said to move. We may have to recognize light as an entity apart from color to explain such concepts as the movement of light.

The issue is whether anything is left if we follow Max Planck in eliminating from the concept of light anything, including its color, that is perceivable by the senses. In Planck's reasoning, the invisible residue consists of the "real, objective phenomena." But where is this unverifiable residue? How can we confirm that it exists if it lies entirely beyond the senses?

Because modern theory presents us with a photon entrapped in a world without time, and movement occurs only in time, we do well to look closely at the concept of the movement of light. If movement is transportation from here to there, the movement of light is not only invisible but dissimilar to the movement of anything else. The question is whether we reasonably call it movement in any conventional sense.

I suspect that the movement of light, originally called the propagation of light, is a figure of speech, words traditionally used to describe a phenomenon that can be conceptualized in simpler terms. Can all phenomena associated with the movement of light be described without using the word *movement* and without using the word *light*? Perhaps *change* is a better word than *movement* in this case; perhaps *color* is a better word than *light*. If this or some equivalent reduction can be accomplished, it may resolve one incon-sistency in modern theory: color is equated with light, which is said to move; yet we never say that color moves.

Drawing Inferences About Light and Color

For Bertrand Russell, "any definition of 'red' which professes to be precise is pretentious and fraudulent" (Russell 1948, 260). We do, however, make definitions. These definitions incorporate popular but confused ideas about the relationship between light and color, ideas that are questionable inferences from the data thought to support them. The definitions and ideas eventually find their way into the sciences where they assume an air of infallibility.

That red can be identified as light with a wavelength of 650 millimicrons is not really true. The statement may be so loose as to be meaningless. *Red* designates a broad class of colors, because this is the nature of color names. Irrespective of whether colors can be correlated with wavelengths, *red*, because it is not one color, cannot be correlated with one wavelength.

To accommodate its status as a range, red can be defined, in Russell's words, "(1) as any shade of color between two specified extremes of the spectrum, or (2) as any shade of color caused by waves having wave lengths between these two extremes, or (3) (in physics) as waves having wave lengths between these extremes" (Russell 1948, 259). Spectrophotometric readings suggest that none of these alternates are adequate either. A surface properly categorized as red reflects varying wavelengths in the red range (about 630-780 millimicrons). It can additionally reflect quantities of orange, yellow, green, blue, or light from any portion of the spectrum.

The phenomenon of multiple reflectance is consistent with commonplace observations when mixing paints. Adding a small amount of blue paint to a large amount of red paint presumably endows the mixture with some ability to reflect blue light. Yet the color of the mixture, although not exactly the same red as previously, will likely still be properly classified as red.

Multiple reflectance is not the only argument against the assumption that red objects are ideal reflectors, either of red light or of rays that match their own color. The color pink, considered to be a type of red, can be mixed from red and white pigments. Because the white pigment nominally reflects all wavelengths, the pink presumably does the same. This suggests a failure of the generality that red colors, as a class, can be correlated with the range of wavelengths identified as red. Particular red colors can be produced that reflect some light from beyond the red range or from any portion of the spectrum. Mixtures of light from the red sector of the spectrum are insufficient if we want to replicate every variety of red.

It is not true that *red*—every individual variation in the range we call *red*—can be defined in terms of light with a wavelength of 650 millimicrons. What *is* true is the opposite of what is asserted. Light with a wavelength of 650 millimicrons looks red in color. Given a particular wavelength, we can make reasonably accurate general statements about the color that light will look to an observer.

If you specify any wavelength in the visible light sector of the electromagnetic spectrum, I will tell you the color of light of that wavelength. I can easily look up the answer in any diagram of the electromagnetic spec-

trum. If a crude approximation suffices, I will provide generic names, such as *red, blue*, or *blue-violet*. If a more exact specification is required, I will look at the light and select a color swatch that matches it as closely as possible.

Problems proliferate when the task is set forth in inverted order. If I show you a particular color, you cannot determine, without elaborate trial-and-error testing, the wavelength or wavelengths that account for that color. At minimum, a spectrophotometer is needed. These instruments are not entirely reliable and are less accurate than eyes when fine distinctions are involved. Although classical theory implies otherwise, most colored surfaces reflect more than a single wavelength of light. The visible light spectrum, which ranges from approximately 400 to 700 millimicrons, includes only variations in hue. Variations other than hue occur among the ten million different colors the National Bureau of Standards contends are individually recognizable.

The stronger generality for the circumstances is that light waves can be defined in terms of their color. No serious argument occurs on the point that light with a wavelength of 650 millimicrons looks red. As if we had fallen into the wonderland of Alice's mirror, what is conventionally asserted is the opposite of what can be seen. Or, as often in the explanation of color, eccentric assessments of visual phenomena survive because they integrate more easily with traditional beliefs and classical theories about the nature of radiant energy, the material world, and human experience.

CHAPTER 13

Light as Symbol and Visual Metaphor I

> Before the time of Newton, white light was supposed to be of all known things the purest. When white light appears colored, it was supposed to have become contaminated by coming into contact with gross bodies. We may still think white light the emblem of purity, though Newton has taught us its purity does not consist in simplicity.
>
> James Clerk Maxwell, Scientific Papers

The visual world can be thought of as a continuum of color or an illusion caused by light. Either mode is adequate for everyday purposes. Each excludes the other, implying a different context for understanding the perceptual universe. Etymology provides clues about how the concepts evolved, why each assumed the forms it took, and how human beings reasoned over the centuries about the phenomena of the natural world.

The word *light* can be traced to the Teutonic root *luh* (to be light), similar in sound to Latin *lumen* (a light) and *lucere* (to shine), Greek *leukos* (white), and Sanskrit *rocate* (he shines). *Color*, from Old Latin *color*, had an original meaning of a covering, from *celare*, to cover or hide. This suggests that color was not given a name at an early date (its name is borrowed from that of another entity), and names for light and light effects must be of earlier vintage. When color was named, it was thought of as the skin or superficial covering of an object, to be differentiated from the essence imagined to lie within.

The conception of color as a surface phenomenon could reasonably have been based on the observation that many objects, especially life forms, have colors on their surfaces that are not continuous throughout their interiors. Although interiors are no less colored than surfaces, this easily escapes attention because interiors ordinarily are not exposed to view. *Celare* can be traced back further to Greek *Kalyptein* (to cover, conceal) and Sanskrit *Śarana* (concealing), roots for English words as diverse as cellar, cell, and hell.

The curious association of color and hell may rest on an association between the sensory appeal of color and hell as a final destination for those who gave themselves to sensual pursuits. The suspicion that excessively bright color is heathen or barbaric is evidently of ancient vintage, persists in Goethe's writings, and is still with us today. We like bright colors not because we consider them genteel but because we have lost interest in gentility.

If, as it seems, interest in value distinctions is of earlier vintage than interest in color, this has an understandable logic. People have practical reasons for bearing in mind the distinction between darkness and light. Human beings, unlike bats, distinguish objects more easily by day than by night. The discovery of fire—artificial light—is legendary and the remains of artificially kindled fires are among the earliest surviving human artifacts. Torches, their remains scattered in Paleolithic caves, originally served the purpose of the flashlights required today before braving the blackness of dark cellars.

Practical considerations are not the whole story. The visual difference between night and day is memorable because environmentally pervasive, more extreme than the differences seen in daylight between individual varieties of color. Seeing the greenness of grass is not the equivalent of seeing nothing else. But at night the color of the darkness gives an impression of being endless.

The etymological record suggests that light, dark, night, and day attracted more attention than color or individual colors and were given names at an earlier date. *Day, night, black, white,* and *dark,* like *light,* cannot be traced to earlier words meaning anything different than they do. Day is from the Anglo-Saxon *daeg,* meaning day. Night is from the Anglo-Saxon *niht* or *neaht,* similar to Icelandic *nott,* Danish *nat,* Gothic *nahts,* Greek *nyx, nyktos,* or Sanskrit *nakti* and *nakta,* all of which mean

night. Dark is from Middle English *dark* or *derk,* and Anglo-Saxon *deorc,* meaning dark.

The names of colors usually derive from the names of objects, and the generic term *color* similarly points to an entity other than itself. If color was regarded as a covering (of objects), this explains why it was associated with them and why so many color names are borrowed from those of objects. Among names for hues, however, *yellow* and *blue* are unique. They alone cannot be shown to be derived from the names of objects and are probably older than other hue names.

Why would yellow and blue have been named or noticed earlier than other hues? The easiest answer is their value contrast, which resembles that between white and black or between lightness and darkness. Spectral yellow is light, like white. Spectral blue is dark, like black. The pairs black/white and yellow/blue occur together in the natural world and might have attracted attention for this reason. The sky, black at night, is blue by day, implying an endless cycle of permutations from black to blue. Sunlight, although usually called white, is also described as golden or yellow. The bifurcated association is reflected in derivatives of *aurum,* the Latin word for gold. In addition to *aureole* (the type of light effects called a halo), these derivatives include *oriole* (the bird) and *aureolin,* the name of a pale yellow (or golden) color.

Although light is likely a more ancient concept than color, no record remains of the date at which the earliest version of either word came into use. Nor do we know why two words became current for what might have been regarded as a single phenomenon in perceptual experience. But light and dark, which refer to the difference between day and night, also describe the quality in colors that became known as color value. A model can be imagined in which human beings originally noticed lightness and darkness and later developed names for the hues, while barely considering that both hue and value are characteristics of the same entity. The phenomena originally called light and darkness could have been explained as aspects of color.

Color value is binary, although hue distinctions are not. The proverbial "difference between night and day" is more extreme, by experiential criteria, than the similarly proverbial "difference between black and white." The difference is between homogeneous and nonhomogeneous color, not simply between one color and another.

The colors that might summarize the difference between night and day, if assumed to be the black of the darkness and the white of light, do not present themselves in orderly transition in the natural cycle. This may explain why few names other than light gray and dark gray have been coined for varieties of gray. As a color phenomenon in nature, the passage from the black of the night to the white light of day is interrupted by the roses, pinks, and yellows of sunrise and sunset. This may have been the phenomenon that suggested to Aristotle or his predecessors that colors were mixtures of the opposites of darkness and light. Bright hues were seen in the sky at the time of transition from darkness to light.

The nonbinary nature of hue is reflected in figures of speech. "As different as black and white" is emphatic. "As different as pink and blue" is not and is rarely used. Among other etymological marks of the disassociation between color value and hue, lightness and darkness are not names of colors. Even black and white may be regarded as noncolors. Yet none of these words can be explained in other than visual terms.

An individual blind from birth can differentiate between night and day if taught, say, that night is the period when clocks indicate that the time is between 6:00 P.M. and 6:00 A.M. Vision is required for the more subtle task of learning to distinguish between black and white or between dark and light. Like color names, words referring to lightness and dark-

ness are taught to children by ostensive definition: by pointing at what the child ought to look at.

The historical record follows the etymological record. Light traditionally has been regarded as the phenomenological reality or primary: as percept rather than interpretation, cause rather than effect. Color, correspondingly, is secondary or superficial, an illusory skin that may be unreal.

The body of symbolism associated with light, like names for light effects, is of ancient vintage. Unlike color symbolism, which is scattered, unsystematic, and probably more recent, the body of symbolic beliefs associated with light is too intensely focused to allow uncertainty about what it represents. The most common association is with a supreme deity or absolute.

The sacred architecture of ancient and medieval peoples provides a virtual encyclopedia of the diverse religious ideas of its builders, including ideas about the importance of light, of its absence, or of the interplay between light and darkness. Among familiar art-historical examples, the Egyptian pharaoh Akhenaton's lost temple at Tell el-'Amarna (Eighteenth Dynasty) is said to have had no roof. This allowed the worshiper to be bathed in the rays of the sun god. The device was evidently a deliberate stylistic deviation from the dimly lit interiors of earlier Egyptian hypostyle temples. Abbot Suger's ideas about the symbolic association of light with God are regularly recounted as a preface to theories about Gothic architecture, especially those that refer to the large stained-glass windows that modulated the light entering cathedrals.

Darkness, the opposite of light and therefore its equal, has proved equally capable of suggesting religious experience. Examples include the hypostyle temple, the Indian cave temple, the womblike darkness of the confessional booth, even the practice of praying or meditating with closed eyes, as if seeking an inner light in the darkness. We rarely reverse the metaphor by wondering whether an inner darkness should be sought in the light.

Architecture has always been an art of spaces, therefore of light and darkness, the two visual conditions for space. The interior space of any building is a vessel into which light can enter or from which it can be excluded. But buildings have exterior as well as interior spaces. Symbolic ideas about light have affected beliefs about where sacred buildings should be located, not just how they ought to be constructed. The recurring idea that the gods speak from high places is said to explain why houses of worship were often elevated. Familiar examples include the Mesopotamian shrine on its ziggurat (intended to symbolize a mountain), the Parthenon on the Acropolis hill, a synagogue in a high place, or a Gothic cathedral towering above other buildings in its town.

I doubt we reach an entire understanding of this passion for heights without reflecting that what verifiably comes down from above is light, stirring thoughts about who could have sent it. A shrine, temple, church, or synagogue in a high place is metaphorically the "first" among buildings in its vicinity to be illuminated. We need not concern ourselves about whether the illumination is by the words of the most holy or by a more earthly light.

Goethe believed "darkness and light have eternally opposed each other, one alien to the other" (Matthaei 1971, 126). The opposition is more likely rooted in language than eternal, a literary concept grown beyond its modest visual foundation. Terms such as enlightenment, elucidation, illumination, and lucidity equate light with understanding and grace. Darkness is the implied opposite in each case, though it has become archaic to refer to the unenlightened as the benighted. A major difference between light and color is the greater ease with which light can be envisioned in terms of parity or polarity. If a foundation for the impulse ought to be sought in the phenomenological world, not-light is capable of ostensive

definition, in the sense that darkness can be exhibited. Not-color cannot be shown, and it is a more ambiguous, possible meaningless, concept. It implies the extinction not only of the visual field (the color domain), but of all memory and knowledge of it.

Although the usual name for not-light is *darkness*, if relative in degree it is called *shade* or *shadow*. Not-color has never been thought to require a name of its own. The closest terms are *colorless* or *transparent*, which are not bona fide names for color conditions because they do not describe surfaces of objects. They denominate the interior (or essential) condition of any object that allows the colors of the objects behind it to be seen. The phenomenon is an exception to the rule that I cannot see behind objects in front of me. If the objects are colorless or transparent, I see whatever lies behind them.

Light and not-light appear as antitheses in the first chapter of Genesis. God's first act is the creation of light, where previously there had been only darkness, a darkness that may or may not have been preceded by a more absolute "nothing." Adding to the uncanniness, light is presented as an entity that preexists radiance from luminous celestial bodies. Day and night, darkness and light, appear on the first day (Genesis 1:3). The sun, moon, and stars are absent until the fourth (Genesis 1:16). A perennial question, discovered by clever children, is what the source of the light could have been during the first three days of creation.

One answer is that Scripture, whether it originates or just perpetuates the paradigm, pays scant attention to the nature of perceptual experience. Biblical personages are identified by reciting their genealogies rather than by descriptions of what they looked like. The orientation of the Bible is nonvisual. Its authors or compilers were indifferent to the sensuous delight of telling about what can be seen. Both Old and New Testaments are devoid of Homeric rosy-fingered dawns, although similes and other literary devices abound. A bride may be compared to a garden. A report about what a bride (or a garden) looked like is less likely to be encountered. The limited worldly splendor evoked is that of perfumed odors and joyous music. Little is said about shapes and colors.

The biblical injunction against graven images is consistent with this context. Those who passed along the prohibition by setting down the words of the Old Testament show little interest in visual experience. Nothing excites them in the task of depicting or capturing, in words or pictures, how anything looks. Their priorities, or their morality, lay elsewhere.

Within this ambience, the opening of Genesis, with its striking imagery of light and darkness, may seem a false note. Light and dark, because the blind see no difference between them, may seem unambiguously visual. Yet the light that opens the first chapter of Genesis is an unusual light. We do not discover this light subsequently illuminating a world to be adored for its magnificence or for the wonders of what we see. The universe of the Old Testament is painted in unrelieved black and white. The differences between the path to be followed and that to be avoided are as great as those between, so to speak, night and day. The faithful are enjoined to love God, who cannot be seen, and not the world, which is visible. This orientation does not encourage valuing of the visual sense.

Disjunction from perceptual reality (from what can be seen) is the point of the supranormal light of the first three days of Genesis: the Ur-light that has no identifiable source other than God. The imagery intimates that light can be envisioned as other than the physical radiance of incandescent objects. Light can be read as a symbol. As such, it acquires a value beyond its inherent worth as an object. At a much later date, Saint Augustine recycled the motif in admonishing that the sun is only a reminder of its maker, of the light greater than itself that lies behind it.

Language rarely transcends religious metaphor, a form of double-speak inherited from its past. Musings about the meaning of light remain a perennially popular, though overworked, form of poesy. Among numerous borrowings in *The Waste Land*, T. S. Eliot reworked a passage in *The Aeneid* in which Virgil describes the light of torches that hang from the ceiling in Dido's palace (Eliot, *Waste Land*, note to line 92). But in "Virgil and the Christian World," Eliot complained that Virgil, unlike Dante, sees light only as a physical entity and overlooks its symbolic possibilities. An absence is noted, in *The Aeneid*, of "*lume*, and all the words expressive of the spiritual significance of light" (Eliot 1957, 147).

Eliot apparently believed that concern for this significance was uniquely Christian, or Judeo-Christian. Yet Christian symbols are often of pre-Christian vintage, as in this case. In the second book of *The Aeneid*, flames appear around the head of the infant Ascanius. The flames are taken as an omen when they are discovered to be illusory. The passage is often cited as an early example of the image of the halo, effectively of the symbolic use of light. We do not know who originated the idea that light could be a sign or an omen, that it could have purposes beyond a utilitarian purpose. The Star of Bethlehem was read as a supernatural omen. So was Halley's comet, when it appeared in the sky in A.D. 1066, just before the Battle of Hastings.

Light as God, Dark as Void

Equating God with light cannot be called anthropomorphism in the most rigorous sense. It differs from conjuring up a mental picture of an old man with a white beard. But it satisfies a similar need to recast the imperceivable in comfortingly familiar form. A parallel compression allows darkness, lightlessness, or blackness to function as a figure for the void: the emptiness from which we hope God will save us. This abyss is to be distinguished from the emptiness that is God. The metaphor suggests, intriguingly, that one can be differentiated from the other.

Visualizing an abyss filled with darkness is not difficult, although it may be too easy. The once immensely popular *"Invictus,"* by William Ernest Henley (1849-1903), is one of many literary works that project a similar epiphany. The radiance of spirit is to dispel an otherwise all-encompassing not-light.

> Out of the night that covers me,
> Black as the pit from pole to pole,
> I thank whatever gods may be
> For my unconquerable soul.
>
> . . . .
>
> I am the master of my fate;
> I am the captain of my soul.

Darkness disappears with the arrival of light, as human experience suggests. For Henley, as for others, metaphysical solace lay in imagining the void as a dark night inflated to macrocosmic dimension.

If the metaphysical abyss is to be a meaningful concept, we need to imagine it as more than just a big pot of black paint. Based on a visually insensitive, although traditional, reasoning about the color black, Henley's metaphysics is atrocious in its own right. The difficult task, before which imagination falters, is to imagine a void filled with *nothing*, a figure for universes beyond human understanding. In the face of the abyss, talk of mastery or illumination is empty, and even darkness and light may be meaningless concepts. If any of us, as Henley optimistically imagines, were truly the masters of our fate, I doubt we would voluntarily choose to die.

Whether or not to trivializing ends, the counterpoint of light and darkness is familiar poesy for marking the limits of human comprehension. That which men and women understand is figuratively illuminated; a deeper darkness enshrouds what escapes us. The metaphor, handed down from the past, long ago degenerated to the tediously platitudinous. We have every reason to understand darkness, at least as well as we understand light. Even though most of us hope to be able to sleep through most of them, the total number of terrestrial nights is exactly equal to the total number of terrestrial days.

Night is different from day. But why is it regarded as mysterious? I suspect what unsettles us is the color field experience, seeing a single homogeneous area of color uninterrupted by other colors.

Light, shadow, and the interplay between them acquire ornate symbolic overtones for adults. The infant may lack a natural sense of these subtleties or even an interest in the phenomenological foundation from which they arise. Arnheim pointed out that young children typically do not include light and shadow relationships in their art (Arnheim 1956, 310). When taught to do so, they acquire an interest in modeling with light and shadow that replaces the earlier emphasis on color.

Because children also need to be taught the difference between right and wrong, I suspect that what is being taught, in either case, is a habit of thinking in terms of opposites, whether light/shadow, black/white, or right/wrong. The child requires an understanding of oppositeness to comprehend the process of reasoning, based nominally on the discipline of logic. We all learn, and often need to unlearn, the strict distinction between true and false that allows no room for what is more or less true. The price of this education is sensitivity to the continuum of the perceived world, including the world of visual experience.

I do not mean that the concept of light and dark is so narrow as to be no more than handmaiden to logic and morality, to the imagined polarity that inspires us to assert a distinction between order and disorder. But it rarely rises far above this primary impress, even in the visual arts. In painting, modeling with light and shadow is inseparable from the representation of three-dimensional form on a two-dimensional surface. The forms of the corporeal world are what light and shadow reveal or conceal.

Rudimentary modeling with light and shade can be seen in some Paleolithic cave paintings, notably at Altamira. But painters of the Roman Empire, possibly preceded by the Greeks, were the first to exploit the device in art consistently. Pre-Roman (or pre-Greek) painters rarely represented light and shadow. Indeed, it plays a subordinate role in virtually all art except European, and European-influenced, art from the early Renaissance until the late nineteenth century. This cannot be because shade or shadow was unimportant to, or unnoticed by, other peoples. More likely, an excessive importance was attributed to it. Long before Robert Louis Stevenson penned "I Have a Little Shadow," folk tales from all over the world equated the human shadow with the human soul. A person's soul could be stolen by seizing his or her shadow.

In Western painting, concern for the naturalistic representation of light and shadow waxes and wanes with interest in perspective drawing and the related device of foreshortening. These tools configured the picture plane in terms of the polarities of near/far and here/there. Without them, the illusionist tradition in Western painting could not have developed or would have assumed a different form.

For Alfred North Whitehead, discovery of how to make "true-to-life" paintings encouraged the development of modern science, which profits from similarly close observation of natural phenomena. Whitehead's point has merit, though it is too idealistic. A long time has elapsed since the scientific study of light implied a disinterested contemplation of sunsets, rainbows, or other natural light phenomena. Humanity has sought its scientific understanding of light, as it sought its gods, in the invisible world. The role of the natural world was only to disgorge evidence that this invisible world might exist.

If a high degree of symbolic significance was attributed to light and darkness at a remarkably early date, the relatively late appearance of representations of light in painting may seem out of character. We cannot assume, however, that paintings always show us what people think is most important. The concept of light, like the concept of soul, was excessively overburdened with metaphysical complexity. It became intimidating or overwhelming. A belief that a phenomenon is significant need not lead to immediate answers to questions that are critical in the art of painting. One question is how the phenomenon can be represented on a two-dimensional surface. Other questions are whether it can be represented at all and how its depiction can be integrated with other artistic goals and limits.

Even today, some light phenomena are rarely represented, because essentially unpaintable. Although the opening chapter of Genesis is famous, Michelangelo's illustration of it on the Sistine Chapel ceiling is exceptional. God's separation of the light from the darkness is awesomely nonvisualizable, therefore rarely depicted in painting. I cannot imagine what the event would have looked like, and no analogies come to mind that might help. The deity of the Sistine Chapel ceiling, poised between a black cloud and a white cloud (the darkness and the light) waves his arms as if he were a magician performing tricks on a stage. Michelangelo's brave effort falls far short of the metaphysical grandeur of the biblical words. Later illustrators of the Bible by and large left that passage alone.

Starlight is another painterly enigma. Dante is famous for evoking it by ending each cantica of *Commedia* with the word *stelle*. But Rembrandt, that great student of all manner of light effects, left no depictions of the stars at night. The scintillation (twinkling) of the stars is temporal and therefore cannot be painted. Dots of white paint displayed on a black curtain fail to evoke the awe that the sky at night has traditionally inspired. Van Gogh painted the night sky with its stars several times. I am tempted to wonder if this is because he was mad. *Starry Night*, that justly famous endeavor, cuts the Gordian knot by abandoning naturalism; the lavish swirls provide, instead, one artist's objective correlative for starlight.

Light and Perspective

Diagrams in textbooks on optics show how rays of light pass through lenses. These diagrams look remarkably similar to perspective drawings, though the vanishing point is replaced by a focal point. Either type of picture is a geometrical construction. What is diagrammed is the manner in which rays of light move from a point of origin to a terminus. If the rays did not travel (radiate) in the manner they do, there would be no such thing as perspective, the progressive diminishing of the visual size of any object as it recedes from a viewer.

In art, perspective drawing and modeling with light and shade supplement one another. The aim of perspective drawing (or mechanical drawing) is to present an accurate two-dimensional projection of the perceived shapes of objects in the physical world. Although elsewhere we doubt the reliability of the visual sense, only this accurate projection of what we see is regarded as a correct or true picture. To make a drawing of, say, a building in proper perspective is held to be synonymous with drawing the building correctly, an assumption rarely disputed even by those who question whether "correct drawing" is necessarily the aim of art.

Students in art schools are known to be generally unenthusiastic about the ubiquitous required course in mechanical drawing, perhaps a reaction to the moralistic tenor. The implied distinction between a right and wrong way to draw is coupled with a demand, in most cases, for a nearly unattainable level of neatness and precision. Yet the rules of per-

spective, codified by the Florentine architect Filippo Brunelleschi (1377–1446) and developed further by Dürer and others, were once regarded as an exciting innovation, a high technology of their day. The laws of perspective revealed that although no object has a constant perceivable size or shape, the relativity of vision has a logic.

Extension in the visual field (size and shape) is relative, in particular ways, to a particular viewer at a particular time and place. Those ways can be determined by an adaptation of geometry or by borrowing the methods of construction used in geometry. In foreshortening, the application of what is essentially a calculus enables an approximation of the perspective of those forms (for example, the human hand) too complicated to be entirely reduced to combinations of simple geometrical shapes.

Virtuoso displays of skill in perspective rendering, and in the foreshortening of the forms of the human figure, are common coinage in Renaissance art. Examples include Botticelli's *Adoration of the Magi* (Washington, National Gallery); Raphael's *School of Athens* (Vatican Palace, Stanza della Segnatura) and *Marriage of the Virgin* (Milan, Pinacoteca di Brera); Mantegna's *The Dead Christ* (Milan, Pinacoteca di Brera) and *St. Jerome Led to Martyrdom* (Padua, Oretari Chapel); Perugino's *Giving of the Keys to St. Peter* (Vatican, Sistine Chapel); Jan van Eyck's *Madonna with Chancellor Rolin* (Louvre); and van der Weyden's *St. Luke Painting the Portrait of the Virgin* (Boston, Museum of Fine Arts).

In these and other works, perspective drawing assumes a fixed viewpoint that is an artificial convention. The question remains open whether perspective really bears a one-to-one correspondence with visual perception. Human beings do not typically see from either a single eye or a fixed viewpoint. The eyes, of which we have two, continually scan. And the world is neither petrified nor a mirror image of ideally frozen forms that transcend its flux.

Light as Symbol
and Visual Metaphor II

> Such also before others are accepted into heaven, and are among those there at the center, because they are in light more than others.
>
> Emanuel Swedenborg, *Heaven and Its Wonders and Hell*

> When Swedenborg's message was revealed to me . . . it was as if light came where there had been no light before; the intangible world became a shining certainty.
>
> Helen Keller, Introduction to *Heaven and Its Wonders and Hell*

Perspective drawing and the rendering of light and shadow can aim for illusionism, which we often equate with visual truth. Either can also become an end in itself if pushed to extremes for dramatic effect. Playing with foreshortening and perspective began in the early Renaissance, and some artists aspired to more than just the obligatory landscape seen through an open door or window. Michelangelo used extreme foreshortening in the figures of nude boys on the Sistine Chapel ceiling. Pozzo used extreme perspective in *The Apotheosis of St. Ignatius*. Both works are tour de force art-historical markers. They show that painters, with perseverance, learned to represent any object from any viewing position in "true perspective."

A more modern conception of perspective occurs in Parmigianino's youthful self-portrait in a convex mirror. What we see depends on the focal length of the lens through which the perceived light passes or of the mirror in which an image is reflected. The artist's large hand and much smaller face prefigure the images seen in fish-eye lenses, Weegee photographs, Picasso paintings.

Although regarded as distortions of the way the world looks, images in curved mirrors and through fish-eye lenses *are* the way the world looks in those mirrors and through those lenses. No object has a normal shape or color that remains the same under all conditions. Colors vary with illumination, and shapes vary with spatiotemporal location. What we see is affected by the color balance of the light illuminating the scene and by the path the light rays travel to reach the eye. A penguin ten feet from me does not have an unchanging size and shape even for me. Size and shape vary according to the lens, or combination of lenses, through which I look. The limit is that no lens can make a penguin look like a kangaroo.

When used to create styles of painting that are not naturalistic or illusionistic, perspective drawing and modeling (light and shade) diverge, evoking different responses. Extreme perspective effects amaze viewers or are regarded as distortions. They rarely seem metaphysical or mysterious. We attribute metaphysical overtones to paintings that include extremes of light and shadow. Artists arrived at an interest in these extremes by a series of steps, by solving one after the other what are now called painterly problems. They saw certain challenges, met them, and moved on to others.

Late Gothic and early Renaissance painters struggled to master the representation of the three-dimensional world on a two-dimensional surface. They wanted to understand forms, which for them meant the anatomical forms of the human body and the perspectival forms of distant landscapes. The edges of forms are precise in, say, van Eyck's paintings, either because he liked the effect of exactness or because he wanted to show how carefully he looked at all the details of what he saw.

Almost as soon as representing forms clearly and exactly was discovered as a significant problem, forms began to get lost again. They disappear into deep shadows in many Mannerist and Baroque paintings. Artists had not given up on the goal of understanding three-dimensional forms. They had passed beyond the goal and no longer saw it as a relevant painterly problem. At a date when any trained artist had learned to draw anything, including the human figure, from any perspec-

tive and in any foreshortening, the skill had become a cliché.

The motif of enveloping shadows, which conceal forms light would reveal, grows with a life of its own. We can trace the iconographical history of forms hidden in semidarkness through the paintings of, say, Masaccio, Leonardo, Caravaggio, and Rembrandt. In El Greco's paintings, shadows that are unusually dark (nearly black) play against illuminated areas that are unusually light (nearly white). The colors of objects are revealed through the middle tones. El Greco forces both light and shadow. Forms bend and twist from the stress. Although El Greco disliked Michelangelo's paintings, his own have a similar tension achieved in a different manner.

Why do we read transcendental intimations into strong light and shadow effects? Artists who rely heavily on light and shadow are not always admired more than others for that reason (figure 14-1). But painters credited with revealing profundities about the human soul are usually those who create shadows that are read as mysterious. Leonardo in *St. John the Baptist* (Louvre) and Rembrandt are prime examples. So is the Abstract Expressionist painter Mark Rothko. Fascination with chiaroscuro, tenebrism, and all manner of light and shadow effects is enduring.

As visual metaphor, the play of light against darkness can be read as confirmation that the world is less a continuum than an interplay of opposites, reducible to what is easily understood. In the cosmic melodrama, a replay of Zoroastrianism, Ahura Mazda, the god of light, enters the lists to joust with Ahriman, lord of the darkness. The outcome of the battle may unveil the mysteries that never were spoken. Having institutionalized the idea of oppositeness (which unfortunately is inseparable from competitiveness), we temper it only insignificantly by allowing that familiar further possibility: perhaps all opposites can be recon-

Figure 14-1. Light and shadow: opinions over the centuries.

Stendhal: "The great fault of the French School of painting is the total lack of chiaroscuro."

John Ruskin: "Now if there be one principle, or secret more than another, on which Turner depends for attaining brilliancy of light, it is his clear and exquisite drawing of the *shadows*."

Eugène Delacroix: "Painters who are not colorists produce illumination, not painting."

Paul Cézanne: "Light does not exist for the painter."

Heinrich Wolfflin: "[Leonardo's Judas] is the only one who sits quietly with his back to the light, and whose features are therefore in shadows."

Horatio Greenough: "He whose eye is tickled by the play of light and shadow, and the merely picturesque projections of the current fashion, will be inclined to flout me when I say these are a jargon and no tongue."

Leon Battista Alberti: "I should hardly ever think of a painter as middling-good who did not know exactly the effect light and shade produce on every surface."

Roger de Piles: "The knowledge of lights and shades, which painting requires, is one of the most important and essential branches of the art."

Charles Alphonse du Fresnoy: "The shining eminence of Corregio consists in his laying on ample broad Lights encompassed with friendly Shadows, and in a grand style of Painting, with a delicacy in the arrangement of the Colours."

ciled eventually. They may paradoxically be one, although not one.

Through the writings of Ogden Rood, who popularized the ideas of Maxwell and Helmholtz, some of the French Impressionists and neo-Impressionists came to regard themselves as researchers into the science of color and light. Seurat, and for a time Pissarro, saw themselves as researchers in the most strictly scientific sense. Whatever respectability they thought science could lend to art, A. S. Eddington later returned the compliment. He explained his conception of the subatomic world by comparing electrons and protons to the color spots in an Impressionist painting: small discrete units that made a whole but were not connected with one another.

No reason exists to suspect that Monet or Seurat had premonitions of quantum theory. Human beings recycle one another's intuitions, including intimations so widely shared as to be societal or collective. The seventeenth cen-tury, like the nineteenth, brought famous advances in the understanding of light in the physical sciences. It was the age of Newton and Hooke. It was also the age of Caravaggio (1573–1610), Artemisia Gentileschi (1597–1651?), Bernini (1598–1680), Rembrandt (1606–69), and Vermeer (1632–75). Interest in light characterizes both painting and the physical sciences at that time. It was part of a broad social paradigm rather than proprietary to any single discipline.

Rembrandt was sixty years old when Newton performed his prism experiments. Rembrandt's passion for finding evidence of God's perfection in the natural world was probably as ardent as Newton's (and, later, Maxwell's) is said to have been. Rembrandt may have been less assured in advance of what was supposed to be discovered. What was found that was new was an absence of hierarchical ranking among human souls, a finding that predates by a century the French Declaration of the

Rights of Man. Old baggage, passed on by Caravaggio, was the habit of viewing light and darkness as extremes.

Most of us have no basis for understanding the proclivities of those who had no electricity to light their homes. We rarely sit indoors in the dark. Newton sat in a dark room watching a single ray of light pass through a slit and a prism before it fell on the wall. Goethe later complained that this was not a reasonable way to study colors. Rembrandt painted illuminated figures emerging from darkness, as if separated by a theatrical spotlight from the surrounding shadows. Whether Rembrandt painted under low-light conditions or just imagined them, the device is an inspired compositional tool.

Human beings (including viewers of paintings) look at light rather than darkness if given a choice. This is not because light symbolizes God, but because light provides better conditions than darkness for seeing colors and structural details. The tendency to look at light can be called instinctual, though I prefer to call it utilitarian. In Rembrandt's paintings, a catalog of what is illuminated (or represented as illuminated) is a catalog of elements the artist wanted looked at, or thought were compositionally important.

The paintings of Rembrandt's maturity mark the end of the road for an idea. Vermeer's interest in light was different from Rembrandt's and prefigured the French Impressionists. His paintings are relatively free of shadows. Light is a fluid flowing through every crevice of the environment and uniting all parts. By bringing out the colors of objects, the light invites consideration of those colors in their own right. The burden of inscrutable darkness has fallen away, along with its symbolic associations. The eye, which finds a light in the darkness in Rembrandt's paintings, travels a more complicated route through the many colors of Vermeer's illuminated environments.

To defend the idea that Vermeer is as great and profound a painter as Rembrandt is not difficult. But the literature suggests Rembrandt is more often praised for offering psychological insights into the human condition. Crucial expectations are satisfied for viewers: that the opposites of darkness and light mark the bounds of experience, that human beings are the measure of all things, the noblest of creations. We remember light and shadow from Rembrandt's paintings, along with human faces. From Vermeer's, we recall fragments of another sort: the reflection in a brass dish of the colors of an Oriental rug, the whiteness of light coming through a window with gold mullions.

If a catalog were compiled of the visual configurations that continue to engage viewers most, the image of light playing against shadow might head the list. Like conventional perspective, this type of imagery plummeted in importance after the Impressionists and Cézanne. From the 1950s onward, it reappeared in new forms. A list of Abstract Expressionist painters popularly credited with proferring metaphysical profundity would lean heavily toward those who use dark, murky, or shadowy colors, especially if unrelieved by lighter tones that might suggest brightness or light. Mark Rothko and Ad Reinhardt are examples.

Great art has been created in the past. But this is not the past. We need new metaphors to replace old ones that have been recycled too often. The unknown is not a big bucket of black paint. Nothing profound or significant is said about the human condition by comparing it to darkness and light or black and white.

New metaphors will be found by looking at the discredited parts of human experience, parts brushed aside because they have labels like delusion, illusion, random, accidental, unreal, or subjective. Color and other items in this class (emptiness, nothingness, randomness, and so forth) do not comfortably fit into our present system. But we have no other seeds for a new system, a new way of understanding the world and ourselves.

Halos

Halos provide a striking example of the symbolic use of light in the visual arts. The several ways of representing them constitute an encyclopedia of ideas about what light looks like or how it ought to be conceptualized. Halos appear in religious art as a radiance around the heads of the saintly, a convention for indicating the touch of the godhead. The larger *mandorla* or body halo appears behind Christ in medieval art, but is not unique to the art of Western Europe. Mandorlas also appear in representations of the Buddha.

Each variation resists explanation in terms of mimesis, the imitation of nature. Halos, like dragons and angels, are not seen in the natural world, though they have their own iconographic history. Halos appear in painting long before artists had acquired illusionistic skill in the rendering of illumination. Many do not look like realistic representations of light. But they were correctly read over the centuries as visual metaphors for it.

In medieval and early Renaissance art, the halo is often a gold or yellow disc, situated behind a head seen frontally. Although light is called white, disc halos are rarely this color. The frequent use of gold leaf suggests, as in the golden skies of Byzantine icons, an intent to let opulence carry the message that could not be conveyed by illusionism. Gold, the color of neither light nor the sky, transforms either into intimations of a world different from this one. Derivation of the word *aureole* (halo) from the Latin *aurum* (gold) suggests halos may have been thought of as golden before they were painted that color in art.

When the human head is represented frontally, with a disc halo behind it, the halo is behind the head both in spatiotemporal terms

and in terms of the picture plane. This congruency is lost if the head is rotated to, say, a profile view. If the halo is still "behind" the head, it is no longer clear what *behind* means.

One of two solutions for the profile view is illustrated by the angel in Botticelli's *Annunciation* (Uffizi). Its halo is a golden pie plate seen from the side. It lies behind the head in, so to speak, real space-time. Because the angel's head does not overlap the halo, the halo is not "behind" in terms of the picture plane.

In the other possibility, the profile face overlaps a frontal halo. The effect is as if the disc had transported itself through real space time to relocate "behind" the head in terms of the picture plane, though not spatiotemporally. Neither option can be shown to be more correct than the other.

As might be expected from the ambiguities that arise in profile view, disc halos rarely or almost never appear on heads seen from the rear. But Giotto, in his *Last Supper* (Padua, Arena Chapel), valiantly takes on the problem. The attempt was, so far as I know, not repeated. If depicted behind the head in real space-time, the disc halo overlaps the head on the picture plane and obscures it. If behind in terms of the picture plane, head overlaps halo. This unfortunate image is indistinguishable from that of a human figure confronting the disc of its own halo. The iconographic habit of placing all participants at the Last Supper (or all except Judas) on the same side of the table, all facing the viewer, sidesteps the problem of depicting haloed heads from the rear.

The lines radiating from Mary's head in Rogier van der Weyden's *Annunciation* (New York, Metropolitan Museum of Art) illustrate an improved type of halo. Although each line is meant as an individual ray of light, the imagery is symbolic rather than illusionistic. Rays of light, though linear, are not lines. Botticelli, who may have been apprenticed to a goldsmith in his youth, develops further variations. The haloes look as if they were made of gold wire or filigree work in his *Virgin and Child with Angels* (London, National Gallery), and *Madonna of the Book* (Milan, Poldi-Pazzoli).

The halo floating above the head of the angel of Leonardo's *Annunciation* (Florence, Uffizi) is a tour de force of perspective rendering and graphic analysis. Seen in side view, it consists of spokes radiating from a center, a combination of disc halo and ray halo. In the even more splendid playings of *The Last Supper* (Milan, Santa Maria della Grazie), Christ is depicted without a halo. But Leonardo has implied its presence in four ways. More exactly, he reduces the halo to four qualia, each presented in isolation.

First, light streaming through a doorway behind Christ surrounds his head, providing the radiance of a halo. Second, the doorway is surmounted by a curved molding shaped like a portion of a circle. If, following the tenets of gestalt psychology, we imagine the circle completed, its location on the picture plane is that which would be occupied by a large disc halo around Christ's head. Or his head is at the center of the implied disc.

Leonardo's third intimation is of a line or ray halo, created by locating Christ's head so that it overlaps the vanishing point of a one-point perspective system. The lines usually said to be receding to that vanishing point might, with imagined reversal of their imagined direction, be thought to proceed from Christ's head to form a world-encompassing ray halo. Leonardo has played cleverly on that truism central to many optical illusions: all lines point in two directions at once, if lines "point."

The fourth intimation is psychological or metaphysical. The miraculous is essentially a condition in which more is sensed than can be seen. Christ's halo is transcendental (or miraculous) in Leonardo's *Last Supper* because although it is not there in one sense, we are able to sense it in another.

Leonardo's degree of complexity is rarely approached. But later artists developed further variations on halos. In Titian's *Savior of Hortelano* (Prado), rays of light shine from Christ's head to form a cross. In El Greco's *Saint Martin and the Beggar* (Washington, National Gallery), curving clouds form a ring-shaped halo behind the saint's head. In Adam Elsheimer's *Baptism of Christ* (London, National Gallery), Christ's halo is created by four airborne cherubim joining arms to form a circle.

The question of who ought to have a halo has been answered differently in different societies. Byzantine emperors and empresses, unlike those of Western Europe, are depicted with halos in art. In Islamic art, halos are dispensed democratically. They appear on the heads of ordinary human beings engaged in good works, sometimes according to a pictorial logic in which the artist seems to dispense them at will.

Halos, like dragons, have literary antecedents that explain why they are depicted in painting though nobody has ever seen one. The prototype for the halo is sometimes identified as the flames that appear around the head of the infant Ascanius in Virgil's *Aeneid*. Among older images, fire is more directly linked to the potency of the godhead in the story of Semiramis, consumed by flames when Zeus grants her request to show himself in his true form. In the Old Testament, when Moses comes down from speaking with God on Mount Sinai, beams or rays of light shine from his face, which he covers with a veil except when speaking with God. (Exodus 34:29–35). The horns growing from the head of Michelangelo's *Moses* brought attention to the passage. The Hebrew word *karnot*, it was pointed out, can mean either rays of light or horns, creating a possibility for mistranslation.

If the theory is correct, which meaning came first? Did *karnot* originally mean horns (a symbol of male sexual power), later adapted to identify rays of light or rays radiating from a human head? Or were the circumstances the reverse? In English, names for light are not usually derived from names of other objects. More often, names for light inspire names for other objects. The word *radius*, as in radius of a circle, comes from the Latin word for ray. The rays in halos are radii of a circle that has the human head at its center. The word "luminary," sometimes used to mean just an important person, is more correctly a person who illuminates the human race, a borrowing from Latin *lume*, light.

The Moses of Exodus becomes an independent radiator of light on Mount Sinai, although with equal literary logic he might have passively reflected the light of God. When the figuration is carried over to the visual arts, rays of light rarely or never shine from faces. They rest behind heads or around them, a variation that more easily lends itself to pictorial representation.

Color Symbolism

By comparison with symbolism of light, color symbolism is diffuse. It probably developed at a later date and exists largely as a supplement to the symbolism of light. Symbolic associations with darkness and light have international roots and appear in many cultures. Associations with the hues, which might have developed during the Middle Ages, seem more closely linked to the moral imperatives of the Old Testament, although color names appear rarely in the Bible.

Symbolic associations with black and white, carried over from those of darkness and light, are based almost entirely on the play of positive against negative. White is a symbol of purity, of the original sexual purity of human life. The symbolism drifts over to pale colors in general, as in the traditional use of very pale pinks, blues, and other tints that approach white for the clothing of sexually innocent

infants. In Renaissance paintings of the Annuciation, white lilies symbolize the purity of the Virgin Mary.

Black, color of death or of mourning, expresses regret for lost loved ones. It also recalls loss of sexual innocence, the event by which, according to St. Augustine's interpretation of Genesis, death was brought into the world. Hence the otherwise curious association of black clothing with funerals but also with sexual provocativeness, as in women's black underwear or the idea that black dresses for women are sophisticated. Black or darkness is associated with prostitution, as in the phrase "ladies of the night." Baudelaire, following the symbolic cue, compared Parisian prostitutes to black cats.

The Bible identifies carnality as the first sin and says that the wages of sin is death. Or so the medieval moralists tell us, taking their cue from St. Augustine. Black is understandably the color of both death and sin, ambiguously both sin generally and sexual transgression. The association is not limited to Judeo-Christian societies. Islamic legend says the sacred black stone of Mecca was white when it fell from heaven. The stone, incorporated today into the masonry of the Ka'aba, became black—rather than blue or green—from the sins of the human beings who touched it. Why was the stone sent? Evidently to remind human beings of the blackness of their deeds, for which they could expect to be punished.

The symbolism of black and white rests solidly on religious metaphor, on its intimation that the greatest death is the death of the soul. The symbolism associated with other colors usually turns on association with objects typified by a particular color. Blue is cool because it is like the sea or because we imagine ourselves turning blue with cold. But red, followed by orange, is closely linked to black and white, to their intimations of sexuality, sin, and death.

Red is passion because it is associated with

the colors of blood and fire. The passion is sexual and gender differentiated. Red dresses, like black dresses, were once thought too daring for presumably virginal young women. Sexually aggressive men are not thought to dress entirely in red. But we might imagine them driving red sports cars and being called red-blooded. Women are not called red-blooded. As in the title of Stephen Crane's *Red Badge of Courage*, red for men has positive connotations and means brave and manly. As in the scarlet woman of Revelations 17 or the title of Hawthorne's *The Scarlet Letter* (the scarlet letter *A* was branded on an adulteress), red for women suggests sexual transgression, associations similar to those for black.

A red flag means war, aggression. A white flag means surrender, including surrender to the will of God. A black flag means piracy, aggression against decent society. The paradigm for the moral associations of red, white, and black is the Biblical story of the Garden of Eden, interpreted by medieval moralists to mean that Eve and her daughters led men astray.

Black, white, and the proverbial touch of red are a popular color combination, juxtaposing a bright hue against both extremes of achromaticity. The taboo against using large areas of red in home decoration, or excessively bright varieties of the color, reiterates the theme that red easily gets out of control. No parallel taboo exists against too much black, although large amounts of black in home decoration or in a young person's clothing might be considered depressing or macabre. In the 1940s, red combined with pink, orange, or purple was regarded as a bad combination; the colors were said to clash. Pink, orange, and purple can each be mixed using red and therefore are red related. The issue, again, is a need to avoid too much red.

Moral associations need not dictate the color of clothing worn every day. When they do, the associations are easy to read, though we need not assume that each member of each group thought about them. Modern prisons are said to have been inspired by the ideas of the Quakers, who thought that incarcerating criminals so they could think about their sins was preferable to hanging them. The traditional black-and-white stripes of prison clothing reminded the miscreant of the need to think about right and wrong. It also served as a reminder of the austerity of prison life, the separation from pleasures including the pleasures of color in clothing. Gray, another popular color for prison clothing, is similarly austere.

Among religious groups for whom the world is a source of temptation, such as the American Puritans, colors other than black and white are often avoided in clothing. The reasoning, presumably, is that black and white have moral associations and other colors do not. Other colors, therefore, serve no religiously useful purpose and can be classified with jewelry and perfume as unnecessary adornments of the body.

Restrictions on the colors of clothing worn by men are more common than those for women, reflecting the traditional idea that the man is a role model as head of the family. Modern Hasidic Jewish men in New York City wear black business suits and white shirts. In rural Pennsylvania Amish men wear black suits or denim work clothes and bright ultramarine blue shirts. Amish women wear blue, green, brown, or violet dresses, avoiding red, orange, and yellow, the warm colors. Dresses are one color only, probably for the same reason snap fasteners are used instead of buttons. To cover the body with clothing is decent, but more than one color in shirts and dresses is not needed.

Rules about allowable colors in clothing are not unique to religious communities. Business suits in dark colors for modern men, a uniform in many large corporations, bespeak dedication to the job, a renouncing of all distractions including bright or light colors in clothing. The Hawaiian shirts in strong colors worn by the president of an innovative computer software company assert a right to other standards. People are sensitive to the messages conveyed by colors in clothing, intolerant if invisible lines are overstepped, and more critical of men's clothing than women's clothing.

Despite a widespread elimination of dress codes and virtually complete freedom in leisure wear, creative costumes in creative colors are not considered appropriate for people in authority or responsible positions. Hawaiian shirts rarely appear during business hours on, say, bank presidents or United States senators, even the senator from Hawaii. A police officer who wore an orange, purple, and green shirt with his uniform would be ordered to change it.

Clothing not criticized for a high school student might annoy a judge if an attorney wore it to court. If the judge felt the colors were too extreme to be consistent with the dignity of the court, the attorney could be removed from the courtroom. Many clients would not be pleased to be represented by an attorney in pink overalls and a green shirt. The president of the United States would be criticized if he wore a vermilion jumpsuit to a summit conference with the Russians. The Russians might be more shocked than the Americans. We still equate dignity with dark or subdued colors, an idea with traditional roots.

Freud pointed out in *Totem and Taboo* that something prohibited on ordinary occasions is often allowed under special circumstances. Priests and ministers often wear black suits or robes with white collars, colors symbolizing their dedication to God or renunciation of the ways of the world. In the Catholic church, cardinals wear scarlet robes; the pope can wear all red or all white. The symbolic message is that higher echelon officers of the church wear bright colors for the glory of God, the same reason angels are shown wearing gorgeous

clothing in early Renaissance paintings. The practical purpose served by colors other than black and white is that when the pope or his cardinals appear in public, the colors of their clothing cause them to stand out from the crowd.

Red is thought of as an active color, hence masculine. Blue is calm or passive, hence feminine. The associations can also be reversed. Red has been characterized as emotional, thus feminine; blue as intellectual, thus masculine. For the clothing of infants, pink is for girls, pale blue for boys. Blue suggests the vastness of blue seas and blue sky, leading to an association with intellect and spirituality and to fascination with blue eyes. Red in its negative aspect suggests wantonness, shame, or infamy, consequences of failure to control the passions. Blue suggests melancholia, an inability to function. Rejected lovers in poems master their blueness or die of broken hearts, a pointing from blue melancholy to the blackness of the grave.

Purple suggests richness or royalty by reminding of robes that ancient kings dyed with Tyrian purple. The color is also associated with extreme rage, perhaps similarly a prerogative of kings. Or it suggests the overly ornate (purple prose). In societies where elderly women were expected to dress in black, pale shades of lavender, mauve, or other purples were often acceptable alternatives.

The Chinese are said to have developed a distaste for milk because all milk products were once reserved for their Mongol conquerors. The similar dedicating of purple to royalty may have achieved a parallel effect. Like orange, the color is not popular and was rarely used in Europe in interior decoration or men's clothing. That purple is employed far more extensively in Islamic art, often in combination with red, added to its aura of the exotic, an aura elsewhere reflected in the modern association of the color with homosexuality, particularly male homosexuality.

Associations with orange are as unfortunate as those with purple. The color is thought to symbolize bad luck in Japan. In the West, orange and black are the colors of witches and Halloween, rarely a popular combination for women's clothing. During the Middle Ages, women with carrot-colored hair—redheaded women—were thought to be witches and often burned at the stake. Later belief held that redheaded women were sexually promiscuous, another way of being a witch. The association was picked up in Renaissance painting. Mary Magdalene, the repentant lady of the night, is traditionally pictured with red (orange) hair, a painterly device for identifying her and alluding to folk beliefs about hair of that color.

Why are people with carrot-colored hair called redheaded rather than orange-headed? Whatever the answer, associations with orange hair follow those for red in being gender specific and sexually allusive. Redheaded men were not thought to be witches or devils in medieval folklore. Only women with hair of this color were characterized as enemies of God (witches) or bewitchers of men who might tempt them to promiscuous behavior. The paradigm, again, is Eve, and the associations rest on a foundation of religious metaphor.

Green is associated with the verdancy of growing things. In its negative aspect, green is linked with envy. Many molds and fungi are green. Unembalmed corpses, if Caucasian, acquire a greenish hue after death. Envy, we are evidently to understand, rots, consumes, kills, or is deathly.

Yellow suggests radiance and joy because associated with sunniness, the yellow of the sun, or the richness of gold. The dense layering of symbolic association for the color may be more complex, even, than that for red. In German, *Gold* is gold, *Geld* is money, and *gelb* is yellow, a similarity of sound that suggests all three are closely associated. Gold (the color

name) appears to have positive connotations, while yellow has negative connotations.

The word *yellow* is avoided in English in metaphors that have a positive aspect. We have golden girls and fair-haired boys, but no yellow people except cowards. People with yellow hair are called blondes. Sunny days are golden, not yellow. Golden replaces yellow in many plant names, even if the flower or fruit is yellow: goldenrod, golden seal, golden bantam corn, golden delicious apples. Silence is called golden to show that we value it. Journalism is called yellow if of a type we do not value. In a thread separate from the gold-yellow link, the negative association of yellow with cowardice must turn on attributing to the frightened a tendency to involuntary urination.

Goethe, in a passage expurgated from Eastlake's translation of *Farbenlehre*, found that, "when a yellow color is communicated to dull and coarse surfaces . . . the beautiful impression of fire and gold is transformed into one not deserving the epithet foul; and the color of honor and joy reversed to that of ignominy and aversion. To this impression the yellow hats of bankrupts and the yellow circles on the mantles of Jews, may have owed their origin. Cuckold yellow is really nothing but a dirty yellow" (Matthaei 1971, 169).

The practices Goethe reports can be related to money as easily as to ignominy. Bankrupts were disgraced because they mishandled money (and therefore were made to wear yellow hats). The color name *cuckold yellow* (no equivalent exists in English) also implies loss of wealth and disgrace because of this mismanagement. The wealth in this case is of another kind. If a man's wife is regarded as his possession, her infidelity suggests the cuckolded husband has allowed himself to lose what is rightfully his.

Jews, barred from many professions during the Middle Ages, were permitted to be moneylenders, an occupation despised because interest was charged. Compelling Jews to sew yellow circles on their mantles suggests, again, that the Christian majority associated this group with money, and in a negative manner. The reasoning was recycled in Nazi Germany, where Jews were compelled to wear yellow identifying stars. The color was meant to be an insult.

The Future of Color Symbolism

Freud said nothing about color symbolism but a great deal about symbolism generally that is pertinent. He pointed out the symbolic content of dreams and fantasies, their hidden sexual content, the creation of symbols by attributing gender to what is not human (blue and the sea are regarded as feminine), and the cloaking of ideas in symbols. His patients preferred not to know what was on their own minds, to avoid feelings of guilt. They punished themselves by developing neurotic symptoms, acting out the need to atone without recognizing why this need was felt.

The proposed therapeutic solution was to interpret the symbols, freeing the patients to understand their thoughts and deal with them directly. Although Freud recognized the traditional nature of symbolism and its appearance in folklore, he failed to follow this thread to its conclusion. Sick patients grow up in a sick society. Color symbolism and other symbolism is traditional, passed from one generation to the next. If symbolism in most cases confuses thought rather than refining it, as seems to be true of color symbolism, little can be accomplished by psychoanalytic treatment of an individual patient.

Freud was pessimistic about human possibilities. Jung saw more positive aspects in symbolism. Symbolic associations were treasures that drifted up from the depths of the collective unconscious. They were the content of that unconscious. Symbolism, Freud and Jung would have agreed, has a literary content. I regard it as excess baggage for that reason, a

legacy we need not accept. Color and the visual arts are visual, adequately understood only on that basis. Most people know whether they like Egyptian art or the art of India before they discover what the symbols in the works mean. Some never care what the symbols mean. Those persons unable to decide what they like until all the symbolism is thoroughly explained, and until they know, say, the pharaoh's name and his wife's name and what the Egyptians ate for breakfast, are not visually oriented. They absorb information like sponges but only information of certain kinds.

I see no danger that color symbolism will inspire pogroms against redheaded women, though taking symbolic ideas about black and white seriously contributes nothing to improving race relations in the United States today. The conceptual problem with color symbolism, as with color theory, is its reliance on simpleminded slogans. Thousands of variations of, say, red exist. Developing visual sensibility to color implies noticing the wide range of variation. The English language unfortunately encourages lumping all variations, no matter how different, under the label *red*. Most people follow the cues and do this. Color symbolism reinforces this oversimplification by reducing the effective aspect of color to nonsense sayings. It deadens people's ability to notice their feelings. Does *every* variation of red make everyone think of passion at all times? Why would this be the case, when reds can be so different one from the other?

The moral thread running through color symbolism is discouraging on other grounds. Subliminal though it be, this morality I do not care to perpetuate. People over the ages read the Bible selectively and remembered what supported their biases. We preserve their mistakes by attributing significance to their symbolic ideas. A conception of morality that regards wrong and right as absolute, comparing them to night and day or black and white, is insensitive. The moral issues facing the human race today have nothing to do with whether scarlet women wickedly seduce men by wearing irresistible black lace underwear, with whether redheaded women are witches and whores.

We will continue to regard red sports cars as sexy, and black lace underwear as devilish. Eliminating traditional symbolic associations with color and light would require deconstructing the English language, which we can-not accomplish. We can and should stop psychologizing about these associations. We have more refined ideas about morality than color symbolism conveys. And we need a more sophisticated understanding of color than can be reached by this route. Colors have no correlation with the sexual behavior of human beings or with human ideas about morality. Why would anyone ever think one could shed light on the other?

Nonvisual Seeing and the Metameric Grays

The Pythagoreans, having constructed matter out of numbers, next proceeded to arrange the main members of the universe according to a plan in which there was a little observation of nature, and a lot of *a priori* mathematical reasoning.

Benjamin Farrington, Greek Science

Color is something we see, rather than something we hear. But the question of whether color can be experienced by nonvisual methods is ancient. The issue is whether human beings can transcend the senses, possibly by the power of pure thought. Classic anecdotes about remarkable gifts are usually offered by narrators who heard the story from someone else. Robert Boyle reports about John Vermaasen, a thirty-three-year-old Dutchman blinded by smallpox at age two, who was reputed to be able to distinguish colors by touch (Boyle [1664] 1964, 42–49). The "Ingenious Person" who told Boyle about the prodigy had tested Vermaasen by asking him to sort black, white, red, blue, green, yellow, and gray ribbons. The test was inconclusive in that "he call'd the White Black and the Red Blew."

Vermaasen said he could identify colors by their relative smoothness. Boyle suspected sensitivity to the smell of fabric dyes, pointing out that Vermaasen "seems not consonant to himself about the *Red*, which as you have seen in one place, he represents as somewhat more Asperous than the *Blew*; and in another place, very Smooth." With the wistfulness of the faithful who missed the miracle, Boyle longed for "the Opportunity of Examining this Man my self, and of Questioning him about divers particulars which I do not find to have been yet thought upon."

The question of whether human beings can see without eyes is moot. Any method of seeing that is nonvisual is, by definition, not vision. Furthermore, we cannot hear with our noses or see with our ears. No sense organ is able to deliver percepts of the type specific to any other. The dream of nonvisual seeing perennially recurs in the media and in journals of psychology, philosophy, and philosophy of science (Hattersley 1970, 55-58; Perkins 1971, 329-37). In academic forums the question often takes the form of whether a hypothetical blind scientist could learn as much about color from instruments as others learn through using their eyes. Can knowing about red equal or exceed knowing what red looks like? Can so much be known about an experience that having the experience adds nothing further? Can thought replace all other modes of human activity? We are never asked to consider whether "knowing about" color is possible without a brain. We assume that the brain and its function are inseparable, an assumption not made about eyes.

Knowing about something implies acquiring knowledge. Knowing what something looks like implies undergoing experience. Because knowledge is not experience, the blind physicist is at a disadvantage. Although knowledge can be acquired from experience, experience cannot be extrapolated from knowledge. The limitation is not surmounted by redefining experience to include empathy, which is said to give people insight into experiences they have not undergone. Empathizing with another's experience, and thereby acquiring an understanding of it, is a bona fide experience for the empathizer. But it differs from the experience with which empathy is sought.

We cannot be more than we are or do more than we do, a constraint that has an objective basis. The criterion for an experience, even an inner experience, is that it occurs. This effectively means it has a spatiotemporal location. If an experience is in the mind, its location is that of the body with which the mind is associated. Arguing in favor of experiences that do not occur or that do not occur at locations appropriate for those experiences is self-contradictory. Feeling as if one had fought in

the Punic Wars is not germane to the question of whether one was there. Blind scientists who feel as if they have seen red and therefore as if they understand the experience are in a no more defensible position. Either they saw the color or they did not. "As if" is not good enough.

The literature expresses greater interest in whether the blind can experience color than in whether the deaf can experience sound. The argumentation is often embellished with technological trimmings, as if they could provide the necessary magic. Feigl asked that his readers imagine "the case of a congenitally blind scientist, equipped with modern electronic instruments who could establish the (behavioristic) psychology of vision for subjects endowed with eyesight. The blind scientist could thus confirm all sorts of statements about visual sensation and qualities—which in his knowledge would be represented by hypothetical constructs" (Feigl 1958, 385).

Feigl's blind scientist could not confirm all statements. He could evaluate those that required knowledge of color, but not those requiring experience. His own experience would be limited to the reading of instruments. This is experience of a different order than the experience of those who see or who apprehend color by looking at it. Given the different experiences of the sighted and of the blind, two different types of knowledge can be derived. This need not imply, except in a gross practical sense, that Feigl's congenitally blind scientist is disadvantaged by comparison with those who are sighted. He cannot understand the experience of seeing. But the sighted, as bias leads us to forget, are unable to comprehend the experience of having never seen.

Feigl's blind scientist differs from a randomly selected blind person. The scientist has unimpeachable professional credentials. As important, he has instruments at his disposal that are both "modern" and "electronic." The instrumentation, although it may include spectrophotometers and colorimeters, is as ideal-ized (or as improbable) as the scientist. No instrument presently in use, no matter how modern and electronic, enables the blind to solve even such simple color tasks as sorting red poker chips from green ones or distin-guishing red lights from green at traffic inter-sections.

The question about instruments for meas-uring color is not really whether they could work miracles for the blind. It is how reliably they perform their intended tasks for anyone. Wright pointed out that in the checking and calibrating of colorimeters, interlaboratory comparisons "have shown a depressingly large spread in colour measurements made with instruments of the same design, iet alone with different types of instruments" (Wright 1962, 3; [1944] 1969, 258).

Kelly, who identified six methods for meas-uring color, found that, for maximum accuracy, "a color should be measured by a spectrophotometer and the result expressed numerically either in terms of the CIE method or a Munsell renotation" (Kelly, 1965, 2). Deane B. Judd of the National Bureau of Stan-dards did not find this was sufficient. Judd arrived at a conference on colorimetry to report he had been unable to complete an experiment as scheduled. The data had been collected with a Beckman spectrophotometer. When an attempt was made to repeat the meas-urements using a General Electric spec-trophotometer, problems arose from "dif-ferences in the spectrophotometric values for the samples obtained respectively by the Beck-man and General Electric spectrophotometers. With the values given by the latter the good agreement previously noted no longer held. Some further work on the spectrophotometry was required" (*Symposium on Visual Prob-lems of Color* 1961, 343). The hazards of switching brands are not to be ignored when measuring with a spectrophotometer. Further-more, how refined is a spectrophotometer?

Forty years ago, Evans found that "the differ-ence in color that can be detected by an expert between two otherwise identical pieces of paper is, at present, smaller than the difference which can be detected by spectrophotomet-ric measurements and calculation" (Evans 1948, 203). No significant change has occurred since that date.

Feigl was not interested in how spec-trophotometers work or how well they work. Like most of us, he took the wonders of mod-ern machines and electronic instrumentation for granted, though instruments for measuring color fall far short of public expectation. What interested Feigl, and what is supposed to be proved by the imaginary blind scientist, is the supremacy of understanding over experience. Feigl's purpose was to defend deductive think-ing, including those deductive techniques applied to the analysis of color that have yielded so little of substance. We do not need more theories of color devised by those who reason and write as if they had never seen color.

Without prejudice to whether hypothetical blind scientists can become experts on color, real scientists with bona fide visual handicaps find the going more difficult. The British chem-ist John Dalton (1766–1844) found he made errors in identifying the colors of chemical solutions and precipitates. After comparing his color observations with those made by others, Dalton concluded his evaluation of red and green was defective. Describing his condition, he wrote the first scientific report on color blindness, for many years called Daltonism after him. Those with whom he discussed his vision must have tried to explain what red or green meant to them. It is not recorded that this cured Dalton. He was precluded from acquiring a type of understanding that could compensate for inability to experience. The kind of superior understanding Feigl imagines simply is not possible, whether for imaginary blind scientists or for real scientists like Dalton.

A less famous example of a scientist with a visual problem is provided by J. Plateau, the scientist who published a book on surface tensions in soap bubbles. In studies of surface tension in thin films, observations of color are important. Soap bubbles show bands of color on their surface, as well as a black area. If the black area is touched, the bubble bursts. But a sharp instrument can pierce other parts of the surface and be withdrawn without breaking the bubble. James Clerk Maxwell, in the review "Plateau on Soap Bubbles," explains how this scientist was able to continue his research after losing his eyesight (Maxwell [1890] 1965, 2:393–99). Like John Milton, who asked members of his family to read to him, Plateau borrowed the eyes of others. Friends and assistants performed experiments under his direction and answered his questions about what had happened.

The experiences of real-life scientists with visual impairments suggest that the hypothetical blind scientist who masters all by the force of intellect, assisted by modern electronics, is just a technocratic conceit. Nobody is capable of perceiving what for him or her is imperceivable. Even if machines were able to think or experience, the perception of color by a machine would be a perception for that machine. A blind person could no more annex the machine's experience than he or she could appropriate the experience of another living human being. Machines cannot live our lives for us, even if it could be shown that machines were capable of a superior quality of life.

Unless a priori knowledge can equal or exceed the scope of knowledge that is a posteriori (I do not think that it can), no blind scientist can understand color in the same manner as a sighted person. A blind scientist arguably cannot confirm *any* statement about color, because verification is inseparable from a need to confront colors, at some point, with a functioning eye. Although the blind scientist might take instrument readings competently if

the scales on the instruments were in braille, who is to set up the instruments? No blind scientist can follow, unaided, a command to select five blue objects to be studied by a spectrophotometer.

The issue of the hypothetical blind scientist is linked to that of whether sense data can be explained in a manner that can support a notational system. Like Aristotle's hypothetical blind man who argued about colors, congenitally blind scientists are precluded from understandings similar to those of sighted persons until this can be accomplished. Sense data must be exhaustively understood and translated into abstract (nonsensual) terms in a manner ensuring that nothing of consequence is lost in the translation.

The claim of contemporary physics is that the task is already accomplished. Colors, or those relatively few colors included on the electromagnetic wave scale, can be notated in terms of the wavelengths of the light they reflect. But too much is lost in this system. Consider the metameric grays. Developed by the Inter-Society Color Council, these grays are visually indistinguishable under specified lighting conditions. Yet they have dissimilar reflectance; therefore, they could never correctly be coded by the same notation in any notational system based on reflectances.

Metamerism is an everyday phenomenon, familiar to all who mix paints. To match the color of a sample, we need not know the colors mixed for the original sample. Two paints that match in color but are mixed from different constituents would have dissimilar reflectances, although whether this would be perceptible to human beings depends on the illuminating light. This is why colors that match under one light may not match under another.

The problem in explaining a metameric relationship between two colors to the hypothetical blind scientist is that the notation for the colors, which confirms dissimilarity in reflectance, would be contradicted by the perceptual experience of seeing them—they would look alike. Under some lighting conditions, a paint made from, say, inherently green pigment might exactly match another paint made from a mixture of blue and yellow pigments. The two paints would have different notations but would look alike in color. How could the blind scientist be edified on what "look alike" means? The term is comprehensible only as a report of an observation by a functioning eye.

Speakers of English can make two classes of statements in which color names are used. Only those statements that refer to language rules can be understood without looking at the colors, or without an ability to see colors. To say two colors look alike is to report a visual experience, a report understandable only to those who have had similar experiences.

Blindness, however, can be considered as a relative condition. Is a person either blind or not blind? The either-or categories reduce the diversity of experience to simpleminded stereotypes. People classified as legally blind can see, though their vision cannot be corrected to better than 20/400. Even the best lenses allow them to see no more at twenty feet than the statistically average observer sees at four hundred feet. Among those who are not congenitally blind, entirely blind, or legally blind, many people need eyeglasses for various visual corrections. Everyone is blind to some extent, in the sense that no human being has unlimited visual acuity.

The metameric grays mark one kind of limit for everyone, the only reasonable explanation for why they look alike although demonstrably different. A species with greater visual acuity than our own might be able to see the differences we can just measure. Our own blindness (what we cannot see, rather than what we can) is what we might describe to the blind scientist to explain the nature of the metameric grays. Under certain lighting conditions, we see no more difference between them than would be seen by the scientist.

An invention as bizarre as the hypothetical blind color scientist may not be needed to reach to the nature of the difference between knowledge and experience. We all have vision that is limited in a variety of ways. I cannot see, for example, cosmic rays. I fail to understand how this limit could be transcended by learning a great deal about cosmic rays, irrespective of how recondite the acquired knowledge or how sophisticated the instruments used to collect it. Knowledge cannot aspire to the complexity of experience and therefore cannot substitute for it.

To suggest that the blind will never see is foolhardy. Those without legs learn to walk. In blindness caused solely by cataracts, vision can be restored in many cases. Among myopics and astigmatics, contact lenses and eyeglasses improve otherwise substandard vision. But this is the realm of the prosthesis, the transplant, and other wonders of modern medicine and optometry. Whether vision can be restored for the profoundly blind depends on whether eye transplants are possible or a functioning artificial eye can be constructed. These are different questions from that of whether the need for a functioning natural or artificial eye can be bypassed through knowledge, color notational systems, electronic instruments, human will, or blind faith.

Whether sensory experience can be eliminated is less important than why anyone would want to prove it to be superfluous. For Planck, eliminating sense perceptions from physics represents a "sacrifice made to pure knowledge." But knowledge is not necessarily more pure than sensory experience, nor is thought necessarily more pure than perception. It leads to results more likely to be regarded as invisible and therefore superior.

What is at issue is a system of morality in which thought is regarded as pure and sensory experience as morally suspect. The hypothetical blind scientist who knows all about color is presented to raise the question of whether sensory experience can be eliminated, whether it performs no useful function. We cannot eliminate sensory experience because its nature is unique. Thought is different, and one cannot be a substitute for the other.

PART THREE

Color and Form

The Eye sees no forms. It only sees that which differentiates itself through light and dark or through color.

Johann Wolfgang von Goethe, Color Theory

The Two-Dimensional World

I think of color as an interval of space—not as red or blue. People used to think of color and form as two things. I think of them as the same thing, so far as the language of painting is concerned.

Stuart Davis, Conversation with James Johnson Sweeney

The question of what causes light and color, that staple of the physical sciences, is matched in philosophy and the life sciences by that of whether color is real. The answer to the first question depends on what causality is understood to imply. The answer to the second turns on the difference, if any, between an entity that really exists and one that just appears as if it might.

Color cannot be shown to be either more or less chimerical than anything else. Thus, the question of whether color is real invites the counter question of whether anything is real.

A less incendiary point is that color is inseparable from both the mode of perceiving it and the domain in which it is encountered. Though this is not immediately obvious, color and vision mean the same thing, just as color and light mean the same thing. They refer to a single phenomenon burdened with more than one name.

Illusion and Reality

Color exists in the visual field. This two-dimensional universe, separate from the three-dimensional world of touch, operates according to rules of its own. The visual field is neither the world nor my entire perception of the world. Beyond the boundaries of visual experience, I can detect tastes, sounds, and smells. I can experience spaces by moving through them. I can experience objects by touching their surfaces. Another class of percepts tells me about myself: whether I feel hungry, tired, disoriented, thoughtful. The visual field has no direct connection to these other perceptual universes. It contains only my apprehension of what the world looks like.

A real chair has not entered my eye when I see one, any more than a real chair has entered my head when I think about one. The visual field contains images, not objects. The English language is poor in forms for describing these images. Language in general encourages the expediency of summarizing experience, including visual experience, in generalized or idealized terms. Perception, unable to encompass this economy, stubbornly wends its own way.

The conceptual imperative is unambiguous: the environment, like every object in it, ought to be envisioned as stable, each a receptacle for its singular identity. The world, although it changes, remains the same world it was yesterday. A yellow chair by the window in my room will not be a different chair if moved to another place tomorrow. The dynamics of vision, however, are relative. In my perception of world or chair, the presumed singularity cannot be confirmed. The way any chair looks is affected by my vantage point, my perspective, or, more formally, my coordinate system.

I notice a chair on Monday from far away; on Tuesday, I see it nearer. On Wednesday, I look at it from a seated position, although I had previously been standing. On Saturday, someone is sitting in the chair and lighting conditions have changed so the chair's color looks different. On Sunday, the chair has been moved to another room. If a camera were to record these sightings, no two photographs of the chair would be alike. They would show different views of the chair. Nelson Goodman used the term *presentations* for these multiple apprehensions of a singular object (Goodman 1957, 127).

Conventional wisdom holds that the multiple presentations are evidence of the delusion of the senses and that the colors of the chair may be similarly illusory. If I were seeing the chair correctly, theory says, the chair would look the same at all times. But the camera, which lacks human fallibility, sees the chair essentially as I do. The similitude is not entire, but the congruency is remarkably close. The camera even sees, in its own way, the colors that may not be real. Either my percepts are less illusory than I have been taught to assume, or the camera mechanistically shares my delusion.

The Real World

Language and acculturation cannot affect people's eyes. But they affect how we interpret what we see. What we are taught in this case is quite odd. The multiple presentations of the imagined chair, or of any other object, are to be accounted for by envisioning, so to speak, an objective object, divorced from any singular experience of seeing it.

The transcendental object—in this example, the objective yellow chair—is assumed to exist each time anyone encounters any of its individual presentations. It still exists (and remains yellow) when no one is present to look at it. This objective chair is conventionally said to be real and to exist in a world of similarly real objects. We are asked to prefer this story about what cannot be seen to what is visually self-evident.

The real world containing the real chair, although regarded as three-dimensional, is not an exact equivalent for the three-dimensional world available to touch. It resembles a matrix superior to the universe of any individual form of sense perception. The objective world includes both corporeality and colors (the objective chair is yellow), although I cannot touch chairs with my eyes or see colors with my hands. Extrapolated from the sum of the perceptions, the real or objective world exceeds the limit of perception. Reality is a useful fiction, as is objectivity. What is the fiction useful for? It is necessary? It is reasonable?

Does it further understanding of color?

As if we had passed through Alice's looking glass, the objects located within the objective world possess unusual attributes. Unlike the particular presentation of a yellow chair that I alone saw on Tuesday, the objective, real, yellow chair, in its objective, real world, can be seen under an infinite number of conditions by an infinite number of persons at an infinite number of times and places. This identifying characteristic remains stubbornly theoretical. Nobody understands how to implement it except the Mad Hatter. No human being is on record with the heroic claim that he or she personally observed any given object from every possible spatiotemporal location. The task might reasonably be accomplished, given all the time in the world. No human being is allowed that much time, a limit we must not ignore.

However ardently I may hope that the real chair exists when I am not looking at it, its presumed existence can only be known through belief, as an article of faith. Knowledge that the chair is still there when I am not looking at it, unlike knowledge that the chair is yellow, is never available through immediate perceptual experience. The profound barrier, as children discover, is that I cannot *see* whether the chair is still there if I am not looking at it. Endeavoring to circumvent this familiar visual limitation, I can solicit testimony confirming the existence of the chair from someone who observed it while I was not looking. This does not speak to the question of what happened to the chair when nobody was looking at it.

Solipsism is feared because human beings need to believe that the world extends beyond human experience of it. Creation myths from all parts of the globe, including the opening chapters of Genesis, throw down the gauntlet with assertions about what is metaperceptual. With few exceptions, they declare that the world was created before human beings inhabited it, a condition that could not have

been confirmed by human beings. An earlier chaos of unspecified form (a darkness on the waters) is said to have preceded whatever form of creation occurred.

That the world is of earlier vintage than human beings is scarcely doubted. Why do we believe this? Some of the faithful cite Genesis. Those who prefer another authority point to the geological and biological record presented by fossils, or to astronomy and cosmology: to look back time and the big bang. But both scientific and religious explanations are elaborate forms of conjecture, neither supported by anyone's immediate experience. No human eye saw the world before human beings were on earth. Because no one saw, no one knows, and we simply make inferences. We hope that our rules for making these inferences are reasonable and that we will remember the difference between inference and observation, between believing and seeing.

Seeing is believing. But we believe in many things nobody has ever seen, including the significance of our ideas. Objectivity (as in "the objective world") and reality ("the real world") are synonymous for most purposes. Either conception relies heavily on tactile elements difficult to reconcile with the visual matrix.

Reality can be loosely defined as all the real objects in the world, along with the empty (but real) spaces between these objects. Each of the objects is said to have a front and back at the same time, though we cannot see both at once. The inconsistency is not genuinely resolved with mirrors. I can no more prove that the world and its objects have the structure attributed to them than I can prove that absolutes exist.

If what is known (or believed to be true) exceeds what any of us can see, this substantiates the familiar claim that differences exist between knowing and seeing. A dog is able to see a yellow chair, with less or greater visual acuity than a human. The dog is not expected to have worked though the philosophical intricacies of whether the chair, or its yellow color, ought to be regarded as real. Does it matter that I have worked them through? What benefit can I expect to derive after I have determined, once and for all, whether the world is real? Is that question significant? What does it mean?

Real and Unreal Chairs

Does the world go away when I close my eyes? The visual answer to the question is that I cannot very well tell with my eyes closed. That human beings have traditionally demanded more of an answer than that has been, I think, a misuse of human intelligence. This misuse fosters reasoning based on the metaphor of an invisible God, in which what cannot be seen is assumed to be more important than what we see. Conjecture loses touch with observation, and ability to reason about observation weakens. The mind is valued more than the senses, a weakness with a direct bearing on theories about color.

Whether a real, objective world still exists when I close my eyes is not a meaningful question. Like the inquiry about how many angels can stand on the head of a pin, it asks for a determination that cannot be made. Worse, the impression of a significant issue is created by a semantic trick, a play on words. Thereafter, the syllogism goes from bad to worse—if I cannot look at the objective world while I am not looking at it, something is wrong with my eyes. Possibly, then, the colors I see are not real, a nonsense issue that has persisted for centuries.

Traditional arguments against the credibility of sense data turn on the distinction between knowing (or believing) and seeing. Sense data is thought to be philosophically disappointing because it fails to confirm what is believed to be true. Because I cannot look at a chair I am not looking at, I cannot directly verify that the chair *is* there when I am not looking at it. Sense data disappoints expectations, but the expectations have not been sufficiently scrutinized.

To explain what the word *chair* means is reasonably simple. To illustrate the scope of the term, a carpenter can be invited to construct some chairs and show how chairs ought to be used. This cannot address the question of what we mean by saying these chairs are "real," "exist," or redundantly even "really exist." The realness attributed to them implies the essential that the chairs are still there when I am not looking at them. Human value judgment is such that this is held to be more significant than the oddity that I am still here (or suspect that I am) when not actively engaged in the act of looking at chairs.

For the philosopher F. H. Bradley, in *Appearance and Reality*, "I can not transcend experience, and experience is *my* experience. From this it follows that nothing beyond myself exists; for what is experience is its &the self'sé states." In assertions about what exists and what does not, the word *exists*, as in Bradley's sentence, is almost impossible to define. Bradley could as reasonably have concluded that nothing beyond himself is himself, a tautology.

Taking Bradley's solipsistic world at face value, objects in this world disappear when not being perceived; only the self can be regarded as real. In another kind of world, the inhabitants might disappear when not engaged in perceiving objects. A universe of either of these two types (or of many other conceivable types) would look exactly like the universe in which we reside. To determine its actual nature would be beyond human capability. I cannot know that unperceived chairs are there or that they are not there. I can be certain only that I cannot see them when I am not looking at them, a visual limit to what I can know.

My hypothetical yellow chair with its green, red, and orange cushion is conventionally called a real object, even though, in the present example, it is only a figment of my imagination. Some people feel strongly about maintaining a proper sense of reality. If I said I had decided to imagine an unreal chair, they would insist this is impossible and that I must be imagining a real chair or a real hypothetical chair—as opposed to an unreal hypothetical chair. Convenient fiction or not, people take reality seriously.

The argument that chairs are real but perhaps their colors are not is familiar. Its problematic aspect is not the unrealness attributed to the colors but the realness attributed to the chairs. The physical sciences, carrying the quest for an ultimate reality one step further, have not contributed to clarity. We are asked to believe that even the chairs are not real, though their electrons and other subatomic constituents are. If Newton's absolute time and absolute space have been discarded in the physical sciences, no foundation exists for the conception of an absolute reality: an objective world in which real chairs (or real electrons) are frozen monoliths, forever unchanging.

Any chair said to be real can be exhaustively explained as a generalized or idealized chair that cannot be experienced in its totality. No matter how often I look at any chair, I cannot encompass the visual experience another person might have when looking at it. I can not see the chair's back while regarding its front. Nor am I able to see it from every conceivable spatiotemporal perspective and under every possible lighting condition.

To refer to "the chair" is a verbal economy, necessary because English is not well adapted to dealing with visual concepts. Using the phrase "the chair," although inexact, requires fewer words than saying "the total of the various ways in which the chair has thus far appeared to me, and to others, on the multiple occasions on which it, or one or another of its presentations, has been observed." One concatenation of words means the same as the other. One is a description of what lies within the realm of individual and aggregate human perception. The other is a brief summary of that data, no more or less meaningful than the original data. Confusion enters when "the chair" is inflated to more than it can reasonably be: when the chair is called real and the sense data unreal, as if one could be severed from the other.

The real or objective chair should not be confused with the Platonic ideal chair, that staple of undergraduate courses in philosophy. Nor is it the generic chair that floats in the mind as a ghostly surrogate for chairs in general. It is, however, as conceptualized and artificial as either. Both the ideal chair and the generic chair consist of those parts common to all chairs. These parts may be elevated, in the case of the ideal chair, to a level of chair perfection.

The notion becomes untenable if we stubbornly plod on to compile a list of what those parts ought to be. Color, as often the case, is at the center of the inconsistencies. The ideal chair and the generic chair must each be some color (the ideal chair is probably an ideal color), because all chairs are colored. But neither chair can be any particular color. No particular color is common to all chairs. Nor is any particular color the ideal color or an ideal color for a chair.

To see or visualize a color that is no particular color (or that is an ideal color) is impossible. Therefore, we cannot imagine what either of these idealized chairs might look like. This is of no practical consequence because we are said to be unable to see them. The reason we cannot see or photograph them is related to their incomprehensible colors.

The real or objective chair, unlike its generic and ideal cousins, is neither an abstract summary of the parts common to all chairs nor a refinement of the symmetry of those parts. We talk about it as if it were a single chair with the potential to be seen from all possible perspectives. The closest analogue for its parts would be to imagine a camera taking photographs of one chair from every available viewpoint, every possible distance, and under every conceivable lighting condition. The photographs would be infinite in number. Any of them might represent the chair as some particular person had seen it as some particular time. But no individual's experience would include all the presentations in the photographs.

Although the generic chair and the ideal chair are respectively no particular color and the ideal color, the real chair can be every color. Certainly a real chair can be painted any color and still remain the same chair. A chair that can theoretically be every color (or any color) is as improbable as the chairs of ideal color or no particular color. The image of a chair that I see, that can be photographed, and that lies within the realm of the senses, can only be (and must be) *some* color or some collection of colors.

Absurdity is a good criterion for whether a statement is a mental construction rather than a report of, or inference from, sense data. The real chair, always *there*, always *the same*, is as inaccessible to the senses as Plato's ideal chair. This objective chair is something we all know, or have entered into a societal conspiracy to sustain. But it is not verifiable. Nobody can see it, or see it in all it aspects. It is not a visual concept.

The camera, because it sees without knowing, reports, presumably correctly, what is available to be seen: a chair looks different in both shape and color from different perspectives. Anyone unreconciled to this sensual phenomenon—in the final analysis, a basic phenomenon of color and vision—is quick to add the qualification "But it is really the same chair." I reply, "But it really looks different." My respondent and I are in engaged in word play, a good-natured jousting with value judg-

ments. The game is to determine whether sense data, including vision and color, ought to be taken seriously. The winner is the individual who is most adept at manipulating the word *real* in support of his or her views.

Much confusion about color and visual experience could be avoided if we more often remembered that the conventional figure of a monolithic real chair with monolithic real colors is a hypothetical construct. We imagined it and never saw it. Because of its all-encompassing nature, the real chair can never be directly experienced in its entirety: no one can see a single chair in "every" possible way. More at home in the mind than among the senses, the real chair is an ideal, a useful fiction. But if it were called an ideal chair, people would confuse it with the Platonic chair, another type of ideal.

In assessing visual experience, we imagine the real chair situated in a universe of similarly real objects to which we attribute responsibility for our perceptions. An analogue for what I see at any moment is a snapshot taken from within that imagined world, a nation with inexact boundaries. We continue to wonder, on occasion, how real objects differ from objects, real chairs from chairs, real truths from truths. A definition of *real* is needed. But the word eludes definition except as the opposite of unreal.

Questions about what is real, including all variations of the questions about color's reality, are questions about how to use language. Regrettably, they are often taken seriously as meaningful or even profound questions about the phenomenological world. Operationally, when an entity is said to be real, a value judgment is implied between it and another item judged to be unreal, therefore of inferior value. In this good-bad classification system, real is always better than unreal. *Real* can even mean wonderful, which is why we have such idioms as "a real human being."

The real world, an object of knowledge,

may be contrasted with the unreal (illusory) world of visual images and their chimerical colors. Imagine that we swept away judgmental code words (*real, unreal*) and demanded a rational explanation for why our conception of a monolithic reality is more significant than visual experience. A convincing argument would not be easy to supply. The immediate facts are only that the visual world floating in front of our faces differs from the real world we imagine. We see a visual universe of observable changes, not conjectured stability, manifested as a succession of different images that may be apprehended by me or by a camera. A discussion of the various presentations of the chair that I see implies a different universe of discourse than discussing what I believe I know about the chair.

Anyone asked to show what is meant by a real chair might reasonably point to a three-dimensional chair as its closest approximation. Because every real object has an unreal twin, the next endeavor should be that of locating an unreal chair. Everyone knows where to look. What is said to be "unreal," in this example, is the two-dimensional image of a chair available to visual perception.

A two-dimensional image of a chair is regarded as unreal because it deviates from the three-dimensional chair (the real chair) assumed to be normative. The word *image*, as in *image of a chair*, is sufficient to suggest an ephemera: an apparition of something else that is the genuine article. By extension, the entire content of the visual field is often called a visual illusion, because what I see is not the world. Instead, it is merely an image, which has two spatial dimensions and cannot be shown to have three. If I close my eyes, the image of the world goes away. But I am told that the real world does not.

The image of a chair is held to be unreal not because we have measured it against something called a real image and found that they did not match. The reason that images of chairs

are not real chairs is that they are images rather than chairs. Furthermore, real chairs are real only by stipulation, because no physical difference exists between a chair and a real chair. I prefer regarding the chair and its image as different objects in different universes, each with its unique set of characteristics. One, to keep peace with those who insist on the designation, is a real (three-dimensional) chair. The other is an equally real (two-dimensional) image.

Whether three-dimensional universes with their objects are real in a manner that two-dimensional worlds with their images are not leads again to the question of whether touch is more reliable than vision. Traditionally people must have believed this to be the case. Our conception of reality is founded on the idea that we confirm whether objects are *there* by touching them. But I wonder why the question arose, as if the senses had to be graded and one found better than the other. We need both touch and vision, and they usually work in harmony.

Possibly mirages led early people to believe that the eye is not always reliable, that visual images can appear without the tactile correspondence expected in that case. Do objects exist that we can bump into yet not see? The black holes that modern cosmologists imagine in outer space meet those requirements. But no black hole has been found so far. Only in stories about the supernatural do people collide with objects that cannot be seen.

Regardless of what inspired the idea that the eye is unreliable, the reasoning is defective. Because of the greater scope of the eye and its ability to perceive colors, we see many things that have no tactile equivalent, ranging from rainbows to the horizon to words printed in books. The idea that three-dimensionality is real and two-dimensionality is illusory leads to a conceptual morass. It obliges us to explain how height and width, illusory when they appear together (as in two-dimensional universes), can become nonillusory (real) when linked with depth.

Because the distinction between real and unreal is hierarchical, the central issue is value judgment. The rhetorical forms built into language encourage us to affirm or assume that three-dimensional universes are significant in ways that those of two dimensions are not. An entity might be described as "only an image"; rarely is anything called "only an object." The syntactical bias toward trivialization of what is not three-dimensional probably can be traced to the accident that, as three-dimensional bodies, we live in the three-dimensional world. The tripartite nature of dimension in our environment can be affirmed by touch, even with closed eyes. It cannot be reached directly by vision, at least not by vision alone. We can only look into, but never enter or touch, that parallel universe of two dimensions suspended before our faces.

The two-dimensional world is devoid of depth. But it includes color, the element suggesting that two- and three-dimensional worlds are discrete. One is not part of the other, any more than the eye is part of the hand. Despite the assumptions made in projective geometry, I see no possibility that one can be regarded as a projection of the other, except in a nominal sense. No element accessible to touch on the surface of a chair—no bump, hollow, or other feature I can feel in its geography—might reasonably be said to produce color if projected on a two-dimensional surface.

Delusion and the Geometry of Visual Space

When we use the words "white color," we must not suppose that what we mean by these words is either something outside the eyes or something in the eyes. We must not suppose it to be any place at all.

Plato, The Theaetetus

The flowers have no colors; they send off physical vibrations, called vibrations of ether, but colors exist only when there are the mind and eye to transform these vibrations.

E. W. Scripture, Thinking, Feeling, Doing

To ask whether what we see, including color, is real or a delusion of the senses is to entertain a curious assumption: that some aspects of the phenomenological world are more illusory than others. The proverbial delusion of the senses avoids solipsism, a belief that the world disappears when not looked at. A more radical possibility is introduced. Perhaps the real portion—only this portion—of the world remains. The unreal or illusory portion, which includes color, removes itself to some other place. The nameless limbo to which it retires is as distant as the limbo containing chairs I am unable to see because I am not looking at them. Can anything be partly real and partly unreal, or more real in some parts than others?

The strange thought that the phenomenological world can be graded in discernibly different degrees of realness is traceable to the pre-Socratic philosophers. For Heraclitus (ca. 536–470 B.C.), the only constants are the variables of motion and change. His universe, like that of contemporary quantum theory, was in a condition of continual metamorphosis. Nothing ever stood still. For Parmenides (470 B.C.), the world was stable and unmoving. Motion was a delusion of the senses. The concept proved to be enduringly popular, though we need not assume Parmenides invented it. Phenomena that we do not know how to systematize, particularly visual phenomena, are still called delusions of the senses.

Parmenides, whose frozen world is otherwise absurd, must have meant to convey a sense of realities other than those that can be seen. The hidden reality is a world that eternally endures, although the world discovered through visual observation is continually passing away. Whether one world is more real than the other has been reduced, in Western thought, to the issue of whether the world is made of forms (corporealities) or events. Is touch, by which we apprehend forms, more reliable than vision, which reveals only the endless permutations of visual space, time, and color? The issue surfaces in the classical question of whether light is a stream of particles or a wave. Particles, at least as the Greeks imagined them, can be caught and held in the hand. Waves cannot be arrested without ceasing to be waves.

In one of his two paradoxes that speak to the question of whether motion exists, Zeno (ca. 490–430 B.C.) asks us to consider the flight of an arrow. The arrow cannot be moving if just resting at an infinite number of points in space. It seems to move, which led Zeno to a conclusion similar to that of Parmenides. Motion is a delusion of the senses. Or it is a greater delusion of the senses than the substantiality of the forms that move. The arrow was there but not moving.

As if cinematography had been predicted by Zeno, any reel of motion picture film of an arrow in flight consists of a sequence of individual still pictures, called frames. In each frame, the arrow appears in a slightly different position. The question raised by Zeno's paradox is whether it is a delusion of the senses when the images appear to move in a motion picture being projected. The answer I prefer is that we ought to know better than Zeno. It is a matter of common knowledge that any reel of film consists of a linked sequence of still photographs. The sequence of pictures exhibits movement when projected, a visual fact that can be explained in terms of the limits of acuity of the human eye.

The film in motion argues for the illusoriness of the motion "that is not there" to no greater extent than it argues for the illusoriness of the forms we see in motion, which are as profoundly not there. Zeno correctly predicted how motion would look when stopped by a movie camera. But motion stopped is no longer motion, although the condition has no separate name.

Hallucinations and Visions

Zeno assumed that what cannot be touched is illusory, even if it can be seen. The assumption, which Ivins regards as central to Greek thought, opens the door to an unmanageable hierarchy of relative degrees of reality. No reliable criteria are available for sorting the real from the more real, the most real, the really real. Whether the physical world is real is a semantic question. No discernible difference exists between an ordinary world and a world dignified by calling it real.

Because the world is one piece, we can build consistent models by saying that everything is real or, as in Buddhism, by saying that everything is unreal. We can consistently regard the universe as paradoxical, entirely real and entirely unreal at the same time. Or models can be built in which the issue of reality is avoided. We can call *reality* just a semantic issue, not meaningful. Confusion ensues when we follow Parmenides in imagining that the world can be partly real and partly unreal. What glue holds the real and unreal parts together? Why did Parmenides not admit the flaw in his theory? He could not explain motion, so he dismissed it by saying it was not there.

Parmenides was not laughed out of town for what could have been viewed as evasive double-talk. The Greeks may have already been partial to the idea that the world is a mixture of illusion and reality, of things that exist and things that just seem to. The real and unreal parts remain stuck together in some cases but float apart in others. The reasoning is by analogy with touch, untempered by what we learn from vision. Touch teaches that we bump into objects but cannot bump into space. Space, consequently, does not really exist, a muddled reasoning that still haunts us today.

From hallucinations to colors, many visual experiences explained in terms of illusion or delusion can be more coherently understood without those concepts. Consider how the following events might be assessed, in terms of illusoriness or absence of it.

- I see a chair.
- I see a hologram of a chair.
- I see a chair. But when I report this, others say I must be hallucinating because they cannot see it.
- I deliberately lie, saying I see a chair when I do not.

Wrong conclusions can be drawn about what we see, as about anything else. But a perception either occurs or does not. The limit leaves no room for the concept of a wrong or mistaken perception: for thinking a chair was seen although this was not the case. In each example except the fourth, I must have seen the image of a chair, though differing statements can be made about the circumstances under which the experience occurred. Any error lies not in the observation, but in supposing that a corporeal, three-dimensional chair is necessarily present whenever anyone sees one.

Quasars, holograms, hallucinations, movie films, still photographs—all give evidence that visual images can be seen in the absence of the three-dimensional objects nominally said to account for the images. Individuals are not committed for psychiatric observation because they do not really see the visual hallucinations they report. Their problem is that they *do* see

such things, under circumstances that give cause for concern. The rest of us do not really see the hallucinated objects and events.

The individual who reports seeing things that cannot be explained in terms of our understanding of the external world elicits a diversity of responses. These responses depend on what was seen and how listeners react to the story. People who believe Moses saw God on Mount Sinai may not believe I saw God at the supermarket. Beyond the subjective interpretations made about hallucinations by persons other than those who have them, these experiences remain private affairs. If William Blake said he saw an angel in a tree, we hazard more in doubting the vision than in doubting that angels exist. No person is privy to another's vision—or visions. We cannot prove that Blake saw a tree, and we cannot disprove that he saw an angel.

Facts provide no authority in this case, because the facts needed are not accessible. The fact that the world contains trees does not speak to the question of whether Blake saw the tree the angel was sitting in. The fact that the world contains no angels does not disprove that Blake saw one. It only indicates that the cause of any perceived image was not, so to speak, a real flesh-and-blood angel who happened to be passing by.

If I believe Blake saw an angel in a tree, I will call his experience a vision. If I disbelieve, I will characterize it as a hallucination. To assume that the tree was seen but the angel was not is the height of presumption. We cannot edit what other people see or even what we see. Although I am able to change my mind, I cannot alter my visual experiences.

Optical Illusions

Hallucinations and visions are private affairs, accessible through reports that are secondhand for persons other than those who experience the hallucinations and visions. Another class of visual field phenomena, the optical illusion, shares with the hallucination the characteristic of evoking metaphysical doubt. It shares with color the interesting characteristic of being subject to verification. More than one person can see the illusions.

The psychologist R. L. Gregory classes some optical illusions as "figures which disturb" the eye, while others are figures that "are seen distorted" (Gregory 1966, 133–36). The unusual aspect of the disturbing or distorting is its universality. A large number of people, viewing an optical illusion, will each provide roughly the same report about how the figure appears. As a result, no criterion can be enunciated for how optical illusions would look to an observer who saw the figures without being confounded. To be confused by optical illusions appears normal, while to remain unconfused is abnormal. Just as no method exists for teaching anyone to see red as blue, no method exists for training an observer to see an optical illusion in an undistorted manner, irrespective of what Gregory might have meant by that term.

If everything we see—the "visual illusion" —should be regarded as phantasmagorical, the optical illusion superimposes a secondary layer of illusoriness that is troubling. If the world is not really the way it looks, what can we mean by singling out the optical illusion as a figure that is not really the way *it* looks? Is everything unreal and a few special things more unreal? Goethe had a simpler idea: only optical truths exist. I believe Goethe is correct, and distorted seeing is a meaningless concept. The defining characteristic of optical illusions is not the illusoriness attributed to them. Each illusion consists of a visual or graphic form that contradicts commonplace intellectual expectations. Most of the expectations are guided by our strange conception of reality, the suprareality in which everything remains the same although this is not what we see.

We expect, for example, that two lines of equal length will always look the same length. But, in the Müller-Lyer arrow illusion, they do not (see figure 17–1). We expect that when two patterns are superimposed, the third pattern they will create can be predicted. But moiré patterns are unpredictable. We expect that straight lines will look straight without regard to the field surrounding them. But, in the Hering illusion, straight lines superimposed on radial patterns look curved.

What is deceived, in these and innumerable other instances, is the predicting mind rather than the perceiving eye. The hidden assumption is that an object ought to look a certain way. It ought to display qualia consistent with conventional expectations about that object. Straight lines ought to look straight under all conditions, if for no other reason than that they *are* straight.

This type of noncontextual reasoning would mean that a ship on a distant horizon should not look like a dot, because everyone knows ships are not dots. The unreasonable and unreasoning expectation is that the visual field ought to correspond to our model of an

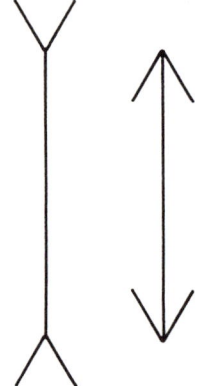

Figure 17-1. The Muller-Lyer arrow illusion. The central line segment is the same length in each figure. It appears longer in the figure with outgoing fins, which is the taller figure.

objective world with a singular identity. We should see what we want to see. Furthermore, we ought to immediately discover for any deviance an explanation that commends itself as conventionally acceptable. Whether or not acceptable, the more reliable explanation typically lies exposed in the putative illusion. As the Hering figure demonstrates, straight lines need not always look straight. Optical illusions teach visual lessons we do not want to learn.

Optical illusions are usually investigated by seeking a real cause for the putatively unreal illusion. The aim is to fit the figures into a conventional understanding of phenomenological reality by finding a way to explain them that will not disturb that understanding, that will not make waves. This leads to psychologizing about an eye that sees incorrectly and a brain that corrects the eye's errors. The literature is thin on consideration of the other possibility: that the eye is seeing correctly but the brain is not thinking very clearly.

The Müller-Lyer Arrows

Among optical illusions, the Müller-Lyer arrow illusion is a frequent object of study (figure 17-1). Gregory has compiled a list of six theories about why subjects take the line in the left figure to be longer than that in the right, although both are equal in length.

1. The eye movement theory "supposes that the features giving the illusion make the eye look in the 'wrong' places," a reasoning further explored by Jean-Paul Sartre (Gregory 1966, 141; Sartre n.d., 46).

2. The limited acuity theory proposes that "we should expect the figure with the outgoing fins to look too long, and the one with the ingoing fins to look too short if the acuity of the eye were so low that the corner could not be clearly seen" (Gregory 1966, 141).

3. The confusion theory "suggests that certain shapes 'confuse' the perceptual system. It

is the kind of 'theory,' alas, all too prevalent in psychology—it is no more than a rather misleading statement of what we wish to explain" (Gregory 1966, 142).

4. The empathy theory "is that the observer identifies himself with parts of the figure . . . and that he becomes emotionally involved so that his vision is distorted rather as emotion might distort an intellectual judgment" (Gregory 1966, 144).

5. The pregnance or good-figure theory, suggested by gestalt psychologists, proposes that illusions "are supposed to be due to pregnance exaggerating the distance of features seeming to stand apart, and reducing the distance of features which seem to stand together" (Gregory 1966, 145; Kohler 1947, 99).

6. The perspective theory proposes that "the illusion figures suggest depth by perspective," an undefined term in this case (Gregory 1966, 145).

Each of these theories makes proposals about the workings of eye and mind but begins from an excessively schematic description of the figure said to be catalyzing those workings. To Gregory, the arrow illusion "is simply a pair of arrows whose shafts are of equal length, one having outgoing and the other ingoing arrowheads at each end. The one with the outgoing heads looks longer although they are both in fact the same length" (Gregory 1966, 140).

More to the point, the line that looks longer occurs in the figure that *is* longer: the figure with the outgoing arrow heads is taller than that with the ingoing heads. The Müller-Lyer arrow illusion is not an error of vision. It is an error in the estimation of length. Any investigation of it ought to seek an understanding of the rules followed in estimating size. That these rules are not efficient is evident. Human beings saw the sun, moon, and stars for millennia without correctly estimating the sizes or distances of these objects.

Double Entendre as Illusion

Optical illusions other than the Muller-Lyer arrows follow a similar pattern of defeating commonplace expectations. Many involve ambiguous figures, which can be read or interpreted in more than one way. These illusions are less illusory than they are parallels to verbal puns, in which a single word is susceptible to multiple interpretations. Some illusions in this class play on the conventions of perspective. Examples include the cubes, ambiguously both concave and convex, that appear to "jump" from one state to the other (figure 17-2).

Which end of the lines forming a contour for the sides of the cubes ought to be regarded as farther away? Alternating the reading, which the viewer can easily learn to do at will, toggles the cube's state between the illusions of concavity and convexity. The fascinating limit—a bona fide visual limit—is that the cubes cannot be seen as simultaneously concave and convex.

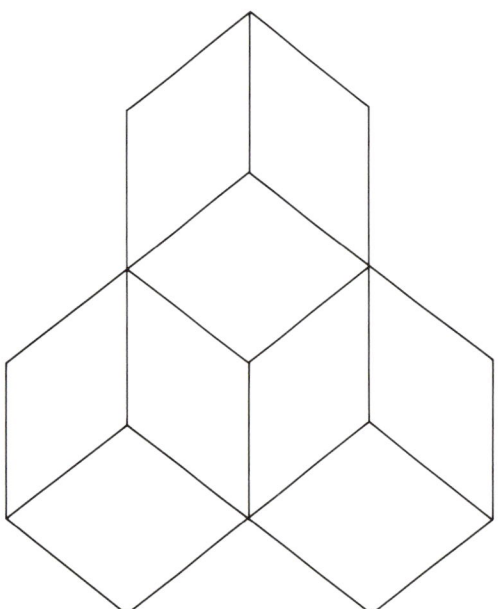

Figure 17-2. Cube illusion. A line drawing of a convex cube is geometrically congruent with a line drawing of a concave cube.

The ability to appear two different ways is not unique to the cube illusion, and it invariably indicates two different interpretations are involved. I have ridden the New York subway when I was in a bad state of mind. Other people in the car looked menacing and dangerous. When I was able to quiet my mind, the people looked ordinary and decent. The people in the car did not change. My eyes did not change. My interpretation changed.

In the cube illusion, we assume the eye is seeing incorrectly in noticing that lines on a planar surface are susceptible to more than one reading. We do not assume the ear is hearing incorrectly in catching homophones, words similar in sound and perhaps also in spelling that nonetheless have different meanings. If a possibility for multiple readings exists, noticing that possibility can scarcely be characterized as an error.

Verbal puns and their mechanisms have been more thoroughly investigated than the visual double entendre often seen in optical illusions. In *Jokes and Their Relation to the Unconscious* (1905), Freud explored the theory that jokes and puns violate psychosexual taboos. Puns more immediately violate language taboos. They confound expectations about how words should be chosen and aggregated into sentences.

The telling evidence that play on words defeats expectation (the expectation that a given word in a given sentence shall have a single meaning) is the degree to which word play annoys some listeners. They lack the sense of humor to feel at ease in a world in which objects stubbornly refuse to behave as they ought to. Spoken syllables can refuse to comply with an expectation that they point to a single word with one meaning. A picture of a concave cube *can* look exactly like a picture of a convex cube, no matter how strongly we feel that it ought to be one or the other.

What expectations are involved in the cube illusion? First, we expect three-dimensional space to behave like a rigid grid in which *near* and *far* never exchange positions. If a camel is farther from me than a penguin and I do not change my position, space cannot "flip" so that the penguin is farther than the camel. Second, we expect pictures on two-dimensional surfaces to behave as if they were counterfeits of the objects they depict. If object *a* has certain qualities, we expect a picture of object *a* to show these qualities. Finally, we expect that if object *a* is not object *b*, a picture of object *a* is not a picture of object *b*.

These expectations seem to have the force of the self-evident. Yet an inadequate conception of the phenomenological world supports them, a conception that fails to properly discriminate between three-dimensionality and two-dimensionality. When dealing with images on planar surfaces, say, a picture of a cube, each of the three expectations is either dead wrong or irrelevant. To deny this by insisting, instead, that the picture is wrong or is seen wrong is untenable. It suggests a reluctance to make peace with visual reality by allowing it to be what it is. It is not conceptual reality, the reality that we imagine.

With regard to the first expectation, is three-dimensional space a rigid grid in which *near* and *far* have fixed positions? The answer is immaterial because the nature of three-dimensional space is not at issue in the cube illusion. Pictorial space, a flat plane, has two dimensions. Because anything flat, such as the surface of a piece of paper, lacks depth, *near* and *far* (which refer to depth) are arbitrary or meaningless concepts.

To prove that *near* and *far* exist only as a matter of interpretation on flat surfaces, draw a straight line on a piece of paper. Which end of the line is farther off in the distance? As no distance exists on the flat surface, choose whichever answer you want: (A) neither end, or (B) whichever you label "more distant."

The second expectation incorrectly assumes a one-to-one relationship between object and image, between a three-dimensional cube and a picture of a cube. But images are not tied to objects by invisible strings. Pictorial images are marks on a surface, entities in their own right and not surrogates for the objects represented. Each of the several forms of the cube illusion is a diagram on a planar surface. Each has the attributes of a diagram, not the attributes of a cube.

Some people resist the idea that, say, a picture of a distant mountain in a Renaissance painting is just spots of paint on a canvas. They want to call the image an illusion of a mountain and theorize about what the term means. I conclude they want a label for the paint spots that includes the word *mountain*. This creates a literary link between the paint spots and their conception of the actual mountain, even if no actual mountain ever existed and the artist imagined the scene. These people know how to think about mountains but not about colors on flat surfaces.

The third expectation incorrectly assumes that because a concave cube is not a convex cube no picture can depict both at once. The expectation is dead wrong in this case, though the error is rarely noticed. An outline drawing of a cube that is convex is absolutely indistinguishable from an outline drawing of a cube that is concave. One can be traced from the other, and the drawing, or diagram, can be read either way.

The reading depends on which edge of the cube is assumed to be farther away. If I want neither end farther, I can read the picture as not a cube at all, just a hexagon with three lines radiating from the center to three angles or vertices. Adding shading to the picture does not eliminate the ambiguity. A rigid three-dimensional surface cannot be both concave and complex from the same perspective. But a drawing or projection of a surface of this type follows another set of rules. A single picture, like a single word, can have multiple meanings, not just many shades of meaning.

Impossible Figures

In Surrealist art, optical illusions, sometimes combined with puns, are gateways to the unconscious for anarchists. They occur in a formalistic manner in Op Art, displayed for our delectation as if mysteries to plumb. In a class of illusion made familiar through prints by M. C. Escher, pictures are drawn of objects that could not be constructed in a three-dimensional world. They confute the laws of structural mechanics just as other objects that can be drawn—unicorns, sphinxes, dragons, angels, and mermaids—confute the laws of biology (figure 17-3).

Irreconcilable with our tactile conception of reality, the structurally impossible figures are linked at a remove with incommensurable numbers, discovered by the Pythagoreans when it was found that lines could be constructed that could not be measured. The Pythagoreans were upset to discover that their expectations had been wrong. To their credit, they did not argue that the unmeasurable lines (say, the diagonal of a square with one-inch sides) were illusions or not really there.

Because the term is used arbitrarily, Escher's impossible figures are called optical illusions and drawings of unicorns are not. The drawings teach us not to expect a two-dimensional world to match a three-dimensional world. They also teach that a two-dimensional universe is not subject to more stringent limits just because it has fewer dimensions. Pictures can be drawn of objects that cannot or do not exist in the three-dimensional world—objects we will never bump into. We all know that from seeing pictures of unicorns, angels, and dragons.

Escher's pictures of impossible figures, like other artists' pictures of unicorns, are real in that they fit the definition of real pictures. Each is a two-dimensional configuration. Their only limit is that the marks on the planar surface depict what could not or does not exist in the three-dimensional world. The impossible figures defeat the arbitrary expectation that what cannot exist in three dimensions (and therefore cannot be integrated with our conception of reality) cannot exist in any form anywhere.

If illusion (or delusion) is a label applied to that which contradicts expectations, the immediate pointing is to the provisional nature of human knowledge. What we know never consists of more than what we think we know at the moment. Picking and choosing our facts, we construct our private and collective pictures of reality. Over the centuries, facts that did not fit, including many about color and vision, were disposed of by labeling them *illusions*. This banished them to a conceptual limbo of facts thought not worth considering.

For Descartes (1596–1650), that objects known to be large look small when seen from a distance was a delusion of the senses. Yet the mechanics of perspective had been understood in the visual arts for a hundred and fifty years before Descartes was born. Because perspective can be given an optical, not simply a mechanical, explanation (the explanation concerns how rays of light pass through a lens), the question is where the delusion lies. We cannot reasonably say rays of light are deluded when they persist in passing through lenses (whether glass lenses or the living lens of the eye) in one manner rather than another.

The assumption that anything ought to look like "what it really is" is baseless, especially since our ideas are often unclear about what things are. Equally baseless is that any object

Figure 17-3. Impossible figure illusion. Just as lines that are incommensurable (impossible to measure) can be constructed, figures that are impossible to construct can also be drawn.

ought to look the same under all conditions, without regard to such variables as viewing distance and changes in illumination, without regard, in short, for the relativistic aspects of visual space, time, and color. Not finding what we expect, we feel comfortable concluding that something is wrong with our eyes. That something is wrong, instead, with our thinking is more difficult to consider.

In the ideal world envisioned by Descartes—indeed, demanded as if it were superior to our deluded domain—nobody would know whether it was day or night, because the colors of objects would remain unchangingly "what they really are." Nobody would be able to judge distances, because all objects would unvaryingly look "the size they really are." And we would all fry to a crisp. The sun, showing itself in this crowded world as large as it really is, would for consistency be as hot as it really is, or as hot as it would feel if not millions of miles away.

I see few advantages in this transcendental nonsense world. Perhaps people could derive moralistic satisfaction from its putative revelation of "what things really are." They might be relieved to discover, at last, a world in which what they saw outside their heads nicely matched up with ideas inside their heads. They could interpret this as a freeing from the delusion of the senses, a flight upward to realms of higher knowledge. Yet the only higher knowledge is that we cannot demand from the world a truth other than that it presents us.

The Geometry of Visual Space

We cannot regard color thoughtfully without realizing that visual space, the space of flat surfaces, is unique. This space has only length and width, and no depth. As optical illusions teach, visual space cannot be understood in terms of rules that apply to three-dimensional space and often fails to conform to our conception of

three-dimensional reality. Visual space is a two-dimensional world with a reality of its own.

Less sensational indicators of the unique nature of visual space are more profound than, say, the Hering illusion. Euclid's fifth axiom implies that any given line has only one parallel passing through a particular point. Therefore, parallel lines never meet. But parallel lines meet, as anyone can see, in railroad tracks receding to a horizon. In perspective drawings, the converging of parallel lines—that they can be nonparallel—is tacitly acknowledged.

Today a ray of light is often regarded as the ideal straight line. Parallel rays of light are not always parallel either. Illustrations in books on optics diagram the diverging and converging of parallel rays of light passing through lenses. Space in Euclidean geometry (a space in which parallel lines never meet) is not consistent with visual space. The inconsistency is not resolved in projective geometry, which undertakes to explain what occurs when shapes on a spherical surface are projected onto a plane. Part of the ambiguity in the Euclidean system, which prevents its reconciliation with the geometry of vision, is the fixed orientation of its picture plane. Like the far walls of rooms in Vermeer's paintings, the Euclidean plane lies perpendicular to the observer's sight line and is presented as incapable of rotation in most cases.

Geometry gives us our conception of three-dimensional space, in which we believe, say, that parallel lines are always parallel. They stay the same (parallel under all conditions) and never meet. Descartes, regarding perspective effects as delusions, was assuming or asserting the Euclid's fifth axiom is right and what we see is wrong. Why is space in geometry inconsistent with space as we see it? Is Euclid's fifth axiom wrong? Does it need further refinement?

After generations of mathematicians had puzzled over whether Euclid's fifth axiom was more properly an axiom or a theorem (derivable from the four axioms that precede it) and whether it could be proved, it was discarded. The gesture opened the door to the non-Euclidean geometries. Carl Friedrich Gauss (1777–1855), János Bolyai (1802–60), and Nikolay I. Lobachevsky (1792–1856) developed hyperbolic geometry. Bernhard Riemann (1826–66) developed spherical non-Euclidean geometry. Felix Klein (1849–1925) proved that these and other alternate geometries were each logically as valid as Euclid's.

The non-Euclidean geometries were not inspired by the meeting of parallel lines at the vanishing point in perspective systems. Nor was the inspiration the meeting of, say, railroad tracks in the far distance in nature. The railroad tracks and other perspective effects are interesting to artists and architects. Art had traveled the same path as mathematics without notice, relying on visual rather than mathematical reasoning. Attempts to represent perspective phenomena in art date back to the Romans, long before development of the alternate geometries. By Descartes's day, books were in print on perspective, and any competent artist understood the system. The remaining question is whether Euclid's basic assumptions, not just the fifth axiom, can be adjusted to more easily reconcile them to what we see.

Point and Line to Plane

In a usual manner of imagining the foundations of geometry, a single point is thought to create a line by moving in space. Nothing need be assumed other than the point, its movement, and the direction of this movement (figure 17-4).

The difficult question is how that line develops into a plane. It might move laterally, creating a plane indistinguishable from an infinite number of parallel lines by lying alongside one another. Like the sheets of paper on which we write our thoughts, this Euclidean

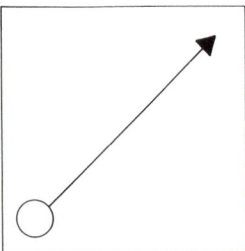

Figure 17-4. A Euclidean point creating a line. A line segment is the path traced by a moving point, which one must assume had an origin. Whether the origin is in space-time or in "infinity" is irrelevant.

plane is rectilinear. Irrespective of whether it has edges, it possesses vertical and horizontal axes at right angles to one another. They correspond to the respective directions of movement of the original point and the line derived from it (figure 17-5).

This familiar means of developing plane from line is unnecessarily complicated. Both ends of the line are assumed to move, yet only one need move. The other can stay fixed. The line's lateral movement is also logically inconsistent. We had intended to follow the travels of *one* Euclidean point through space. The line's lateral movement compels us to assume

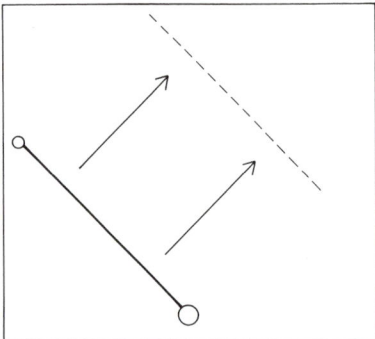

Figure 17-5. A Euclidean line creating a plane. An infinite number of parallel lines lie alongside one another to form the Euclidean plane, as if the original line had moved laterally, with neither end fixed.

an infinity of other Euclidean points, required to explain the infinity of parallel lines that form the plane. Each of these lines is distinct from the original line, in that it passes through no points on the original line.

In one way of imagining the construction, the infinity of additional points is required to provide points of origin for the infinity of parallel lines. In another way, the infinity of points are those through which, respectively, each member of the infinity of parallel lines passes. In either case, the infinity of additional points is inconsistent in a system that proposed to begin with one point and never explained why more were needed. More troubling, each of the infinity of parallel lines extends infinitely. How can the lines all extend to a single infinity if they never meet? We are compelled to accept an infinity of infinities, a messy conception.

Imagine a different way of creating a plane. Only one end of the line moves. The end corresponding to the point of origin remains permanently fixed. Movement, given these limits, can only be radially around the point of origin, as if the line were a spoke on a spinning wagon wheel moving radially around the hub (figure 17-6). In everyday terms, an automobile (the moving point) starts out from Washington (the fixed point). The car drives down a perfectly straight road as far as, say, New York (any distance will do), and then decides to change direction. The car moves in a huge circle that finally brings it back to New York. Washington is the center of the circle. The distance from Washington to New York is the radius of the circle.

A plane produced in this manner is curvilinear, again without regard to whether it possesses edges. One of its "axes" corresponds to all possible radii of a circle. The other consists of an infinite number of concentric circles moving outward from the original point. Whether or not axes of a coordinate system in a usual sense, each of these respective axes

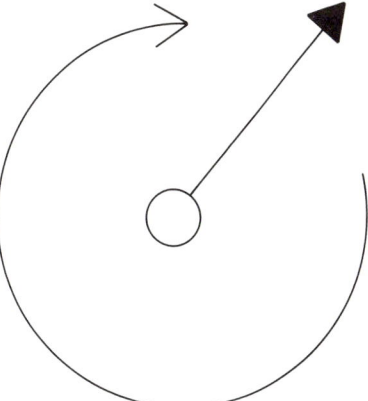

Figure 17-6. A non-Euclidean plane. If the line is assumed to remain fixed at its point of origin, its movement is limited to circumambulating that point. The plane created (or traversed) has curvilinear rather than rectilinear coordinates. It can be more easily reconciled with visual (phenomenological) events and with the rules of mechanical perspective.

corresponds to the respective directions of movement of point and line (linear, radial).

If the process of rotating the line around its fixed point of origin is extended to three dimensions, the volume created is spherical, an outgrowth of both the fixed point that forms its center and the great circle of its cross section. Returning to the moving automobile, assume that Washington (the fixed point) is floating in outer space. The automobile (the moving point) has driven as far as New York, also floating in space. The automobile is tied to Washington by a taut, unbreakable chain. The automobile, which can fly through the air, is given the task of driving through every point in space that will keep the chain taut. The volume described will be a sphere.

The archetypal Euclidean volume is cubic rather than spherical. The cube is created when the Euclidean plane, that infinity of parallel lines, moves at a right angle to itself through an additional infinity of parallel lines (figure 17-7). Thus, a troubling aspect of geom-

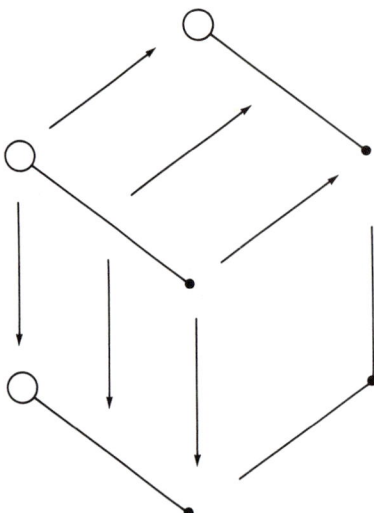

Figure 17-7. Euclidean volume (a cube). The prototypical Euclidean volume is the cube, formed when the plane repeats the line's motion in moving laterally through space. Its infinite parallel lines never meet, or they meet only at an infinity that is metaphysical because it can never be reached.

etry is its inconsistency on the question of how a cube (cubic space or cubic volume) can be created at all. If a Euclidean plane is synonymous with an infinity of parallel lines, we cannot reasonably have more than this infinity of lines. Yet this excess of infinities must be assumed to extend the plane into a third dimension.

The problem is avoided in creating a sphere because one end of the moving line remains fixed at its initial point of origin. Constructing a sphere requires an infinity of lines radiating from a fixed center. But we need neither more lines than this infinity nor fewer lines (figure 17-8).

While lip service is paid to Euclidean geometry, we ignore its tenets in imagining models of the world. The big bang theory, for example, proposes that the universe was originally a singularity: a point that preceded time and space. We are asked to imagine the explosion

of the universe as we know it out of this singular point. I doubt anyone envisions the Ur-point moving due south to form a line; thence the line traveling east-west to form a plane; thence up-down to constitute a cubic volume, with the requisite x, y, z coordinates. If only because more consistent with what we know about explosions, the easier image is of radiation in all directions from a center.

Visual Space as a Circularity

Parallel lines in railroad tracks meet in the distance less because the senses are deluded than because the logic of Euclidean geometry, which directs many of our expectations about the nature of the world, falls short of providing a reliable picture. Irrespective of whether this is the sense in which space is said to be curved in theoretical physics, space as we see it behaves as if it were spherical: a radiation from a fixed point, or vanishing point, toward

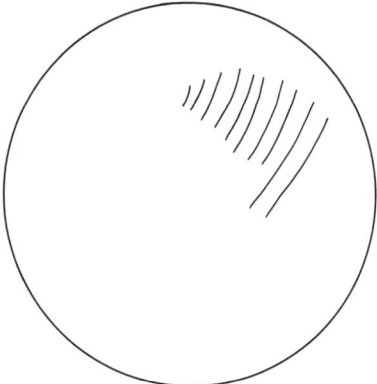

Figure 17-8. Non-Euclidean volume (a sphere). The sphere, the prototypical volume for non-Euclidean space, is formed when the line, with one end fixed, moves through all possible points in space other than this fixed point of origin. In spherical (visual) space, parallel lines meet at an infinity identifiable as the center of the sphere, the vanishing point of a perspective system, or the point from which the Ur-line originated.

which receding parallels converge. That no tactile equivalent can be found for this visual converging is immaterial. The reason I cannot obtain verification that parallel lines really meet at vanishing points on a horizon is that my arms are not long enough to reach the horizon. And the horizon recedes as I move closer to it.

Vanishing points, which lie on the horizon or above it, are assumed in systems of perspective drawing. What is a vanishing point (a point at which railroad tracks meet) in terms of the phenomenological world? Although more easily understood as an optical manifestation than through geometrical analogy, the vanishing point is not an entirely subjective phenomenon. Just as I cannot see red as blue, I cannot by effort of will relocate the vanishing point from where it happens to be. But neither can I turn my back on it. Railroad tracks that recede to a vanishing point in the east, when I look in that direction, will recede to a vanishing point in the west when I look the opposite way.

As if space were the ultimate fluid, or as if no privileged coordinate system existed, the vanishing point is always central to my visual field, controlled by the direction in which I look. It can even be more than one point, as in two-point and three-point perspective systems. In the great sphere of visual space, any point, anywhere, can function as a center depending on which way I look.

I conclude that the vanishing point, though prospectively any and all points in space, is a single point. The likely candidate (because I can move it around at will) is the focal point of the lens in my eye, projected outward as if it existed in a far distance rather than on the visual plane. The focal point of any lens is an attribute of that lens. We need to look through the lens to be aware of it. Yet the focal point never appears to reside in the interior of the lens.

The spherical nature of visual space, which allows parallel lines to meet at a vanishing point, might be regarded as an outward projection of the spherical shape of the human eyeball and the focal point of its lens. Possibly, in a world where intelligent beings had eyeballs shaped like cubes, Euclidean space would be more consistent with visual space and parallel lines would never meet. That world would require different optical laws than ours, and I will not conjecture about what they might be.

Nonconverging Parallels

We cannot leave the subject of parallel lines without acknowledging the many occasions on which they fail to converge. Railroad tracks viewed from an airplane flying above them look parallel, which raises the question of how to explain the vanishing of the vanishing point. Imagining it relocated above my head as I look down from the airplane is not a satisfactory solution. It says nothing more than that the vanishing point cannot be found within my field of vision.

In a better model, imagine an opaque plane lying perpendicular to the line of sight—the orientation assumed for the picture plane of Euclidean geometry. This opaque plane blocks the vanishing point from view by preventing our seeing the distance into which parallel lines might recede. Like Newtonian physics, Euclidean geometry represents a limited case, the single case in which the spherical geometry of vision is occluded by the Euclidean wall.

If we always looked down on railroad tracks from airplanes, the tracks would never meet at a vanishing point on the horizon. Euclidean space would correspond to visual space, and the fifth axiom would hold. Euclidean geometry is excessively idealized, which is why its concepts confused Descartes. I find it odd that this also means Euclidean geometry gives its best explanation of the world we see when applied looking down from airplanes. Its conception of space no longer works when the airplane lands.

Everything we see, as has often been said, presents itself as both color and form. Yet conceptually, or through long habit, we separate one from the other, relying on geometry to tell us about shape and perspective (regarded as objective) but not about colors (regarded as subjective). The distinction is artificial. The horizon and the vanishing points of perspective systems (and of perspective geometry) have no phenomenological reality as objects that can be touched. Both, like color, are subjective, two-dimensional manifestations never exactly the same for two observers or two cameras. The horizon *is* a color phenomenon, perceivable only as an abutting of the colors of the sky with those of the earth.

Might we, reasoning from this, develop a new geometry that began with the colors we see; that assumed straight lines are paths traversed by rays of light, and that moved on to deduce the rules of geometry as we know them? This would be a strange kind of geometry, blending phenomena we now regard as psychological with others we now regard as mathematical. Or it might be regarded as a joining of two kinds of geometry. The Munsell and Ostwald systems for organizing colors, like many simpler systems that preceded them, envision color solids that are geometrical constructions. If color relationships can be explained, at least to an extent, in geometrical terms, then why cannot this explanation be incorporated into Euclidean geometry or into any of the several non-Euclidean geometries?

Extension in the Visual Field

As you ramble on through life, brother,
Whatever be your goal,
Keep your eye upon the doughnut
And not upon the hole.

Mayflower Coffee Shops

Color is unique to the visual field, in that it cannot be seen perceived anywhere else. It is also the basic element in the visual field. Images of objects are made of color. So are images of the spaces in and around them, a difference between what we touch and what we see. In three-dimensional terms, a doughnut from a bakery shop is a three-dimensional object. Its hole is a volumetric space that is empty. The two-dimensional world of visual imagery has no doughnuts, but it has images of doughnuts. We call these images *doughnuts* as an expediency, and the expediency sometimes causes confusion.

Holes and Spaces

Visually, the hole in the doughnut (or in any image of a doughnut) looks like an area of color, as does the doughnut itself. The colors of the hole are attributable to the plate, table, or other objects lying behind or beyond the doughnut. Although conceived of as empty in three-dimensional terms, holes never look empty in the visual field. Color uniformly permeates the images of both objects and the spaces between them. Everything we see, as has been repeated, is some color or collection of colors.

That the visual field is devoid of holes or empty spaces means we cannot see them as such. A visual gap, by its nature, is visually imperceptible. We need not, in pondering this mystery, rely only on the example of the nonemptiness of images of doughnut holes. A blind spot is known to exist at the center of the retina. The evidence, which is compelling, is that no rods or cones are found at the junction of optic nerve and retina. But the eye's blind spot is invisible: without phenomenological consequence as a visual field phenomenon. What we see has no gap, hiatus, or empty place in its center. The visual field, in other words, does not ordinarily give the impression of looking like a doughnut.

A geometric or topological logic underlies the absence of holes in the visual field, causing the all-pervasiveness of its color. Holes always go somewhere, whether into things, under them, or behind them. In the three-dimensional world, holes are experienced as such because things can be put into them, an experiential confirmation of their emptiness. Doorways into a third dimension, holes remain for this reason inconceivable (and also imperceptible) in a planar, or two-dimensional, realm. Nothing lies behind the images of the mirror, the eye, the photograph, the movie film, or the picture plane of a painting. A hole in the two-dimensional continuum of any image has no place to go.

The three-dimensional world in which volumetric forms are located is a discontinuous domain of objects and empty spaces. The two-dimensional realm of images is both immaterial and homogeneous in this immateriality. As Maurice Denis remarked about the picture plane of a painting, images in general are aggregates of color spots. If not recognized as such, they are misunderstood as windows in a wall. The viewer assumes an imperative to look into, or through, the imagined window toward an imagined third dimension, a charming but insubstantial idea.

The colored images of objects cannot be pierced to gain access to any metaphysical essence hidden behind the skinlike surface. Whether the images are those of the visual field or of the picture planes of mirrors, photographs, and paintings, we cannot look through a two-dimensional configuration because nothing lies behind it. Anything behind an image, like anything in front of it, is not part of the image, the limitation that defines imagery as two-dimensional.

I sometimes think the idea that breaking a mirror brings bad luck is promoted to discourage inquisitive children from smashing mirrors to determine whether this is the way to get inside. Expectation is offended by the discovery that images have a front but no back, an outside without an inside. As human beings, we remain forever outside the image, in front of it and never behind it. Or images are always in front of us. We lose touch with them if they move behind us or to any other location. I cannot see what I am not looking at. I cannot look at what is not in front of my face.

The obdurateness of surface is not confined to the surface we know as the visual field. What we are able to touch, in the three-dimensional world, is confined in most cases to the curved planar surfaces of objects. These surfaces, because two-dimensional, have little in common with the volumetric forms that they cover, which in a sense cannot be reached. Cutting an apple in half is less a journey inside the apple than a creation of additional exterior surfaces, a revelation of further aspects of the apple's image. Like the surface of the outside of the apple, the surface of the inside is colored, in this case not in the same colors.

The Extension of Color and Form

Within the visual field, the most striking characteristic that color and two-dimensional (visually perceived) shapes have in common is dimension or extension, the ability to vary in age and size. Objects, including perceived color spots or aggregates of color spots, become older through extension in time. They become larger through extension in space. Spatial extension is reversible in theory. Anything that expands can contract. Temporal extension is more complex. In theoretical physics, Feynman diagrams show electrons and other particles moving backward and forward in time. But in the everyday world, what has been called the arrow of time points in one direction only, a message conveyed by the nature of death. All life moves onward to die, and the dead do not return. The future, in simpler terms than ordinarily used to define it, is when we will die. The past is where those already dead can be found.

The changes we explain by attributing them to the passing of time may need a better explanation. To ask whether time moves forward or backward in the everyday world is meaningless. No criterion exists for the difference. In vision, as in the corporeal realm, change or the passing of time cannot be halted. Among visual pathologies, both physiological and psychosomatic, no such thing occurs as a person afflicted by a selective inability to see motion. Cinematographers can freeze a single frame and theoretically hold it forever. The functioning eye cannot similarly escape time, which behaves in vision as in the world of three dimensions. Either we see in terms of time (the forms that are seen move), or we do not see at all.

Every object appears to have constraints to its potentiality for spatiotemporal extension. Human beings rarely grow taller than seven feet or live longer than a century. Jain mythology attributes a spiritual significance to these limits. In the first descending period of the Jain cycle, human beings are said to have been six miles tall; they had 256 (or 28) ribs. In the second period, their height was reduced to four miles, their ribs to 128 (27); in the third period, two miles and 64 (26) ribs. Progressive shrinkage reduced human beings to the size of our era. In future, people will shrink to eighteen inches, have 8 ribs, and live fewer than twenty years. After this, the order of the epochs will reverse. Men and women will grow progressively larger, with more ribs and longer life spans.

A familiar science-fiction plot toys with the related idea of a world endangered by something devoid of constraints on its extension. The malevolent (or Malthusian) animal, plant, insect, virus, rock, or substance threatens to grow larger or reproduce itself (a way of increasing) until it crowds out forms of life other than itself. *The Incredible Shrinking Man*, a classic science-fiction tale made into a movie, imagines extension in a reverse direction: the protagonist shrinks smaller and smaller, apparently ad infinitum.

Extension as Becoming

Extension is dependent on becoming, which implies absolute fluidity. Its implied opposite is being, which suggests absolute stasis. Although the objects of the everyday world become older, larger, or smaller, Zeno's paradox can be expanded to argue that extension, like motion, is impossible. No movement exists if we merely rest at various points in time. Nor, by a similar reasoning, can objects become larger or smaller. They are just one size at one point in time, another size at another.

Pursuing this reasoning leads to a model of the universe based on a reel of motion picture film. Each frame, separate from any previous, is an entirely new picture. The world would be in a unique state of being every instant, never the same as a moment ago nor connected to any worlds of the past. This vision is the ultimate existential extension of Hooke's argument that Newton's prism manufactured the spectral colors.

Despite its intuitive appeal and precedents in religious and philosophical thought, this vision has rarely commended itself in the West. Stability cannot be presumed for scientific laws unless inherent in the world to which these laws apply. From a scientific point of view, we find it expedient to think of the world as always the same (or always the same even though it changes), rather than continually different. When regarded as immutable despite change, the world acquires a history, a record of the past and a key to predicting the future, a talisman against terrors and uncertainties. The cost of the talisman is loss of sensitivity to those aspects of the experiential world difficult to conform to the system.

Assuming that extension exists, the extension of the visual field is limited. Unless I turn my head, change location, or use a mirror, I cannot see objects behind me. Nor can I see behind objects in front of me. Constrained by the human condition, I see the objects in front of my face and only that portion of the surface of each object that happens to be facing me.

The limits of the visual field are measurable and fairly stable for any individual. Measuring from the pupil of the eye, the average human being sees about sixty-five degrees on the nasal side, ninety degrees on the temporal side. In a small number of subjects, the size of the visual field varies from day to day, for some reason that has not been determined (Fuchs [1908] 1924, 256). In hemianopsia, caused by pituitary abnormalities, half the field for each eye ceases to function (Fuchs [1908] 1924, 263).

The fish-eye lens and other wide-angle camera lenses have a more inclusive field of view than the human eye. But, just as writing an exhaustive autobiography is impossible because the author will have more experiences after the autobiography is completed, for any eye or lens to see everything in its surroundings is impossible. Optical and conceptual difficulties prevent our even imagining an eye or lens with such an all-encompassing field of view that it could observe itself observing itself.

The 360-degree fish-eye lens is as constrained as any other. We cannot see what we are not looking at, and the fish-eye lens is not looking at itself. Nor is the lens of a human eye that may be looking through the fish-eye lens on the camera. Pictures made with fish-eye lenses often include the photographer's feet but never the photographer's face.

Mirrors, which the Etruscans and other ancient peoples buried with the dead to ward off evil spirits, partially transcend these optical limits. I can look at myself looking at myself in a mirror. Mirrors are preferred as light-gathering devices for large telescopes precisely because they do that work more efficiently than lenses. Even a mirror is unable to see what lies behind itself, an insurmountable physical limit. A sphere with a mirror surface, reflecting everything around it, is unable to reflect its own interior.

Axiomatically, nobody can see what is not being looked at, and looking at everything is impossible. Something always exists that is not being looked at, a limit integral to lenses and mirrors, not a peculiarity of the human eye. Traditionally, the ability to see everything, or everything at the same time, has been attributed to God or the gods, probably because no all-seeing eye, lens, camera, or mirror exists. Why do the photographers' faces not appear in pictures taken with 360-degree fish-eye lenses? Why do we have to stand in front of a camera, not behind it, to take pictures of ourselves? I suspect that the limit could be expressed in mathematical terms and could be shown to relate to the number of dimensions in our world. Transcending it might require a world with a greater number of dimensions, in which, say, a circle could have more than 360 degrees. From our world, we know only that the 360 degrees swept by the fish-eye lens does not reach everything.

Images have other limits that refer directly to dimension. Images in a mirror, whether regarded as illusions or as reflections, refer to a three-dimensional world but are planar (two-dimensional) themselves. Volumetric space is unable to function as a mirror of an analogous kind, for no three-dimensional mirrors exist that are capable of reflecting four-dimensional space. Nor do we have one-dimensional mirrors that reflect two-dimensional space.

Extension and Size

In tactile terms, the perceived size of an object is the size felt by a moving hand. In visual terms, because of the phenomenon of perspective, a translation is needed. The extension, or perceived size, of any object seen by the unaided eye is accounted for by two factors: the real size of the object and its distance from the viewer. From ten feet away, one person may look larger than another because he or she is larger. But a person five hundred yards in the distance looks smaller than another six feet away, regardless of the size of the people.

Our estimates of the physical size of objects begin with extension, the perceived size of the object relative to other objects in the visual field. An assessment is made of the degree to which visual size is determined by distance, and of the degree to which visual size is determined by the actual dimensions of the object. For very distant objects, color and brightness provide clues to distance, though the clues are neither easy to read nor reliable. A distant mountain appears veiled by blue haze to a greater extent than another mountain nearer the viewer, but the amount of haze varies from day to day. Distant stars look more dim than those nearer, but a bright star can be farther away and larger than a small, dim, nearby star.

Because the environment provides visual clues to size, input into the system can be manipulated. The clues can be tampered with. The colonnade with false perspective by the Baroque architect Francesco Borromini creates an illusion of greater depth than is present.

The Distorted Room, constructed by the American psychologist A. Ames, tempts the observer to wrong conclusions about the real sizes of objects (Gregory 1966, 178–179; Ittelson 1952). Its playing with perspective invites incorrect estimation of viewer–object distance.

The misestimation has a subjective aspect. As the Belgian Surrealist René Magritte learned from Hieronymus Bosch, a sense of the uncanny is created when objects look greatly out of scale with the size we expect them to be.

Like the Ames room, the depth perception experiments of James J. Gibson shed less light on the nature of perception than on rules for reasoning about what is perceived (Gibson 1950, 1968). If the distance of an object is incorrectly estimated, an inversely related mistake about its real size cannot be avoided. The ancients Greeks believed the fixed stars were small and relatively close to the earth. We believe them to be large and at enormous distances. At issue are differing game plans for rationalizing extension: for balancing the books by explaining the size that the stars appear to be in the visual fields of human beings looking at them.

We have no subjective sense of the absolute size of a visual image on the retina of the eye, which must be exceedingly small. If I saw the page of a book no larger than the fraction of an inch the image occupies on the retina of my eye, the print would be too small to read. Because a sense of the absolute size of visual images on the retina is absent, a sophisticated algorithm for juggling ratios is likely involved in estimating sizes and distances. The process never intrudes on consciousness as mathematical, and animals judge sizes and distances that interest them as competently as human beings.

The microscope and the telescope increase the visual size of objects, their extension within the visual field. The microscope enlarges objects otherwise too small to be seen. The telescope enlarges those too distant (therefore, too small) to be seen. In either case, lenses and curved mirrors supplement, or increase, the focal length of the lens in the eye of the human being using the instrument. The mechanism suggests that the experimenter cannot be separated from an experiment.

Whether anything is seen through a microscope or telescope, and what is seen, depends on the lens of the eye looking through the instrument, a vital part of the machinery when an observation is made. The limit is not overcome by replacing the eye with a camera because a human eye is still required to look at what the camera records.

Enlarging is not always sufficient, or required, when an object is difficult to see. To see large bodies in their entirety, a mechanism is needed to make them look small enough to fit within the visual field within a single moment. Astronomers and cosmologists, confined by this limit, can offer no more than conjecture, however sophisticated, about the shape of the universe. Direct visual verification, if possible in any ordinary sense, could be provided only by an individual observing the universe from its outside, from a sufficient distance to see the entire system at once.

Because systems cannot be seen from the outside by an observer located inside, human beings had no way to confirm the roundness of the earth visually until the twentieth century. Astronauts see this roundness from outer space, and we see the photographs they took. Descartes's opinion to the contrary notwithstanding, delusion of the senses was always a poor explanation for why the round earth looks flat to creatures living on its surface. The barrier is topological or perspectival and relates to the nature of coordinate systems.

How any object, including the earth, looks depends on the perspective from which this object is seen. We cannot reasonably expect that an object viewed from a point on its surface will look the same as it would if observed from a point beyond or outside that surface. Different conditions—different points in a coordinate system—suggest differences in how things look. Rather than deceiving us, vision probably provides very keen insight into the nature of the phenomenological world, its

mathematical bases and constraints. We do not know how to read the signs, how to arrive at a sufficiently sophisticated understanding of what we see.

The conception of an arrow of time, in the physical sciences, expresses the idea that time moves in one direction only. An arrow of vision exists and is also one-directional, though this second arrow receives no attention. I can look in only one direction at one time. I cannot be inside a system looking out at the same time that I am outside the system looking in. I cannot be behind a camera lens and in front of it at the same time. Photographers' faces do not appear in photos taken by fish-eye lenses for the same reason that the earth when seen from its surface looks different than when seen from outer space. The issue is the arrow of vision, which allows us to look into a coordinate system in which we see as far as the vanishing point of that system. I can choose to look east. I can choose to look west. I am not given the choice of looking east and west at the same time.

The Edge of the Visual Field

Color and form display dissimilar attributes when extended to the edges of the visual field. Color behaves as if it were a substance rather than an object. In an important visual dynamic, seeing nothing but a single color is possible, as in seeing the darkness of the night. We cannot see, or imagine seeing, nothing except a single form.

The behavior of two-dimensional forms in planar universes differs from that of three-dimensional forms in volumetric space. In figure 18-1, a small black disc grows progressively larger in its white field. At maximum extension the disc, which fills the field entirely, is no longer identifiable as such; it is now a black rectangle. No visual clues exist to its original nature, which can only be understood

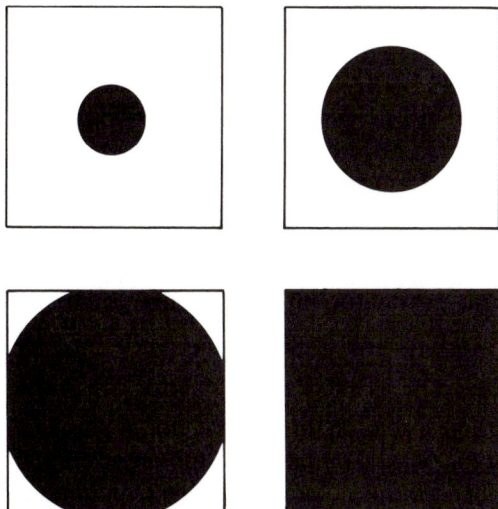

Figure 18-1. A form growing larger in a field. A form that expands to breach the perimeter of its field merges with that field, or becomes indistinguishable from it. The form cannot be measured "within" the field.

by knowing its history. In effect, it no longer has that nature, which was simply a temporary attribute.

Although the black rectangle gives no reason for suspecting it might have been part of a circle, a person asked to draw a rectangular segment that is part of a circle would be compelled to arrive at the figure of a rectangle. A form extended to fill any planar field, or to exceed its limits, is no longer identifiable as the original form. For this reason, the black circle is no longer a circle in the final drawing of figure 18-1. Its color, which has undergone no corresponding change, remains black throughout. In two-dimensional universes, form behaves in extension as a variable, or is metamorphic. Color behaves as a constant, or is immutable.

Traditional intimations that the constancy of color holds in both time and space can be accounted for by the difficulty of imagining any other condition. Genesis proceeds from the separation of light and darkness to tell about the creation of a multitude of forms and spirits. We are not told that God created colors, numbers, or himself. Nor are clues provided about how any member of this threesome came into being. Either all three always existed, or another creation story explains them. Why are we not told how these three items were created? I see a relationship among them on two levels, a relationship that might have interested mystics, although I know of no evidence that it did.

On the first level, the darkness of the primordial void is unimaginable without a prior assumption of color (through which its extension might have been perceived) and number (by which it might have been measured). Although we never think of the writers of the Old Testament as logicians, a good logical argument might be made that color and number are first things, the necessary prior assumptions that allow us to assume the primordial void. How would God have known the void was there had he not been able to see it (color) and take its measure (number)?

At a second level, relationships among the three uncreated elements point to the kind of paradox that delighted medieval theologians. Or they suggest the children's game that asks whether rock, fire, or water is strongest. Is number greater than color? Is color greater than number? Number, we might say, exceeds color, because we cannot know the color of numbers. But color exceeds number, because we cannot know the number of colors. The deity of the Old Testament, limitless and superior to all else, fits nicely into the picture, perhaps too neatly. Because immeasurable, God exceeds number; because invisible, his "colorlessness" is similarly absolute. In another way of understanding the linkages, Genesis presents us with two voids, the classical antithesis between matter and spirit. The void containing darkness and light, from which the world was made, is matched by the limitless void which is God himself.

Genesis probably hides clues we no longer understand about the reasoning that led human beings to conclude that a colorless, limitless God existed. If this God was discovered by analogical reasoning, the analogy was with empty space. Whether in Genesis or in the modern physical sciences, human beings find it easier to imagine empty space giving birth to forms than forms giving birth to empty space. Thought moves more easily in that direction for two reasons. First, space, which has only extension, is a simpler element than matter, which has both extension and mass. Second, empty space is needed to allow motion, including the gesture of creating a world. No creation myth exists that declares the universe was originally, say, a solid block of stone (or, for that matter, a spot of color). In Buddhism, the idea of forms emerging from empty space is carried to the next logical plateau: the forms, we are told, are illusory, no more substantial than the space from which they arose.

Color, like space, has extension without mass and might be thought of as a visual correlative for the tactile experience of feeling nothing. The link is noticed by modern writers, more often by those writing on color than by those writing on space. It rarely comes to the surface in myth and legend. No creation story tells us, say, that the creator deity was a large blue spot. Genesis comes closest to dealing with color through its two voids: the invisible, colorless void which is God and the other void we imagine as black, or black and white.

Fragmentation

A blue spot that grows larger loses its original size but can retain its original color. The behavior of color as a constant in extension and of two-dimensional form as a variable leads to several visual consequences. Among them, the overall character of a form (unlike the overall character of a color) cannot be determined from small parts of the original unit. The fable of the blind men and the elephant strains too hard at a point that could have been made economically. One blind man feels the ear of the elephant; another, its trunk; the third, its tail. Each generalizes from limited experience, arriving at wrong conclusions. The three blind men are unable to agree about what an elephant looks like.

The protagonists of the story need not be blind. Sighted observers are prone to similar error if similarly unfamiliar with entire elephants. An elephant's ear, which does not feel like an elephant, also does not look like an elephant. Details of a form, even visually perceived details, cannot convey complete information about the form as an entirety. The Egyptians and other early peoples showed a strong preference for depicting human beings and animals in their entirety in art. The preference had an informational aspect. Most animals are bilaterally symmetrical, allowing us to assume that the left side of, say, an elephant's head will look like a mirror image of the right side. No further axes exist, and nobody ever learned what an elephant looks like from seeing only its head.

As if there were a geometry of vision, the limitation has a structural or topological dynamic. Figure 18-2 shows what occurs when the expanding black circle of figure 18-1 disappears into its own field. When the circle passes beyond the perimeter, it can no longer be measured within that field. If we assume that the black field of figure 18-2(A) is part of a large black circle, no criterion exists for determining whether the circle is as shown in 18-2(B) or as in 18-2(C) or otherwise.

Breaching of the perimeter is the significant factor, irrespective of whether the field is entirely filled. In figure 18-3, a black object lies partly inside and partly outside of a white field.

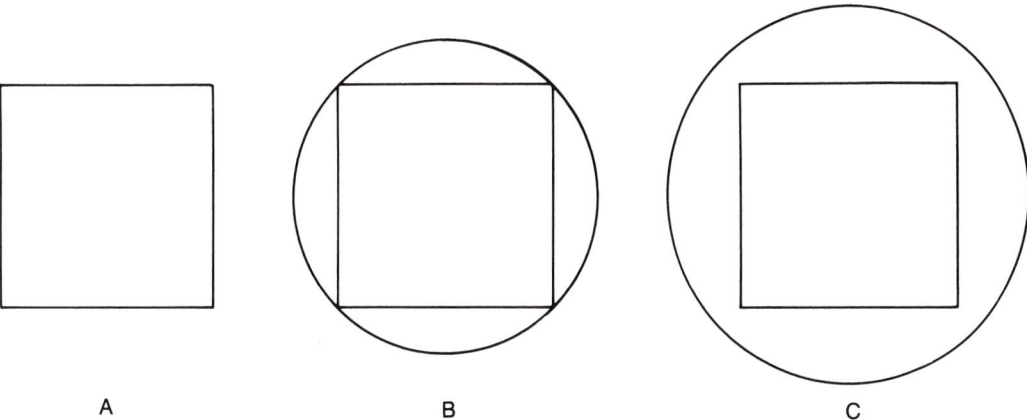

A   B   C

Figure 18-2. A form disappearing into its field. If limited to the confines of the field, we have no criterion for judging the nature of what lies outside. Noncongruent forms may appear visually congruent.

An observer inside the white field, unable to see beyond its edges, cannot determine the surface area of the black object. The observer has no way to discover the shape or size of those parts of the black object that are not accessible, that lie outside the white field. Figures 18-3(B) and 18-3(C) show two possibilities from a limitless number.

Although this is rarely taught as a mathematical rule, areas cannot be measured unless their edges can be located. Nor can volumes be computed unless their surfaces can be found. This is why we have a more exact knowledge of the volumetric size of the earth than of the volumetric size of the universe. Nobody can predict how large a horse is, or what it looks like, from seeing its black tail. But if the horse is known to be a single color, we may correctly infer from the color of the tail that the horse is similarly black. If an area of color is a homogeneous blue, any fragment is as blue as the whole.

Extension has no effect upon color. Nor does fragmentation, reversing the process of extension by dividing an area of homogeneous color into smaller areas. Accommodating this constancy of color, the English language does not encourage referring to the parts, or

details, of, say, blue, green, or lavender. We think of forms, but not colors, in terms of entire forms and details, topologically different categories. If a form is larger than the field in which the form is being viewed, what appears in that field is a detail. Only part of the form is seen, and it may not look like the entire form. We see details of the universe when looking through telescopes, not the entire universe at once. The cosmological principle, which is actually a cosmological assumption, takes a bold conceptual leap. It tells us to assume that the universe looks pretty much the same in all parts. How could anyone be sure of this unless all the parts were seen?

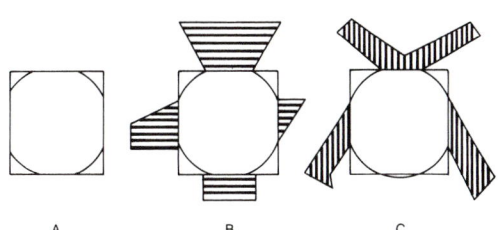

A   B   C

Figure 18-3. Form and area. We cannot measure an area outside a field from within the confines of that field because the edges of the area to be measured cannot be located.

Color in Fragmentation

The division of a drop of water cannot make it less watery, a constancy that holds, in theory, until the molecular level. The division of a blue color spot similarly yields two blue color spots, not two spots each half as blue as the original. But no molecules of blue exist, to be reduced to atoms of something else. And we are not encouraged to ask how long the process of dividing a blue color spot can be continued. A tiny particle of blue paper too small to be seen by the unaided eye would still look blue, I am sure, if examined by a microscope, as blue as it would continue to look if blown up to fill the universe entirely.

Beyond the lower limits of the microscope, the question is whether, like magnetism and thought, subatomic particles, presently known to us through their tracks in cloud chambers, are to be imagined as absolutely inaccessible to vision. Any possibility of seeing them directly implies seeing their colors, because anything that has no color cannot be seen. If the feat is a technological possibility, the easier assumption is that the photons responsible for blue might look blue, rather than some other color. No basis exists for conjecture about the colors of electrons, protons, or neutrons.

Few models exist to guide us on how to reason intelligently in this direction. Because color is correlated with wavelength of light in the physical sciences, conventional wisdom in the sciences holds that color cannot exist for anything, say, an atom, that is smaller than the wavelength of visible light. We need to assume, in that case, that violet objects can be smaller than red objects, because violet has a shorter wavelength. In favor of the assumption, colors fade out in the depths of the ocean in this manner: violet rays penetrate deeper than those of other colors, and the ability of rays of the spectral colors to penetrate ocean water is correlated with wavelength.

A similar phenomenon may occur in air. Although aerial perspective is not customarily explained in this manner, assume that blue and violet rays, known to have a greater power to penetrate deep into water, also penetrate farther than other rays when moving through air. We could then conclude that although objects reflect rays of all colors, only the blue or violet rays reach a distant observer, the reason distant objects look bluish gray. Carrying the thought further, the rays reaching a distant observer may be predominantly ultraviolet, which has a shorter wavelength than violet, looks bluish gray, and ought to have a greater penetrating power than the spectral colors if penetrating power is correlated with wavelength.

Despite these correlations, I am dubious about the wisdom that color cannot exist in objects smaller than the wavelength of visible light. The sticking point, as often, is the status of black and the blackness of the night sky. We assume that we are able to see *nothing*, the name applied to the black color of interstellar space. It would be surprising if the "somethings" imagined floating in the nothing—the subatomic particles suspended in the vacuum—were not similarly colored, even if only similarly black in color.

If a portion of the blackness between the stars were repeatedly subdivided, would it cease to look black? I see no way in which the wavelength of light can have any bearing on the question. Black is not correlated with wavelength and is called an absence of wavelengths. Assume that a portion of the blackness of the space between the stars would continue to look black, no matter how often divided. Would the same be true for a naturally black substance, say, coal?

We cannot, at these frontiers of conjecture, rely on such conceptions as the threshold of vision. The microscope offers evidence that although color is seen, it is more than something seen. Even exceedingly small objects have colors of their own, revealed when the microscope brings them into our field of vision.

CHAPTER 19

Complementarity in the Visual Field

Objects are colored shapes, but one perceives the shapes only because they are colored.

Charles Edward Gauss, The Aesthetic Theories
of French Artists

As is familiarly noted, anything that can be identified as a visual element can be reduced to an aspect of color or form or both. Brightness is color variation. Lines are the edges of forms or occur within them. Motion is an event that happens to forms, a meaningless concept in a formless void.

Should color and form be regarded as complementary classes within the visual field? The concept of complementarity, derived from logic, tells us that complementary classes are disjoint and exhaust their field. This implies three essential conditions. First, no item can belong to both of two complementary classes. Second, every item belongs to one or the other class. Third, the sum of the two complementary classes equals the universal class.

If form and color are complements, this might be represented as in figure 19-1, modeled after the Venn diagrams used in symbolic logic. In the elaborate conventions for reading diagrams of this type, the area of the square inside the circle (identified as form) is the complement of that outside (identified as color). The exploded view reveals the further relationship that is critical: within the visual field, nothing can be both a form and a color if form and color are complements.

A substantial barrier exists to reasoning farther in this direction. *Every* visually perceptible entity, with a single exception, manifests itself as both form and color at the same time. Arnheim observed that a form is visible because its color differs from the color of its environment (Arnheim 1956, 222). The

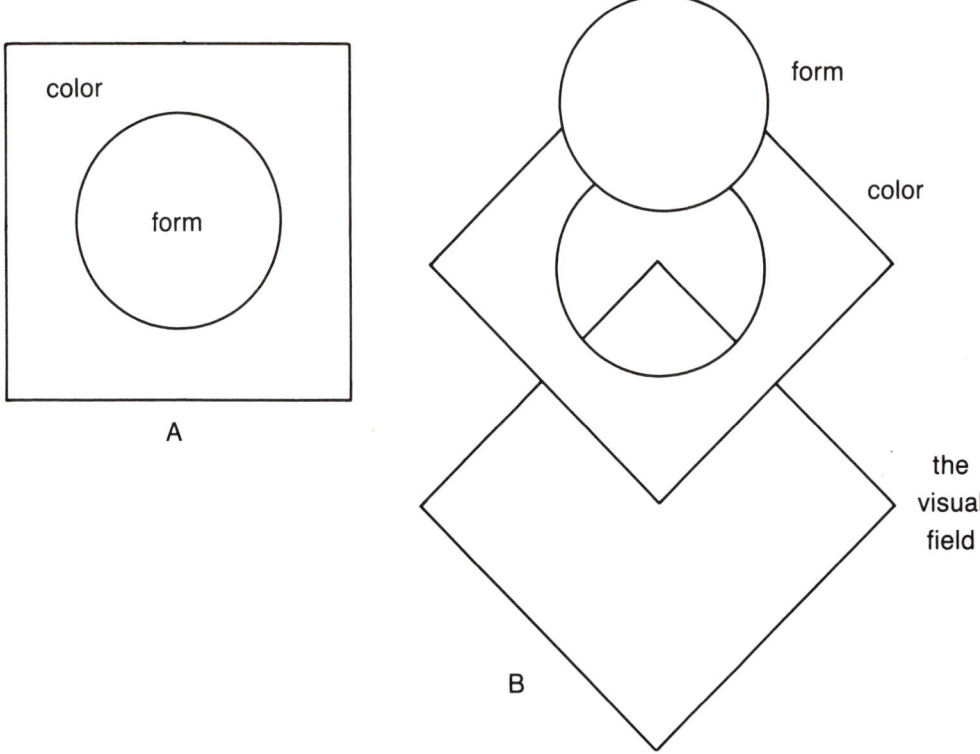

Figure 19-1. Form and color as complements. If form and color are complements, every visual experience can be classified as one or the other, and no visual experience can be both.

printed shapes of black letters on a page in a book are seen because they differ in color from the white page. A form indistinguishable in color from its environment is visually imperceptible as a form, which is why we cannot see objects in the dark. In figure 19-2, a black circle, visible against a white background, cannot be seen against a field of similar black. Isolation (or nonisolation) of a two-dimensional form from its surroundings is a function of its color.

That every visually perceptible form is distinguished because of its color amounts to saying that any two-dimensional form "has" a color, "is" some color, or "is colored." Form and color are not mutually exclusive and therefore cannot be complements. Although no dictionary would define a form as a color or

equate one with the other, the distinction has no correlative in vision. When we speak of seeing a spot of color, that spot is taken to have a discernible form or shape, the attribute that allows it to be identified as a spot. Colors, however, are not invariantly perceived as spots. The exceptional case is the color field. In this phenomenon, color appears dissociated from form, though visual form cannot appear without color.

The color field is an area of any single homogeneous color extending as far as the observing eye can see at that moment. This translates, in experiential terms, to the experience of seeing nothing but, say, light green. The most familiar color field is the dark of the night if the stars cannot be seen, or the similar blackness of an enclosed, darkened

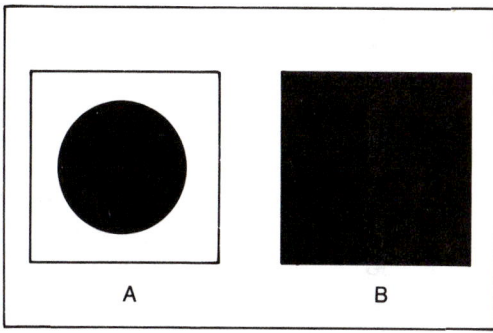

Figure 19-2. Form and field colors. A black form, visible against a white background, is invisible against a field of a similar black.

room. No method exists for remaining in a darkened environment yet also seeing around the edge of the darkness. In a parallel phenomenon, no way exists of seeing around, or behind, the edge of the image in a mirror.

Color field conditions can be simulated in experiments. In nature they are approached in a group of rare visual pathologies collectively known as the chromatopsias. Similar in effect rather than in cause, the chromatopsias lead to discoloration of the jellylike humors inside the eyeball. The result is to overlay the visual field with abnormal hues, although the condition is self-limiting by its nature. For vision to be possible, the humors in the eyeball must remain transparent, and any color they assume must remain transparent.

In erythropsia, the field of vision looks red. A white wall would present that color, as if being viewed through a pane of red glass. In xanthopsia, caused by jaundice, the overlay color is yellow. In cyanopia, it is blue; in ionthinopia, violet; and in chloropia, green. Several ophthalmological explanations are given for the chromatopsias (Fuchs [1908] 1924, 247).

Apart from the darkness, which is a genuine color field, and the overlays of the chromatopsias, which approach the condition, the experience of seeing colored fields is less com-

mon in nature than seeing colored objects. But we can extrapolate by relying on either of two analogies. A red color field might be thought of as similar to the darkness seen at night, although it is red in color rather than black or gray. A red color field can also be thought of as the homogeneous red of a red color swatch, extended as far as the eye can see.

Models of color fields are easily constructed, and the term is familiar from critiques of color-field painting. A sheet of red paper provides a convenient model, a miniature of a red color field. The sole limit of the paper is its scale. The color of the paper ends at the edge of the paper, not the edge of the visual field of a viewer. What occurs when we see, or imagine seeing, nothing except a single color?

For a color-field experience to occur, stimulation must be spatially uniform and temporally continuous. If, during an interim, what I see changes from all red to all yellow, then I have not seen a red color field continuously in that interim. What has been seen instead is a red color field for part of the time, a yellow field for the rest.

The number of possible color fields is limited only by the number of possible colors. The statement "I see nothing except . . ." can be completed with the name of any color. The statement is meaningful and unique irrespective of the color name used. The experience of seeing nothing but yellow differs from seeing nothing but blue, brown, purple, silver, or white. Each color is capable of forming a perceptible field of its own unique color, which we may see, imagine, or model.

I can imagine seeing nothing but mauve, the color field that is exclusively mauve extended to the point where it obliterates anything else I might see. I cannot, to show the limits of imagination, conceive of a color field that, at one and the same time, is both entirely mauve and entirely vermilion. Vision has constraints, many noticed by Aristotle, which we cannot surmount. These constraints are assumed but rarely discussed, and they bear on theories about color.

Although, say, every part of the visual field is colored, no part can be more than one color at the same time, the reason a color field can not be both entirely mauve and entirely vermilion. Seeing color without form is a possibility, as in the color field. Seeing form without color is not possible. The tactile sense fills the gap by allowing us to touch objects in the dark, though we cannot identify their colors by touch. If the laws of the physical world allowed intelligent beings to exist who had no tactile sense, these beings would be unable to see objects in the darkness and would be unable to touch them either.

Form as Discontinuity

Color is capable of assuming two modes. It can occur as either a color field (in which the color is continuous) or colored forms (in which the color is not continuous). Because nothing can be both continuous and discontinuous, no perceptual experience can consist of both at the same time. If I see nothing but continuous yellow, I cannot perceive, at the same time and place, a yellow disc situated in blue, gray, or multicolor surroundings.

Forms, if this line of reasoning is continued, can be defined as color discontinuities within otherwise homogeneous color fields. They disrupt the continuum of uniform color (or of formlessness) that would exist in their absence. Seeing forms requires seeing more than one color.

The model of color in the visual field as either continuous or discontinuous is similar to the classical conception of the three-dimensional world as a discontinuous domain of substance and emptiness: of corporeal forms interrupting what would otherwise be the continuousness of the spaces surrounding them. Discontinuities in the two-dimensional universe, however, consist solely of transitions from one color to another, as in a meeting between redness and blueness.

I conclude that two-dimensional form is an attribute of color, though rarely explained in this manner. We perceive spots of color and infer that some spots can be understood as forms. Color is the percept; form, the interpretation. Form (or forming) is an event that happens to color, paralleling the manner in which motion (or moving) is an event that happens to forms. No motion can exist without forms, and no forms can be seen without colors. In visual terms, colors create forms and are not applied to them. The phenomenon can be demonstrated by using models of color fields.

COLOR FIELD MODEL I

If two-dimensional (visually perceptible) forms are disturbances of color fields, this implies they ought to be regarded as events, as patterns of the moment. It also implies they can be created through work: the physical act of disturbing. A sheet of uniformly red paper is an adequate model of a red color field. It differs from the largest possible field only in its scale: in the observer's ability to see what lies beyond its edges.

Imagine that this paper is wrinkled into a ball. It is then spread as flat as its wrinkled condition allows. Applying force to wrinkle the paper constitutes the performance of work. In its "worked over" condition, the paper no longer looks flat. Its surface is covered with wrinkle forms that look like minute hills and valleys.

The color of the paper is affected by creation of these forms. Color discontinuities have been introduced into the surface. If they were not there, the forms of the wrinkles would not be seen. Although the paper is still properly described as red, the red is no longer uniform. Parts of the wrinkle forms are in shadow. Taking readings from an ordinary photographic light meter will confirm that the shadow areas are darker (a darker color). Other parts of the wrinkle forms catch the light and are lighter (a lighter color).

A more sophisticated test is to paint a picture of the wrinkled paper, recording what it looks like as faithfully as possible. The task cannot be performed with a single color, not even a color exactly matching the red of the original, unwrinkled paper. At minimum, a second, darker color is required for those areas of the wrinkles in shadow. Or a second, lighter, color is required for the areas that catch the light. Applying physical force to the paper—in this example, wrinkling it—creates both discernible forms and color discontinuities.

COLOR FIELD MODEL 2

A more complex model of a color field is provided by a movie screen in a dark room. Its viewing surface is perceived as a continuous field of uniform color, if only because any object in the dark appears nominally black. If observers were to watch this screen forever, no change would occur in its color as long as the room remained dark. The color is effectively in a state of equilibrium. No physical effort is required to maintain the black color of the screen, other than that the life support systems of the observers must keep them alive so they can continue looking at the screen.

Conditions change if a projectionist enters the room and turns on a movie projector. The immediate effect is disruption of the black surface of the screen. It now appears to consist of a variety of shapes in different colors. When this process (the ordinary showing of a movie film) begins, the observers see images of people, houses, trees, automobiles, and other objects. These screen images so closely resemble the visual appearance of natural objects that many people cannot distinguish a photograph of a photograph from a photograph of an object. Cinematographers, for this reason, often film live actors playing out their roles against backgrounds that consist of slides or

films rear-projected on screens. When the film is released, audiences rarely notice that they are seeing photographs of the actors and actresses combined with photographs of photographs of the scenery.[1]

Disturbing the black continuum of the movie screen to project a motion picture parallels wrinkling the sheet of red paper. In either case a field of homogeneous color is disturbed by the application of force: by work in a physical sense. The difference is that the moving forms of the motion picture imply more complex types of work. Miles away, a generator system creates power to drive the projector. Electric mains deliver this power to the projector motor. Film moves through the film gate. Light passes through this film, which is coated with an emulsion of variable color and density. The projector bulb must continue to burn. A breakdown in any part of this system causes the film to stop. The colors that create moving forms disappear as the screen reverts to its earlier equilibrium of uniform darkness.

In the examples of the wrinkled paper and the movie film, physical work is performed and energy expended to create discontinuities in what had initially been a field of uniform color. Only after the discontinuities are created can we say that forms exist in those respective two-dimensional fields. Visually perceived forms can be explained, in the examples and generally, as color discontinuities in an otherwise uniform field. If a blue disc appears in a field of yellow, the disc is visible because its blueness is color-discontinuous with the yellowness of the field. If no discontinuity appears and the field remains uniformly yellow, we may properly conclude no blue disc is at hand that anyone might report seeing.

Color as Surface

The visual world can be imagined as a colored film or surface. The events occurring among the colors of that surface result in the images we see. Although the syntax is unavoidably awkward, those events are adequately defined by assuming that colors "take form."

To imagine, instead, that colors are applied to forms would require showing that two-dimensional forms are capable of preexisting their colors. This is exactly what cannot be demonstrated. No such thing exists as a two-dimensional form devoid of color. We see color even when looking at colorless objects, because the transparency of these objects allows the colors of objects behind them to be seen.

Thus, on the question of whether form or color comes first, color unambiguously preexists two-dimensional form. To see nothing but turquoise blue, or nothing but yellow, is possible. Seeing the color of the dark of the night is possible and commonplace. These experiences expose us to color fields uninterrupted by forms. They thus give evidence of color preexisting form.

Two-dimensional forms, which are made of colors, are a special category of forms, accessible only through vision. The tactile sense, though it provides information about three-dimensional space, is blind to the two-dimensional world, to images that appear on surfaces. This is why touch cannot differentiate between a one-dollar bill and a twenty-dollar bill. Braille books for the blind make use of dots raised from the surface of the page, not because the blind are unable to read ordinary books by touch, but because nobody is able to do so.

The Coordinates of Vision

Visual imagery creates the impression of a film or surface, a commonplace idea. It inspires the equally commonplace questions of where the images are and whether I am only imagining them. Geometry may provide the key to why questions about whether the visual field exists—exists in the sense of possessing coordinates in three-dimensional space—dissolve into troubling inquiries into the nature of existence.

Three points are sufficient to locate any object in three-dimensional space, a familiar lesson of high school geometry. Space, for the purpose, is imagined as a grid or coordinate system with intersecting x, y, and z axes. Given the required coordinates, I can locate myself relative to any other three-dimensional object in the universe.

The lesson has a corollary important to an understanding of color. Unless all three coordinates are available, an object cannot be located in three-dimensional space. And the third coordinate cannot exist for any manifold that is two-dimensional. The two-dimensional space in which images exist is logically independent, sufficient unto itself. It cannot be located in, or by reference to, any system that assumes three-dimensionality.

Art historians and critics have popularized the concept of the illusion of space, an illusion said to appear in the two-dimensional picture planes of naturalistic paintings. But visual space is not volumetric, because it is two-dimensional. It cannot be equated with three-dimensional space, if only on the argument, drawn from geometry, that an area (in this case, the area of a picture plane) cannot be congruent with a volume (in this case, a volume of space).

Experience confirms the uniqueness of two-dimensional universes. I can measure the distance between myself and a table, but the distance between myself and the image I see of a table is as profoundly unreachable as the beginning of time, hence the argument (which misses the point) that the image of a table exists only on the retina or only in the brain. We might as reasonably argue that three-dimensional tables exist only on the fingertips of the hands that touch them or on the skin of those that bump into them.

The difference between two-dimensional and three-dimensional matrices bears on studies of binocular vision, or of the unfortunately named "perception" of space and depth. No convincing evidence is available that this purported perception, examined by gestalt and perceptual psychologists, is a perception at all in any reasonable sense. It is better explained as an inference from the relative size and location of forms within the field of vision.

Visual clues to depth in images typically lack correlation with phenomena in the three-dimensional world, a characteristic they share with color. In either case, the noncorrelation is evidence of the fundamental two-dimensionality of the phenomenon. Among a variety of depth clues, overlapping or occluding is the partial "cutting off " of, say, an image of a table by that of a person standing in front of the table. On examination, the actual table, which has not been cut off in any three-dimensional sense, will be discovered undamaged. In this and a thousand other cases, we cannot assume that what happens to images also happens to objects.

Perspectival effects are similarly disjoint from three-dimensional phenomena. In three-dimensional terms, a mountain is far away if walking to it takes a long time. In two-dimensional terms, the mountain is far away if it looks small. Although objects in the distance may look small, this never implies that they are small, another sign of the dissimilar destinies of images and objects. Vanishing points, lines receding to vanishing points, and other elements that are constituent parts of systems of mechanical drawing or perspective drawing similarly have no correlates in the three-dimensional world. The vanishing point can be seen but not touched.

The horizon on which the vanishing point lies is meaningful only in visual or two-dimensional terms. Horizons appear in paintings as lines of demarcation where the colors of the landscape meet those of the sky. But no ridge or hollow can be found on the surface of the earth that can be identified as the horizon or that a blind person can touch to learn about horizons. We cannot reach the horizon ourselves, despite its psychological importance to us. Like the vanishing point resting on it, the horizon continually recedes when approached. Like color, it has no determinable location in the three-dimensional world.

In the world of thought, the horizon separates day from night. Disorientation in the darkness grows directly from the absence of a horizon or "eye level" that can be used as a focus. Indoors in the daylight, we do not see the horizon as a separation of earth and sky. But its aptly named correlate, the eye level, performs the same function. Receding lines on objects below my eye level recede upward, receding lines of objects above my eye level recede downward. The complex job of orienting myself in space depends on reading these signs, seen in the daylight and not in the dark.

Because language and culture encourage the confusion, two-dimensionality is often regarded as a fragment of the three-dimensional world, rather than a universe independent from it or parallel to it. The argument subordinating the two-dimensional to the three-dimensional proceeds as follows. The top of a table is planar, as is the front of a mirror. Each of these surfaces, although two-dimensional, has a location in three-dimensional space. Its existence at that location can be confirmed by touch.

As in the many connections between plane and solid geometry, which become less convincing when color is introduced into the picture, the reasoning has hidden limits. The only thing that can be confirmed about planar surfaces in three-dimensional space is where they are, how shaped (the two-dimensional surface of an egg may be curved), and how large relative to other objects in that space. This information pertains to the environment around the surfaces, not to their interior or essential condition. We cannot confirm, by touch or measurement, what colors the surfaces are or what images, if any, appear on them. The blind, for this reason, cannot identify the images in a mirror or determine whether a glassy surface is a mirror.

The flaw in the confusing literature on depth perception is its insensitivity to relationships among visual elements. The visual field is finely tuned to its function. Its elements have more profound purposes than just to help us understand depth. Perspective is often called an illusion. I regard it as a magnificent algorithm, a formula that enables a larger number of elements to be crowded into the visual field than otherwise would be possible. The visual miniaturizing of distant objects solves the problem of how to squeeze more into a limited box.

One result is an enormous increase in the speed with which information can be processed. This increase largely accounts for the superiority of vision to touch. I can look at three chairs more quickly than I can investigate then by touch. If the chairs are in the same room, all three can be looked at together. On a starry night, we see celestial objects too far away to be touched and at astronomical distances from us. The colors of objects allow one object to be distinguished from another and allow objects to be distinguished from their environments.

The eye must have developed from cells sensitive, as indeed all cells are, to radiant energy or its absence: to heat or cold. Mutation can be imagined in which some cells became sensitive to that aspect of radiant energy we call light and color. The human skin to this day has a primitive photosensitivity, suggesting that the tactile and the visual can be traced to a single source. Skin tans in response to ultraviolet rays but not to rays of other wavelengths.

Although a surface phenomenon, color is more complex than the superficial covering it was traditionally taken to be. In life forms it operates as a code integrated with the genetic code. The chlorophylls, for example, have been shown to absorb primarily the red and blue wavelengths of daylight. Familiarly they appear green because they reflect, rather than absorb, light in that wavelength (Govindjee and Govindjee 1974). This implies that the catalyst of photosynthesis is not really light. Instead, it appears to be the programming of chlorophyll to utilize some colors of light but not others, a programming indicated by chlorophyll's greenness and inseparable from the substance.

Color Fields and Colored Forms

In one place [Chevreul] remarks that "red isolated appears differently than when juxtaposed with a white, black, blue, or yellow surface." We should very much like to know how Chevreul *isolated* his colour. A colour can only be isolated by considering a surface so large that the whole of the retina is occupied, and in this case it can not be used directly for purposes of comparison.

George Field, [Field's] Chromatography

I f the visual field is to be divided into complementary classes, form and color are unmatched because they lack an ability to be similarly independent. Any color can be seen in isolation from forms, the experience of seeing a color field. But two-dimensional forms cannot be seen (which means they do not, or cannot, exist) in isolation from color. Rather than functioning as a complement to form, color meets the condition of a visual field universal. We may properly assume, as has often been observed, that all visual imagery includes color.

Following after this assumption, a bona fide complementarity can be identified in the visual field. But it is not between form and color. With more defensible logic, the complementary classes are colored forms, and colored fields. Every visual experience can be identified as one or the other, and no visual experience consists of both at the same time. I cannot see a black square on a scarlet ground at the same time and place I perceive a continuous field of undifferentiated scarlet.

The Union of Form and Field
An interesting objection arises to a classification system in which form and field are regarded as alternate modes in which color makes itself manifest. The objection is that form must be separable from field to establish true complementation. Yet forms are said to be unable to exist without fields. Objects, in other words, reside in environments rather than being surrounded by nothingness.

In a two-dimensional matrix, a form is an area enclosed by a perimeter; in three dimensions, a volume enclosed by a surface. In either case, no matter how large the form, it is always possible to imagine fields or spaces lying beyond. A form cannot be removed from surroundings. It can only relocate from one set of surroundings to another.

As if the world were a collection of Chinese boxes, the environmental field surrounding a given form may be nested within larger fields. The totality of these nested or concentric fields provides a linkage between the smallest possible enclosed form, which is finite, and the universal continuum, which presumably cannot be exceeded. In a simple example of the mechanism of environment, which functions in both three dimensions and two, I am located in my room. My room is in, respectively, my house, the city, the country, the earth, the universe, and any enclosures that exist beyond that. Because a field is environmental to anything and everything within it, the earth is the environment for my city and not merely for me.

The night sky is imagined as a field without edges when human beings wonder if its blackness continues forever. The stars are forms lying within it. The primary difference between forms and fields, alternately called figures and grounds, is that fields need not be enclosed. The unenclosed field, which is limitless, is evidently the paradigm for all fields. There is no other way of explaining why geometry books, which give instructions about how to construct various enclosed forms, offer no corresponding recipes for constructing edges of fields. Perhaps it is tacitly recognized that fields with edges are actually forms.

Any entity with a finite boundary (archetypally, a form) retains a potential for enclosure within that which is infinite in extent (archetypally, a field). That the converse is not true is merely a way of saying that the word *infinite* means uncontainable by the finite. In phenomenological (or topological) terms, no form can be, at one and the same time, both inside and outside a perimeter, or both inside and outside a surface.

An exception exists to the rule that it is always possible to imagine a field larger than even the largest form, an environment more enormous than the most gigantic object in it. The exceptional case is the universe, which effectively means interstellar space and the celestial bodies suspended in it. Two puzzling questions concern its status as object in environment, if in fact it enjoys such a status. The first is what lies outside, an outside apparently as inaccessible as the back of a reflection in a mirror. The second is whether the universe, whether in steady state or expanding, could be uniquely an object with no environment surrounding it.

If the universe, from microcosm to macrocosm, is a continuum of nested environmental fields, there are only three final possibilities. Each requires the concept of infinity. There may be an infinite number of these fields (each enclosed in a field larger than itself). Or the last field may be unenclosed, and therefore infinite in extent. Or both conditions may be true at the same time.

The modern conception of the universe as finite implies a finite number of fields, with the last field finite as well. But it appears to be merely a variation of the second case, and the concept of infinity has been displaced rather than genuinely eliminated. What is infinite in an enclosed, finite universe with nothing outside is the exterior "nothing," unbounded unless a way can be found to identify its limits.

Children sometimes ask where the end of the world is and what lies beyond. The questions are easily expanded into others for which adults similarly have no answers. How can we identify nothing when we see it, if it is something we cannot see? If it cannot be seen or identified, how could a determination be made about whether nothing surrounds the universe? Even a mathematical conception of the nature of the universe, which led, for example, to the idea that it was finite but had no environment, could not eliminate the question of how this nonenvironmental *nothing* could be identified or defined. What is implied is not merely an absence of subatomic particles but an absence, as well, of the empty spaces between them, the *nothing* of the universe in which we live.

The inconsistency in the reasoning is that we are apparently asked to assume the existence of two distinctly different types of *nothing*, unrelated to one another. The first lies within the universe and is variously identified with either empty volumetric space or the color black (as in the perceived blackness of the spaces between the stars). The second *nothing*, outside the universe, is among other things an absence of the first, because the conception of a universe with nothing outside does not allow for exterior spaces. The second *nothing* presumably cannot look black. If it did, we would be compelled to imagine a universe afloat in a sea of that particular color.

These and similar questions are applicable to worlds of two dimensions, rather than unique to those of three. It might even be argued that their origin lies in the attempt to understand perceptual experience at the edge of the visual field, a frontier that similarly defies efforts to reach beyond it. What I see at any given moment is finite but never all there is to see. Like the images in mirrors, what remains to be seen apparently has no end. Metaphorically, I might want to imagine that it reaches to the end of the world.

The perimeters that define two-dimensional forms also provide the boundaries at which form and field visually meet. For example, I might imagine exhibiting a blue disc so large you would be unable to see either its edges or the environment surrounding it. The disc, for you, would be a field, not a form. On similar reasoning, the darkness of a starless night is

field rather than form within human perception. Irrespective of whether the darkness has a perimeter, the human observer confined to a fixed place lacks the capacity to see it or to see beyond it.

Form and field, as this suggests, are essentially contextual. A form in one environment may function as an environment for another form enclosed within itself. The question of how to separate form and field, if they can be separated, turns essentially on location. Or it turns on location respective to a perimeter.

Separating Form and Field

A black disc against a gray background in a two-dimensional matrix provides a simple example of a form in a field, a configuration psychologists often refer to as a figure on a ground. Whether the figure is regarded as on its ground or in it varies, but it is a question of topological interest. Koffka preferred *on*: "The left cross can appear either as a blue cross on a yellow ground, or as a yellow cross on a blue ground. . . . The ground is unaffected by the contour and is partly hidden by the figure. . . . No visual figure can occur without a ground on which it appears" (Koffka 1922, 551). Kohler preferred *in* or *within*: "The threshold for a patch of color has been found to be higher in the area of a figure than within a ground of the same objective color" (Kohler 1947, 120).

That any figure might lie *on* its ground is a dubious assumption, because the word implies *superimposed on*. In a two-dimensional universe, nothing can consistently be assumed to be superimposed on anything else. Koffka's further assumption that a ground (or field) might continue "without interruption" behind a figure (or form) is as monumentally unverifiable. A black cross in a gray field or ground cannot be lifted to investigate whether the gray continues behind it (figure

---

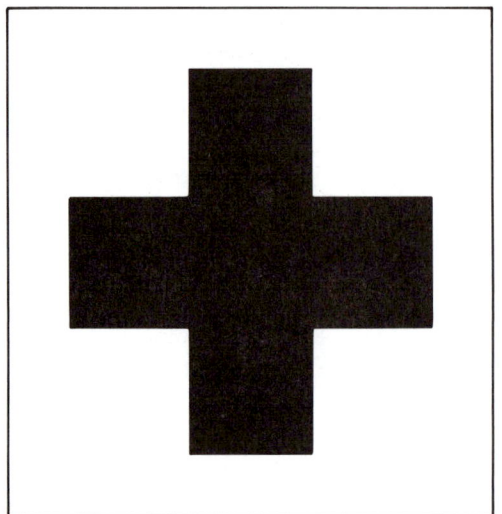

Figure 20-1. A black figure on a gray ground. If superimposition of one form "on" another cannot be assumed in a two-dimensional universe, figures (forms) must lie "in" grounds (fields), rather than on them.

20-1). There is no "behind" in a planar universe, because any term that relies on the concept of a third dimension is experientially meaningless when that dimension is absent. The question of whether a given human observer exhibits sensibility to visual phenomena reduces in large part to the question of whether that point is understood or denied.

A model of the black cross and gray ground can be constructed by cutting the shapes out of colored paper. Figure 20-2 illustrates three methods. Although indistinguishable from one another when completed, the gray field is constructed differently in each. In the first two, the ground continues, as Koffka imagines, behind the figure. In the third it does not. In the second model, a square hole occurs in that part of the field concealed by the black cross.

The third is the only model that accurately represents either a two-dimensional universe or the manner in which form and color are seen in the visual field. The other models are

implicitly three-dimensional. The gray field passes, in each, behind the black cross, an impossibility in vision because the images we see have no depth.

The subtleties of *on* versus *in* may seem abstruse. But most people have an excellent practical understanding of the structure of two-dimensional fields. Imagine, for example, that the black cross in gray field was to be enlarged, to be painted on the side of a building. It

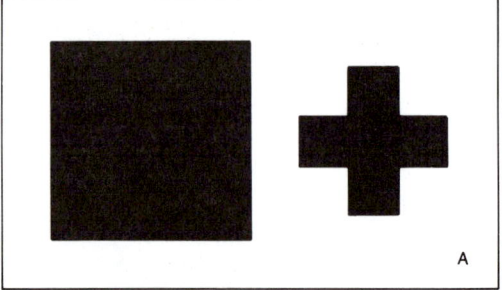

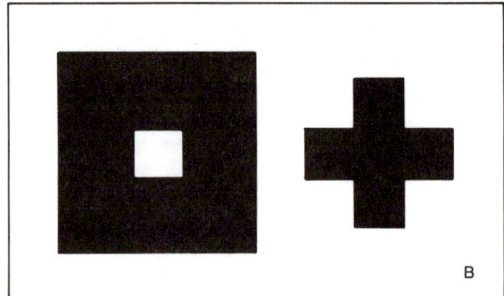

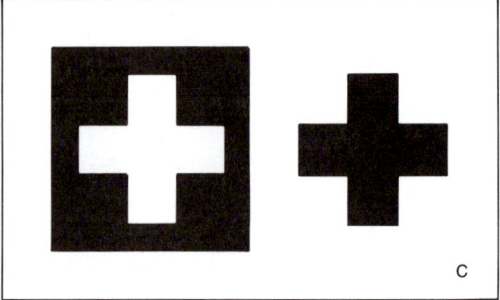

Figure 20-2. Three models of a figure in a ground. The three models of a black cross on a gray ground look visually similar but differ in construction. Only C is genuinely two-dimensional.

would be necessary to calculate how many gallons of gray paint would be needed. Even children, given the problem, are able to understand that the final visual effect will be the same whether or not extra paint is used to continue the gray area "behind" the black cross. The practical solution is as in figure 20-2(C). Gray paint is not needed for that portion of the field occupied by the black cross.

The computations for the gray paint point to a method for separating form from field (or figure from ground). The gray area of figure 20-2(C), although likely to be regarded as a continuous field (passing, perhaps, even behind the figure), is actually discontinuous. The discontinuity consists of the hole in its center, corresponding to the space occupied by the black cross. The gray shape is only nominally a field, more correctly a form. Like any form, it consists of a fractional part of a field, and has a perimeter or limit. Its perimeter is identical with that of the black cross.

As this suggests, the type of configuration misleadingly classified as a form in a field (or a figure on a ground) is more coherently understood as two forms. One is the negative shape, or complement, to the other. Although Euclidean geometry, oblivious to negative space, fails to make clear the dynamics, forms can only be seen two or more at a time, because every form effects disruption of a field. In that truism familiar in the visual arts but often overlooked in studies of perception, every form has a negative shape to itself. And the figure on ground is actually two figures, another way of expressing the idea that objects possess environments.

Colored forms can be defined, in visual terms, as fractions or portions of colored fields. What I see at any given moment, if blue, is either all blue (a colored field) or partly blue (a colored form). In the illustration, the entire configuration consists of two forms. One is gray; the other, black. Each is a fraction of a field, with edges within the domain that con-

tains it, and the two forms share a common set of edges. The exterior edges of the black cross are the interior edges of the hole in the center of the gray shape.

This suggests that fields (by which I mean uninterrupted fields) are unable to coexist with forms. Colored forms and colored fields are bona fide complements within the confines of the visual field, although form and color are not. Anything that can be seen is either color-continuous or color-discontinuous. It is either a colored field or a collection of at least two colored forms.

Noninterpenetrability

No contemporary understanding of oppositeness explains Aristotle's assertion that " 'grey' and 'white' do not apply at the same time to the same thing, and hence their constituents are opposite" (*Metaphysics*, book 5). It is true, however, that two colors cannot occupy the same visual space at the same time. Colors are noninterpenetrable. Among conditions that follow from this, no entity, including a perceived color spot, can be both entirely red and entirely blue at the same time.

The noninterpenetrability of colors suggests an attribute often assumed to be exclusive to material objects. Just as two colors cannot occupy the same visual space at the same time, two corporeal objects cannot occupy the same physical space at the same time. Colors, however, are devoid of mass, the quality likely to be cited to explain the inability of three-dimensional objects to interpenetrate. The mass of a corporeal object, it seems reasonable to believe, is what cannot move into the space occupied by the mass of some other object.

This raises the question of what we mean by saying that objects have mass and colors do not. Beyond that, I am interested in whether mass is really necessary to noninterpenetrability. A more likely answer might be surface.

Even a child learns to understand the difference between colors and objects and, indeed, must do so to learn how to use color names. Chairs, apples, and airplanes are accessible to multiple senses; they can be both seen and touched. Colors are available to a single sense. They can be understood only through visual means. If mass is an essential difference between a color and an apple, the word appears to apply exclusively to extension within a third dimension; to the type of extension that can be touched.

I am going to move from this to propose that whereas mass is associated with extension into a third dimension, noninterpenetrability is as intimately associated with two-dimensionality. I include among two-dimensional entities not only planar universes (for example, the visual field or the picture plane) but also the shaped and colored two-dimensional surfaces of three-dimensional objects. Each of these surfaces can be defined as a two-dimensional plane meeting itself in every direction, the characteristic that enables it to enclose what we identify as the volume of the object. Its analogue in the two-dimensional world is *perimeter*, a line that meets itself to enclose an area rather than a volume.

Surface is the two-dimensional (planar) aspect of any three-dimensional form. Perimeter is the one-dimensional (linear) aspect of any two-dimensional shape. The hierarchy can be carried further by noting that length is the null-dimensional aspect of any line, null-dimensional because it does not include width.

Surface, perimeter, and length are absolute delimiters. I mean by this that any three-dimensional object can be defined as the volume enclosed by its surface; any two-dimensional form, as the surface enclosed by its perimeter. Any line can be defined in terms of its length, which in fact is how we define lines. Surface, as this further suggests, is common to both two-dimensional and three-dimensional forms. It delimits in one case and

constitutes that which is delimited in the other. Because noninterpenetrability and surface are common to both two- and three-dimensional universes, it seems reasonable to ask what the relationship is between them.

Displacement

That familiar catechism of elementary school science class, that two objects cannot occupy the same space at the same time, suggests that what is being attributed to corporeal objects is as likely to be a property of space. Apparently nothing can move into a space that is not empty, much as nothing can be put in a box that is full. An occupied space becomes available for use only if its contents are moved or displaced. In a familiar example used to illustrate the nature of displacement in the three-dimensional world, I settle into my bathtub, causing the water level to rise. Following a principle said to have been enunciated by Archimedes in his own bath, the water has been displaced by me. Because matter is noninterpenetrable, two objects cannot occupy the same space at the same time.

Color displacements that occur in the visual field are similar to displacements in the physical world in that they similarly serve to sustain the constancy of the field. But they cannot be explained by a similar analogy, in part because the visual field lacks empty spaces to which displaced colors might migrate. As a simple example of visual field displacement, I might imagine observing a field of yellow into which an orange disc has been introduced. Because I cannot see yellow where I see orange, the orange color of the disc displaces a portion of the yellow. In operational terms, while looking at the orange I cannot see the portion of yellow nominally behind it. The area lost to view, or displaced, is identical in size and shape to the occluding disc.

It is not possible to say where the occluded color has gone. It cannot be genuinely behind the disc, a meaningless term in a universe with only height and width. Unlike the water in Archimedes' bathtub, it has not moved elsewhere to displace some other item. It has merely been displaced from the field of vision, vanished into a world of interphenomena. It was visible once; in some cases it may appear again. But it is not there (or anywhere) now, in any perceivable or conceivable sense. There is no answer to the question of where what we see goes when for any reason it is no longer seen.

The primary difference between visual displacement (of colors) and physical displacement (of matter) is that one is a series of transformations; the other, a series of motions. Displacement, in the physical world, resembles a game of musical chairs. The path of each displaced item can be traced, to show it has merely moved on to displace something else. At least ideally, when I step into the filled bathtub, my body displaces water, which in rising displaces air. That air moves to fill the void I had occupied before getting into the tub.

The bathtub model has limits. It might be construed to incorrectly imply, for example, that no order determines what displaces what. Yet I cannot sink into my bathtub if its water is frozen into a block of ice. And if an ordinary drinking glass is pushed, bottom up, into water, the water will be unable to displace the air in the glass. What displaces what, and under what circumstances, is contextual. It is also associated with surface, the attribute common to both three-dimensional objects and color. What allows my body to displace water more easily than ice is that water has a less resisting surface than ice.

Constancy of Color

Many questions that have been regarded as significant when asked about universes with three dimensions are rarely or never asked about those that have two. The amount of matter and energy in the universe, for example, is said to be constant. We have no idea whether this is also true with regard to the amount of color. Imagine, to illustrate the nature of the question, that a green table burns to black ash. Although the pile of ashes is smaller than the table, the chemist is prepared to account for the permutations of every molecule, to prove that nothing was really gained or lost.

No similarly exhaustive audit can be provided for the metamorphoses of color. Where did the green of the table go? Where did the black of the ashes come from? Insofar as motion is implied in either case—and it is virtually impossible to describe the phenomenon without that metaphor—the journeying of the greenness of the table differs from the travels of its atoms. Unlike motion in the corporeal world, it is not a journey from here to there, because there is remarkably elusive. Like light, which similarly "travels" without necessarily arriving any place in particular, colors can apparently move on to an ambiguous destination. Or, like the blackness of the ashes that we formerly knew as the greenness of the table, they can appear as if by spontaneous generation.

The question of why noninterpenetrability ought to exist at all comes easily to mind. Solid objects are said to actually consist primarily of empty space in which subatomic particles float at relatively enormous distances from one another. If the table we see and touch is not genuinely solid, why does it persist in behaving as if it were? Why cannot the cloud of molecules that constitutes one object pass, ghostlike, into, or through, the cloud of molecules that constitutes another?

A common explanation compares the motion of molecules in an object to the action of a moving airplane propeller, effectively barring access to the space in which the movement occurs. This explanation cannot be extended to colors (there are no molecules on which to hang the propellers), which suggests the analogy is weak. But it is amusing enough to pursue to a point. If the molecules of an object are imagined to be equipped with the hypothetical propellers or comparable mechanisms, these devices would not necessarily be required throughout. They could most efficiently be attached solely to the molecules on the surface of the object. That surface, which incidentally displays the object's color, is what most immediately encounters the surfaces of other objects, offering more or less resistance to intrusion.

Color as Surface

Unlike the surface of an onion, that of an image cannot be peeled away. This evidently accounts for the tenacity of color in the visual field or for its remarkable constancy. I cannot add to, or subtract from, the totality of what I see, the exact reason I cannot see both red and blue at the same time and place.

One reason for suspecting that displacement may be a function of surface, consequently of two-dimensionality, is its more radical nature in the visual world. Displaced color spots are obliterated, rather than being transferred from one place to another. Furthermore, resistance to displacement in the three-dimensional world can be correlated with the character of an object's surface more easily than with other physical aspects of the object.

In the continuum of resistances, gases, which have no surface, present no barrier to mingling with one another. Although an atom of chlorine presumably cannot occupy the spatiotemporal location of an atom of oxygen, this does not, as a matter of fact, prevent a cloud of chlorine gas from mixing with a cloud of oxygen, evidence that three-dimensionality per se is not a barrier to penetrability except at the molecular level. On a planet so hot that all elements were gaseous, all could presumably intermingle. Liquids display what is called surface tension, often resisting other liquids

until the tension is broken. Soap facilitates the mixing of oil and water by weakening this tension.

Surfaces constitute a large part of the integrity of any object. By surface I mean the actual two-dimensional shaped plane, irrespective of what lies beneath it. Life forms resemble complex combinations of liquids and jellies rather than gases or genuinely dry solids. Most or all possess specialized surfaces designed to protect their interiors from, among other things, dehydration. The loss of a large amount of skin is fatal to higher organisms, just as destruction of the cell wall is fatal to an amoeba. Human epidermis, an example of surface in a life form, has an outside (the actual surface) and an inside. It cannot function correctly if grafted to a human body so that its outside is inside.

Although the surface tension of liquids can be broken, that of solids displays a remarkable integrity. In a homogeneous substance, it typically cannot be weakened, divided, or destroyed. If a piece of stone is broken into smaller pieces, each fragment has as hard a surface as the original. The homogeneity is similar to that of a color field, in which, for instance, any portion of a field of homogeneous green is as green as the whole. Whether because of the nature of two-dimensionality (surface) or for some other reason, extension, for either objects or colors, appears to imply extension of the capacity for being noninterpenetrable.

It would be regarded as a retreat into solipsism to assume that the world did not exist other than in the form of the colored images I see. But perhaps this trivializes the issue. The visual field is a surface, a planar matrix composed of color which, as such, has certain characteristics. Beyond this, the entire world is a surface, including those aspects accessible to touch. A hologram looks more convincingly three-dimensional than an ordinary photograph, apparently solely because it more fully records the nature of the surfaces of objects.

The external world, as has been said of the picture plane of a painting, is a surface that shuts us out, compelling each of us to remain in his or her assigned place. The essence or interior of any object remains perennially inaccessible. The limit is only transcended in dreams, fantasies, and myth. Ghosts, apparitions, and spirits, as we imagine them or depict them in movies, pass into or through solid objects, an expression of the idea that other worlds may not be subject to the limitations of this one. Lovers, imitating Hermes and Aphrodite, may imagine merging with one another. Mystics can yearn for union with God, in whatever form they imagine that union.

The figures of ghosts and ghostlike objects, probably invented after looking at clouds and fogs, suggest ways of imagining what it might be like if two objects were able to occupy the same space at the same time. But nothing helps in the case of colors. I cannot even imagine what it would be like if something I saw were entirely blue but also entirely green at the same time. The limit is not genuinely transcended by imagining the colors mixed together.

Geometry of Surface

In an alternate geometry based on vision, any two-dimensional form, including a perceived color spot, might be defined as the area enclosed by its perimeter; any three-dimensional form, as the volume enclosed by its surface. No object can be both two-dimensional and three-dimensional at the same time, which essentially means that enclosed volumetric forms cannot maintain linear perimeters. Imagine, to illustrate the mechanism, that a black bowling ball is painted green. The small area of green paint used to begin the task has an identifiable perimeter. But when the entire surface has been covered with green paint, the perimeter of the green area disappears. This phenomenon has a bear-

ing on the artificial lines we invent in making outline drawings of objects. The circle I draw to depict the moon is not the moon's perimeter. It is, however, the perimeter of that portion of the moon's surface I am able to see at the moment, an essentially two-dimensional configuration.

Perimeters and surfaces are inversely related to the quantity of what they enclose, a relationship that cannot be altered. Cutting a square piece of paper in half does not reduce the total area of the two pieces; but their aggregate perimeter is increased by 50 percent. Smashing a brick into fragments does not affect total volume or weight. But the total amount of surface area in all the fragments vastly exceeds that of the original brick.

Because surface and perimeter are basic physical functions of the forms they delimit, we cannot alter them without changing the forms. Peeling the outer layers from an onion does not create an onion without a surface. It produces only a somewhat reduced onion with a smaller, but entire, surface of its own.

Perimeters

Forms and fields can be visually perceived if, and only if, composed of color. Forms have outer boundaries or perimeters, which cannot be true of fields if they extend to infinity. Because the enclosed forms of plane geometry are described by telling how to construct their perimeters, an alternate to imagining them as shapes is to envision them as locations.

A triangle, for example, is any enclosed area located within a perimeter composed of three straight lines. The area outside a triangle's perimeter (the expanse from the perimeter to infinity) is not called a triangle. But it is limited at its interior edge by the perimeter it shares with the triangle. Axioms for a two-dimensional universe might be as follows:

1. A perimeter is a line that returns to its starting point.

2. Perimeters cannot be seen unless the areas they separate differ in color.

3. Forms are areas marked off by perimeters.

4. Fields are areas devoid of perimeters.

5. No positive shape can be its own negative shape (or no figure can be its own ground), because nothing can be located both inside and outside of a given perimeter at the same time.

6. Because nested, or concentric, perimeters are possible, a figure that lies in a ground can serve as a ground for another figure lying within itself.

PART FOUR

Color and Culture

I am persuaded . . . that no two colours produce together a positively unpleasant effect.

William Benson, Principles of the Science of Colour Concisely Stated to Aid and Promote Their Useful Application in The Decorative Arts

CHAPTER 21

Hue, Color, and Culture

Hue can be described as the property which gives color its name—blue, blue-green, red, etc.—the name, that is, by which it is distinguished from other colors in the visible spectrum.

J. Scott Taylor, A Simple Explanation of the
Ostwald Color System

Children in the lower grades are taught to memorize the word sequence "red, orange, yellow, green, blue, violet" but not because a special value exists in knowing the order of the colors of the spectrum. The names also identify the hues, the major varieties of color other than black and white. The use of a single set of names for both purposes reflects the belief that the hues are found in their purest or most typical form in the spectrum. A person asked what pure blue looks like can point to the blue portion of the spectrum. Spectral blue is regarded as either pure blue or its closest approximation.

Can a blue that is more pure or more intense than the blue of the spectrum exist? The question asks whether we can imagine such a blue, perhaps located in Plato's world of ideal forms palely reflected in the forms of everyday experience. The question turns back on itself, dissolving into nonsense. The English language offers no syntactical barrier to placing the words *pure* or *ideal* before the name of any color. A world of ideals, if it exists, might seem likely to include pure blue, as well as pure (or ideal) varieties of other pure or impure colors. The inconsistency is that blue is a perceptual experience, and ideals are usually thought to be beyond perceiving. Dreaming of ideal perceptions that can never be perceived, ideal experiences that can never be experienced, becomes self-contradictory.

Nevertheless, *pure*, when applied to color, is a popular descriptive term. Almost everyone understands the implied antithesis between pure and impure or between perfect and imperfect. In descriptions of color, as elsewhere, *pure* and *perfect* pass as ad hoc synonyms for *beautiful*. Sometimes *pure* is an alternate for *bright*. Rarely is the word applied to colors that are not spectral hues or close to the hues. We do not speak of, say, pure olive drab, pure medium gray, pure brown, or pure navy blue.

Before acquiring its additional meanings, purity was a traditional parameter for grading color. Its less judgmental modern descendant, *chromaticity*, means saturation (or proportion) of hue. As chromaticity or hue content drops, colors become, in the vernacular, paler, darker, duller, or muddier.

Children encouraged to recite the names of the hues are usually encountering their first, and unless they study art, their last, formal instruction about color. Students and teachers are likely to describe the exercise as learning the names of the colors rather than those of the spectral hues. The blurring of distinction perpetuates the confusing practice of using *color* to mean, ambiguously, either all colors or only the hues. The looseness of language has an acrimonious history. Goethe criticized Newton for devising a theory of color based only on the colors of the solar spectrum. The limitation might be defended if the spectral hues could be shown to enjoy special status, or if colors absent from the spectrum are not really colors.

An otherwise inexplicable body of formal and informal argumentation addresses exactly this issue. We are told that, for example, black, white, gray, metallic colors, fluorescent colors, and iridescent colors are not really colors in the same sense as the spectral hues and their derivatives. The argument proposes a class of items that effectively are not really colors. Yet each of the *not really colors* is a color by the criterion of exclusion.

Assume that a color is an entity endowed with spatiotemporal location in the visual field. We learn, by seeing, that this color excludes all other colors from its location. I conclude that colors not included in the spectrum, say, silver, gold, black, white, and the iridescent colors, are not substantively different from red, blue, or green. They differ in color but not in whether they are colors. For experiential as well as conceptual reasons, we cannot have a category of colors that are *not really colors*.

Colors can be regarded as objects of perception, thus objects. They are more often called properties of other entities to which they are said to belong. Dictionaries often report, say, that red is a property of one portion of the solar spectrum. This means that both red and a particular portion of the spectrum can be seen at the same time and place. By this ill-considered criterion, red can be linked to anything that is red. Red is the color of blood, of red flowers, of red laser beams. That red and the other hues are found in the solar spectrum is scarcely more useful than the information that penguins, giraffes, and elephants are found in zoos. It tells us where, from time to time, the hues are located, but not what they are.

The word *red* can be defined in a less confusing way. We can call it a name conventionally conferred on a portion of the spectrum, rather than a quality belonging to the spectrum or to some part of it. This eliminates any need to explain the nature of a quality or to justify drawing a distinction between a quality (or property) and an object. Although the object-or-quality conundrum has persisted throughout the history of color theory, the differences between objects and qualities relate to human value systems rather than to the phenomenological world.

Reasoning about the nature of color and light is often argumentation about their place in a hierarchy, a subjective concern.[1] White light can be divided into colored rays, which Newton offered as evidence that light is not a quality. Light enjoys, Newton argued, a higher status than qualityship can confer. His curious logic is that no quality possesses qualities. Yet color is said to have the qualities of hue, value, and chroma. Color can be, say, moderately dark, very light, bright, dull, or glossy, all similarly called qualities. We would have less need for adverbs if qualities could not be further qualified. Every quality possesses qualities, including the quality of being present or not present.

Newton's purpose is more interesting than his argument. He wanted to take issue with the assumption that material objects are of special significance, a significance we attribute to them by calling them real. Light, color, empty space, and other immaterial entities are less significant, not entirely real, an idea with ancient roots. For Plato, geometrical forms were worth discussing. The empty spaces around them were not. A more modern conception of space pictures it as a system of coordinates, never wholly empty because it includes these coordinates. But any coordinate system depends on an arbitrarily selected center from which its axes originate. No fixed center is available in the universe, therefore no absolute center for a universal coordinate system. The modern idea that no coordinate system is privileged is close to Aristotle's argument that location is an artificial concept. I may well be convinced that a chair is there. But *there* effectively means at an indeterminate place. It remains as mythic as *once upon* a time, which means at an indeterminate time. The looseness of *there* has a bearing on arguments meant to prove that chairs and other material objects are there but colors are not.

The ambiguity of location or the arbitrariness of coordinate systems is not the whole story. Light passes any designated point in space with a rapidity once thought to be evidence of instantaneous propagation. Because it never stops moving, light cannot be said to reside at a certain fixed distance from some other object. Neither, however, can light be separated from visual phenomenology. No theory of forms is sufficient to explain the difference between day and night, a difference that is the locus for our ideas about both light and time.

Newton may have meant to elevate light to the status of virtual object, a way of saying he thought light was important. At earlier dates, other people said essentially the same thing. During the twelfth century, Abbot Suger thought light was a symbol of God or an emblem of God's works. The association appears in the Bible. Ancient peoples were probably more impressed by the effects worked by light than by any attributable to the surface colors of objects. Light causes growth. In excess, it destroys. It can be concentrated through lenses to start fires. We know today that objects are not passive reflectors. Plants grow not just because of the light of the sun but because their green pigment, chlorophyll, reflects some rays while absorbing others. And the dangerous aspects of ordinary sunlight are matched by those of a ruby laser, a concentration of one wavelength or color to the exclusion of the rest.

For ancient peoples, the rainbow could be construed to provide a reason for according a special status to the hues. It comes and goes in the sky without human intervention, suggesting colors belonging to God or the gods. When it appears in myth, as in the Bible, we find it accorded a special place. In myths of India, Indra carries a thunderbolt, like the Greek god Zeus, but also the rainbow. Part of a creation myth says the gods and titans churned a primeval ocean of milk. Airavata, a sacred milk-white elephant whose name means rainbow, was one of the first creatures born from the churned milk (Zimmer 1946, 104).

The idea that the rainbow and its hues have a special significance, feeding on itself over the centuries, made the hues easy to overestimate. For Goethe, the German language "has the advantage of possessing four monosyllabic names no longer to be traced to their origin, viz., *gelb, blau, rot, grun* (yellow, blue, red, green)" (Matthaei 1971, 249). Goethe was too sophisticated to argue that the hues were more important than other colors because God had put them in the sky in the rainbow. But he assumed it would make sense if the names of hues had always been constant in meaning.

Red is not blue, or the name *blue* is used incorrectly if applied to colors that ought to be called *red*. The group of colors that speakers of English call *red* can be designated by any other name, and the conventions for segregating colors can be modified. Red can be defined as a larger class, a smaller class, or eliminated entirely. Its relationship to other colors, including white, can be regarded differently.

Among speakers of English, pink is considered a variety of red. The name is applied to colors that can be matched by mixing red paint and white paint, especially if a high proportion of white is needed. Intelligent beings from another galaxy might argue that pink should not be classified as a type of red, because pinks look different from reds. The argument is irrefutable. The visual difference is the very reason we segregate certain pale reds by calling them pinks.

Red is called pure because a hue. White is called pure for other reasons. Pink is not usually called pure, though made from two "pure" colors. What rules do we follow in deciding a color is pink, and in deciding whether pink is pure? Any pink can be replicated by a mixture containing some red, though this is also true of any purple or any orange. Purples and oranges are neither called pink nor categorized as types of red. I conclude the red component of pink is not the issue, though pink is called a type of red. The critical factor is our often confusing conception of white, matching our confusing conception of black.

White is called "not a color," though also, "light of all colors," or even "every color." Each of these propositions is dubious, and they make no sense as a group. Newton's prism experiments justify the assertion that white light is composed of rays of the spectral colors. But the rays in aggregate are not, as Newton called them, "all colors." The metallic colors, for example, are not matched by spectral rays of those colors. White (light) is not synonymous with white (the color), and generalizations about the whiteness of light do not hold for the whiteness of other objects. White paint is not composed of paint of all colors, any more than white shoes are composed of shoes of all colors.

Does white light separate into colored rays because it is white or because it is light? Light, not white, is what passes through prisms, the only known instance in which anything white can be shown to be composed of colors. That white is not a color is as faulty as the assumption that white is all colors, except to the limited extent that white is not a spectral hue. I cannot see white, just as I cannot see yellow, at the same time and place I see blue.

White is regarded as pure in a different sense than the spectral colors because it is also called colorless. James McNeil Whistler responded angrily to the art critic P. G. Hamerton, who complained that Whistler's *Symphony in White No. III* was not an entirely white painting: "Bon Dieu! did this wise person expect white hair and chalked faces?" (Whistler 1890, 45). Hamerton was insensitive but not incorrect, and his readers probably understood him. Speakers of English are rarely challenged for the assumption that white, because pure or not a color, ought to be wholly untinged by other colors.

The reasoning carries over into racial designation, an elaborate code that only nominally refers to skin color. Nobody's skin is actually black, white, yellow, or red. Because white and black also are used as figures for good and bad, the English language is heavily endowed with idioms that can be mistaken for (or turned into) racial slurs. Lily white intentions are pure; black motives are evil.

The idea that white is, or ought to be, pure or untinged by any other color is often expressed by calling it *colorless*, an ill-considered usage because "colorless" is best reserved for designating transparency. Between water and milk, we all know which is white in color and which is colorless. Yet for Greenough, "the absence of color in the teeth is as beautiful as its presence in the lips" (Greenough 1962, 90). White teeth are neither colorless (transparent) nor the same color among different individuals. Indeed, matching a cap to an adult's teeth usually means finding the right shade of ivory, and dentists routinely use charts of human tooth colors.

Greenough's remark implies that white, because not a color, does not count. The wide currency of a similar belief must explain why any pink is more likely to be thought of as a type of red than a type of white, even if its white component exceeds the red: the white is not counted as a color. Or, as in the politics of race, *white* is used as if the word meant entirely white, a standard not applied to other colors.

Hue weighs more heavily than chroma or value in our assessment of color but appears to be arbitrary. The classical Greeks named the colors of the rainbow as red, yellow-green, and purple (Wallace 1927, 24), a close approximation for how the colors appear in modern photographs of spectra produced by diffraction gratings (Hoyle 1957, 183). Wallace argued, on evidence of a rainbow she had seen, that the Greek naming of its colors was more accurate than our own (Wallace 1927, 76):

A magnificent double rainbow that lasted about half an hour was seen in London, at 6:30 P.M., Sept. 12, 1925. The present writer (X) and another observer (Y), whose appreciation of color values is very accurate, independently recorded the colors observed, in order from the top to the bottom (i.e., theoretically from red to violet) of the uppermost or clearest arc. These observations are recorded below. The colors in italics are those that seemed to stand out most plainly. As the bow was visible so long, these observations are the result of careful judgment. Their disparity shows: 1. the variation in what is seen by the eyes of different individuals and in the interpretation their minds make of what they see; 2. that the rainbow does not consist of seven ordered bands or distinct colors; 3. that the ancient descriptions of it as red, yellow-green and [purple] were nearer what one actually sees, than are the spectral colors.

X	Y
Violet	Wide *orange*
(*Rose*)	band
(Orange)	(Bright yellow)
Yellow (very plain)	(Light *green*)
	Blue
Green, blue and *indigo*	Red
(indistinguishably blurred)	
Antique purple	Violet
Red	

In Islamic cosmology, the colors of the spectrum are identified as "red, yellow, green, and blue, corresponding to the four elements" and linked to celestial bodies (Nasr 1978, 86–91). Mars is associated with red, the sun with yellow, Jupiter with green, and Venus with blue. Saturn and the moon are respectively linked with black and white.

Modern ways of dividing the spectrum are as arbitrary as those of prescientific peoples. Newton, who expected the objects of the world to be ordered in sets of seven, saw seven colors in the solar spectrum. In England the colors are still named as he saw them (indigo is retained as a major hue), probably because Newton was English. In the United States, color wheels usually include six hues, perhaps in deference to American practicality. As we learn in high school geometry, a circle can be divided into six equal sectors by marking off the radius on the circumference. Only a compass is needed. A protractor is required to divide a circle into seven sectors. Furthermore, seven is an odd number, which complicates the task of dividing colors into pairs of complements.

Divisions within hue classes are set for similarly eccentric reasons. Perceptible differences inconsistent with preferred sorting criteria are ignored. By a visual standard, a bright red may resemble a bright orange more than a dark maroon resembles a pale pink. Yet the first two, because hue is the preferred criterion, will be said to belong to different color classes. The last two will be assigned to the same class, because both are varieties of red. A visual standard for color similarity is the simplest of all standards. We need to determine from looking at the colors how easily one can be distinguished from the other. At a distance, or under poor illumination, navy blue can be confused with dark green more easily than with pale blue. I conclude that navy blue does not look like pale blue as much as it looks like dark green.

The criterion for calling colors blue is not that they look alike but that they share a common hue component. Bias in favor of the hue parameter is built into everyday forms. If asked to describe a dark blue color, the respondent is thought to be correct if the color is identified as blue. It cannot be called merely *dark*, a term that is not a bona fide color name. But dark blue is dark as much as it is blue.

Conventions in color naming, like other conventions, are not necessarily consistent among themselves. Pink is a special name for light reds, baby blue, a less frequently used name for light blues. Light green is sometimes called mint green. Light yellows are sometimes called cream color, and two observers may disagree about whether cream is a type of light yellow or a type of yellowish white. Brown and gray are enormous color classes that cut across the boundaries of hue. Some browns tend toward orange, others are yellowish, greenish, or reddish. But all are cataloged as browns. Pale brown is usually called tan or beige. Brown with a high blue component may be called gray. A wide range of colors intermediate between brown and gray has no particular name.

CHAPTER 22

Prime Minister Gladstone and the Blues

By that same way the direfull dames doe drive
Their mournful charett, fil'd with rusty blood.

Edmund Spenser, The Faerie Queene

Nothing is phonemically, morphemically, or expressively significant about the group of sounds that form the spoken word *red* or the group of letters by which the name is written. In German, *rot* and *Rot* (respectively, the adjective and noun forms) are used. In Spanish, red is *rojo*; in French, *rouge*; in Dutch, *rood*; in Italian, *roso*; in Polish, *czerwony*.

No matter the language, the color class red is thought self-evident. A range of colors belongs in the class, the individual shades in this range look similar according to a universally acknowledged sorting criterion. Only the name of the class (its spelling and pronunciation) would be expected to differ from one language to another. If, however, no universal sorting criterion exists (if sorting by hue is just conventional), no common understanding can occur among the peoples of the world about what the terms *similar* and *dissimilar* mean when applied to color.

In the social sciences, Segall, Campbell, and Herskovits reported that the topic of " 'racial' or cultural differences in color perception and in color vocabulary, has the longest and most sustained research history in the culture and perception area" (Segall, Campbell, and Herskovits 1966, 38). The grandfather of the substantial literature is William Ewart Gladstone (1809–98), Queen Victoria's prime minister. Gladstone was an amateur philologist and student of the classics. A study of the *Iliad* and *Odyssey* led him to believe that Homer (ca. 800 B.C.) applied color names inappropriately. Citing such phrases as "black blood," Gladstone argued that the usage could only be understood by assuming that Homer, traditionally said to have been blind, was instead colorblind. Consequently, Homer thought blood was black. The poet's contemporaries are not known to have questioned the usage, inspiring Gladstone to argue, further, that the ancient Greeks as an entire people had little or no ability to perceive color (Gladstone 1858, 3:457– 99; 1877).

If Gladstone was correct, the ability to discriminate colors had developed only within the past three thousand years. This indicated Darwin had been wrong in supposing that biological evolution proceeded slowly. Until about 1924, when interest faded, the topic was heatedly discussed. Color blindness was conjectured to afflict many ancient and modern authors, as well as enormous sectors of the population of the world.

Geiger, among many who were captivated, applied Gladstone's reasoning to the Upanishads, the Eddas, and ancient Chinese works. He saw evidence that ancient peoples had an inability to distinguish blue. They also had difficulty with green and perhaps with yellow (Geiger [1871] 1880).

Dr. Hugo Magnus, an ophthalmologist and classical scholar from Breslau, "with an Aristotelian obliviousness of the possibility of testing his statements by experiment before publishing them," carried the argument further.[1] He contended that a defective color vocabulary characterizes most non-Europeans. According to him, various visual inadequacies are the cause, of which an inability to see blue is most common.

Christine Ladd-Franklin, whose writings on color are more widely known than those of others in the group, theorized that ability to distinguish colors is correlated with racial superiority (Ladd-Franklin 1929). Members of advanced societies see all colors. Nonurban peoples ("primitives") perceive the world in black and white. Or, in the variation more common in anthropological circles, they have defective acuity for blue (possibly also green), which they confuse with black.

Gladstone and his followers took counts of the number of times color names are used in ancient and modern literary works. Attention was paid to usage that seemed uncommon. Employing the same name for more that one color was taken to be a sign of inability to distinguish between the colors. In Beowulf, which dates from the early eighth century (Wallace 1927, 69), the 3,183 lines of the poem include sixteen terms descriptive of color, which occur a total of thirty-nine times. Most refer to color value, including such words as dark, bright, and pale, together with black, white, and gray.

Among early dissenters, Grant Allen sensibly argued that art is a more reliable indicator than language of ability to discriminate colors. What were being regarded as deficiencies in color vocabulary are not unique to ancient and tribal languages. Nor are they indicators of atypical vision (Allen 1879, 202–21). Allen pointed to Julius Caesar's report "that the ancient Welsh stained their bodies blue," evidence they were not insensitive to the appeal of that color. Allen distributed a twelve-part questionnaire to "missionaries, government officials, and other persons working amongst the most uncivilised races." He asked every question he could think of ("Have they separate names for green and blue? for green and violet?"). Allen concluded that it is not disinterest but "love for color which distinguishes the real savage."

Field workers set out to get to the bottom of the matter firsthand. W. H. R. Rivers, a member of the Cambridge anthropological expedition to the Torres Strait, which lies between Australia and New Guinea, collected data on color naming among Murray Islanders. He concluded they could not distinguish between blue and black (Rivers 1901, 44–58).

At the St. Louis Exposition of 1904, the psychologist R. S. Woodworth administered tests for color blindness to eleven hundred persons of diverse racial backgrounds. They were asked to match dark shades of colored paper with pale tints of the same color. Woodworth, who failed to recognize this as a test for inclination to sort by hue, regarded it as an examination of fineness in color discrimination. He found that "Filipinos, and indeed all races examined, were inferior to whites in this test. Negritos did better than many more advanced races" (Segall, Campbell, and Herskovits 1966, 44).

Though the assumptions of the researchers seem ridiculous, and they were often misled by their own racism, fallout from the great color-blindness controversy lingers. A folklore dictionary of recent vintage reports that, "not because they are color-blind, but because they have no use for a finer distinction, some primitive peoples see no more than three or four colors in the world around them. They have no terms for many of the colors other peoples see" (*Standard Dictionary of Folklore, Mythology, and Legend*, 1:242). For the authors, *see* implies *having a name for*, a gross though common misapprehension.

Everyday experience reveals that linguistic differences are not signs of genetic or racial differences in ability to distinguish colors. Americans of diverse ethnic backgrounds all use color names similarly. They all distinguish blue from green, and both from black. The uniformity would not occur if the ability to discriminate colors could be explained by reference to ethnicity.

The views of Gladstone and his followers were subjected to a slowly gathering tide of scrutiny. Rivers had given color-vision tests to Murray Islanders in an old missionary house without artificial illumination. The results were compared to those obtained from British observers tested in a well-lighted laboratory. The two sets of findings are not comparable, as Titchener complained fifteen years later

(Titchener 1916, 204–36). Colors look different under different illumination. Rivers was probably moved by expediency: artificial illumination may not have been available on the islands in the Torres Strait in 1901. But Rivers saw no connection between the light provided to his subjects and how well they were able to make fine color discriminations. The oversight speaks to the issue of his own understanding of color.

Natives of the Murray Islands, Rivers reported, had no name for blue and were unable to make clear discriminations when shown the color (Rivers 1901, 44–58). Titchener argued that Rivers misunderstood the similes Murray Islanders used to identify colors. *Golegole*, for example, is the name of the cuttlefish and a color. Rivers translated *golegole* as "black," assuming it refers to the black fluid secreted by the animal. Titchener contended *golegole* makes more sense as an allusion to the cuttlefish's variegated color. If Titchener's reinterpretations are accepted, the Murray Islanders made fewer errors in color naming than Rivers believed. And they never identified colors as black that were not black. If they had grouped blue and black together, what would the significance of the classification have been? Goethe saw the visual similarity between these two colors, though the researchers did not.

The theories of Gladstone and his followers are interpretations imposed on what were assumed to be peculiarities unique to non-Indo-European languages. If a people applied a common name to both green and blue, the question asked was whether they were visually insensitive to the difference between these hues. Because syntax encourages the oversight, speakers of English are forever forgetting that any color name refers to a range, not to a few shades of color. Given that the number of discernible shades of color (about ten million) greatly exceeds the number of color names in any known language, vastly different colors will inevitably be called by the same name. Brown is an example in English.

We commonly see differences in color without bothering to say what they are. An English-speaking observer may appropriately use the name *green* for both an extremely pale yellowish green and an extremely dark blue-green. Only when asked, or compelled by circumstances, do we go beyond the economies of everyday word usage to seek terms to express the greater number of color subtleties that can be seen. Language is poorly designed for succinctly explaining the range of variation in continua, including the color continuum. The difficulty in finding names for exact shades of color is known and often complained of.

The research of Gladstone and his followers was flawed in allowing for only two conclusions. The first was that primitive and ancient peoples were afflicted by inferior color vision. The second was that they possessed inferior color vocabularies by comparison with our own. A pathology was invented to explain Homer's "black blood." But no comment was offered on "black hearted," "yellow coward," and similar metaphorical forms in English. Wallace felt "tempted to wonder whether Gladstone was not a bit 'colorblind' himself to have appreciated so little the poetic metaphors embodied in Homer's color epithets" (Wallace 1927, 5). The theorists also did not notice that dried blood, as a matter of fact, looks black.

Why did variant systems for naming colors attract so much attention? Except among mathematicians, less interest was taken in the unusual methods of counting, often derived from bases other than ten, discovered in many parts of the non-European world. The answer may be that ascription to others of inferior conceptions about color is a challenge to their taste. Or it is an assertion of the superiority—not least of all, the moral superiority—of one's own taste. Behind this embarrassing cultural imperialism lies suspicion of the strangeness of the stranger, the unexamined assumption

that because we are sane the rest of the world must be crazy.

Gladstone, though forgotten as a color theorist, opened a chapter in the history of taste that winds along circuitous paths to settle again on the issue of taste in color, not just the preferences of natives in New Guinea but everyone's conception of what constitutes color harmony and how colors ought to be used. The taste of an era is not necessarily that of prime ministers and anthropologists. But in this case it was. Signac praised Delacroix because "he incited painters to dare everything and not to fear that a harmony can be too brightly colored" (Rewald 1943, 16). That, however, was radical talk. From the eighteenth century until well into the twentieth, expressions of a more conservative norm are typical.

Goethe thought it "worthy of remark, that savage nations, uneducated peoples, and children have a great predilection for vivid colours; that animals are excited to rage by certain colours; that people of refinement avoid vivid colours in their dress and the objects that are about them, and seem inclined to banish them altogether from their presence" (Matthaei 1971, 221).

Santayana reminded us that "children and savages, as we are so often told, delight in bright and variegated colors" (Edman 1936, 39). Moholy-Nagy similarly found that "children and primitives are particularly attracted to vivid, vital primary colors, especially red and yellow (Moholy-Nagy [1921] 1947, 155). Africans, Hawaiians, and Puerto Ricans have each been accused, at various times and by various accusers, of suspect taste for gaudy combinations of hue, though what is deplored as vulgarism at one time may become au courant at another.

Taste in color is inseparable from taste in art, which is why certain color combinations, say, pink, orange, and purple, are defended by pointing to painters (in this case, Matisse) who used these combinations. At about the time

Rivers was testing the Murray Islanders to see what could be wrong with their eyes, Oceanic, African, and American Indian art was being collected by the European and American ethnographic museums in which much of it still reposes. Its interest was thought to be just sociological. It was not regarded as art, because it looked different from European art. So did some European art. Demons were within, not just on foreign shores: artists whose work was deviant but who could not always be written off as charlatans or mentally unbalanced.

The ophthalmologist Ernst Fuchs resisted explaining art in terms of pathologies of the eye. Predicting the effect of these abnormalities is risky because there are, "for example, color-blind painters, whose work even with regard to color stands among the highest in the art. . . . It would be a great mistake to impute the peculiarities in coloration or drawing that are constantly exhibited by certain artists to any deficiency in their visual sense" (Fuchs [1908] 1924, 244). The argument had to be made because a web of ophthalmological interpretations had developed. Fuchs was not impressed by their Victorian pretension to verity. But others were and continued to be. The human figures in El Greco's paintings, an optician confided while fitting my eyeglasses, are long and thin because the artist had an astigmatism. Van Gogh's *Sunflowers*, the same optician confided, is painted primarily in yellow because the artist, who had better-documented ailments, was afflicted with xanthophilia or xanthopsia, because of which everything looked yellow. The condition must have been in remission on those days when van Gogh used other colors in his paintings.

What would my optician say if I told him I had no time for an eye exam? I could offer to send along one of my paintings, for his use in updating my eyeglass prescription. Even persons unfamiliar with the arts need not feel intimidated by an aesthetic theory that is so simple. Given the premise that an artist is sick

(the evidence for sickness is the art), the remaining task is to diagnose the affliction. Anyone is qualified to do this, and no examination of the patient is required.

The sickness of an artist who made unloved art or the sickness of persons with unusual taste in color was not always thought to be ophthalmological. The issue of moral fitness drew attention and continues to be intrusive in color theory today. Vanderpoel, observing that "the use of agreeable and harmonious colors tends to the sanity of the whole body by strengthening the nerves," reported "a few cases on record where all sensation of color is wanting, everything appearing in differing shades of grey" (Vanderpoel 1903, 73). Although hereditary in some instances, vice could not be overlooked because the defect "is also brought on by the excessive use of tobacco, alcohol, and other stimulants."

Jean-Martin Charcot (1825–93), the French specialist in nervous diseases, took an interest. Medical science was obliged to contribute where possible to understanding of the etiology. As Vanderpoel reported, "Dr. Charcot and his school in Paris have made many examinations into visual disturbances, and through these examinations much of the peculiar coloring and mannerism of some of the modern painters of the so-called impressionist, tachist, mosaist, gray-in-gray, violet colorist, archaic, vibrist, and color orgaist schools have been explained. The artists tell the truth when they say that nature looks to them as they paint it, but they are suffering from hysteria or from other nervous derangements by which their sight is affected" (Vanderpoel 1903, 6).

Vanderpoel knew enough about color to be publishing a book on the subject. Charcot was uninformed about color or art. Despite the extensive theorizing of the Impressionists, that artists are motivated by their ideas about art, not by nervous derangements, was not a possibility he considered. Why did Vanderpoel overlook Charcot's limitations? In one of two possible answers, his prejudices meshed with her own, a meeting of minds that makes strange allies. In the other, his credentials as a physician, a scientist, led her to assume he could offer superior insights even in areas far from his field of expertise.

Charcot's opinion, much quoted, was a watershed in the explanation of taste in color, color in art, and art. In the early twentieth century, those who looked to pathology for the key to deviant taste usually cited psychological imbalances rather than moral or ophthalmological defects. Or moral concern was expressed by wondering if the offenders were psychologically ill, a method expanded to answer any question. Despite his fascination with the creative process, Freud (who studied with Charcot in 1885) became adept at inventing a fatal flaw to devalue everything from artistic genius to altruism to the psychic life of women.

Freud also extended the scope of the method and took more interest in artists acknowledged to be great than in those who attracted a narrow audience. Art became the neurosis and the artist became the patient, summoned to the couch from beyond the grave in most cases. The ad hominem aspect of this reckless aggression is smoothed over today. In the hands of Freud and his followers, the methodology is called a form of literary criticism or art criticism. But writers and artists are the targets of investigation, not literature and art. The assessments offered become, at their worst, a high-flying version of the tabloids that reveal the secret vices of movie stars and public figures. Rarely are admirable qualities found in creative workers, or found worth discussing.

The innocuous, though unfruitful, idea that pleasing colors and great art have a moral value is of earlier vintage than Gladstone. He and his followers turned the idea upside down. They set the style of suspecting that what displeases or puzzles any viewer is immoral, depraved, or pathological. Whether among the islanders of the Torres Strait or in Leonardo da Vinci, taste and creativity, a human birthright, are reinterpreted as a festering cesspool of abnormalities of eye, mind, or soul.

Freud rarely used color names in his writings. Gladstone, when writing on topics other than Homer's color vision, probably used fewer than are found in *Beowulf*. The lapse raises questions about Freud's and Gladstone's eyesight if we ought to apply the reasoning used by Gladstone himself, by Geiger, Magnus, and Ladd-Franklin. In the study of human psychology, others filled in the gap. The Swiss psychiatrist Hermann Rorschach, rounding out Charcot's suspicion, found that French Impressionist painting indeed could be equated with "colors" (Rorschach 1964, 109). On the Rorschach inkblot test, undue interest in color at the expense of form is held typical of Impressionist painters and "epileptics, manics, imbeciles, paretics, scattered schizophrenics, or notoriously hot-headed, hyper-aggressive and irresponsible 'normals' " (Rorschach 1964, 33).

The message behind this madness is an autocratic determination to root out nonconformity, to set standards. Whether moral standards alone are the appropriate canon for color and the arts was never certain. Gustav Fechner and Wilhelm Ostwald, both trained in the physical sciences, were the most influential of those who hoped to prove that harmony of color and beauty in the arts were governed by scientific laws. The issue of morality could be laid to rest on the basis that scientific law by its nature is moral, a reasoning that led directly to modern color theory.

No responsible commentator argues today that color in Impressionist painting is best explained in terms of nervous derangement. Nor is defective color vision thought to be typical of contemporary artists and heathens beyond the pale of what Jung called "the white civilized world." But these indiscretions are not entirely behind us. Segall, Campbell, and Herskovits indicated the great color-blindness controversy "persisted unresolved" in the social sciences at least through 1966 (Segall, Campbell, and Herskovits 1966, 247). It would be comforting to find that lack of reliable information about anomalous color vision contributed to the confusion. But information was not lacking. It was ignored by the researchers, a classic example of self-deception in scientific research.

Ernst Fuchs, author of a standard text on ophthalmology (1908), and professor of that subject at the University of Vienna, held views on anomalous color vision substantially similar to those current in professional circles today. Fuchs found color blindness more difficult to diagnose than the anthropological literature of his day suggests. Rivers, for example, tested Murray Islanders by asking them to sort Holmgren wools. But Fuchs found "the wool test is unsatisfactory," a conclusion with which the Optical Society of America more recently concurred. The test "has been criticized as detecting only about half of the color defectives examined, as failing quite a number of over-anxious normals, and as permitting very easy practice improvement" (Fuchs [1908] 1924, 245; Optical Society of America 1953, 140).

Another instrument Rivers employed, the Lovibond tintometer, is not a tool for testing for color blindness and went unmentioned by Fuchs. Its usual use is in grading colors of industrial materials by comparing light reflected from a sample to light transmitted through colored glass filters. Industrial users criticize the tintometer because the erratic densities of its filters (red, yellow, and blue) make it difficult to calibrate and therefore unreliable (Optical Society of America 1953, 330). Rivers adapted the machine as a source of colored patches that the subject was asked to "recognize and name correctly" (River 1901, 44–58).

Rivers's tintometer would not have passed muster with Fuchs, who contended "we should not . . . undertake to test the color sense by setting colored objects before the person and asking him the name of the color." The problem is that "an uneducated man will not infrequently call the colors wrong" (Fuchs [1908] 1924, 247). Titchener, according to R. L. Gregory, "did a study at Cornell in which respondents were required to name the colors of bits of paper without the use of abstract color names, using instead the names of concrete objects. Analyzing these data in a manner analagous to Rivers, Titchener obtained specious evidence of an insensitivity to blue" (Gregory 1966, 46).

Fuchs named Nagel's anomaloscope as the standard clinical instrument. In conjunction with the Stilling test, it provided "the simplest and most satisfactory means of determining the presence of color blindness" (Fuchs [1908] 1924, 246). Gregory indicated that the anomaloscope, although the usual explanation of its functioning "must be wrong," remains a standard test instrument today (Gregory 1966, 125–29).

The anomaloscope was not mentioned by Rivers. Nor was the Stilling test, available at the time and apparently familiar to the nonmedical public. Grant Allen, before taking issue with the views on color vision propounded by Gladstone, Geiger, and Magnus, had tested his own eyes to be sure he was not color-blind himself. Without prejudice to what Fuchs would have thought about self-testing and self-diagnosis, he would have approved of Allen's report that the test was conducted by means of "Dr. Stilling's Tables for the Examination of the Colour-Sense" (Allen 1879, 206).

Judd noted four standard tests for color blindness used today (Judd 1979, 204). In the Holmgren wool test, the subject is asked to match pieces of wool to larger skeins that are red, green, and rose. In the Nagel charts, color spots are placed in a ring on different cards.

The subject must say which cards are of a single hue and which have several hues. On the Stilling charts, spots are arrayed and colored so that they form a digit that can be read by the normal observer. In the Ishihara charts, an improved version of the Stilling charts, some digits can be read only by normal observers (trichromats), others only by dichromats. Some of the Ishihara cards have two digits, one of which will be read by a normal observer, the other by a dichromat.

The findings produced by Gladstone and his followers were as bizarre as their methods. The type of color blindness they most often attributed to entire populations was insensitivity to blue, sometimes said to extend to include green and dark colors in general. The remote inspiration may have been Goethe, who had conjectured that two people he knew were unable to see blue.

Inability to distinguish blue, as a pathology, fits uneasily into either current ophthalmological theory or that of the early twentieth century. Fuchs identified three types of anomalous color vision: protanopia, deuteranopia, and tritanopia. He defined the first two as insensitivity to, respectively, red and green. In tritanopia, "probably the primary sensations of yellow and blue are wanting, but red and green are present. This condition, which is hence called blue-yellow-blindness (Hering) or violet blindness (Helmholtz), is so rare that it has been but insufficiently investigated" (Fuchs [1908] 1924, 243–44).

Gregory agreed that "tritanopia is extremely rare" (Gregory 1966, 127). The Optical Society of America distinguished between tritanopia, which is weakened perception of blue and yellow (and is rare), and tetaranopia, in which "the blue and yellow sensations are absent," the known condition that most closely approximates the blue blindness hypothesized by Gladstone, Magnus, Ladd-Franklin, and Geiger. Tetaranopia "is exceedingly rare, since only five cases have ever been described" (Optical Society of America 1953,137). Yet Geiger hypothesized a universal and total insensitivity to blue—tetaranopia—among all ancient peoples, while Magnus and Ladd-Franklin thought it was common to most or all non-Europeans.

I conclude, from reading Fuchs, that Rivers, an anthropologist, and Woodward, a psychologist, were unqualified to diagnose or assess visual anomalies. They should not have been testing anyone's eyes. They knew too little about color and color vision and had never consulted the ophthalmological literature of their day. Fuchs's opinions about anomalous color vision have stood the test of time better than theirs.

Like Rivers, modern researchers in the social sciences often devise their own tests, which hopefully do not incorporate as many misconceptions. Yet misconceptions will remain difficult to avoid until more people are trained to think visually, to reason in an orderly manner about what they see. The aestheticizing of color encourages dilettantism, an assumption that personal feelings are infallible and need not be subjected to scrutiny. A thread can be traced, in the history of theories about color, from Gladstone and his followers through Charcot and his followers to Wilhelm Ostwald and his followers. Research can be dead wrong, yet have an effect over a prolonged period. If it fails to contribute to a solution, it becomes part of the problem.

Bassa, Shona, and Ibo

Biologically speaking, there seems little doubt that our colour sense
was evolved from our tone sense. Originally the eye perceived only
degrees of light. Those who are completely colour-blind show a
reversion to this state.

Adrian Stokes, Colour and Form

Gladstone and his followers might be
written off as ethnocentric, a common shortcoming in nineteenth-
century scholarship. The researchers were
unsophisticated about color and insensitive to
the arbitrary nature of language. They questioned societies with different systems for
naming colors, though no system is more correct than another. Yet why should differences
exist between languages if language does not
drive perception? We all see the same thing.

Similarities lie behind linguistic differences.
Commenting on color-naming practices in
African languages, the modern linguist H. A.
Gleason, Jr., reminds us that the spectrum is
"a continuous gradation of color from one end
to the other. That is, at any point there is only
a small difference in the colors immediately

adjacent at either side. Yet an American
describing it will list the hues as *red, orange,
yellow, green, blue, purple*, or something of
the kind. The continuous gradation of color
which exists in nature is represented in language by a series of discrete categories. . . .
There is nothing inherent either in the spectrum or in human perception of it which
would compel its division in this way. The
specific method of its division is part of the
structure of English" (Gleason 1961, 4).

Bassa and Warm/Cool

Bassa and Shona, spoken in Liberia and Zim-
babwe, illustrate other ways of classifying
colors. The Bassa language is unusual in dividing the spectrum into just two main types of

color and their subvarieties. The divisions, *ziza* and *hui*, correspond to what are called warmness and coolness in English. The warm colors (*ziza*) are red, orange, and yellow. The cool colors (*hui*) are green, blue, and violet.

Gleason found an advantage to the Bassa system for one purpose, simple though the system may seem. Western botanists have discovered that our method of dividing the spectrum into six major hues "does not allow sufficient generalization for discussion of flower colors. Yellows, oranges, and many reds are found to constitute one series. Blues, purples, and purplish reds constitute another. These two exhibit fundamental differences that must be treated as basic to any botanical description. In order to state the facts succinctly it has been necessary to coin two new and more general color terms, *xanthic* and *cyanic*, for these two groups. A Bassa-speaking botanist, under no such necessity, would find *ziza* and *hui* adequate for the purpose. They divide the spectrum in approximately the way necessary" (Gleason 1961, 5).

What do speakers of Bassa notice that prompts them to group colors in this way? They attribute significance to the qualities we call warmness and coolness, ill-formed and confusing concepts in English. Warm colors (those with longer wavelengths) are said to advance visually. Cool colors (shorter wavelengths) are said to recede visually. Children and earnest art students often puzzle, to no conclusive end, over whether, say, a red color spot "comes forward" more than a blue spot does.

Red, orange, and yellow, the warm colors, indeed have a greater tendency to attract the eye, especially when set off by dark or dull colors. But we should not confuse subjective states of mind with action by external agencies: Because the visual field is a two-dimensional matrix, colors cannot advance or recede. No movement in a third dimension can occur. The red spot that seems to come for-

ward in, say, a watercolor painting, will be found seated as firmly on the paper as all other color spots if the painting is touched.

The advancing of color from its plane is a misleading figure of speech. I submit a less problematical explanation. In vision, the eye makes sense out of an array of color spots by seeking extremes. We look for the lightest spot, the darkest, the brightest, the area of greatest contrast. The colors we call warm usually attract the eye more than those we call cool. Poussin often used bright red at the focal point of the composition of his paintings, a color effective in drawing the viewer's attention.

Cool colors, given the right circumstances, compel attention as effectively as warm colors. In Renoir's *Madame Charpentier and Her Children* (Metropolitan Museum), most of the painting is in warm tones of orange and orange-brown. Two color areas stand out because of their contrast with this scheme. The pale blue of the children's clothing—a cool color—attracts attention for its difference from the painting's general tonality. The effect is strengthened by the nearby black and white in the dog and the mother's dress and by Renoir's virtuoso brushwork in the children's hair. We notice the people and the dog as Renoir intended, but particularly the children in their blue dresses.

In most cases, warm colors, especially red, attract attention more quickly than cool colors. The key, again, is relationship to a background. In the natural world, the most common colors in the environment are the tertiary colors, tones of brown and gray. The cool hues of the short-wavelength end of the spectrum—blue, green, and violet—look visually similar to the tertiaries and tend to get lost among them. For this reason, color schemes limited to cool colors and tertiary colors—say, a room decorated in blue, green, brown, and gray—run a risk of being considered dull. The colors are recognized as similar, perhaps too similar.

Warm colors provide a higher degree of contrast with the general background tonality.

Bright red usually attracts the eye more quickly than bright yellow, though yellow and black are a high-contrast pair in traffic signs and the yellow stands out. Whether or not seen against black, we probably equate yellow with white, because yellow and white are both light. Bright red, by default, is the color that looks most different from other colors, from the background tonality of the natural world. The popular combination of red, white, and black—strong hue against strong value contrast—changes in character if bright yellow is substituted for the red. The similarity between yellow and white becomes apparent.

Bassa divides color into *ziza* and *hui* without attributing warmness or coolness to these classes. No analogy is drawn between color and temperature. The colors at the long-wavelength end of the spectrum just look different from those at the short-wavelength end. In English, *warm* and *cool* are not regarded as color names, the exact reason botanists coined *xanthic* and *cyanic*. Yet the words warm and cool function in the same manner as, say, *red* or *blue*. Warm colors can be sorted from cool colors as easily as red from blue.

The English language, unlike Bassa, is structured to downplay the importance of warmness or coolness, though the qualities are seen and acknowledged. If asked the color of a red object, the observer is thought to have given a wrong answer if *warm* is supplied. *Warm* and *cool*, like *light* and *dark*, are not color names in English other than in a de facto sense. A speaker of Bassa would find this strange.

Shona
In the Shona language, *cipswuka* identifies reds and purples, grouped together on the basis of visual similarity. *Citema* is used for black, blue, and blue-green. *Cicena* identifies white, yellow, yellow-green, and green. In addition to

cipswuka, citema, and *cicena,* its main generic terms for hue or hue/value, Shona, like Bassa, contains names for more refined variations, subvarieties within the class. These correspond to English words such as crimson, scarlet, or rose.

The Shona name *cipswuka* probably would not puzzle speakers of English. Red and violet are at opposite ends of the spectrum. But reds and violets look similar, and a range of red-violet colors exists "between" red and violet. The use of *citema* for both blue and black, of *cicena* for both yellow and white, is more surprising. The practice of applying a single name to both a range of hue and either black or white is found in several languages. A cause of controversy in anthropological research, it largely accounts for erroneous reports of color blindness to blue or of inability to distinguish blue from black. Color blindness to black was never suggested as an explanation, a sign of the narrow channel in which the researchers' thoughts flowed. Reports of confusion between white and yellow were also rare, apparently because the researchers saw the visual similarity between white and yellow more easily than that between black and blue.

A single name for blue and black is precluded in English because colors are segregated by hue, and hue is separated from value. Blue is classified as a hue. Black, white, and gray are identified as values. Speakers of Shona treat hue and value as equal in importance, or prefer value. This leads to a system with its own refinements. The average speaker of English, shown spectral blue and spectral yellow, identifies the pair as *blue* and *yellow*, which fails to take account of the darker value of blue. Because "the strongest yellow pigment is by nature much lighter, or higher in value, than the strongest blue pigment" (Munsell 1969, 25), giving correct answers in English compels the speaker to identify one aspect of the blue/yellow relationship while ignoring another.

To argue that speakers of English, who rarely point out the greater darkness of spectral blue, are unable to see lightness and darkness would be absurd. No more reliable basis exists for the once popular supposition that speakers of languages such as Shona, with a single generic name for blue and black, see no hue difference between these dark colors. Human experience is richer than human language, and when language is used to report experience, more is left out than can be included. Language compels speakers to extrapolate, which is both its strength and its weakness. A speaker of English who never used the word *blue* without mentioning that blue is darker than yellow would be regarded as eccentric. People would have no idea why the information was being offered.

Segregating hue, the custom in the West, is consistent with Newton's theories about color. But Newton had a conception of color before developing his theories and may have tailored the theories to this conception. In Third World cultures studied before the advent of television, a tendency to group blue with black is neither unusual nor surprising. Blue and black look similar, especially if the blue is dull or dark. In *The Tibetan Book of the Dead*, five major colors are associated with deities "enhaloed in radiance of rainbow light" in a mandala (Evans-Wentz [1927] 1966,127). The colors are white, red, yellow, green, and blue. Black is absent from the rainbow mandala, and blue is the only color of the rainbow lights with a negative connotation. The soul is warned not to be "attracted towards the dull blue light of the brute-world . . . wherein stupidity predominates" (Evans-Wentz [1927] 1966, 130).

In the United States, the art of "singing the blues" emerged in a population of African descent. Feeling blue, in the original form of the idiom, was attributed to the blue devils. Other phrases that metaphorically equate blue with sadness may have an independent origin.

Although blue ribbons are awarded as prizes, blue is also equated with negative feelings and conditions similar to those associated with black. Blue laws are puritanical (the Puritans dressed in black) and designed to curb those who do not respect the Sabbath.

Ibo

In Ibo, a language spoken in Nigeria, color is initially classified as either o-*ji* or o-*cha*. O-*ji* identifies colors that are blackish or dark. O-*cha* identifies colors that are whitish or light. O-*ji* and o-*cha* are not equivalent to the Shona *citema* and *cicena*, because no separate class exists for red-violets. Nor can *citema* and *cicena* be adequately translated as *dark* and *light*, because different conventions govern their use.

The speaker of English, asked to sort light colors from dark ones, assumes a command to ignore hue. Light blues are placed in one pile, dark blues in another. In Ibo, o-*ji* and o-*cha* refer to the value range of the spectral color, taken as a norm for that color in certain cases. Blue is always o-*ji*, a dark color. Yellow is always o-*cha*, a light color. Purple and green can belong to either class. A dark purple or green is o-*ji*, light varieties are o-*cha* (figure 23-1).

The initial division is supplemented by a simile citing an object familiar to Ibo speakers. An orange object is described by remarking that its color is o-*cha* and like palm oil (which is orange). Red is compared to blood, black to charcoal, green to leaves, blue to the sky, and so forth. *Melemele*, an alternate name for blue objects, is an exception to the preference for simile, and identifies blue objects without comparing them to anything else.

Despite the significance attributed to hue in English, our ability to describe colors would be severely limited if words referring to lightness and darkness were lacking. The English language includes phraseology similar in con-

Figure 23-1. Hue (major color) classifications in Ibo. Unlike English, which segregates by either hue or value but not both at the same time, the Ibo language uses a combined hue/value system.

o-*cha*	o-*ji*
(light colors)	(dark colors)
white	black
red	blue
yellow	green
orange	purple
purple	
violet	
green	

tent to the Shona and Ibo terms though syntactically quite different. *Pastel* resembles *cicena* in identifying the class of light colors, including pale pink, pale blue, pale yellow, and pale green. *Light colors* and *dark colors* are used to group in a syntactically similar manner.

Tint, tone and *shade* are more formal. They too refer to value irrespective of hue, though not to value alone. *Tint* identifies a color that is light expressly because it contains white. Spectral yellow, though light, is not a tint. *Shade* identifies a color that is dark because it contains black. *Tone* identifies a color containing gray. Spectral blue, though dark, is neither a shade nor a tone. Yellow, purple, green, or any other color becomes a tint if mixed with white, a shade if mixed with black, a tone if mixed with gray. Because *shade* also means variety or kind (as in "the exact shade of blue"), *tone* is sometimes used for a color mixed with either black or gray.

Although English provides a facility for classifying colors according to lightness or darkness, whether this constitutes classification according to color is messy. As in the case of warmness and coolness, English includes words that function as color names though we say they are not color names. Colors can be sorted according to whether pastels, tints,

tones, shades, warm colors, or cool colors. Pastels are a range of pale (or whitish) colors, a continuum as easily surveyed as the range or continuum of colors called red. Yet *pastel, tint, tone*, and *shade* are not regarded as names of colors. Neither are *dark colors, grayed colors, pale colors*, or other similar constructions. I will be understood if I ask a salesperson to show me dresses in pastel colors. If asked the color of a pink dress, I cannot correctly answer "pastel," which is not the name of a color.

A word, say, *red*, qualifies as a color name in the English language if it identifies a range of colors classified by chromatic difference without regard to lightness or darkness. But the use of hue as a sorting criterion is not the whole story. A color name can also be a word that identifies any achromatic range from which hue is excluded (black, white, gray, light gray, dark gray). What cannot be a color name is a label for any range of colors in which value is the sorting criterion but chromatic differences are allowed. *Black, gray*, and *white* are color names. *Tone, tint*, and *pastel* are not. The imperative is to isolate chromatic differences from value differences, to avoid mixing one with the other.

The bias probably existed in English, or in earlier languages from which modern English is derived, well before the hue circles and gray scales of modern color theorists presented the separation of hue and value as a discovery. But it was not the original method in English. Words such as *pale, light, dark*, and *bright* appear more often in *Beowulf* than hue names. The primal color names adopted at some later point might have been regarded as a better system for naming colors. Evidently, the primal names came to be classified as the only bona fide names for colors. Words like *light* and *dark* continued to be used, but were regarded as not really color names.

Ibo offers insights into why so many color names in the English language are compressed similes, borrowings from the names of objects.

In Ibo, a color might be identified as, say, light and like a lemon. English has the apparatus for similar constructions, and we find the apparatus, though not the constructions, in *Beowulf*. "Light, and like a lemon," easily reduces to lemon colored or just lemon.

In English, the separation of value from hue shores up the idea that black and white should be regarded as opposites, a moral agenda linking the colors with good and bad. The idea has no meaning in visual terms, because the purported oppositeness—as opposed to just differentness—cannot be seen. Filling out the picture by grouping the hues into pairs of opposites as well is of more modern vintage, familiar from nineteenth-century literature on the hues and their complements. Despite a century of argumentation about color complementarity—about which hue is opposite to which—we still interpret moral differences in terms of black and white, rather than in terms of, say, red and green, or orange and blue.

English is syntactically inconsistent in including words that identify ranges of color yet are not considered real color names. *Pastel* is a de facto color name because the word identifies a range of related colors. Its meaning, like that of any color name, can only be taught ostensively. The congenitally blind can learn to say that pastel colors are pale, just as they learn to say that grass is green. They can have no conception of what either statement means in visual terms; they cannot sort color samples according to whether pastel or green.

A moral agenda, where it exists, is based on literary concepts. Hue is separated from value to preserve symbolic associations that link white and black with good and evil. Amorality or immorality has been attributed to bright hue, which lacks the moral associations of black and white. I am not surprised that the American Puritans and the Calvinists dressed in black and white, that Santayana believed only children and savages liked bright colors, and that

Goethe thought persons of refinement showed a distaste for bright colors. Liking colors is not quite mainstream, a preference attributed to women, artists, and aesthetes. I find these ideas wrongheaded because they grow from a mingling of things that do not belong together. Good and evil are in the human mind, as are ideas about human sexual mores. Colors, like trees, rocks, and clouds, are neither good nor evil. Although the literary (I do not mean literate) cast of the English language prompts us in this direction, burdening colors with inappropriate symbolic associations becomes a form of collective baby talk.

The baby talk is not always harmless. A clear definition of what constitutes a color name in the English language would be helpful for, say, evaluation of the visual agnosias, the condition in which patients are said to have forgotten color names. Developing a definition is complicated by the double standard, by the presence of *pastel, tone, shade, warm, cool* and other words that are not considered color names though each names a range of colors. The words cannot be eliminated because we need them.

A more subtle harm is the coarsening of visual sensibility. The Shona doubtless have a system of morality, evolved without clouding the issue of whether *cicena* and *citema* are color names. It would be interesting to know whether their moral system is quite as black and white as ours.

The differing values of the spectral hues are acknowledged in the Ostwald and Munsell systems. Both systems make clear that, say, no bright yellow can be as dark as a bright purple. But both systems segregate hue from value. In a more innovative diagram of color relationships developed by Kandinsky, white is associated with yellow because both are light, and black is associated with blue because both are dark (figure 23-2). Kandinsky may have been led to this arrangement by the idea that white is a combination of all spectral hues,

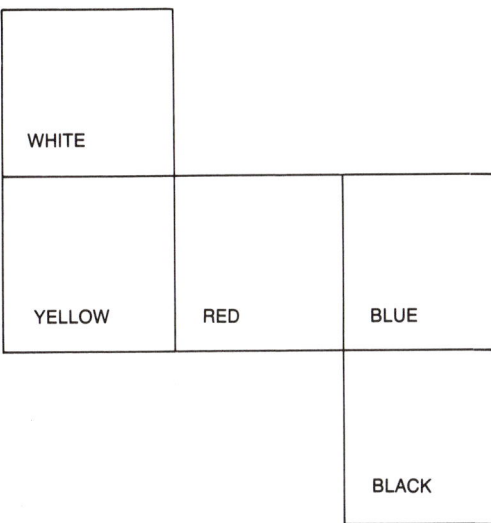

Figure 23-2. Kandinsky's hue/value scale. Over a period of time, Kandinsky gradually refined his palette to black, white, red, yellow, and blue, presumably because these colors could be regarded as pure, simple, or spiritual. His diagram of relationships among these colors assumes a hierarchy in which hue and value are combined.

while black is the absence of light (a presence of no hue). Completing the syllogism, each spectral hue might fall on a continuum between these extremes. If Kandinsky's stepped boxes are rearranged into a straight line, the result is a combined hue/value scale, an integrated system similar to that of the Shona.

In another kind of combined hue/value scale, the colors can be arranged in a circle (figure 23-3). Reading clockwise from center bottom (white to black), the colors grow progressively darker. The pairs on the axis show maximum contrast: of value in the case of black and white, of hue in the case of red and green. In this scale no color lies opposite the color identified as its complement on a conventional color wheel. But each lies opposite another of high contrast to it. The high contrast pairs are white and green, yellow and blue, orange and violet, red and black.

Although yellow and blue, for instance, are presumed to be less different than the conventional complements of yellow and purple, I am not convinced that this is the case. How can a child be taught yellow is "more different" from purple than from blue? If a visual criterion cannot be identified, complementarity has no meaning in visual experience.

Unlike the Shona, we regard blue and black as categorically dissimilar. Signs that the colors are visually related are taken as oddities when noticed. Using, say, Winsor & Newton oil paints, rose madder and black can be mixed to form a series of purples. In mixtures of black and yellow, black similarly behaves as if it were blue and produces dull olive greens, though not bright greens. A table of reflectances of artists' pigments, condensed from a compila-

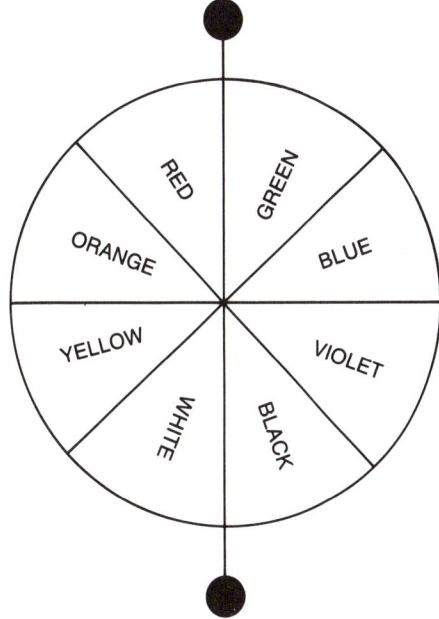

Figure 23-3. Hue/value scale. In this alternative arrangement of a color wheel, pairs of high-contrast hues lie opposite each other but are not complements in the traditional sense. Reading around the circle from white to black, the colors grow progressively darker in value.

Figure 23-4. Reflectances of artists' pigments. From
"Technical Studies," 1939, Cambridge, Massachusetts.
Fogg Art Museum, Harvard University.

Pigment	Dominant wavelength (millimicrons)	Reflectance (percent)	Purity (percent)
Alizarin crimson	628.0	6.6	57.2
English vermilion	608.1	22.3	59.9
Cadmium red	604.8	20.8	67.3
Venetian red	599.2	13.1	50.2
Burnt sienna	598.5	7.6	40.1
Burnt umber	589.5	5.1	34.2
Cadmium orange, medium	586.9	42.2	86.9
Raw sienna	584.2	20.0	61.3
Chrome yellow, medium	581.6	63.1	81.8
Zinc yellow	575.8	32.6	79.7
Zinc white	569.5	94.9	1.5
Chrome green, medium	552.4	16.0	34.7
Emerald green	511.9	39.1	22.8
Ivory black	494.5	2.2	1.7
Cobalt blue	474.6	16.8	65.5
Cobalt violet	560.3c	9.3	48.5
Manganese violet	553.7c	27.0	21.6

c = colors that cannot be matched by monochromatic spectral light.

tion by the Fogg Art Museum, indicates that the dominant wavelength reflected by ivory black is in the blue range (figure 23-4). The paint appears black because so little light is reflected.

As the table also indicates, the perceived color of paint is not always consistent with the dominant wavelength reflected. Alizarin crimson is a bluish or purplish red rather than an orange-red. Yet its dominant wavelength lies in the orange or red-orange range. The dominant wavelength of Venetian red, a dull orange red, is in the yellow or yellow-orange, rather than red-orange, range.

Black can be mistaken for blue more easily than for any other color, a sign that the colors look similar. If an area of pale gray (made by mixing black and white) is next to an area of value-similar pale blue (made by mixing blue and white), the colors are difficult to distinguish from a distance. The combination would be a poor choice for, say, traffic signs. The effect of merging cannot be replicated using pale yellow and pale gray, or pale yellow and pale blue. The colors in these sets look differ-

ent, even if matched closely in value and seen from a distance. Among darker varieties of color, black and navy blue are more easily confused from a distance than, say, black and dark maroon. The reason for confusing them is that they look similar.

Goethe wrote of blue's "affinity with black." He found that if "darkness is seen through a semi-transparent medium, which is itself illuminated by a light striking on it, a blue colour appears," an observation bearing on the Tyndall blues (Matthaei, 1971, 223). Furthermore, "blue gives an impression of cold, and thus, again, reminds us of shade."

Goethe's belief that blue is cold need not have come solely from its visual affinity with black. In English we speak of feeling blue with cold. And the evolutionary scale, ascended, seems to show a bias toward muted variations on the warm colors, suggesting positive (good, warm) affinities for these colors. Although blue eyes in human beings and in Siamese cats are among the exceptions, blue, violet, and green are rare colors among mammalian forms. Among the warm hues, bright red, orange, and yellow are less often seen among mammals than among birds, reptiles, insects, and plants. Muted forms of these colors are common: umbers, russet-browns, tans, yellow-browns, and so forth.

Color in Nature

Attempts to understand color by observing its occurrence in nature were largely abandoned after Newton. They were briefly revived by Goethe, who pointed to Robert Boyle as his model. In biological forms, color guides a selective ability to absorb light and determines the wavelengths absorbed. This color selectivity is integral to the life process, and perhaps it was crucial to the origin of life.

The oldest fossil organisms thus far discovered resemble modern blue-green algae (Myxophyceae), which possess blue pigments in addition to the green chlorophyll found in other plants. The ancient algae, if also blue-green, reflected blue and green rays while absorbing and utilizing those in the red, orange, and yellow range. The sea in which they lived is also blue-green, more greenish near coasts. The rays the algae needed penetrate the sea, but only to shallow depths, as Rachel Carson pointed out in *The Sea Around Us* (Carson 1958).

Red, orange, and yellow rays are available to a depth of two hundred to three hundred feet. Greens fade out somewhat lower, and blue penetrates to one thousand feet. Violet rays may reach another thousand feet. Beyond that, all is dark. The red, yellow, and orange rays used by blue-green algae are available primarily near the surface, limiting the depth at which the algae can live.

Carson found the colors of animals in the sea generally related to depth. Fish that live near the surface are often blue or green. Closer to a depth of one thousand feet, many creatures are transparent. Between one thousand and fifteen hundred feet, common colors are

silver, red, brown, black, and violet. At depths greater that fifteen hundred feet, "all the fishes are black, deep violet, or brown, but the prawns wear amazing hues of red, scarlet and purple." (Carson 1958, 43). Half the fishes that live in dark waters are luminescent, and some are blind. In deep-sea fishes the cones of the retina tend to atrophy while the rods, which give low-light vision, increase (Carson 1958, 44). Evidently these fish, because they have the retinal cones that provide color vision, descended from ancestors who lived at shallower depths. When the fish moved into darker, deeper waters, low-light (rod) vision became more useful.

Even in clear ocean water, no plants live below six hundred feet, and most live in the upper two hundred feet. The green pigmentation in plant cells, chlorophyll, found in small globular bodies called chloroplasts, is color-programmed to require rays of the warmer colors. Although various explanations have been given for the phenomenon, chlorophyll, when dissolved in ether, shows a bright red fluorescence even if the exciting light is blue or yellow. (Govindjee and Govindjee 1974). The fluorescence is close to the color of human blood, in which hemoglobin, which is red, plays a role similar to that played by chlorophyll in plants.

Why have no ocean plants adapted to life in the dark depths? Some land plants, such as mushrooms and fungi, live in the dark. A probable reason is the coldness that accompanies absence of light. Although polar bears, penguins, and seals live in the Arctic, plant life disappears at low temperatures. That polar bears have fur is incidental to the more basic color programming of life forms. In higher plants and animals this turns on the greenness of chlorophyll and the redness of hemoglobin.

Among plants that live on the land, chlorophylls are found in conjunction with other pigments including the carotenoids, which are red, orange, or yellow. Chlorophylls absorb primarily in the red, orange, blue, and violet ranges. Carotenoids, which account for the color of carrots, absorb mainly blue wavelengths. The carotenes, a class of carotenoids, are converted to vitamin A in the mammalian liver. Chlorophyll and the several other pigments associated with it absorb, in aggregate, light from most of the wavelengths of the solar spectrum. Houseplants often do poorly under artificial light, which lacks many of these wavelengths. They improve under lights balanced to more nearly approximate the colors of light from the sun.

The close chemical similarity between chlorophyll and hemoglobin, the substance that gives mammalian blood its red color, is one of the most curious color phenomena in nature. When cited as an argument in favor of a vegetarian diet, the assumption is that chlorophyll can be easily converted to hemoglobin because the molecules are identical except for one atom. A porphyrin ring that forms a sort of head for the chlorophyll molecule has an atom of magnesium at its center. The corresponding porphyrin ring in hemoglobin contains an atom of iron instead of magnesium.

Unlike the chloroplasts of plants, red blood cells are not exposed to direct sunlight. Mammalian blood moves through the closed channels of a circulatory system. But sunlight penetrates mammalian tissue through the skin, as in the process by which it stimulates calcium metabolism and synthesis of vitamin D.

Interior parts of the body can also be affected by light entering through the eye. Sexual maturing in mammals, known to be stimulated by light, is delayed in congenitally blind individuals. Richard J. Wurtman, studying other light-driven biological rhythms, found that many were color-driven. Green light is most effective in shifting the body-temperature rhythm in rats and in suppressing activity of the pineal gland (Wurtman 1975, 75). Jaundice in premature human infants can be cured by exposing the child to light, and blue light works better than other colors.

Coloration in animals, including the redness of mammalian blood, gives every sign of a biological purpose, as does the greenness of plants. Color also seems to have a function in the absence of light, although we know little about this. Human beings assume that color has no purpose in environments in which human beings would be unable to see it. This idea is ill-considered. Red prawns live deeper in the ocean than red light waves penetrate and ought to look black to other fish—if the fish perceive the prawns as we would. The parchment worm (*Chaetopterus pergamentaceus*) is strongly luminescent. Yet it lives buried, just its two ends slightly protruding, in a tube it builds on the sea bottom. No other creature ever sees its orange light.

Unless invisible, every object is some color, even if just transparent or black. We have no grounds for assuming that for creatures living in darkness black is a better color than, say, red or orange. Interior parts of the human body are not black, even in dark-skinned peoples. Yet these parts are not exposed to light.

The redness of mammalian blood implies absorption of wavelengths in the blue and green range, a different way of operating than that catalyzed by the greenness of chlorophyll in plants. Although lower animals lack red blood cells and some algae are red, one question is whether plants differentiated from animals according to whether they utilized primarily the longer or shorter wavelengths of the solar spectrum. Whatever the answer, the life process is intimately associated with the colors of the pigments carried by organisms, not just by light. That coloration is not biologically casual is also implied by its genetic basis. Each organism, like each part of that organism, is limited to some colors and not others. Daisies are never black; human hair is never blue or green. Although some living creatures are small and others are transparent, no organism is invisible, another kind of color constraint. Where life exists, it has a color condition.

Robert Boyle conjectured that white animals would be more prevalent in Arctic climates, as protective coloration in snow or because less light was available to "bring out" their colors. Rarely do assumptions as simple as the second prove out. And the mechanisms of nature often do not conform to what color theory suggests. For example, dark objects are better absorbers of light than light objects, which suggests that dark skin would be better for cold climates.

Alternatively, people in cold climates might have developed fluorescent or luminescent skin, since fluorescent and luminescent colors store light and release it later. People in hot climates might have evolved silver skin. Silver is excellent at reflecting light. Or all human beings might have developed transparent bodies. In the tropics, transparency would pass light through. In the Arctic, people could use the transparency of their bodies to focus light, starting fires whenever they wanted. Nature, in the designing of human skin, operates by another logic. Silver, along with luminescence, fluorescence, and transparency, never appears in mammalian forms, though common in fish and insects. The amount of melanin, a dark pigment, determines the color of human skin.

Protective coloration in animals has been studied. But no organized body of scientific research as broad as, say, cosmology, assesses the function of color as we perceive it throughout the physical world.

Whether the universe is one or many, breaking down or developing, biological evolution has led to progressively more complicated forms, with more complex requirements about the ways in which light or color or both are used. To grow complex, however, is to grow vulnerable, because complicated machines have more parts that can break. Against this background of change, color in life forms was evidently always genetic. The ancient blue-green algae were all the same color, programmed by this color to live under certain conditions. Why were the earliest life forms not black, capable of absorbing all wavelengths? Why is neither chlorophyll nor hemoglobin that color, although dead leaves and dried blood turn brown or black?

We rarely associate purpose with the inanimate world, because the concept suggests consciousness. Yet I doubt that the apparently purposeful nature of color is unique to life forms. Crystals have their molecules arranged in an orderly fashion and are often transparent. The transparency, which passes light, minimizes the deteriorating effect of sunlight. Do inanimate substances have certain patterns they tend to preserve? If so, a law is suggested similar to the law of inertia or Darwin's concept of the preservation of species.

Transparent plastics deteriorate rapidly, largely from the effect of ultraviolet wavelengths. While doing so, some turn yellow, a color effective at reflecting or blocking ultraviolet. The lens of the human eye, which filters out ultraviolet, also acquires a yellowish cast with age, as if this additional assistance was needed to protect a retina more fragile than in youth. Coal, buried in the ground, is black, the best absorber of radiant energy. Is this a source of the heat needed to transform coal into diamonds?

We know much more about the effect of, say, vitamins than about how different colors or wavelengths of light affect the human body. The damage to the earth's ozone layer has been an unpleasant reminder that excess ultraviolet causes cataracts and skin cancer. The yellow-brown smog over large American cities shifts the color balance of sunlight passing through, to what public health effects we do not fully know.

The color of electric lights is so different from sunlight that the same color camera film cannot be used to record both accurately. Except that grow lights are available for plants, no effort has been made to correct this. Yet we know that blue light, weak in indoor illumination, cures jaundice in premature infants. The correlation bears on the sallow complexion attributed to those who work indoors.

Newton left us the idea that the objects of the world can be regarded as reflectors of light and themselves colored only for that reason. This does not explain the mechanism of selectivity in reflectance, of why these objects are many colors, or colored by a variety of pigments. If every object reflected every wavelength of light, we would live in a world of monochrome white, a reversal of the nominal blackness of the night. Nature may tell us more about color theory than color theory can tell about nature.

CHAPTER 24

Tristimulus Theory and Metamerism

These persons, as may be gathered from what has been stated, saw fewer colors than other people: hence arose the confusion of different colours. They called the sky rose-colour, and the rose blue, or *vice versa*. The question now is: did they see both blue or both rose colour? did they see green [as] orange, or orange [as] green?

Johann Wolfgang von Goethe, Farbenlehre

Color blindness, a condition that provokes controversy among theorists, is no longer cited to support beliefs about ancient and primitive cultures. We do not believe grossly defective color vision afflicts entire populations. Anomalous color vision remains of interest to colorimetrists for its bearing on tristimulus theory, an elaboration of the idea that three primary colors exist.

Tristimulus Theory

Tristimulus theory is loosely based on ideas originally put forth by Thomas Young (1773–1829), James Clerk Maxwell (1831–79), and Ewald Hering (1834–1918). Young, an English physician, discovered that most spectral colors (not all) could be matched by a mixture of three properly selected lights of different colors. He concluded that the eye needed only three receptors to enable all colors to be seen. Maxwell developed a coordinate system for plotting the three lights that became known as the Maxwell triangle (figure 24-1). Hering, who believed the receptors might each be sensitive to a range, identified these ranges as red to green, yellow to blue, and white to black (light to dark).

Modern tables of tristimulus value list the relative proportions of red, green, and blue light required to match monochromatic lights in the spectral colors for a statistically determined standard observer (see figure 11-2). But the varieties of anomalous color vision that occur in human populations cannot be entirely correlated with what tristimulus theory

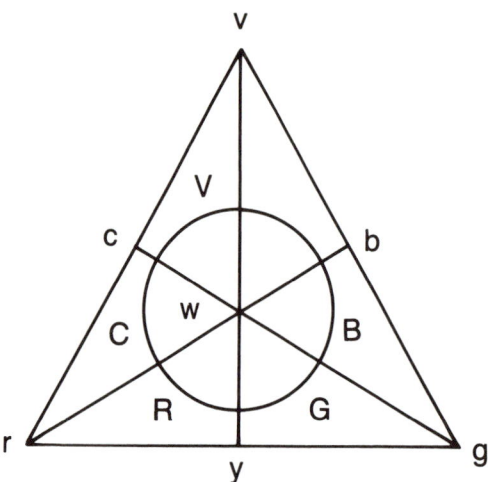

Figure 24-1. The Maxwell triangle. All hue variations can be plotted on the Maxwell triangle between the extremes of red, violet, and green (the corners). White lies at the center. (After Maxwell [1890] 1965, 121.)

implies. The most common type, popularly called red-green blindness, is an inherited, sex-linked characteristic. The condition is sometimes attributed to 10 percent of all men. Judd provided a more conservative estimate of 3 percent, along with one-tenth of 1 percent of all women (Judd 1979, 198). No other type of defective acuity for color shows evidence of a genetic basis.

Atypical acuity for red and green would appear to be a serious impediment to recognizing traffic lights. Judd contended this was not so, because a "traffic signal red is a yellowish red, seen as yellow by the red-green blind; many of the green traffic signals have purposely been made bluish green so that red-green blind observers would see the signal as weak blue and so be able to tell it from the red signal" (Judd 1979, 198). For Fuchs, however, "bluish green appears to [the color blind] a colorless grey" (Fuchs [1908] 1924, 243).

Because yellow light is said to be a mixture of red and green light, how a traffic light could be "seen as yellow" by those with impaired

acuity for green and red is unclear. If, as in pigments, green is a mixture of yellow and blue, normal acuity in the yellow/blue range is inconsistent with impaired ability to see green. Conjectures about what the color blind seen tend to be more confusing than helpful, and the condition is as poorly described as the visual agnosias.

Relying on Young's three receptors, three basic types of color vision are identified. These are *trichromatism, dichromatism,* and *monochromatism.* Individuals in these groups require, respectively, three, two, or one color(s) of light to match any color they see. Trichromatism (three lights) is considered normal. But anomalous trichromats, who are otherwise asymptomatic, require different proportions of the lights than those found to be statistically average. Anomalous trichromats may be no more genuinely anomalous than individuals who require, say, a different amount of sleep than is statistically average. But questions would arise about tristimulus theory if we could show that anomalous trichromats do not, in fact, see colors differently.

Monochromatism

The monochromat can match any color with one light, which varies in brightness but not in hue. An individual limited in this manner sees fewer colors than average and is assumed to distinguish solely between darkness and lightness (black/white). Monochromatism receives less attention in the literature than dichromatism. But the condition is easier to reconcile with modern theory about the function of the retinal rods and cones.

The rods, which provide low-light vision, differentiate primarily between light and dark, the reason colors become progressively more difficult to distinguish in the evening. If the cones were to become nonfunctional, vision might be limited to dark/light (black/white) sensations. The eyes of fish that live in the depths of the ocean, where little or no light reaches, often have atrophied cones.

Theory is not prepared to explain why monochromatism, once attributed to large sectors of the world's human population, and today to dogs and cats, does not occur in isolation in human beings. Vision limited to differentiation between light and dark appears pathological, rather than an otherwise normal functioning devoid of hue discrimination. It usually occurs in conjunction with photophobia (oversensitivity to light) and low visual acuity (Fuchs [1908] 1924, 244).

Given these conditions, absence of ability to distinguish hue is less an anomalous form of color vision than a symptom of serious visual impairments that include inability to distinguish forms. The legally blind man or woman who can distinguish only degrees of light and darkness and who has little or no perception of form is more frequently encountered than the classical monochromat: the individual, if any, who sees the world as if it were a perfectly clear black-and-white photograph.

The human eye without viable cones may be as unable to function in a normal manner as the circulatory system without viable red blood cells. Yet what constitutes normal functioning is arguable in this case. A progressive degradation in acuity is a feature of vision under low light conditions. As evening progresses, we lose the ability to see objects clearly, not just the ability to see their colors. Rod vision is less acute than cone vision and may resemble the vision of creatures lower on the evolutionary scale. Some amphibians perceive only movement, the reason for the folk advice to stand perfectly still in the presence of a snake.

Creatures able to see only movement must perceive a monochromatic world of fleeting shadows, a condition we would characterize as impaired vision if it occurred in a human

being. At an even lower evolutionary level, photosensitivity, the primitive response to light or its absence, can occur even in organisms without eyes. The phototropism of plants, which causes them to grow toward the light, is a photosensitivity of this sort.

Not Seeing Light and Dark

Popular beliefs about color infect theory because they are shared by the theorists. Where shall we place diminished acuity for colors regarded as "not colors"? Lessened ability to distinguish black from white (dark from light) is rarely or never singled out as an impairment of color vision. Yet the condition actually exists and is far more common than classical monochromatism, which may not exist at all.

If we forget that form cannot be isolated from color in visual experience, we are liable to assume that color vision functions like the tinting applied to black-and-white photos. Transparent glazes of color are imagined to overlay black-and-white shapes that could maintain their integrity without the colors. The model is implicit in the reasoning of Gladstone and his followers but marginally appropriate even for low-light vision in the evening. Under daylight illumination, the superior analogue is the color photograph, devoid of black and white shapes in the sense that the layers of dye on the film are red, yellow, and blue.

Irrespective of how vision ought to be modeled, diminished acuity within the black/white range is as legitimately a defect of color vision as impaired acuity for hue. The condition is commonplace and the subject of an extensive literature. Popularly called night blindness (hemeralopia), it consists of more than normally diminished visual acuity under conditions of low illumination. Apparently caused by reduced functioning of the rods, night blindness is often attributed to vitamin A deficiency. But it can be symptomatic of other conditions, and it occurs with the aging process (Fuchs [1908] 1924, 249-51). Although not classified as a form of anomalous color vision, night blindness implies a lessened ability to distinguish between black and white, particularly in low-light environments. It coexists with apparently undiminished acuity, under daylight illumination, for red, yellow, blue, green, and other colors.

Those afflicted by night blindness, or by its milder form manifested by slow visual adaptation to the dark, see the darkness. Their difficulty is limited to distinguishing light, a white blindness unaccompanied by black blindness. If the condition is caused by impaired functioning of the rods, no impairment should occur under daylight illumination. I suspect the condition occurs both by day and by night. I notice, as I grow older, that my eyes adapt more slowly to the dark. But I also need brighter light for reading at any time. The aging eye may grow progressively less sensitive to light, in a manner too complex to reconcile with Hering's three simple sets of receptor pairs. The elderly do not lose acuity for some colors while maintaining acuity for others. If the three receptor pairs exist, can they all age or degrade at exactly the same rate?

Dichromatism

Colorimetric theory holds that dichromats, who require a mixture of two lights to match any color they see, distinguish black from white. They also differentiate either blue/yellow or red/green, but not both of these ranges. Because red and green light are said to mix to form yellow light, the condition is curious as described. Diminished vision for the yellow end of the yellow/blue range is inconsistent with full acuity for red and green.

Nothing in tristimulus theory provides a basis for predicting that insensitivity to blue/yellow (or to black/white) would occur less often than faulty distinction between red and green. But the disparity is considerable. Red/green maladaptivity is common. Blue/yellow maladaptivity is rare (the literature is divided only on how rare) and associated with degenerative diseases of the eye.

The question of whether blindness to blue is possible for an otherwise normal eye turns on whether any visual pigment can be shown to be uniquely sensitive to blue. If no such pigment exists, there cannot be a pathology—blue blindness—brought about by its absence. The question remained controversial as recently as 1957.[1]

Setting aside weakened and absent acuity for the blue/yellow range, respectively tritanopia and tetaranopia, dichromatism usually implies anomalies limited to the red/green range. Red/green dichromats are divided into *protanopes* and *deuteranopes*. Both are said to distinguish only between light/dark (black/white) and blue/yellow. But protanopes also show an abnormal brightness distribution. To the statistically average viewer, the brightest part of the spectrum lies at about 555 millimicrons (yellow/green). For protanopes, it occurs at 550 to 590 millimicrons (yellow/orange).

Judd contends that people with anomalous color vision, although classified as impaired, ought to have superior ability to make fine color discriminations in the yellow/orange range (Judd 1979, 199). But can we assume that the human eye makes the finest discriminations of hue in that sector of the spectrum seen as brightest or lightest? Although some correlation exists, reading or matching colors under overly strong light is as difficult as doing so under dim light.

Seeing Colors Differently

The names people use for colors reflect more than just what is seen. A color identified as *viridian* by one person can be called *dark blue-green* by another and *green* by a third. This gives no ground for concluding that the three observers are having different visual experiences. The presumption is reasonable, however, that anyone who sees colors differently will have difficulty understanding how to use color names.

F. H. G. Pitt asked three deuteranopes and two protanopes to identify the colors of the spectrum, and he compiled a table of the names that were used (figure 24-2). The table would be more informative if we knew whether the subjects were shown spectral lights, colored lights, or colored papers thought to reflect certain wavelengths. And Pitt's own predilections may have contributed to the extent to which colors were incorrectly identified as yellow. For example, some hue intermediaries are included, notably yellow-orange (golden yellow, 583-600 millimicrons) and yellow-green (greenish yellow, 567-578 millimicrons). But others, such as red-orange and blue-violet, are omitted. Even allowing for this imbalance, an unusually large number of colors are called yellow. For Judd, "the naming of colors by a dichromat gives virtually no clues to what he is seeing" (Judd 1979, 200).

Deuteranope number three applied *orange-green*, a term meaningless to most people, to shades of orange and yellow. The coinage bespeaks confusion about language rules for construction of compound color names. Orange-green's relatives are topazy yellow and blackish white, the terms that inspired Munsell and the ISCC to demand more rational systems of color naming. Confabulations of this type may come from people who pay insufficient attention to how other people use words. But I doubt that the confabulations can be dismissed as just incomprehensible. Deuteranope number three may have followed some private logic in concluding that certain colors looked somewhat like orange and somewhat like green.

Pitt's companion chart of *confusion colors* predicts names that might be used for specific wavelengths or colors by "confused" protanopic and deuteranopic observers (figure 24-3). A wavelength of 502 millimicrons, for example, is recognized by a normal observer to be blue-green in color. Pitt predicts that protanopic observers will call the color Nile green, cream, brown, or purple-brown, because all of these colors look alike to them.

Pitt's confusion colors show little or no correlation with names used by the dichromats. One protanope identified 502 millimicrons as the area of transition between blue and royal blue. The second identified colors

Figure 24-2. Color naming by five dichromats (three deuteranopes, two protanopes). (Adapted from Judd 1979, 201, after Pitt 1935, xiv.)

Description by Normal Observer	Wavelength (millimicrons)	Remarks by Dichromats				
		D1	D2	D3	P1	P2
Red	658-780	yellow	orange	yellow-green	dark color—red?	orange
Orange	600-658	yellow (warm)	yellow	orange-green	yellow	lemon
Golden yellow	583-600	yellow	yellow	orange-green	yellow	lemon
Yellow	578-583	yellow	yellow (orangy)	orange-green	yellow	yellow
Greenish yellow	567-578	yellow	yellow (orangy)		yellow	yellow
Green	524-567	greenish-yellow	yellow-white	yellow	yellow nearly gone, maybe red?	light yellow to white
Blue-green	502-524	whitish	pink	yellow	yellow gone, nearly green	blue
Blue	431-502	blue	mauve	blue	green	royal blue
Violet	390-431	blue	blue	blue	dark color	violet

Figure 24-3. Confusion colors for red-green color blindness. Conjectures about what the color blind see are not testable. The color names used by Pitt's dichromats are not those predicted as "confusion colors." (Adapted from Judd 1979, 202, after Pitt 1935.)

Normal Colors Names for Colors of Nearly Identical Chromaticity for Protanopic Observers

Wavelength	Color Name
496	Light blue, gray
499	Green, ivory, fawn, light stone, pink
502	Nile green, cream, brown, purple-brown
505	Mid-Brunswick green, middle stone, deep cream, crimson
509	Sea-green, bronze green, deep stone, primrose, buff
515	Light Brunswick green, red
525	Yellow, orange

Normal Color Names for Colors of Nearly Identical Chromaticity for Deuteranopic Observers

Wavelength	Color Name
500	Light blue, gray
504	Green, ivory, light stone, fawn, pink
506	Nile green, brown
508	Mid-Brunswick green, cream, middle stone, purple-brown
511	Sea green, deep cream
514	Light Brunswick green, bronze green, primrose, deep stone
517	Buff, crimson
530	Yellow, red

in the blue-green range by the names *yellow that was nearly green* or *green*. Both protanopes named a broad range of colors as yellow or lemon, spanning what the testers identified as the continuum from orange through green. Otherwise, they did not give similar answers. And for protanopes, as for anyone else, calling many colors yellow does not mean that all colors given that name look exactly alike. One protanope identified both extremes of the spectrum (red, violet) as dark, but thought the red might be red. The other correctly identified violet, but referred to red as orange, suggesting that the color looked relatively red, but not red enough.

Decades of wild conjecture about what "primitives" see suggest that inadvisability of speculating about what anyone sees, a lesson applicable to predictions about the vision of deuteranopes. An individual of normal vision—a trichromat—is said to require three colors to match any color he or she sees. This is not exactly a demonstration that three colors are needed to produce color vision. Color can be seen by looking at any of the three lights in isolation and the color black is seen when no light is present. Because more mixtures (therefore more colors) can be made with three lights than with two, we might conclude the trichromat sees a greater variety of colors, perhaps ten million rather than seven million. Even that modest assumption was challenged by Edwin Land, inventor of the Polaroid camera (Land [1959] 1961).

Land performed experiments in which two black-and-white positive transparencies were made in a split-beam camera. One was taken through a standard photographic filter that passed wavelengths longer than 585 millimicrons (red filter, Wratten 24). The other passed wavelengths shorter than 585 millimicrons (green filter, Wratten 58). Because of the filters, yellows, greens, blues, and violets looked unusually dark in the first photo, while reds and oranges looked dark in the second.

Using two projectors, each fitted with a polarizing filter that could be rotated, the transparencies were projected on a screen in registration with one another. The long-wave transparency was additionally passed through the red filter used in taking it (Wratten 24). The composite image appeared on the screen in full color. When the red filter was moved to the projector with the short-wave image, the colors appeared in reverse (red became green, and so forth). For Land, "The departure from what we expect on the basis of colorimetry is not a small effect but is complete. . . . Color in images can not be described in terms of wave length and, in so far as the color is changed by alteration of wave length, the change does not follow the rules of color-mixing theory" (Land [1959] 1961, 388).

The gauntlet was thrown down. Judd responded in "Appraisal of Land's Work on Two-Primary Color Projections," admitting that even three-color systems fall short of reproducing all colors. For this reason, four-color reproduction (red, yellow, blue, black) is preferred in the graphic arts. But, Judd complained, two-color primary systems are not new. And none reproduces as full a range of colors as a system with three primary colors: "for example, if the scene shows a man in an olive-drab uniform (Y 4/4), next to a bed of purple iris (RB 4/6), with green grass (GY 5/8) in the foreground, and blue sky (B 9/4) in the background, about the best that this scene could be rendered by all possible mixtures of red light with incandescent-lamp light would be to show a man in a brown uniform (YR 4/4), next to a bed of purplish-black (RB 1/1) iris, with blue-green (BG 5/8) grass in the foreground, and pale green (G 7/4) sky in the background" (Judd 1979, 485).

Judd's color codes are Munsell notations. His point is that a reproduction system using two primaries results in unacceptable photographic quality. But this is how many photos look, notably those produced by Polaroid and Instamatic cameras. We tolerate them as passable, if not pleasing, "reproductions" of the scenes that were photographed. The compromise has led to user-friendly cameras that no longer need the hours of exposure time required by early black-and-white films. Faster film has resulted, however, in progressive degrading of photographic quality over the past 150 years. We have grown resigned to accepting bad photographs, blurred video images, and the downright ugly colors of color television. The Polaroid camera was immensely successful, because it gave instant gratification, not quality photography.

The history of color photography diverges from that of black-and-white photography. Early black and white photographs, taken with slow film, amazed people by the fineness of their detail. They matched the acuity of the human eye, and all details that could be seen were captured in the photos. Later, fast films and high-speed lenses produced pictures that exceeded the acuity of the human eye. They stopped the action of galloping horses and hummingbirds' wings.

The camera, people said incredulously, never lies. Photographs are regarded as good evidence in a courtroom. Yet the color photograph always lies. No color film has ever been capable of refined replication of the colors of objects. This is why painters often complain about photographs of their work. In theory, the three layers of dye used in color camera film ought to make matching "all colors" possible. In practice, this does not work.

If, as Judd said, a two-primary system produces such colors as "purple-black iris with blue-green grass," this bears on what dichromats see. Theirs is a system that lacks a third primary. Inconsistently, Judd and others have insisted that "the colors perceived by protanopes and deuteranopes are the grays and all kinds of blues and yellows" (Judd 1979, 466). An equally likely possibility is a color universe slightly skewed from our own, a world that looks like a Polaroid print. Fuchs found that "many of those afflicted with red-green blindness are not aware of their defect, and are much grieved or affronted if they are charged with it. . . . In ordinary life, they rarely make mistakes in naming colors" (Fuchs [1908] 1924, 245).

Metamerism

To match the color of a paint sample other than a metallic of dayglo color, we need not use the colors mixed for the sample. The phenomenon, familiar to anyone who mixes paints, is called *metamerism* in the colorimetric literature. The question about anomalous color vision is why some observers cannot distinguish between colors that look different to other observers. Metamerism brings the absolute limits into focus. Some pairs of colors cannot be distinguished by any observer. These colors appear to match under some lighting conditions but do not match under others. They are mixed from different constituents and can be shown to have dissimilar reflectances.

What makes colors look alike that are not alike? The color quality of illumination is a likely candidate. All objects look the same color in the dark, although this goes unrecognized as metamerism. An object that ordinarily reflects a certain wavelength of light cannot do so if no light of that wavelength is present. But metamerism is a function of perspective and not just illumination, which implies a mathematical basis. Given sufficient distance, no observer can distinguish red from green. A building made of, say, red and green bricks appears to be one color when observed from a sufficient distance.

Metameric materials developed for use in colorimetric experiments include a pair of green textiles (prepared by E. I. Stearns) and the Granville grays, created by Walter Granville in 1949. In an experiment designed primarily to determine the effect of viewing distance (angular subtense) on color matching, Kenneth L. Kelly showed two of the Granville grays to thirty-nine viewers (figure 24-4). The paint used for one of the panels (the simplex gray) was a mixture of black and white. That for the other (the complex gray) was a mixture including yellow, green, purple, and white. Because of the dissimilar pigments, the panels reflect light differently (figure 24-5). Their colors look alike under some lighting conditions but not under others.

Kelly's subjects were asked to describe the colors of the panels, first at an angular subtense

Figure 24-4. Metamerism: observer differentiation between simplex and complex Granville grays. The Granville grays have dissimilar reflectances and therefore look alike under some viewing conditions but not under others. (Adapted from Kenneth L. Kelly, "Observer Differences in Colour-Mixing Functions Studied by Means of a Pair of Metameric Grays," in *Symposium on Visual Problems of Color*. [New York: Chemical Publishing Company, 1961], pp. 345-63.)

Observer (sex, age)	Eye and Hair Color	Simplex at Angle of 10%	2%
M 55	blue, brown	red	green
M 45	hazel, brown	red	green
F 56	brown, brown	red	green
M 27	hazel, dark brown	pink	pink
M 44	blue, brown	red	green
F 39	blue, dark brown	red	green
M 51	dark brown, black	slightly pink	green
M 41	blue, blond	pink	green
M 38	blue, red	pink	green
M 21	hazel, auburn	pink	green
F 50	hazel, brown	pink	slightly pink
M 39	blue, blond	pink	pink
M 62	blue, brown	pink	green
M 34	blue, brown	red	green
M 46	blue, brown	pink	green
M 29	dark brown, black	pink	green
M 34	dark brown black	pink	pink
M 47	blue, brown	match	green
F 44	brown, dark brown	pink	green
M 42	brown, brown	pink	match
M 48	brown, brown	pink	green
F 37	dark brown, dark brown	lavender	green
F 37	brown, brown	pink	pink
F 19	brown, brown	lavender	lavender
F 29	blue, brown	red	match
F 25	hazel, light brown	lavender	match
M 53	blue, brown	match	green
M 52	brown, brown	match	green
F 42	dark brown, dark brown	pink	slightly pink
M 66	blue, brown	green	green
M 68	blue, brown	green	green

M 21	hazel, blond	red	green
M 36	blue, blond	red	green
F 18.5	hazel, brown	pink	pink
M 28	green, blond	pink	pink
M 38	brown, light brown	pink	pink
M 56	blue, brown	red	green
M 31	dark brown, black	pink	pink
M 77	blue, brown	green	green

of 10 percent and then at a farther distance, 2 percent. Introducing an additional variable that should have been saved for another experiment, the lighting was gradually stepped down. Subjects were asked to say when it had been reduced to a point that caused the two grays to look alike. Notations were made of the exact voltage. Any two colors look alike if seen from a great enough distance. And any two colors look alike if the lighting is stepped down sufficiently, even though, in the case of some colors, illumination must be stepped down to complete darkness.

Predictions based on the 1931 standard observer (a statistically determined entity) had been that "the complex gray will appear greener in daylight than the simplex, and the reverse will be true" at a color temperature similar to that of incandescent light, 2,854°K (Kelly 1965, 350). Because the testers believed that change in angular subtense was equivalent to a change from daylight to artificial illumination, the simplex gray was predicted to look more reddish at 10 percent (closer distance); more greenish at 2 percent (farther distance). Whether the predictions were accurate is not clear. The experiment, which could have been simpler, included various manipulations with filters.

Kelly reports that younger observers are more likely to "describe the simplex gray as redder than the complex at both the 10% and 2% positions," an effect attributed to increase of ocular pigmentation with age (Kelly 1965, 357). Eye color shows a closer correlation, with blue-eyed observers more likely to deviate from the predictions. The 1931 standard observer evidently did not have blue eyes. Twenty-five percent of the responses by women offer more detail than the testers

Figure 24-5. Spectral directional reflectances of simplex and complex Granville grays. (After Kenneth L. Kelly, "Observer Differences in Colour-Mixing Functions," in *Symposium on Visual Problems of Color*, [New York: Chemical Publishing Company, 1961], pp 345-63.)

Wavelength	Simplex Gray	Complex Gray	Wavelength	Simplex Gray	Complex Gray
380	0.317e	0.305e	580	0.343	0.287
390	0.324e	0.307e	590	0.345	0.306
400	0.331	0.309	600	0.346	0.342
410	0.338	0.310	610	0.347	0.389
420	0.337	0.304	620	0.347	0.425
430	0.336	0.301	630	0.347	0.452
440	0.335	0.305	640	0.347	0.480
450	0.334	0.306	650	0.347	0.504
460	0.334	0.316	660	0.348	0.517
470	0.332	0.373	670	0.347	0.516
480	0.331	0.488	680	0.347	0.500
490	0.330	0.528	690	0.348	0.484
500	0.330	0.497	700	0.348	0.483
510	0.331	0.441	710	0.348	0.502
520	0.331	0.391	720	0.347	0.528
530	0.332	0.357	730	0.346	0.556
540	0.334	0.337	740	0.346	0.589
550	0.336	0.311	750	0.345	0.626
560	0.338	0.289	760	0.344e	0.627e
570	0.342	0.281	770	0.343e	0.627e

e = extrapolated

required, though limited in this small sample to "lavender," or "slightly pink" rather than just pink. Some of the female subjects evidently took greater care in making discriminations about color or were trying harder to do what they believed was expected.

A Model for Color Blindness

During the Second World War, Judd replied with polite exasperation to letters from interested citizens. They suggested that if dichromats "see colors differently," they might be asked to assist the war effort by looking through camouflage impenetrable to the normal eye. The inquiries, in all their zaniness, are understandable. Neither the technical nor the popular literature provides a clear model of how anomalous color vision ought to be understood. Tests are available to reveal the condition. They need to be supplemented by other tests for fineness of color vision among the general population.

Color matching is a commonplace task at which some people are better than others. Human beings vary in the required acuity, especially under less than optimal conditions. We can learn much about how to design tests by considering those available for nearsightedness (myopia) and other defects in form discrimination or focus.

Given sufficient distance, nobody is capable of reading the letters printed on an eye chart in an optometrist's office. The myopic individual has difficulty at near distances. This nearsighted observer has no difficulty comprehending the difference between *E* and *F*. But the shapes of the letters blur into their surroundings, interfering with form discrimination. Understanding the difference between maroon and brown is similarly no guarantee against difficulty in distinguishing between them at a distance or under poor light.

A test for acuity in differentiating colors might present a set of graded, progressively more difficult, conditions. Imagine that subjects are able to identify, from a distance of eighteen inches, which of two swatches is black and which is navy blue, or which of two yellow-green swatches is more greenish. If progressively fewer make correct discriminations from distances of four, fifteen, or twenty-five feet, which would likely occur, a basis is afforded for standards of acuity in differentiating colors. The grading system, like the test, can be modeled after that for anomalies of focus. Normal eyesight is labeled 20-20 vision, and other conditions are identified as deviations from that. Thus, 20-400 vision indicates an ability to see at twenty feet what those of unimpaired vision see at four hundred feet.

Difficulty in discriminating between red and green is more extreme than difficulty in discriminating, at a distance, between two similar dark greens. Whether some, or all, dichromats are completely unable to differentiate between any red and any green under any circumstances is by no means clear. The literature often implies this is the case. But an individual absolutely unable to see a difference between red and green would use the same name for both colors. The dichromats tested by Pitt did not respond in this manner, and no simple pattern emerges from their errors (see figure 24-3).

What dichromats see, if they see colors differently, is a complex issue. Confusing red and green implies confusion about any color in which either is a component. It implies some degree of confusion about every hue range, one of several ambiguities the colorimetric literature does not address. Among others, the assumption that black and white are not colors breeds the confusing idea that a color sense is not needed to recognize them. Confusing purple with black is classified as inability to recognize purple, not inability to recognize black. Although theory does not preclude the condition, we are not asked to consider the possibility of monochromats who see only blue and yellow, rather than only black and white. Nor are we told of dichromats with normal acuity for red, green, yellow, and blue, but none for achromatic tonalities. We are not told why the conditions that actually exist match up so poorly with what tristimulus theory predicts. What the investigators have found gives every sign of being conditioned by what they were looking for.

Should we assume that an individual lacking red/green receptors is effectively as blind under red light as the normal individual would be if trying to see by gamma rays? Relying on Judd's description of how the color blind see traffic lights, the answer is no. Those of anomalous vision see a different color or range of colors, a surrogate for any range they are unable to perceive. The supposition leads to thorny questions. How can receptors sensitive only to blue and yellow do double duty by perceiving red (they would perhaps perceive it as blue) for an eye otherwise incapable of seeing that color? If this occurs, the nominal blue/yellow receptors should be reclassified as de facto blue/yellow/red receptors.

Inability to see red or confusing red with green are conditions as loosely defined as the visual agnosias. Vision, contrary to what is assumed in tristimulus theory, is not a set of discrete cubbyholes in which some can be closed off without affecting others. Because any hue name refers to a range, all reds cannot be indistinguishable from all greens by even the most extreme dichromat. Between pale pink and dark green, a value difference is evident, and the dichromat is said to have no difficulty distinguishing between light and dark.

A more subtle issue is that any color, including red, can be mixed with any other. In many cases, the resulting color would not be identified as red, even if red were one of its constituents. This presents a serious impediment to imagining a confusion about red, or about the range from red to green, which is not potentially a confusion about any or every other color range. How will a dichromat see, say, the color of a can of blue paint into which a quarter can of red paint has been blended? In theory, the dichromat should see the blue as if the red had not been added to it. This amounts to a difficulty in seeing blue.

CHAPTER 25

Color and Form in Art

Painting as it is now promises to become more subtle—more like
music and less like sculpture—and above all it promises *color*.

Vincent van Gogh, Letter #528

The formal relationships within a work of art and among different
works of art constitute an order for, and a metaphor of, the entire
universe.

Henry Focillon, The Life of Forms in Art

W e learn about images by looking at them. We learn about ourselves by observing how people react to imagery. In his monograph on Michelangelo's *Moses*, Sigmund Freud offered his insights into a piece of Carrara marble carved to resemble a man. Michelangelo's shaping of the stone cannot have endowed it with human character or personality. Freud would not have cared to defend the idea that psychoanalytic techniques could be applied to inanimate objects. The inconsistency cannot be smoothed over by the conceit that Freud was trying to look "through" the stone surface to the person who had been represented. Because Moses was not the sitter for this portrait, whose face could have peered back is conjectural. We often imagine images to be transparent to our probings; to be surrogates for what they represent.

Long before Freud, ancient peoples are said to have superstitiously suspected that an object and its image shared a common destiny. They were linked by what Sir James George Frazer identified as "sympathetic magic" and deconstructed in the many volumes of *The Golden Bough*. We join Frazer in scorning such quaint notions, but we cannot put them entirely behind us. I would not enjoy watching a friend destroying a photograph of me.

Psychologists, no more immune than the rest of us to the disease of confusing images with objects, are often disturbed by the familiar dinner plate on a table (Kohler 1947, 48–51). The plate persists in looking elliptical, although everyone knows plates are round. The mind, when quiet, remembers perspective and its explanation through optics or projective geometry. No entity can occupy two different spatiotemporal locations at the same time, nor can noncongruent configurations be the same. An image and what that image looks like cannot be identified with the object that is imaged. Yet we often behave as if we suspected that this should not be the case.

The issue of what constitutes an image or representation grows increasingly complex, driven by technological advances that force us to see what was previously unnoticed. Photographs can be taken of photographs, producing imitations of imitations of imitations in the Platonic sense. This kind of layering is not necessarily aesthetically inferior. W. H. Auden's *The Old Masters* is more interesting, rather than less so, because the Breughel painting that inspired the poem was inspired by a passage in Ovid's *Metamorphoses*. Elsewhere, our understanding of northern Renaissance art is colored by whether we share the artists' interest in the fantastic imagery of the biblical book of Revelation.

As Cézanne recognized, art grows from previous art, from what we see today in museums. Studies of iconography in the visual arts, like studies of literary sources, propose to inform us about who imitated what. They tell us about the long chain of what the imitated in their turn are discovered imitating.

Living among images of images of images, we become confused about how to sort one from the other. Australian aborigines were long ago regarded as naive for wondering whether the camera that photographed them would capture their souls. Are we more sophisticated in assuming that the camera captures the aborigines' facial expressions. I think not. Cameras do not capture anything. Their function is to form images, a process that should not be personified.

A color photograph can be taken of anything that can be seen, because the visual world can be coded as an array of spots of color in a two-dimensional matrix. For Maurice Denis, a painting was an arrangement of spots

of paint on canvas (Denis [1890] 1966, 509). Thus, a distinction could be made between a painting and its imagery. The painting, a physical object, could be weighed on a scale. Its imagery (or its picture plane) could not be weighed, because two-dimensional matrices have no mass. Nor have they secrets behind them to be unveiled. There is no "behind" to the imagery of the eye, the mirror, or the picture plane of a painting. Nelson Goodman was correct in raising the question of how an artist can paint the world the way it "is" (Goodman 1968, 6–10; Gombrich 1960, 297). The task cannot be accomplished. Images are separate from the three-dimensional world. They neither capture it nor flatten it out so that it can be glued to a surface.

The history of art might be read as a debate on the nature of imagery, a dialectic about color and form relationships. I suspect the conception of image making evolved from the discovery of constellations in the sky, from imagining lines that made pictures by connecting the dot of one star to the dot of another. Easy steps lead from seeing pictures in the sky to imagining pictures drawn on surfaces. Dots can be made on a surface to replace the dots of the stars in the sky, or the dots can be eliminated entirely. Each can be remembered only as a point at which a line changes direction.

Early peoples would not have picked out the constellations had the sky been without stars, a link between images and the celestial objects that inspired them. The development of astrology, probably by the Babylonians, rounds out the picture, elaborating on the idea that some of the constellations, the starry images, are meaningful. They affect human destiny. No vast conceptual leaps are required to move from the idea of imagining images in the sky to the modern, though literary, conception that images are connected with objects and have significant stories to tell.

Is this the process that actually occurred, or just a process that might have been possible? We cannot know. But the ancient practice of prophesying through looking at the livers of animals, criticized by Ovid in *Metamorphoses*, similarly seeks to extract meaningfulness from the random images of nature. Pictures exist in artists' minds before being set down on surfaces. Where could these pictures have come from, except from what was stored, seen, and conceptually rearranged?

Paleolithic cave painting, the earliest surviving art set down on surfaces, is usually explained in terms of hunting magic. If the explanation is correct, the idea that images are connected with objects is of earlier vintage than the conviction that they ought to be. Yearning for a lost paradise pervades the Greek tales of Pygmalion (who carved a statue that came to life) and Zeuxis (who painted grapes so realistically that birds wanted to eat them). Nobody living today has seen these fabulous works of art. Nor can we locate the portrait with the painted nose on which Giotto's painted fly looked so lifelike that Cimabue tried to brush it away.

The message of these ancient and medieval stories is that an image *can* aspire to the condition of an object. Somewhere in this world is the looking glass into which Alice can step. The magic looking glass differs from all others in that the world behind it is spatially similar to the world in front of it and is equally accessible.

Lewis Carroll may have been just telling little girls what he thought they wanted to hear. But his inspired stream of consciousness is related to Leonardo da Vinci's musings. For Leonardo, in the notebooks, the visual world was a window into, or mirror of, the three-dimensional forms of the natural world. A collection of recipes is set forth for imitating the appearance of three-dimensional objects. Leonardo's self-imposed task was to look "through" the two-dimensionality of imagery to a three-dimensional matrix presumed to lie behind. Color, insofar as it entered the picture,

was largely an attribute of forms, a skin that covered them. Leonardo set down his thoughts about the colors of objects and about effects independent of material objects such as solar spectra and aerial perspective.

The parallel style of criticism, which can be traced back to Plato, was overripe by the time of Giorgio Vasari (1511–74). Paintings were evaluated by assessing the degree to which the artist imitated or captured the shapes and colors of natural objects. Like Zeuxis' grapes and Giotto's fly, paintings were good if they "looked real," if the two-dimensional image seemed a slice of the three-dimensional world. Here is Vasari on Leonardo's cartoon for *The Battle of Anghieri*:

> Leonardo began a cartoon representing the story of Nicolo Piccinino, captain of the Duke Filippo of Milan, in which he drew a group of cavalry fighting for a standard, representing vividly the rage and fury both of the men and the horses, two of which, with their forefeet entangled, are making war no less fiercely with their teeth than those who ride them. We cannot describe the variety of the soldiers' garments, with their crests and other ornaments, and the masterly power he showed in the forms of the horses, whose muscular strength and beauty of grace he knew better than any other man (Vasari [1550] 1957, 154).

The critical inability to separate image from object, to recognize that each has different attributes, is an inability to think abstractly about visual phenomena. As a form of art criticism, the genre descended to bathos in the nineteenth century; to near hysteria, where it survived, in the twentieth.

Stendhal's negative review of Delacroix's *Massacre of Chios* (Louvre) prefigured the modern idea that if we have the criticism, perhaps we do not need the art:

With the best will in the world, I cannot admire Delacroix and his *Massacre of Chios*. This work always appears to be a picture that was originally intended to depict a plague, and whose author, after having read the newspapers, turned it into a *Massacre of Chios*. I can only see in the large animated corpse which occupies the middle of the composition an unfortunate victim of the plague who has attempted to lance his own boils. This is what the blood appearing on the left side of this figure indicates. Another fragment that no young painters ever omit from their pictures of the plague is an infant who tries to suckle at the breast of his already dead mother; this can be found in the right-hand corner of Mr. Delacroix' painting. . . . There should have been a fanatical Turk, as handsome as Girodet's Turk, slaughtering Greek women of angelic beauty and menacing an old man, their father, who will in turn, succumb to his blows.[1]

Neither Delacroix nor Stendhal had attended a massacre. Yet we are asked to consider whether the critic's expectations about what massacres really look like are preferable to those of the artist. What could have led Stendhal, "after having read the newspapers," to the gaffe of imagining that his own imaginings could stake out a superior claim to truth? The critic, who should have known better, was demanding a right to supervise the artist, though this is not the whole story.

In Stendhal's world, as in Leonardo's or Vasari's, images are conventionally read as surrogates for what they represent. Any critic without firsthand experience of what was represented was compelled to use imagination to bridge the gap. No other way was available to discharge the obligation to enter into the game of make-believe. The discouraging result is a world in which it is considered infantile

for a child to imagine a toy soldier coming to life but not for an adult art critic to conjecture about what might transpire if a soldier made of spots of paint swung his sword.

Yarn spinning of this type is not venal. But it fosters confusion. Toy soldiers do not come to life. Painted soldiers do not swing swords. As Freud failed to remember, stone men neither move nor have human souls. A stone may well have a soul in some animistic sense of its own. But that is not the kind of soul Freud was seeking.

The idea that art copies nature may just mean that it ought to. That it really does is a dubious conclusion from, so to speak, the available database. Of, say, the thousands of paintings in museums of the crucifixion of Christ, not one was executed by an artist who had been at the scene. Many premodern works of Western art are literary in inspiration. They illustrate stories from books, most often the Bible, Homer's *Iliad* and *Odyssey*, Ovid's *Metamorphoses*, Virgil's *Aeneid*, and Dante's *Commedia*.

If two-dimensional matrices are regarded as windows into a third dimension, the expectation follows that color in paintings ought to look real, appropriate to the objects represented. Some liberty was allowed as a sort of visual poetic license. That it was limited can be seen in early objections to the arbitrary use of color in French Impressionist and German Expressionist painting. The artists exceeded poetic license, straining the unspoken rule that pictorial imagery ought to approximately adhere to the real colors of objects. Paintings imitate nature, nature imitates the ideal. The universe is pictured as if a hall of mirrors, not a collection of separable, self-sufficient items and events.

A review by Pierre Wolff suggests that the "unnatural" use of color, rather than the now-famous broken color, was the disturbing element for unfriendly early critics of French Impressionist painting: "Just try to persuade

M. Pissarro that trees are not purple, or the sky the color of butter; that the kind of things he paints can not be seen in any country; and that no real intelligence could be guilty of such excesses. . . . Try to explain to M. Renoir that woman's torso is not a mass of rotting flesh, with violet-toned green spots all over it, indicating a corpse in the last stages of decay."[2]

Pissarro never painted purple trees. Wolff was unable to read the purple as shadow. Or he was led by rancor to pretend he had missed the point. His objection, in any case, is both to the colors used in rendering objects and to the presumed excess of painting what "can not be seen in any country." At a much later date, Earle Loran showed, in *Cézanne's Composition*, that when Cézanne's paintings are compared to photographs of the scenes, they look different. By that time, nobody was surprised.

I cannot see the history of western art, prior to the twentieth century, as a quest for a copy of nature. Rather, a nature that had never existed was invented. For Leonardo da Vinci, the cracks in a plaster wall could stimulate a painter to imagine pictorial scenes and images, a form of free association that precedes the Rorschach inkblot test by several centuries. The American painter Ralph Albert Blakelock (1847–1919), reasoning similarly, is said to have based the composition of *Brook by Moonlight* on the reticulated patterning of paint cracks in an old zinc bathtub. Neither Leonardo nor Blakelock argued that aggregates of lines could be interesting in their own right or need not point to a three-dimensional world lying beyond.

At issue is a hierarchical conception of form that subordinates it to content or meaning. As in the writings of Johannes Itten, who taught a color class at the Bauhaus, modern thought was often not modern on this point: "In the study of color, I eliminated all searching for form. . . . The students usually started by drawing the outlines of spots and coloring them afterwards. They paid attention to form and not to color. As early as 1917 I made the students use the chessboard division for most exercises in order to free the study of color effects from associations of form" (Itten 1963, 41). Itten's conception of what constitutes form was limited to configurations invented by his students or executed with a degree of deliberation. The squares of the chessboard do not count. Similarly, the critic Clive Bell's praise of "significant form" implies that some varieties are not significant. Used in this value-laden sense, *form* becomes an accolade rather than a descriptive label. The usage justifies asking, elsewhere, whether any form exists in Walt Whitman's *Leaves of Grass* or in Abstract Expressionist painting.

For those who make the distinction, what justifies a sorting of significant form from form that is less significant? Alas, it is usually literary content. For Henri Focillon, form had to be more than form, more than configuration or how things look. It had to be adorned with ancillary content, meaning, or purpose. How things look was not considered interesting. What counted was the significance the critic found behind the surface. A firm foundation was laid for the conception that we do not need art if we have the ideas of critics about art.

Roger Fry was Clive Bell's contemporary. Yet Fry's ideas were often more visual, more modern. Fry's remarks on Cézanne's *Houses by the Marne* are art criticism of a different nature from the remarks of, say, Vasari or Stendhal: "Behind, a tree divides the composition in half with the rigid vertical of its trunk, above which its foliage forms an almost symmetrical pyramid, which is completed and amplified by the group of houses behind. Only to the right is there a very unaccentuated suggestion of a diagonal movement" (Fry 1958, 61).

Arnheim's thoughts on El Greco's *The Virgin with Santa Ines and Santa Tecla* were similar: "The attitudes of the Virgin and the child create a slanted axis. The tilt from the upper right toward the lower left connects the figures in the clouds more directly with the saint to the left" (Arnheim, 1956, 358). The critic looks at the painting rather than beyond it. A world is found sufficient unto itself, the coordinate system of the picture plane. A painted tree on that picture plane can be the compositional axis of the painting, although a three-dimensional tree is rarely or never the axis of anything.

Fry's variety of criticism follows the paradigm of the sciences. His remarks derive their validity from their verifiability. If the tree divides Cézanne's composition in half, then Fry is correct. If it does not, he is incorrect. Stendhal's remarks on *Massacre of Chios*, based on different assumptions, amount to a pleading that the reader support the critic in opinions that are finally unverifiable. For those who agree that no picture of a massacre is convincing without violated damsels, Stendhal's criticism is valid. For those who disagree, it is not. What Stendhal sees in the mirror of art is himself, although he may have been passionately convinced it was a mirror of the world.

Cézanne, proverbial father of modern art, is praised for his patient conviction that an order can be found in nature. Yet the insight is scarcely original. A belief that nature is orderly is central to Western thought and in all probability inspired the builders of Stonehenge. Cézanne's break with traditional rhetoric was more radical, as in his observation that natural forms all can be seen as constructions based on the sphere, cone, and cube (Fry 1958, 52). Objects are separated from what they mean to us and tied to the cool world of geometry rather than the emotional hothouse of content. The world is spheres, cones, and cylinders, as well as trees, cows, and people.

Is the geometry two-dimensional or three-dimensional? A representational painting is not usefully regarded as a translation of a three-dimensional world into the two-dimensional world of the picture plane. The visual field is a two-dimensional matrix in its own right. Teaching drawing implies a redirecting of attention—teaching students to forget about how they think things really are. Learning to observe how things really look is difficult, a battle against acculturation, which teaches a nonvisual method of reasoning.

CHAPTER 26

Subjectivity and the Number of Colors

The fact that the higher vertebrates, and even some insects, distinguish what are to us diversities of colour, by no means proves that their sensations of colour bear any resemblance whatever to ours.

Alfred Russel Wallace

Every child probably wonders how many colors exist and decides there is no way of knowing. Estimates by adults span a wide range. Moses Harris believed there were fewer than 660 colors. Birren found

there are two different answers. . . . If colors and color variations are to be judged and measured in terms of wavelengths, luminance, degrees of reflectance, and the like, there are *millions* of colors. But if colors are to be judged by the eye and clearly distinguished by the eye, the variation of colors is remarkably limited in number—and probably to not more than a *few thousand*. In pure spectral light, for example (as seen in a spectrometer or in

a beam of light refracted through a prism), a number of studies have obliged scientists to admit that the eye cannot distinguish more than about 180 different hues! (Birren 1969, 50).

Segall, Campbell, and Herskovits, citing Triandis, reported that "man can discriminate some 7,500,000 colors" (Segall, Campbell and Herskovits 1966, 47; Triandis 1964). And the National Bureau of Standards estimated "there are about ten million surface colors distinguishable in daylight by the trained human eye" (National Bureau of Standards Circular, n.d. *a*. 4). The question of how many steps of gray can be visually identified between black and white similarly yields broad estimates, ranging from only 5 or 10 (Sargent), or 9 (Birren), to

44 (Itten), 214 (Chandler), several hundred (Ostwald), or about 700 (Freeman).[1] How would one go about taking a count of one's own, in effect as a type of thought experiment?

A tally can be taken of the number of colors, or of the number of grays, only if that number is finite. It is neither finite nor infinite if the question is metaphysical, like that about the number of angels able to stand on the head of a pin. A count of the angels cannot be made, not merely because nobody has ever seen an angel. The more immediate barrier is that nobody knows where to look for one.

If the number of colors is infinite, the process of counting them is without end. If color cannot be located, the counting process can have no beginning. Entities are countable only if the domain in which they exist can be located.

Locating Color in Light

Colors differ from angels in that people regularly see them, or imagine seeing them. The major uncertainly concerns where the sighting occurs, an uncertainty that has inspired an extensive literature. Color may be located in light, the world, the eye, the brain. It may exist in some, all, or none of these places. It may even be located, as I have suggested elsewhere, in a two-dimensional universe unique unto itself.

Etymology suggests that color was originally regarded as a skin or covering that hid the essences of objects, therefore, as an attribute located with those objects. Newton relocated it in light. Or he assumed that color is light, a reasoning irreconcilable with the proposition that color is caused by light. In a universe in which causality (external agency) is assumed, no phenomenon can be its own cause. The assertion that color is light, in other words, cannot consistently be supported by the arguments that color is caused by light.

Newton's locating of color in light relied on his experimental discovery, reported to the Royal Society (1671), that "when any one sort of Rays hath been well parted from those of the other kinds, it hath afterwards obstinately retained its colour, notwithstanding my utmost endeavors to change it" (Whittaker [1910] 1951, 1:18). Newton construed this as evidence that each individual ray was elemental in the color it displayed. But this immutability is not unique to spectral rays. Many or most chemical substances exhibit a color that cannot be changed. Chlorine gas, for example, is green; crystals of copper sulfate are blue. Each retains its color as long as it retains its form, suggesting no privileged status for the spectral rays in behaving similarly. Newton's data merely suggests that colored light rays are colored. More is needed to argue convincingly that light can be equated with color.

There are other objections to locating color in light (or to equating one with the other). Consider, for example, the proverbial explanation that color is seen because rays of light enter the eye after being reflected from objects. The explanation assumes corporeal objects and eyes: it thus suggests that even if color is light, it cannot be light in isolation.

Another objection is that the objects light encounters before entering the eye are not neutral reflectors. Each displays a selectivity in reflectance that determines its color. The selectivity in reflectance is an attribute of the object, rather than of the light. It can even be changed by modifying the object. A green table burned to gray ashes no longer looks green, even if no change is effected in the quality of light falling on it.

Among other reasons no explanation of color vision relies on light alone, the electromagnetic scale is merely a scale of hue variation. It cannot explain other components in color, and the greater number of colors are neither assigned places on it nor correlated with particular wavelengths. For example, explanations for metallic and iridescent colors typically assume that these colors can only be seen by observing metallic or iridescent objects (rather than metallic or iridescent light waves).

Although locating color in light is far from satisfactory, the behavior of light presents the primary obstacle to locating it in objects. The color of any object varies according to environmental lighting. In effect, no object has a fixed color independent of the light shining on it.

Many of these difficulties fall away if I am only required to count the colors I see, perhaps because counting itself is a subjective process. Deferring for the moment questions about the nature of subjectivity. I shall assume that color is located in the human eye. This is, after all, the only theory that allows us to explain why the blind are unable to see.

Color Seen by the Eye

The assumption that color is visual in origin implies that it never exists unless generated by a functioning eye, or pair of eyes. Because eyes cannot function without brains, an ancillary neurological apparatus is implied. Through its association with brain and eye, the visual field is a subjective phenomenon. If the total area seen by a pair of eyes, it ought to consist, in theory, of a pair of circular arenas, each the field of vision for a single eye. The evidence for circularity is that light enters the eye through the pupil, an opening that is circular. The lens of the eye, through which light passes before reaching the retina, is similarly round.

Receiving rays through these orifices, the eye evidently either edits or possesses a degree of insensitivity. The portion of the visual field seen by both eyes does not appear to be substantively different, in either brightness or intensity, from the portion seen by only one eye. The field of vision for a single eye is not perceived as round. Nor is that for both experienced as overlapping discs.

Beyond the fact that the visual field does not look the way it might be expected to look, questions about its shape elude answers. Fish, unlike humans, have eyes that look in opposite directions. According to the theory of binocular (two-eyed) vision, this ought to preclude any ability to judge distance. But fish do not forever go about bumping into things. Some insects have multifaceted eyes, in effect, dozens or hundreds of eyes. All of these creatures must have visual fields subject to different limits than those of humans, which cannot, however, tell us what they actually see.

The dragonfly's eye, like my own, probably merges the images from its separate lenses, a reminder that what is actually or verifiably in the visual field is not necessarily congruent with what is seen. An excellent example is provided by the default condition for human vision, which mercifully relieves me of the tedium of continually regarding my nose or the edge of my cheek. Although those anatomical protuberances extend into the field of vision, I need not notice them if I would rather not. Vision, like thought, can be focused by giving or withholding attention.

The phenomenon of the leading eye similarly suggests that consciousness edits, although the process is not wholly under conscious control. Because my leading eye is the left, what I see with both eyes is approximately similar to what I see with only the left eye. I can verify this by aligning a distant object with my extended forefinger and comparing what is seen with right eye, left eye, or both eyes. I can no more will myself to make the right eye lead than I can will myself to be ambidextrous. And everyone has a leading eye, just as everyone is either left-handed or right-handed.

Among a few certainties about vision, I know I cannot see everything, sufficient evidence that the field of vision is not limitless. I cannot see what I am not looking at, including what is behind me. Nor can vision's range be extended beyond what is popularly called the corner of the eye. Straining to look beyond that corner, I encounter nothing tangible to report. There is only the subjective sense of a machine refusing to operate beyond predetermined limits, unmoved by human effort to compel more.

The eye has a variety of other limits, many familiar primarily because methods have been found for overcoming them. The telescope and microscope show what is otherwise too small to fall within the scope of vision. Eyeglasses correct for imperfect curvature of the lens of the eye, improving visual-field acuity. Stop-action photography and slow-motion cinematography reveal how fast-moving objects (for example, a hummingbird's wing) would look if the unaided eye could see them.

The apparently insurmountable barrier is that the visual field can neither be isolated nor studied directly. Access is solely through report of the person who sees, although reports can be tested in some cases. An optometrist takes note of the error if a patient reading an eye chart incorrectly identifies a letter *E* as letter *D*. The same patient's report of discomfort from new eyeglasses is more difficult to assess.

If the visual field is limited or finite, it can accommodate only a finite number of colors. This perhaps explains one of the more striking differences between the color continuum and the number continuum. Whether or not because infinitely numerous sets are singular, no integer in the number series replicates any other. Although I have five fingers on each hand, this merely implies I have two sets of fingers, not that there are two number fives.

Although Wilhelm Ostwald argued to the contrary, color is not singular in the same sense as number. Any given color can occur more than once, as in the case of a particular shade of vermilion seen at more than one time and place. These multiple occurrences are conven-

tionally ignored in cataloging colors. The question of how many different reds exist is understood to be a question about how many discernibly different varieties can be found, not how many individual red spots exist in the natural world.

Number also suggests that an infinite series cannot be closed, and the spectral hues in this sense cannot be infinite in number. In figure 26-1, numbers on the right side read counterclockwise, increasing from 1 to infinity; the series is 1, 2, 3, 4 . . . n. The circle cannot be closed. There is no final term for n, hence none for $1/n$ either. Seemingly, we cannot count to 1 beginning with the smallest fraction, just as we cannot count from 1 to the end of the number series, which is essentially linear.

The figure comes to mind in connection with color value, particularly on such questions as whether absolute white or absolute black can be reached. It is inapplicable, however, to hue. The hue circle can be closed, as in the familiar color wheel, and apparently has no gaps.

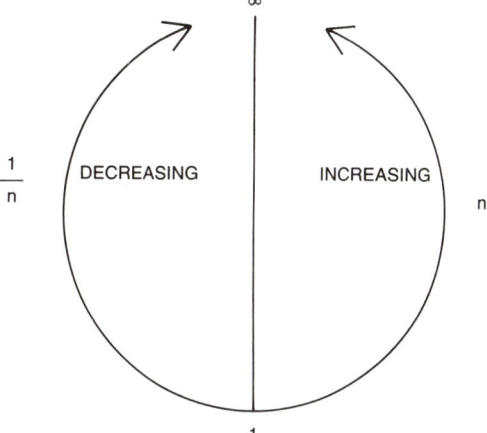

Figure 26-1. An infinite series cannot be closed. Traveling up the right side from the 6:00 position, numbers increase in the series 1, 2, 3, 4 . . . n from 1 to infinity. They decrease from one to infinity along the left side, where the series is 1/1, 1/2, 1/3, 1/4 . . . 1/n. In neither case is infinity reached.

Differentiating Colors

To count colors, we need to know more than merely where to locate them and that their number is finite. Criteria are needed for distinguishing between one color and another. They can be easily extrapolated from the crude practical methods used in color matching.

A primitive test might be whether the same name seems equally appropriate in each case. If one object can be called *light yellowish green*, but another must be qualified as a *slightly darker light yellowish green*, the two colors are merely related rather than exactly the same. The limitation of the test is that two colors properly called by the same name need not necessarily match. Because *dark bluish red*, for example, is the name of a class or range of colors, one dark bluish red need not necessarily match another.

Color matching is usually accomplished by placing two colored objects in juxtaposition to one another. It implies addressing the question of whether their colors can be visualized as homogeneous: in effect, as a continuum. If two pieces of green paper are regarded in this manner and no subjective sense of discontinuity is reported by the individual making the judgment, both swatches are identified as the same green, either for that observer or for observers in general.

We might imagine combining color matching with a variation of the bubble sort used in computer programming. An ideal observer, shown two colored objects, could be asked to decide whether their colors were the same. Subsequently, the color of a third object might be compared to those of the first two. At least in theory, every object in the world could be looked at if the process were continued for a sufficient length of time. The total number of colors could be determined by taking a tally after eliminating any color found to be the same as some other.

There is no ideal observer, and individuals vary in visual acuity. If two colors look alike to one observer but different to another, the question arises as to whether they should be counted as two colors or one. Would it be proper, for example, to count infrared as a visually perceptible color if it were discovered that a single individual was able to see it?

Standards already exist that suggest an answer to the question. The individual who excels or sets records is the marker for assessing human capability. The mile, we say, can be run in less than four minutes. This merely implies that at least one person has done so, even if only once.

Relying on the familiar figure of the record setter, a tally of all perceptible colors might reasonably include all that anyone was able to see, even if certain fine differences could be distinguished only by a single observer, and by that observer only under certain conditions.

The criterion of exclusion (I cannot see color A when and where I see color B) provides a standard for what constitutes a perceptible color. It also speaks to the issue of color sameness. If color A and color B can be seen at the same time and place, both are the same color. In practical application, if a certain color swatch is the color of my shirt and also the color of my neighbor's shirt, then my neighbor and I have the same color shirt.

Beyond these relatively easy questions lies another, more troubling: that of the relationship between your perception and mine.

Subjectivity

A popular question about the visual field is whether its sensitivity is similar among all human beings or even among all higher vertebrates. Does everyone see the same thing when looking at blue?

Given that no two persons have identical noses, ears, genes, pulse rates, or electrocardiograms, it seems fatuous to maintain any expectation of identical eyes, identical retinas, or identical neurological processing of visual percepts. Even in a single individual, as any optometrist and most wearers of eyeglasses can confirm, both eyes may not function similarly. One is often more nearsighted, farsighted, or astigmatic than the other.

Some people claim to see color differently with one eye than with the other. Research confirms the existence of this condition, even to the extreme defined as pathological. Judd reports thirty-seven cases of individuals colorblind in one eye but not in the other.[2]

No proof can be devised that blue looks the same to everyone because no way exists of determining how it looks to anyone. This is sometimes said to be an impassable barrier to the development of a coherent theory of color. How can we communicate with one another about blue if your perceptual experience of the color cannot be proved identical to mine?

One answer is that no body of theoretical or practical knowledge rests on a foundation of proven experiential similitude. It has never been considered an impediment to the development of geometry that no proof is available that a triangle looks the same to everyone. Nor has dentistry suffered from absence of proof that everyone's toothache feels the same.

Alfred Russel Wallace, credited along with Darwin for formulating the theory of evolution, pointed out that we cannot assume animals see colors as humans do. Because the visual pigments that enable the eye to see are known to differ in chemical composition among different animal species, the probability is that they do not.[3] Wallace's reasoning was expanded by Gladstone, Ladd-Franklin, and other color theorists who sought to prove that primitive peoples see colors differently.

Although the theories may seem bizarre today, it is not always easy to agree with those who originally opposed them. Grant Allen went so far as to contend that "over the whole known world, among the most civilized and the most savage races alike, the perception of colour now appears to all competent observers exactly identical" (Allen 1879, 221). The question is not whether Allen's assertion is true, but how the alleged determination could have been made. We can do more climb into one another's brains to investigate private percepts than we can investigate private thoughts.

The question of whether everyone sees the same thing when looking at color is only nominally innocuous. Many find it difficult to consider coolly because it bears directly on the nature of the human condition. Or it is about what visual experience can reveal concerning that condition.

If you and I do not see the same thing when looking at green, we share no common perceptions. Thus, we have no genuinely common experience about which to communicate. We are utterly isolate from one another, beyond possibility of meeting.

To put the question to the test, imagine two observers. Each is asked to look at an apple on a table in a room. The apple, which has a wormhole, is partly red, partly green. The table, perhaps, is blue.

Three questions can be asked about the event. Will both observers see the room interior in the same way? The apple? The color of the apple? The answer to each question is no. Visual experience is contextual and singular.

The room as an entirety will look different to each viewer. Two observers cannot stand or sit in the same place at the same time and thus cannot see from the same perspective. For a similar reason, two cameras at separate locations in the room will not produce identical photographs.

An apple, like a room, cannot provide two observers with identical visual experiences. Nor can the limit be transcended. Imagine, for example, that observer X stands first at position *a*, seeing an apple that looks unblemished. A wormhole is discovered by X when he or she moves to position *b*.

Observer Y, traveling a reverse circuit, occupies *b*, then *a*, and is led to a different set of inferences. The viewer who initially sees the unblemished side of the apple will be compelled to revise his or her estimate of its wholeness. The viewer who initially saw the wormhole makes an assessment requiring no later revision.

The question of the apple's color follows that of its wholeness. One observer, because of his or her vantage point, may conclude that the apple is mostly green. The other discovers it to be mostly red. Even if the apple's color is uniform, the illumination throughout the room will not be. Perhaps the side with the wormhole is illuminated by strong light. Its color appears reddish orange, approaching vermilion. The side with no wormhole is in shadow; it looks alizarin. Two viewers will not see the same color, any more than they see the same apple. I perceive a reddish orange apple with a wormhole; for your, it is reddish purple with no hole.

If the visual field is assumed to resemble a color movie passing before the eyes of the observer, each individual sees a unique movie shared with nobody else. Two viewers looking at the same apple might as well be living in different worlds. For all practical purpose, they actually are. Each perceives a different apple, or a different presentation of the same apple. Each incorporates the perception into a different context of past visual experiences. Even if it were possible to assume an identical neurological apparatus, it is no more possible for two persons to have identical visual experiences than it is for two identical movie cameras, filming from different locations, to produce identical film footage. The limitation is a matter of mechanics before any consideration of human psychology.

The popular suggestion is that we all see the same thing but individually impose different interpretations on the common perception. Actually, we all see different things; there are no common perceptions. Interpretation creates the comforting illusion that we all see the same thing, are sufficiently similar to understand one another's experiences, or even share a world of experience (including visual experience) in common.

Human experience happens only to individuals and is limited to individual location in times and spaces. I cannot share your experience because I cannot share your flesh or be at the same place and time where and when your experiences happen to you. I cannot be you. Nor can I see the color of an object exactly as you do. The red apple can be a topic of conversation, not because you and I have each seen the same thing, but because we each know the conventions for using the words *red* and *apple*.

As this incidentally suggests, language has an inherent ambiguity that cannot be eliminated. *Red*, or any other color name, identifies a range, never a single variety or a single spot of color. But this is also true of *the apple on the table*. In the range of visual experiences implied by the term, mine can never be exactly the same as anyone else's.

Object or Attribute

We say that something looks heavy or dry or cold, although the eye
in fact is unable to know these sensations. But, it is important to
notice that we never say anything feels red.

William M. Ivins, Jr., Art and Geometry

My well-worn *American College Dictionary* shows that *color* has twenty-eight meanings, while *form* has forty-one. *God* has only six meanings. *Good* has twenty-six; *bad*, fifteen; *goodness*, five; *virtue*, eleven; *beauty*, three. *Faith*, *hope*, and *charity* boast, respectively, nine, eight, and six. Even among words with many meanings, an unusually large number of meanings, not always consistent with one another, are assigned to only two words.

The Words *Form* and *Color*

Form can refer to two-dimensional or three-dimensional forms, prompting us to forget they have dissimilar attributes. The possibility for confusion is compounded by application of the word to a concept as removed as etiquette (good form). *Color* can be used as a label for color in general or the hues, a limited range. The word can identify all the hues (seen on the color wheel) or the hues exclusive of the reddish violet range (the hues of the solar spectrum).

The looseness creates a need for vigilance on the issue of which of our many beliefs about color hold for all colors, not just for certain subgroups. The statement that color can be correlated with wavelength is meaningful in the case of those hues assigned places on the electromagnetic scale. The idea disintegrates into nonsense when applied to color in general.

In the case of *form*, an ad hoc method for resolving the ambiguous dimensionality is to select another word for two-dimensional forms. *Shape* is a common choice, used in plane geometry. Or we can just live with the ambiguity and with the shortage of terms applicable to two-dimensional universes. *Space-time continuum* implies time and three-dimensional space. No comparable term is available for labeling time and two-dimensional space, the space-time continuum of the visual field.

We learn to decipher, in most cases, how *form* or *color* ought to be understood in a particular sentence. The task can be difficult, and dictionaries offer only limited help. Dictionaries list formal meanings rather than what words suggest—that tangled web of associations reflecting societal value judgments. A painter or poet whose work is called formless (as in critiques of Walt Whitman's *Leaves of Grass* or T. S. Eliot's *Waste Land*) is not being praised in most cases. The logic underlying that use of the word is not made clear in dictionaries.

At a further remove from the scope of the dictionary, words acquire personal associations that impel each of us to do what we must, as if following private directives understood by nobody else. Kandinsky's rejection of the representational form as a subject for painting is surely linked to the passion for colors he traced to his infancy (Grohmann 1958, 29). The form/color relationship had a personal meaning for Kandinsky beyond what it might mean to the rest of us.

Language communicates through syntax as well as content. On the syntactical level, *color* follows different rules than *form* or *shape*, though each term can be used as noun or verb. For *form* and *shape*, the verb names the process by which the noun comes into existence. Forms (shapes) result from work, thus are the end result of a process. *Color* (verb) does not name a process by which *color* (noun) is created. *Forming* is an appropriate answer to the question of how forms are

created. *Coloring* does not answer the parallel question about colors. Forming (shaping) bespeaks the making or modifying of forms (shapes). Coloring only implies the application of preexisting colors to a preexisting receiving surface.

Through this distinction, forms imply a past in which the process of forming occurred. Colors do not, compelling us to regard them as givens, existing entities without a history explaining how they came to exist. A fractional nanosecond after the big bang, cosmologists conjecture, forms as we presently know them did not exist. Did color exist? The theorists imply, as does the Bible, that the early universe probably looked black (not green or "imperceptible"), a curiosity requiring further comment. Are we to assume that black, as ancient as time and space, came into being with them at the moment of creation? If not, what later process accounts for formation of this primeval color?

The primal color names follow syntactical rules similar to that for *color*. Red is the result of reddening (of a surface); yellow, a result of yellowing; black, of blackening; tan, of tanning (of the skin). White is the result of whitening; gray, of graying; brown, of browning. Compound color names and nonprimal color names are rarely used in this manner. Graying has a commonplace meaning; light graying and dark graying do not. Crimsoning is occasionally used, but not, say, mauving or tauping. Other exceptions occur. Green is rarely called a result of greening, although the usage is permissible. The laundry substance called bluing is intended to whiten clothes, not make them blue.

For syntactical parallelism with *color, form,* and *shape*, we can turn to *element, compound,* and *mixture*, basic terms in chemistry. The chemical elements are primal or given. Mixtures and compounds are derivatives created by combining elements. The syntax for *mixture* and *compound*, like that for *form* and *shape*, presumes performance of physical work: a process leading to a result. The syntax for *element*, as for *color*, does not.

The syntactical forms imply that visually perceived forms and shapes (like chemical compounds and mixtures) are made of more primal substances; that colors (like chemical elements) are modules composed solely of themselves. The hierarchy reverses that of everyday understanding. Historically, color has been regarded as a secondary to some primary other than itself. Colors are called unreal or subjective, relative to a presumed realness or objectivity in forms. Color has been regarded as a skin on the surface of objects, an attribute of form or of light.

Rules for Naming Forms and Colors

Rules for naming forms are difficult to identify, other than that in geometry a regular polygon with more than four edges, say, an octagon, is named by reference to the number of its edges. The implication is that the number of regular polygons is as great as the highest number in the number series. Among rules for naming colors, the borrowing of color names, say, *rose*, from object names rests on an equally simple rationale. Forms that we see are always associated with color; particular objects or forms are associated with particular colors or ranges of color. People began using object names for color names because whenever they looked at objects, they saw the colors of those objects.

That few objects are named after colors— reversal of the mechanism is rare—also has its primitive visual logic. Naming an object after a color other than its own color is tantamount to naming the object after an attribute of some other object, a senseless endeavor. But naming an object after its own color—as in calling a blue chair a blue—sows confusion about the distinction between color names and object names. Calling a blue chair a blue raises the question of what to call chairs that are not blue. Calling a banana a yellow misleadingly implies that yellow is found only in bananas. The French, in an exception, order black coffee as *un noir* (a black).

Nouns and Adjectives

Any color name can be used as a noun or an adjective, a form of syntactical doubling. Model phrases and sentences can be constructed illustrating the alternate usages. Stress may differ in each pair but meaning remains approximately similar. "The red of the apple" conveys the same meaning as "the red color of the apple."

Nouns are the names of primaries: of forms, objects, or objectifiable entities. Adjectives label secondaries: attributes, characteristics, or qualities that describe forms, objects, or objectifiable entities. The language conventions echo, rather than answer, the question of whether colors are objects or attributes. Colors can be regarded as objects within the confines of the two-dimensional universe of visual experience. If imagined to exist in a real, three-dimensional universe reaching beyond the visually perceptible, they become less than objects. Colors lack the three-dimensionality necessary for objectivity (self-containment) in a three-dimensional world.

Color, though regarded as a perception, might be thought of as a third dimension that joins height and width in the planar world of vision, or a fifth dimension in four-dimensional space-time. The concepts of perception and dimension blur into one another, a sign that one or both may be poorly explained. Width, height, and depth, the three spatial dimensions, are initially available as tactile perceptions. The twentieth-century conception of time as a dimension departs from the traditional idea that a dimension is measurable in miles, meters, or other units of length marked on a ruler. Time is what clocks measure. Color is what the eye measures.

Color Names as Adjectives

Whether regarded as attributes or as objects, colors are significantly different from other members of their class. Adjectives are the names of attributes, which are said to belong to objects but to be other than objects in their own right. If attributes, color ought to show family resemblances to other items in that class. Consider, however, the following phrases:

The tall, beautiful green tree.
The tall, beautiful green person.

The adjectives *tall* and *beautiful* are relativistic, for they refer to value judgments by an observer. A tall person is not the same height as a tall tree or building, and no criterion for tallness is equally applicable to each. The measure of a person is taken relative to other people, not relative to trees.

I conclude that *tall* means tall by comparison with other items in a class. *Beautiful* is similarly fluid, as are canons of beauty. Standards that explain what is meant by a beautiful man or woman are not applicable to a beautiful automobile. A beautiful tree is ranked by comparison with other trees, not by comparison with horses.

Greenness, unlike tallness, implies comparison as to color, but never among objects in a class. The color of a green person can exactly match that of a green tree, automobile, or horse. Because a green tree is green according to an independent color standard, a chart (or swatch book) of greens can be assembled, but not a chart of tallnesses or beauties. To see nothing but green is possible. To see nothing but tall or tallness is not possible, for these terms acquire meaning only in relation to objects: tall people, tall trees, tall buildings.

The nonrelativistic function of color is shared by number, substance, and various other classes of attributes that can be separated from objects. A large cat can be called a small

animal, which implies the cat is large in one sense but not in another. Nothing can be green in one sense yet not green in another. Nor can a house have ten windows in one sense but not in another or be built of stone in one sense but not in another.

Color, number, substance, and other separable attributes challenge the convention of assuming the subordination of attributes to objects, a convention reflected in the philosophical distinction between primary and secondary qualia. Consider a stone house. Speakers of English are not permitted to call it a *house stone*, because the order of the words is important. If a house is made of stone, why is this less significant than its having the shape of a house? For better or worse, we prefer shape to substance or color, because shapes can be understood in terms of geometry.

Color Names as Nouns

Nouns can be divided into two groups. Some identify material objects (such as, *dog* or *house*). Others point to entities that are abstract, that lack physical substantiality (*size, patriotism*). The groups overlap at two points, because the border between the concrete and the abstract is as vague as that between substance and vacuum.

At the first point of overlap, we can imagine any material object as a member of a class of similar objects. To accommodate this, any noun that labels an object can be used or adapted to identify the genus. Dogs are particular animals in "my two dogs are barking," but a class in "dogs bark." The class containing all dogs is as abstract as the concept of virtue. Although we can make statements about classes, the classes often cannot be reached. What is nominally research on the dog is usually data collected by studying three, three thousand, or some limited number of dogs.

At a second point of overlap, abstract ideas

can be talked about as if they had attributes of the kind unique to corporeal objects. Worries can be called heavy, a figure of speech. Abstract concepts are not isolated from the world of corporeal objects, and most can be explained as inferences from that world. Eternity is the longest possible duration; duration is an inference from changes in objects. These include changes human beings observe in themselves, which they attribute to the aging process.

Color lacks three-dimensionality, which encourages our regarding it as an ephemera. The temptation is to group color names with nouns that identify abstract ideas. The classification is untenable if the defining characteristic of an abstraction is that it can be explained as an inference from objects. The class of red colors can be explained as an inference, drawn from individual red colors rather than from individual red objects. Any single shade of red eludes summarization in this manner. What would one have to look at to infer a particular shade of red?

To the extent that the answer is a particular red object, we *perceive* redness rather than inferring it. Inferences are interpretations built on previous perceptions. Because colors lack mass, they impress us as categorically dissimilar to dogs, chairs, and other physical objects. Among shared characteristics, *blue*, like *chair*, names an entity we perceive and do not infer.

As sense perception, color is subjective or intrapersonal, a special category. We might argue that the referends of color names are neither concrete nor abstract. Perceptions are not material objects, not concrete. Neither are they abstract, because a perception is not an inference. We understand the meanings of *concrete* and *abstract* by reference to an external world, and color is not located in that world. Perhaps, as has been suggested, colors are located in people's heads.

If we follow this path, every sensory experience other than color or visual experience can be reduced to a common denominator locating it in the world of physical objects. This common denominator is the movement of objects. When taste, smell, sound, or tactile sensation occurs, an object in the physical world will be found to have changed its position. Criteria can be established for what an outside observer sees and can measure if a study is made of a person experiencing one of these perceptions. The observer would not share the perception. But sharing is not required for verification. I need not fall off a ladder with a friend to confirm that he or she fell off a ladder.

Tactility, taste, and smell, the three most primitive senses, are the easiest to assess. Tactile sensation occurs when an object in the physical world contacts the perceiver's body, often the skin of the hands. The touched object moves or is moved into proximity with the perceiver, or the perceiver relocates to the vicinity of the object. If I stand ten feet from a table and neither I nor the table move, any outside observer can verify that I have not touched the table—no tactile perception has occurred.

Forces touch us and are often reducible to a flow of particles, as in the movement of air molecules called the wind. If an amoeba buffeted by Brownian motion is able to feel, it feels the particles striking it. We look through a microscope, see motion, and infer the force activating the particles. Gravity fits uneasily with this pattern, because moving particles have not been identified. I doubt that human beings have a direct tactile apprehension of gravity in an ordinary sense of the word. I determine whether I am standing in water or floating (a form of weightlessness) by whether my feet touch the bottom. A feeling of pressure in my ears as an airplane descends might be attributed to gravity, again not directly. I do not recall ever feeling gravity or its absence, as one might feel the wind or its cessation.

Taste and smell, specialized forms of touch, share its affiliation with movement. A tasted object must contact the perceiver's tongue, a meeting that can be externally verified. In the case of smell, small particles that can be weighed and measured (they have mass) must contact the mucous membrane of the nose.

The kinesthetic sense, a superior form of the tactile sense, is sometimes equated with empathy or with extrasensory perception. Kinesthesia enables me to feel "in my bones" how to perform the steps of a dance or respond to the rhythm of events. Testing an individual experiencing a kinesthetic sensation would reveal, I am sure, changes in muscle tone, blood pressure, brain waves, and other neurophysiological indicators.

Explaining hearing in terms of motion is more complex. Sound is regarded as a movement of sound waves that cannot be seen. What is seen (and can be verified) is movement in the object that is the source of the sound. A hammer strikes a table, a tuning fork vibrates, an automobile engine begins operating. Scientific explanations of sound imply that an object in motion establishes a second type of motion in a second object. A hammer striking a table sets up sound waves in air. The sound cannot exist without the waves. But the sound waves require the hammer blow.

Hearing indirectly implies two objects in motion, one affecting the other. The motion of the first object, the source of the sound, can be seen and provides a basis for prediction. I can predict you are not hearing a car engine if I see that the engine is not running. If a hammer strikes a table near you, I can predict that any sound you perceived was of a hammer hitting a table. Many objects, from engines to piano wires to vocal cords, are capable of making sounds when they move, yet they create none when at rest. In a world without motion, no sound would be heard. In such a world, would it be possible to see colors?

Touch, taste, smell, and hearing are understandable in terms of simple mechanics, for their source can be traced to the motion of objects. No explanation of these classes of sensory experience is complete without assuming a physical world in which motion is possible and in which objects move. Whether an individual perception consists of tactility, taste, odor, or sound depends on what object moves and what part of the perceiver's body is contacted. In the variety of experience I call kinesthetic, events occur under the skin. The stomach churns, muscles tense or relax. The subjective impression is of movement within the body, more definitively assessed by instruments than by an external observer.

Although the brain is sent information by all of the sense organs, machines record some forms of sense data more effectively than others. We have no machines for recording tastes, smells, and tactile perceptions. The tasks are unimaginable, impossible. But recorded sounds, say, bird songs, can be indistinguishable from the original sounds of the natural world. Sound waves are recorded, and quite successfully. No waves are associated with taste, smell and tactility.

What we see can be captured, though not as faithfully as what we hear. A legend about the Greek painter Zeuxis says that birds thought the grapes he painted looked exactly like real grapes. Human beings have more intelligence than birds. Human beings know the difference between grapes and a painting of grapes, between birds and a photograph of birds. Holograms record more information than photographs, yet not enough.

Human vision—the perception of color—differs from other senses in its scope. Touch, taste, and smell require that the perceived entity touch the part of the human body that perceives it. I cannot touch or taste what is in the next room. Sounds in daily life similarly originate in nearby objects. Unless explosives are detonated or bombs dropped, hearing a sound five miles away is unusual. Clouds and stars, which we see, lie at much greater distances. Vision is the sense most delicately adapted to working across large spatial expanses. Indeed, the conception we form of empty space is visual, though we learn about the emptiness of spaces through tactile experience.

Imagining what an empty room looks like is easier than imagining how pacing off the distance around the room would feel. For envisioning larger empty spaces, perspectival effects come to mind. We might imagine, say, a landscape with a river flowing toward a distant mountain, an image familiar from the backgrounds of Renaissance paintings. To imagine vast spaces, we think of the black of the night sky, which never ends though it may be finite. Or we remember the black within which we see with closed eyes, another figure for empty space.

Why does our conception of empty space take the form of visual images if three-dimensional space is tactile? One answer is that memory is poor for tactile experience. I have no clear recollection of how empty space feels, and the hand is less efficient than the eye in gauging distances between objects. Another answer is that the eye may have an ability, albeit limited, to "think," to process the perceptions of the hand and provide objective correlatives. If so, it functions like those computer peripherals, say, printers, that have small built-in memories of their own to supplement the main memory of the computer. This decentralized arrangement could offer practical advantages. Pictorial information is complex, a probable reason for the thickness of the optic nerve. On a computer, manipulating and storing graphics, say, a page of pictures, requires far more memory and disc space than a page of words. A limited ability by the eye to preprocess, to put information in order

before sending it, would ease the burden on the brain.

A third possibility is that the brain stores visual and tactile memories in the same area, in effect jumbling them together. This could explain why our conception of empty space takes the form of visual images and why visual images emerge when we consciously try to retrieve memories of tactile experience. Whenever I try to recall how velvet feels, I also remember what velvet looks like. A common box for items that ought to be separated may seem a bad idea, a mistake. Among possible purposes, the meld of visual and tactile memories may feed the kinesthetic sense, a blending of vision and tactility in which thought flows in the opposite direction. Watching dancers learn their steps, I feel how I plan to perform those steps. I do not see a mental picture of how I will look while doing so.

Technologically sophisticated experiments have provided much information about the neurological functioning of the brain, an unexplored territory. We still know little about the relationship of thought to vision and other senses, about human ability to reason. Can a brain kept alive without a body think? Deprived of sensory experience, what would the brain think about?

Western philosophy assumes a categorical difference between the mind and the senses. The process of reasoning has traditionally been explained somewhat as follows. The senses, which are never able to do anything right, transmit the misinformation they collect. The mind or brain, like an autocratic paterfamilias, sorts what is wrong from what is right. How does the brain know what is right if the information coming to it is wrong? Well, it just knows. The system sounds irritatingly inefficient. In the technocratic countertheory, the brain, like the CPU of a computer, is just a central processing unit manipulating input conveyed from peripherals. If this technocratic vision is correct, artificial intelligence is possible and human intelligence is overrated.

Either scenario is depressing. In one, human intelligence is a metaphysical assumption. In the other, uniquely human intelligence does not exist. More optimistic theories are possible. Is the brain built on the same model as the eye, which sees black when unstimulated by light? If so, it too should be self-activating, capable of functioning when "nothing" is sent to it. This small possibility gives life to our conceptions of intelligence, memory, conscience, soul, spirit, human dignity. In its favor, the electroencephalogram of a person in a coma indicates brain activity, though that of a dead person is flat.

The Movement of Light

Any machine, natural or man-made, needs an external agency to switch it on and off. The switch for eye and brain, the self-activating organs, is life and death. We begin seeing and thinking at birth or in the womb. At death, the brain no longer sends impulses to the electroencephalograph needle. The eyes, though they may remain open, no longer see.

Eyes and eyesight can be lost during life without causing the death of the individual, a difference between eye and brain. But the brain, bilaterally symmetrical like the ocular system, can be grievously injured and continue to function. In some people, half the brain has been removed, usually to control epileptic seizures. The question of why we see blackness when "nothing" exists to be seen reduces to a double line of inquiry. The question asks whether "empty space" is empty, but also why the eye is self-activating.

The function of eye and brain cannot be explained according to the model applicable to sense organs other than the eye. We cannot identify objects in the natural world that cause seeing and thinking, that turn switches on and off. I can decide, by an effort of will,

not to listen to the beating of my heart. In a dark room, I cannot decide not to see the color of the darkness. Color, however, is explained in terms of light, an explanation that associates vision with the movement of light. This is inconsistent with the idea that the eye never switches off, that vision differs from the other senses because it cannot be correlated with motion of any object in the external world. How are these discrepancies to be resolved?

I would prefer to eliminate the word *light* from the English language and use *color* instead. A single phenomenon is confusingly known by two different names, and *color* is the more useful name in this case. Setting that issue aside, light unquestionably plays a role in vision. This need not mean that light moves, or that we aptly characterize what it does as a motion. The *movement* of light is a misnomer, as is *movement* through time. Each is a traditional conception, colorful, poetic, confusing. We do not need either one. The habit of saying that light moves creates confusion about color (which is unmoving), and obscures the more significant issue of what light (and time) actually do if move is not the right word.

The familiar litany of state-of-the-art information about light has been much popularized in the past twenty years and can be concisely recited. The speed of light is a constant. Nothing in the universe can move faster. Measurements of the wavelength of light are extraordinarily accurate, for Loeb and Adams, "among the most accurate physical measurements known" (Loeb and Adams 1933, 440). It thus "becomes readily apparent that in the wavelength of light we have a standard of length which is absolutely invariable and exact" (Loeb and Adams 1933, 445). The length of the standard meter has even been redefined "in terms of what we now believe to be an invariable unit, the wavelength of light" (Jenkins and White 1957, 255).

Unlike the movement of a tuning fork, the movement of light waves or photons cannot be seen. The movement of light is an abstraction, an inference from instrument readings. If light moves in any ordinary or experiential sense, its behavior should be similar to other entities in motion. A reasonable qualification is that human beings are unable to see this movement because it is too fast, occurs on too small a scale, or for some similar reason lies beyond the scope of human perception.

If these conditions cannot be met, the movement of light is significantly different from the movement of other objects. It may not be movement as the term is generally understood. Imagine a world in which everything else moves but light is immobile. Would this world look different from our own? How can we tell whether an object has moved?

The reasoning by which we infer that objects have moved implies measurement. A chair that has moved or been moved presently stands, say, five feet from where previously located. The mode by which it was transported is irrelevant. The chair, like a traveling car, might have been continuously visible throughout its journey. As permissibly, its behavior might have resembled that of an electron jumping between orbits, or the science fiction voyagers teleported in "Star Trek": the chair magically disappeared from one location and appeared at another. Transportation from here to there is the sole necessity for motion. Here and there must be separated by a measurable distance.

Because movement is transportation rather than transformation, a moving object is assumed to retain its physical integrity. A chair can move without losing a leg. Movement implies a change of location and that the object grows older during the moving interim. This aging, conventionally disregarded, is a meaningless conception for a ray of light. If time slows to a halt at the speed of light, rays of light do not grow older.

If we reasonably expect movement to involve relocation from here to there, demonstrating movement for light is quite difficult. Light cannot be measured unless the measuring instrument affects it. To say that light is now here means an amount has been apprehended by an eye or a measuring instrument. The observed portion, because it enters the eye or instrument, is precluded from traveling onward to there. Interfering with its travels to (or from) there is the only way to prove light is here.

Seeing light is not evidence that the light is in transit, any more than seeing blue is evidence that blueness is in transit. To confirm movement, the same object must be sighted in two places, impossible in the case of light. The portion that finally arrives there is a residue never halted (observed) at any previous here. If one chair is seen in Connecticut on Monday, another in New York on Tuesday, we do not properly infer that a chair moved from Connecticut to New York.

I am mindful of the nature of waves as they travel through, say, water. If a tidal wave breaks on a beach, we need not assume that the molecules of water on the wet beach were part of the wave at its point of origin. The critical point is that waves in water can be seen without halting their motion from here to there. This cannot be accomplished with light. The movement of light implies a parallelism with the movement of objects. Beyond this, what the term means is unclear, as are the details of the journey of light between its present here and a past or future there.

The Movement of Time

Light and time are inseparable in modern theory in the physical sciences. In past centuries the movement (propagation) of light was believed to be instantaneous, and time was thought to continue forever. In modern theory the speed of light is finite. Time slows down as it approaches this velocity, "stopping" when the speed of light is reached.

Time, along with space, is held to date back no earlier than the big bang (Hawking 1988). Despite these revisions, we continue to assume that time moves from past through present into future. Is the movement of time, like the movement of light, a misnomer, a semantic confusion? I think it is, and that some of the ambiguities in our reasoning about color can be traced to oddities in our conceptions of time and light.

Nothing moves in an absolute vacuum, because nothing is present that might move. Movement is an event. The event happens to (or requires the presence of) forms, objects, or material particles, however materiality or corporeality might be defined. Attributing movement to time and light is peculiar, though the conceptions are traditional. In neither case can a movie camera photograph the movement in slow motion, as might be done with, say, the movement of a galloping horse. Time involves no particles that might move and has no origin or destination. It lacks the verifiable here and there needed to demonstrate movement in the usual sense of the word.

Language facilitates talking about past and future as if they were other times. But we are unable to reach or transport ourselves to either. The only time that exists for living human beings is the present, from which we cannot escape. The admonition to live in the present is unnecessary. We have no choice. Time travel is a science fiction fantasy, possibly because no time exists other than our own.

We do not know where the present goes when no longer the present, or where a light goes when turned off. The most painful conundrum posed by our conception of time is rarely discussed but may lie behind the yearning to understand the nature of time. Human beings have never understood what happens to the dead, where they go, or whether they or the past exist in any understandable sense.

We have as little idea of where the future is, because past and future are ancient human inventions, symbols, fables, games with words. They shore up the argument that time moves, which makes time and change more understandable, less threatening. The metaphor is born out of a human will to fend off the incomprehensible. The conception of time moving casts a powerful spell. People imagine they hear it moving in the ticktock of a clock.

Attributing movement to time anthropomorphizes it, makes it seem more like a human being. In art and folklore, time is further reduced to Father Time, an old man with a white beard. If we could plumb a collective unconscious to learn the source of the concepts—time, past, future—I suspect the underlying issue is death. We explain why death occurs by saying each person has an allotted time and time passes; time runs out for that person. The past must have been invented to explain where the dead go. The future can be defined as our fate, our own deaths. The words *fate, fatal*, and *fatality* all have the same root. The three Fates, in Greek mythology, were not concerned about the future of the universe. Their job was to spin and cut threads that represented the life and death of individual human beings. We have not experimented with the idea of jettisoning these metaphorical security blankets and confronting the incomprehensible without preconceptions.

Nobody has ever seen time or observed it moving. But movement has positive connotations in human terms. It separates the quick from the dead, suggests progress and mastery, provides important metaphors. People act officially at formal meetings by making motions. The papers filed to commence a lawsuit are moving papers. Experiences that affect us are also called moving. Life is metaphorically called a journey, a movement rather than a series of changes. We deplore people whose lives "go nowhere," who have "no direction." Human beings want to feel that the human race is on the move, going somewhere, marching along with time, keeping up with the times.

Time has a single here, which is now, and a double there, the past and the future. The "arrow of time," a modern coinage, expresses the idea that the movement of time is not reversible, though subatomic particles, we are told, can move in a reverse direction through time. Early human beings may have found the arrow of time less significant than we do. Their myths, collected by Sir James George Frazer in the many volumes of *The Golden Bough*, stress the cyclical nature of life, not the idea that the world moves on. In the cyclical conception, an analogy drawn from the cycles of the natural world, people, animals, and vegetation live and die. New life emerges from the remains of the old, a series of changes in which nothing changes.

Human beings search for a purpose in life, suggesting that any purpose is not easily obvious. In Buddhism, the world of changes is regarded as *Maya*, illusion. All forms, past, present, and future, are illusion. Effectively, the only time is this instant, in which we are experiencing the illusion. The Judeo-Christian tradition and the humanistic tradition, unlike in many ways, identify the future as the significant time, the time when the purpose of life will be fulfilled. If the future is a convenient fiction, a figure of speech, both are lost in a dream. For the believer, the future is the moment when each of us will be judged by our creator. For the humanist, the future is the time when human beings will have fulfilled human potential, completed the self-appointed task of mastering the universe.

Interesting questions arise about time in connection with scientific proof. If white light passed through a prism is separated into the spectral rays, anyone at any time should be able to repeat Newton's experiment to confirm this. Proof, in the physical sciences, means the original experiment can be repeated to yield the same result.

How can we prove that Newton performed his prism experiment in 1666? We cannot recall the past to demonstrate that if the year 1666 were recycled, Newton would perform the experiment "again." Historical events can be documented, not replicated. Theories about the past, including Darwin's theory of evolution, are constrained by the same limit. They cannot be proved or disproved according to the standards of proof for laboratory experiments.

Ornate theories about the nature of proof have sought to reconcile this discrepancy. The simpler answer is difficult only because it cuts across many disciplines. I suspect we cannot prove things about the past or the future because past and future do not exist. Time does not move, or move from one to the other. A more apt term is needed to describe what time does, or to explain what we mean by time. Light does not move and probably cannot be shown to exist as an independent entity separate from color. If the word *light* were eliminated from the English language, our ideas about it could be rephrased by talking about color. Some adjustment would be necessary, but no loss in clarity would occur. Clarity, I think, would increase. We would refine thought by eliminating nonvisual concepts, by bringing our ideas more into harmony with the phenomenological world.

The conception of time and space as a continuum is a triumph of twentieth-century thought. It implies that time and space both move or neither moves. We are forced to choose either of two models for time. In the simpler model, assume that the matrix we call the present includes all time and all space. Time does not move (nor does light), because no past exists that time could come from, no future to which it could be going. Clocks can exist in this world, but an interval must be defined as a specified number of ticks of a watch. The ticks can be counted, though no explanation can be given for what happened to the ticks already heard. The present, in this conception of time, has features similar to those of the black holes imagined by modern cosmologists. Nothing escapes from the present, certainly not light. Tomorrow never arrives. Like the horizon, it keeps receding, and we draw no closer to it. Tomorrow and yesterday are fables, like the pot of gold under the rainbow.

For the alternate model, assume that past and future are meaningful concepts, rather than convenient figures of speech. We can imagine time racing from one to the other as if it were the Orient Express. In that case, space cannot consistently be static. If time and space are a continuum—stuck together—space must move into the past in stately tandem with time. We shall have to accustom ourselves to talking about the arrow of space (a parallel to the arrow of time) and to thinking of space moving, as does time. I find this model too confusing. It burdens us with an infinity of space-time continua, one existing in the present and the others at points in the past and future that we can never reach.

Stephen W. Hawking identifies three arrows of time, each pointing in the direction in which time is moving. These arrows are our evidence, from the physical sciences, that time is moving.

We remember the past, not the future, the *psychological* arrow. This arrow, which of the three has the greatest appeal to the imagination, can be misleading. Sometimes we do know what will happen in the future (I know tomorrow will be Tuesday), but this is not called "remembering the future." We do not remember the past entirely, and no person can remember another person's memories. In the life of the individual or the race, more is forgotten than remembered. Some things that are remembered never happened.

The *thermodynamic* arrow identifies the future as a period of greater disorder than the past. Its foundation is the second law of thermodynamics, which holds that disorder (entropy) always increases in systems. The second law of thermodynamics once meant that everything breaks down sooner or later; no perpetual motion machine can exist. If it is evidence of the direction that time is moving—or that time is moving—we need to know in which direction the arrow should point. One person's idea of order is another's conception of disorder. If the early universe was an ocean of radiation and quarks, why is this state more orderly than its present state, with intelligent life on earth?

The second law of thermodynamics makes sense in its original form. If adapted to tell where to find the future, it makes less sense. My car is not 100 percent efficient; it wastes energy. From the perspective of the entire universe, however, the energy wasted by my car is recycled, as will also eventually be the case with my car. Furthermore, systems break down, but not like the wonderful one-horse shay that deteriorated at the same rate in all of its parts. If a car breaks down because, say, its brakes fail, the rest of the car can look perfect. If I wanted to monitor the signs that the universe will not endure forever—the signs at which the thermodynamic arrow is pointing—where are these signs, and what are they?

The third arrow of time, the *cosmological* arrow, points in the direction the universe is expanding. Whether time will run backward if the universe contracts has been asked. Unless we know the universe will expand forever, the cosmological arrow is not a reliable guide to where the future is located. We can consistently believe that the universe is expanding and also that time does not move, that no time exists except the present.

Fermions and Bosons

The Copenhagen interpretation of quantum theory allows us to imagine multiple realities and sometimes requires that we do so. These multiple realities can take the form of, say, swarms of ghost electrons that exist in the form of probabilities and coalesce into a single electron when observed. Universes may exist parallel to our own, in which what might have occurred has occurred.

These are wonderful conjectures. They do not touch on the multiple realities we live with every day: the three-dimensional world of touch, the two-dimensional world of vision or color, and thought, devoid of spatial extension although we regard it as existing in time. Can a three-dimensional universe include other universes that are not three-dimensional? If it can, why is it impossible to tell the color of an apple touched in the dark? If touch, vision, and thought are parallel realities, what glue holds them together?

Possibly, the visual field is three-dimensional, or usefully regarded in that way. We can assume that the third dimension is color, a substitute for the depth of the world of touch. The distinction between fermions and bosons, in quantum mechanics, speaks to the issue of why we have no organ that can both see and touch. Fermions, named after the statistics developed by Enrico Fermi and Paul Dirac, obey what is known as the Pauli exclusion principle. They move incrementally, from one quantum state to another. Protons, electrons, and neutrons are fermions. Bosons (after the Bose-Einstein statistics), do not obey the Pauli exclusion principle and can occupy the same energy state. Photons, the massless particles that account for color and light, are bosons.

The distinction—roughly, a distinction between matter and energy—suggests that the two-dimensional world of vision (color) is a universe of bosons; the three-dimensional world of touch, a universe of fermions. Human beings evidently lack a neurological apparatus capable of relating to both at once. No single sense both touches and sees, perhaps because different types of receptors are required to relate to the two types of particles.

Object or Attribute

Vision differs from other perceptual experiences in that the colors we see cannot be explained in terms of an immediately verifiable movement of objects. If light moves, we do not see the movement. Relying on current conceptions in the physical sciences, color and vision are boson related. Other sense perceptions are fermion related. Different classes of particles are involved.

If we assume that color exists in a world of its own—a parallel reality like those of the physical sciences—the question of whether color is attribute or object can be answered. Assume that objects can be isolated, can exist independently. Isolating implies separating an entity from other entities in its class, though not necessarily from those in other classes. Colors are separable in this sense. Blue is distinct from red, which is why I cannot see both at the same time and place. Any individual color can be isolated from other colors. In this sense, all colors are objects. We may want to avoid confusion by calling them *objects of perception*.

Are colors separable from three-dimensional objects? The blueness of a chair cannot be severed from the chair. We cannot transport the chair to one location and its color to another. To explain this limit, we might regard the color as if it were glued to the chair. I think this is an insufficient model. Any chair can be located in three-dimensional space by means of the *x, y, z* coordinates familiar from high school geometry. Its color cannot be placed in that manner, because vision is limited to two spatial dimensions. I conclude that the color of a chair is not part of the chair in a three-dimensional sense, and that this is why nobody can determine by touching a chair whether its color is red or blue. The color is in another world from the chair, in a different coordinate system. Color lies in the two-dimensional image of the chair that we see rather than in the three-dimensional chair that we touch.

Certain traditional questions about color, visual imagery, and vision devalue them in subtle ways. We are asked to consider, say, whether color is real, whether images are ephemera, whether our eyes deceive us. These questions have been asked for centuries. I suspect their slant reflects societal attitudes about two-dimensionality. Plane geometry is not regarded as inferior to solid geometry, an exception. In most other cases, two-dimensionality impresses us as less significant, less real, than three-dimensionality. As a result, the English language is not rich in terms that encourage sensibility to two-dimensional matrices, to the abstract aspects of visual experience. And metaphors that refer to flatness or two-dimensionality almost always have negative connotations.

Being without depth or having nothing below the surface is not admired in poetry, people, or ideas. Being without substance is also bad, although being spiritual is good. Novelists are criticized if their characters are two-dimensional. Voices without expression are flat, as are musical notes sung off key. Yet seeing objects is as important as bumping into them.

Conveying Information about Color

The Munsell System, as adapted to problems of color notation and description, has become the most highly developed 'tool' to be developed anywhere. Thanks to the cooperation of numerous scientists, to the work of scientific committees, to the endeavors of such organizations as the Inter-Society Color Council, the Optical Society of America, the National Bureau of Standards, the System today is pre-eminent.

Faber Birren, A Grammar of Color

Many color names exist, and new coinages are introduced daily. But the primal terms have remained stable over an extended time. Few generalizations can be made about the large body of names that are not primal, other than that most are borrowed from the names of objects. The primary rule for learning color names derived from object names is that the viewer can refer to the object if uncertain about the color. The meaning of any color name is best clarified by ostensive definition, by showing a sample of the color or color range. A swatch or sample is mandatory if a color is to be matched. Despite claims to the contrary by color theorists and colorimetrists, no scientific nomenclature for color exists. Nor does any system approach one.

Nomenclatures and Notational Systems

Familiar examples of scientific nomenclature are found in chemistry and the biological sciences. Each consists of an alternate set of names for objects identified differently on an everyday basis. For the chemist, table salt is sodium chloride. For the ornithologist, the Eastern robin is *Turdus migratorius migratorius*. The technical terms are derived from Greek and Latin, a mechanism intended to prevent their being confused with ordinary English words.

Within a nomenclature, each individual scientific name is a code, conveying information about relationships among objects in the system. The terms *sodium chloride* and *sodium hydroxide* indicate that each of these compounds has sodium as a constituent, a family resemblance unrevealed when the substances are identified as salt and lye. Biological names provide similar clues. Robins and bluebirds are related, because both belong to the family Muscicapidae.

When Munsell developed his notational system for colors, he apparently intended to provide color with a nomenclature similar to that used in chemistry. The same path was followed by Ostwald, who was trained as a chemist. But the Munsell and Ostwald notational systems, like those of their followers, fail to provide a distinctive set of alternate names. The color known in ordinary language as *red* has no scientific name other than *red*. When James Clerk Maxwell and other physicists describe light of various wavelengths, they identify the colors by such everyday terms as red, green, and scarlet. These terms are of limited usefulness. Adults rarely make errors in identifying objects as, say, red or blue. Yet, as Munsell complained, confusion reigns when we want to convey the minute color differences between a particular shade of blue and hundreds of others that are similar but not exactly the same.

Because no scientific nomenclature for color exists, describing the exact color of a beam of monochromatic spectral light is as difficult as describing the exact color of any other colored object. Arnheim, citing a listing compiled by Hiler, notes that the color of light with a wavelength of 600 millimicrons "has been described by various authors as Orange Chrome, Golden Poppy, Spectrum Orange, Bitter Sweet Orange, Oriental Red, Saturn Red, Cadmium Red Orange, and Red Orange" (Arnheim 1956, 348). No scientific way to use color names exists, because no scientific color names exist.

The shortcoming of the major cataloging systems is less an absolute lack of names (the ISCC gives names for 267 major color classes) than the character of the names that were chosen. These names are variations on ordinary

language names and not sufficiently different from them. The names range from Munsell's *blue-green* to the National Bureau of Standards's *moderate bluish green* and *light grayish reddish brown*.

Although similar names are used in the several systems, they are not applied to colors in a similar manner. No international agreement has been reached on whether one system is preferable to another. In the United States, the Inter-Society Color Council and the National Bureau of Standards have evolved a standardized system based on Munsell's (ISCC-NBS). In Great Britain, the comparable system is founded on Ostwald's methods and names. Standard blue is not the same standard, and not the same blue, on both sides of the Atlantic.

When names in a nomenclature system differ from those used every day, this insulates them from the loose and changing usage of ordinary language. Ambiguity, for example, is not unique to color names. Nor is the tendency to proliferate. Many plants and animals are known by dozens of different popular names. The same name may be used to identify different species by people in different locales. A single species may thus acquire several names.

What has been understood in developing the nomenclature of the biological sciences is that trying to edit or organize popular names is an exercise in futility. The names, as a group, have no sense or order and usually developed in a random manner. With sufficient effort, much could be learned about how people use the terms *cattail* or *bluish green*. But this is not the expeditious way to systematize information about plants or colors. Assigning the botanical name *Typha latifolia* to the cattail and providing a description of what the plant looks like places it in the nomenclature of botany without opening that other can of worms: the question of whether people always call cattails *cattails* and consistently use the name only for that plant.

Colors, admittedly, are a special case. We

cannot describe what they look like and thus cannot pair descriptions with names. The visual difference between blue and yellow eludes words, although a botanist can concisely state the difference between a cattail and an oak tree. Colors are said to have fewer than half a dozen qualia, a probable reason for the difficulty of the task. Hue, value, chroma, and glossiness are most frequently mentioned. Plants have a greater number of defining attributes. Many of these attributes are countable and measurable, including the number of lobes to a leaf and the manner of branching of stems.

The defining characters of plant species would not be recognized as such by an untrained, though interested, observer. Yet they can be pointed out by the technically trained. Whether colors can be described depends on whether they have qualia beyond those usually cited and whether these qualia are countable or measurable. We also need to reassess those situations in which measurement is thought to have occurred. Whether anything pertinent has been measured is questionable if we do not know whether light with a wavelength of 600 millimicrons is "Orange Chrome, Golden Poppy, Spectrum Orange, Bitter Sweet Orange, Oriental Red, Saturn Red, Cadmium Red Orange, [or] Red Orange."

Munsell Color Notation

Among familiar chemical symbols, Na, Fe, O, H, and Cl respectively identify atoms of sodium, iron, oxygen, hydrogen, and chlorine. In chemistry, these and symbols for the other elements can be combined into formulas that display the result of chemical combination. The chemical notation for water, H_2O, indicates that the molecule consists of two atoms of hydrogen (H), one of oxygen (O).

In Munsell's notational system, following the format used in chemistry, letter symbols are provided for each of ten major hues. These are supplemented by numerical indications of value and chroma, measured on a scale devised by Munsell and specified for each color in his system. A typical notation might be R 5/10, identified by Munsell as a shade of vermilion (Munsell [1905] 1961, 20). The hue symbols are as follows:

R	red
YR	yellow-red
Y	yellow
GY	green-yellow
G	green
BG	blue-green
B	blue
PB	purple-blue
P	purple
RP	red-purple

A chemist on the East Coast can send a chemist on the West Coast the formula for a chemical substance. In a similar manner, one colorimetrist can write to another thousands of miles away. Munsell notations can be used to identify a color being discussed. Munsell hoped to convince us that the chemist mailing a formula and the individual posting a Munsell notation are engaged in similar activities. But the respondent receiving the Munsell notation will be unable to determine, by reading it, what the intended color looks like. A copy of the Munsell color book is required to locate the swatch corresponding to that notation.

This is the fatal flaw in the system, which provides ostensive definition, masquerading as an abstract notational system. A chemical notation, say, NaCl, tells what a substance is. A Munsell notation, say, R 5/10, does not tell what a color looks like. It just indicates where to look to find out. The Munsell notation resembles a literary citation. It tells where to locate information but does not provide the information directly.

The entire tedious notational system that Munsell recommends can be eliminated by sending a color sample. All concerned can be mercifully relieved of any need to look up swatches in books. Even if the books are retained, a notational system is not necessary for identifying individual swatches. Each of the 1,200 samples in Munsell's *Book of Color* can be assigned a number from 1 to 1,200. A swatch labeled number 376 is as clearly identified as another marked R 5/10. Swatches can be equally useful if labeled, say, "page 5, second row, third swatch from left."

In the glossary of *A Color Notation*, Munsell contends his system provides "an exact and specific description of a color, using symbols and numerals, written HUE/VALUE/CHROMA" (Munsell [1905] 1961, 59). Elsewhere, the claim of precision is qualified. Color notation is just "a very convenient means for recording color combinations, when pigments are not at hand" (Munsell [1905] 1961, 28). The system would be more convenient if not tied to the availability of the *Munsell Book of Color*.

Munsell argued that his notation provided an "exact and specific description of a color." But an additional requirement must be met to develop an abstract notational system. The description must not be ostensive or must be direct rather than indirect. Identifying a particular color as the blue used in the wallpaper of the master bedroom at the White House in Washington, D. C., is admirably exact and precise. This wallpaper, like the *Munsell Book of Color*, is available for public examination by those who find a reason to take an interest. We understand, however, the prudence of not sending respondents far afield to study swatch books or wallpapers. Those who want a color matched exactly will send a sample. If color combinations must be recorded and "pigments are not at hand," the pigments are easier to come by than the *Munsell Book of Color*.

The avoidance of Greek and Latin coinages in systematizing the naming of colors was meant to cater to the presumed limitations of the industrial user, a figure whose shadow looms large in color theory. Theorists from Goethe onward pleaded the relevance of their ideas about color to dyers and other practical persons (Eastlake [1840] 1970, 289). The untutored wisdom of the simple soul was asserted against the authority of science. This wisdom was also to stand against the obdurateness of artists, who were not unanimous in their gratitude for color systems. Goethe's praise of the dyer Jeremias Friedrich Gülich is unaccompanied by any clear explanation of what is praiseworthy in the ideas Gülich published (Eastlake [1840] 1970, 291). I suspect Goethe was no more deeply interested in dye technology than in the chemistry of ceramic glazes. Goethe had no praise for Newton and praised Gülich instead.

The modern industrial user, still courted in literature explaining why the ISCC-NBS system is needed, is more sophisticated than the simple dyer of Goethe's day or the honest tailor to whom Chevreul dispensed advice on the use of color in clothing (Chevreul [1845] 1980, 165–79). This industrial user is not well served by any of the systems. Imagine a scenario in which a hypothetical manufacturer is sent a Munsell notation. This industrial user is instructed to ensure that all sweaters made in the factory match the color indicated by the notation. Having located, in the handy *Munsell Book of Color*, the swatch to which the notation is keyed, the manufacturer must determine how to proceed.

Removing the swatch from the book to pass it along to the dyers means it will be unavailable if needed again. Sending the entire expensive book means *it* will be unavailable and may be mislaid. If I were the manufacturer, I would make up color swatches or have them made. How is time or effort saved by the notation?

The communicator bears certain burdens in the art of communicating. If I wanted another person to understand an unfamiliar word I was using, I would explain what the word meant. I would not hand the person a dictionary. If I wanted the person to understand exactly what color I had in mind, I would pass along a sample of the color. I would not send the *Munsell Book of Color* or expect a copy to be procured. Munsell turns this societal norm upside down with no benefit that I can see.

The purported usefulness of Munsell notations to industry rests on the assumption that the chain of command consists of only two people, each of whom has on hand the requisite book of color swatches. In manufacturing anything, many people are involved, and any of them may need to know the color of the object. Supplying each with the *Munsell Book of Color* is uneconomical and unnecessary. If samples of only one color are needed for the job at hand, no reason exists for every person involved to have samples of twelve hundred colors.

Color Standards

Even if Munsell's proposals were not questionable on theoretical grounds, implementing them would not be easy. Commercial and technological factors complicate the task of making color standards available. Modern VGA monitors for computers are capable of displaying 256,000 colors, a small number compared to the ten million colors that the National Bureau of Standards computes can be visually distinguished. Paper swatches of standardized colors are expensive to produce and do not reproduce well in ordinary books. The limitations of color printing technology are part of the difficulty. Despite the vigilence of museums, we are all accustomed to seeing, printed in books, reproductions of famous paintings in which the color reproduction is dreadful.

Beyond the crudity of photolithography

and related printing processes lies the crudity of color photography. Perhaps because color sensitivity in camera films has been sacrificed for speed, color films in wide usage (Kodachrome, Ektachrome, Kodacolor, and so forth) have narrower sensitivity than the human eye to color nuance. Even the best color photographs fall short of matching the colors in paintings or in color swatches. Silk-screened swatches tipped into books by hand provide a better opportunity for color control, therefore greater potential for accuracy. Like other colored materials, these swatches are affected by time and exposure to light.

Do chemical substances exist that reflect a single wavelength of light? Could, say, a standard yellow be defined as the color of crystalline sulfur? These directions have not been explored, and the standardizing of color has not been related to the standardizing of, say, the standard meter. The standard meter, a platinum bar kept in Paris, has been redefined in terms of the speed of light, regarded as invariant. A meter is now the distance light travels in 0.000000003335640952 seconds. If light is just another name for color, the standard meter has been redefined in terms of color. We rarely think of length in these terms.

To standardize the colors of the spectrum in a manner similar to that used for metric length, a single wavelength might be chosen as, say, standard red. To dispose of Goethe's complaint that light is not color, a standard red *color* might be defined as the color of this light reflected from a standard white surface, say a surface coated with barium sulfate or titanium oxide. Difficulties intrude in this process. If a wavelength in the red range were arbitrarily chosen as standard red and that light reflected from a white surface, the illumination in the room would have to be specified as well. Also, red light is defined in physics as a range. Yet no two texts give exactly the same numbers for the limits of this range in terms of wavelength. Physicists, like the rest of us, have no clear conception of standard red or pure red.

Color Notation and Ostensive Definition

Graphic symbols, including those used in notational systems, are shorthand substitutes for words. Therefore, whether an abstract color notational system can exist independent of ostensive definition depends on whether colors can be described without resort to simile. The modern fashion among compilers of dictionaries is to identify green as a color like that of a portion of the spectrum. The method is no more sophisticated than that of the proverbial Ur-primitive who identifies green as the color of leaves. It is an inferior description, despite resort to a more esoteric object.

Most leaves are green. A visitor from another galaxy could look at leaves to discover which color was meant. The spectrum is less helpful to the uninformed, because most portions of it are not green. An a priori understanding of what green looks like is necessary to determine which is the green portion. For exactly this reason, nobody ever learned to identify green from a dictionary.

If colors cannot be described in words or by means of abstract notational systems independent of ostensive definition, this need not imply that color is shamefully tainted by the purely subjective. Its condition may parallel that of numbers and other conceptual primitives. *Six*, like *red*, has no scientific name and is called *six*, written as *six* or *6*, in technical treatises as in ordinary language.

Similarly, no abstract notational system has been developed for *up, down, left,* and *right*. Like color and number, they can only be explained ostensively. We cannot explain what *six* means other than by displaying six objects, just as we cannot explain the meaning of yellow other than by exhibiting an item of that

color. I conclude that language is insufficiently refined for some tasks or incapable of accomplishing them altogether. We need to seek a better understanding of those entities that can only be explained by pointing at them.

Showing Colors

We talk about things by mentioning their names, the reason for complaints about the ambiguity of color names. In an ideal language, every object in the world would have a name, and no object would have two names. This ideal is difficult to implement, for color or anything else. Although no two Americans have the same Social Security number, we would be hard pressed if required to address other people by their Social Security numbers. Fewer names are available than Social Security numbers, which we tolerate in the assumption that the law of probability protects us. Undoubtedly an excessively large number of Jane Smiths and John Smiths live in the United States. We trust that no single person will have to deal with several of them at the same time.

Providing every citizen, among 200 million Americans, with a unique name would be a formidable task. By estimate, only ten million colors exist, though the problem is similar. Nobody would be able to remember ten million names, even if every individual variation of color had its own.

We manage to communicate about color, despite these complications, because communication is not limited to speech and writing. Communication also encompasses a variety of gestures, and human beings can communicate by showing things to one another. Although regarded less favorably than telling, showing is not a primitive ceremony. As is necessary in all modes of communication, common acculturation links the active subject (who shows) and the passive object (to whom something is shown). Rules determine what may be shown, to whom, when, and in what manner.

Among objects that can be shown, color swatches are displayed to make clear how a particular color name ought to be understood or what color should be selected for a particular purpose. Because the swatches convey information by requiring that something be looked at, they resemble diagrams, charts, and graphs, specialized offshoots of written language that are conventionalized and contextual. Graphs, for example, are not intended as representational pictures of what they "represent." A black bar can denote the aggregate of people who, according to context, purchased new cars, live west of the Rocky Mountains, or are registered Democrats.

Color swatches differ from diagrams, charts, and graphs in that what is shown consist of colors rather than lines or shapes. The color swatch can be combined with other forms, as in a layout for a two-color newspaper ad. The colors of swatches may be understood as samples, which implies they ought to be matched closely or exactly. Or, functioning more in the manner of a code, they can be taken to indicate only a broad class of color. Workers in a given industry, familiar with its conventions, rarely find it necessary to discuss how a swatch, sketch, or layout ought to be interpreted.

The textile manufacturer who wants to key a dyed fabric to a painted piece of paper may find dyes are not available to match the colors exactly. A subjective determination is made of when a sufficiently close approximation has been achieved. Looser standards are involved when a newspaper or magazine production person, working from a red and black layout of a two-color ad, "matches" the red of the layout by specifying any available red ink. Color swatches and samples speak a silent language of their own. Their colors are meant to be matched. But how closely depends on the circumstances.

Describing Colors

Describing the colors of objects, like showing samples of the colors, follows everyday rules. In describing movable objects, we conventionally tell what the object looks like, not where it is located. Describing, say, Picasso's *Night Fishing at Antibes* implies something other than specifying, however meticulously, where the painting is situated relative to the elevators at the Museum of Modern Art in New York City. The spatiotemporal coordinates of a portable object, because subject to change, are not regarded as integral to the object. Yet identifying where an object is located can be legitimate, sometimes uniquely for the circumstances. A trucking company sent to pick up *Night Fishing* might be more interested in locating the painting in the museum than in locating it within the history of art. At times, green paint is justifiably called the can on the top shelf.

In daily affairs, colors are described by methods not acknowledged in dictionaries. The colors of, say, house paints vary between manufacturers, even if labeled by the same name. If part of a room has been painted in Benjamin Moore ivory, and more paint is required, the hardware store clerk should be told the brand name as well as the color.

Some of these ad hoc forms for identifying colors reflect the built-in limits of manufacturing processes. Photographic film varies in color sensitivity from one emulsion lot to the next, a matter of importance to cinematographers. Knitting yarns vary in color from one dye lot to the next. Specifying emulsion numbers and dye lot numbers ensures color consistency between original and subsequent purchases. Use of lot numbers is common in industries that involve dyeing processes. The variables of dyeing, which include the length of time an object is immersed, are such that color consistency often cannot be guaranteed from one batch to the next.

An emulsion number printed on a box of movie film is a code. It tells nothing about the color sensitivity of the film other than that it is similar to that of other boxes of film bearing the same number. The emulsion number does not, interestingly, guarantee that the film is properly balanced for color sensitivity, and it may warn that it is not. Boxes of film may carry a notation, say, that all rolls with emulsion number 1,174 should be used with a cyan filter of a particular density.

Chemical Names as Color Names

Codes and names are not always easy to separate, because names can be used as codes. Many commercial color names for artists' paints, say, *cadmium red*, are adapted from the chemical names of the pigments used in the paints. *Cadmium red* is a red paint in which the pigments are cadmium sulphide and cadmium selenide. Pigments are a specialized type of object, and the practice of naming colors after objects is commonplace.

For a chemist, the difference between zinc sulfide and cadmium sulfate might turn on the difference between a sulfide and a sulphate. When chemical names are adapted to identify pigments, a more important consideration is that zinc sulfide (zinc yellow) is a pale greenish yellow pigment or color. Cadmium sulfate (cadmium yellow) is also yellow, but brighter and not so greenish.

Although many names for artists' pigments are borrowed from chemical nomenclature, their use is not consistent with that nomenclature. The chemical names acquire an operational meaning as the names of colors. A piece of fabric described as cadmium red is understood to be a particular color. We are not required to assume that cadmium salts were used to dye the fabric. For anyone familiar with names of pigments, *cadmium red dark* conveys more information about the intended color than alternatives such as red, dark red,

dark bluish red, and so forth.

Dictionaries rarely acknowledge operational usage, which bypasses ordinary rules. In its formal meaning, a chemical name such as zinc sulfide identifies a substance, not its color. But scientific terms often drift into ordinary language by acquiring everyday meanings inconsistent with technical usage. These meanings can identify how an item is used, rather than what it is. Fluorides become popularly known as ingredients in toothpastes; bromides, aids to digestion; chlorine, a killer of germs in swimming pools; iodine, a household antiseptic.

No chemistry book would define hydrogen as a substance used in bombs or neon as a gas used in neon signs (which in most cases are filled with gases other than neon). By a similarly operational rationale, the chemical names of pigments used to apply color to surfaces acquire a secondary meaning as the names of those colors.

When chemical names acquire a secondary meaning as color names, different rules apply than when the names are used within the parameters of chemical nomenclature. Zinc yellow paint from two different manufacturers is likely to differ in color, method of manufacture, and such variables as ratio of pigment to vehicle. Yet both will be called zinc yellow. By extension, the name can be applied to any yellow that looks similar to zinc yellow, whether or not attributable to that pigment. We need not investigate the chemical composition of the glaze used for dinner dishes before describing the color of the dishes as zinc yellow, cobalt blue, or cadmium red. The chemist, grading a batch of zinc sulfide, finds chemical purity, an absence of adulterants, significant. For the paint manufacturer, the primary question is whether adulterants affect color.

Patterns emerge from operational usage. The names of modern dyes (mauve is an exception) seldom inspire color names. Many of these dyes have no ordinary language names and are identified by chemical names that are polysyllabic and difficult to remember. Color names adapted from the chemical names of pigments refer to those of modern vintage, including cadmium red, cadmium yellow, and titanium white. Traditional pigments tend to retain their original names: vermilion, emerald green, burnt sienna, yellow ocher, and so forth.

Colors and Numbers

Most modern color cataloging systems use numbers as well as names. In the ISCC-NBS system, ten million colors are divided among 267 classes, while finer distinctions are indicated numerically. The English language does not contain ten million color names. If it did, nobody would be able to memorize them. The advantage of numbers is that anyone who understands the system can extend it indefinitely. Counting to ten million does not require the prior memorizing of ten million numbers.

Like the ISCC notational system, Munsell's combines names with numbers, though in a different manner. Hue (major color class) is described by name, say, red. For notational purposes, each hue name is abbreviated to a letter (R, in the case of red). Value and chromaticity are indicated by numbers. The net effect is to address the problem that any given color name—for example, *light gray green*—can be shown to be applicable to a broad range of colors. Particular colors or shades of color in the range can be efficiently designated by any of a wide variety of name and number combinations, by such constructions as *light gray green 1, light gray green 2, light gray green 3*, and so forth. The device eliminates any necessity for coining individual names for each shade or variety of light gray green.

Although numbers are often used as qualifiers in this manner, I know of no system of color cataloging that relies on number alone. In an entirely numerical system, each of the ten million ISCC colors might be assigned a number between one and ten million. In theory, we could then include in ordinary language statements such as ''I like color number 965,873.'' Assuming that the ISCC is correct in computing ten million visually distinguishable colors, no ambiguity would occur about which color is meant. The barrier is the limitation of human memory, considerable in this case.

Human beings are unable to commit colors to, or retrieve then from, memory with exactitude. This is why the wise, when asked to decide whether two colors match, insist on looking at both colors at the same time, in close proximity to one another. We lack a memory for color and also lack the computer's ability to manipulate long strings of numbers without error. Although my friends cannot be expected to remember my Social Security number, the proliferating computers in which it is entered always print out the digits correctly. In the case of color, nobody would remember, or be able to visualize, the difference between, say, color number 965,873 and color number 965,874. Yet the difference, if between ISCC colors, would be noticeable when swatches were examined.

Modifications to numerical systems can make them easier to remember. The following set might be used as the basis for a system of coding the spectral hues.

HUE	CODE
red	6
orange	5
yellow	4
green	3
blue	2
violet	1

In this system, a blue-violet, intermediary between blue (code 2) and violet (code 1), might be designated by an intermediary number carried out to any required number of decimal places, for example, 1.5. The terms 1.1, 1.13, 1.28, 1.47 might designate a series of blue-violets that tend increasingly toward blue, a system that ought to be workable whether the number of colors is infinite or not. The system resembles a clock, which enables us to divide time into hours, minutes, seconds, and other other neat packets, though we believe time itself is a continuum and possibly infinite.

We easily lose track of the passage of time, the reasons watches and clocks are needed to issue reminders. No reminder is needed of what red looks like. Color is a more intimate concept than time, more closely tied to perceptual experience. Perhaps for this reason, a sense of discomfort interjects itself when 6/4/2 or any other arbitrary group of numbers is proposed as an alternate set of names for red/yellow/blue. One argument against an entirely numerical system for coding colors is as follows.

The number continuum cannot reflect the differences in color quality between different sectors of the spectrum. Blue is fundamentally dissimilar to orange. This is not made clear if blue is called 2 and orange is called 5. Numbers are insufficiently expressive. The visual difference between, say, blue and orange is what they fail to express or communicate.

The demand for expressiveness through names is not consistent. Number is apparently acceptable when something is thought to have been measured. The prime example is the defining of red, in physics, as light with a wavelength of 650 millimicrons, violet with 400 millimicrons, and so forth. The quantitative relationship that exists between the frequencies raises the question of whether a parallel quantitative relationship can be assumed between the colors. Probably it cannot be, or the assumption is not useful. There is no way in which violet is approximately two-thirds of red, other than that this is the ratio between their respective assigned wavelengths.

Munsell's notation for what he called a typical maroon is 5R3/4. *R* stands for red. 5, 3, and 4 refer to hue, chroma, and value for that maroon. Less ornate constructions are possible. Typical maroon can as easily be identified as 534, 435, or 999. The sole requirement for an internally consistent code is that a single number apply to no more than one color. What offends in identifying colors by numbers are meaningless numbers, which code without purporting to measure. If 5 is used as a designation for orange, or 534 for maroon, the numbers are as arbitrary as those in the Dewey decimal system used for library cataloging. They are also potentially as useful—and less ponderous than the systems at hand.

Among available color atlases, the *Munsell Book of Color* contains over twelve hundred different swatches. Its utility is not impaired if each swatch is renumbered according to position in the book. Whether the numbering commences at the first or last page is of no importance. A designation such as 534 is as useful as 5R3/4. It may even be more helpful, because it does not create the misleading impression that something measurable has been measured.

Thinking of orange as, say, 5 seems strange. But this is just a matter of acculturation. Arbitrary numbering systems are used to describe perceptual continua in which sectors differ as greatly as orange and blue. The thermometer measures the temperature continuum in terms of arbitrary degrees. Understanding what the numbers on a thermometer mean implies a complex interpretive process. Changing from one method of measuring temperature to another, say, Fahrenheit to Celsius, becomes confusing because a new system of interpretation must be superimposed on an old one. We eventually learn to remember that 100°C is hotter than 200°F and 0°C is warmer than 20°F.

For those familiar with the conventions, −20°F means unbearably cold; 125°F means unbearably hot. In-between numbers indicate conditions that are called cool, bracing, cold, pleasantly warm, unpleasantly warm, very hot, or chilly. We become adept at interpreting the numbers and know what they imply. Temperature readings, in turn, impress by their seeming exactness, and may people prefer them to verbal description. To hear that the temperature rose to 90° seems to communicate more than just being told it is hot. If colors were coded numerically, people would similarly learn to interpret the numbers or would come to regard them as meaningful.

A system that measured some aspect of color (and reported the measurements) might seem preferable to one in which arbitrary numbers were assigned. When numbers represent measurements, they "really mean something," in that they communicate information beyond themselves. If a person is six feet tall, the measurement conveys information about the individual: that he or she is tall. Except to personnel in the Social Security system, that the six-foot tall person's Social Security number is 683-97-0014 conveys nothing except the information that this is the number.

We have many systems that purport to measure color or some aspect of it. But the urge to measure is not sufficient to ensure that measurement really takes place, or that the numbers are interpreted in a sensible manner. Munsell grades the grays on a value scale ranging from 0 (black) to 10 (white). This scale represents "the averaged results obtained by seven experienced observers" (Munsell [1905] 1961, 63). On this scale, gray 4 is darker than gray 8. Whether twice as dark is a meaningless question, because the ratio between the respective grays (8/4 = 2) points to nothing that is perceptually verifiable. Calling one color twice as dark as another is as meaningless as calling one day twice as hot as another.

Measuring differs from counting. Often no operational criteria can be established to explain what *twice as much* means. It can mean twice as large a measurement on an arbitrary scale and nothing further. The reading from the scale fails to correspond to any identifiable aspect of the object and is less a measurement than an ornate code.

According to the Fahrenheit thermometer, the temperature at which water boils is $6\frac{5}{8}$ times as high as the temperature at which it freezes. But 212 °F cannot be $6\frac{5}{8}$ times as hot as 32°F in any demonstrable sense. The ratio fails to hold if readings for boiling and freezing water are taken from Celsius thermometers. When readings are taken from arbitrary scales, the readings cannot be regarded as measurement, and reasoning based on numerical ratios is meaningless.

In measurement of another type, something can be perceptually verified. That one box contains twice as many apples as another can be factual, verifiable by counting the apples in the boxes. A ten-pound box of apples can be shown to weigh as much as two five-pound boxes. But to say that one color is twice as dark, or twice as blue, as another is arbitrary. No way exists of verifying the statement or explaining what it means. Similarly, a temperature of 80° cannot be shown to be twice as hot as a temperature of 40°. I conclude the reason for the difference is that apples can be isolated for counting. Darkness, blueness, and warmth cannot be isolated as objects, which bears on the limited nature of the measurements we make of them.

A main argument for coding colors by assigning arbitrary numbers to them is that the alternative of measuring (assigning meaningful numbers) may not be available. Some sort of Dewey decimal system for colors might be preferable to arbitrary numbers disguised as measurements of hue, value, chroma, or whatnot. Orange as 534.7 is ultimately less objectionable than 5R3/4.

CHAPTER 29

On Ambiguity in Color Names

It must not be supposed for a moment that the colors on this chart represent the colors of all the birds of eastern North America. . . . It should be clearly understood, therefore, that when greyish brown, for example, is mentioned, it does not follow that the feathers to which the term is applied are of exactly the same color as the plate, but that they are nearer to this color than to any other in the plate. Used even in this general way, the plate will prove a far more definite basis for description than if everyone were left to form his own idea of the colors named.

Frank M. Chapman, Handbook of Birds of Eastern North America

Florence Elizabeth Wallace compiled many examples of failure of parallelism between color names in English and those used by ancient Greek authors (Wallace 1927). Homer had no label for the color modern speakers of English call *bright yellow*. The Greeks regarded orange as three classes of hue, corresponding to our red-orange, orange, and yellow-orange. Although common between one language and another, skewings of this type create difficulties for translators. *Bright yellow* cannot be rendered in classical Greek if this variety of hue has no name in that language. The Bassa color name *ziza* cannot be translated into a single nontechnical English word if we want to avoid *warm colors* and the class to which *ziza* refers includes reds, oranges, and yellows. Alternately, if *ziza* is a color name, but its nearest equivalent in English, *warm colors*, is not, translations are confusing and misleading.

Failure of parallelism between languages cannot fully account for the frequency with which color names are mistranslated, poorly defined, inconsistently used, and misused in English by great translators, great scientists, compilers of dictionaries, and educated adults. Although taught to choose words carefully, we are careless with color names. Nobody makes the mistake of identifying pink as green. Primal color names are usually remembered, as are the more familiar symbolic associations with these colors. Misused or confused names are usually those of the second echelon, familiar enough to be remembered but not familiar enough to be remembered entirely, say, magenta, vermilion, scarlet, lavender, crimson, or viridian.

Color names of this kind are not obscure words. Most are sufficiently familiar to be appropriately included in a spelling bee for children. An educated adult can spell them and has a general impression of what each means, though they remain capable of causing uncertainty. Consider the Italian word *vermiglia* in several translations of Dante's *Commedia*. *Vermiglia* is identified as a cognate for the English *vermilion* in many Italian-English dictionaries. Cognates, where they exist, are the preferred translations for foreign language terms, unless a word changes meaning in passing from one language to another. Yet in major translations of *Commedia*, *vermiglia* is often not translated as *vermilion*. It is not even translated to the same English color name in each occurrence.

In the Temple Classics edition of *Inferno*, *vermiglia* is *crimson* in one passage, *red* in a second, and *fiery red* in a third (*Inferno* iii, 132; *Inferno* vi, 16; *Inferno* xxxiv, 39). John Ciardi translated *vermiglia* as *red* in the first two passages and as *fiery red* in the third (*Inferno* xxxiv, 39). In the Reverend Henry F. Cary's translation of *Inferno* (1805), *vermiglia* is *vermilion* in the first and third of the passages but *red* in the second (*Inferno* vi, 16).

Ezra Pound and others have written about the philosophy of translation as it applies to poetry. I suspect that Pound's erudite considerations are not the issue in this case. Dante is highly effective in his use of color names. Assuming that he had the same color in mind each time he used *vermiglia*, we must look to the translators for an understanding of the inconsistencies. They were uncomfortable with the color name *vermilion* or thought that their readers would be.

The lack of consistency or refinement in the substitutions is a more subtle defect. Among terms selected, crimson and red are not synonyms for vermilion. Fiery red is without grace, because all bright reds are fiery. The term suggests, redundantly, "more fiery than most (fiery) reds." As if colors were not worth concerning ourselves about, we use color names in a haphazard manner. Dictionaries list many scientific names and place names but are less comprehensive with color names, the reason specialized dictionaries of color names have been compiled. Even scientific theories about color tend to be more slapdash, less carefully considered, than theories of other kinds.

Some color names are inherently vague. With the best will in the world, nobody could learn how to use them. *Violet, purple,* and *lavender* are not regarded as synonyms. Each refers to a different color, intermediary between red and blue. Ranking and range are uncertain. Is violet more bluish than purple? Is purple more reddish than lavender? Is purple a variety of violet? Alternately, is violet a variety of purple?

Answers vary among those imprudent enough to risk opinions. For Wallace, *violet* meant bluish purple and was not the correct English word for translating two Greek color names used by Homer that refer to reddish purples (Wallace 1927, 74). Answers are not that simple. In English, consensus cannot even be found about whether the color at the short extreme of the spectrum is more properly called purple or violet.

The human eye shows greatest sensitivity to fine differences of color in the yellow-green range. Yet second-echelon color names for reds and purples outnumber those for yellow-green or any other range of color. Examples include maroon, scarlet, crimson, vermilion, cochineal, magenta, cerise, heliotrope, violet, lavender, purple, fuchsia, and rose. Why do we have so many names for reds and purples? Does a cultural preference for those colors exist?

A cultural aversion is more likely. The colors inspire apprehension, which does not explain why this should be associated with a more-than-usual number of names. Conventional canons of taste dictate that color schemes are dull if limited largely to brown, gray, blue, and green. More definite disapproval is reserved for uses of red and purple considered excessive, excessive because too large an area of the color is used or the shade is too bright. Too much red is considered vulgar. Too much purple is thought bizarre. The association of purple with homosexuality (it less often carries, today, connotations of royal robes of Tyrian purple) is incidental to its being considered (as is orange) inappropriate for many purposes, ranging from men's business suits to bathtubs to wallpaper.

Names can be regarded as surrogates for the named object, the reason human beings dislike having their names mispronounced, misspelled, or forgotten. They read the lack of attention as an insult, and a common way of devaluing anyone or anything is to pay no attention to the name. The more-than-usual ambiguity in names for purples is undoubtedly a side effect of societal ambivalence toward the color over a period of centuries. People who like purple clothing often say they like the color because it is "different."

Orange, regarded by the Greeks as three colors, has a controversial history and is said to be disliked in Japan. Munsell, arguing that orange is not a color, rechristened it *yellow-red*. Ostwald restored it as *orange*, whether or not following Moses Harris, who had defended the integrity of orange centuries earlier.

Magenta and Fuchsia

The greater number of color names in English are borrowed from object names, from objects of that particular color. The system sounds simple, but leaves room for confusion about which object ought to be pointed out as an example of a particular color. Compilers of dictionaries become as confused as anyone else. My *American College Dictionary* (1953), for example, encounters this difficulty with several color names of the second echelon. These include *magenta, fuchsia, blue, indigo,* and *violet*, a cluster of overlapping names for related ranges.

Magenta is defined as (1) the dye fuchsin, and (2) a reddish purple color. The expectation is that *fuchsin* will be properly identified, in its place, as reddish purple (magenta) in color. My dictionary's entry for *fuchsin* calls it a dye that forms deep red solutions and derives its name from the fuchsia flower, which it resembles in color. Is the fuchsia flower (resembling fuchsin in color) magenta, reddish purple, or deep red? The entry for *fuchsia* identifies it as the name of a *crimson* flower.

The reader is left to puzzle over whether *magenta* means reddish purple, deep red (like the dye fuchsin, with which the color is identified), or crimson (like the fuchsia flower that fuchsin resembles in color). Greater tangles are avoided only because this edition of the dictionary declines to hold forth on what *fuchsia* means when used (as it often is) as a color name.

Blue, Indigo, Violet

My *American College Dictionary* defines *spectrum* by listing the colors as Newton identified them. The last three are blue, indigo, and violet. The entry for *indigo* calls it a deep violet-blue between blue and violet in the spectrum. Among blue, indigo, and violet, the reader is to understand that violet is the least bluish (most reddish) color. The compilers have forgotten this ranking in a third entry, which says that *violet* means bluish purple. A fourth entry explains *purple* as any color containing red and blue.

Munsell, who regarded purple as a "more appropriate" name for violet, would have objected to the third and fourth entries. They imply that in the color class *purple* the more bluish (not the more reddish) varieties are called *violet*. The dictionary identifies the last color in the spectrum as *violet*. Munsell called it *purple*. Newton, followed by twentieth-century colorimetrists, reserved the name *purple* for mixtures of red and violet, the extremes of the spectrum. In Newton's arrangement purples were always more reddish than violets.

My dictionary parts company with Munsell in indicating that *lavender, violet,* and *mauve* are bluish purples, and *lilac* is reddish purple. Munsell characterized each of these colors as a purple that is neither reddish nor bluish (Munsell [1905] 1961, 56). The few certainties in this morass are not those identified by my dictionary. *Purple* and *violet*, as Munsell argued, are virtual synonyms. People use whichever they prefer for the name of, say, the last color of the spectrum. *Violet* names a broader range of color than that of the flower.

What color names mean, how people use and misuse them, and which colors are preferred is an aspect of popular culture. Many people have favorite colors and color combinations. They regard the preferences as personal taste. But many ideas about the use of color are traditional and crop up again and again. Black and white color schemes, we say, are improved by a little red. Yet too much red is garish or in poor taste.

Dressing entirely in red is thought to convey a message of aggression, though only in certain contexts. British soldiers wore red uniforms in the 1700s and became known as redcoats. Modern male corporate raiders and real estate developers, no matter how aggressive, do not wear red suits. A man's red suit might be thought acceptable for an artist, actor, singer, or anyone in an occupation where standards are thought to be different. A vase of red roses is not thought of as aggressive. Red sports cars are thought of as daring. Black sedans are regarded as conservative.

I received a mail-order catalog offering shirts for men and women in a choice of thirty different colors. All colors were offered for both sexes, except that the vendor had no pink shirts or lavender shirts for men. Readers were expected to understand why. With a "dare to be different" attitude, Brooks Brothers, the department store, once offered pink Oxford button-down collar shirts for men. Pink, I conclude, is not a color for men. Even in this era of androgynous rock stars and unisex clothing, pink is associated with baby girls. But if a pink shirt comes from a fashionable haberdasher, the ordinary rules do not hold.

Pink button-down shirts from Brooks Brothers were popular for many years. Violet shirts were not offered. A timid person is called a shrinking violet. Pale shades of violet and lavender were once thought to be appropriate colors for clothing for elderly women. Market researchers find, I am sure, that violet shirts for men do not sell well. These ideas survive because people sense an inner logic, often without knowing how to explain the logic. Taste in color, like taste generally, grows from a set of expectations.

Orange, Purple, Yellow-Green

We expect the colors of the spectrum to be "pure," which means both bright and unique. The color uniqueness of red, yellow, blue, and green is rarely questioned. Orange is said to resemble red, which may cast aspersions on its purity. Purple is said to resemble blue. Along with bright yellow-green, bright orange and purple are not ordinarily used as a basis for decorative schemes, whether in room interiors or clothing. The combination appears in Art Nouveau and other styles that aspire to be different.

Yellow-green, like yellow-orange, is probably regarded as an impure yellow, less than unique because it resembles another color. In its muted form, as olive drab or khaki, yellow-green is perennially fashionable, as is rust, a muted form of orange. Bright yellow-green is disliked and regarded as unflattering in clothing. Few secondary color names exist in English for colors in the yellow-green range, far fewer than for reds and purples. Yet yellow-green is the range in which the eye shows greatest acuity.

Identifying Colors on Color Wheels

Anthropologists and linguists have long been interested in where the points of division between colors of the spectrum are imagined to lie. How colors are named bears on the question of how acculturation affects interpretation of visual experience. V. F. Ray, listing the basic color terms used in ten North American cultures, found little uniformity in the terms used or the parts of the spectrum to which they apply (Segall, Campbell and Herskovits 1966, 47; Ray 1953). The point can be made without investigating whether any ten American Indian tribes name the major colors in the same way or whether we do it as the classical Greeks did. No two modern experts on color agree with one another, even on issues as fundamental as the names of the major classes of color, the names of the colors of the spectrum, or the way hues should be arranged on color wheels.

On Albert H. Munsell's wheel, the colors of the spectrum are arranged to read clockwise from the color of longest wavelength (red) to the shortest (violet). Perhaps to stake out a claim to product uniqueness, Wilhelm Ostwald's is designed to read counterclockwise, moving, again, from red to violet (Munsell [1905] 1961; Jacobson 1948, 26; Munsell 1969, 82; Ostwald [1916] 1969, 83). The color Ostwald identified as blue is the range popularly called royal blue. Munsell included a similar color among the major hues but called it purple-blue; it is not, in other words, blue. Munsell's blue, more toward green, looks like the color Ostwald called turquoise. Thus, Ostwald names a royal blue as blue; Munsell names a turquoise blue so different from Ost-

wald's blue that the two could never be taken one for the other.

Beginning from this difference about what constitutes blue, each theorist presents a system for naming the major hues grievously skewed in comparison to the system of the other. Munsell includes ten colors in his wheel. Ostwald switches to eight, incommensurable with ten. Newton, on numerological reasoning, had identified seven. Moses Harris preferred six; Johannes Itten, twelve. The question is how many ways a pie can be sliced. The Rational Color Circle, published by Faber Birren in 1934, is divided into thirteen slices and is asymmetric. The slices radiate from a point halfway between center and edge, rather than from the center (Birren 1969, 25).

In Munsell's system for naming his ten hues, red, orange (which is called yellow-red), and yellow occupy 30 percent of the wheel and by implication constitute 30 percent of the spectrum. In Ostwald's system, these colors are allotted 37.5 percent, an amount 25 percent larger than that allowed by Munsell. Two of Ostwald's color classes, leaf green and purple, together occupy approximately 25 percent of his color circle. Munsell's corresponding colors, yellow and green-yellow (the range corresponding to leaf green) and purple and red-purple (corresponding to purple) occupy 40 percent of the total color circle, an amount 60 percent larger than that allocated by Ostwald.

Ostwald must have believed that Munsell underestimated the number of discernible variations of color in the range identified as leaf green to purple. But Ostwald's reasoning goes unexplained. The confusion caused by the skewing is worsened by inconsistency in naming. Munsell and Ostwald were not of a single mind about the qualities that make a color name appropriate. Munsell, who "decried such vague terms as pea green, evergreen, invisible green" (Munsell 1969, 71), left no message about whether he also decried sea green and leaf green, which in Ostwald's system name two of the eight major hues. *Sea green* is a traditional name, rather than a coinage by Ostwald or his translators. The cube of colours by William Benson includes the names *sea-green green* and *sea-green blue* (Benson [1868] 1930). No plain green occurs in the Ostwald system. Hopefully, intermediaries between sea green and leaf green are not to be designated by such constructions as *sea greenish leaf green,* or *leaf greenish sea green.*

As the Munsell and Ostwald systems stand, large numbers of statements about particular colors can be constructed that are true according to one system but not the other. And any naming of colors correct according to the Munsell system will be incorrect according to Ostwald. These ornate systems, incompatible with one another, are similarly incompatible with less fully developed systems suggested by Newton, Moses Harris, Johannes Itten, Faber Birren, and others.

PART FIVE

Color Theory

Various contrivances have been proposed under the titles of Tables, Scales, Colour-Circles, Chromatometers &c., for representing either by numbers or a rational nomenclature, colors and their modifications. They are generally founded on these three propositions:—1. There are three primary colors. 2. Equal portions of these colours being mixed, produce pure secondary colours. 3. Equal portions of the three primary colours produce black.

But, 1. We know of no substance which exhibits pure colour; that is, which reflects only one kind of coloured rays, whether pure red, pure yellow, or pure blue.

2. Since it is impossible to procure pure colouring matters, how can it be said that orange, green, and violet are composed of two simple colours mixed in equal proportions? Or that black consists of a mixture of equal parts of three simple colours?

M. E. Chevreul, The Principles of Harmony
and Contrast of Colors

CHAPTER 30

Systematizers
and Systems

The earlier assumption of six principal colors and three fundamental colors is incorrect.

Wilhelm Ostwald, The Color Primer

The invention of the color wheel is usually attributed to Newton, though occasionally to the painter Moses Harris (ca. 1766). We do not know who originated the idea of arraying all the colors in a three-dimensional color solid, an activity popular from the seventeenth century onward. Relationships among colors were diagrammed on triangles, spheres, cones, cubes, and other geometrical shapes.

The diagrams are usually symmetrical, reflecting dreams of a neatly ordered universe that offers mute testimony to the tidiness of God's housekeeping. Theorists assumed that natural relationships, including those among colors, could be reduced to mathematically regular measures. The tone had been set by Newton, whose numerological interests led

him to conclude that the planets, the musical notes, and the hues of the spectrum must all match in number and had all been created in sets of seven.

Mathematical conceptions of order continue to hold sway in the natural sciences. But the computations have grown too complex to be understandable to a wide audience, and the practice of assuming simple correlations has long fallen out of favor. The search for simple measures continued longest among those who believed that the arts followed laws comparable to those of the sciences. A search for morality was the hidden agenda, a determination to define beauty and stamp out the unbeautiful. Well into the twentieth century, many seekers appeared to believe that the arts, especially music and the visual arts, could not be considered genuinely respectable unless laws could be found that explained them and defined their purposes.

If color harmony and other forms of beauty could be shown to have a rational basis, the arts would be revealed as more than just aesthetic. They would assume a position among the verities, an expression of natural law. Only then could they be thought to be touched by the moral (or perhaps masculine) nature of the Creator, who ordained order by bestowing the laws by which creatures and phenomena were bound.

The ceremonial sense of high ethical concern was pronounced by the early 1900s, more in theories about the mathematical basis of color harmony than in application of similar reasoning to other areas of the arts and aesthetics. Color theory, in the popular mind, remains largely chained to these fancies. We do not know, however, whether natural law has a mathematical or symmetrical basis, whether tidiness has a superior claim to moral virtue, or whether the universe is tidy.

Alfred Hickethier's *Color Mixing by Numbers* includes illustrations of eighteenth- and nineteenth-century color diagrams (Hickethier 1963, 15–17). The German astronomer Tobias Mayer (1723–62) developed a three-part color triangle of earlier vintage than the Maxwell triangle adapted by modern colorimetrists. The mathematician J. H. Lambert (1728–77) invented a color pyramid. Goethe, who conducted color experiments for twenty years, drew a variety of color circles and triangles. The Romantic painter Philip Otto Runge (1777–1810) developed a color sphere adapted by Albert H. Munsell and later by Wilhelm Ostwald. In Runge's sphere the hues lie at the equator, black and white at the poles. M.E. Chevreul (1786–1889) arranged the colors on a hemisphere and the hues in a circle. Wilhelm von Bezold (1876) put the colors in a cone grading toward a black apex. Ogden Rood (1831–1902) devised a double cone, black at

one apex, white at the other; Charles Blanc (ca. 1873), a six-pointed star. A. Höfler (1905) diagrammed a double pyramid with black, white, red, yellow, green, and blue at its vertices. Other mappings came from Charpentier (1885) and from Athanasius Kirchner (1671), the German Jesuit better known for his interest in mechanical methods of musical composition.

The search for symmetry has parallels in other areas of design, the visual arts, and music. Jay Hambidge's dynamic symmetry, based on measurements of the Parthenon, gave prescriptions for inherently beautiful proportions, the proverbial lost formulas of the ancients. Joseph Schillinger (d. 1943), professor of mathematics at Columbia University, attempted to reduce beauty, and through it, the arts, to mathematics. Schillinger said George Gershwin composed *Porgy and Bess* according to the Schillinger system of musical composition (Schillinger 1941; 1948). We know it was used by Heitor Villa-Lobos, whose *New York Set to Music* (1946) was advertised as a translation of the New York skyline "from silhouette to music notes with the help of the Schillinger system of Musical Composition." In *Mathematical Basis of the Arts*, Schillinger offers formulas for devising harmonious color schemes. The formulas emphasize regularity but otherwise bear little resemblance to earlier recipes by Munsell and Ostwald.

Whether color harmony and beauty of proportion follow mathematical laws is uncertain, and the terms are difficult to define. The proportions of the golden section have been called beautiful but would become boring if we used them for everything. Arguing in favor of an association between mathematics and music is easier, because ratios exist among vibrating strings. Louis Wilson's ophthalmic color scale is based on an assumption that rules for musical harmony can be directly adapted to create pleasing color combinations (see figure 34-1). Indeed, color harmony is a concept of musical origin, as are the chords and intervals mentioned in the writings of Munsell, Ostwald, Birren, and other color theorists.

Analogies between colors and musical notes are vague, and Arnheim questioned their relevance (Arnheim 1956, 338). Benjamin Whorf criticized "what is often rather inaccurately called the 'music' of words," as well as *synesthesia*, the process by which "we speak of 'tones' of color, a gray 'monotone,' a 'loud' necktie. . . . Colors are conjoined with feelings for the analogy to concords and discords." Whorf called for a more refined aesthetic sense, an end to synesthetic "confusion of thought" (Whorf [1956] 1967, 156, 267).

Systems for composing music, like those for combining colors, were perennially controversial. Well before the twentieth century, however, they boasted of practical benefits. The late-eighteenth-century London music publisher Welcker announced a "tabular system whereby any person, without the least knowledge of music, may compose ten thousand minuets in the most pleasing and correct manner." Martin Gardner (1974) traced the steps by which this interest led to the question of whether a computer can be programmed to compose symphonies without human intervention.

Is the core of the arts human intelligence, as Piet Mondrian thought was the case with the art of painting? Can a chimpanzee, pounding randomly on a typewriter, eventually compose Milton's *Paradise Lost*? We less often ask whether the chimpanzee, given a brokerage account and a pin to stick randomly in the stock market page, will eventually make a killing on Wall Street. In the visual arts, paint-by-the-number sets and coloring books speak to the yearning for easy fixes among a popular audience, as do books on how to get rich. Modern coloring books for grown-ups project undertones of irony, as if a recognition that filling in blanks, systematically or not, is a simpleminded activity for an adult.

Systems for selecting harmonious colors never sank entirely to the vulgarity of forgotten schemes for creating musical masterpieces. The emergence of color styling as a profession provided an incentive for minimizing claims that no sensibility to color is needed if the right recipes for using it are at hand. Ratios comparable to those between musical notes do not exist between colors or among their wavelengths. In musical notation, B-flat is a single note. Red is a range of thousands of colors. If red is to be explained in terms of wavelengths, many wavelengths are involved.

Classic works in the history of color theory include Boyle's *Considerations Touching Colours* (1664), Newton's *Opticks* (1704), Goethe's *Farbenlehre* (1810), and Chevreul's *De la loi du contraste simultané des couleurs* (1845). None was widely circulated among a popular audience, and the issues they raise are technical and complex. The most popularly influential and commercially successful of modern theorists were Albert H. Munsell (1858–1918), Wilhelm Ostwald (1853–1932), and their interpreters including Faber Birren. Although Munsell was an art educator and Ostwald a physical chemist, their reasoning about color was similar. Each conveyed a simple message carried directly to the marketplace. The two men met in Boston in 1905, that fruitful year in which Picasso made the first Cubist paintings and Einstein and Freud began publishing their ideas.[1]

Munsell, educated at the Massachusetts Normal Art School, taught at the Normal Art School in Boston until 1915. In 1879, he read Ogden Rood's *Modern Chromatics* (1871), a popularization of Maxwell's ideas. Rood's book was read by the French Impressionist painters, along with Chevreul's.

In *A Color Notation* (1905), Munsell outlined his system for regularizing the understanding of color and ensuring good taste in its use. The system was later expanded by the Inter-Society Color Council (National Bureau of Standards). Dorothy Nickerson, Deane B. Judd, Kenneth L. Kelly, and others who worked on the ISCC-NBS system have also been contributors and consultants to later editions of *Color Notation*.

Ostwald, born of German parents in Latvia, studied at the University of Dorpat (Estonia) and held the post of professor of physical chemistry at the University of Leipzig (1887–1906). Retirement to Saxony enabled him to devote his time to the study of color and natural philosophy. The first of Ostwald's several books on color, *Die Farbenfibel* (Color Primer) was published in 1916.

The Munsell and Ostwald systems are incompatible. We cannot take the recipes for harmonious color schemes offered by one system and apply them to the other. But both systems follow the same format. Each offers a gray scale displaying a series of steps between white and black, a hue circle identifying the major spectral hues, a color solid that theoretically can be expanded to include all colors except the metallics, and a color manual that displays the colors of the solid in book form. Each of these items is presented in the form of paper standards: colored swatches in various arrays.

Both theorists regulated the naming of colors, developed systems for writing color notations, and set forth formulas for creating harmonious color schemes. A different set of parameters is used in each system. Munsell located colors according to the coordinates of hue, value, and chroma. The Ostwald coordinates are hue content, black content, and white content. Ostwald's system, patterned after Munsell's also drew on the theories of Gustav Fechner. The logarithmic gray scale, one of Ostwald's applications of Fechner's ideas, has been incorporated into recent editions of Munsell materials.

Both theorists founded companies that disseminated their ideas to a wide audience. In 1918, the year of his death, Munsell organized the Munsell Color Company (Baltimore), which still actively merchandises industrial and pedagogical materials. Birren recommends, as "of particular interest and value . . . certain teaching aides offered by the Munsell Color Company. These are reasonable in cost and have been widely used in color and art education. Available are a number of charts and chart sets on which color chips may be mounted. There is a hue, value/chroma chart showing Munsell's five principal colors and five intermediate colors, a nine-step gray scale, and a seven-step chroma scale for red. In addition there are sets of constant hue charts for Munsell's key hue. . . . There is a teacher's demonstration kit and special large wall charts" (Munsell 1969, 796).

Ostwald's corresponding venture into industry, including the education industry, was "known as 'Ostwald Energie,' and this organization not only reached the entire German educational system but offered to extend counsel to German business and industry" (Ostwald [1916] 1969, 5). Ostwald's *Color Science* was translated into English by J. Scott Taylor. More widely circulated in the United States than Taylor's two-volume translation are adaptations of Ostwald's ideas by Egbert Jacobson (1942, 1948), Faber Birren (1969), Charles N. Smith (1965), Rudolph Arnheim (1956, 335–38), and others.[2] Egbert Jacobson, formerly an art director for Container Corporation of America, supervised that company's publication of *The Color Harmony Manual*, a set of standards based on Ostwald's theories. Jacobson's major work in his own name is *Basic Color* (1948), an interpretation of the Ostwald system showing ways of applying it to industrial styling and the fine arts. Birren, a color consultant and founder of Faber Birren and Company, was born in Chicago (1900) and studied color theory with Walter Sargent in the School of Education at the University of Chicago (Sargent [1923] 1966). While Jacobson is an interpreter of the Ostwald system, Birren is the system's exegete, an author of many books on color and color systems.[3]

Creating harmonies by means of the Ostwald system is simple, outlined by Jacobson in *Basic Color*. Familiarity with the arrangement of the color solid is required. Sets of colors are selected from the solid according to formulas Ostwald prescribes. Any set chosen by this technique is harmonious; ostensibly it is more harmonious than an equal number of colors chosen at random.

Because they stress symmetry and mathematical regularity, Ostwald's formulas could be easily translated into a computer program. Sets including every third, sixth, or twelfth of the twenty-four colors in the hue circle are identified as harmonious. Indeed, "neatly spaced intervals anywhere on the color solid lead to harmony" (Ostwald [1916] 1969, 66). When colors are spaced equidistantly, the ratio of their distances is unity, the ratio Plato held to be perfect or beautiful. Some of Ostwald's formulas, such as the ring star, are complex, although similarly regular. The Ostwald formulas cannot be applied to the Munsell solid because Munsell arranges the colors differently.

Color schemes for industry were devised by the Ostwald and Munsell systems, although interest declined after the 1940s. Jacobson listed numerous examples, including fabrics woven by Herbert G. Antin (Jacobson 1948, 198). Projects recommended for art students include painting Ping-Pong balls in harmonious Ostwald colors and pinning the balls together to look like molecules. That activity too has passed into obsolescence.

The criticisms that should be offered are obvious. By now, many have been made. Arnheim, doubting that color harmonies used by painters can be shown to follow simplistic rules, wisely pointed out that any given set of colors can be used to create either a good painting or a bad one (Arnheim 1956, 337). Stuart Davis, who regarded the defining characteristic of modern art as its manner of using color, rather than its abstractness, complained that monotony in the spacing of intervals in the color solid implies monotony of colors (Sweeney 1945, 34). Matisse, a major colorist, said he devised his color schemes intuitively, and denied using a system. Van Gogh, said to have chosen the colors for his paintings by playing with scraps of colored knitting yarn, might have wondered why such an elaborate technological superstructure was needed.

In the Ostwald and Munsell systems, as in later adaptations, color is not recognized as contextual. Proportion is ignored. We are encouraged to conclude that a properly selected set of harmonious colors, without regard to the proportion of each color used, is pleasing for any purpose at any time. Harmony is implicitly an absolute, as if color usage occurred in a vacuum divorced from the affairs of the world. Birren, studying Ostwald's formulas, found, for instance, that "a pale green looks better with a deep navy blue than a pale blue looks with a deep green or olive. Pale yellow looks better with maroon than pink looks with a deep citron" (Birren 1969, 46). These dicta are not arbitrary, because, "a number of studies in the field of psychology have verified the observation of Chevreul that colors look best (a) when they are closely related or analogous, or (b) when they are complementary or in strong contrast" (Birren 1969, 35).

I mistrust grand generalizations, and so should the unidentified psychologists who did the studies. We cannot determine, once and for all, which color combinations "look best." An entirely yellow-and-maroon world would be oppressive, because any combination of colors can be overused. Cannons of absolute harmoniousness cannot be reconciled with human propensity for growing tired of anything at some point. People like variety, at least in our society.

Munsell's and Ostwald's theories of color harmony also have a serious technical defect not remedied in improvements to the systems. The mathematical ratios held to define sets of colors as harmonious do not correlate with anything visual. In the Ostwald system (Munsell's is similar), a set of colors is identified as harmonious if, and only if, its members are spaced in one of several prescribed manners. The determining factor is location in Ostwald's color solid. The harmonious sets, as a result, show no perceptible family resemblances. Assume that a thousand harmonious and a thousand nonharmonious color combinations are created from the Ostwald color solid. A viewer will be unable to sort one group of sets from the other by eye, although in theory harmonious combinations ought to look better.

Because location, rather than color, is crucial, and no two theorists arrange the colors within solids in the same manner, a harmonious set of colors according to the Ostwald system is not a harmonious set in the Munsell system. Nonvisual criteria are presented for assessing visual phenomena, an eccentric aesthetic principle. The educated eye is a meaningful concept. We can learn from Japanese art, Islamic art, and African and Amerind textiles that individuals and whole societies have been unusually refined in their use of color. We cannot assume that all creative colorists use the same combinations of colors or kinds of combinations.

Color Clash

Credible evidence is difficult to find about which color combinations look best. A well-defined body of popular belief purports to identify which look worst. Combinations at the bottom of the hierarchy for harmony are said to clash. Clashing, like harmoniousness, is a musical analogy. With lurid intimations of clanging cymbals and cacophony, it implies that some color combinations are comparable to musical discords, or that certain colors are wrong in juxtaposition to one another.

Color sets busy clashing in the 1940s (most no longer clash) included blue and green, pink and orange, pink and purple, orange and purple, and red and green. Why do some colors clash? We need not look for some oddity of eye or brain that might cause certain color combinations to look inherently unpleasant. The coinage tells about the beliefs of the observer, not about the phenomenological world. Goethe pronounced the combination of blue and green "repulsive" (Matthaei 1971, 260). He never bothered to explain why we are not offended by the blue sky and green grass.

Tastes change. *Clash* was thought to identify a significant aspect of the offensiveness of some color combinations. The word provided a way to convey the message that certain colors were not to be used together. It gave viewers the comforting feeling that objective reasons existed for their taste. The arbitrary nature of the concept was veiled so successfully that neurophysiological and psychological explanations of color clash are still sometimes sought.

Baudelaire identified good taste as conventional taste, intolerant of deviation from its canons. What was liked or disliked about color in the past is less interesting than the vehemence with which taste is defended. Red, said to enrage bulls, was for several centuries provocative to human beings. The color was regarded as offensive if used in excess, in excessively bright variations, or in the wrong places. Goethe was certain "it may be safely assumed, that a carpet of a perfectly pure deep blue-red would be intolerable" (Matthaei 1971, 172). Ostwald objected to large areas of red in Pompeiian wall paintings although today, as Arnheim pointed out, we find Matisse's *Red Studio* unobjectionable (Arnheim 1956, 338).

Taboos about red are often disguised societal taboos about sensuality. Fashion once decreed, for example, that mature married women might wear bright red dresses but young girls should not. We correlate black and white with wrong and right, including wrongness and rightness in sexual behavior. The association of red with passion is more indirect. We link red with blood, because blood is red. Blood was once regarded as the seat of the passions, one of the four cardinal humors thought to explain human disposition. Human behavior can be described as hot-blooded or cold-blooded, and the Passion of Christ is linked with his blood. Men are called red-blooded, or brave and virile. Women are rarely called red-blooded.

Other vagaries of taste can be similarly traced to symbolic associations with colors. These associations surface even in works on the occult. In a 1924 course of instruction of how "to become acquainted with the several astral colors perceived by psychic vision," C. Alexander contended that the adept can see astral bodies around human beings. The colors of these auras reveal the conditions of souls through familiar symbolic associations: "Astral White is the antithesis and absolute opposite of Astral Black. . . . Love gives out the astral color of Crimson. . . . The Astral Color of Blue represents thoughts and feelings of the class generally known as 'spiritual' or 'religious' " (Alexander 1924, 33–40).

Symbolic associations with colors differ in different societies and thus are unlikely to have an instinctual basis. As psychoanalysts and literary commentators have taught us, anything can be a symbol of anything, requiring only a rationalization sufficient to link symbol with symbolized object. Black is the color of mourning in our society; white has been used in China. The usage can be explained in each case. I see no barrier to a society in which other colors served the purpose. Red might be the color of mourning, on the basis that shedding blood can be equated with death; blue because the dead go to a heaven located in the sky; green because grass grows on graves.

Neuroses, as Freud described them, are sys-tems of private symbolism devised by patients who do not recognize or will not say what they really think. This is a comment on the nature of symbolism, not just mental health. Societal systems of symbolism, like private versions, say things in roundabout ways. Traditional color symbolism provides an illusion of a link to a past that does not exist. It helps us make sense of the world by using the tools earlier peoples used to make sense of it. "Red means passion," a student tells me, proud to be recycling an old saw current for hundreds of years.

I wonder if anything that distracts attention from the present is wholesome. The secret of great colorists may be an ability to look at colors without preconceptions, without concern for what was thought about color in the past. The social aspect of color symbolism is invidious. Can racial harmony be achieved in a society that equates good and bad with white and black, also uses white and black to code people, and has too many literary ideas about the special status and purity of white?

If people are to be sorted by skin colors, the actual colors should be used. Citizens can fill in questionnaires by identifying themselves as members of the *somewhat pinkish medium beige* race, the *darker burnt sienna with a yellowish cast* race, the *pale ocher* race, or whatever color name best describes the exact skin color of that individual. This would give us many more races. Perhaps no two people would belong to the same race. The situation would be humorous, ridiculous. But we need the reminder to think carefully about what we take seriously.

For Birren, "Munsell's work is in every way classical. It has developed permanent values in the art and science of color" (Munsell 1969, 6). For Florence Elizabeth Wallace, Munsell's *Color Notation* was "an unscientific, metaphysical, but interesting little book" (Wallace 1927, 1). Munsell was not a scientist. He did something original by assembling and grading a large collection of colors, fascinating to look at. Ostwald was a physical chemist whose ideas about color were often based on what was scientifically obsolete or scientifically questionable.

The theories of Munsell and Ostwald, hailed by advocates as "doctrines" (Ostwald [1916] 1969, 79), survive today as a foundation for much of what is taught about color in art schools. They also survive as a mystique. Birren, an impassioned interpreter of the mysteries, rarely failed to include respectful capitalization when mentioning "The System" or the "Principles of Albert H. Munsell" (Munsell 1969, 70–71).

The rambling aesthetic of either system is vague and ambiguous. Birren found it was "Munsell's contention that order assures beauty" (Munsell 1969, 69). Ostwald added that we can "establish this basic law: Harmony = Order" (Ostwald [1916] 1969, 65). Wearing his own hat, Birren expanded these insights into a series of incantations to be taken to heart rather than subjected to scrutiny: "*There is harmony in white, grey, black. . . . There is harmony in pure color, shade, black. . . . There is harmony in tint, tone, black. . . . There is harmony in shade, tone, white . . .* " (Birren 1969, 54–62).

"The Principles" too often lead to discouraging results. Jacobson, following the Ostwald system, analyzed the use of color in twelve well-known paintings.[4] He concluded that "the great painters have long used, and that Ostwald has at last accurately described, the fundamental principles of harmony" (Jacobson 1948, 157). This is the unconscious advocate argument, a variation on argument by appeal to authority. Favored by the followers of Freud, the argument holds that a theory can be validated by showing its relevance to great artists of the past or to their work. The artists may have been unaware of what they were doing and may have expressly said they were doing something else. The staying power

of the argument lies in its circularity. Those who do not conform can be dismissed as not really great artists. The theorist is certain to be right although the artist may be wrong.

Jacobson devised a system for keying the general type of color used in a painting. Among fifty works listed under "key" categories, Renoir's *Madame Charpentier and Her Children*, El Greco's *View of Toledo*, and Botticelli's *Three Miracles of Saint Zenobius* (all three in the Metropolitan Museum of Art), are said to be in the same color key. Matisse's *The Blue Window* (New York, Museum of Modern Art), van Gogh's *La Berceuse* (Boston, Museum of Fine Art), Gauguin's *Tahitian Woman* (Chicago Art Institute) and Giotto's *The Epiphany* (New York, Metropolitan Museum of Art) are similarly placed in a single key.

The rankings are disheartening to anyone familiar with the paintings. The differences in color usage between *Madame Charpentier and Her Children* and *View of Toledo* are more worth reporting than whatever similarities Jacobson believed can be found. A theory compelling a conclusion that Renoir and El Greco use color in the same way, that Matisse's use can be equated with Giotto's and Vermeer's, or that Gauguin's colors are similar to van Gogh's is worth rejecting on that account alone. We know a great deal about the color theories of Renoir, Gauguin, and van Gogh. They were not using the Ostwald system.

Jacobson wanted to prove that all color in all art is the same, unvaryingly a type of color Ostwald would have approved. But all color in all art is not the same. Artists have had a wide variety of ideas about color. *Harmony in Blue*, the Matisse painting analyzed by Jacobson, was seen in a color reproduction. Commercial color reproductions of paintings, like color photographs, rarely match the colors in the original work of art. Matisse, in any case, said he did not use a color system.

Problems of a more practical order arise from the limited number of samples available.

Jacobson found in El Greco's *View of Toledo* "some greens that are several shades darker" than any in Ostwald's manual (Jacobson 1948, 162). Richard F. Brown noted that the colors in Pissarro's paintings seldom match the chips in the Ostwald manual "because of the unavoidably limited number of samples in the manual," although it is nonetheless true that "a judgment made by means of a carefully specified and standardized color system is certainly more reliable than one made independently by an eye subject to all the deceptions of surroundings, colors, changing illumination, etc." (Brown 1950, 12).

For Birren, " 'natural laws' of color harmony exist without question," a compelling argument for systematizing the use of color (Birren 1961, 39). In "Functional Color in the Schoolroom" (1949), Birren outlined what he described at that time as the science of functional color. The application of the purported science was to the designing of classrooms, because "a sober study of school children and school environments will stress the need for an objective approach to color rather than a subjective one" (Birren 1949, 136–38). Color functionalism has a well-defined set of rules, and although "a relatively new science, its progress has been rapid, for the benefits of its application may be definitely proven through research studies and clinical tests. While individual accomplishments in the fine arts are often difficult to evaluate, functional color stands or falls on its measurable results."

The message of color functionalism in 1949 was to avoid high chromaticity, because it is "difficult to read a book against the competition of bright colors." Bright colors also lead to eyestrain, and as the child twists to avoid this, the twisting "may affect posture and have an adverse effect upon the growth of young bones." Furthermore, technical advances in modern illumination render "the glare of white walls intolerable," although white is one of the most popular colors used for apartment walls

in cities today.

For the classroom, Birren advised two types of color, each calculated to tranquilize, because "it is one thing to make children happy and quite another to serve the best interests of child vision and child welfare." For elementary schools "pale yellow, pink, and peach" were advised. For high schools cool green, blue, or gray set a more intellectual tone. "Ivory and pale yellow have been found excellent for corridors," but in the classroom, "the two best hues have been found to be pale blue-green and peach." Reds must be avoided because "*red is inciting to activity.*" Birren's preferred choices elsewhere became known as institutional ivory, institutional green, institutional peach, institutional gray.

These ideas, for a period, were widely influential. In 1948, "Faber Birren developed manuals of standard color practice for the shore establishments, surface vessels, and submarines of the U.S. Navy. This was followed in 1952 by a similar report for the Coast Guard, and in 1966 by a report for the U.S. Army." In 1955 the U.S. State Department "sent him as an expert on functional color to an International Congress in Rome on work productivity and safety" (Birren 1969, 8). Governments by their nature are the keepers of morality, conservative in color theory as in much else.

The science of functional color faded when Birren incorporated his ideas into a movement he called Perceptionism, "an advanced art of color" (Birren 1961, 63), and "a joy to study because it deals with human reactions" (Birren 1961, 97). Birren exhibited Perceptionist paintings at the National Arts Club in New York in 1948, and the movement presented its own rules, laws, principles, and copying exercises. Those who knew were always Perceptionists at heart, and "many of the great artists of history have understood Perceptionism and The Law of Field Size or Proportion—perhaps not in a scientific way but through an innate genius" (Birren 1961, 69.)

For beginning students, Birren's *Creative Color* includes color charts and diagrams to be imitated, although, "frankly, these preliminary exercises bear resemblance to the playing of scales in music and to the parsing of sentences in grammar" (Birren 1961, 9). Trickier copy work for the advanced student includes reproductions of thirty Faber Birren paintings that "are meant to speak for themselves, as original and striking examples which point to new directions" (Birren 1961, 10). Anyone "may copy them if he wishes," although Birren reminds us that "from experience I doubt if even a skilled artist could take a look at these illustrations and then, on his own, do as well" (Birren 1961, 96). An appendix, entitled "The Faber Birren Palettes," assists the aspiring copyist by providing listings of the colors used in each painting.

Elsewhere, Birren displayed a reproduction of a Jackson Pollock painting, an example of the bad ends awaiting those "without discipline" (Munsell 1969, 43). Printed opposite the offending Pollock is a work by Andrew Wyeth, who exemplifies "conservatism, tradition and discipline in American art and color expression." For Birren "a musician needs to know a great deal about the elements of music before he can compose. Then he can forget the rules. The same with color harmony and the principles of Albert H. Munsell" (Munsell 1969, 70). Problems begin when those without the imprimatur of genius break the rules.

In art schools and college art departments, the pedagogical posture that confounded neatness, following instructions, and careful copying with discipline survived longer in the teaching of color than in the teaching of drawing or painting. It was not limited to those practitioners on the fringes. During the 1920s coloring diagrams was an integral part of the color class taught by Johannes Itten at the Bauhaus. Exact imitation was the pedagogical goal. In one exercise, "all three basic colors must be clearly represented, checked by the teacher, and painted into the three parts of an equilateral triangle" (Itten 1963, 41). In addition to color triangles, color stars and color circles (Itten's had twelve sectors) were used.

The pedagogical model tells us to imitate our betters rather than trusting our ability to learn by observing. Few other formats for teaching about color have been fully explored, and genuine inventiveness, I fear, is limited to the more or less mad. Brooding over the colors of his scraps of knitting yarn, van Gogh must have learned something. Another eccentric, Dr. Barnes, became a collector of the work of Matisse after becoming wealthy from the invention of Argyrol, a vile-tasting swab used on children's throats. The listings Dr. Barnes compiled of the colors in Matisse paintings may appear pointless to scholars (Barnes and de Mazia 1933). They show, however, that Dr. Barnes looked carefully at the colors.

CHAPTER 31

The Logarithmic
Gray Scale

In the case of the Ostwald Color Solid, we have visually adjusted intervals according to Fechner's Law of Sensation which states briefly that in order to change visual perception arithmetically the stimulus intensity must be changed geometrically.

Charles N. Smith, Student Handbook of Color

A gray scale is a chart of color swatches. It has black at one end, white at the other, and a series of graded grays in between. A scale can be constructed by collecting many samples of achromatic gray and ranking them from lightest to darkest. In the finest possible scale, the difference in value (degree of lightness or darkness) between one gray and the next is so slight as to be nearly imperceptible. From sufficient distance (a small distance in this case), the scale looks like an unbroken continuum blending from white through gray into black. A scale with many small gradations approaches this continuum more closely than another with fewer and larger steps.

We rarely need a gray scale with thousands of small steps; eight or ten larger steps are usually enough. This abbreviated gray scale can be abstracted from a finer scale by selecting, say, every tenth, twentieth, or hundredth step.

Wilhelm Ostwald proposed a more ornate methodology for constructing gray scales, based on the Weber-Fechner law. Intervals between grays (measured in terms of their reflectances of light) are logarithmic. The reasoning that led to this widely circulated scale illustrates in miniature the manner in which unnecessarily convoluted reasoning about color overwhelms simpler, more visual, understandings.

Gustav Theodor Fechner (1801–87), who inspired Ostwald's marriage of color with logarithm, was trained in biology and became professor of physics at the University of Leipzig. After 1843, Fechner, whose major work was *Elemente der Psychophysik* (Elements of Psychophysics), turned to the study of philosophy, experimental aesthetics, and psychophysics. He hoped to demonstrate that aesthetics and the arts were governed by scientific laws.

Fechner's philosophy was influenced by Friedrich von Schelling (1775–1854) and Johann Herbart (1776–1841). He believed that animate and inanimate objects have souls comparable to those of human beings. All souls are animated by a greater world soul similar (although Fechner did not use this comparison) to the Atman of Hindu philosophy. Natural law is the revelation of God's perfection, therefore perfect itself, a dubious though once-popular syllogism, dubious in that this perfect God created imperfect men and women and may have also made an imperfect universe governed by imperfect laws.

The German philosopher Arthur Schopenhauer (1788–1860) had defended Goethe's theory of color. Schopenhauer understood Goethe to mean that colors, as Aristotle concluded, are composed of mixtures of the opposites of darkness and light (Bosanquet [1892] 1957, 366). Herbart, closely associated with Schopenhauer, added the call for "a science of color harmony, like that of harmony in music" (Bosanquet [1892] 1957, 370). The science was to determine which color combinations were beautiful and provide scientific proof of its findings.

Unlike Schopenhauer and Herbart, Fechner experimented, though his experiments and purposes were often not greeted warmly. The Italian philosopher-statesman Benedetto Croce (1866–1952) complained about Fechner's assiduous discovery of too many so-called laws that too neatly supported his scientific aesthetic. Croce wondered why Fechner experimented at all if he knew in advance what he wanted to find (Croce [1909] 1968, 394). An oft-cited experiment persuaded Fechner

that human beings find the proportions of the golden section more beautiful than any other proportions. Fechner had discovered this aesthetic law by asking subjects which of ten rectangles of different proportions they liked best. Bosanquet, like Croce, was unpersuaded, arguing that the actual tendency was "to prefer a form that was not extreme in a given series," and that "most of the persons began by saying that it all depended on the application to be made of the figure, and on being told to disregard this, showed much hesitation in choosing" (Bosanquet [1892] 1957, 382).

In 1839, in a disastrous experiment designed to uncover the nature of colored afterimages, Fechner stared too long at the sun. He lost his sight for three years and, on recovering it, claimed to be able to see the souls of plants. The experience led to Fechner's turning from physics to psychophysics, and to publication of *Nanna, or the Soul Life of Plants* (1848).

Fechner attracted a heterogeneous following, which included the philosopher-psychologist William James. P. D. Ouspensky, Gurdjieff's major follower in the United States, described his own views as essentially similar to Fechner's (Ouspensky 1947, 188). Ouspensky was attracted by the transcendental cast of Fechner's writings. Psychologists drawn to Fechner were more interested, as was Ostwald, in schema that promised methods for measuring sensation. If sensation could be measured, the door could be opened to a mathematical understanding of subjective experience, of the human condition.

Proposing an equation for the relationship between stimulus and sensation, Fechner said that the intensity of sensation is proportional to a multiple of the logarithm of the stimulus. This equation might apply to, say, stimulation of the eye by light waves that cause a sensation of seeing red:

$$\text{sensation intensity} = C \log \text{stimulus intensity}$$

C is a constant to be experimentally determined for each sense modality. Because the German anatomist and physiologist Ernst Heinrich Weber (1795–1878) had proposed a similar constancy in 1834, the formulation is called the Weber-Fechner Law. It has been criticized on logical grounds, and experimental evidence fails to support Fechner's claim that this is a law of universal applicability.

Weber experimented primarily with touch and to a lesser extent with sound. The Weber-Fechner Law became popular among researchers in vision and hearing. Through Wilhelm Ostwald, it was introduced to color theorists, with dubious results in the construction of gray scales. An example often used to illustrate the application of Fechner's law to visual experience asks that we imagine a darkened environment in which a faint light gradually grows brighter.[1]

When the light reaches an intensity strong enough to be noticeable, it is said to have reached the threshold (of vision). The threshold varies among individuals and may vary for any individual at different times. At a further increase of intensity, the light becomes observably brighter, by the smallest amount of noticeable difference. A third increase of specific intensity again causes the viewer to report awareness of an increase in brightness.

By continuing sequential increases, a scale can be constructed. Between any two of its steps, a just noticeable difference in brightness of that light exists for that observer. Fechner held that the increases in intensity required to produce the steps grow progressively larger and show a logarithmic progression. When light is faint, a tiny increase makes a difference. As the light becomes brighter, progressively greater amplifications are required to produce a noticeable difference.

Fechner was a physicist, familiar with the use of logarithmic units on scales for measuring radiant energy. In texts on optics, the entire electromagnetic scale is often shown as a logarithmic scale, a convention with no known bearing on vision (Blaker 1969, 1). Beyond this, the hypothetical experiment includes no provision for sorting out an ill-considered hodgepodge of factors. As the light grows progressively brighter, the viewer will grow progressively more tired from the unnatural task of sitting in the dark looking at it. If progressively greater stimulation is required to produce a similar brightness change, is eye fatigue a contributing factor? A determination might be made by running the experiment backward, stepping down a bright light until it is no longer seen. If eye fatigue is not significant, the decreasing steps (when the experiment runs backward) should match the increasing steps (when the light changes from dim to bright).

A confrontation between a human being and a gradually intensifying light source involves several visual thresholds. Fechner recognized just one, perhaps because the proposed experiment cannot be carried out from full darkness to full light—ethical and safety factors intervene. Yet the entire gamut is needed to understand the scope of the phenomenon. Beyond the level of tolerable intensity, light causes, progressively, eyestrain, pain, temporary blindness, permanent blindness, and death, each a threshold of another order. Human beings tolerate radiant energy only within circumscribed limits, and a series of changes of state can be anticipated in the eye viewing the light.

Similar limits can be seen in exposing camera film. At a point depending on the speed (light sensitivity) of the film, maximum overexposure is reached. The film, depending on whether negative or reversal, produces an image either all black or all white. Further increases of light intensity create no further change in the image recorded, unless the increase is so great that it generates enough heat to destroy the film.

The eye, damaged by too much light, is also

unable to tolerate the coherent light of a laser beam. Despite human passion for order, we are fortunate that atoms under ordinary circumstances do not act in lockstep unison in emitting radiant energy. The pure beam of the laser results when stimulated emission is used to cause them to do so.

At the lower reaches of Fechner's experiment, one of the first visual thresholds to make itself manifest is between scotopic and photopic modes. The eye sees in the dark by means of the rods near the perimeter of the retina (scotopic vision). In a lighted environment it sees largely with the cones surrounding the blind spot at the retina's center (photopic vision). The point at which the environment is experienced as lighted, signaling the transition from rod to cone vision, varies among individuals. In the dark the central portion of the retina is blind because its cones are inactive.

Whether or not an evolutionary relic, scotopic vision is crude, allowing limited perception of fine detail. It does not allow a dim star or other faint light to be seen in the dark if the viewer looks directly at it. The viewer must look, instead, about twenty degrees to the side of the light, a phenomenon known as *averted vision*. Unlike the bright/dim of the automobile headlight, the eye's two systems for seeing differ in the way that each functions. One question is whether a just noticeable difference in photopic vision is registered as just noticeable in scotopic mode. Because of the greater crudity of scotopic vision, I suspect it is not.

Visual thresholds beyond those for scotopic and photopic vision include those for eyestrain and pain, both of which point to the limits of visual acuity. Within the hypothetical experiment, eyestrain would occur at two points. The first is when the amount of light is less than optimal. The second is when the light is so bright that the viewer experiences it as glare.

Other thresholds for eyestrain, although not germane to Fechner's experiment, are encountered every day. Common causes include looking at fine detail, looking at lights that blink (rapid changes from high to low intensity), or an environment combining several intensities of illumination. Eyestrain from reading with insufficient light probably comes from stressing the eye in scotopic mode by presenting finer detail than it can comfortably accommodate.

Each of these visual thresholds marks a transition from one state to another when a light is stepped up or down. None of them can be equated with the single threshold Fechner labels the *threshold of vision*, a threshold that does not exist. Fechner's concept is unfortunately framed, because the point at which a faint light is first seen in the dark is only a threshold for seeing that light. No absolute threshold of vision exists for the functioning eye. At no point do we stop seeing.

Feeling no pain is possible, as is hearing no sound. Genuine thresholds exist for those sensory experiences. Silence has no visual analogue, and no threshold exists for vision or color. During periods of consciousness, the functioning eye unceasingly engages in seeing, even if watching just the nominal black of the night. An extension of the brain, the eye never turns off, and REMs (rapid eye movements) have been shown to occur during sleep.

Differences between pigments and lights were pointed out by Goethe in his criticism of Newton and later were much discussed by late-nineteenth-century painters. Looking at lights in the dark, as in Fechner's proposed experiment, is not comparable to looking at colored pigments or colored objects in daylight. The brightest white pigments are less intense than the brightest white lights, which bears on the representation of light effects in art. The sun can never look as bright in a painting as in actuality. For Ralph M. Evans, the distinction between pigments and lights invalidates Ostwald's adaptation of the Weber-Fechner law, for in Ostwald's "practical reduction of [Fechner's] theoretical considerations to a set of material paper standards it was necessary to use actual pigment colors, and they departed so widely from the theory as to represent a different system" (Evans 1948, 216).

Fewer thresholds must be taken into account if the Fechnerian experiment can be adapted so that colors are used instead of lights. Unfriendly critics of the early twentieth century insisted that the colors in French Impressionist paintings were too bright and might injure the eyes of viewers. But material objects, including spots of pigment, are less than perfect reflectors. Their colors rarely injure eyes. Strong light of any color has that potential, whether direct sunlight (as Fechner painfully learned), when rays are brought into focus through a lens to start a fire, or in the coherent beam of a laser. If, in the case of light, each threshold represents a shift of gear in the visual apparatus, seeing colors in daylight has only one gear.

An abridged English translation of Ostwald's *Die Farbenfibel* is edited by Faber Birren, and the system is also outlined in Jacobson's *Basic Color* (Ostwald [1916] 1969; Jacobson 1948). In adapting Fechner's theories to the construction of a gray scale, Ostwald began with a white surface and a black surface. The white is assigned a reflective index of 100 percent. This is a nominal index. Ostwald explains elsewhere that no white surface reflects 100 percent of the light falling on it. Ostwald's black surface absorbs nearly all the light falling on it and is assigned a reflective index of 1 percent. Why the less-than-ideal black receives an index of 1 percent, rather than a zero, while the less-than-perfect white receives an index of 100 percent, not a lower number, is not clear.

Proceeding from these givens, it might seem that the gray midway between the black and the white ought to have a reflective index of 50.5 percent, an average between the extremes. Ostwald argues that it will be universally agreed 50.5 percent looks too light. The proper gray, "halfway" between white and black, shows a reflective index of 10 percent (Jacobson 1948, 195; Ostwald [1916] 1969, 25). Thus, "if one were to arrange [the steps of the gray scale] according to equal (arithmetic) steps of contents of white, one would obtain too many steps at the white end and too few at the black end" (Ostwald [1916] 1969, 29). The reflective index of any gray b, intermediate between two others (a, c) can be found by the formula $a/b = b/c$.

If gray a has a reflective index of 1 percent (black), gray c a reflective index of 100 percent (white), then intermediate gray b has a reflective index of 10 percent ($1/10 = 10/100$). This is a geometrical progression, and Ostwald found that "where brightness differences form a geometrical progression, only then do we experience corresponding grays as being visually equidistant" (Ostwald [1916] 1969, 26). Ostwald found that the total "number of distinguishable steps of gray under normal conditions amounts to several hundred," though other writers have given numbers ranging from five or ten to seven hundred.

Whether Ostwald conducted tests or just made his own guesses about what most people would guess, determining an average is not accomplished by taking a vote. The midpoint between indices of 1 and 100 is 50.5, a matter of computation. If inconsistent with what most people estimate, we need to know more about most people's competence at estimating reflective indices.

Lightness and *darkness* are inherently imprecise terms, and *half as dark* has no firmer meaning. An observer shown black, white, and a single gray has no basis for answering such

Figure 31-1. A geometric progression.

100	79	63	50	40	32	25	20	16	12.6
10	7.9	6.3	5.0	4.0	3.2	2.5	2.0	1.6	1.26

ill-conceived questions as whether the gray is "halfway" between the black and the white. The question can only mean halfway on a properly constructed gray scale. All steps of the scale ought to be shown. Although an untrained observer may not be sensitive to the issue, judgments about colors are made most effectively if all colors in question are seen. If an observer moves progressively farther away from the scale, a point will be found at which any two given successive steps no longer look sufficiently different to allow them to be identified as two different grays. If this critical viewing distance is the same for all steps, the steps are properly balanced and the middle step is correct.

More exactly, the steps of the gray scale are properly balanced for a particular viewer. We do not know whether a universal gray scale is possible: a scale balanced so that, for any viewer, a single point can be found at which discriminating between successive steps is no longer possible. For a given individual, is ability to discriminate among dark colors equal to ability to discriminate among light colors? People who suffer from night blindness have a reduced ability to see in semidarkness. They might have greater difficulty distinguishing fine differences among dark grays than among light grays.

Ostwald used several steps of computation to arrive at the final indices for his logarithmic gray scale, a scale widely circulated today though its logic is rarely understood. Ostwald began with a scale of twenty terms, a geometric progression (figure 31-1). The scale has ten descending steps between 100 and 10; another ten between 10 and 1. Each term in the series (Ostwald's numbers have been rounded off) can be arrived at by multiplying the previous term by 0.79.

The ratio of any three consecutive terms is $a/b = b/c$, a ratio that also holds for any three terms equidistantly spaced. For the first, third, and fifth terms: $100/63 = 63/40$. For the second, sixth, and tenth: $79/32 = 32/12.6$.

Ostwald's next step, for which I see no purpose (it shuffles numbers without changing relationships), was to take the mean between all terms in the series (Ostwald [1916] 1969; 26; Jacobson 1948). This leads to twenty-five norms of gray, keyed to all letters of the alphabet except j (figure 31-2). Because the geometric progression contains twenty terms, only nineteen means are available between successive terms. The six additional means (u–z) were apparently arrived at by computation. Ostwald later deleted them without explaining why they were added. They inconsistently imply blacks of less than 1 percent reflectance. Ostwald had said the scale could include no black surface that reflected less than 1 percent of the light failing on it.

Ostwald's next step was to abbreviate the norms of gray by removing every alternate term (Ostwald [1916] 1969, 27). This resulted

Figure 31-2. Norms of gray.

89	71	56	45	36	28	22	18	14	11	8.9	7.1	5.6
a	b	c	d	e	f	g	h	i	k	l	m	n

4.5	3.6	2.8	2.2	1.8	1.4	1.1	0.89	0.71	0.56	0.45	0.36
o	p	q	r	s	t	u	v	w	x	y	z

Fig. 31-3. The practical gray scale.

89	56	36	22	14	8.9	5.6	3.6	2.2	1.4	0.89	0.56	0.36
a	c	e	g	i	l	n	p	r	t	v	w	x

in a construction he called the practical gray scale (figure 31-3). The explanation for abridging the norms of gray was that a scale of twenty-five steps is too long to be practical. Its steps are unnecessarily narrow, and thirteen grays will suffice (Ostwald [1916] 1969, 23–27).

To make the practical gray scale more practical, Ostwald discarded 38 percent of it: the last five of the scale's thirteen steps were deleted, dispatched to some limbo from which they will not emerge. The result is a scale ending with p, said to be equivalent to the reflective index of black printer's ink (3.6 percent), because "a deeper black than p could not be created by normal printing processes" (Ostwald [1916] 1969, 27). Ostwald's final eight-step gray scale has reflective indices as shown in figure 31-4. Values for grays a to p, marked off on a ruler or other arithmetic scale, will not fall equidistantly. On a logarithmic scale they fall equidistantly. For Ostwald, "a thorough examination of this gray scale shows that the distances are indeed experienced as being equally spaced to the eye. Only the lower steps give a more crowded impression, in view of the circumstances that the law of geometric progression no longer exactly represents the facts among dark colors approaching black" (Ostwald [1916] 1969, 27).

Figure 31-4. The gray scale.

a	c	e	g
89%	56%	36%	22%
i	l	n	p
14%	8.9%	5.6%	3.6%

In the completed scale, the reflective index assigned to each gray locates it within the range from white (100 percent reflectance) to black (1 percent reflectance). The ability of, say, gray e to reflect 36 percent of the light falling on it accounts for its appearing to be that particular shade of gray. Whether Ostwald is using an absolute or a normative standard for reflectance is often unclear. If absolute measurement is implied, a particular gray is illuminated by a known quantity of light. The amount of light reflected is measured, and a ratio calculated between input and output. By this standard, a surface with a reflective index of 100 (100 percent reflectance) reflects 100 percent of the light shining on it.

More likely, Ostwald's reflective indices are normative or nominal, a detail easy to overlook in the welter of confusing computations. Ostwald pointed out that the closest approximation to ideal white is a dull coat of barium sulfate, the surface taken as a norm 100 (Ostwald [1916] 1969, 24). The actual reflective index of this surface, which is unspecified, may be 80 percent, 96 percent, or some other number. White of 100 percent reflectance, by this normative standard, matches the reflective capacity of barium sulfate. A gray of 36 percent reflective index is measured by deviation from barium sulfate, not in absolute terms.

Why is this unnecessary complication included? If the actual reflective index of barium sulfate is, say, 85 percent, this number could have been used. Adjusting at this point would require recomputing all of Ostwald's reflective indices, to what entire effect is unclear. The logic of the scale—its mathematical logic—is a greater problem. No reproduction will be found in print showing the grays that correspond to Ostwald's entire scale of logarithmical reflective indices. The sector of the logarithmical gray scale that is shown usually runs from a to p. The entire scale cannot be reproduced, because it has no lower end. The numerical progression on which the scale is based continually diminishes at its lower (black) end, but never reaches zero (see figure 31-1). The equation $a/b = b/c$ cannot be solved if c is zero and a and b must be greater than zero.

If the limit is appropriate for the circumstances, scales can be one-ended. The Kelvin scale, measuring temperature, has a lower end at absolute zero ($0°K$) but no upper end. We do not know what the highest temperature would be or if a highest possible temperature exists. The numerical progression used for Ostwald's logarithmical gray scale, running from 100 to 0 but never reaching 0, makes sense if Ostwald believed that some natural substances have a reflective index of 100 percent (absolute white), but none have a reflective index of 0 percent (absolute black). He believed the opposite. He never saw the inconsistency of his computations, or he said nothing in his zeal to prove that color could be reduced to simple mathematical symmetries.

Barium sulfate is assigned an index of 100 based on Ostwald's argument that this is the most reflective surface known, and absolute white does not exist. No surface reflects all light falling on it. Ostwald is more confident about absolute black. He describes a method for creating it. Under laboratory conditions, "a black that will not reflect any light can be produced by making a 4-inch cube-shaped box of dull black painted cardboard, with the black surface facing inside, then cutting an opening about 3/4-inch square in the center of one side" (Ostwald [1916] 1969, 24). The viewer looking into this hole sees an absolute black reflecting no light. The problem about this black of 0 percent reflective index is where to put it. Ostwald's logarithmic gray scale approaches, but never reaches, zero.

Ostwald's instructions for creating an absolute black are those for building a blackbody in physics, a model of interest to Max Planck between 1895 and 1900. In the laboratory a blackbody (which need not be black) consists of a hollow sphere or a tube with closed ends. It has a small hole in its side. The assumption is that radiation entering the hole will bounce about on the curved interior walls until absorbed, with little or no probability of bouncing out through the hole again. The hole is a perfect absorber (or transmitter) of light.

During the nineteenth century, the distribution of radiation from a heated blackbody was found to be inconsistent with the laws of classical physics. To explain this, Planck proposed what later became known as the quantum and laid the foundation for quantum theory. The blackbody also serves as a model for the black holes cosmologists believe may exist in outer space, regions of gravitation so intense that even light is unable to escape (Hawking 1988).

Because of interest in the blackbody in physics, we need not look further for the source of Ostwald's assumption that complete absorbers of light can be created. Why a mirror was not suggested as a perfect (or the most nearly perfect) reflector of light is unclear. Whatever the case, Ostwald's scale of reflective indices would be more compatible with his beliefs about absolute white and absolute black if it were turned upside down to become a scale of absorptive indices. Absolute black would be represented by 100 (it absorbs all light). Absolute white (0 percent absorption) would have no place on the scale, given that the logarithmic progression on which the scale is based never reaches 0. But this is consistent with Ostwald's assertion that there is no white with a reflective index of 100 percent (0 percent absorption), and its closest approximation is a coat of barium sulfate.

This adjustment would not resolve another inconsistency. A midpoint is a place equidistant between fixed extremes. A scale with only one end has no midpoint. Ostwald undertook to develop a gray scale that would identify the midpoint between white and black, the gray half as light as white and half as dark as black. The logarithmic gray scale, offered as a superior solution, suggests no solution is possible. As the scale is extended to progressively greater lengths, its predictions grow progressively more absurd. If long enough to include all of Ostwald's norm grays from *a* (white) to *z* (black), the Ostwald gray scale predicts that the median point between them is gray *n* (5.6 percent reflectance). But gray *n*, by Ostwald's report, is just one step lighter than the black of the blackest printer's ink. I conclude Ostwald amputated the sector of the scale beyond *p* (3.6 percent) because the scale looks ridiculous if seen at its entire length. The printing industry, he said, uses no ink of less than 3.6 percent reflectance.

White and Black

Ostwald contended that if human vision were sufficiently acute, we would be able to see that no two gray spots in the world are exactly alike in value (Ostwald [1916] 1969, 21). The proposition implies that if a sheet of paper is painted a uniform gray, cutting the paper in half establishes a difference in darkness among previously value-identical halves. It also implies that only one color spot in the world is, say, absolute white, and does not address the issue that at twilight this spot might look grayish rather than perfectly white. Ostwald gives insufficient attention to simple visual phenomena. No object, including a color spot, looks the same color under all kinds of lighting conditions. We cannot make broad generalizations about what color objects, including color spots, really are. Because of the phenomenon of optical mixture, a dark gray and a light gray can be indistinguishable—will look alike—at a sufficient distance.

Light (in color) means approaching white. *Dark* means approaching black. In neither case do we know how closely, which makes the words imprecise. The names *white* and *black* have another kind of ambiguity. They tend to be applied to extremes, often to the lightest and darkest colors in an environment. A movie screen that observers in an illuminated room agree is white looks less so if compared to the whiteness of a beam of light falling on it. Subjective understanding of what constitutes white varies. The color class is relativistic or arbitrary, a limit difficult to reach beyond. In theory, absolute white can be defined as the maximum amount of light the human eye is able to tolerate without damage. We have no exact idea of what that amount is.

The darkness of night, though the lightest as well as the darkest color of that hour, is not called white. We call it black, without reference to whether it looks like an absolute black. The elusiveness of white and black has its counterpart in other color ranges. Identifying a color as black, white, or red, we forget having seen blacker blacks, whiter whites, redder reds.

What is forgotten is that any color name identifies a range rather than a single tonality. I can imagine ways to program a computer so that the machine would always be aware of when I meant a single shade of, say, pale blue-violet and when I meant a range of thousands of varieties of that color. Communicating with human beings is more difficult. The English language is not structured to encourage speakers to make the distinction and offers few easy forms for doing so.

Forgetting that colors are ranges is encouraged by language and by the constraints of human memory, which is poor for exact shades of color. Unless two pieces of navy blue fabric are seen at the same time and place, in close proximity to one another, we remain uncertain about whether their colors exactly match. People take wallpaper samples to paint stores because how two colors look together, and whether they match, cannot be decided unless both are seen at the same time. Most of us have learned the humble wisdom of trying on clothes and looking in a mirror before deciding whether to buy them. Seeing, we know. Making assumptions without looking leads us astray.

Why memory for color is poor is uncertain. Preparing the mind for attention to the present implies suppressing the past, an aspect of the existential nature of the human condition. This alone is insufficient to explain why events, feelings, and words impress themselves upon us more indelibly than the small nuances among colors so easily forgotten by both trained and untrained observers. This weakness of memory coexists with a high degree of perceptual acuity. If shown the individual colors in a series, most people can efficiently arrange them in order, whether by hue, value, or chroma. Most people are similarly adept at sorting a series of achromatic grays from lightest to darkest.

Despite its refinement, the ability to rank by hue, value, or chroma has limits. It disappears at the threshold for optical mixture. If two spots of color, which can mean two grays, are seen from sufficient distance they appear to fuse, as in the case of the building of multicolored bricks that looks like a single color from far away.

The logarithmic gray scale has become standard, following Ostwald's scale or the Munsell Company's adaptation of it. Is the central gray too dark, an imbalance inspired by Ostwald's concern that it might be too light? In putting the question to the test, let us assume that the just noticeable difference between two grays is constant for a given viewer under controlled lighting conditions and proportional to the distance between viewer and object. If I can see a just noticeable difference between two grays at a distance of ten inches, this difference will not be visible from a hundred feet away.

A critical distance exists at which consecutive steps are perceived as continuous. The eas-iest way to test a gray scale is to walk away from it until this critical distance is found. Optical mixture takes over; each gray visually merges with those adjacent to it. If grays *a* and *b* differ by "the same amount" as grays *c* and *d*, this can only mean that each approaches a continuum equally closely, with the number of intermediary grays distinguishable between *a* and *b* equal to the number between *c* and *d*. The distance at which *a* and *b* look alike (become continuous) should match the distance at which *c* and *d* look alike. In a properly balanced scale, the distance at which adjacent steps look continuous should be the same for all steps, for the lighter grays and for the darker grays.

A convenient gray scale for testing is used by photographers and published by Eastman Kodak (Eastman Kodak 1966, 11). Its steps match those of the Munsell gray scale (Munsell Student Chart, Hue/Value/Chroma), suggesting logarithmically determined steps. An advantage to the Kodak gray scale is that each rectangle of gray touches the grays on either side of it, a necessary condition for testing balance. Most other gray scales are printed with a separation between the steps. If the Kodak gray scale is viewed from gradually increasing distances, differences between the lighter grays remain visible at a greater distance than differences between the darker grays. The center gray is too dark, a monument to Ostwald's foray into logarithms.

The imbalance of logarithmically determined steps rarely attracts attention, as several ill-considered conventions are followed in printing gray scales. Most have a separation or band between one step and the next. A gray scale is easier to evaluate if each step touches the steps alongside it, an extension of that basic axiom of color matching. Whether two colors match, or the degree to which they do not, is most accurately estimated if the colors are placed so that they touch one another.

Most gray scales are printed on white paper,

another distraction. Any color is affected by the colors surrounding it, Chevreul's law of simultaneous contrast. In the usual format for gray scales, the color surrounding the scale (the white of the paper on which it is printed) is also the color of one extremity. The viewer involuntarily reads the contrast between each gray and its white environment (no way to avoid seeing it), although ostensibly focusing attention on the degree of difference between successive gray steps. Substituting a black background is no solution, though any gray scale looks different if its background is black instead of white. What is needed is no background at all, or a background color different from black, white, or gray, and neither light nor dark. In the first case, each step can touch the next, and the steps can extend to the edge of the paper. In the second, each step should touch the next and the band of background color surrounding the scale should be, say, vermilion.

A second reason gray scales are rarely looked at closely is that most people sense how poorly they reproduce in books, where ideas about color and color value are difficult to illustrate. The Ostwald gray scale is reproduced in *The Color Primer* and in Jacobson's *Basic Color*. The scales in the two books do not look alike. In *The Color Primer*, one pair of illustrations shows the relative whiteness of zinc white and chalk white (Ostwald [1916] 1969, 24). Although chalk white (80 percent reflectance) is darker than zinc white (92 percent), it looks lighter in the illustration. Two diagrams identified as 80 percent gray do not look equally dark and are darker than a third gray the text identifies as 56 percent gray. (Ostwald [1916] 1969, 24, 25, 28).

Ostwald was a leading scientist in late-nineteenth-century Germany. In 1909 he received the Nobel Prize in chemistry for discovering how to oxidize ammonia to yield oxides of nitrogen. His color system, though it followed Munsell's closely, was superior to

it in many ways. Yet his adaptation of the Weber-Fechner Law to construct a gray scale was not a happy experiment. The logarithmic gray scale—by which I mean the entire scale—is not successful in predicting the median gray, and makes progressively more absurd predictions as its darker end is approached.

Ostwald's excising of 38 percent of the steps at the dark end of the scale makes the defect less noticeable but does not remove it. What should have been jettisoned was the insistence that the scale be logarithmic, that it conform to preconceived ideas that were mathematical rather than visual, that meant to prove a point about whether scientific explanations could be provided for visual experience. I suspect we shall have our scientific explanations at some future date. A more advanced science will be needed than is presently available. Certainly a more advanced science will be needed than that offered by Ostwald and Fechner.

Today a sophisticated literature explores the nature of scientific proof. Whether natural laws can be found to explain color, beauty, the arts, or aesthetic experience is not an interesting issue, though still occasionally raised by some psychologists. We smile at the excesses of those late-nineteenth- and early-twentieth-century thinkers, including Fechner and Ostwald, who expected to find a simple scientific law for everything and to finish the job by next Tuesday.

We still use the logarithmic gray scale and have too few answers of our own for the questions Ostwald addressed. Constructing a visually balanced gray scale is a worthwhile endeavor for the National Bureau of Standards, a scale balanced so that each gray merges with the grays adjacent to it at the same viewing distance or angular subtense. A greater need is for standardized tests to allow collecting reliable information about visual acuity for color relationships and color value (lightness, darkness) relationships in a normal population.

Tests for color blindness identify those whose vision is so grossly atypical that we characterize it as defective. These tests were not designed to measure variations in acuity for color among those with normal vision. Tests for fineness of acuity for small color differences, including small differences between grays, would be easy to construct, administer, and evaluate. They could be created by adapting tests and methodologies already available and would not be difficult to standardize.

Trained observers are often used in colorimetric studies, raising the question of whether training improves the ability to distinguish fine differences in color. We do not know that it does. The ability may be inherent. The issue can be avoided if the ordinary eye chart is adapted as a test instrument. Letters in different values of gray could be printed on a medium gray background. The test of whether the individual could discriminate between gray 1 and gray 2 could be whether he or she was able to read, at various distances, letters printed in gray 1 on a background of gray 2. Except for the difference in the chart, the test is exactly that presently used for nearsightedness and farsightedness.

Statistical methods already exist for determining an average from individual variations. These methods are applied to tasks as diverse as determining average life expectancy or average ability to see the forms of letters on an eye chart. Twenty/twenty vision is the ability to see at twenty feet what a statistically determined average person sees at that distance.

Similar scales could be established for ability to distinguish between colors close in hue, value, and chroma. The index of, say, 10/20 could mean the ability to see, at a distance of ten feet from the chart, a difference between two colors, or two grays, that most people can distinguish from a twenty-foot viewing distance.

We do not know whether a correlation exists for a given individual between the just-noticeable difference for different colors. Imagine that a hundred people are in a high percentile for ability to notice small differences between steps of gray. Whether they will share a similarly high level of acuity for small differences among reds, blues, lavenders, and each of the other colors is difficult to predict. Explanations of anomalous color vision are based on the assumption that no such correlation should be expected.

A commercial incentive exists for testing for nearsightedness and farsightedness. Eyeglasses can be fitted to improve acuity—at a charge. No such incentive is available to test for acuity in color discrimination. We know no way to improve substandard acuity. If information about color acuity were collected from a large population, it would prove its usefulness, I think. The information would provide a clearer picture of what to expect from the normal eye and would place color blindness in context. It might help prevent blindness by showing how to look for early warning signals. Certainly it would help in establishing standards for an adequate level of color value discrimination when driving a car at night.

Primary, Secondary, and Tertiary Colors

In the *De Coloribus* another writer of the Peripatetic school, probably not Aristotle, names three elementary colors, black, white, and yellow and by most fantastic reasoning he derives all other from them.

Florence Elizabeth Wallace, Color in Homer and Ancient Art

One purpose of color theory is to predict the results of color mixture. Orange, for example, is predicted (or defined) as the color that results from mixing red paint and yellow paint. The technical aspect of color theory covers questions about how orange and other colors are mixed and behave in mixtures. The aesthetic aspect of color theory is an inquiry into the harmoniousness of orange and other colors in combination with one another. We are told how to combine colors and which colors to combine.

The technical side of color theory is a set of rules about how the gray scale, the color wheel, and the color solid ought to be interpreted, what each implies about color relationships. The *primary colors* are an important concept common to modern color systems and earlier efforts. Primary colors are simplex or modular units that enjoy the status of an initial assumption. The conceptual model resembles that of chemistry, which explains a large number of compounds as chemical combinations of a much smaller number of elements. What is a primary color?

Two definitions are given, neither satisfactory. The first says that the primary colors are a set of colors from which all other colors can be mixed. The reasoning is a variation on Aristotle's belief that colors are mixtures of the opposites of darkness and light. A problem arises with the first definition. Four-color process printing can create the illusion of iridescence or metallic hues. But we cannot take red, yellow, and blue paints and stir them together to create paints in silver and other metallic colors, dayglo colors, fluorescent colors, or iridescent colors. The argument that these colors are not really colors is not helpful. Each visually excludes other colors, the criterion for identifying a color.

The second definition sidesteps the issue of how to mix silver and the other problem colors. A primary color is defined as a color that cannot be mixed from others. This is dangerous ground. If silver cannot be mixed from other colors, as was the original problem, then silver must be recognized as a primary color. This, I think, was not the intent.

By combining primary colors, *secondary* colors and *tertiary* colors are created, according to whether the mixture includes two primary colors or three. In theory, we proceed from a few basic units to every conceivable color.

The assumption that a set of primary colors exists can be traced to antiquity. Aristotle reduced all colors to combinations of darkness and light, effectively his set of primary colors, though he did not use that label. Because colors can be mixed from other colors, the idea persisted that all colors could be mixed from a small set of basic colors. What colors ought to be included in the basic set has not been clear. Leonardo da Vinci listed the primary colors as black, white, blue, yellow, green, umber, purple, and red (Rigaud 1957, 138). He contended, although few modern theorists would agree, that none of these colors can be mixed from others.

The twentieth-century citizen asked to identify the primary colors usually names red, yellow, and blue. Some people say red, yellow, blue, and green. Others say red, green, and purple, or red, green, and blue. Those who exclude yellow do so on the reasoning that red and green lights can be mixed to make yellow light. Yellow therefore is not a primary color.

Correlating the primary colors with other elementary units was a once popular pastime.

In *Principles of the Science of Colour*, William Benson, following Maxwell, identified the primary colors as red, green, and blue, linked with *do, mi, sol* in the musical scale (Benson [1868] 1930, 38). Benson proceeded to one of those tortured comparisons between music (a product of human artifice) and color (a natural phenomenon) that were once thought to shed light on the nature of color. The practice of comparing colors and musical notes can be traced to Plato, who regarded the homogeneous quality of a musical tone extended in time, or of a color extended in space, as examples of unity. Both, therefore, were beautiful, as were geometrical forms.

The English physician and amateur Egyptologist Thomas Young (1773–1829) is often said to have provided a scientific foundation for the belief that a set of primary colors exists. Young, theorizing about color vision, reasoned that each point on the retina cannot contain an infinite number of receptors, each attuned to one among an infinite number of colors. Each point must contain a limited number of receptors keyed to a small set of basic primary colors. Colors other than these primaries are seen when multiple receptors are stimulated in unison. Various ratios of stimulation account for the entire range of perceptible colors.

Young initially believed that red, yellow, and blue were the primary set. He later preferred red, green, and purple. Fascination with primary colors lingers, promising to reduce a complex phenomenon to easily understandable terms. But Young's theory is obsolete today as an explanation of color vision. The set of color-keyed retinal receptors was never located. Modern research has identified two basic receptor types: the rods and cones, named after their respective shapes. The rods, sensitive to differences in color value (light and dark) account for vision under conditions of low illumination. The cones, sensitive to hue or chroma, either cease to function or play a subordinate role when little light is present.

The rods and cones, also called opsins, contain several visual pigments, including rhodopsin (visual purple), porphyropsin, iodopsin, and cyanopsin. Each pigment bleaches in the presence of light. Absorption maxima for rhodopsin and porphyropsin have been shown to differ from one animal species to another. This may mean, as has been suggested, that all species of animals do not see the same colors. But the structure of the eye may not explain how and what people and animals see. The rods of the human eye lie around the periphery of the retina. The cones, necessary for color vision, are clustered near the center. Yet we have no sense that color vision is better near the center of the eye. We sense no difference in acuity for color in different parts of the visual field, although such differences may actually exist.

Young is remembered primarily for two experiments. In the first, light sent through two slits to a screen fell in an interference pattern of alternating bands of light and shadow. This suggests light behaves like a wave, although Newton had regarded it as a stream of corpuscles. An adaptation of Young's double-split experiment became a cornerstone of quantum theory when it was shown that the behavior of a beam of electrons, passing through one or both slits, could not be explained by the laws of classical physics.

Young based his theory of color vision on the second experiment. He demonstrated that if three properly spaced light frequencies are selected from the spectrum, all other spectral colors can be created by mixtures of these three. Various sets of colored lights can be used. But each must contain no fewer than three lights. Young's experiment was performed with colored lights, which do not behave similarly to colored pigments. It provides an experimental basis for the claim that many three-color sets of lights are primary.

From the colors in any of these sets, all other spectral colors can be mixed.

This is not equivalent to demonstrating that one set (rather than multiple sets) of lights can be used to mix all colors (not just the spectral hues). Also, Young's belief that he had mixed all of the spectral colors flies in the face of Newton's findings. Newton contended that when rays were mixed to create green, this green was not a color match for the singular ray of spectral green. An unanswered question is whether Young obtained different results or was just less discriminating in his observation of colors.

Young's experiment suggests that the issue is spacing, not color. If all or most colors of the spectrum can be matched by mixing rays in any set of three properly spaced colors, the number of sets of primaries is too large for the word to have any meaning. None of these sets is primary in the sense of being a unique set. The experiment was never properly assessed in the haste to use it as evidence that a set of primary colors exists. We need to know why spacing is important.

The logic of the usual argument from Young's three lights leaves much to be desired. Assume that every spectral color can be mixed from the primary colors in any set in which it is not included as a primary. Let A, B, and C be the colors in a primary set. Let X, Y, and Z be the colors in another primary set. If the colors A, B, and C can be mixed in various proportions to create every other spectral color, each much be a primary. But A, B, and C are not primary colors if it is true that they can be mixed from X, Y, and Z, the colors in another primary set. Young's experiment, said to show that a set of primary colors exists, is better evidence that no set of primary colors exists. Young showed that all or most spectral colors (not all colors) could be mixed from various sets of three colors (not a single set). To press further is an improper generalization.

Primaries Cannot Be Mixed from Other Colors

A primary set of colors is not a necessary assumption, and the logic of the second definition is no better than that of the first. Assume that a primary color, say, red, cannot be mixed from other colors. Let A and B be colors, which may or may not be red. Let red_1, red_2, and red_3 be various shades of red, a color that is primary. Let $\neq$ mean "cannot be mixed to make."

$$B + A \neq red_1$$
$$A + red_2 \neq red_1$$
$$red_1 + red_2 \neq red_3$$

The first proposition is that red cannot be mixed from A and B, because a primary color cannot be mixed from other colors. Two propositions follow, according to whether A, B, or both are red. Are any of the propositions true?

Although the first proposition is ensconced in color theory and popular belief, each proposition is untrue. Colors can be mixed to form red. The only requirement is that one or more of the colors in the mixture be red. The second proposition, a special case of the first, shows how to mix red. Imagine a large amount of red paint to which a small amount of paint of any other color is added. The red paint, though not exactly the same as previously, will in most cases remain red. To change red paint (or red light) to another color, more is required than admixture of a color other than red. The proportions of the mixture must be such that redness is no longer visually dominant. If more and more of, say, black paint is added to red paint, the color changes to blackish red, a variety of red. The paint ceases being red at the point when so much black has been added that we ought to classify it as reddish black (a shade of black) rather than blackish red (a shade of red).

The third proposition represents a type of mixture that also results in red. Both components are red, although neither is the shade of red obtained as an end result. Everyone knows that if two reds are mixed together, the result is a third red, different from either of its components although still red. This is a genuine contradiction of the assertion that no mixed color can be red.

Secondary Colors

The edifice of color theory, like a tower of Babel, rests on the wobbly assumption that a set of primary colors can be isolated or is already known. The secondary colors, the next layer of elaboration, are obtained when two primary colors are mixed. If the primary colors are assumed to be red, yellow, and blue, the secondaries are orange (red plus yellow), green (yellow plus blue), and purple (blue plus red).

Variation is available through adjusting proportions. A large amount of red and a small amount of yellow yields some shade of red-orange, an orange tending toward red. Reversing the ratio yields yellow-oranges, oranges tending toward yellow. Proportion is critical in color mixture, though ignored in color theory. It could be taken into account in color notation by adapting the subscripts used in chemistry. In chemical notation, H_2O is water and H_2O_2 is hydrogen peroxide. The subscript numbers acknowledge that each molecule has a different ratio of hydrogen atoms to oxygen atoms. Following this method, red_{10} + $yellow_3$ might indicate a mixture of ten parts red, three parts yellow. Attention to proportion brings into focus the excessively schematic nature of color theory. Indeed, red and blue make purple in some cases. But if a tiny amount of red paint is added to a large amount of blue paint, purple is not the result. For a second example, if the red is close to orange, the blue is greenish, and the colors are mixed in equal amounts, most people will call the product color brown.

Tertiary Colors

The tertiary colors result when all three primary colors are mixed. One way is to mix the primary colors, say, red, yellow, and blue, directly. A second way is to mix any two colors in the secondary (orange/green/purple) set. Because each secondary color is made from two primary colors, a mixture of two secondary colors includes all three primary colors.

The tertiary range is usually identified as brown, a simplification. It includes, depending on the proportion of each primary component, a large variety of russets, olives, browns, grayish browns, and bluish grays. The color schemes in Rembrandt's paintings are based on a wide variety of tertiary colors. Some bluish grays in the tertiary sets are so dark that they approach black or near black. As a result, people are sometimes uncertain about whether brown or black is the result of mixing paints of all colors.

Surfaces absorb the colors (wavelengths) of light that they do not reflect. The tertiary colors, because they have more components, usually absorb more colors of light than primary or secondary colors. Brown surfaces, which absorb many wavelengths (colors) of light, and black, which absorbs all wavelengths, are the most common colors in the natural world. Nature's balance favors conditions that allow the absorption or passage of light. The hues, as the least mixed, purest, brightest, or most reflective of all colors, suggest maximum deviation from this de facto norm. We do not know, however, whether the fascination of human beings with pure hues has a biological basis.

All colors cannot be mixed from a set of primary colors unless the primary/secondary/tertiary set includes all colors. It does not. Excluded ranges of color include metallic colors, fluorescent colors, iridescent colors, and dayglo colors. Paint in any of these colors can be mixed with paint of any other color.

Color theory has nothing to say about mixtures of this sort, an unexplored frontier.

Color variations based on surface sheen are also excluded. Yet shiny black, for all practical purposes, is a different color from dull black. No object can be both shiny black and matte black at the same time. Ultraviolet constitutes another excluded class, though ultraviolet light can be seen by some people. Because the light can be seen, it can also be mixed with light of other colors. Paint that reflects ultraviolet wavelengths can be mixed with paint of other colors.

Black and white are excluded from the primary/secondary/tertiary set. But black paint and white paint are frequently mixed with paint in those colors. The colors the Inter-Society Color Council standardized as ISCC blackish red and ISCC reddish black can be matched by mixing black and red. Mixture of a primary, secondary, or tertiary color with black yields colors described as grayed, darkened, or blackish. More formally, these varieties of color are called *shades* or *tones*.

Mixed colors with a strong white component are called *pastels* or *tints*. Distinctions are rarely drawn, although they might be, between pastel primary colors (say, pink), pastel secondaries (pale green), and pastel tertiaries (tan). The omission suggests the coexistence, without fraternization, of two separate sets of language rules for naming colors. Some pastels have names of their own: pink, tan, beige, eggshell, cream, maize, pistachio, mint, baby blue. Pastels that have a black component as well as a white component are usually called grayed pastels or whitened tones.

Purity and Muddiness

The ranking of colors as primary, secondary, and tertiary is hierarchic, based on the presence of one, two, or three primary components. The hierarchy is limited to colors that in theory can be reduced to primary colors.

A color made by mixing, say, silver paint and yellow paint has no place in the system. It cannot be ranked.

The linguistic tilt of the ranking system implies that the primary colors are primal or elemental. As the least mixed colors, they can be regarded as pure. The tertiary colors are the most mixed or least pure. Following this ranking, many idiomatic expressions refer in judgmental terms to purity or lack of purity in individual colors. Browns, although many people like them, may be called murky, muddy, or dirty, rarely a term of admiration. When a primary or secondary color is called murky or muddy, this usually implies it tends toward brown. It falls short of an expectation that reds, yellows, blues, greens, and violets should be bright or "pure." A dark blue, say, navy blue, is rarely called muddy. The term is reserved for blues with yellow and red components, blues that tend toward the tertiary range.

Why is muddiness bad in a color? I suspect the issue is human passion for order, expressed in a desire for cleanliness that goes back to an early date. The Old Testament sorts animals into clean and unclean groups and forbids eating unclean animals, rules still followed today by Orthodox Jews and Muslims. Unclean animals are often associated with mud: the pig because it wallows in mud, the carp because it gets its food from the mud at the bottom of ponds. Human beings, we are told, are made of the dust of the ground or of dirt, a humble origin. We were not made, as the angels may have been, from heavenly or ethereal matter.

As in the case of many popular ideas that carry over into our judgments of colors, an irrational bias runs through this dislike for mud. Early human beings in Mesopotamia built their houses out of mud brick, a material used since the New Stone Age. Clay, a variety of mud, is the basis of the ceramic arts. People might have praised this wonderful material, although the Bible does not. The Greek myth of Anteus, whose mother was the earth, says he could not survive unless he touched the dirt from time to time. When a person returning from abroad kneels to kiss the earth of the homeland, we understand what is meant and regard it as very emotional.

Muddiness or dirtiness, when attributed to a color, implies chromatic mixture: deviation from an ideal of chromatic purity that calls for fewer than three primary components. People who say they like purity in colors are rarely discovered to mean pure brown or pure olive green. Colors without spectral components such as silver and bronze are rarely called pure or impure colors.

Taste in color changes and sometimes is volatile. Modern designers of clothing and home furnishings notice the difference between, say, this year's olive green (which is fashionable) and last year's olive green (which is not). Long-term trends lie behind styles of the moment. Over the past forty years, people have come to prefer bright colors, now widely used in clothing, home decorating, office furniture, automobiles, pots and pans, and bedsheets. The long-term change in taste was probably caused by the use of strong color in modern art, or the influence on modern art of designers. Other twentieth-century influences are American Indian and African textiles and the comic-strip colors of color television and video games.

Muted colors, like other colors, go in and out of fashion. When fashionable, brownish blues or olive greens are thought of as subtle rather than dull or dirty. The reinterpretation leaves the point of reference unchanged. A tertiary color is called subtle in appreciation of its subtle deviation from the norm of either the primary colors or the spectral hues.

The reputation for purity of the primary and secondary colors is as ancient as that of the tertiary colors for lack of it. Again the roots lie in religious metaphor. The primary colors, we say, cannot be made from mixture. Red, yellow, and blue are pure in that sense. The reputation of the hues for their own type of purity comes partly from their brightness. Spectral green is brighter than olive green. Also, the spectra in which the hues appear are created by light, pure because it is incorporeal. Divorced from the materiality associated with the corporeal world, incorporeality—including the incorporeality of light—suggests the realm of the creator rather than that of his creations.

Although comets and eclipses of the sun might have seemed more amazing, thunder and the colors of the rainbow seem to have been the events in the sky that most impressed ancient peoples. Zeus, the Greek king of the gods, carried a thunderbolt. In India, the rainbow and the thunderbolt were symbols of Indra. The Bible said the rainbow was set in the sky after the flood as a sign of God's covenant with human beings. The rainbow is a familiar figure for purity or resurrection, and the search for purity, or mourning for its loss, is a potent theme in Western literature.

In the visual arts, rainbows and other light effects are popular in painting from the late Renaissance through the nineteenth century. But the idea that some colors are more pure than others was not forgotten in the twentieth century. The use of color in the paintings of Piet Mondrian turns on an association of purity with "pure colors." Mondrian's search for an art that was to be spiritual or pure and that, for consistency, had to be created with pure colors, led to a gradual paring of his palette. The pinks, browns, and other mixed colors found in Mondrian's early paintings gave way to a palette limited to primary and achromatic colors: red, yellow, blue, black, white. No other colors, apparently, were sufficiently spiritual, pure, or elemental.

The gorgeousness of Mondrian's combination of red, yellow, blue, black, and white seems to come from the uniqueness of each color, different from any other in that set. Red, white, and black (or red, light, and dark), an unusually popular combination in Renaissance and Baroque painting, similarly relies on a set of colors in which each is distinctly different from the others. The color scheme cuts across boundaries of style and time. Van Eyck used it in *The Man with the Red Turban* (London, National Gallery), as did Rubens in *Diana and Actaeon* (New York, Metropolitan Museum of Art).

Is this juxtaposing of strong hue with strong value contrast inherently beautiful? Do we like sets of colors in which, as in Mondrian's paintings or in the rainbow, each color looks very different from the others in the set? Perhaps. But Rembrandt, considered a great colorist, offered tertiary schemes built on small color variations within a limited range. The appeal of Rembrandt's colors lies in the similarity of one color to another. Rembrandt and Mondrian are often called spiritual, an effect attributed to the colors in their paintings. Yet Mondrian used unmixed primary and achromatic colors. Rembrandt used a wide range of subtle tertiary variations.

Why do certain colors or combinations of colors create a sense of religious awe? Why did Mondrian's interest in the spiritual lead him to simple colors? I suspect the issue is speechlessness, the condition of having no words to describe what we see. We have no idea how to translate into words the nature of blueness or its differentness from redness or whiteness. Speechlessness by its nature approaches religious awe, as if the inexplicability of color were an objective correlative for the inexplicability of the absolute.

Much earlier than the paintings of Mondrian, we can turn to Sumerian and Byzantine art to see color used for religious purposes, though not the colors Mondrian chose. Sumerian and Byzantine art, both from the same part of the world, relied heavily on the gorgeousness of gold leaf and silver leaf, materials with distinctive colors. After the Middle Ages, these and other metallic colors were rarely seen in painting until the 1960s. Gold and silver came to be thought of as not really colors and went unmentioned in books that advised on how to combine and mix colors.

Turning the System Upside Down

Hierarchical rankings that are disguised value judgments can be turned upside down without gain or loss of interior logic. We need not assume that complex substances, say, the tertiary colors, are less pure than substances that are simplex, say, the primary colors. Imagine reversing the system. The complex units, the tertiary colors, shall be the norm.

Rather than grading colors from pure to impure, we shall rank them from complete to incomplete. Brown, because it includes all the primaries, will be described as a complete color. Red, because it does not, will be called incomplete. A reversal in public taste would occur. People would assume that the brighter variations of color were distressingly incomplete rather than gratifyingly pure. The conventions of language would encourage the new assumptions.

A grading from complete to incomplete is no better or worse than a ranking from pure to impure. Either makes sense if ranking is to be according to the number of components. Assume that red, yellow, and blue are coded as A, B, and C. The primary, secondary, and tertiary colors can be notated in the following manner.

Set 1: A, B, C (red, yellow, blue)
Set 2: AB, AC, BC (orange, purple, green)
Set 3: ABC (brown)

Our choice is whether to assign the greater value to the extreme of the scale which is most complex or that which is least so.

Why do we feel compelled to reason in either of these judgmental manners? The boring exercise of defining one color in terms of another, like the boring exercise of defining women in terms of their differences from men, interferes with what might otherwise be a less self-deceiving vision of the nature of the experiential world. Red, blue, brown, silver, dayglo green, yellow, pale lavender, and all other colors are each equally unique, each best appreciated for its individual qualities.

In the type of metaphor passed along to us by earlier peoples, the world, divided, is a series of fragments to be reassembled into hierarchies, each resembling a king ruling over the subjects beneath him. We need more refined metaphors, less autocratic images. A better exercise is to imagine dividing a blue spot of color in half. This division does not make the spot less blue and suggests that the whole is inherent in every part. All colors are beautiful, in the sense that all people are beautiful. This is not the message of color theory, with its rankings that are rarely either logical or consistent with perceptual experience.

Complementary Colors

Each color is closely related to another called its complement.

Walter Sargent, The Enjoyment and Use of Color

In pigments, complementary colors mixed together will cancel each other out, creating a neutral tone of gray or black.

Joshua C. Taylor, Learning to Look

In logic the complementary class to red can be identified as not-red. In color theory complementary has a specialized meaning and applies to the sets below. One color in each set is a primary color. Its pair is the secondary color made by mixing the two remaining primary colors.

- red and green   (green is yellow and blue)
- blue and orange   (orange is yellow and red)
- yellow and purple   (purple is red and blue)

In a three-primary system, here assumed to consist of red, yellow, and blue, the complement to any primary is the secondary made by

mixture of the other two primaries. Color wheels are arranged so that each primary lies opposite its complement. The concept can be extended to any hue variation with appropriate shifts. The complement of an extremely yellowish red is an extremely bluish green. As the balance of the red shifts toward yellow, that of its complement rotates in an opposite direction.

This traditional arrangement of color wheels implies that an equal number of intermediaries lies between any two major hues. Yet we do not know whether the number of, say, blue-greens the average observer can distinguish is matched by an equal number of yellow-oranges. Symmetry in distribution seems unlikely. The eye shows variations in sensitivity and discriminates with greater fineness in the yellow-green range. The symmetry implied by the color wheel probably does not exist and is never the same symmetry with any two theorists.

The Ostwald wheel has eight basic colors. Purple and leaf green (more yellowish than sea green) occupy 25 percent of the hue circle. The arrangement implies, though Ostwald may not have thought about it, that 25 percent of distinguishable hue variations lies in this sector. On the ten-sector Munsell wheel, 40 percent is occupied by the colors that look most similar: red-purple and purple (together corresponding to Ostwald's purple), and green-yellow and yellow (corresponding to leaf green). What percentage of visually distinguishable hue variations lies in the yellow-green through purple range? Is it 25 percent (Ostwald) or 40 percent (Munsell)? Without knowing, we cannot determine whether each color has been paired with its correct complement.

Treated at some length in Helmholtz's *Physiological Optics*, the concept of color complementarity—that each color can be paired with an opposite color—is widely assumed to have a rational or scientific foundation. Yet it can have no such foundation unless a unique set of primary colors can be identified. This primary set must include one exact shade or wavelength of, say, red, not just the range of reds generally.

Carried over into the concept of color complementarity is the familiar baggage of misconceptions about color that have persisted for centuries. Complementarity does not apply to those colors, say, black, that are assumed to be not really colors. Complementarity is to be understood as a function of hue, of the primary and secondary colors, or of sets of those colors. Black and white are not conventionally included in a listing of complementary sets, though black is often called the opposite of white, and "no light rays" is defensibly the logical complement to "all light rays." Similarly excluded are all colors that lack a hue

component. No answer can be given to the question of what colors are the complements to silver and bronze. The tertiaries are bypassed, with less logic. If any given brown is to be regarded as some ratio of red, yellow, and blue, we can ask that an opposite ratio be identified. We can also ask what color (presumably another brown) corresponds to this opposite ratio.

The question of whether complementarity can exist among grays, even though not between black and white, turns on the distinction between achromatic grays (made of black and white only) and those tinged with hue. Among the achromatics, light gray is not called the complement of dark gray. But theorists usually agree that the complement of a reddish gray is a greenish gray. The Ostwald color solid is constructed to compel this identification.

The universe of discourse for complementarity is the hue component of the set of primary colors. Yellow is called the complement of purple because the issue in complementarity is hue rather than value (lightness or darkness). We are asked, in making the identification, to ignore the lightness of yellow and the darkness of purple. Even though lightness and darkness are said to be opposites, this variety of oppositeness is not considered in this case.

Injunctions to learn the complementary colors abound, which presupposes a value in doing so. For Sargent, "one who uses colors should know the exact hues of the more important pairs of pigment complements" (Sargent [1923] 1966, 115). For Bragdon, "complementary colors should be learned and committed to memory, just as a musician recognizes and remembers consonant musical tones" (Bragdon 1932, 117). Guptill "cannot over-emphasize the importance of these complementary hues in work with pigments. You should memorize the principal pairs" (Guptill n.d., 87).

Like the admonition to study opposites, the

dicta are impossible to follow. The particular shades of color opposite one another are never the same from one color theorist's wheel to the next. This leads to too many answers to the question of what the complements are. Too few answers exist to that other question of how the determinations were made. Ranking colors in pairs of opposites sows confusion and leads to no useful insights.

Camille Pissarro, asked to define Impressionism, identified two principles: "study the complementaries" and "don't mix pigments." Pissarro's color system, diagrammed by Brown (1950), included ten major classes of hue grouped in five complementary pairs:

- red and blue-green
- yellow and blue-violet
- green and red-violet
- blue and orange
- violet and yellow-green

The number of alternative arrangements is as large as the number of theorists offering opinions. Figure 33-1 shows the complementary pairs according to Munsell, Ostwald, Birren, Ross (who followed Chevreul), and Trautman. If asked to name the complement of blue-green, the respondent should reply "red" according to Pissarro or Munsell. On Birren's wheel, the answer is red-orange. For Trautman, the color is green-blue rather than blue-green; its complement is purple-red. The complement of yellow, according to the theorist, is variously blue-violet, purple-blue, ultramarine, or violet. The differences between systems reach beyond naming to the placement of hues.

For Birren all theorists were equally right, not equally wrong, because "generalities alone are important," and "whether yellow finds its true complement in ultramarine blue (Ostwald), in purple-blue (Munsell) or as [in Birren's system] is of no great consequence" (Birren 1969, 81). But if color complementarity is a meaningful concept, agreement is

Figure 33-1. The complementary colors identified by five theorists. Given the absence of firm criteria for complementarity, the colors identified as complements vary from one theorist's wheel to another's. And similar names need not imply similar colors. (Complementaries from the color wheel devised by Fritz Trautman after Bragdon 1932, 123. Ross complementaries after Ross 1919, 3.)

OSTWALD (8 major hues)
red and seagreen
orange and turquoise blue
yellow and ultramarine
leaf green and purple

MUNSELL (10 major hues)
red and blue-green
yellow-red and blue
yellow and purple-blue
green-yellow and purple
green and red-purple

BIRREN (12 major hues)
red and green
red-orange and blue-green
orange and blue
yellow-orange and blue-violet
yellow and violet
yellow-green and red-violet

ROSS (12 major colors)
red and green
red-orange and green-blue
orange and blue
orange-yellow and blue violet
yellow and violet
yellow-green and violet-red

TRAUTMAN (16 major hues)
redness and blueness
red-orange and blue-indigo
orange and indigo
orange-yellow and indigo-violet
yellow and violet
yellow-green and violet-purple
green and purple
green-blue and purple-red

needed on more than the principle that colors have complements. The perennial question about complementarity is what the term means in relation to color. Unless it can be linked to perception—correlated with something people see—complementarity remains a conceit, a label that provokes endless argument because it has no intelligible meaning.

Complementarity as Negation

What can I see in two colors that shows me they look opposite to one another? A common answer is that complementary colors negate one another. This negating is not the same as mutual exclusivity. Although the blue I see might be said to have negated the red I cannot see at the same time and place, this leads to no more than the conclusion that any color is a complement to all colors other than itself.

Evidently mixtures of colors can be ranked according to whether negation occurs. Blue and orange, because complements, would negate one another when mixed. Blue and yellow (noncomplements) would not. Most developments of the negation theory specify a third color to be obtained when complements are mixed. What color?

A mixture of two complementary colors includes all three primary colors. Thus, we would expect the mixture to look brown, whether or not the same shade of brown in each case. In the several explanations of complementarity, however, the product color is variously identified as brown, white, gray, or black. We need more information about this product color, the criterion for whether a mixture of two colors causes them to negate one another, whether the colors are complements.

The Maxwell Disc Test

One of the more technologically ornate explanations of negation holds that the colors in any complementary pair spin to gray on a Maxwell disc or color top. James Clerk Maxwell invented the device, popular for many years in the schools. The Maxwell disc is a disc on a spindle caused to revolve by a motor or other mechanical means. Maxwell's original instructions for making one have been updated by later authors (Maxwell [1890] 1965; Jacobson 1948; Smith 1965). A modern Maxwell disc can be made of cardboard, cut to the size and shape of a phonograph record, and spun on the turntable of a record player.

To test colors A and B for complementarity, papers of these colors are fastened to the disc. Whether each paper should cover half the disc's surface is unclear. In one variation on the theory, when the disc is spun, it ought to look gray if A and B are true complements. The mutual negating is a negating of chromaticity, which in this case results in an achromatic gray.

Given that every theorist structures the color wheel with that theorist's chosen set of complements, two outcomes are possible: most sets will not pass the test, or the test is unreliable. If the idea of color complementarity has a meaning (it may not), five or more different shades of orange cannot each be identified as the exact complement of a particular shade of turquoise blue. If $a + b = c$, and a and c are known, multiple values do not exist for b.

Claims of ability to pass the disc test are common, and at odds on critical details. We are not told what proportion of each color should be used, or whether the same value of gray results in each case. If red and green spin to achromatic gray, and yellow and purple also do so, will the gray be equally light or dark in each case? Birren contended that if complementary Munsell colors are "combined in equal 50-50 percent proportions and spun on a motor, the resultant visual mixture would be a neutral gray" (Munsell 1969, 54). T. M. Cleland, an associate of Munsell, required that the colors be mixed in proportion to their chroma (Munsell 1969, 28). The prescription is so vague as to be meaningless, and it is not the recipe Birren advised for spinning Munsell colors. Ostwald claimed the complements identified on his wheel spin to "yield a neutral gray," though in unspecified proportions (Ostwald [1916] 1969, 35).

Smith used Maxwell discs to assess the accuracy of the eight Shiva maximum complementary colors. These paints were "designed to mix in equal proportion by weight to a middle gray in pairs of complements," though the relative weight of a pigment or paint has no known correlation with its color (Smith 1965, 91). No pair passed the test. One of the four pairs spun to a violet-gray, another to a yellowish gray. The other two failed to spin to the same gray. The ratio of color areas required to produce any gray was never 50 percent/50 percent. It ranged from 21/79 percent to 30/70 percent. Smith concluded that although Shiva's maximum complementary colors "show a highly unsatisfactory performance record when mixed on the Maxwell wheel," they are a "set of true complements" (Smith 1965, 91). Is the problem the Maxwell disc mixture, the maximum complementary colors, or both?

Guptill was not enthusiastic about Maxwell discs, saying "this method of color mixture was for many years more confusing than helpful. Although the fascinating little device blended colors to produce innumerable hues, it never quite proved out with either the Brewster or Young-Helmholtz theories of color mixture" (Guptill n.d., 18). Listings from Cholet indicate that colors mix on a Maxwell disc in a manner inconsistent with any theory about mixtures of either colored pigments or colored lights (figures 33-2 and 33-3). Sargent reported that, "in fact, we find that the color which with another produces gray when mixed with paints, is seldom if ever the same hue that produces gray with it when the mixture is made with disks, on the color-top, or with colored light. . . . When we mix violet and yellow pigments we can approximate a neutral gray. When, however, we spin the top with violet and yellow disks no adjustment of their proportions will give us an exact neutral. The gray will be slightly pinkish. . . . Blue and yellow disks produce gray when rotated. In pigments, however, blue and yellow produce green. . . . In order to produce gray with paints, the color which must be mixed with blue is orange, but with the color top the blue and orange disks give a violet purple" (Sargent [1923] 1966, 111).

Maxwell believed that the color "produced by fast spinning [of a Maxwell disc] is identical with that produced by causing the light of the different colours to appear on the retina at once" (figure 33-4). This is unlikely in light of what we know today. Color results obtained by disc mixing are not those predicted or obtained from either light or pigments. The factors that probably account for the disparity are multiple reflectance and metamerism, a visual similarity between colors with dissimilar sources or constituents. Pigments and dyes, including those used to manufacture colored papers, usually reflect more than one wavelength of light. Even if the color of a piece of red paper visually resembles that of a beam of monochromatic light of a specific wavelength, the paper is unlikely to be reflecting light of only that wavelength. The beam and the paper cannot be regarded as equivalents.

The Benham disc, a cousin of the Maxwell disc, is black and white while at rest but red and blue in motion. The behavior of the Ben-

Figure 33-2. Comparative results of Maxwell disc mixture and pigment mixture. Maxwell believed that mixing colors on spinning discs could be equated with mixing beams of colored light. But this is not the case. Results in Maxwell disc mixture are also typically dissimilar to results from mixing pigments. (After Cholet 1953, 22).

Pigments	Maxwell Disc Mixture	Pigment Mixture
Violet-carmine and Hooker's green	yellow-gray	brown
Violet-carmine and gamboge	pale yellow-gray	sepia-gray
Violet-carmine, Prussian blue and gamboge	green-gray	gray
Violet-carmine and Prussian blue	blue-gray	blue-gray
Violet-carmine and carmine	pink-purple	dull red-purple
Gamboge and Prussian blue	pale green-gray	dull blue-green
Carmine and Hooker's green	yellow-orange	brick red
Carmine and green	pale red	dark red

Figure 33-3. Mixtures on Maxwell discs required to match mixtures on palette. Colors obtained by mixing on discs can be correlated only uneasily with those from mixing pigments and require different proportions. (After Cholet 1953, 22.)

Mixture on Palette	Mixture by Rotation
50 violet + 50 Hooker's green	21 violet + 22.5 Hooker's green + 4 vermiiion + 52.5 black
50 violet + 50 gamboge	54 violet + 20 gamboge + 26 black
50 violet + 50 green	50 violet + 18 green + 32 black
50 violet + 50 Prussian blue	47 violet + 49 Prussian blue + 4 black
50 violet + 50 carmine	36 violet + 37 carmine + 8 ultramarine + 19 black
50 gamboge + 50 Prussian blue	12 yellow (gamboge) + 42 Prussian blue + 41 green + 4 black
50 vermilion + 50 ultramarine	21 vermilion + 20 ultramarine + 51 black + 9 white
50 Hooker's green + 50 carmine	23.5 yellow green (Hooker's green) + 8 carmine + 52 vermilion + 16 black
50 carmine + 50 green	50 carmine + 24 green + 26 black

ham and Maxwell discs suggests that hue can be created, modified, or destroyed by motion, a phenomenon unexplained by any present theory of color. Would the color seen on a disc spinning at a particular velocity be modified if the disc were accelerated or slowed down? We do not know. Like the slit phenomena explored by Thomas Young, disc phenomena are little understood.

The Product Color Test

Whether Maxwell discs perform as predicted is of small interest except for the issue of complementarity. If complementary colors cannot be shown to negate one another by spinning to gray on the discs, how can we identify pairs of complementary colors? Variant versions of the theory do not rely on Maxwell discs. They suggest colors other than gray to be obtained under various circumstances. Complementarity between two colored lights is said to be proved if they can be mixed to form white light. Proportions for the mixture are not specified, nor is it clear whether the white will be identical with that of a beam of natural white light.

Mixtures of pigments of complementary colors are said to form, variously, brown, gray, or black. Proportions, again, are unspecified. If brown, this is not a test of complementarity. Brown is elsewhere identified as the color

of any mixture including three primaries, irrespective of whether these primaries were ever arranged to form a pair of complementary colors. Because a tertiary color can be made from two secondary colors, brown is the predicted result of mixing, say, orange and green, orange and purple, or purple and green. None of these pairs are complements.

If black, gray, or any color other than brown, this conflicts with the definition of a tertiary color. Mixtures of complements include all three primaries, and are consequently predicted to produce brown. They cannot at the same time produce gray or black. The gist of the inconsistencies is that brown cannot be a test of complementarity, yet must be the test. The color is the predicted end result when any mixture includes all three primaries.

This leads to a negative test of sorts: if a mixture of two colors does not produce brown, the colors are not complements. We must therefore eliminate black or gray. Mixing two pigments to produce black or gray proves the colors are *not* complements. Brown is the end result of mixing complements, although also an end result of mixing various color pairs that are not complements.

To test the logic of the various theories, let A, B, and C be primary colors. Let ABC be brown, the predicted color of any mixture that includes A, B, and C. Let AB be the secondary color complementary to primary color C. Let Z be any color other than brown. The definition of a tertiary color then implies the following about any pair of complementary colors.

$$AB + C = ABC$$
$$Z \neq ABC$$
$$AB + C \neq Z$$

The result of mixing complementary colors must be brown and cannot be any other color. Yet brown is not a test for complementarity, because the color is predicted for any mixture including three primaries. Mixtures including three primaries exist that are not mixtures of complementary colors.

$$AB + BC = ABC$$
$$BC + AC = ABC$$
$$AC + AB = ABC$$
$$A + B + C + ABC$$

Other Tests

Other explanations of how to test for complementarity verge on the incoherent. Fuchs offered the thought that "the complementary colors are mutually destructive, each excluding the other from sensation" (Fuchs [1908] 1924, 242). Ostwald put his faith in the "law of least resemblance." This is said to determine that "there exists for every hue in the hue circle another that is most different from it, which is called its complement" (Ostwald [1916] 1969, 34). That less resemblance exists between, say, yellow and purple than between yellow and red is largely a matter of opinion. Ostwald provided no further information about the workings of this convenient, elsewhere undocumented, law.

Sargent reported, "by looking at the afterimages of all our (colored) disks we can

Figure 33-4. Construction of Maxwell discs. Maxwell discs, in their day, were popular in both the schools and scientific laboratories.(From Maxwell [1890] 1965, 122.)

The colored paper is cut into the form of discs, each with a small hole in the center, and divided along a radius, so as to admit of several of them being placed on the same axis, so that part of each is exposed. By slipping one disc over another, we can expose any given portion of each colour. These discs are placed on a little top or teetotum, consisting of a flat disc of tin-plate and a vertical axis of ivory. This axis passes through the center of the discs, and the quantity of each colour exposed is measured by a graduation on the rim of the disc, which is divided into 100 parts.

By spinning the top, each colour is presented to the eye for a time proportional to the angle of the sector exposed, and I have found, by independent experiments, that the colour produced by fast spinning is identical with that produced by causing the light of the different colours to fall on the retina at once.

By properly arranging the discs, any given colour may be imitated and afterwards registered by the graduation on the rim of the top. The principal use of the top is to obtain colour-equations. These are got by producing, by two different combinations of colours, the same mixed tint. For this purpose there is another set of discs, half the diameter of the others, which lie above them, and by which the second combination of colours is formed.

The two combinations being close together, may be accurately compared, and when they are made sensibly identical, the proportions of the different colours in each is registered, and the results equated.

These equations, in the case of ordinary vision, are always between four colours, not including black.

From them, by a very simple rule, the different colours and compounds have their places assigned on the triangle of colours. The rule for finding the position is this:—Assume any three points as the positions of your three standard colours, whatever they are; then form an equation between the three standard colours, the given colour and black, by arranging these colours on the inner and outer circles so as to produce an identity when spun. Bring the given colour to the left-hand side of the equation, and the three standard colours to the right hand, leaving out black, then the position of the given colour is the centre of gravity of the three masses, whose weights are as the number of degrees of each of the standard colours, taken positive or negative as the case may be.

In this way, the triangle of colours may be constructed by scale and compass from experiments on ordinary vision.

find the color that is the complement of each'' (Sargent [1923] 1966, 104). The technique is not reliable. Afterimages are too faint to allow precise discriminations of hue to be made. *A Color Dictionary* (The North American Society of Arts, Inc., 1931, unpaginated) reported that ''as two opposite colors (such as blue and orange) are brought together, one neutralizes the other until the brightness or chroma of each changes from the most intense to the dullest stage.''

Beyond the circus of capriciousness exhibited by color systems and their champions, experiential reasons can be cited for wondering whether color complementarity is a meaningful concept. No child can be taught ostensively that red looks more different from green than from black, yellow, blue, white, silver, or any other color. Ostwald's law of least resemblance refuses to make itself manifest in any visual form that can be exhibited. It can only be communicated as a decree or accepted as dogma.

Complementary Wavelengths in Light

Arnheim noted the ''Babylonian confusion that reigns once we pass beyond what is said to be verifiable: that mixtures of certain spectral colors are said to create an impression of achromaticity for the average observer,'' effectively, that complementary wavelengths of light mix to form white (Arnheim 1956, 348). Is even this verifiable? One difficulty is in

determining which colors correspond to these wavelengths. If the colors cannot be firmly identified or are inconsistently named and identified among observers, the assertion that the wavelengths are those of complementary colors has no foundation.

Delving more deeply into the technical literature does not resolve the inconsistencies, a pervasive condition in color theory. Helmholtz, followed by Arnheim, identified wavelengths of 607.7 and 489.7 millimicrons (respectively, yellow-orange and blue) as an achromaticity-creating pair of complements (figure 33-5). Kries, Frey, König, Dieterici, Angier, and Trendelenburg disagreed, as does nearly every other authority (figure 33-6). The Optical Society of America found that the complementary wavelength to 489.7 is 605, not 607.7 (figure 33-7). Ostwald's diagram of complementary wavelengths indicates that 482 or 483 (not 489.7) is complementary to 607.7 (figure 33-8).

The difference between Helmholtz and Ostwald looms larger than the small numerical discrepancy suggests (see figure 33-8). Between three and four of the twenty-four Ostwald hue steps are involved, 15 percent of that circle. Further, according to Ostwald's computation, 489.7 millimicrons is one of several wavelengths devoid of any complement, a condition indicated by the gap on the right side of Ostwald's hue circle. A wavelength of 607.7 millimicrons corresponds to yellow-orange or orange, depending on the theorist.

Figure 33-5. Complementary wavelengths in light. Because mixtures of light give results that differ from mixtures of pigments, complementary wavelengths in light cannot be correlated with complementary colors in pigments. (After Helmholtz [1909] 1962, 2:126.)

Color	Wavelength	Complementary Color	Wavelength	Ratio of the Wavelengths
Red	656.2	Green-blue	492.1	1.334
Orange	607.7	Blue	489.7	1.240
Golden yellow	585.3	Blue	485.4	1.206
Golden yellow	573.9	Blue	482.1	1.190
Yellow	567.1	Indigo-blue	464.5	1.221
Yellow	564.4	Indigo-blue	461.8	1.222
Green-yellow	563.6	Violet	433.0	1.301

Figure 33-6. Complementary wavelengths listed by seven observers. Agreement is rarely found among observers identifying complements, in the technical as well as the popular literature. (After Helmholtz [1909] 1962, 2:128.)

Helmholtz		Kries		Frey		Konig		Dieterici		Angier		Trendelenburg	
656.2	492.1	656.2	492.4	656.2	485.2	675.0	496.5	670.0	494.3	669.3	490.0	669.4	491.2
607.7	489.7	626.0	492.2	626.0	484.6	663.0	495.7	660.0	494.0	654.6	489.0	654.9	490.5
585.3	485.4	612.3	489.6	612.3	483.6	650.0	496.7	650.0	494.3	641.2	490.2	641.3	490.4
573.9	482.1	599.5	487.8	599.5	481.8	638.0	495.9	635.0	494.0	628.1	487.9	628.4	489.2
567.1	464.5	587.6	484.7	587.6	478.9	615.3	496.0	626.0	493.1	616.2	487.4	616.2	487.9
564.4	461.8	579.7	478.7	586.7	478.7	582.6	483.6	610.0	492.2	604.8	487.0	604.8	487.3
563.6	433.0	577.0	473.9	577.7	473.9	578.0	476.6	588.0	485.9	593.8	484.7	593.9	485.7
.....	.....	575.5	469.3	572.8	469.3	576.0	467.0	585.7	485.7	583.3	480.6	583.5	482.8
.....	.....	572.9	464.8	570.7	464.8	574.5	455.0	578.0	476.6	572.9	473.3	572.4	469.1
.....	.....	571.1	460.4	569.0	460.4	573.0	450.0	575.6	470.0	.....	.....	.....	.....
.....	.....	571.0	452.1	568.1	452.1	.....	.....	571.5	455.0	.....	.....	.....	.....
.....	.....	570.4	440.4	566.3	440.4	.....	.....	571.3	448.0	.....	.....	.....	.....
.....	.....	570.1	429.5	566.4	429.5	.....	.....	571.4	442.0	.....	.....	.....	.....

Figure 33-7. Complementary wavelengths for given source C.
(After Optical Society of America 1953, 307.)

Wavelength	Complementary	Wavelength	Complementary	Wavelength	Complementary
380	567.0	488	596.5	590	485.9
400	567.1	489	600.9	591	486.3
420	567.3	490	607.0	592	486.7
430	567.5	491	616.8	593	487.0
440	568.0	492	640.2	594	487.3
450	568.9	568	439.3	595	487.6
455	569.6	569	450.7	596	487.9
460	570.4	570	457.9	597	488.1
465	571.5	571	463.1	598	488.4
470	573.1	572	466.8	599	488.6
471	573.6	573	469.7	600	488.8
472	574.0	574	471.9	605	489.7
473	574.5	575	473.8	610	490.4
474	575.1	576	475.4	615	490.9
475	575.7	577	476.7	620	491.2
476	576.4	578	478.0	625	491.5
477	577.2	579	479.0	630	491.7
478	578.0	580	480.0	640	492.0
479	579.0	581	480.8	650	491.2
480	580.0	582	481.6	660	492.3
481	581.2	583	482.3	670	492.3
482	582.6	584	482.9	680	492.4
483	584.1	585	483.5	690	492.4
484	585.8	586	484.1	700	492.4
485	587.8	587	484.6	780	492.4
486	590.2	588	485.1		
487	593.0	589	484.5		

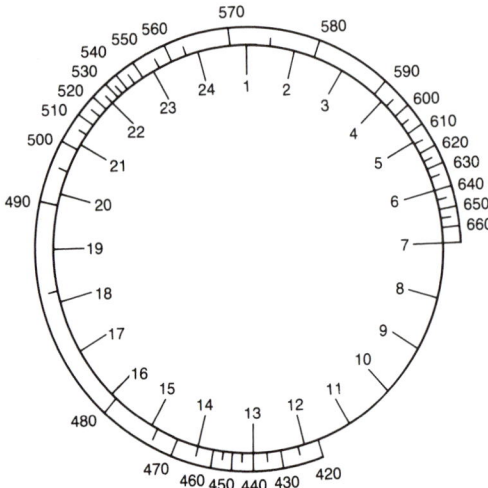

Figure 33-8. The Ostwald complements. The Ostwald complements differ from those of Helmholtz and the observers he cited. Colors in the red-violet range are shown without assigned wavelengths.

A wavelength of 489.7 probably falls in the blue range but is identified in some systems as blue-violet.

A test for complementarity that is independent of the color obtained by mixture is noted primarily in the technical literature. As Helmholtz and Arnheim observed, complementary wavelengths are said to have a roughly similar ratio: approximately 1.25 (Arnheim 1956, 348). This cannot mean, however, that the complement of a wavelength can be determined by computation. Given lack of agreement on the particulars of which wavelength (or which color) complements which, how a reliable table of ratios can be developed is unclear.

Whether the 1.25 ratio is even significant is debatable. According to Ostwald, the wavelengths for visible light range from about 420 to 660 millimicrons, a narrow range (see figure 33-8). Between these extremes, no two numbers can have a ratio to one another of less than 1.00 (660/660 = 1) or more than 1.58 (660/420 = 1.571). According to Helmholtz, the range of wavelengths for visible light runs

from 433 to 656.2 millimicrons. The complementary wavelengths Helmholtz identified show ratios from 1.19 to 1.334, within a possible range of approximately 1.00 to 1.52 (656.2/433 = 1.52).

In the technical literature, as in popular works and school texts, the persistent issue is verifiability. How Ostwald determined that the complement to a wavelength of 607.7 millimicrons was 482 or 483 millimicrons is unclear. Nor do we know how others arrived at other numbers. The complementary sets in the Ostwald system are dissimilar to those shown by Munsell or by anyone else. Each arrangement impressed its advocates as correct, though we are not told why.

Munsell and Ostwald Complementaries

Inches can be translated into centimeters, although the two cannot be mixed in the same computation. The skewing between the color wheel of one theorist and that of another is of such a nature that no comparable form of translation is possible. The Munsell hue circle, divided into ten basic colors that have names, uses a decimal system to provide a total of 100 hues. The order of the spectral colors (red to violet) reads clockwise. In the traditional manner, colors thought to be complements lie opposite one another.

The Ostwald hue circle includes eight basic colors with names. Two intermediate colors placed between each provide a total of twenty-four hues. These are numbered from one to twenty-four, beginning with yellow. The order of the spectral colors (red to violet) reads counterclockwise (For the Munsell wheel, see Munsell [1905] 1961; 1969, 82. For the Ostwald wheel, Jacobson 1948, 26; Ostwald [1916] 1969, 83). Ostwald identified three hundred hues as an absolute maximum that can be included in a hue circle. Beyond that number, differences in steps are held to be so minute as to be no longer visually discernible. In the

Ostwald circle, as in Munsell's, "perfect visual complements lie opposite each other. . . . Such pairs will cancel into gray if mixed on a [Maxwell disc]" (Ostwald [1916] 1969, 84).

In books, different printings of Ostwald and Munsell hue circles show noticeable color variations and an inferior level of color control by industrial standards. Noticeable color differences are more likely to occur in two printings of the Munsell hue circle than in two American flags made by different manufacturers (Compare Munsell hue circles in Munsell 1969 and the Munsell Company's Munsell Student Chart; Ostwald hue circles in Jacobson, 1948 and Ostwald [1916] 1969). Adjusting for this limitation of commercial printing, the sets Munsell identified as complements cannot be reconciled with the Ostwald complements in either color or name. As previously noted, on Munsell's wheel, red, orange (called yellow-red), and yellow occupy 30 percent of the circle. On Ostwald's, these colors occupy 37.5 percent, a difference of 25 percent. Another 25 percent of the Ostwald wheel is occupied by the color classes leaf green and purple. Munsell's corresponding colors, yellow and green-yellow (corresponding to leaf green) and purple and red-purple (corresponding to purple) occupy 40 percent, a difference of 60 percent.

Among the consequences of this skewing, both theorists may show the same pair of colors as complements, designated by dissimilar names. Munsell identified as complements colors he labeled *yellow* and *purple-blue*. Two colors that look similar to this pair appear in Ostwald's circle, similarly as complements. The Ostwald colors, however, are labeled *yellow* and *blue*, respectively hues 1 and 13.

Some colors look so dissimilar that no comparison can be made. Examples include blue and the green with the highest yellow component. The same name may be used for dissimilar colors, or different names for the same

color. Although *yellow* and *blue* (hues 1 and 13) are complements in the Ostwald system, Munsell yellow and blue are not. Nor is Munsell's blue the same color as Ostwald's. Munsell blue is closest to the Ostwald color called turquoise. The color Ostwald calls blue is identified by Munsell as purple-blue.

Colors opposite one another on one wheel are in many cases not opposite on the other. Munsell's blue and yellow-red are complements. The question of which Ostwald colors look most similar to them is complicated by color variations in different reproductions of the Ostwald wheel. The closest match is probably either Ostwald's turquoise 16 and orange 4 (Jacobson 1948) or turquoise 16 and yellow 3 (Ostwald [1916] 1969). The Ostwald pairs appear to be one step off of complementarity.

Munsell's red and blue-green are complements. The closest match in Ostwald's wheel are red 7 and turquoise 17. The Ostwald colors are indicated to be two steps away from complementarity (8 percent). Munsell's red-purple and green, a complementary pair, are difficult to correlate with any of the colors on Ostwald's wheel. The closest match may be Ostwald's red 9 and leaf green 22, one step off of the complement. Munsell purple and green-yellow are complements. The closest match appears to be Ostwald purple 11 and leaf green 24, one step off of the complement.

Complementarity and Harmony

Whether or not a meaningless concept, color complementarity has a rich mythos. For Birren, "a number of studies in the field of psychology have verified the observations of Chevreul that colors look best (a) when they are closely related or analogous or (b) when they are complementary or in strong contrast" (Birren 1969, 35). Elsewhere Chevreul, who questioned whether complements could be identified, was credited with discovering that "the complementary assortment (of colors) is superior to every other" (Birren 1969, 38).

For Jacobson, complementarity headed a list of six modes of color harmony (Jacobson 1948, 56). Analyzing twelve paintings, he found that "the amazing accuracy of the complementary colors in these paintings is a final indication that great artists are almost as sensitive to color differences as modern spectrophotometric instruments" (Jacobson 1948, 56). Color discriminations made by eyes, which need not be the eyes of great artists, are *more* refined than those made by instruments (Evans 1948, 203). Beyond this, Jacobson's criterion for accuracy is unclear. Colors opposite one another on Ostwald's wheel, because believed to be complements, will not lie opposite one another on Munsell's.

As Chevreul pointed out, color complementarity falls by the wayside unless absolute primaries can be identified. This requires demonstrating that, say, a particular red is the primary red, meeting conditions that cannot be met by any randomly selected bright red. Until a primary set can be identified or shown necessarily to exist, no foundation exists for the conception of absolute secondaries or complements.

The elusiveness of primaries, secondaries, and complements accounts for the differences between Munsell's system and Ostwald's and for the lack of agreement between any two theorists on any point other than the importance of color theory. It accounts for the offset between one theorist's wheel and the next, a skewing that ensures the exact green opposite a particular red will not be the same in any two systems. Birren's argument that all color systems are equally correct is not convincing. I conclude the systems are all equally incorrect.

Color Mixture

Mixtures of blue and yellow as lights produce white. Blue and yellow [Maxwell] discs produce gray when rotated. In pigments, however, blue and yellow produce green.

Walter Sargent, The Enjoyment and Use of Color

Mixed colors look similar to their components in some cases, though not always. Reddish gray resembles red and gray. Green resembles neither blue nor yellow. We cannot always judge, by looking at colors, how they will look when mixed. The color wheel allows results to be predicted approximately, but not with precision, the limited truth behind the truism that blue and yellow make green. Nobody can select, from a chart of thousands of shades of green, the exact shade that will be produced by mixing four parts Prussian blue, one part cadmium yellow, and two parts white. Human beings work effectively when assessing a mixed color they see, less effectively guessing the colors of mixtures not available for viewing. Given paint to match, the trained person accomplishes the task by eye, with no exact knowledge of how the original paint was mixed.

The answers to questions about color were once sought by studying music (figure 34-1). In a reversal used to explain color mixture, we are often asked to consider differences between musical chords and mixed colors, as if those differences were not to be assumed. Maxwell mused that in a mixed color "we cannot directly recognize the elementary sensations of which it is composed, as we can distinguish the component notes of a musical chord" (Maxwell [1890] 1965, 2:271). Gregory concurred (Gregory 1966, 119). For Wright, "there is nothing corresponding to [color mixture] for sound, since the ear does not synthesize the aural response in the way the eye integrates the visual response. When a chord

313

Figure 34-1. Ophthalmic color scale correlating colors with musical notes, developed by Louis Wilson. Wilson's scale is apparently based on the assumption that colors will be pleasant to look at if the musical notes to which they are keyed create a musical combination that is pleasant to hear. (After Bragdon 1932, 120.)

Color	Musical Note(s)
purple	C, B sharp
purple-red	C sharp, D flat
red	D sharp
red-orange	D sharp, E flat
orange	E, F flat
yellow	F, E sharp
yellow-green	F sharp, G flat
green	G
green-blue	G sharp, A flat
blue	A
blue-violet	A sharp, B flat
yellow	B, C flat

the criterion, the person can be asked to mix colors to match, say, a particular green. Unfortunately, if the task is accomplished, we are not free to conclude that the components of the original mixture were correctly identified.

A color can be matched without knowing its components. Many ways exist to replicate any mixed color, the phenomenon colorimetrists call metamerism. A medium gray can be made by mixing black with white. It can also be made by mixing light gray with dark gray. A set of yellow-greens that match one another can be obtained by mixing various proportions of yellow with blue, blue-green, or green. What is indeterminable from looking at a mixed color is which of a range of possible combinations accounts for the mixture. Using any combination in the range, the color can be replicated. The nearest parallel is number. Ten is the sum of nine and one, and also the sum of six and four.

Except in laboratory experiments, laser shows, and theatrical lighting, mixing colored lights is an infrequent activity. Mixing colors to match other colors usually involves mixing paints or dyes. The task, mysterious to the uninitiated, is a commonplace skill on which industry routinely relies. Mixing and matching colors, like drawing the human figure, can be taught to almost anyone, usually in a brief time.

Although not as confusing as comparisons between color and music, those between color and sound are similarly limited. Optical mixtures differ from aural mixtures. Sounds, including musical notes, are considered mixed if the components occur at the same time in near proximity to one another. The location from which individual sounds originate is irrelevant, provided the sounds can be heard. The same chord has been played whether one musician strikes its three notes or three musicians each strike one note. Sound mixture is a subjectively oriented concept. It refers to what the listener hears. If one note is audible, while two others are struck simultaneously in

of music is struck, the listener, especially if he is trained, can identify the individual notes comprising the chord" (Wright [1944] 1969, 69).

The reasoning, by now, is pro forma. We should not need to be told that strong similarities rarely occur between systems created by human beings (say, music) and natural phenomena (say, color). Musicians identify the notes in a chord because they know music, which has a limited range and strict rules about what sounds can be used and how they can be combined. No amount of training enables anyone to separate the components in a mixture of sounds, as in the merging of voices heard as the roar of a crowd.

Nontraditional music is similarly resistant to instant analysis, for it more nearly approaches the complexity of combinations of natural sounds. Rarely can one listen to computer-generated music and deduce the program by which it was generated or the sounds that went into the mixture if these sounds were not conventional musical notes.

Although the components cannot be identified in a mixture of colored lights, imagine an observer asked to make the attempt. How can we evaluate the correctness of the observer's answers? Adopting replicability as a soundproof enclosure, no chord has been heard by that listener.

Visual phenomenology includes no such thing as a simultaneous occurrence (mixture) of two colors in which an observer sees only one of the colors. A possible exception is that some theories of color blindness imply that this might occur. These theories leave us wondering whether a mixture of red and black would look black to an individual with deficient sensibility to red.

A mixture of colors, unlike a mixture of sounds, occurs only if two or more colors are seen at the same time and place. The requirement for simultaneity in space and time appears to violate the principle that colors cannot interpenetrate. Identifying a green object as a mixture of blue and yellow is inconsistent with the idea that nothing is both entirely blue and entirely yellow. Or nothing can be both blue and not-blue.

Mixture is a troublesome term in the explanation of light in the physical sciences. For Jenkins and White, the theories of Gouy and others raise "the question as to whether Newton's experiments on refraction by prisms, which are usually said to prove the composite nature of white light, were of much significance in this respect . . . the view that the colors are manufactured by the prism, which was held by Newton's predecessors, may be regarded as equally correct" (Jenkins and White 1957, 223).

For Whittaker, though Newton's prism experiments demonstrated that "ordinary white light is really a mixture of rays of every variety of color. . . . The word *mixture* must not be taken to imply that the rays of different colours, when compounded together, preserve their separate existence and identity unaltered within the compound, like two constituents in a mechanical mixture. On the contrary, as was shown by Gouy in 1886, natural white light is to be pictured, in the undulatory representation, as a succession of short *pulses,*

out of which any spectroscopic apparatus such as a prism manufactures the different monochromatic rays, by a process which is physically equivalent to the mathematical resolution of an arbitrary function into periodic terms by Fourier's integral theorem" (Whittaker [1910] 1951, 1:17). Fourier's integral theorem asserts that any periodic function of a single variable p, which does not become infinite at any phase, can be expanded in the form of a series consisting of a constant term, together with a double series of terms, one set involving cosines and the other sines of multiples at the phase.

White light as a mixture of colored rays is a figure of speech. Color mixture is as elliptical, though we can assess the issue without Fourier's integral theorem. Mixing colors is impossible, because colors cannot be isolated from objects. Whether these objects are colored lights or colored pigments makes no difference. I cannot take blue chairs and put the blueness in one pile and the chairs in another. Nor can I accomplish this separation with blue pigments or blue lights.

Any statement about color mixture involves an ellipsis. If yellow and blue make green, this can only be verified by demonstrating that when yellow *pigment* is mixed with blue *pigment* the *pigment mixture* looks green. Pigments, rather than "colors," have been mixed; and pigment particles, rather than colors, have intermingled.

Green need not be thought of as a mixture of blue and yellow colors. It is more adequately identified as the color presented by a mixture of blue and yellow pigments. Or it is the color of a mixture of those pigments in some cases. If the pigments consist of large chunks, each half an inch in diameter, a mixture does not look green. It looks like a mixture of pigment chunks in which some are blue and some yellow.

For mixtures of light, we do well to follow Whittaker with appropriate modification.

White is not obtained in light by a mixture of colors. Instead, white is the color of what "is to be pictured, in the undulatory representation, as a succession of short *pulses*, out of which any spectroscopic apparatus such as a prism manufactures the different monochromatic rays, by a process which is physically equivalent to the mathematical resolution of an arbitrary function into periodic terms by Fourier's integral theorem."

Statements about mixing colors refer to the color of a mixture of something other than color: of light, pigment, or other substance located in the three-dimensional world. Colors are indeed mutually exclusive and cannot interpenetrate. A green object is singularly green. Its greenness may or may not have been created by mixing blue and yellow pigments. Color mixing is a misnomer, not a breach of the visual limit that I cannot see blue at the same time and place I see yellow.

Mixed Colors Without Mixture

A compelling reason exists for identifying green as the color of some mixtures, rather than a mixture in its own right. Many greens are not mixtures in any understandable sense. Green grass is not a mixture of blue and yellow grass. The green chlorophyll that gives grass its color is not a mixture of blue chlorophyll and yellow chlorophyll. Many green substances, including green pigments, are inherently green, therefore not open to explanation as mixtures in any sense.

Examples of traditional green pigments used by artists include chrome green, Hooker's green, and viridian. The colors of some of these green pigments (such as cadmium green) are difficult or impossible to replicate by mixture of blue and yellow pigments. Newton found a comparable phenomenon in light. Mixing blue and yellow spectral rays, he produced a ray of green. This, however, was not the same green as a ray of unmixed

(monochromatic) green spectral light. *Blue + yellow = green* is not a reversible equation. *Green = blue + yellow* is not necessarily true.

Because of the ellipsis in any assertion that colors are mixed, any color name possesses a double referend. *Green* properly identifies materials that are inherently green. It can also apply to mixtures of blue and yellow materials, though only if they look green. A jar of blue marbles and yellow marbles is not a jar of green marbles. Although the familiar recipes of color theory suggest otherwise, green cannot be reduced to blue + yellow. Nor is blue + yellow necessarily green.

Using the Color Wheel to Predict

Color is located in the two-dimensional visual realm that we, as three-dimensional bodies, are unable to enter physically. We are limited to looking into it or at it, unable to mix colors because colors cannot be reached or touched. I cannot will piles of red and blue pigments to intermingle as a single pile of powders. Nor can I will myself to perceive the respective redness and blueness of two color spots combined into a single mixed color. We live in one world while looking into another, or the human condition is indistinguishable from that model.

What is nominally called *mixing colors* is an action undertaken in the three-dimensional world, a combining of pigments, lights, or other colored materials. If the term is understood in this limited sense, any color can be mixed with any other. More exactly, any two colored materials can be mixed, unless they repel or destroy one another. The question of how many ways colors can be mixed reduces to that of how colored materials can be combined.

Maxwell identified seven ways of mixing colors (Maxwell [1890] 1965, 126–54). I have added eight others to his list. Among the fifteen, only two are ordinarily considered in explanations of color mixture. We are told what to expect from mixture of colored lights and from mixture of colored pigments.

The traditional narrowness of focus suggests that pigments and lights have been regarded as paradigmatic, as symbols of the material and immaterial aspects of the three-dimensional world. But it was also a genuine discovery, surprising when first made, that colored lights and colored pigments rarely behave similarly in mixtures. White light can be synthesized from rays of the spectral colors, or it can be separated into them. As was known long before Newton, these accomplishments cannot be imitated with paints.

Color mixing can involve both lights and pigments. A blue light might be allowed to fall on a yellow object. The object, under that set of circumstances, looks neither blue nor yellow but some combination of the two. The blending of colors on spinning Maxwell discs, which Maxwell pronounced equivalent to the blending of rays of colored light, eludes classification as either pigment mixture, light mixture, or a combination of the two.

The chart of results when mixing colored lights in figure 34-2 is adapted from Helmholtz, who warned that "mixed pigment does not give at all a colour that would be the resultant of mixing the two kinds of lights that are reflected separately from each of the ingredients" (Helmholtz [1909] 1962, 2:122). Helmholtz's chart indicates that red and cyan blue lights mix to form light that is pale pink. Orange and green mix to form yellow. Green-yellow and violet produce white. Red and green make pale yellow. Golden yellow is a result of mixing red and green-yellow. Even allowing for the ambiguity of color names, these results are distinctive, different from those obtained with pigments or Maxwell discs.

The greater number of color wheels in print are designed to teach color-mixing principles to art students. They show what can be expected in mixing paints (pigments). This is

Figure 34-2. Results of mixing light. The results of mixing lights of different colors are rarely similar to those obtained by mixing pigments or by mixing colors on Maxwell discs. (Adapted from Helmholtz [1909] 1962, 2:129.)

1. red + violet = purple
2. red + indigo-blue = dark pink
3. red + cyan-blue = pale pink
4. red + blue-green = white
5. red + green = pale yellow
6. red + green-yellow = golden yellow
7. red + yellow = orange
8. orange + violet = dark pink
9. orange + indigo-blue = pale pink
10. orange + cyan-blue = white
11. orange + blue-green = pale yellow
12. orange + green = yellow
13. orange + green-yellow = yellow
14. orange + yellow = (?)
15. yellow + violet = pale pink
16. yellow + indigo-blue = white
17. yellow + cyan-blue = pale green
18. yellow + blue-green = pale green
19. yellow + green = green-yellow
20. yellow + green-yellow = (?)
21. green-yellow + violet = white
22. green-yellow + indigo-blue = pale green
23. green-yellow + cyan-blue = pale green
24. green-yellow + blue-green = green
25. green-yellow + green = (?)
26. green + violet = pale blue
27. green + indigo-blue = water blue
28. green + cyan-blue = blue-green
29. green + blue-green = (?)
30. blue-green + violet = water blue
31. blue-green + indigo-blue = water blue
32. blue-green + cyan-blue = (?)
33. cyan-blue + violet = indigo-blue
34. cyan-blue + indigo-blue = (?)

a historical oddity: the invention of the wheel is attributed to Newton, who used it to show his ideas about light. To Newton's surprise, the spectrum that fell on his wall was not circular, but oblong, a narrow rectangle, with a width approximately five times its length. The oblong familiarly had red at one extreme, violet at the other.

Newton's rearranging of the spectral band into circular form became accepted practice because it provided a more complete account of visual experience. A continuum of reddish violet colors lies "between" red and violet. This range is absent from the spectrum or rainbow, which does not include the full gamut of hue. To explain the discrepancy, the argument is sometimes offered that the solar spectrum is really circular as it emerges from a prism, although it looks linear. For Gordon Lynn Walls, "the spectrum really has no ends—it only seems to have, due to the way in which a prism forms it. Really it is a closed entity, for red and violet are adjacent, psychologically—their mixture results in purple, which lies outside the spectrum but fills the gap between red and violet in a spectrum which we might imagine bent into a ring" (Jacobson 1948, 116).

We too often accuse our eyes of misleading us, and Walls's proposition is unconvincing. In visual experience, a distinction cannot be made between the ways color phenomena really are and the way they (really) look. The color wheel, Newton's mangled solar spectrum, remains popular because reliable, to a degree, in is predictions about color mixtures. Children can be taught such formulas as "blue mixed with yellow makes green."

Because of its idealized nature, the wheel communicates ideas about color mixture that are wrong along with some that are roughly right. Two bright colors, when mixed, may not produce a third that is similarly bright. Among artists' pigments, phthalocyanine blue and lemon yellow form a bright green. Ultramarine blue and cadmium yellow medium, an equally bright pair, form a duller green with an olive cast. Some bright blues and yellows yield a product color approaching the outer limits of what anyone might want to call green.

Blue and yellow make green when mixed, but only in the limited sense that they will not produce pink or orange. The predictions made by the color wheel are approximate. They appear to have greater applicability for secondary colors near the red end of the spectrum (orange), less for those near the violet or purple. Among available red and yellow pigments, many pairs exist in which, when that particular bright red pigment is mixed with that particular bright yellow pigment, a bright orange is obtained. Rarely is a mixed orange dull if mixed from a bright red/yellow pair.

A smaller proportion of instances exist in which bright blue pigment can be mixed with bright yellow pigment to produce a genuinely bright green. Sometimes the green is dull or drab. It deviates from any variety that would be widely identified as "a really good green."

Among available red and blue pigments, a small proportion of instances exists in which mixture of the colors in some red/blue set will provide a "good" (bright) purple. The dull purples often obtained from mixtures of red and blue have a grayish look. Although just two colors are involved in a red/blue mixture, the grayish cast recalls the tendency of tertiary (three-color) mixtures with a high blue or purple (blue/red) component to look more like grays than like browns. Blue has an affinity with black and gray.

Orange, the only secondary color mixed without blue, comes closest to following the prediction of the color wheel that primary colors ought to mix to form secondary colors no less bright than they are. Mixed greens and purples, which require blue, deviate from this standard. Why is it easier to mix bright oranges than bright purples? Although the phenomenon is rarely recognized or discussed, I think we can find an answer.

The English language encourages an emphasis on hue when identifying colors, a stress that downplays the value component of the primary colors. Spectral yellow is lightest, closest to white. Spectral blue is darkest, closest to black. Imagine ranking red, yellow, and blue by assigning numbers that grow higher as the color grows darker:

yellow	0
red	1
blue	2

We can next assign to each secondary color a numerical value that is the average of the numbers assigned to the two primaries mixed to obtain it.

orange	0.5
green	1.0
purple	1.5

For the secondary colors, the higher the number, the more chance that mixing bright primaries will lead to a dull, grayish, or darkened version of that secondary. The value component of the primary colors evidently plays a role in color mixing that reflects some physical or optical law.

Methods of Mixing Pigments

Among the seven methods of color mixing listed by Maxwell, the most familiar is the mechanical mixture of colored powders. These are usually in the form of pigments. Although a mixture of household cleanser and face powder has little value as a pigment, it illustrates, as easily as can be shown by pigments, the mechanics by which dry powders enter one another's interstices.

The traditional method for making paint was invented in the Paleolithic era and is as old as the art of painting. It was used in the Altamira and Lascaux caves. Particles of colored material (pigment) are suspended in a paste or liquid vehicle. Without a vehicle to bind them, powdered pigments cling to a surface with difficulty, a limit familiar to artists who make drawings with chalk or pastel. The paints applied to the walls of Paleolithic caves appear to have been made from dried and pulverized clays, as well as other powders. These powders were probably mixed with animal fats. Vehicles popular at later times include egg yolk, gum arabic, wax, oil, varnish, and acrylic medium.

Because a vehicle is present, mixing paints usually involves combining colored liquids, pastes, or gels, a process uneasily characterized as mixing pigments. Pigment powders are not present in all modern paints. Some, including fluorescent paints, are made with liquid dyes. The process of making paints from dyes can include a secondary vehicle that behaves as a pseudopigment though not inherently colored itself. M. G. Martindill, a pigments and coating consultant, described a method by which "synthetic fluorescent dyes can be dissolved at low concentrations in a transparent liquid, usually a resin, and the mass than solidified to form a solid solution which can be ground to form a pigment" (Martindill 1988, 188).

Modern manufacturers also add powders that affect the color of the paint, yet are neither carriers of coloring material nor pigments in a conventional sense. In modern alkyd and polyurethane house paints and varnishes, a transparent, light-diffusing powder sinks to the bottom of the can when the paint stands. This powder accounts for the difference between flat and matte varnish; between gloss black and flat black; between shiny paint and the same color with a nonglossy surface.

Many characteristics of paints have more to do with the vehicle than with the pigment. Egg tempera looks paler than oil paint and dries faster, although the same pigments are used in both. Water-base paints look darker when wet, complicating the problem of matching colors. With house paints, which are not intended to last as long as artist's paints, matching is difficult if a color has changed by exposure to light or air. Repainting woodwork is preferred, for this reason, to touching up spots where old paint has chipped.

Mixing Lights

Maxwell identified four methods of mixing lights without regard to the source of the lights. These include superposition of beams of different colors on an opaque screen, uniting beams by passing them through a prism, and uniting two or more beams through a doubly refracting prism. In a fourth method, originated by Helmholtz, beams are united by a transparent surface that reflects one and transmits the other. In this method two colored wafers lie on a table with a glass plate between them. The glass is placed so that the reflection of one colored wafer corresponds with the image of the other seen through the glass. Because a reflection on glass is faint, the technique is similar to looking at a colored object through the afterimage of another object.

Optical Mixture

Two methods of mixing color offered by Maxwell play on the limits of acuity of the human eye. In one, different colors can be successively presented to the retina, as on spinning Maxwell discs. In the other, a different color is presented to each eye by, say, asking a subject to wear eye glasses with one red lens and one green lens. In either of these methods, which cannot be explained solely in terms of laws of color mixing, any mixture occurs in the subject's eye.

Maxwell discs, and Maxwell's scientific ideas transmitted through the writings of Ogden Rood, inspired the French Impressionist painters to their thoughts on broken color, small spots of color meant to mix optically in the eye of the viewer. In Maxwell's second method, the red and green eyeglasses, mixture may not occur in any ordinary sense. The respective perceptions of redness and greenness would be directed to different sides of the brain, which might accept the reading of a dominant side. The result would be perception of either red or green, not both at once or any third color that could be called a mixture of the red and green.

Experiments with eyeglasses and goggles have been undertaken by G. M. Stratton, Theodor Erismann, and James J. Gibson, using colored lenses and prisms that modified curvatures, created rainbow fringes around objects, turned the visual field upside down, and created other distortions. In an experiment

closer to that suggested by Maxwell, Ivo Kohler devised goggles with lenses tinted blue on the left half and yellow on the right half (Kohler 1972, 111). Observers saw through blue glass when looking to the left, through yellow when looking to the right. Subjects adapted to these devices. They learned to ignore the bisected color field presented by Kohler's goggles, much as wearers of bifocals learn to ignore a field of vision split horizontally.

Because the eye, or the mind, edits without conscious intervention, ease of adaptation is a common phenomenon. For example, many years ago, I noticed that straight lines looked curved. The condition was diagnosed as astigmatism and since then has been corrected by eyeglasses. I often wonder what purpose is served by the correction. Straight lines soon ceased looking curved whether or not I wore my eyeglasses. I could not make the lines look curved when I tried. Yet the astigmatism, a fault in curvature of the lens of the eye, has not gone away and is regularly discovered in eye examinations.

Many parallel mechanisms exist. The normal eye ignores the blind spot that exists at its center and has no conscious awareness of the overlap of the visual fields for right and left eye. Elderly people rarely complain that everything looks yellow, though the lens of the eye becomes yellowish with age. Kohler contended the eye's ability to adapt can be overloaded, a plausible supposition. The condition called eyestrain is effectively an overload of the eye's ability to adapt to difficult conditions. The issue, in adaptation of the eye, is that a one-to-one correspondence does not always exist between what we see and what is available to be seen. We need to know more about how and what the eye edits, and under what circumstances.

Other Methods

I have added the following methods for mixing colors to Maxwell's list, though the compilation is still not exhaustive.

A colored object or pigment can be illuminated by a colored light, as when a blue light shines on a yellow table. The technique is used in theatrical lighting and cinematography. In the black light shows popular in the 1960s, the illuminating light was ultraviolet.

A colored object can be viewed through colored liquid, as when a lemon is immersed in a glass tank of blue copper sulfate solution.

Two colored liquids can be mixed, as in combining green ink with blue ink.

Colored objects can be looked at through anything transparent that is colored: colored glass, colored liquid, colored gelatin filters. Practical application of the technique can be seen in sunglasses, stained-glass windows, and the filters used by photographers. The squid, in a variation, squirts black ink to destroy the transparency of water and wraps itself in an artificial night.

Small dots of one color can be placed among small dots of another until the surface is covered. In art, the device appears in the broken color of the Impressionist painters, refined to the smaller color spots of the pointillist technique used by Seurat and the neo-Impressionists. Modern three-color and four-color process printing, used to reproduce color illustrations in books and magazines, is a more recent adaptation.

Fabric weaving, discussed by Chevreul, provides a related medium for color mixing. In a fabric woven with red woof and yellow warp, the small spots of color fuse to a single color if looked at from a sufficient distance or if the yarns are very fine. In nature, a distant multicolored object, say, a building of bricks of several colors, fuses to a single color. We cannot anticipate the color the building will look from six blocks away if 30 percent of its bricks are red, 12 percent are tan, and 58 percent are yellow. The color wheel is not successful in predicting results of optical mixture.

In traditional oil painting techniques, mixed colors can be produced by glazing and scum-

bling. In glazing, a layer of oil paint, thinned to transparency or semitransparency by the use of varnish, is superimposed on an opaque underlayer of another color. The technique is used in Renaissance and Baroque painting, sometimes over a monochrome underpainting in which white is mixed with the olive green pigment called terre vert (green earth). As in the opalescent skin tones in Rubens's paintings, the color of the underpainting is visible through, but modified by, the layers of glaze. In scumbling, a thin layer of fairly opaque paint does not completely veil, and blends with, the color over which it is applied. The once-popular technique of tinting black-and-white photographs simulates the uses of glazes in oil painting.

Colors can be mixed by using movie film and a projector. Film can be projected in which blue frames alternate with yellow ones. This would have to be done at higher speed than the normal twenty-four frames per second, which create an impression of blue flashes alternating with yellow flashes.

Chemical substances, as the alchemists knew, impart characteristic colors to flames. The phenomenon is the basis of spectroscopy, which enables modern astronomers to study the colors of the light of distant stars. The gas in kitchen stoves burns with a blue flame, although wood fires tend more toward red, orange, and yellow. Copper and its salts turn flames green, and so forth. A fine mixture of powders, each imparting a different color, should give flames of several colors or a mixed color when burned.

Teaching About Color Mixture

One argument in favor of the limited type of color theory diagrammed in color wheels is that learning about primary, secondary, and tertiary relationships imparts understanding of how to mix colors. To the extent that art students and others are to be educated about mixing paints, what ought to be taught is largely inconsistent with what the color wheel implies. Consider the proposition that red paint, yellow paint, and blue paint can be mixed to form brown paint. Does anyone do this? Should the procedure be recommended?

Commercially available brown paint, including that intended for artists, is not made from a mixture of red, yellow, and blue pigments. The pigment, or coloring matter, used in its manufacture is inherently brown. No incentive exists for a manufacturer, or anyone else, to turn to alternate procedures. Pigments that approach the spectral hues in color are costly. Brown pigments are inexpensive in most cases. A large and important group of traditional brown pigments, the earth colors (for example, umber, sienna, ocher) are the least expensive of all pigments. As the name suggests, these pigments are made from earth, which varies in color in different locales because of differences in composition.

The best advice for an art student confused enough to contemplate mixing brown from, say, cadmium red, cadmium yellow, and ultramarine blue is to abandon the project. Buying brown paint is more cost-effective. The narrower assertion that blue and yellow make green is equally limited in scope. The equation is not true if reversed. Green is not necessarily composed of blue and yellow in the strict sense that H_2O must include hydrogen and oxygen. Green paint is usually manufactured from inherently green pigments, not those that are blue and yellow.

A person who wants to paint a chair in a green of his or her choosing is ill-advised to begin with yellow and blue paints. The procedure of choice, more easily controlled, is to make fine adjustments to the available green paint closest to the required color. This paint can be lightened, darkened, made more yellow, modified as desired. Anyone who asks how to mix red paint ought to be told, as the color wheel implies, to buy a tube of red paint. The person also should be reminded, though this is not clear from color wheels, that if two different reds are on hand, a variety of others can be made by mixing them.

We are not advised to manufacture our own water just to prove it can really be synthesized from hydrogen and oxygen. Knowing which colors mix to form brown has a negative value as an admonition to stay away from these mixtures. Pissarro's advice *not* to mix colors is meant to remind that mingling bright colors from different hue ranges results in a brown or tertiary, which may not be the end desired.

Mixing purple is as ill-considered an endeavor as mixing brown, though for other reasons. Inherently purple pigments are available and are brighter than purples mixed from the more commonly available reds and blues. At the same time, an interesting range of purples and violets can be created by mixing rose madder with any black, though color theory allows for this range only when red is mixed with blue. Limiting its pedagogical usefulness, the color wheel provides answers that are too short, too simplistic, too certain, as if all the answers were known. It was never intended for the purpose of instilling in students the confidence to ask questions about color and to reason about what can be observed.

Additive/Subtractive Theory

The theory of the additive and subtractive varieties of color mixing still stands uncontested today.

Maurice Grosser, The Painter's Eye

White light, as Newton showed, can be produced by recombining the spectral rays derived (or manufactured) from it. The effect cannot be replicated with paints, where no mixture of colors yields white. Not can it be achieved with Maxwell discs, or by any form of mixture that involves both lights and pigments. Newton's discovery will not support the broad generalization drawn from it. White paint, unlike white light, is not a mixture of colored components. The discrepancy is inconvenient because it undermines the proposition, in popular belief and the physical sciences, that color can be understood in terms of light.

To smooth over the difficulty, the thought is sometimes offered that if white paint cannot be made by mixing colored paints, this must be because paint is less pure than light. I do not know what *pure* means in the context, or why paint ought to be regarded as impure because different from light. How is the explanation to be extended to Maxwell discs? The discs are as naughty, or as impure, as pigments. They too refuse to behave as we think they ought to.

Those seeking a more satisfying technical explanation can turn to what is loosely known as the additive/subtractive theory, familiar to most people who have studied art. The general form of the theory varies among proponents, but it begins with the proposition that rules regulating colored lights have an inverse relationship to those governing colored pigments.

When lights of two colors are combined, the theory asserts, their wavelengths (expressed in millimicrons) are added together. The wavelengths of the third color obtained from the mixture is equal to the sum of the wavelengths of the two constituent colors. This charming nonsense compels an untenable conclusion. It implies that mixing red lights of two different wavelengths—say, 645 millimicrons and 650 millimicrons—would yield light with a wavelength of 1295 millimicrons, As figure 35-1 indicates, this is beyond the upper extreme of the visible light sector of the electromagnetic scale. In everyday language, the fallacious prediction is that mixing two slightly different shades of red light would yield a third color human beings could not see. It would lie in the infrared range. If we mix, say, seven or eight colors, and have more wavelengths to add together, the sum can carry us beyond infrared to the ranges for radar and radio waves.

When colored pigments are mixed together, the theory doggedly continues, the wavelength (in millimicrons) of one color is to be subtracted from the wavelength (in millimicrons) of the other. The wavelength of the third color obtained from the mixture is equal to the difference between the wavelengths of the two constituent colors. Presumably the smaller wavelength is to be subtracted from the larger, to avoid negative wavelengths. The theory assumes that any mixed color is limited to no more than two components, which need not be the case. If a mixed color has three, eleven, or nineteen components, how can anyone determine which wavelengths to subtract from which? Additive/subtractive theory hazards no opinion.

Limiting the task to just two colors, subtracting wavelengths is as dubious as adding them. We are to understand that mixing, say, red pigments of two slightly different wavelengths (645 and 650 millimicrons) would yield pigment of a color corresponding to 5 millimicrons. This lies beyond the lower extreme of the electromagnetic scale for visible

Figure 35-1. Wavelengths of the spectral colors. Wavelengths of the spectral colors are given variously by various authors. But the range is generally from approximately 380 to 780 millimicrons. (After A. C. S. Van Heel and C. H. F. Velzel, *What is Light?* [New York: McGraw Hill, 1968], p. 39.)

Spectral Color	Wavelengths (in millimicrons)
red	780-630
orange	630-600
yellow	600-570
green-yellow	570-550
green	550-520
blue-green	520-500
blue	500-450
violet	450-380

wavelengths. In everyday language the fallacious prediction is that mixing two slightly different shades of red pigment, no less than mixing two slightly different shades of red light, would yield a third color human beings were unable to see. The theory is exceedingly strange.

In books dealing with color and visual perception, the additive/subtractive theory is alluded to more often than explained, and rarely examined in embarrassing detail. Like many strange propositions in color theory, its foundation is said to lie in physics, with no exact pinpointing of provenance to be reached. Bertram Cholet skims over the theory lightly, as does the psychologist R. L. Gregory (Cholet n.d., 10-14; Gregory 1966, 119). Recent books mention no particular problem with it and, if they ignore it, offer no new theory. References to adding and subtracting light waves and to additive and subtractive primaries (the primaries in pigment and light) are still common.

One of the more painfully detailed explications is found in *Light and Vision*, a volume prepared in the late 1960s by the science editors of *Life* magazine. The *Life* editors introduce an additional embroidery in their explanation of the discrepancy outlined:

The answer to the riddle [of why white paint cannot be mixed from colored paints] lies primarily in the totally different ways colors are achieved with light and pigments. The differences are analogous to addition and subtraction in mathematics. All spectral colors can be created by *adding*, in varying degrees of intensity, different amounts of three primary components of light. Pigment colors, on the other hand, are arrived at by subtraction. . . . Green is relatively short [in wavelength], about 500 millimicrons; red is extremely long, about 700 millimicrons; red is extremely long, about 700 millimicrons. The eye averages these two wavelengths and sees one of 600 millimicrons, which is in the yellow sector of the spectrum. (Mueller and Rudolph 1966, 98).

Because the explainers change premises in midparagraph, whether the wavelengths of two colors of light should be added or averaged to arrive at the wavelength of the mixed color remains unclear. The question is whether either adding or averaging makes sense.

Black and white pigments mix to form gray, a phenomenon not to be explained by any adding, subtracting, or averaging of wavelengths. The achromatic colors are without assigned wavelengths, other than that black is loosely called "no" light (no wavelengths), and white "all" wavelengths. Gray is presumably on a continuum between. Because *all* has no numerical equivalent (*none* might be understood to mean 0), no computations can be performed. Thus, additive/subtractive theory provides no predictions about mixtures involving colors that lack assigned wavelengths, that are not included on the electromagnetic scale. The excluded colors consist of the achromatics and all other nonspectrals, in aggregate a larger class than the spectral colors.

The additive/subtractive theory is operationally impossible to apply. It never specifies proportions for the colors to be used and has

no mechanism for adjusting the calculations to take account of different proportions. Red and yellow make orange, but only in the sense that orange is a range of colors rather than a single shade. A continuum of variations, ranging from reddish orange through yellowish orange, can be created from any given red and yellow by varying proportions.

A very yellowish orange and a very reddish orange cannot be expected to have the same wavelength, though each can be mixed from the same red and yellow. If each shade of orange is assumed to have its own wavelength, additive/subtractive computations must lead to a range of wavelengths, not a single averaged wavelength. Any theory that predicts the result of color mixtures by computations involving wavelength must lead to more than one numerical answer in order to take account of proportion.

Other absurdities in additive/subtractive prediction derive from its failure to take account of the circular relationship among the hues, of the two continua between red and violet. Mixtures of red and violet paint yield red-violet paints, which cannot reflect averaged wavelengths. The range of red-violet colors is not included in the electromagnetic scale and is consequently devoid of assigned wavelengths. Furthermore, additive/subtractive theory, as understood by the science editors of *Life*, incorrectly predicts that red and violet will mix to form yellow (580 millimicrons), which has a wavelength representing the average of the respective wavelengths of red (780 millimicrons) and violet (380 millimicrons).

Among other nonsensical predictions from taking the average of wavelengths, green (525 millimicrons) is incorrectly predicted as the result of mixing violet and orange (450/600). Blue-green (500) is incorrectly predicted as the result of mixing violet and yellow (400/600). In both of these examples, adding or subtracting yields a result as absurd as averaging.

If wavelengths ought to be added for light, red light (761 millimicrons) is incorrectly predicted as the result of mixing two violet lights (380 and 381 millimicrons). If wavelengths ought to be subtracted for pigments, bluish violet (400), rather than reddish violet, is incorrectly predicted as the result of mixing red pigment (780 millimicrons) with violet pigment (380 millimicrons). Mixing orange and blue (630/450) or green and yellow (550/570) is incorrectly predicted to yield results completely off the scale, whether one wavelength is added to or subtracted from the other.

The faulty predictions of additive/subtractive theory derive from its questionable logic, too eccentric to patch or repair. Assume that any color can be correlated with a numerical notation indicating its wavelength in millimicrons. X is the numerical value of the wavelength of a primary color. A and B are the numerical values of the wavelengths of two colors that may or may not be primary. C is the wavelength of the color that results from mixing A and B. These objects exist in a common medium, whether pigment or light.

The additive/subtractive theory predicts, according to its major versions, one of three results when A and B are mixed. (1) The numerical values of A and B will be added to provide the wavelength of product color C. (2) The numerical values of A and B will be subtracted, one from the other, to provide the wavelength of color C. Or, (3) the numerical values will be averaged, again providing the wavelength of product color C. The possibilities can be notated as follows.

$A + B = C$ = additive mixture (light)
$A - B = C$ = subtractive mixture (paint)
$(A + B) / 2 = C$ = averaging (light or paint)

Primary color X, by definition, cannot be made by any type of mixture of any other colors. Certain negative formulas can be given. They state that color X, because primary, cannot be made by mixing A and B. Nor can its wavelength be obtained by adding, subtracting, or averaging the wavelengths of any other two colors.

$$A + B \neq X$$
$$A - B \neq X$$
$$(A + B)/2 \neq X$$

The two sets of formulas are not consistent. Term X represents wavelength (in millimicrons) of a primary color. No number X exists that cannot be expressed as the sum of two other numbers, the difference between two other numbers, or the average of two other numbers. Either the result of color mixture cannot be predicted by arithmetical computations on the wavelengths of the colors or primary colors do not exist. A third possibility is that additive/subtractive theory is wrong and no primary colors exist.

Mathematical sophistication is not required to understand why the predictions are absurd when wavelengths are added or subtracted. The numerical value for the wavelength of mixed color C must lie between 380 and 780 (millimicrons), the visible light sector of the electromagnetic scale. But the numerical values for A and B lie in the range from 380 to 780. Among solutions for the formula $A + B = C$, where A and B are each more than 380 but less than 780, over 90 percent of the value for C exceed 780.

The problem with subtraction is similar. The value for C cannot be less than 380 if it is to correspond with a wavelength in the visible light sector of the electromagnetic scale. Among solutions for $A - B = C$, where A and B are each more than 380 but less than 780, a large number of values for C will be less than 380.

The main problem that intrudes in averaging is different. In physics, the relationship among the hues is diagrammed in a linear manner. The wavelength in millimicrons of yellow (580) is an average between the extremes of red and violet, 780 and 380. This solves the equation, but gives a wrong answer. We do not obtain yellow by mixing red and violet.

$$(A + B) / 2 = C$$
$$(780 + 380)/2 = 580$$

Two continua exist between red and violet, because the relationship among the hues is circular, not linear. The color wheel, though it has shortcomings, diagrams this in a correct manner. Red-violet is the color obtained by mixing red and violet. It lies on the second continuum, the continuum absent from the line diagram used in electromagnetic theory. The formula for averaging $(A + B)/2 = C$, would have to be expanded to provide for two answers, sufficient to indicate which continuum we ought to look on to locate a given color C lying halfway between A and B. Either $(A + B)/2 = C_1$ (the color on continuum 1), or $(A + B)/2 = C_2$ (the color on continuum 2).

The theory cannot be patched to accomplish this end. The circular nature of hue relationships cannot be accommodated in electromagnetic theory. No range of wavelengths exists for reddish violet colors, no second continuum. The electromagnetic scale, a linear scale, cannot be adjusted to provide one. Nor does any way exist to compute an arithmetical average that would allow for two different results.

Another arithmetical limit is that wavelength range for violet (450 to 380) is less than that for either blue (500 to 450) or red (780 to 630). Although violet is the result of mixing red and blue, no average of wavelengths in those ranges can ever fall in the violet range. If $(A + B)/2 = C$, C cannot be less than $A/2 + B/2$. All values for C, in this case, fall considerably below that limit.

The author of additive/subtractive theory is mercifully anonymous. The theory apparently came into being when a chain of assumptions were made that were not tested by studying the results of the proposed computations. The starting point was probably the observation that white light can be explained as a mixture of colored rays. It was assumed that white paint ought to be open to a similar explanation, an assumption for which no basis exists. Mixing pigments of every hue yields brown, gray, black, or near black. Because pigment mixture and light mixture could not be shown to be similar, they were assumed to be opposite. White is popularly called the opposite of black.

A probable reason for concluding that wavelengths of light had to be added is that the result of mixing all the colors of light was supposed to be white, loosely identified as all wavelengths, an infinity of wavelengths. A probable reason for concluding that wavelengths of pigments had to be subtracted is that the result of mixing every color of paint was supposed to be black (loosely identified as a nullity, or no wavelengths). The theory was programmed for absurdity. A hodgepodge of unexamined popular misconceptions about color was accepted at face value. They were assumed to have a rational or scientific foundation, and a scientific explanation was diligently constructed.

Less diligence was applied to examining the results of the proposed computations or the problems at hand. Three difficulties are insurmountable. First, mixing two colors never yields a single product color, one reason additive/subtractive theory can never work. Any two colors can be mixed in various proportions and yield a continuum or range of product colors. Second, all colors do not have assigned wavelengths. The electromagnetic scale includes only the hues and their intermediaries with the exception of the red-violet range. Third, two roads lead from red to violet, and we need to know which road to take, which direction to travel in the hue circle. Orange, yellow, green, and blue are between red and violet, as on the electromagnetic scale. The range of red-violet colors is also between red and violet, a phenomenon electromagnetic theory cannot accommodate. In mixing red and violet paints, the result is red-violet. The color does not average out to yellow. As for the purported oppositeness of light mixture and paint mixture, Helmholtz identified purple—not yellow—as the result of mixing red and violet lights (see figure 34-2).

When adding and subtracting of wavelengths is tested, the computations yield nonsense. This must have been apparent to the first person who tried the computations. Somebody likely assumed that a wrong form of computation was being used. The sensible question, not asked, is why we believe anything significant can be discovered about color mixture by arithmetic computations involving wavelengths.

Sensing the futility of adding and subtracting wavelengths, the editors of the *Life* science series turned to averaging as an aid to producing more satisfying computations. The proposal that the eye averages wavelengths demolishes any possibility of explaining in terms of wavelengths why mixtures of pigments yield different results from mixtures of lights. It implies that the eye perceives an average among wavelengths whether lights or pigments are involved. No computational opposite to averaging is available to shore up the proposal that mixtures of lights operate according to opposite rules from those governing mixtures of pigments.

Averaging has its own problems, doggedly overlooked. Additive/subtractive theory had acquired a reputation for being scientific, technically unimpeachable, before it came to the attention of the editors of the *Life* science series. The question, as often in color theory, is how so ill-conceived an idea survived for so long.

Notes

Chapter 1: Learning to Use Color Names

1. On ostensive definition, see Russell 1948, 63. On ostensive learning of color names, see Rhees 1969.

2. *Webster's Second International Dictionary* traces *yellow* to the Old English *geolu*, which means yellow or yellowish. *Blue* is from Middle English, Old High German, and Old English words that appear to have had no meaning other than bluish. *White* has no known root earlier than *hwit* (Old English), which means white. *Black* and *gray* are from *blaec* and *graeg* (Old English), meaning black and gray. *Brown* from the Sanskrit *bhru*, apparently always meant brown.

Chapter 3: Understanding Color Names

1. For analysis and modifications of the Munsell system, see J.J. Glen and J.T. Killian, "Trichromatic Analysis of the Munsell Book of Color," *J. Opt. Soc. America* 30 (1940): 609; W.C. Granville, Dorothy Nickerson, and C.E. Foss, "Trichromatic Specification for Intermediate and Special Colors of the Munsell System," *J. Opt. Soc. Am.* 33 (1943): 376; K.L. Kelly, K.S. Gibson, and D. Nickerson, "Tristimulus Specification of the Munsell Book of Color from Spectrophotometric Measure-

ments," *J. Research NBS* 31 (1943): 55; S. M. Newhall, "Preliminary Report of the OSA Subcommittee on the Spacing of the Munsell Colors," *J. Opt. Soc. Am.* 30 (1940): 617; S.M. Newhall, D. Nickerson, and D.B. Judd, "Final Report of the OSA Subcommittee on the Spacing of the Munsell Colors," *J. Opt. Soc. Am.* 33 (1943): 385; D. Nickerson, J.J. Tomaszewski, and T.F. Boyd, "Colorimetric Specifications of Munsell Repaints," *J. Opt. Soc. Am.* 43 (1953): 163.

Chapter 5: Knowing How to Identify Color

1. See Geschwind 1969. For a more detailed report on this same patient, see Geschwind and Fusillo, *Arch. Neurol.* 15 (1966): 66. For an earlier report on a case of this type, see H. Lissauer, *Arch. Psychiat. Nervenkr.* 21 (1889): 222.

Chapter 7: Light and Dark in Perspective

1. For seventeenth-century publications on the spectrum that predate Newton's report of his experiment, see Marcos Antonio de Dominis, *De radiis visus et lucis in vitris perspectivis et iride tractatus (Venice, 1611); Rene Descartes, "Dioptrique" and "Météores" (Leiden,*

1637); *Marcus Marci, Thaumanthias, liber de arcu coelestri deque colorum apparentium natura* (Prague, 1648); F.M. Grimaldi, *Physico-mathesis de lumine, coloribus et iride* (Bologna 1665); Robert Boyle, *Experiments and Considerations Touching Colours* (London, 1664); Robert Hooke, *Micrographica; or, Some Physiological Descriptions of Minute Bodies Made by Magnifying Glasses* (London, 1665).

Chapter 8: Newton

1. Newton stated: "To the same degree of Refrangibility ever belongs the same colour, and to the same colour ever belongs the same degree of Refrangibility. The species of colour, and degree of Refrangibility proper to any particular sort of Rays, is not mutable by Refraction, nor by Reflection from natural bodies, nor by any other cause that I could yet observe. When any one sort of Rays hath been well parted from those of other kinds, it hath afterwards obstinately retained its colour, notwithstanding my utmost endeavors to change it" (Whittaker [1910] 1951, 1:14).

2. "In the end it was shown that everything in physics can be explained either on the particle hypothesis or on the wave hypothesis. There is therefore no physical difference between them, and either may be adopted in any problem as may suit our convenience. But whatever is adopted, it must be adhered to; we must not mix the two hypotheses in one calculation" (Russell 1948, 23). See also: "Take, for example, the question of waves versus particles. Until recently it was thought that this was a substantial question: light must consist either of waves or of little packets called photons. But at last it was found that the equations were the same if both matter and light consisted of particles, or if both consisted of waves. Not only were all equations the same, but all the verifiable consequences were the same. Either hypothesis, therefore, is equally legitimate, and neither can be regarded as having a superior claim to truth. The reason is that the physical world can have the same structure, and the same relation to experience, on the one hypothesis as on the other" (Russell 1948, 256).

Chapter 9: The Cause of Color and Light

1. For scattered experimental evidence that questions the classical correlation between colors and wavelengths, see Land: "Color in images cannot be described in terms of wave length and, in so far as the color is changed by alteration of wave length, the change does not follow the rules of color-mixing theory" (Land [1959] 1961, 388). For a refutation of Land's views, see Judd (1979). For observations of the color blind that suggest conclusions inconsonant with classical color theory, see C.H. Graham and Y. Hsia, "Some Visual Functions of a Unilaterally Dichromatic Subject," in *Symposium on Visual Problems of Color* (New York: Chemical Publishing Company, 1961), 283–97.

Chapter 10: Red-Violet, Blue, Brown, and Optical Mixture

1. Bertrand Russell stated: "Physics is an empirical science, depending for its credibility upon relations to our perceptive experiences (Russell 1948, 256).

Chapter 19: Complementarity in the Visual Field

1. For a description of the cinematographic techniques, see Raymond Fielding, *The Technique of Special Effects Cinematography* (New York: Hastings House, 1968), 259–321, which also includes a bibliography of eighty-two articles dealing with the process.

Chapter 21: Hue, Color, and Culture

1. "A 'red object' is an object which is otherwise known than by the quality red; it is an object which has been given a determined place in an order. The sensation is an object which has not yet thus been placed. It is incorrect, then, to say that we can have sensations of redness; redness is a concept; or to say that we have sensations of red. The sensation is of a red *something*, a red spot or area. And the discovery that the cause of the sensation is a pathological irritation does not affect the objectivity of the sensation in the least. The red 'that' was there, and the fact that the object cannot be further defined and verified does not make it any the less object" (Eliot 1964, 62).

Chapter 22: Prime Minister Gladstone and the Blues

1. See Wallace 1927, 5. See also H. Magnus, *Die geschichtliche Entwicklung des Farbensinnes* (Leipzig, 1877); and H. Magnus, *Untersuchungen über den Farbensinn der Naturvolker* (Jena, 1880). For other authors on the use of color words in Homer and ancient authors, see: J. Soury, *De l'evolution historique du sens des couleurs* (1878); J. Lorz, *Die Farbenbezeichnungen bei Homer mit Berücksichtigung der Frage über Farbenblindheit* (1882); A. de Keersmaecker, *Les sens des couleurs chez Homere* (1883); Edmund Veckenstedt, *Geschichte der griechischen Farbenlehre; das Farbenunterscheidungsvormogen, die Farbenbezeichnungen der griechischen Epiker, von Homer bis Quintus Smyraneus* (1888); A. Clerke, *Familiar Studies in Homer* (1892), 294–302; N.P. Benaky, *Du sens chromatique dans l'antiquité sur le basé des dernieres descouvertes de la prehistorie, de l'etudé des monuments écrits des anciens et des données de la glossologie* (1897).

Chapter 24: Tristimulus Theory and Metamerism

1. See W.A.H. Rushton, "The Cone Pigments of the Human Fovea in Color Blind and Normal," *Symposium on Visual Problems of Color* (New York: Chemical Publishing Company, 1961), 107. Rushton was challenged by Wald, who complained that although "Dr. Rushton had faithfully refrained from saying anything about a foveal blue-sensitive pigment it was nonetheless there."

Chapter 25: Color and Form in Art

1. Stendhal, Article 7, *Journal de Paris*, 9 October, 1824.

2. Review of Durand-Ruel exhibition of Impressionist paintings, by Pierre Wolff for *Le Figaro*. Reprinted in Jean Renoir, *Renoir, My Father* (Boston, Little, Brown & Co., 1962),158.

Chapter 26: Subjectivity and the Number of Colors

1. See Sargent: "Experiments show that, without training, our eyes perceive easily about five degrees of value (i.e., gray), beginning with white and ending with black. . . . With a little training we can recognize and assign to their place in the scale about twice as many" (Sargent [1923] 1984, 62). See also Birren: "Psychological study has shown that the average person will readily distinguish about nine steps from black to white" (Birren, 1961, 24). See also Itten: "I have had many interested and gifted students who were able to make visible up to forty-four tone gradations between black and white" (Itten, 1963, 19). See also Chandler 1934, 69–70. See also Ostwald: "The number of distinguishable steps of gray under normal conditions amounts to several hundred" (Ostwald [1916] 1969, 23).

2. See D. B. Judd, "Color Perceptions of Deuteranopic and Protanopic Observers," *J. Res. Nat. Bur. Standards* (1948): 247–71. See also C.H. Graham and Y. Hsia, "Some Visual Functions of a Unilaterally Dichromatic Subject," in *Symposium on Visual Problems of Color* (New York: Chemical Publishing Company, 1961), 283–97.

3. See Wald 1961, 27.

Chapter 30: Systematizers and Systems

1. Ostwald lived in the United States at the time, although the university at which he was lecturing is given differently by different authors. Birren (Ostwald [1916] 1969, 8) identifies it as M.I.T. Jacobson (1948, 1) lists it as Harvard, where Ostwald was visiting professor of physical chemistry and Ingersoll lecturer on the immortality of man.

2. Ostwald's other works include *Er und Ich* (Leipzig, 1936), *Der Farbkorper* (Grossbothen, 1919), *Die Harmonie Der Farben* (Leipzig, 1918), *Die Farbenfibel* (Leipzig, 1916), *Der Harmonthek* (Grossbothen, 1926), *Levenslinien* (Berlin: 1927), *Letters to a Painter* (trans. A. W. Morse: New York, 1906), *The Ostwald Colour Album*, (trans. J. Scott Taylor; London, 1932–35). For textbooks based on the Ostwald system, see O.J. Tonks, *Colour Practice in Schools: A Graded Course in Color Seeing and Using for Children Between the Ages of Five and Fifteen* (London, 1934); J.A.V. Judson, *A Handbook of Colour: A Textbook for Students, Teachers of Art, and All Interested in Color* (Leicester, 1935); Arthur B. Allen, *Colour Harmony for Beginners* (London, 1936); Arthur B. Allen, *The Teaching of Colours in Schools* (London, 1937).

3. Birren's books include *Color in Vision* (1928), *Color Dimensions* (1934), *The Printer's Art of Color* (1934), *Functional Color* (1937), *Monument to Color* (1938), *The Story of Color* (1941), *Selling with Color* (1945), *Color Psychology and Color Therapy* (1950), *New Horizons in Color* (1955), *Creative Color* (1961), *Color for Interiors* (1963), *History of Color in Painting* (1965), and *Principles of Color* (1969). He edited works by Chevreul, Ostwald, Munsell, and Moses Harris, sometimes heavily. An edition of Ostwald's *Color Primer* is prefaced by Birren's editorial assurance that the original text is "more or less intact" (Ostwald [1916] 1969, 17). Munsell's *A Grammar of Color*, though a "magnificent volume," is pared to six pages, augmented by seventy-five contributed by Birren and others. The explanation is that "Munsell was not much of a writer, and though he could think and speak clearly and coherently, to all indications he found the task of author a difficult one. The best presentations of his views are by others" (Munsell [1921] 1969, 40).

4. The paintings Jacobson discussed are Giotto's *The Epiphany*, Picasso's cubist *Fruit Dish*, El Greco's *View of Toledo*, Rousseau's *La Cascade*, Botticelli's *Three Miracles of Saint Zenobius*, Vermeer's *A Girl Asleep*, van Gogh's *Bedroom at Arles*, Picasso's *Red Tablecloth*, Matisse's *Harmony in Blue*, Gauguin's *Mahana No Atua*, Renoir's *Madame Charpentier and Her Children*, and Cézanne's *Still Life with Apples*.

Chapter 31: The Logarithmic Gray Scale

1. See, for example, Cholet: "[Fechner's law of the threshold] indicates that between black, or the absence of light, and white, or the presence of total light, our perceptions are stimulated by logarithmic progression. This means that for us to discriminate between black and a perceptible gray or the first presence of white added to the black requires a very small amount of stimulus indeed. This is the absolute threshold. To discriminate between this first gray and a second gray requires an amount increased by a small fraction of the threshold amount of white light and to discriminate between the second gray and a third gray requires a further increase by the same fraction and the amount increases as a logarithm up to total white. From these studies a gray scale was organized by Wilhelm Ostwald and the grays were termed achromatic colors. Their reflectances plot at equal intervals on a logarithmic graph" (Cholet 1953, 18).

Bibliography

Albers, Josef. 1963. *Interaction of Color*. New Haven: Yale University Press.

Alexander, C. 1924. *The Real Inner Secrets of Psychology*. Vol. 5 of *Astral-Plane Phenomena*. Los Angeles: C. Alexander Publishing Company.

Allen, Arthur B. 1936. *Colour Harmony for Beginners*. London: Frederick Warne & Company.

———. 1937. *The Teaching of Colours in Schools*. London: Frederick Warne & Company.

Allen, Grant. 1879. *The Colour-Sense: Its Origin and Development*. Boston: Houghton, Osgood, and Company.

Aristotle. *Physics*. Loeb Classical Library.

———. *Metaphysics*. Loeb Classical Library.

Arnheim, Rudolph. 1956. *Art and Visual Perception*. Berkeley: University of California Press.

———. 1966. *Toward a Psychology of Art*. Berkeley: University of California Press.

Asher, Harry. 1961. *Experiments in Seeing*. Greenwich, Conn.: Fawcett Publications.

Bacon, J. 1925. *The Theory of Colouring: Being an Analysis of the Principles of Contrast and Harmony, In the Arrangement of Colours, With Their Application to the Study of Nature and Hints on the Composition of Pictures, &c.* 24th ed. London: George Rowney and Company, Ltd.

Barasch, Moshe. 1978. *Light and Color in the Italian Renaissance Theory of Art*. New York: New York University Press.

Barnes, Albert C., and Violette de Mazia. 1933. *The Art of Henri Matisse*. New York: Charles Scribner's Sons.

Barr, Alfred H., Jr. 1951. *Matisse: His Art and His Public*. New York: Museum of Modern Art.

Benaky, N. P. 1897. *Du sens chromatique dans l'antiquité sur le base des dernieres descouvertes de la préhistorie, de l'étude des monuments écrits des anciens et des données de la glossologie.*

Benson, William. [1868] 1930. *Principles of the Science of Colour Concisely Stated to Aid and Promote Their Useful Application in the Decorative Arts*. London: Chapman & Hall.

Beveridge, W. M. 1939. "Some Racial Differences in Perception." *British Journal of Psychology* 30:57–64.

Birren, Faber. 1949. "Functional Color in the

Schoolroom." *Magazine of Art* 42 (April): 136–38.

_____. 1961. *Creative Color*. New York: Van Nostrand Reinhold.

_____. 1969. *Principles of Color*. New York: Van Nostrand Reinhold Company.

_____. 1976. *Color Perception in Art*. New York: Van Nostrand Reinhold Company.

Blaker, J. Warren. 1969. *Optics*. New York: Barnes and Noble.

Boas, Franz. [1927] 1955. *Primitive Art*. New York: Dover Publications.

Bosanquet, Bernard. [1892] 1957. *A History of Aesthetic*. New York: Meridian Books.

Bowie, Henry P. 1911. *On the Laws of Japanese Painting*. San Francisco: Paul Elder & Company.

Boyle, Robert. [1664] 1964. *Experiments and Considerations Touching Colours: First Occasionally Written. Among Some Other Essays, to a friend: and now suffer'd to come abroad as The Beginning Of An Experimental History Of Colours (1664)*. London: The Sources of Science.

Bragdon, Claude. 1932. *The Frozen Fountain*. New York: Alfred A. Knopf.

British Colour Council. 1934. *Dictionary of Colour Standards*. 2 vols. London: British Colour Council.

_____. 1938. *Horticultural Colour Chart*. London: British Colour Council.

Brown, Richard F. 1950. "Impressionist Technique: Pissarro's Optical Mixture." *Magazine of Art* 43 (January): 12–15.

Bruno, Vincent J. 1977. *Form and Color in Greek Painting*. New York: W. W. Norton Company.

Burnet, John. 1950. *Greek Philosophy: Thales to Plato*. London: Macmillan and Company, Ltd.

Burris-Meyer, Elizabeth. 1938. *Historical Color Guide*. New York: William Helburn.

Capra, Fritjof. 1975. *The Tao of Physics: An Exploration of the Parallels between Modern Physics and Eastern Mysticism*. New York: Bantam Books.

Carnap, Rudolph. 1966. *Philosophical Foundations of Physics*. Edited by Martin Gardner. New York: Basic Books.

Carson, Rachel L. 1958. *The Sea around Us*. New York: Mentor Books.

Chakravarti, Tapo Nath. 1978. *The Universe of Colour: Modern Western and Ancient Indian Perspectives*. Calcutta: Putul Chakravarti.

Chandler, Albert. 1934. *Beauty and Human Nature*. New York: n.p.

Chapman, Frank M. [1895] 1966. *Handbook of Birds of Eastern North America*. New York: Dover Publications.

Chevreul, M. E. [1845] 1980. *The Principles of Harmony and Contrast of Colors*. New York: Gar-land Publishing. Originally published as *De la loi du contraste simultané des couleurs*.

Cholet, Bertram. 1953. *Color Digest*. New York: Higgins Ink Company.

Clerke, A. 1892. *Familiar Studies in Homer*.

Cohen, I. Bernard. 1958. *Issac Newton's Papers and Letters on Natural Philosophy*. Cambridge: Harvard University Press.

Cohen, Walter. 1957. "Spatial and Textural Characteristics of the *Ganzfeld*." *American Journal of Psychology* 70:403–10. Reprinted, 1966, in *Experiments in Visual Perception*, edited by M. D. Vernon. Baltimore: Penguin Books.

A Color Dictionary. 1931. New York: The North American Society of Arts, Inc.

The Color Tree. n.d. New York: Interchemical Corporation.

Crick, Francis. 1981. *Life Itself: Its Origin and Nature*. New York: Simon and Schuster.

Croce, Benedetto. [1909] 1968. *Aesthetic: As Science of Expression and General Linguistic*. Translated by Douglas Ainslie. New York: Noonday Press.

Cutler, Carl Gordon, and Stephen C. Pepper. 1923. *Modern Color*. Cambridge: Harvard University Press.

Denis, Maurice. [1890] 1966. *Definition of Neo-Traditionalism: From the Classicists to the Impressionists*. Edited by Elizabeth Gilmore Holt. New York: Doubleday, Anchor.

Descartes, René. [1664] 1972. *Treatise on Man*. Translated by Thomas Steel Hall. Cambridge: Harvard University Press.

Dickie, George. 1962. "Is Psychology Relevant to Aesthetics?" *Philosophical Review* 71:285–302.

Doerner, Max. [1921] 1934. *The Materials of the Artist and Their Use in Painting, with Notes on the Techniques of the Old Masters*. Translated by Eugen Neuhaus. New York: Harcourt, Brace and Company.

Eastlake, Charles Lock, ed. 1970. [Goethe's] *Theory of Colours*. Translated by C. L. Eastlake. Cambridge, Massachusetts: MIT Press.

Eastman Kodak. 1966. *Kodak Color Dataguide*. Rochester, New York: Eastman Kodak.

Eddington A. S. 1933. *The Nature of the Physical World*. New York: Macmillan Company.

Edman, Irwin, ed. 1936. *The Philosophy of Santayana*. New York: Random House.

Efron, Robert. 1969. "What is Perception?" In *Boston Studies in the Philosophy of Science*, edited by Robert S. Cohen and Marx W. Wartofsky, Vol. 4. Holland: D. Reidl.

T. S. Eliot. 1957. In *On Poetry and Poets*. New York: Noonday Press.

_____. 1964. *Knowledge and Experience in the Philosophy of F. H. Bradley*. New York: Farrar,

Straus and Company.

———. 1967. *Poems Written in Early Youth*. New York: Farrar, Straus and Giroux.

Emerson, Ralph Waldo. [1836] 1969. In *Selected Poetry and Prose*, edited by Reginald L. Cook. New York: Holt Rinehart Winston Inc.

Evans, Ralph M. 1948. *An Introduction to Color*. New York: John Wiley.

Evans-Wentz, W. Y., ed. [1927] 1966. *The Tibetan Book of the Dead*. New York: Oxford University Press.

Faulkner, Waldron. 1972. *Architecture and Color*. New York: Wiley-Interscience.

Fechner, Gustav Theodor. [1860] 1966. *Elements of Psychophysics*. New York: Holt, Rinehart and Winston.

Feigl, Herbert. 1956. Minnesota Studies in the Philosophy of Science, vol. 1, edited by Herbert Feigl and Michael Scriven.

———. 1958. "The 'Mental' and the 'Physical.'" In *Concepts, Theories and the Mind-Body Problem*, vol. 2 of *Minnesota Studies in the Philosophy of Science*, edited by Herbert Feigl, Michael Scriven and Grover Maxwell, 385. Minneapolis: University of Minnesota Press.

Feigl, Herbert, Michael Scriven, and Grover Maxwell, eds. 1958. *Concepts, Theories and the Mind-Body Problem*. Vol. 2 of *Minnesota Studies in the Philosophy of Science*. Minneapolis: University of Minnesota Press.

Field, George. 1858. *Rudiments of the Painter's Art; or, A Grammar of Colouring*. London: John Weale.

———. 1885. *Field's Chromatography, A Treatise on Colours and Pigments for the Use of Artists*. Modernized by J. Scott Taylor. London: Winsor and Newton.

Fielding, Raymond. 1968. *The Technique of Special Effects Cinematography*. New York: Hastings House.

Focillon, Henri. 1948. *The Life of Forms In Art*. New York: Wittenborn, Schultz.

Frank, Philip G., ed. 1956. *The Validation of Scientific Theories*. Boston: Beacon Press.

Freud, Sigmund. [1905] 1960. *Jokes and Their Relation to the Unconscious*. New York: W. W. Norton Company.

Fry, Roger. 1958. *Cézanne*. New York: Noonday Press.

Fuchs, Ernst. [1908] 1924. *Textbook of Ophthalmology*. Translated by Alexander Duane, M.D. Philadelphia: J. B. Lippincott Company.

Gallant, Roy A. 1961. *The ABC's of Astronomy: An Illustrated Dictionary*. New York: Doubleday and Company.

Gardner, Martin. 1974. "Mathematical Games: The Arts as Combinatorial Mathematics, or How to Compose Like Mozart with Dice." *Scientific American* 231 (December): 132–36.

Gauss, Charles Edward. 1966. *The Aesthetic Theories of French Artists*. Baltimore: Johns Hopkins Press.

Geiger, L. [1871] 1880. *Contributions to the History and Development of the Human Race*. Translated by D. Ascher. London. Originally published as *Zur Entwicklungsgeschichte der Menschheit*.

Geschwind, Norman. 1969. "Anatomy and Higher Functions of the Brain." In *Boston Studies in the Philosophy of Science*, edited by Robert S. Cohen and Marx W. Wartofsky, 4:98–136. Holland: D. Reidl.

Gerstner, Kare. 1986. *The Forms of Color*. Cambridge, Massachusetts: MIT Press.

Gibson, James J. 1950. *The Perception of the Visual World*. New York: Houghton-Mifflin.

———. 1968. "What Gives Rise to the Perception of Motion?" *Psychological Review* 75 (July): 335–46.

Gjertsen, Derek. 1986. *The Newton Handbook*. London and New York: Routledge and Kegan Paul.

Gladstone, W. E. 1858. *Studies on Homer and the Homeric Age*. 3 vols. Oxford: Oxford University Press.

———. 1877. *The Colour Sense*.

Gleason, H. A., Jr. 1961. *An Introduction to Descriptive Linguistics*. New York: Holt, Rinehart and Winston.

Gogh, Vincent van. 1958. *The Complete Letters*. Greenwich, Conn.: New York Graphic Society.

Gombrich, Ernst. 1956. *Art and Illusion*. Princeton: Princeton University Press.

Goodman, Nelson. 1957. *The Structure of Appearance*. New York: Bobbs-Merrill.

———. 1968. *Language of Art*. New York: Bobbs-Merrill.

Govindjee and Rajni Govindjee. 1974. "The Absorption of Light in Photosynthesis." *Scientific American* 231 (December): 68–82.

Greenough, Horatio. 1962. *Form and Function: Remarks on Art, Design and Architecture*. Berkeley: University of California Press.

Gregory, R. L. 1966. *Eye and Brain: The Psychology of Seeing*. New York: McGraw-Hill Book Company.

Gribbin, John. 1984. *In Search of Schrödinger's Cat: Quantum Physics and Reality*. New York: Bantam Books.

Grohmann, Will. 1958. *Kandinsky: Life and Work*. New York: Abrams.

Grosser, Maurice. 1959. *The Painter's Eye*. New York: Bantam Books.

Guilman, Maxine Kraut. 1967. "Writings on Color

in Sixteenth Century Italian Art Theory." Master's thesis, Department of Art History, Columbia University.

Guptill, Arthur L. n.d. *Color Manual for Artists*. New York: Van Nostrand Reinhold Company.

Hahn, Hans. [1933] 1966. "Logic, Mathematics and Knowledge of Nature." In *20th-Century Philosophy: The Analytic Tradition*, edited by Morris Weitz. New York: The Free Press.

Hamlin, D. H. 1949. "The Ridgway Color Standards with a Munsell Notation Key." *Journal of the Optical Society of America* 39:592.

Harris, Moses. [1766] 1963. *The Natural System of Colors by Moses Harris*. Edited by Faber Birren. New York: Whitney Library of Design.

Harrison, Bernard. 1973. *Form and Content*. Oxford: Blackwell.

Hatt, Joseph Arthur Henry. 1925. *The Colorist: Designed to Correct the Commonly Held Theory That Red, Yellow, and Blue Are the Primary Colors, and to Supply the Much Needed Easy Method of Determining Color Harmony. Together with a System of Color Nomenclature and Other Practical Information for Artists and Workers or Designers in Color*. New York: D. Van Nostrand Company.

Hattersley, Ralph. 1970. "Do You Have Eyes in Your Skin?" *Popular Photography,* March, 55–58.

Hawking, Stephen W. 1988. *A Brief History of Time: From the Big Bang to Black Holes*. New York: Bantam Books.

Hay, D. R. 1845. *The Principles of Beauty in Colouring Systematized*. London: William Blackwood and Sons.

Helmholtz, Hermann von. [1909] 1962. *Helmholtz's Treatise on Physiological Optics*. Ed. James P. C. Southall. 2 vols. New York: Dover Books.

Henri, Robert. 1923. *The Art Spirit*. Compiled by Margery Ryerson. Philadelphia: J. B. Lippincott.

Hering, Ewald. [1905–20] 1964. *Outlines of a Theory of the Light Sense*. Translated by Leo M. Hurvich and Dorethea Jameson. Cambridge: Harvard University Press.

Heron, Patrick. 1955. "Space in Color." *Arts Digest* 29 (March 15): 8–11.

Herrington, Donald E. 1968. *How to Read Schematic Diagrams*. Indianapolis: Howard W. Sams and Company, Inc.

Hickethier, Alfred. 1963. *Color Mixing by Numbers*. New York: Van Nostrand Reinhold Company.

Hiler, Hilaire. 1942. *Color Harmony and Pigments*. Chicago: Favor, Ruhl and Company.

Hodson, Geoffrey. 1976. *Music Forms: Superphysical Effects of Music Clairvoyantly Observed.* Wheaton, Ill. Theosophical Publishing House.

Hofmann, Hans. 1948. *Search for the Real*. Andover, Mass.: Addison Gallery.

Howard, Frank. 1838. *Colour as a Means of Art, Being an Adaptation of the Experience of Professors to the Practice of Amateurs*. London: J. Thomas.

Hoyle, Fred. 1957. *Astronomy: A History of Man's Investigation of the Universe*. New York: Crescent Books.

Imperial Chemical Industries. 1971. *ICI Colour Atlas*. London and Cleveland: Imperial Chemical Industries.

International Printing Corporation. 1935. *Three Monographs on Color*. New York: Research Laboratories of the International Printing Corporation.

Ittelson, W. H. 1952. *The Ames Demonstrations in Perception*. Princeton: Princeton University Press.

Itten, Johannes. 1963. *Design and Form: The Basic Course at the Bauhaus*. New York: Reinhold.

Ivins, William M., Jr. 1946. *Art and Geometry: A Study in Space Intuitions*. Cambridge: Harvard University Press.

Jacobson, Egbert. 1942. *The Color Harmony Manual and How to Use It*. Chicago: Color Laboratories Division, Container Corporation of America.

————. 1948. *Basic Color: An Interpretation of the Ostwald Color System*. Chicago: Paul Theobald.

Jenkins, Francis A., and Harvey E. White. 1957. *Fundamentals of Optics*. New York: McGraw Hill Book Company.

Judd, Deane B. 1979. *Contributions to Color Science*. Edited by David L. MacAdam. Special publication 545 prepared for the National Bureau of Standards.

Judson, J. A. V. 1935. *A Handbook of Colour: A Textbook for Students, Teachers of Art, and All Interested in Color*. Leicester: The Dryad Press.

Katz, David. 1935. *The World of Color*. London: K. Paul, Trench, Trubner and Company, Ltd.

Keersmaecker, A. de 1883. *Les sens des couleurs chez Homere*.

Kelly, Kenneth L. 1965. "A Universal Color Language." *Color Engineering* 3 (March–April). Reprinted by National Bureau of Standards, NBS Circular 553.

Koffka, K. 1922. "Perception: An Introduction to Gestalt-theorie." *Psychological Bulletin* 19:551–85. Reprinted, 1966, in *Experiments in Visual Perception*, edited by M. D. Vernon. Baltimore: Penguin Books.

————. 1935. *Principles of Gestalt Psychology*. London: Kegan, Paul.

Kohler, Ivo. 1972. "Experiments with Goggles." In *Altered States of Awareness*, edited by Scientific American. San Francisco: W. H. Freeman and Company, 1972.

Kohler, Wolfgang. 1947. *Gestalt Psychology*. New York: Mentor Books.

Koyré, Alexander. 1965. *Newtonian Studies*. London: Chapman and Hall.

Ladd-Franklin, Christine. 1929. *Colour and Colour Theories*. New York: Harcourt, Brace and Company.

Land, Edwin. [1959] 1961. "Color Vision and the Natural Image." In *Symposium on Visual Problems of Color*. New York: Chemical Publishing Company.

Léger, Fernand. 1946. "Modern Architecture and Color." Translated by George L. K. Morris. American Abstract Artists exhibition catalog. New York: Ram Press.

Leland, Nita. 1985. *Exploring Color*. Cincinnati: North Light Publishers.

Leonardo da Vinci. [1802] 1957. *The Art of Painting*. Translated by John Francis Rigaud. New York: Philosophical Library.

———. 1939. *The Notebooks of Leonardo da Vinci*. Translated by Edward MacCurdy. New York: Reynal & Hitchcock.

Lewitt, Sol. 1975. *Lines and Color*. Zurich: Annemarie Verna.

Linton, W. "A List of the Principal Colours Used in Painting." *Art Journal* (London) 2:271.

Loeb, Leonard B., and Arthur S. Adams. 1933. *The Development of Physical Thought*. New York: John Wiley.

Luckiesh, Matthew. 1938. *Color and Colors*. New York: Van Nostrand.

Maerz, A., and M. Rea Paul. 1930. *A Dictionary of Color*. New York: McGraw-Hill Book Company.

Magnus, H. 1877. *Die geschichtliche Entwicklung des Farbensinnes*. Leipzig.

———. 1880. *Untersuchungen über den Farbensinn der Naturvolker*. Jena.

Magnus, Rudolph. 1949. *Goethe as a Scientist*. New York: Henry Schuman.

Malevich, Kasimir. 1971. "An Attempt to Determine the Relation between Colour and Form in Painting." In *Malevich, Essays on Art 1915–1933*. New York: Wittenborn.

Martindill, M. G. 1988. "A European Eye on Luminescence: Fluorescent and Phosphorescent Colours for the Visual Artist." *Leonardo: Journal of the International Society for the Arts Sciences and Technology* 21 (2): 187–90.

Matthaei, Rupprecht, ed. 1971. *Goethe's Color Theory*. Translated by C. L. Eastlake, with notes by R. Matthaei. New York: Van Nostrand Reinhold Company.

Maxwell, James Clerk. [1890] 1965. *Scientific Papers*. Edited by W. D. Niven. 2 vol. New York: Dover Press.

Moholy-Nagy, L. [1921] 1947. *Vision in Motion*. Chicago: Paul Theobald.

Mueller, Conrad G., and Mae Rudolph. 1966. *Light and Vision*. New York: Life Science Library.

Munsell, A. H. [1905] 1961. *A Color Notation: An Illustrated System Defining All Colors and Their Relations by Measured Scales of Hue, Value and Chroma*. Baltimore: Munsell Color Company.

———. 1942. *Munsell Book of Color*. Baltimore: Munsell Color Company.

———. 1969. *A Grammar of Color*. Edited by Faber Birren. New York: Van Nostrand Reinhold Company.

Nasr, Seyyed Hossein. 1978. *An Introduction to Islamic Cosmological Doctrines*. Boulder, Colo.: Shambhala.

National Bureau of Standards. Inter-Society Color Council. n.d. *a. The ISCC-NBS Method of Designating Colors and a Dictionary of Color Names*. NBS circular 553.

———. n.d. *b. The ISCC-NBS Color-Name Charts Illustrated with Centroid Colors*. Supplement to NBS circular 553.

Newton, Sir Issac. [1704] 1952. *Opticks, or a Treatise of the Reflections, Inflections & Colours of Light*. 4th ed. New York: Dover Publications.

Optical Society of America. 1953. *The Science of Color*. New York: Thomas Y. Crowell Company.

Osborne, Roy. 1980. *Lights and Pigments: Colour Principles for Artists*. New York: Harper and Row.

Ostwald, Wilhelm. 1906. *Letters to a Painter*. Translated by A. W. Morse. New York: Ginn & Company.

———. 1916. *Die Farbfibel*. Leipzig: Unesma.

———. [1916] 1969. *The Color Primer*. Edited by Faber Birren. New York: Van Nostrand Reinhold Company.

———. 1931–33. *Color Science*. Translated by J. Scott Taylor. 2 vols. London: Winsor and Newton.

———. 1932–35. *The Ostwald Colour Album*. Arranged by J. Scott Taylor. London: Winsor and Newton.

Ouspensky, P. D. 1947. *Tertium Organum: The Third Canon of Thought, A Key to the Enigmas of the World*. New York: Alfred A. Knopf.

Perkins, Moreland. 1971. "Sentience." *The Journal of Philosophy* 67 (June 3): 329– 37.

Pitcher, George, ed. 1969. *Wittgenstein, The Philosophical Investigations: A Collection of Critical Essays*. New York: Doubleday, Anchor Books.

Pitt, F. H. G. 1935. "Characteristics of Dichromatic

Vision." In *Report of the Committee on the Physiology of Vision*, xiv. Special report series, no. 200. London: Medical Research Council.

Planck, Max. n.d. *A Survey of Physics: A Collection of Lectures and Essays*. Translated by R. Jones and D. H. Williams. New York: Dutton.

Plateau, J. 1873. *Statique expérimentale et théorique des Liquides soumis aux seules Forces moléculaires*. Paris: Gauthier-Villars.

Plochere, Gladys and Gustav. 1948. *Plochere Color System: A Guide to Color and Color Harmony*. Los Angeles: Fox Printing Company.

Poling, Clark V. 1986. *Kandinsky's Teaching at the Bauhaus: Color Theory and Analytical Drawing*. New York: Rizzoli.

Portmann, Adolph, et al. 1977. *Color Symbolism: Six Excerpts from the Eranos Yearbook, 1972*. Dallas: Spring Publications.

Ray, V. F. 1953. "Human Color Perception and Behavioral Response." *Transactions of the New York Academy of Sciences* 16:98–104.

Rewald, John, 1943. *Georges Seurat*. New York: Wittenborn.

Rhees, R. 1969. "Can There be a Private Language?" In *Wittgenstein, The Philosophical Investigations: A Collection of Critical Essays*, edited by George Pitcher. New York: Doubleday Anchor Books.

Ridgway, R. 1886. *A Nomenclature of Colors for Naturalists*. Boston: Little, Brown.

———. 1912. *Color Standards and Color Nomenclature*. Baltimore: Hoen.

Rivers, W. H. R. 1901. "Primitive Color Vision." *Popular Science Monthly* 59:44–58.

Robinson, Daniel Sommer. 1947. *The Principles of Reasoning: An Introduction to Logic and Scientific Method*. New York: Appleton-Century Crofts, Inc.

Rood, Ogden N. [1879] 1913. *Student's Textbook of Color, or Modern Chromatics with Applications to Art and Industry*. New York: D. Appleton & Company.

Rood, Roland. 1941. *Color and Light in Painting*. Edited by George L. Stout. New York: Columbia University Press.

Rorschach, Hermann. 1964. *Psychodiagnostics*. Translated by Paul Lemkau, M.D. 6th ed. New York: Grune & Stratton.

Ross, Denman Waldo. 1919. *The Painter's Palette: A Theory of Tone Relations, An Instrument of Expression*. New York: Houghton Mifflin.

Royal Society of London for Improving Natural Knowledge. *Philosophical Transactions: giving some Accompt of the present undertakings, studies and labours of the Ingenious in many considerable parts of the world*. 1664–1832. London: The Royal Society of London for Improving

Natural Knowledge.

Rucker, Rudy. 1984. *The Fourth Dimension: A Guided Tour of the Higher Universes*. Boston: Houghton Mifflin Company.

Russell, Bertrand. 1948. *Human Knowledge, Its Scope and Limits*. New York: Simon and Schuster.

Sapir, Edward. 1921. *Language: An Introduction to the Study of Speech*. New York: Harcourt, Brace and World.

———. 1949. *Selected Writings in Language, Culture, and Personality*. Berkeley: University of California Press.

Sargent, Walter. [1923] 1964. *The Enjoyment and Use of Color*. New York: Dover Publications.

Sartre, Jean-Paul. 1950. *The Psychology of Imagination*. New York: Philosophical Library.

Schillinger, Joseph. 1941. *The Schillinger System of Musical Composition*. New York: Carl Fischer, Inc.

———. 1948. *The Mathematical Basis of the Arts*. New York: Philosophical Library.

Scripture, E. W. 1895. *Thinking, Feeling, Doing*. New York: Flood and Vincent.

Segall, Marshall H., Donald T. Campbell, and Melville J. Herskovits. 1966. *The Influence of Culture on Visual Perception: An Advanced Study in Psychology and Anthropology*. New York: Bobbs-Merrill.

Skinner, B. F. 1972. *Beyond Freedom and Dignity*. New York: Bantam Books.

Smith, Charles N. 1965. *Student Handbook of Color*. New York: Van Nostrand Reinhold Company.

Société Francaise des Chrysanthemistes and R. Oberthur. 1905. *Répertoire de Couleurs pour Aider à la Détermination des Fleurs, des Feuillages et des Fruits*. Paris: Libraire Horticole.

Soury, J. 1878. *De l'evolution historique du sens des couleurs*.

Standard Dictionary of Folklore, Mythology, and Legend. 2 vols. New York: Funk and Wagnalls.

Stokes, Adrian. 1937. *Colour and Form*. London: Faber and Faber Ltd.

Strathmore Paper Company. 1921. *A Grammar of Color*. Westfield, Massachusetts: Strathmore Paper Company.

Sullivan, J. W. N. 1965. *The Limitations of Science*. New York: Van Nostrand Reinhold Company.

"Surangama Sutra, The". 1942. In *The Wisdom of China and India*, edited by Lin Yutang. New York: Random House.

Swedenborg, Emanuel. [1758] 1965. *Heaven and Its Wonders and Hell*. Translated by John C. Ager. New York: The Citadel Press.

Sweeney, James Johnson. 1945. *Stuart Davis*. New York: Museum of Modern Art.

Symposium on Visual Problems of Color. 1961. New

York: Chemical Publishing Company.

Taylor, H. D., L. Knoche, and W. C. Granville. 1950. *Descriptive Color Names Dictionary*. Chicago: Container Corporation of America.

Taylor, Joshua C. 1961. *Learning to Look: A Handbook for the Visual Arts*. Chicago: University of Chicago Press.

Taylor, J. Scott. 1935. *A Simple Explanation of the Ostwald Colour System*. London: Winsor and Newton Ltd.

Textile Color Card Association of the United States, Inc. 1941. *Standard Color Card of America*. New York: Textile Color Card Association.

Titchener, E. B. 1916. "On Ethnological Tests of Sensation and Perception with Special Reference to Tests of Color Vision and Tactile Discrimination Described in the Reports of the Cambridge Anthropological Expedition to the Torres Straits." *Proceedings of the American Philosophical Society* 55:204–36.

Tonks, O. J. 1934. *Colour Practice in Schools: A Graded Course in Colour Seeing and Using for Children Between the Ages of Five and Fifteen*. London: Winsor and Newton Ltd.

Triandis, H. C. 1964. "Cultural Influences on Cognitive Processes." In *Advances in Experimental Social Psychology*, vol. 1, edited by L. Berkowitz. New York: Academic Press.

Vanderpoel, Emily Noyes. 1903. *Color Problems: A Practical Manual for the Lay Student of Color*. New York: Longmans, Green and Company.

van Gogh, Vincent. *See* Gogh, Vincent van.

Vasari, Giorgio. [1550] 1957. *Lives of the Artists*. Translated by E. L. Seeley. New York: Noonday Press.

Vernon, M. D., ed. 1966. *Experiments in Visual Perception*. Baltimore: Penguin Books.

Wald, George. 1961. "Retinal Chemistry and the Physiology of Vision." In *Symposium on Visual Problems of Color*. New York: Chemical Publishing Company.

Wallace, Florence Elizabeth. 1927. *Color in Homer and Ancient Art*. Smith College Classical Series, no. 9. Northhampton, Mass.: Smith College.

Walls, Gordon Lynn. 1942. *The Vertebrate Eye*. Bloomfield Hills, Mich.: Cranbrook Press.

Whistler, James McNeil. 1890. *The Gentle Art of Making Enemies*. New York: John W. Lovell Company.

Whitehead, Alfred North. [1925] 1953. *Science and the Modern World*. New York: Mentor Books.

Whittaker, Sir Edmund. [1910] 1951. *A History of the Theories of Aether and Electricity*. 2 vols. New York: Harper Torchbooks.

Whorf, Benjamin Lee. [1956] 1967. *Language, Thought and Reality: Selected Writings*. Edited by John B. Carroll. Cambridge: MIT Press.

Wilson, Anton. 1970. "Film Feedback." *Filmmaker's Newsletter* (September): 32.

Wittgenstein, Ludwig. 1958. *The Blue and Brown Books: Preliminary Studies for the "Philosophical Investigations."* New York: Harper Torchbooks.

————. 1967. *Remarks on the Foundations of Mathematics*. Edited by G. H. von Wright, R. Rhees, and G. E. M. Anscombe. Cambridge: MIT Press.

Wright, W. D. [1944] 1969. *The Measurement of Colour*. New York: Van Nostrand Reinhold Company.

————. 1962. *Proceedings of the Conference on Optical Instruments and Techniques, 1961*. London: Chapman and Hall.

————. 1968. *The Rays Are Not Coloured: Essays on the Science of Vision and Colour*. New York: American Elsevier Publishing Company.

Wurtman, Richard J. 1975. "The Effects of Light on the Human Body." *Scientific American* 233 (July): 68–77.

Young, Thomas. 1802. "On the Theory of Light and Colours." *Philosophical Transactions of the Royal Society* 92:20–71.

Zeishold, Herman. 1944. "Philosophy of the Ostwald Color System." *Journal of the Optical Society of America* 34 (July).

Zimmer, Heinrich. 1946. *Myths and Symbols in Indian Art and Civilization*. Edited by Joseph Campbell. New York: Pantheon Books.

Index

Achromaticity, 54
Additive/subtractive theory, 323–328
Agnosias. *See* Visual agnosias
Airglow, 49
Allen, Grant, 10
Anomaloscope, 199
Aristotle, 3, 62–63
  light effects versus color effects, 103
Art, color and form in, 224–229
Artists, use of light, 114–120
Astronomy, relation to color, 58–61

Bassa language, 201–203
Bible, 34
Birren, on color clash, 279–280
Black, 88–91
  as an absolute, 53–54
  Goethe's views, 208
  as light absorber, 91
  relation to nothingness, 50–52
  symbolic, 120–122
Blue
  ambiguous names for, 265
  astronomy related to, 59
  describing ultraviolet rays, 85
  Goethe's views, 208
  moderate, ISCC chart, 19

symbolic, 120, 122
  Tyndall, 62
  visual affinity for, 54
Bosons, 248–249
Boyle, Robert, 62
  cause of color theory, 74
Brain damage, relation to color information, 40
Brown, cause of, 85–86

Cantor, Georg, 11
Carnap, Rudolph, 13, 14
  theorem weaknesses, 23
Chapman's color swatches, 24–25
Charcot, Jean-Martin, 197–198
Color. *See also specific colors*
  achromatic, 54, 88
    tristimulus values, 95. *See also* Black; White
  in art, 224–229
  cause of, 73–78
  causing light, 97–98
  chimpanzee studies, 41
  chroma, 14
  clash, 276–280
  coding, by wavelengths, 93–94
  complementary, 301–303
    harmony and, 311–312

Maxwell disc test, 304–306
    Munsell wheel, 310–311
    as negation, 303–304
    Ostwald wheel, 310–311
    product color test, 306–308
    wavelengths in light, 308–310
  as a continuum, 11–12
  created by light, 62
  describing, 257–258
  differentiating, 234
  doubting, 34–36
  experience, 41
  fields
    constancy, 181–182
    displacement, 180–181
    noninterpenetrability, 179–180
    perimeters, 183–184
    separating form and, 177–179
    surface, 182–183
    surface geometry, 183
    union with form, 175–177
  form and, 237–239
    naming, 239–244
  games, by Ludwig Wittgenstein, 29–31
  generic, 14–15
  hell associated with, 107
  hue, 14, 187– 192

Other Books from Design Press

PRINCIPLES OF VISUAL PERCEPTION—2ND EDITION
by Carolyn M. Bloomer

How and why do people's perceptions of a work of art differ? Combining psychology and art theory, artist and educator Carolyn M. Bloomer explores how we construct meaning from visual information and how the physiological aspects of visual perception are influenced by culture and experience. Making reference to the problems of creating and teaching art, Bloomer offers practical applications for the ideas of each chapter with studio projects designed for both classroom and individual practice.

Hardcover $27.45 Book No. 50004

SYMBOLS SIGNS LETTERS
by Martin Andersch

Elegantly designed, exquisitely produced, and winner of a gold medal at the International Book Art Exhibition (Leipzig, 1989), this collection presents the art of calligraphy at its finest and most innovative level. It combines professor of design Martin Andersch's observations on the state of lettering in the twentieth century with extraordinary work done by students in his seminars. **Fine Print** magazine says, "It is a beautiful book, with inspiring pictures and ideas for teachers, students, and laymen . . ."

Hardcover $74.00 Book No. 50006

LOGIC AND DESIGN
by Krome Barratt

Perception and communication specialist Krome Barratt examines key principles of design and their relationship to art, mathematics, and science in this unique combination of text and graphics. A sourcebook of ideas from a variety of disciplines, all concerned with innovation and problem solving, it covers such topics as number, ratio and scale, rhythm and harmony, and similarity and contrast, and suggests ways that the designer can creatively apply them.

Paperback $16.60 Book No. 50012

*Prices subject to change without notice.

Ask for Design Press books at your local bookstore or write

Design Press
P.O. Box 40
Blue Ridge Summit, PA
17294-0850

TO ORDER TOLL-FREE: 1-800-822-8138